ADVENTISTICA

Studies in Adventist History and Theology – New Series

Series Editors:
Johannes Hartlapp, Daniel Heinz,
Stefan Höschele, Rolf J. Pöhler

PUBLISHED BY
THE INSTITUTE OF ADVENTIST STUDIES
OF FRIEDENSAU ADVENTIST UNIVERSITY

Volume 3

ROLF J. PÖHLER

DYNAMIC TRUTH

A STUDY OF THE PROBLEM
OF DOCTRINAL DEVELOPMENT

FRIEDENSAU
ADVENTIST
UNIVERSITY

ADVENTISTICA
Studies in Adventist History and Theology – New Series
Editors: Johannes Hartlapp, Daniel Heinz, Stefan Höschele, Rolf J. Pöhler

Volume 3
Dynamic Truth: A Study of the Problem of Doctrinal Development

Author: Rolf J. Pöhler
Editorial Assistant: Philip Nern

Cover: © rasani.design Leipzig

© 2020 Institute of Adventist Studies
Friedensau Adventist University
(Theologische Hochschule Friedensau)
39291 Möckern-Friedensau, Germany
Internet: www.thh-friedensau.de
E-Mail: ias@thh-friedensau.de

Printed by: BoD - Books on Demand, Norderstedt

This title is also available as an e-book.
ISBN e-book: 978-3-935480-55-0

ISBN Print: 978-3-935480-54-3

TO MY STUDENTS

who scrutinize my beliefs
and prompt me persistently
to reexamine their foundations
in the search for "present truth"

Contents

Part I
Continuity and Change in Christian Doctrine: A Preliminary Inquiry

Preface: "Another Leap Forward"

Rolf J. Pöhler, a pastor in his native Germany, earned a Master of Divinity degree *summa cum laude* at Andrews University in 1975. A paper he wrote during 1978 on Adventist history caught my attention, causing me to expect further quality studies from him.[1] Inasmuch as pastoral and administrative duties engaged Pöhler for another dozen years, it took him until 1995 to complete a Doctor of Theology program at Andrews University, with a dissertation entitled "Change in Seventh-day Adventist Theology: A Study of the Problem of Doctrinal Development."

UMI Dissertation Services of Ann Arbor, Mich., claim to make available "almost every doctoral dissertation accepted in North America since 1861." So I read Pöhler's dissertation with deep interest. It is now more accessible as two handsome volumes. These books blend the sensitivity of a pastor, the didactic skills of a teacher and the rigor of a scholar. Pöhler is a conservative in the best sense: he is so deeply committed to the faith and the values of his church that he tends to understate rather than overstate problematic issues. Yet the tenacity of his research leads him to a wealth of material and his faithfulness to truth constrains his analyses. The result is a joy to read even though it challenges often-heard assumptions.

Pöhler has done his homework so well in Christian thought for his first volume that he comes to the study of Adventism with a tentative set of expectations, most of which prove to be apt. His dissertation cites 31 master-level and doctoral studies that deeply inform his enquiry into Adventist history. He is thoroughly acquainted with the published work of historians and theologians whose writings are germane to his topic. But Pöhler does his own thorough investigation into the primary sources; indeed, his bibliography runs to 94 pages. While his conclusions are congruent with those of his colleagues, they extend the analyses of Seventh-day Adventist doctrinal development that are currently available from other sources.

After reviewing the evidence, no one can truthfully deny the fact of doctrinal change within Christianity in general and Adventism in particular. But a more important question to ask is how the processes of change can be understood and described effectively. That exercise calls the community of faith to develop safeguards to protect itself from irresponsible change even as it welcomes change that brings it closer to Scripture. Pöhler is able to handle sacred issues and controversial matters with such care and calmness that most unbiased readers will applaud his findings.

---

1 "'... And the Door Was Shut.' A Study of the Doctrine of the Open and Shut Door as Related to the Sabbatarian Adventists in the Decades after the Disappointment of 1844," Manuscript 1978 (192 S.)

For its mastery of sources, the quality of its analyses and the balance of its propositions, this groundbreaking study is an outstanding achievement. In that its cutoff point is 1985, it lays an effective foundation for continuing exploration.

Perhaps the most important chapter in Pöhler's dissertation is, surprisingly, the shortest. Entitled "Prophetic Authority and Doctrinal Change: An Analysis,"[2] it concludes with the claim that Ellen White "exerted a significant influence on the development of Adventist doctrines, being actively involved in the formation, preservation, and revision of the teachings of the church." More than that, "she herself participated in various types of theological change, encompassing not only theological maturation and doctrinal growth but, at times, even doctrinal adjustments and revisions." Therefore Pöhler can affirm, cogently: "To a considerable degree, she shared in and fostered the process of theological growth and doctrinal development which the Seventh-day Adventist Church experienced during her lifetime."

Not only did Ellen White surpass her fellow believers in the depth of her understanding "but also in striking a balance between the need for theological continuity and substantial identity, on the one hand, and the possibility of theological revisions and doctrinal changes, on the other." Her genius was, in part, to tirelessly warn the church against two perils: "the careless rejection of precious 'old light' and the stubborn resistance to much-needed 'new light'." The moral is clear, and well stated: "This concept can still provide guidance for the church faced by the perennial dangers of theological immobilism and doctrinal revisionism. Seventh-day Adventists may do well to emulate the example of their prophet who served both as a strong factor of doctrinal continuity and a constant catalyst of doctrinal change." Pöhler finds Ellen White's concept of doctrinal development intriguing: "The truths of redemption are capable of constant development and expansion."

A decade or two after their completion, a few dissertations are seen to tower above the many. Pöhler's dissertation is on my short-list of those in Adventism that will be seen increasingly as thorough, illuminating and constructive. I await with keen anticipation the fulfilment of his promise about "upcoming work." One who has enabled Adventist studies to take another significant leap forward must continue to share his giftedness with the church at large.

Arthur Patrick†, DMin, PhD[3]

---

2   In the manuscript, chapter 6 had 32 rather than 21 pages. At the request of the dissertation committee, the "Examples of Ellen White's Participation in Doctrinal Change" were left out. Likewise missing in the book of 2000, they are reinserted in the present volume.

3   Arthur Patrick (1934-2013) was an esteemed Australian pastor, teacher, and author. He was the first director of the Ellen G. White/Seventh-day Adventist Research Centre in Australia. Just months before he succumbed to a fight with cancer, he invited me to preach and lecture at Avondale College and in Sydney. I remember him as a Christian gentleman, a gifted scholar, and a personal friend. As a tribute to him, his review of my doctoral dissertation is published here with the kind permission of his widow Joan.

Author's Preface

When I took up advanced theological studies at Andrews University in the 1970s, the development and even change of the doctrines of the Seventh-day Adventist Church immediately caught my attention. The early history of the denomination, in particular, provided a rich field for studying its theological growth and adjustments. It also raised some intriguing questions regarding the possibilities and limits of theological development. Research into the unique sanctuary doctrine soon led me to the intricate problem of the "shut-door" teaching. The latter, in turn, made me aware that doctrinal readjustments were not only a historical fact but constituted a theological challenge that should not be underrated nor ignored by scholars and churches alike, including my own Seventh-day Adventist denomination.

From this insight it was only one step to the realization that the problem of doctrinal development required the serious attention of trained theologians. What was needed were detailed and precise information as well as adequate methodological tools for dealing properly with the historical facts as well as the contemporary challenge of doctrinal change. The latter had received renewed attention under the impact of Vatican Council II's clarion call for the aggiornamento of the Roman Catholic Church (1962-1965).

Relating the issue of doctrinal continuity and change to my own church and its history resulted in an innovative and quite extensive study on "Change in Seventh-day Adventist Theology: A Study of the Problem of Doctrinal Development." It was accepted as doctoral dissertation for the ThD degree at Andrews University (Michigan, USA) in 1995. The 600pp-study consists of two parts of unequal length: Part I offers a concise and preliminary inquiry into the issues of continuity and change in Christian doctrine, laying the foundation for Part II, which presents a detailed historical investigation of continuity and change in Adventist theology.

In 1999 and 2000, respectively, the dissertation was published by Peter Lang in a slightly adapted form in two books, specially geared to historians and theologians studying doctrinal change, on one side, and interested Adventist readers (teachers, students, and laypersons alike), on the other. The last copy sold early this year, which raised the question of whether or not a republication was called for.

Several reasons suggest it. Firstly, the book is still used as a textbook in Adventist schools (including Friedensau Adventist University), regarded by some as a definitive text for students of Adventist history and theology. Secondly, the high selling price was forbidding from a student budget's perspective. Thirdly, the publication in two volumes left both wanting in a sense like an unfinished artwork. For these reasons, the dissertation is now published again in unabridged form as an inexpensive reprint. The reissue as print on demand and as e-book makes it also economically suitable.

But is this volume still up-to-date, considering that its research was undertaken several decades ago and that it uses 1985 as the cut-off date for its historical analysis? Actually, *Dynamic Truth* was not only the first Adventist study of doctrinal development, but still is the only extensive academic investigation of its kind. Apart from George Knight's commendable *In Search for Identity* (2000), no Adventist theologian has traced the various phases of Adventism's theological journey in a monograph. And no one at all has studied the various Adventist responses to change in the light of the different models and theories on doctrinal development developed by Christian theologians over the centuries.

While the first part of the book as well as the concluding chapters 5 and 6 – dealing with Adventist conceptions of doctrinal change including Ellen White's view on it – are unparalleled in Adventist literature, chapter 4 may be considered somewhat outdated. Not only is its historical survey on Adventist doctrinal developments limited to about a dozen examples of growth and change, none of them reaching beyond 1985. Since then, quite a number of research papers and even doctoral dissertations have been written, bringing to light further details on these case studies and discussing other doctrinal topics as well.

However, the case studies presented in this volume still serve as illustrations of its main points, amply demonstrating the reality, extent, nature, and direction of doctrinal development in Adventist history. They should be supplemented with, and amplified by, other studies, which will further strengthen the argument of this book.

Dynamic Truth is presented in the hope of further contributing towards the much-needed theological reflection on the multifaceted and complex issue of doctrinal development, particularly within the Seventh-day Adventist Church. In view of the challenges posed to the Christian faith by secularized societies, relativistic world views, and pluralistic theologies, it is essential to have a clear understanding of both the issues involved in, and the options available with regard to, the perennial and intricate problem of doctrinal continuity and change. Beyond that, it may also serve as a case study on doctrinal development from the perspective of a relatively young Protestant denomination. To note how a conservative church is grappling with unexpected and considerable doctrinal changes may be eye-opening, not just for its own adherents, but for the wider Christian community as well. It is to this end that *Dynamic Truth* is published.

I am particularly thankful to my student assistant, Philip Nern, for his editorial help; to my colleague, Stefan Höschele, for his perusal of the manuscript; and to the Institute of Adventist Studies for supporting the project. As with the original manuscript, the most important acknowledgment is due to the abundantly gracious and inexhaustible Source of all life and achievement. *Soli Deo Gloria.*

Rolf J. Pöhler, MDiv, ThD
Professor of Systematic Theology
Friedensau Adventist University
July 2020

Introduction

I would exchange a thousand errors for one truth!

John Nevins Andrews

From the beginning of my studies I have made it a rule that
whenever I come to know a sounder opinion on an issue, I will
gladly and humbly give up the first opinion knowing that what
we know is very little in comparison to what we do not know.

Jan Hus

Background and Context

As in the life of individuals, so also in the corporate existence of institutions and
groups, churches and nations, crisis situations may develop that have an up-setting
and disconcerting effect upon the people involved. From its inception, the history
of the Christian church is replete with examples of this, one of the best known being
the Protestant Reformation and its aftermath of the sixteenth century.

In spite of its recent origin, the Seventh-day Adventist Church has not been
exempt from such times of crisis. Some of these involved controversies regarding
doctrines whose traditional understanding was questioned by some within the
community of faith. Apart from the years following the great disappointment of
1844, the most important and best known of these periods is tied to the year 1888.
In this century, similar crisis situations occurred when some Adventists[1] challenged
certain historic beliefs of the church.[2]

This study was written in the wake of another, more recent one of these
theological controversies that proved quite traumatic for a number of Adventists
involved in it.[3] Judged from the past, similar crises should rather be expected in the

---

1   The short term Adventist(s) as a synonym for the longer, and more accurate, phrase Seventh-
     day Adventist(s) is used in this study, except when dealing with the Millerite phase of the
     Advent movement.

2   During the first decade of this century, J. H. Kellogg and A. F. Ballenger caused a major stir
     in the church involving pan(en)theistic notions of God and the uniquely Adventist doctrine
     of the heavenly sanctuary. In the 1930s, the Australian pastor W. W. Fletcher and the
     European church leader L. R. Conradi fell out with their denomination when they openly
     rejected the authority of the prophet Ellen White. For more details, see below, pp. 231-232,
     and 235.

3   The controversy centered on the doctrinal views of former Adventist Robert D. Brinsmead,
     theologian Desmond Ford, and pastor Walter T. Rea. In the main, it involved questions of

future. However that may be, what usually seems involved in such conflicts is the theology, the authority, and the identity of the Seventh-day Adventist Church.

In other words, what we are dealing with is a threefold challenge and potential crisis situation: (1) a crisis of theology challenging the traditional and distinctive body of beliefs the church has inherited from its founding fathers; (2) a crisis of authority questioning whether the powers that be are indeed ordained of God to exercise their role in a given manner in the church; and (3) a crisis of identity putting in question the historic and unique self-understanding of the church.[4] It has become rather commonplace for Adventists in some parts of the world to speak of the existence of an identity crisis in the church.[5]

What lies at the bottom of this threefold challenge is, in fact, a crisis of change. The widening gap between the movement's founders and their spiritual descendants, the growing sense of history and cultural change, and the discovery of certain modifications in the church's heritage of faith over the years are raising nagging questions as to the timeless validity and continuing relevance of the message, mission,

soteriology, prophetic interpretation, and the authority of Ellen G. White. More than 100 pastors left the ministry, or even the church, either voluntarily or under pressure; several thousand church members went into open or inner emigration by withholding their assent to certain church teachings or even founding new congregations. However, the long-term effects of this crisis on the Adventist Church seem not to have been very significant. The situation was reflected in the titles of several publications dealing with conditions in the church. See, e.g., Arthur LeRoy Moore, *Theology in Crisis: Or Ellen G. White's Concept of Righteousness by Faith as It Relates to Contemporary SDA Issues* (Corpus Christi, Tex.: Life Seminars, 1980); "Must the Crisis Continue?" *Spectrum* 11:3 (1981): 44-52; Richard Emmerson, "The Continuing Crisis," *Spectrum* 12:1 (1981): 40-44; "Adventist Colleges Under Siege," *Spectrum* 13:2 (1982): 4-18; Desmond Ford and Gillian Ford, *The Adventist Crisis of Spiritual Identity* (Newcastle, Calif.: Desmond Ford Publ., 1982); and Alexander LaBreque, "Adventism in Crisis," *Evangelica*, March 1983, 17-18.

4   As in the case of an individual, a community (like a family or a church) needs a clear and healthy sense of identity which involves at least the following five dimensions: self-acceptance (Who am I?), relationships (Where do I belong?), origins (Where do I come from?), purpose/mission (What am I here for?), and goals (Where am I going?).

5   N. Gordon Thomas, for example, openly declared in the general church paper, "We Adventists face an identity crisis ... This identity crisis may be a major factor behind the attempted reinterpretation and reevaluation that now disturbs our church" ("The Almost Chosen," *AR*, 14 January 1982, 4). Already in 1969, James J. Londis had applied this expression to Adventists ("We Don't All Worship the Same God," *RH*, 23 October 1969, 5). See also Thomas Steininger, "Adventistische Identität," *Adventecho*, 1 April 1983, 4-5. More recently, Clifford Goldstein asserted, "Adventism today is suffering an identity crisis, a theological crisis, and a spiritual crisis" (*False Balances* [Boise, Idaho: PPPA, 1992], 16). Similarly, Jack W. Provonsha reflected on "the crisis of identity" that the church currently faces; he concluded that "the Seventh-day Adventist movement, at least in the First World, may be facing its greatest crisis since the disappointment of 1844" (*A Remnant in Crisis* [Hagerstown, Md.: RHPA, 1993], 7, 166).

and self-understanding of the church.[6] These tensions are heightened by the fact that Western societies have largely become secular and pluralistic segments in a heterogeneous world making it all the more difficult for any Christian denomination to maintain unity of faith, conformity of practice, and singularity of purpose.[7]

Thus, any new generation of believers needs, in a sense, to establish anew its relationship to the inheritance received from its spiritual progenitors.[8] But can, or should, these traditions be modified and adapted to new situations? Must they perhaps even be discarded and replaced by new beliefs? Is change necessary for the growth and advancement of the church, or rather does it constitute an impediment to it threatening its very existence and self-identity? These are questions raised among Seventh-day Adventists today.

Psychologically speaking, people generally tend to resist change.[9] Besides, in matters of religion, doctrinal adaptations and revisions seem to stand in irreconcilable conflict with the concept of an eternal and revealed truth.[10] At the same time, however, the winds of change have repeatedly been blowing with force, if not on the

6   This issue was addressed in a book prepared for the delegates to the 53d Session of the General Conference of SDAs, Dallas, Texas, 1980. See Gottfried Oosterwal et al., *Servants for Christ: The Adventist Church Facing the '80s*, ed. Robert E. Firth (Berrien Springs, Mich.: Andrews University Press, 1980). For a perceptive description of the "chasm between faith and history of faith" and of the "bridge-building that is essential to care for the chasm," see Arthur N. Patrick, "Does Our Past Embarrass Us?" *Ministry*, April 1991, 7-10. "Too often we tend to forget the ups and downs of the past, and imagine that our doctrines have been static. This failure to perceive the nature and extent of historical development of faith, doctrine, and practice in the Adventist Church has caused a chasm of misunderstanding between the faith of many Adventists and the realities of their heritage" (ibid., 8).

7   That Adventists are becoming increasingly aware of the secular and pluralistic character of the contemporary world is indicated by several publications. See Humberto M. Rasi and Fritz Guy, eds., *Meeting the Secular Mind: Some Adventist Perspectives*, Selected Working Papers of the Committee on Secularism of the General Conference of Seventh-day Adventists 1981-1985, 2d ed. (Berrien Springs, Mich.: Andrews University Press, 1987); Caleb Rosado, *Broken Walls*, North American Division Series on Church Leadership (Boise, Idaho: PPPA, 1990); Rolf J. Pöhler, "Religious Pluralism: A Challenge to the Contemporary Church," in *Cast the Net on the Right Side: Seventh-day Adventists Face the "Isms,"* ed. Richard Lehmann, Jack Mahon, and Borge Schantz (Newbold College, Bracknell, Berks, England: European Institute of World Mission, 1993), 81-89; and Michael Pearson, "The Problem of Secularism," ibid., 90-101. See also below, pp. 243-245.

8   "It is of the essence of Christian theology, from its very beginning, that it investigate ever anew its relevance to the world and its identity in Christ" (Jürgen Moltmann, "Christian Theology and Its Problem Today," *Reformed World* 32 [1972-1973]: 6, 5-16).

9   "No one really likes the new. We are afraid of it" (Eric Hoffer, *The Ordeal of Change* [New York: Harper & Row, 1952/1963], 3).

10   "The changing Church poses a problem to the abiding character of the christian [sic] faith. Many people are troubled by the changes going on in the life and teaching of the Church. They wonder how they can still cling to the unchanging truth of the christian [sic] faith" (Gregory Baum, *Faith and Doctrine: A Contemporary View* [Paramus, N.J.: Newman Press, 1969], 9).

Adventist church premises, then certainly throughout Christendom in general – not to the least in recent decades.[11]

There are those who see this not merely as a dangerous threat but rather as a welcome opportunity for the Christian church.[12]

> Crisis is a part of life – of that which is vital, dynamic, moving forward ... It is a peak point of decisiveness which either ushers in a significant spurt of growth or a retardation that ranges from stagnation to disintegration or extinction.[13]

So, in spite of the possible risks involved, the Christian church in general, and the Seventh-day Adventist Church in particular, should face the issue of doctrinal change unhesitatingly – at least, if they want to provide reliable answers to the questions raised by the crises of change. In the view of a renowned church historian, "no task confronting Christian theology today is more vital than the demand that it face this issue squarely."[14] It is in response to Pelikan's challenge that this work was written.

Scope and Purpose

In order to be prepared for and properly respond to the periodic challenges of change, the church needs to understand the circumstances as well as the possible reasons and driving forces behind them.[15] To this end, an analysis of doctrinal developments in

---

11 "Every age in human history is an age of transition, but in some ages the transition is more abrupt and disconcerting than in others" (F. F. Bruce, "The Kerygma of Hebrews," *Interpretation* 23:1 [1969]: 17, 3-19). Especially since Vatican Council II (1959-1965), the Roman Catholic Church has experienced such a crisis of change. What was hailed by some as the long-overdue *aggiornamento* (updating and renewal) of the church was strongly opposed by others who feared that the walls of doctrinal certainty and authority were crumbling before their very eyes. (See George A. Lindbeck, *The Future of Roman Catholic Theology: Vatican II: Catalyst for Change* [Philadelphia: Fortress Press, 1968]; Langdon Gilkey, *Catholicism Confronts Modernity: A Protestant View* [New York: Seabury Press, 1975]; and Raymond E. Brown, *Biblical Reflections on Crises Facing the Church* [New York, and Paramus, N.J.: Paulist Press, 1975]). In the 1970s, the Lutheran Church-Missouri Synod got involved in a dispute over its doctrine of inspiration; it was interpreted by observers as a crisis of change (Robert W. Jenson, "Missouri and the Existential Fear of Change," *Dialog* 14 [1975]: 247-250).

12 Interestingly, the Chinese word for crisis contains two characters, one denoting danger, the other opportunity.

13 Mary-John Mananzan, "Crisis as a Necessary Impetus to Spiritual Growth," in *Traditio – Krisis – Renovatio aus theologischer Sicht*, Festschrift Winfried Zeller zum 65. Geburtstag, ed. Bernd Jaspert and Rudolf Mohr (Marburg: N. G. Elwert, 1976), 560-561. Cf. Bernd Jaspert, "'Krise' als kirchengeschichtliche Kategorie," ibid., 24-40; and Paulus Gordan, "Identitätskrise und Kontinuität," ibid., 454-462.

14 Jaroslav Pelikan, "Theology and Change," *Cross Currents* 19 (1969): 384.

15 "To stay relevant, the church must not only respond to change; it must also anticipate change, for change challenges leadership to deal more effectively with differences" (Rosado, 120).

the history of the Seventh-day Adventist Church and of the various theological positions regarding doctrinal continuity and change could contribute significantly.

More specifically, this document pursues a twofold objective. In the first place, it discusses the problem of doctrinal continuity and change as treated in theological literature in general in order to gain a full understanding of both the issues involved and the possible solutions available for them. By studying Seventh-day Adventism in the wider context and in the light of the history of Christian theology as a whole, the study provides an interpretative framework that may help both Adventists and those studying Adventism to better understand the history and development of the denomination (Part I).

In the second place, the study investigates the extent, nature, and direction of doctrinal developments that have occurred in the history of the Seventh-day Adventist Church from its inception until recent years. Over against this backdrop, the document then analyzes the reactions to whatever doctrinal changes were occurring and the conceptions of doctrinal development advanced within the church (Part II). It is hoped that this provides an adequate and solid foundation on which a hermeneutical concept of doctrinal development may be built within the particular context of Adventist theology.

In order to avoid possible misunderstandings and false, or exaggerated, expectations, it may also be helpful to indicate at the outset what this study does not intend to accomplish.

First, the historical analysis of doctrinal developments does not investigate the manner in which the various Adventist teachings originally came into existence. Instead, it examines how and, to some degree, also why certain of these teachings developed and changed after they did already exist in some, however rudimentary, form. As is shown in Part One, the term doctrinal development as used in theological hermeneutics denotes not the mode of formation but the successive transformation of a doctrine. In other words, it deals with the modification and growth of a teaching following its inception or birth.

Second, this work does not provide an exhaustive treatment of the struggle for doctrinal continuity and change within Seventh-day Adventism. Neither does it discuss all the published or unpublished views advanced in this international and, indeed, worldwide denomination, nor does it analyze the many instances where proposed doctrinal changes were resisted and the historic understanding of the church was confirmed. Its focus lies rather on selected doctrinal modifications and their interpretation within the church insofar as they shed light on the theological problem of development.[16] In order to keep a proper perspective, the year 1985 has been chosen as the cut-off date for the historical investigation of doctrinal change.[17]

The historical importance of American Adventism for, and its continuing influence on, the teachings and policies of the denomination provides the rationale for limiting this work, in the main, to the purview of English-speaking North America. Occasionally this horizon is widened by the input from the author's personal Western European background. Today, both of these regions together represent approximately 12% of the worldwide membership of the Adventist church.[18]

Third, it should also be clear that the historical analysis of doctrinal developments within Adventism does not provide a criterion for possible doctrinal changes in the future. While such an analysis may and, most likely, will have implications for a theology of doctrinal development, any challenge to the teachings of Seventh-day Adventists must be evaluated separately and on its own ground. In other words, doctrinal changes in the past do not, of themselves, provide any justification for doctrinal revisions in the present or in the future.[19]

Finally, it should be noted that this study does not attempt to develop or present an Adventist theology of doctrinal development. As needed as this may be, its requirements would go beyond the limits of this investigation and must, therefore, await another opportunity.[20]

16 In other words, the study does not so much discuss the problem of continuity, for doctrinal continuity and identity are not the crucial issues but rather to be expected in Christian faith. Instead, it addresses primarily the question of doctrinal development and change because this is where the knotty problem actually lies.

17 Choosing the year 1985 as the cut-off date for this study allows consideration of both the 1980 General Conference at Dallas (which endorsed a new version of the Fundamental Beliefs of SDAs) and the 1980 Glacier View Conference (which discussed a number of doctrinal issues important to SDAs) as well as the aftermath of these historic meetings. Because of the inherent artificiality of any cut-off date, reference has been made, in a few cases, to views publicized in even more recent years. In general, however, the 1980 Statement of Fundamental Beliefs of SDAs is treated as the *terminus ad quem* of this investigation. To venture upon any judgment regarding doctrinal developments during the last decade would be rather speculative and, possibly, premature. It could also result in a confusion of tentative ideas and passing theological trends with lasting doctrinal changes.

18 As far as Adventist doctrines are concerned, they still reflect a strong influence of Western thinking. They are, however, officially affirmed by the representatives of the world church convened at a General Conference.

19 While history clearly demonstrates the reality and possibility of doctrinal developments, it says nothing about the desirability or even necessity of particular doctrinal changes. For a discussion of the importance of the scientific study of history for an adequate theology of doctrinal development, see below, pp. 37-45.

20 Originally, it had been my intention to add a third part to the dissertation entitled "Towards an Adventist Theology of Doctrinal Development: Hermeneutical Reflections." This idea was given up, however, because it would have about doubled the size of the study. I therefore decided to limit myself to the present two parts, especially as I consider them foundational to any hermeneutical reflection on the issue of doctrinal continuity and change.

Methods and Presuppositions

In dealing with its subject matter, this book proceeds in a triad of objective information and clarification, historical illustration and demonstration, as well as critical interpretation and evaluation.

Part I provides the background and foundation of the study. It contains a preliminary inquiry into the many-faceted problem of doctrinal change (chapter 1), followed by a historical-genetic survey of the scholarly and involved debate on doctrinal development (chapter 2), as well as a systematic-typological classification of the numerous theories of doctrinal continuity and change (chapter 3).

Part II constitutes the center and crux of the study. First, it presents a historical investigation and analysis of some noteworthy theological developments within Seventh-day Adventism as well as of certain sociological factors that seem to have been involved in them (chapter 4). Then, it surveys and assesses what Adventist authors up to now have written on the issue of doctrinal continuity and change (chapter 5). Finally, it takes a closer look both at Ellen G. White's involvement in doctrinal development and her views on doctrinal continuity and change (chapter 6).

In brief, then, this work proceeds inductively by means of historical description and critical analysis.[21] However, insofar as there are certain basic and unavoidable premises influencing all scholarly research, this study openly acknowledges that it has been written from the perspective of an involved and committed "insider"[22] whose loyalty to his church is only surpassed by his desire to follow truth wherever it may lead. Combining historical criticism and personal faith, I aim at unbiased objectivity but make no claim to detached neutrality.[23]

To approach one's own denomination in a scholarly fashion is beset by several risks. On the one hand, scholars may be tempted to treat the history and theology of their church in a too benign fashion by failing to discuss unpleasant historical facts, glossing over obvious weaknesses, or downplaying questionable theological notions – all in the name of scholarly neutrality. In the attempt to avoid such hidden partisanship, they may, on the other hand, adopt a hypercritical stance denouncing

---

21 "To write history of any sort is to render judgments of some sort" (Mark A. Noll, "Rethinking Restorationism: A Review Article," *Reformed Journal* 39 [November 1989]: 20).

22 "All judgment in history is 'sectarian' in that it depends upon some larger conception of what is true and what is false" (ibid.).

23 The beauty of the stained-glass windows of a cathedral can be fully appreciated only when they are looked at from inside the building while the light of the outside world is shining in. Similarly, to understand the value of one's own churchly traditions, one has to analyze them from within but in the light of the Scriptures and of theological scholarship at large. For a thoughtful essay on the meaning of "objectivity" in the context of historical scholarship and on the possibility of reconciling it with religious commitments on the part of the Christian scholar, see M. Howard Rienstra, "History, Objectivity, and the Christian Scholar," in *History and Historical Understanding*, ed. C. T. McIntire and Ronald A. Wells (Grand Rapids: Eerdmans, 1984), 69-82.

seeming historical blunders and attacking alleged theological aberrations – again in the name of scientific objectivity.

Serious scholarly works will avoid both of these pitfalls. As historians, scholars will analyze the sources carefully and critically and then describe what the facts appear to be as objectively as possible. As theologians, they will meticulously reflect on the data and take a stand without hiding the premises influencing their thinking. They will not try to please friend or foe but serve the truth to the best of their ability. This book makes a deliberate attempt to live up, as far as possible, to this goal.[24] After all, Adventists have been told,

> we have nothing to hide in our history. We have a heritage worth protecting. The best way for the church to protect it is to deal candidly with the controversial and problematic before we are forced to do so by critics. In the long run, the scholars who have the sources, the courage, and the competence to deal with all the evidence can do most for the cause of truth and the nourishment of faith.[25]

24 For an elaboration of this methodology in the context of historical studies on Seventh-day Adventism, see Rolf J. Pöhler, "The Adventist Historian between Criticism and Faith [1990]," TMs; publ. in B. Oestreich, H. Rolly, and W. Kabus, eds., *Glaube und Zukunftsgestaltung: Festschrift zum hundertjährigen Bestehen der Theologischen Hochschule Friedensau.* Aufsätze zu Theologie, Sozialwissenschaften und Musik (Frankfurt, Berlin, New York: Peter Lang, 1999), 203-210.

25 *A Discussion and Review of Prophetess of Health* (Washington, D.C.: Ellen G. White Estate, General Conference [of SDAs], 1976), 15.

Part I

Continuity and Change in Christian Doctrine

Chapter 1

The Problem of Doctrinal Development

All things move and nothing stands still.

Heraclitus of Ephesus

Doctrine belongs to God, not to us; and we are called only as its ministers. Therefore, we cannot give up or change even one dot of it.

Martin Luther

Introduction

Among the many issues that theologians have addressed through the centuries, there may be few possessing greater ramifications than the intricate problem of the development of Christian doctrine. Its universal scope, its complex nature, and its hermeneutical crux are placing Christian theology in a predicament from which it could escape only at the price of tampering with either historical facts or biblical truths.

Still, many Christians, being unaware of its true import, do not seem to perceive the seriousness of the problem. In fact, until the eighteenth century even theologians apparently did not understand the true nature of this puzzling question. It was only with the rise of historical consciousness and the ensuing study of history that the problem of doctrinal development became known in its full extent and was seen as an object of serious theological research.

In recent decades, an avalanche of literature on the issue has hit the libraries of universities and theological seminaries providing students with a wealth of historical information and thoughtful reflection, which render the neglect of this vital theological question almost inexcusable.[1] Continuity and change, development and progress, doctrine and theology – these are some of the key terms used in the discussion of the issue. As they are also crucial for this study, it is advisable first to clarify and define these terms.

It is the purpose of this first chapter to explain and define the problem of doctrinal development as well as to demonstrate its close relationship to the scientific study of history.

---

1   For examples, see the bibliography; cf. also below, p. 46, n. 63.

Clarification and Definition of Key Terms

Continuity and Change

If we were to characterize our contemporary world, it could wittily be done by the familiar phrase "Subject to change without notice." Unquestionably, we live in an age of rapid and radical change. Scientific discoveries and technological break-throughs, the sudden destabilization of political and economic systems, the trans-formation of the social structures of society, and the abandonment of traditional patterns of thought and behavior – all are occurring today in such rapid succession and with such velocity that, in the minds of many, change seems to have become almost the only certain and constant factor of modern life.[2] One is reminded of the ancient dictum of Greek philosophy – πάντα ρεῖ – according to which "all things are in flux."[3] A discerning observer of modernity has expressed this widespread feeling in the following way:

> Change is the basic reality of history; it is in some way the character of whatever being there is. The flux of becoming, not the changelessness of being, characterizes our exis-tence and that of our world. All is in process through time, and nothing stands still.[4]

And yet, even the disturbing idea that there is nothing permanent except change, which so succinctly summarizes much of modern man's experience and thought,

---

2   "The only continuity modern man knows," J. G. Lawler writes, is "the continuity of discontinuity" ("The Future of Belief Debate," in *New Theology, No. 5,* ed. M. E. Marty and D. G. Peerman [New York: Macmillan, 1968; London: Collier-Macmillan, 1968], 183). Among the large variety of changes experienced by humankind are those of a political, economic, technological, scientific, ecological, demographic, organizational, institutional, social, cultural, religious, moral, psychological, behavioral, attitudinal, personal, and existential nature; thus, theological and doctrinal changes are only two out of many possible types of change. For an excellent discussion on the philosophical notion of change, see Milic Capek, "Change," *Encyclopedia of Philosophy,* 1967 ed., 2:75-79. For a succinct description of the modern and contemporary sense of change, see Langdon Gilkey, "Theology and the Future," *Andover Newton Quarterly* 71 (1977): 250-257.

3   Actually, this phrase does not quite accurately represent the thought of the Greek philosopher Heraclitus of Ephesus (about 500 B.C.) to whom it has been ascribed. For Heraclitus' ob-servation, "upon those who step into the same rivers different and again different waters flow" (Fragments on the Cosmos, No. 12), instead of implying that all things are in constant flux, served rather to illustrate the fact that stability underlies all change. But while Heraclitus wanted to emphasize the coincidence of continuity and change, Plato and all successive ancient interpreters of Heraclitus took his river analogy to mean that all things are constantly changing. Still, their error was one of emphasis, not of principle, as Heraclitus apparently held that everything must eventually change. See Heraclitus, *The Cosmic Fragments,* ed. with an Introduction and Commentary by G. S. Kirk (Cambridge: University Press, 1962), 366-384.

4   Gilkey, *Catholicism Confronts Modernity,* 5.

clearly implies that there does exist something like permanence and continuity, if not sameness or identity.[5] In fact, in most instances where change occurs, it happens to something that remains in a very real sense the same, though changing some of its characteristics.[6] This is the case whenever we speak of growth and development, advance and progress, movement and transition, and even transformation and metamorphosis.

The only occurrences of total or absolute change, i.e., of change without continuity, are creation out of nothing *(creatio ex nihilo)* and total annihilation, instances of change from being to non-being, and vice versa. This means that the ideas of continuity (which implies a certain permanence, stability, and even a degree of sameness or identity) and change are not, in fact, mutually exclusive but rather complementary categories of thought – except for the instances of complete identity and total change, respectively.

Almost from the beginning of the attempt to systematically analyze and understand the world in which we live, humanity has been wrestling with the problem of permanence and development, identity and change. One can even say that Western philosophy originated in the endeavor to explain the reality of a constantly changing universe without abandoning the notion of constant and unchanging truth.

There were three basic answers given by the ancient Greek philosophers to the problem of continuity and change.[7] On the one hand, *Heraclitus* (c. 500 B.C.) saw the world in a state of flux marked by continuity and change; he denied that in reality anything remained ultimately unchanged.[8] On the other hand, *Parmenides* (born c. 510 B.C.), the founder of the Eleatic school, rejected the idea that everything eventually changes, teaching instead that nothing changes. Holding to the concept of an eternally changeless and motionless universe, he regarded the phenomenon of change (i.e., of motion, becoming, and multiplicity) as an illusion, as mere appearance without reality or being. This rejection as absurd of the very concept of change was continued by Parmenides's disciple *Zeno* (born c. 489 B.C.) by means of his four famous arguments.[9]

---

5   The term identity is derived from the Latin word *idem*, meaning "the same." For a helpful and succinct discussion of the philosophical notion of identity, see Avrum Stroll, "Identity," *Encyclopedia of Philosophy*, 1967 ed., 4:121-124.

6   Ibid., 121: "It seems a matter of logic that when someone truly asserts of something that it is changing, he thereby implies that there is a 'something' which remains unchanged and unaffected by the transformations 'it' undergoes." This can be illustrated by the everyday exclamation "Oh, have you changed" which expresses both surprise at someone's transformation and recognition of his identity.

7   The following summary is based, in part, on Samuel Enoch Stumpf, *Socrates to Sartre: A History of Philosophy*, 2d ed. (New York: McGraw-Hill, 1975), 3-113 passim.

8   This view gave *Protagoras* and the other *Sophists* the philosophical rationale for their skepticism and moral relativism.

9   They are the paradox of the racecourse, of the flying arrow, of the three passenger cars, and of the race between Achilles and the tortoise. Mention should also be made of some other Greek philosophers of the 5th and 4th centuries B.C. who further contributed to the philosophical

Plato (428/27-348/47 B.C.), the father of Western philosophy, presented a kind of intermediate position by distinguishing between two separate and distinct levels of being: the changeless, spiritual world of intelligible things and the transitory world of sensible things. In his doctrine of ideas, Plato expressed this distinction between immutable, unchangeable reality and changeable appearances in classic form.

Plato's most famous and influential disciple *Aristotle* (384-322 B.C.) rejected the Platonic notion of the separate existence of changeless forms and mutable things. Instead, he defined substance as a composite of unchanging matter (an enduring, underlying substratum) and changing form.[10] This, in turn, led him to distinguish between two types of change: (1) accidental change in which there occurs either a qualitative, quantitative, or local alteration while the essential nature of a thing remains identical; and (2) substantial change in which the primary essence of a thing changes into something else.[11] Thus, at the zenith of ancient philosophy there existed an elaborate theory of continuity and change that would decisively influence Christian theology in later centuries.[12]

discussion of change. They either synthesized the contributions of their predecessors (Empedocles) or presented an essentially materialistic worldview according to which reality is nothing but atoms moving in space (the atomistic school of Leucippus and Democritus).

10   See *Aristotle Dictionary*, ed. Thomas P. Kiernan (New York: Philosophical Library, 1962), s.v. "On Generation and Corruption," and "Metaphysics." Aristotle's view – according to which matter is never found without form (contrasting with Plato who argued that eternal Ideas exist quite independently of any particular appearances) – as well as his insistence on the idea that the objective reality of a thing's substance exists only in the concrete things themselves can possibly be of major importance in a discussion of the relationship between divine revelation and the human expression of revealed truth.

11   According to Aristotle, accidental change includes alterations/modifications in color, size, and shape, as well as the processes of growth, increase, diminuation, aging, development, and motion, while generation (coming to be) and annihilation (ceasing to be) are incidents of substantial, fundamental, or radical change. Aristotle's distinction between matter and form as well as his differentiation between accidental and substantial change may be of special interest in the attempt to distinguish between the essential content and the nonessential form of a doctrinal statement. It should also be noted that according to an Aristotelean model, a doctrine may quantitatively as well as qualitatively change while still being substantially the same.

12   See below, pp. 56-64. On the other hand, mediated through A. N. Whitehead's (1861-1947) process philosophy, which is reminiscent of Heraclitus, the notion of permanent change has gained widespread recognition among contemporary theologians. Whitehead denied the existence of fixed essences in nature and rejected the medieval philosophy of Being. To him, reality consists of continually changing entities devoid of permanent identity but rather always in the process of becoming. His three main speculative works on metaphysics are *Science and the Modern World* (1925), *Process and Reality* (1929), and *Adventures of Ideas* (1933). What is true of contemporary philosophical thought can, thus, also be said of today's Christian theology, viz., that "although the dialogue between Parmenides and Heraclitus is still going on, the former is now much less favored than the latter" (Capek, 79).

In this book, the term change is used in the sense of a variation or mutation[13] that modifies certain characteristics of a thing without thereby destroying the substantial identity of the object in its changed or unchanged state.[14] Continuity, in turn, refers to some kind of permanence and sameness short of complete identity.

As can readily be seen, change may occur in varying degrees of intensity ranging from being almost imperceptible to being radical. In distinction from totally discontinuous, absolute changes from being to non-being, and vice versa, the expression radical change is employed here in the sense of essential alterations of an object, with continuity being limited to non-essential or accidental features.

In brief, continuity and change are treated here, not as mutually exclusive, but rather as contrasting terms which, in most cases, imply each other by expressing the complementary concepts of perpetuity (i.e., of remaining) and alteration (i.e., of becoming different).

Development and Progress

While the philosophical concepts of continuity and change had already been developed by the ancient Greek thinkers of the fifth and fourth centuries B.C., the related ideas of development and progress did not receive full attention until the eighteenth and nineteenth centuries A.D. It was then that, sparked by the growing awareness of the process of time and history, there arose such diverse movements as romantic and objective idealism (Schlegel, Hegel), scientific evolutionism (Darwin), positivist scientism (Comte), and dialectical materialism (Marx). They all resorted to the metaphors of development and progress in order to come to grips with intellectual, social, or natural history by giving meaning and direction to its fluctuating process.

The importance of the new sense of history for the study of doctrinal development and the impact these movements had on the discussion of the problem of change are described later.[15] What is of interest here is the meaning of the terms development and progress in contrast to the related notion of change.

To begin with, both progress and development presuppose the possibility of changes occurring in time and history; in fact, they imply that some change has indeed taken place. For, to speak of development is *nolens volens* to speak of change, however narrowly one may wish to define the latter. This means that whoever accepts

---

13 *Mutatio* is the Latin word for change. Thus, to speak of the immutability of dogma is to deny the possibility of any true doctrinal change.

14 We are, of course, only interested in real changes, i.e., modifications in an object itself, and not in apparent changes, which simply refer to alterations in the observing subject's relationship to a thing.

15 See below, pp. 37-45, 64-79. It should be noted that just as there is a necessary correlation between change and time (for it is only in time that change can occur), so it was only with the growing realization of the flow of time and history that the related idea of development took hold upon philosophical and theological thought.

the concept of doctrinal development cannot with any logical consistency rule out the idea of doctrinal change *in toto*. At the same time, the terms progress and development imply a substantial degree of permanence and identity. For this reason, they can even be used as rough equivalents to the expression continuity and change.

On the other hand, progress and development differ from each other in that the first refers to the quality and direction of change, while the second more specifically deals with its manner and mode. For instance, change may not always lend itself to an optimistic appraisal in terms of progress and advance. Rather it may have to be described in a more pessimistic way as regression, decline, or degeneration. In other words, to speak of progress is to interpret a certain development positively as a forward-moving improvement or a change for the better in contradistinction to both its neutral description in terms of mere change and its negative evaluation as a backward-moving deterioration or maldevelopment.[16]

The idea of development, commonly regarded as synonymous with the notion of progress connoting advance and improvement, more exactly has to do with the way in which changes take place. For to develop means literally to unfold or unwrap something that had been wrapped up or enveloped. Thus, development carries the connotation of making something invisible/hidden visible/manifest by bringing out its latent characteristics or possibilities.

---

16   The notion of decline seems to have been common to all ancient civilizations. It is found, e.g., in the biblical story of creation and the fall as well as in Hesiod's (c. 700 B.C.) view of a bygone golden age. Similar views of successive deteriorations of the state of the world can be found in Hinduistic and Parsee thought (see Helmuth von Glasenapp, *Die nichtchristlichen Religionen* [Frankfurt: Fischer Bücherei, 1957], 158-159, 294-296) and in apocalyptic writings (see, e.g., Dan 2). In the Far East, Confucianism asserted that older is better. Later the notion of decline became typical of reform movements within Christianity, shaped Protestant thought for centuries, and also characterized Harnack's view of *Dogmengeschichte*.

On the other hand, the modern philosophical idea of progress, which can be viewed as a secularized form of the Christian belief in divine providence, has roots in Hellenistic (Epicurean and Stoic) philosophy, Judaism, and Christian eschatology (chiliasm). In spite of its general decline, due to the shock of World War I and its aftermath, it has been gaining new ground among Christian thinkers, not to the least under the influence of the French Jesuit scientist and theologian Teilhard de Chardin (1881-1955). For in-depth treatments of the meaning and development of the philosophical notion of progress, see John Baillie, *The Belief in Progress* (New York: Charles Scribner's Sons, 1950); J. B. Bury, *The Idea of Progress: An Inquiry into Its Origin and Growth* (New York: Macmillan, 1932; reprint, New York: Dover Publ., 1955); Ludwig Edelstein, *The Idea of Progress in Classical Antiquity* (Baltimore: Johns Hopkins Press, 1967); W. R. Inge, *The Idea of Progress* (Oxford: Clarendon Clarendon, 1920); Robert Nisbet, *History of the Idea of Progress* (New York: Basic Books, 1980); W. Warren Wagar, ed., *The Idea of Progress since the Renaissance* (New York: Wiley, 1969); and idem, *Good Tidings: The Belief in Progress from Darwin to Marcuse* (Bloomington, Ind.: Univ. Press, 1972). Though practically synonymous in meaning, the terms progress and progression can also be distinguished in that the first clearly implies the idea of betterment while the latter may be used in a more neutral sense to indicate simply the onward-moving nature of a thing. Cf. *Webster's New Dictionary of Synonyms* (1984), s.v. "Progress."

Such an *explicatio*, however, may take place in various ways – through growth (ontogenesis), differentiation, maturation, metamorphosis, macroevolution (phylogenesis), microevolution, and the like. Therefore, the mere term development, while indicating that change takes place through explicating some implicit quality or potential, is still too vague linguistically to determine the exact manner and intensity in which the unfolding is thought to occur.[17]

The concept of doctrinal development can be understood, therefore, in widely divergent ways, depending not only on whether change is thought to occur in a minute, moderate, or radical way, but also on whether specific developments are regarded as an improvement or corruption of Christian doctrine.[18] Unless further qualified in a quantitative or qualitative way, the expression doctrinal development is used, in the following, as equivalent to the phrase doctrinal continuity and change.

Doctrine and Theology

The concept of doctrinal development calls not only for a clarification of the meaning and connotations of the term development but also for a definition of the qualifying adjective doctrinal. There are two distinct though closely related senses of the term

---

17 For instance, the notion of personal maturation (which implies a process of completing refinement) differs substantially from the concept of natural evolution (passing through many successive stages of mutation and producing virtually an endless variety of new species). Thus, while the terms evolution and development are synonymous on semantic grounds (both denoting literally an act of unwrapping), they often carry diverse connotations regarding the degree of change thought to be involved (see *Webster's New Dictionary of Synonyms* [1984], s.v. "Development, Evolution"). I disagree, therefore, with Jan Hendrik Walgrave who merely sees "different shades of meaning" between the two terms as "development is an historical category and evolution a category of natural science" *(Unfolding Revelation: The Nature of Doctrinal Development* [Philadelphia: Westminster Press, 1972], 17-19).

There exists an interesting correlation between the concept of doctrinal development and the theory of natural evolution in that acceptance of the latter seems to have prepared the ground for a more radical view of the former. Conservative denominations have traditionally rejected the idea of a large-scale evolution, both with regard to natural science and concerning Christian theology. More liberally oriented churches, on the other hand, that came to accept the evolutionary theory have generally tended towards more progressive views on doctrinal development. For concise discussions of the term development, see G. Mühle and K. Weyland, "Entwicklung," *Historisches Wörterbuch der Philosophie* (1791-), 2:550-560; Walter Brugger, "Development," *Philosophical Dictionary* (1972), 92-93; M. Stomps, "Entwicklung," *Evangelisches Kirchenlexikon,* 2d ed. (1956), 1:1095-1096; F. F. Centore, "Evolution (Some Philosophical Dimensions)," *NCE,* Supplement (1974), 16:175-177; and S. M. Daecke, "Entwicklung," *Theologische Realenzyklopädie* (1982), 9:705-716.

18 Thus, the term development may be qualified by such adjectives as genuine or authentic, on the one hand, and wrong, spurious, or erroneous, on the other.

doctrine depending on the relative strictness or looseness of one's understanding of Christian teaching.[19]

In its narrow and restricted sense, doctrine[20] denotes a religious affirmation that a church teaches by virtue of its perceived divine authority and that it expects all members to accept as a revealed truth of faith. For instance, in the Roman Catholic Church, teachings that have been officially defined by the magisterium as divinely revealed truths are regarded as irrevocably fixed, absolutely binding, and infallible doctrines. In this sense, doctrine coincides with the rather modern notion of dogma.[21]

Divested of such absolutist claims, this restricted view is reflected in the confessional writings of the Reformation and was typical of Protestant orthodoxy. It has also been the classic view of the nineteenth-century historians of dogma who concentrated on the public and binding doctrinal affirmations of the Christian church.[22] It is held still today by those denominations that regard their creedal statements or other ecclesiastical teachings as normative formulations and authoritative interpretations of biblical revelation.[23]

19   See Walgrave, 38-40; Bernhard Lohse, "Was verstehen wir unter Dogmengeschichte innerhalb der evangelischen Theologie?" *Kerygma und Dogma* 8 (1962): 28-35; and James Orr, *The Progress of Dogma* (London: Hodder and Stoughten, 1901), 12-13.

20   The term doctrine (Latin: *doctrina*) is derived from *docere* meaning "to teach."

21   See Michael Schmaus, *Katholische Dogmatik*, 6th enl. ed. (Munich: Max Hueber, 1960), 1:69; and Michael Schmaus, Alois Grillmeyer, and Leo Scheffczyk, eds., *Handbuch der Dogmengeschichte*, 4 vols. (Freiburg, Basle, Vienna: Herder, 1951-), vol. 1, pt. 5, *Dogma und Dogmenentwicklung*, by Georg Söll (1971), 20, 50. It should be noted that this narrow and rather technical understanding of dogma developed only during the 19th century when Roman Catholicism attempted to thwart rationalist as well as modernist tendencies through an increased emphasis upon ecclesiastical and, particularly, papal authority. Besides, even today there exists no comprehensive and formal Roman Catholic definition of dogma – the closest to it being the statement of Vatican Council I on Dogmatic Definition and the object of divine faith (see *DS* 3011 [Denzinger-Schönmetzer, eds. *Enchiridion symbolorum ...*]). Cf. Winfried Schulz, *Dogmenentwicklung als Problem der Geschichtlichkeit der Wahrheitserkenntnis: Eine erkenntnistheoretisch-theologische Studie zum Problemkreis der Dogmenentwicklung*, Analecta Gregoriana, vol. 173 (Rome: Gregorian University Press, 1969), 7-16; and Walter Kasper, "The Relationship between Gospel and Dogma: An Historical Approach," in *Man as Man & Believer*, Concilium: Theology in the Age of Renewal, vol. 21, ed. E. Schillebeeckx and B. Willems (New York, and Glen Rock, N.J.: Paulist Press, 1967), 161-163.

22   In this sense, Friedrich Loofs (1858-1928) defined dogmas as "diejenigen Glaubenssätze, deren Anerkennung eine kirchliche Gemeinschaft von ihren Gliedern, oder wenigstens von ihren Lehrern, ausdrücklich fordert" *(Leitfaden zum Studium der Dogmengeschichte*, 6th ed., ed. Kurt Aland [Tübingen: M. Niemeyer, 1959], 9).

23   Cf. Peter Lengsfeld, *Überlieferung: Tradition und Schrift in der evangelischen und katholischen Theologie der Gegenwart*, Konfessionskundliche und kontroverstheologische Studien, vol. 3 (Paderborn: Verlag Bonifatius-Druckerei, 1960), 203. Louis Berkhof sees the difference between the Roman Catholic and the Protestant notion of dogma in the question of origin (Scripture vs. tradition) and authority (infallibility vs. non-infallible authority) but

In its wider and more comprehensive sense, the term doctrine applies to any theological statement or interpretation of truth insofar as it expresses and reflects the common belief of a church. As such, it is synonymous with the term teaching understood as that which a church holds to be taught in, as well as on the basis of, the word of God. Doctrine, in this view, is equivalent to theology, not in the sense of the views or speculations of individual theologians, but as signifying the commonly held understanding of revealed truth. Thus, doctrine is not limited to irrevocable dogmas or creedal formulations but includes those theological reflections that express a denomination's corporate experience, as well as knowledge, of the faith.[24]

Though it is possible to differentiate between doctrine in the narrow sense of dogma and doctrine as the common theology and teaching of a church, the propriety of such a distinction for a discussion of the problem of doctrinal development may be challenged on several grounds.

In the first place, even in Roman Catholic thinking it is not altogether clear where exactly the line has to be drawn between divinely revealed dogmas, defined propositions (Catholic truths), or ecclesiastical doctrines. Besides, the distinction between absolutely certain, infallible dogmas to be held with divine faith and absolute assent, on the one hand, and certain but non-infallible doctrines to be believed with ecclesiastical faith and inner assent, on the other, is largely juridical and of little practical relevance for Roman Catholic Christians. There is also an ambiguity for Catholic theologians in that dogmatic theology deals with binding dogmas as well as with the reformable teachings and theological reflections of the church. In fact, according to contemporary Roman Catholic theology, even dogmas possess the potential for growth and development and, consequently, remain open to reformulation and reinterpretation.[25]

regards dogma positively as "a religious truth based on authority and officially formulated by some ecclesiastical assembly" *(The History of Christian Doctrines* [London: Banner of Truth, 1937], 16-17).

24 In the third volume of his monumental history of the development of Christian doctrine, Jaroslav Pelikan uses the term theology in this sense and in accordance with medieval usage as a near synonym for church doctrine *(The Christian Tradition: A History of the Development of Doctrine,* vol. 3, *The Growth of Medieval Theology (600-1300)* [Chicago and London: University of Chicago Press, 1978], vii-viii, 5-6).

25 See Avery Dulles, "Dogma as an Ecumenical Problem," *Theological Studies* 29 (1968): 397-416; and Thomas B. Ommen, *The Hermeneutic of Dogma,* American Academy of Religion Dissertation Series, no. 11 (Missoula, Mont.: Scholars Press, 1975). Schulz points out "[dass] es nirgendwo eine authentische oder sonst verbindliche Aussage über die Anzahl der Dogmen gibt; ja, die tatsächliche Dogmatisiertheit bzw. Definiertheit in einigen Fällen unter den katholischen Theologen kontrovers ist" (Schulz, 270, n. 36). Cf. Karl Rahner, "Magisterium," *Sacramentum Mundi,* 1968 ed., 3:351-358; idem, "Dogma I. Theological Meaning of Dogma," ibid., 1968 ed., 2:95-98; H. Vorgrimler, K. Rahner, and W. Lohff, "Dogma," *LThK,* 2d ed., 1959, 3:438-446; H. Bacht, "Dogmatische Tatsachen," ibid., 3:456-457; Frederick E. Crowe, "Dogmatic Theology," *NCE,* Supplement, 1974, 16:132; and Thomas P. Rausch, "Development of Doctrine," *New Dictionary of Theology,* 1987 ed., 280-283.

Second, the Protestant rejection of the idea of infallibly defined doctrines leaves no room for a substantial difference between official dogmas, creedal statements, ecclesiastical teachings, and commonly held theological beliefs. Their difference is merely one of degrees respecting their relative authority and finality with which they are invested by the church. Besides, public doctrinal affirmations are inseparably linked, both historically and theologically, with the entire theological heritage and teaching of a church. And, as far as doctrinal change is concerned, the process of development is virtually the same whether a doctrine remains on the level of an unofficial but common teaching or results in a strictly defined and binding dogmatic formulation.

Finally, viewed from the perspective of those Protestant denominations that know neither dogmas, nor creeds, the distinction between dogma, on the one hand, and ecclesiastical teaching and theology, on the other – valid as it may be in itself – is of little use, if not irrelevant.

For these reasons, the term doctrine is employed rather comprehensively in this work to encompass not only the official teachings of the Christian churches but also other theological concepts expressing commonly held beliefs, even though they may not have been officially formulated as church doctrines at any time. For, as Jaroslav Pelikan has succinctly defined it, "what the church of Jesus Christ believes, teaches, and confesses on the basis of the word of God: this is Christian doctrine."[26]

In summary, then, the expression doctrinal development signifies that process as a result of which the common theology and teaching of a church changes in some way or other.[27] Such modifications may be expressed in creedal or creed-like statements, in representative or official publications, in the public proclamation of the church, and so on. In any event, when doctrinal development occurs, it involves

---

26 Pelikan, *The Christian Tradition*, 1:1-5. Without wanting to set rigid boundaries, Pelikan identifies the various modalities of Christian (1) faith, (2) teaching, and (3) confession, respectively, as (1) devotion, spirituality, and worship; (2) proclamation, instruction, and churchly theology; and (3) polemics, apologetics, creed, and dogma (ibid., 4). See also idem, *Historical Theology: Continuity and Change in Christian Doctrine* (Philadelphia: Westminster, 1971), 93-98, for an elaboration of his threefold view on doctrine which he sees reflected in Rom 10:8-10.

27 "Wenn man Theologie als die rationale Reflexion des Glaubens auf sich selbst und seine Gegenstände auffasst, muss man darum auch sagen: Dogmenentwicklung geschieht notwendigerweise immer als Entwicklung der Theologie" (Karl Rahner, "Überlegungen zur Dogmenentwicklung," in *Schriften zur Theologie*, 16 vols. [Einsiedeln: Benziger, 1954-1984] 4:30). According to the New Testament understanding of *didache* and *didaskalia*, Christian doctrine encompasses both the theological indicative of the gospel and the ethical imperative of exhortation. It was only in modern times that doctrine was separated from ethics and both were subsumed under the heading of Systematic Theology. In this study, doctrine is used in its more restricted modern sense without, however, denying the close and inseparable connection between dogmatics and ethics. See K. Wegenast, "Teach," *The New International Dictionary of New Testament Theology* (1978), 3:759-775; cf. Pelikan, *The Christian Tradition*, 1:1-3.

some change in the community's reflective understanding and conceptual expression of divinely revealed truth that is due to an enlarged, or at least modified, perception of the meaning of the word of God.

In other words, doctrinal continuity and change refer to historical and objective developments; they are to be distinguished from personal and subjective changes that merely involve deepening insights on the part of believers into the meaning of divine truth or the teachings of the church.[28] It is the discovery of this phenomenon of the development of doctrine within the Christian church to which we now turn.

Doctrinal Development and the Study of History

Almost from the beginning of Western philosophy the questions of continuity and change, permanence and discontinuity, being and becoming, were given serious attention by reflective thinkers. But it was not until the nineteenth century that the related ideas of progress and development gained prominence as basic principles common to virtually all major philosophical concepts and scientific models of the time.

Closely related to this was the emergence of a strong historical consciousness, which led to the outburst of historical studies in virtually all major areas of human life and thought and resulted in the discovery of the inexorable reality and pervasive nature of change in human history. From now on, theology could no longer ignore history. While not to be stifled by it, it nonetheless had to listen to it.

The Rise of Historical Consciousness

The first steps toward the gradual emergence of modern historical thinking[29] and its concomitant evolution of a new (historical) method of dealing with change were

---

28   Cf. Walgrave, 45-46, 64-65.
29   Pelikan provides a succinct and helpful overview of "The Evolution of the Historical" in his *Historical Theology*, 33-67.   Equally insightful are Josef Nolte, *Dogma in Geschichte* (Freiburg, Basle, Vienna: Herder, 1971), 90-120; and Langdon Gilkey, *Reaping the Whirlwind: A Christian Interpretation of History* (New York: Seabury Press, 1976), 188-208. For detailed studies on the notion of history and the emergence of historical consciousness, see R. G. Collingwood, *The Idea of History* (Oxford: Clarendon Press, 1946); Friedrich Meinecke, *Die Entstehung des Historismus*, 2 vols. (Munich and Berlin: R. Oldenbourg, 1936); and Stephen Toulmin and June Goodfield, *The Discovery of Time* (New York: Harper and Row, 1965). See also Gerhard Ebeling, *Studium der Theologie: Eine enzyklopädische Orientierung* (Tübingen: J. C. B. Mohr [Paul Siebeck], 1975), 71-76, where the author gives a succinct overview of the classic Roman Catholic idea of church history (the church is essentially untouched, though surrounded, by historical changes), the dominant Protestant and Pietist concept (Catholicism equals deformation; Protestantism means reformation), and the 19th-century idealistic view (dynamic development and growth replaces the static conception of the immutable church).

made during the time of the Renaissance and the Reformation. While the historio-
graphers of Renaissance humanism laid the foundation of modern historical studies[30]
the historians of the Reformation and the Counter-Reformation introduced the
historical argument as a polemical weapon in the mutual attempt to convict the other
side of having introduced theological novelties and, thus, of being guilty of heretical
departures from the true and unchanging faith. Though their approach was marred
by dogmatic ends, they contributed nonetheless to the growing awareness of the
historical phenomenon of doctrinal change.[31]

However, it was only in the wake of the *Aufklärung* that the factuality of change
in history including the history of Christian doctrine came to be widely, if not
universally, recognized. Rationalism and Enlightenment led to a "revolution in
historical thinking."[32]

Starting with *Leibniz* (1646-1716), German thought began to interpret history
in terms of the ideas of development and progress. Following his lead, *Voltaire*
(1694-1778) and *Rousseau* (1712-1778) in France, *Hume* (1711-1776) in England,
and *Lessing* (1729-1781), *Kant* (1724-1804), and, particularly, *Herder* (1744-
1803)[33] in Germany shaped a new approach to history characterized (1) by the
comprehensive and consistent application of the ideas of development and progress
to both nature and human society, (2) by systematic and painstaking historical
research, and (3) by the critical examination of the sources and the questioning of
authorities whose credibility was to be judged by the autonomous historians
themselves.[34] By means of probing questions, inductive research, and imaginative
thinking they attempted to reconstruct the past as objectively as possible.[35]

---

30 Lorenzo Valla's (c. 1406-1457) proof of the spuriousness of the "Donation of Constantine"
    and his critical investigation of the allegedly apostolic origin of the Apostles' Creed are prime
    illustrations in point.

31 Outstanding examples of this combination of historical interest and polemical zeal are the
    Magdeburg Centuries (1559-1574) produced under the leadership of Matthias Flacius
    Illyricus and their refutation in the *Annales ecclesiastici* (1588-1607) of Caesar Cardinal
    Baronius. See Robert L. Wilken, *The Myth of Christian Beginnings: History's Impact on
    Belief* (Garden City, N.Y.: Doubleday, 1971), 104-118.

32 See Alan Richardson, *The Bible in the Age of Science* (Philadelphia: Westminster Press,
    1961), 32-51.

33 Herder's four-volume work *Ideen zur Philosophie der Geschichte der Menschheit* (1784-
    1791) was a landmark achievement in historical science. According to romanticism's vision
    of the world, history is an eternally continuing and unfinished process encompassing both the
    realms of nature and human society.

34 Edward Gibbon's *History of the Decline and Fall of the Roman Empire* (1776-1788)
    illustrates this newly emerging rationalistic and critical approach to history.

35 For instance, the famous historian *Leopold von Ranke* (1796-1886) regarded scholarly detach-
    ment, unbiased objectivity, and concern for the pure facts of history ("wie es eigentlich
    gewesen ist") as the hallmark of proper historical science. See his "Preface to the History of
    the Latin and Teutonic Nations," in *The Varieties of History,* ed. F. Stern, 2d ed. (London:
    Macmillan, 1970), 55-62.

Following this historical and critical method, a variety of new historical disciplines claiming independence of ecclesiastical dominance and dogmatic presuppositions set out to investigate with scientific scrutiny past history in its own right and for its own sake.[36] The importance of the rise and growth of this new historical consciousness and methodology, both for human thought in general and for the problem of doctrinal change in particular, can hardly be overestimated.[37]

The Historical Study of Doctrinal Development

It was in this general intellectual climate characterized by the unfolding sense as well as science of history that, at the turn of the nineteenth century, there arose a new theological discipline that is perhaps best known by its German name *Dogmengeschichte.*

Founded by *Wilhelm Münscher* who, in 1797, published the first of his four-volume *Handbuch der christlichen Dogmengeschichte,* this division of church history was concerned with the historical study and analysis of the rise, development, and change of Christian dogmas.[38] Hampered, in its early stages, by the rationalistic[39] or idealistic[40] bias of its representatives, the new discipline reached its brightest period toward the end of the nineteenth century when, within the short span of a dozen years, there appeared three monumental textbooks on the history of dogma, which are still widely regarded as authoritative and unsurpassed compendia of Christian *Dogmengeschichte.*[41]

36 Among the disciplines that developed during this period are the histories of philosophy, religion, theology, dogma, law, literature, and church history. It was also the time when biblical and theological studies became increasingly shaped by the historical-critical method.

37 Alan Richardson has noted that "even today many remain unaware that the historical revolution is of greater significance for human self-understanding than the scientific revolution itself" ("History, Problem of," *Dictionary of Christian Theology,* 1969 ed., 156).

38 The history of dogma is distinguished both from general church history and from other specialized fields of study in ecclesiastical history, such as the history of missions, liturgy, and canon law.

39 Loofs, 2-3: "Vor allem aber war bei Münscher und seinen Nachfolgern der ungeschichtliche Subjektivismus des Rationalismus ein Hemmnis." Cf. Alfred Adam, *Lehrbuch der Dogmengeschichte,* 2d ed. (Gütersloh: Gerd Mohn, 1970), 1:16: "Ein wirklich geschicht-liches Verstehen konnte innerhalb dieser Frage der rationalistischen Betrachtungsweise nicht aufkommen."

40 Ferdinand Christian Baur (1792-1860), the founder of the Tübingen School of New Testament criticism, greatly contributed to the new discipline through the consistent application of the idea of development to the history of dogma. However, his rigid application of Hegelian dialectic to doctrinal development has often been criticized. See Friedrich Wilhelm Kantzenbach, *Evangelium und Dogma: Die Bewältigung des theologischen Problems der Dogmengeschichte im Protestantismus* (Stuttgart: Evangelisches Verlagswerk, 1959), 114-130.

41 *Dogmengeschichte* was not only the product but also the domain of German Protestant scholarship during the 19th century. For brief introductory surveys of the history of the

Defining dogma in the strictest possible sense as only those ecclesiastically sanctioned doctrines that developed under the assumed impact of Hellenistic philosophy on Christian thinking, *Adolf von Harnack* (1851-1930) in his famous study on the history of dogma, primarily focused on the Trinitarian and Christological controversies of the fourth and fifth centuries A.D.[42] Characteristic for his approach to dogmatic development during the Patristic era is the theme of Hellenization and the objective of tracing the progressive dissolution of dogma in the course of history (*Entdogmatisierung*).

Harnack's famous aphorism according to which "dogma both in its conception and in its development is a work of the Greek spirit on the soil of the gospel"[43] reflects his view of a radical antithesis between personal faith and creedalized belief, biblical thinking and Hellenistic philosophy, kerygma and dogma.[44] Based on the idea of the progressive distortion of Christianity under the influence of Hellenistic culture, Harnack regarded the development of dogma as the story of a colossal error and as an antiquated stage of Christian history. Consequently, he called for the radical revision, if not the dissolution, of both the idea and the content of dogma.

Rejecting both Harnack's *Verfallsidee* and his one-sided concentration on ancient Christian dogma but in many respects still following his lead, *Friedrich Loofs* (1858-1928) published his own presentation of the development of Christian doctrine in 1889,[45] soon to be followed by *Reinhold Seeberg's* (1859-1935) well-

discipline, consult Loofs, 1-8; and Adam, 1:15-30. An extensive account of this is provided by F. W. Kantzenbach.

42   Adolf von Harnack, *Lehrbuch der Dogmengeschichte*, 3 vols. (Freiburg: J. C. B. Mohr, 1886-1890). For Harnack's view of the definition and task of the history of dogma, see ibid., 2d enl. ed. (Freiburg: J. C. B. Mohr, 1888-1894), 1:3-22. Cf. also idem, *[Grundriss der] Dogmengeschichte*, 5th ed. (Tübingen: J. C. B. Mohr, 1914), 1-23. According to Harnack, dogma as the center and focus of religion had long since been replaced in the Eastern church by the cultus, in Roman Catholicism by the ecclesiastical institution, and in Protestantism by the gospel. Technically, the development of dogma ended with the seventh Ecumenical Council (787) as far as the Eastern church was concerned, but reached until the Vaticanum (1870) for Roman Catholicism. The history of Protestantism, however, lay within the purview of the discipline only insofar as this was required for an understanding of its deviation from Catholic dogma. Thus, the study of *Dogmengeschichte* terminated with the description of its threefold end in (post-)Tridentine Catholicism, anti-Trinitarian Socinianism, or else the churches of the Reformation.

43   Harnack, *Lehrbuch*, 2d ed., 1:18: "Das Dogma ist in seiner Conception und in seinem Ausbau ein Werk des griechischen Geistes auf dem Boden des Evangeliums."

44   For Harnack's view on the gospel and on the essence of the Christian faith, see ibid., 54-66; and idem, *Das Wesen des Christentums* (Leipzig: T. C. Hinrichs, 1900). The latter contains 16 lectures presented in Berlin during the winter semester 1899-1900, which immediately attracted widespread attention. Harnack used the results of his historical research as building blocks in the attempt to define the lasting value of the Christian faith. Viewed from another perspective, Harnack here spelled out the (liberalist) theological presuppositions undergirding his historical research into *Dogmengeschichte*.

45   Loofs, *Leitfaden zum Studium der Dogmengeschichte*.

known textbook.[46] Common to these three classical studies of the history of dogma was the reduction of the scope of the discipline to those doctrines that had received official sanction by the ecclesiastical authorities, thereby becoming normative and binding for all believers.[47]

More recent studies on the history of dogma have generally tended to broaden the narrow limits of *Dogmengeschichte* as set by its three masters, Harnack, Loofs, and Seeberg. In addition to defined dogmas and official creeds, they encompass also other doctrinal traditions and ecclesiastical teachings that are expressive of the common and prevailing faith, and some have altogether abandoned the distinction between doctrine, theology, and Christian thought.[48]

As a result, designations such as history of dogma, history of doctrine, history of theology, and historical theology can be used almost interchangeably for the historical study of doctrinal development and are, in fact, used in this way by many who are engaged in this field of study today.[49]

But no matter how narrow one may wish to define the subject matter of that subdivision of church history that investigates the historical origins of the doctrines of the church and traces their subsequent developments,[50] it seems difficult, if not

---

46   Reinhold Seeberg, *Lehrbuch der Dogmengeschichte,* 2 vols. (Erlangen and Leipzig: A. Deichert, 1895-1898). This textbook was twice revised and also enlarged to four volumes. Cf. also idem, *Grundriss der Dogmengeschichte,* 4th rev. ed. (Leipzig: A. Deichert, 1919). For Seeberg's critique of Harnack's *Verfallsidee,* see idem, *Lehrbuch,* 1:2-3.

47   In the words of Loofs, "Dogmen [sind] nur die kirchlich als verbindlich anerkannten Glaubenssätze" ("Dogmengeschichte," *Realencyklopädie,* 1898 ed., 4:760).

48   See, for example, Walther Köhler, *Dogmengeschichte als Geschichte des christlichen Selbstbewusstseins,* 2 vols. (Zürich: Max Niehans, 1951), who presented a phenomenology of Christian theology and thought from a *religionsgeschichtliche* perspective; Otto W. Heick, *A History of Christian Thought,* 2 vols. (Philadelphia: Fortress Press, 1965-66); Pelikan, *The Christian Tradition,* whose view of doctrine as churchly theology has already been noted; and the *Handbuch der Dogmen- und Theologiegeschichte,* 3 vols., ed. Carl Andresen (Göttingen: Vandenhoeck & Ruprecht, 1980-1984), which consistently treats the history of theology as part of the development of dogma.

49   According to Pelikan, the designation "history of Christian thought" is a more inclusive term encompassing also social, political, and ethical thinking and should not be used, therefore, as a synonym for either doctrine or theology *(Historical Theology,* xiv-xviii).

50   For an understanding of the different ways in which both the term and the task of *Dogmengeschichte* have been perceived, consult Harnack, *Lehrbuch,* 2d ed., 1:3-22; Loofs, *Leitfaden,* 8-11; idem, "Dogmengeschichte," 4:760-764; Seeberg, *Lehrbuch,* 1:1-6; Adam, *Lehrbuch,* 31-35; Pelikan, *Historical Theology,* 83-98; idem, *The Christian Tradition,* 1:1-10. For further reflections on the problem of the history of dogma, see K. Aland, "Dogmengeschichte," *Die Religion in Geschichte und Gegenwart: Handwörterbuch für Theologie und Religionswissenschaft,* 3d ed., 1958, 2:230-234; J. Auer, "Dogmengeschichte," *LThK,* 2d ed., 1959, 3:463-470; Lohse, "Was verstehen wir unter Dogmengeschichte innerhalb der evangelischen Theologie?"; W. Schneemelcher, "Das Problem der Dogmengeschichte: Zum 100. Geburtstag Adolf von Harnacks," *Zeitschrift für Theologie und Kirche* 48 (1951): 63-89; Ernst Wolf, "'Kerygma und Dogma'? Prolegomena zum Problem und zur Problematik

impossible, to deny the fact that Christian doctrine has indeed developed and changed during the course of time. It is the achievement of the discipline of *Dogmengeschichte* not only to have demonstrated with increasing accuracy and unreserved candor the undeniable reality of doctrinal change but also to have provided a number of outstanding attempts at a coherent presentation and balanced historical interpretation of development in Christian doctrine.[51] In doing this, the historians of dogma have hurled the problem of doctrinal development into the arena of Christian theology. Indeed, as Pelikan has observed, "among all the theological implications of history of doctrine, the most far-reaching is the question of doctrinal change."[52]

As long as scholars did honestly believe that true doctrine was immutable and eternally fixed, they could reserve the study of doctrinal changes for the realm of polemical debates with their theological opponents whom they considered self-condemned by their doctrinal variations and novelties. But when it was seen that the phenomenon of change did involve even their own doctrinal heritage, the whole issue of the development of Christian doctrine began to appear in a new light demanding the serious attention of apologetic and constructive theology.[53]

Now that the factuality of doctrinal change had raised perplexing questions with regard to the truthfulness and historicity of Christian doctrine, and doctrinal development had come to be looked at as a real and involved problem, the search was on for a conceptual framework that would account for the historical data and provide coherent and meaningful answers to the questions raised.[54]

der Dogmengeschichte," in *Antwort: K. Barth zum 70. Geburtstag* (Zollikon-Zurich: Evangelischer Verlag, 1956), 780-807; and Kantzenbach, 251-311.

51 Cf. Berkhof, 20: "The one great presupposition of the History of Dogma would seem to be that the Dogma of the Church is changeable and has, as a matter of fact, undergone many changes in the course of its historical development." This also helps explain why until the 20th century *Dogmengeschichte* remained an almost exclusively Protestant science, for Catholic theology by and large maintained the traditional idea of the immutability of dogma. On the Roman Catholic attitude towards *Dogmengeschichte*, see Adam, 1:24-27; and Josef Ratzinger, *Das Problem der Dogmengeschichte in der Sicht der katholischen Kirche* (Cologne and Opladen: Westdeutscher Verlag, 1966). The best contemporary Roman Catholic presentation of the history of dogma is the comprehensive, five-volume *Handbuch der Dogmengeschichte*. Following the *Lokalmethode*, it comprises about 50 books.

52 Pelikan, *Historical Theology*, xx.

53 "With the dawn of the modern historical outlook and the comparative study of different periods of Christian history it became apparent that although Christians could still speak of an unchanging gospel they could not mean by this exactly what their ancestors had done. There had been development, and the question was how to distinguish true from false" *(Dictionary of Christian Theology*, [1969], s.v. "Development, Doctrine of").

54 Cf. Jaroslav Pelikan, *Development of Christian Doctrine: Some Historical Prolegomena* (New Haven and London: Yale University Press, 1969), 24: "The nineteenth and twentieth centuries have been preeminently the age of historical study in theology. They have therefore been the time when the problem of doctrinal development has forced itself increasingly upon the attention of theologians."

The Importance of History for Theology

As is noted below in chapter 2, it is only since the nineteenth century, when the reality of doctrinal development had become increasingly obvious, that serious thought was given to the theological issues involved. Thus, historical theology has fulfilled an important function by demonstrating the weakness of the notion of doctrinal immutability, which until then had appeared as an unquestionable fact to theologians of practically every shade. As Pelikan has noted,

> the history of Christian doctrine is the most effective means available of exposing the artificial theories of continuity that have often assumed normative status in the churches, and at the same time it is an avenue into the authentic continuity of Christian believing, teaching, and confessing.[55]

Historical research does not serve to demonstrate only the factuality of doctrinal change. By investigating the extent and nature of the development of Christian doctrine, it can also be of invaluable help in the search for an adequate theological response to the problem of change. For instance, no theological interpretation of the problem of doctrinal development may be regarded as valid or acceptable that does not take into consideration the results of historical investigation into the kinds of changes that have actually occurred, the directions they have taken, and the forces that have helped to produce them.[56]

At the same time, it should be pointed out that because of the nature of their task, historians (including the historians of dogma) may generally be more inclined to emphasize the changes they observe than the stability that underlies the fluctuations of history. Yet, even the discovery of far-reaching doctrinal changes does not, in itself, require the repudiation of the concept of doctrinal continuity, nor the notion of unchanging truth. While history means becoming and changing and, therefore, implies flux as well as relativity, it is not, on principle, opposed to being and remaining and, thus, to sameness or identity.

Moreover, it should not be overlooked that insofar as the science of history is descriptive rather than prescriptive, it cannot itself provide the categories by which the fluctuations it observes are to be interpreted. The evaluation of doctrinal developments necessarily proceeds on the basis of philosophical or theological categories – such as the idea of progress or the notion of decline – which are not objectively derived from history itself but are superimposed by interpreters on the basis of their subjective pre-understanding.[57]

---

55 Pelikan, *The Christian Tradition*, 1:9.
56 Change can be defined as motion resulting from applied force. In the process of doctrinal development the external (political, social, economic, and cultural) conditions may act as stimuli and, therefore, as contributing factors of doctrinal change.
57 Though the historical-critical method is now almost universally acknowledged (with the exception of a number of conservative scholars) as an indispensable tool of serious historical research, in recent years it has come under heavy criticism even by some of its supporters,

Harnack's interpretation of the results of his historical research may serve as an illustration of this fact. There can be little doubt that during the early centuries of the Christian era, the doctrines of the Christian church were cast into the language and thought forms of Hellenistic philosophy in an attempt to render them understandable to the Greek mind.[58] But whether this process of Hellenization constituted a tragic distortion and implicit denial of the Christian gospel (as Harnack saw it) or an unavoidable act of translation through reconceptualization that actually protected the church from serious heresies[59] is not simply a matter of historical

partly because of its strong ties to an outdated rationalism and an worn-out historicism with its naturalist and positivist point of view. It has also been clear for a long time that the supposed objectivity of historical criticism was a serious fallacy that ignored the inevitable presuppositions of all human thought. Among the critical voices regarding the adequacy of the historical-critical method are Friedrich Beisser, "Irrwege und Wege der historisch-kritischen Bibelwissenschaft: Auch ein Vorschlag zur Reform des Theologiestudiums," *Neue Zeitschrift für systematische Theologie und Religionsphilosophie* 15 (1973): 192-214; Gerhard Ebeling, "Die Bedeutung der historisch-kritischen Methode für die protestantische Theologie und Kirche," *Zeitschrift für Theologie und Kirche* 47 (1950): 1-46; Floyd V. Filson, "Method in Studying Biblical History," *Journal of Biblical Literature* 69 (1950): 1-18; Ferdinand Hahn, "Probleme historischer Kritik," *Zeitschrift für die neutestamentliche Wissenschaft und die Kunde der älteren Kirche* 63 (1972): 1-17; Martin Hengel, "Historische Methoden und theologische Auslegung des Neuen Testaments," *Kerygma und Dogma* 19 (1973): 85-90; Ernst Käsemann, "Vom theologischen Recht historisch-kritischer Exegese," *Zeitschrift für Theologie und Kirche* 64 (1967): 259-281; idem, "Zum Thema der Nichtobjektivierbarkeit," in *Exegetische Versuche und Besinnungen* (Göttingen: Vandenhoeck & Ruprecht, 1964), 1:224-236; George Eldon Ladd, *The New Testament and Criticism* (Grand Rapids: Eerdmans, 1967); Wolfhart Pannenberg, "Heilsgeschehen und Geschichte," in *Grundfragen systematischer Theologie: Gesammelte Aufsätze* (Göttingen: Vandenhoeck & Ruprecht, 1967), 1:22-78; Peter Stuhlmacher, "Neues Testament und Hermeneutik: Versuch einer Bestandsaufnahme," *Zeitschrift für Theologie und Kirche* 68 (1971): 121-161; idem, "Thesen zur Methodologie gegenwärtiger Exegese," *Zeitschrift für die neutestamentliche Wissenschaft und die Kunde der älteren Kirche* 63 (1972): 18-26; and Helmut Thielicke, *Der Evangelische Glaube: Grundzüge der Dogmatik*, vol 1, *Prolegomena: Die Beziehung der Theologie zu den Denkformen der Neuzeit* (Tübingen: J. C. B. Mohr [Paul Siebeck], 1968). For other critical reactions to the methods of historical criticism, see Gerhard F. Hasel, *Biblical Interpretation Today* (Washington, D.C.: Biblical Research Institute, 1985), 78-99; and Bruce Malina, "The Received View and What It Cannot Do: III John and Hospitality," *Semeia* 53 (1986): 171-194.

58 On the issue of Hellenization, see T. P. Halton, "Christianity and Hellenism," *NCE*, 1967 ed., 3:653-654; P. DeLetter, "Theology, Influence of Greek Theology On," ibid., 14:51-61; Paul Henry, "Hellenism and Christianity," *Sacramentum Mundi*, 1968 ed., 3:10-16; A. Grillmeier, "Hellenisierung und Judaisierung des Christentums als Deuteprinzipien der Geschichte des kirchlichen Dogmas," *Scholastik* 33 (1958): 321-355, 528-558; and Leo Scheffczyk, *Tendenzen und Brennpunkte der neueren Problematik um die Hellenisierung des Christentums* (Munich: Verlag der Bayerischen Akademie der Wissenschaften, 1982).

59 So, e.g., Justo L. González, *A History of Christian Thought*, vol. 1, *From the Beginnings to the Council of Chalcedon* (Nashville: Abingdon, 1970), 393-395. Similarly, Pelikan maintains that "the Trinitarian and Christological dogmas were as much a fundamental

judgment. Inasmuch as historians venture into that kind of interpretation and value judgment, they cease to speak merely on the basis of objective historical research and become proponents of a philosophical or theological viewpoint.[60]

In other words, while historical research is an indispensable prerequisite to an adequate treatment of the question of doctrinal development, it cannot of itself provide the answers demanded by the problem of doctrinal change; for these necessarily reflect some theological *a priori* not simply derived from historical study but rather foundational to it. Thus, history has the important function of providing accurate information on the reality, nature, extent, and direction as well as on the various forces of doctrinal change. But it is the constructive task of theology to furnish an adequate model by which the problem of doctrinal development can find a meaningful explanation without having to take recourse to an unhistorical notion of doctrinal immutability. Pelikan has succinctly described the relationship between historical research and theological reflection in these words: "The tough questions in the development of Christian doctrine will not finally be settled by any historical research, but they can be faced theologically only when such research has done its job."[61]

The Dilemma of Doctrinal Development

According to *Webster's New Dictionary of Synonyms,* a dilemma is "a predicament from which one can escape only by a choice of equally unpleasant or unsatisfactory alternatives."[62] Considering the historical reality of doctrinal changes, this seems to be the very situation in which Christian theology finds itself. To ignore the fact of doctrinal development would mean to close one's eyes to reality. But to admit it could possibly lead the church into the dismal swamp of doctrinal relativism where faith loses its hold on objective truth and may, eventually, drown in a morass of subjectivism and skepticism. How to relate and properly respond to this dilemma is the real issue behind the problem of doctrinal development and the concern of every model proposed for its solution.

Before taking a closer look at these endeavors, it may be important to state succinctly what is meant by the problem of doctrinal development. This can be done by analyzing the threefold predicament of the universality, the complexity, and the hermeneutical crux of the problem of doctrinal development.

refutation of hellenism *[sic]* as they were some sort of 'adaptation of hellenic *[sic]* concepts'" (Jaroslav Pelikan, "The Past of Belief: Reflections of a Historian of Doctrine on Dewart's *The Future of Belief*," *Theological Studies* 28 [1967]: 353).

60   Cf. Seeberg, *Lehrbuch,* 1:2: "Die Geschichte ist an sich nicht Kritik der Geschichte." In the case of Harnack, his *a prioris* came to full expression in his famous essays on the essence of Christianity. See above, p. 40, n. 44.

61   Pelikan, *Development of Christian Doctrine,* 53.

62   *Webster's New Dictionary of Synonyms,* 1984 ed., s.v. "Predicament, Dilemma, [et alii]."

The Universal Scope of the Problem

A look at the enormous amount of literature on the issue of doctrinal continuity and change can easily give the impression that this is largely, if not exclusively, a Roman Catholic plight. The overwhelming majority of books and articles treating the development of dogma from a theological perspective (in distinction to the historical approach of predominantly Protestant *Dogmengeschichte*) has been written by Roman Catholic authors, particularly since the promulgation of the Dogma of the Assumption of Mary in 1950.[63] After all, to dogmatically define as divinely revealed a teaching that apparently can be found neither in Scripture nor in the oldest Christian tradition must of necessity raise the question of how the dogmas of the church can be said to be contained in either the written or the unwritten apostolic tradition, when the latter seems to be totally ignorant of, or even opposed to, such a teaching.

What makes this question particularly difficult to answer for Roman Catholic apologists is the assumption traditionally shared by Christian theology that public revelation ceased with the death of the apostolic eyewitnesses of the divine disclosure in Jesus Christ.[64] But if revelation can be neither changed, nor enlarged or added upon, then doctrinal development can only be a process of making explicit what from the beginning had somehow been implicitly contained in the deposit of revelation. Thus, from a Roman Catholic perspective,

> the problem centers around the dual question of how a comparatively recent teaching can be said to be implied in Scripture (or the apostolic tradition) and how it can be derived from it through a process of development and unfolding.[65]

---

63 "At present, it is almost exclusively a Catholic question – you can look in vain in most of the great Protestant works of doctrine for even a mention of the question" (Frederick E. Crowe, "Development of Doctrine: Aid or Barrier to Christian Unity?" in *Proceedings of the Twenty-First Annual Convention,* by the Catholic Theological Society of America [Yonkers, N.Y.: Catholic Theological Society of America, 1967], 16). For extensive bibliographies on the problem of doctrinal development, see Walgrave, 403-412; Karl Rahner, "Dogmenentwicklung," *LThK,* 2d ed. (1959), 3:457-463; Schulz, xv-xxxi (good on Italian, Latin and German works); Carlo Colombo, "Lo sviluppo del dogma: Bibliografia," in *Problemi e orientamenti di teologia dommatica* (Milan: Marzorati, 1957), 1:381-386; Johannes Feiner and Magnus Löhrer, eds., *Mysterium Salutis: Grundriss heilsgeschichtlicher Dogmatik,* vol. 1, *Die Grundlagen heilsgeschichtlicher Dogmatik* (Einsiedeln, Zurich, Cologne: Benziger, 1965), 783-787; Herbert Hammans, *Die neueren katholischen Erklärungen der Dogmenentwicklung,* Beiträge zur neueren Geschichte der katholischen Theologie, vol. 7 (Essen: Ludgerus-Verlag Hubert Wingen, 1965), ix-xxii (includes a cross section of works on the Marian dogma of 1950); and Schmaus et al., eds., *Handbuch der Dogmengeschichte,* vol. 1, pt. 5, *Dogma und Dogmenentwicklung,* by Georg Söll, 219-222 (lists 20th-century authors in chronological order), hereafter cited as Söll.

64 Cf. *DS* 1800, 1818, 1836 (Vatican Council I).

65 Schulz, 68.

Based on the assumption that authoritatively defined dogmas share the quality of infallibility and are, thus, substantially immutable, Roman Catholic theories of doctrinal development are, therefore, in the main *a posteriori* attempts to explain and justify the dogmas of the church as legitimate explications of divinely revealed truths contained in the apostolic *depositum fidei.*[66]

As Karl Rahner has stated, Roman Catholic theology faces "the task of demonstrating that the identity of the later, 'developed' doctrine submitted to faith with the apostolic deposit of revelation given in Christ is possible as a matter of principle and actually existing in any particular instance."[67] Likewise, Winfried Schulz has observed that "the proof of this identity between those dogmas which have developed in and through history and the original revelatory truth of the apostolic deposit of faith is the basic problem of the phenomenon of doctrinal development."[68]

Over against the Roman Catholic acceptance and defense of allegedly infallible dogmas even in the absence of any direct biblical support, Protestants have traditionally emphasized the *sola scriptura* principle, affirmed the scriptural grounding of their doctrinal beliefs, and rejected Catholic theories of doctrinal development as *ex post facto* rationalizations of dogmatic deviations from the Bible. It comes as no surprise, then, that Protestants have generally considered themselves above the need

---

66 "Any theory is only an attempt to account for these successive doctrines, to explain the facts of history. The 'proof' for any theory is its capacity to explain the past facts" (Peter Chirico, "Religious Experience and Development of Dogma," *American Benedictine Review* 23 [1972]: 60).

67 "Es besteht in der Aufgabe, die Selbigkeit der späteren, 'entwickelten' Glaubensvorlage mit der in Christus ergangenen apostolischen Vorlage der Offenbarung als grundsätzlich möglich und in den einzelnen Fällen als vorhanden nachzuweisen" (Rahner, "Dogmenentwicklung," 3:458). Cf. Hammans, 6: "Die [römisch-katholische] Theologie geht von der heutigen Kirchenlehre aus und sucht diese aus den Offenbarungsquellen zu beweisen."

68 "Der Erweis dieser Selbigkeit hinsichtlich der sich in der Geschichte und durch die Geschichte entwickelt habenden Dogmen mit der ursprünglichen Offenbarungswahrheit des apostolischen Glaubensdepositums ist aber auch das Grundproblem des Phänomens der Dogmenentwicklung" (Schulz, 2). In his just-quoted article, Rahner also elaborates on the three basic types of doctrinal development within Roman Catholicism: (1) the church defines as dogma a teaching that has always been believed and taught materially though not formally; (2) the church reformulates a biblical or traditional teaching in the attempt to clarify its meaning over against possible misunderstanding or heretical misinterpretation (as, e.g., in the case of the Trinitarian and Christological definitions of the Ecumenical Councils of the 4th and 5th centuries); and (3) the church teaches and defines dogmas that have no explicit scriptural foundation and were unknown in (post-)biblical times. As Schulz has pointed out, only the third type of development is problematic as it alone involves an actual progress of dogma (*Dogmenfortschritt*). "Bei dieser Entwicklung stellt sich dann aber das Problem der Explikation des implizit immer schon Vorhandenen in seiner ganzen Schärfe" (Schulz, 69; cf. 40, 91-92). Cf. also Hammans, 1-2.

to justify either traditional doctrines or contemporary statements of faith with the help of a theory of doctrinal development.[69]

However, Protestant theology cannot take lightly or even ignore the issue of doctrinal development – and this for at least two reasons.

In the first place, the very existence and acceptance of various creeds containing authoritative doctrinal formulations and interpretations not explicitly stated in the Scriptures pose the question of the validity and binding character of such teachings vis-à-vis the Bible.[70] For it must be asked how later formulations of Christian belief relate to the authoritative expression of the faith in the biblical canon.

Secondly, the critical interpretation of the Scriptures, which has become common with many Protestant churches, has tended to widen considerably the gap between primitive Christian belief and its present-day understanding. As a result, biblical expressions are used either with a new sense attached to them or reformulated to correspond with modern ways of thinking. But as soon as Christians reinterpret or re-express their faith with the help of contemporary modes of thought and expression, doctrinal development becomes an issue that cannot be ignored.[71]

Though the problem of doctrinal development may seem less difficult for Protestant churches as they claim no infallible authority for dogmas obviously lacking biblical support, still,

69   "It is significant that, generally speaking, Protestant theology has not occupied itself intensely with the problem of development of doctrine. Two facts may help in understanding this ... Although according to orthodox theology there is a core of dogmatic tradition that will in fact forever survive the test of criticism because it so clearly agrees with the teaching of Scripture, no doctrine is in principle absolutely beyond criticism. Second, there is the Pietist tendency of dogmatic relativism which stresses the *sola fide* in such a way that the inner decision or experience of faith and conversion become the only thing that really matters" (Walgrave, 181-182).

70   The Trinitarian and Christological dogmas of the ancient creeds, which are widely accepted among Protestants, are examples of this. Less conspicuous are some of the anthropological (original sin, immortal soul), soteriological (law, election, predestination), ecclesiological (sacraments), and eschatological (eternal punishment) statements of the historic Protestant creeds. Creedal statements can be found in virtually all branches of Protestantism: In Lutheran and Reformed churches (Augsburg and Westminster Confession), in Anglicanism (Thirty-Nine Articles), and in the Baptist and Methodist tradition. See John H. Leith, ed., *Creeds of the Churches,* rev. ed. (Atlanta: John Knox Press, 1973).

71   Gregory Baum has observed that "the tension between past and present is the crucial problem of all the churches today" *(The Credibility of the Church Today* [New York: Herder & Herder, 1968], 145). E. Schillebeeckx has noted that the problem of the development of doctrine constitutes the Catholic pendant to what Protestant theologians call the hermeneutical problem *(Gott – die Zukunft des Menschen* [Mainz: Matthias-Grünewald, 1969], 12-13). Cf. John R. Morris, "The Convergence of Doctrine: Hope of Ecumenism" (Th.D. dissertation, Graduate Theological Union, 1976), 5-10, 162-243, 345-349, 361-368. Seen in this light, the extensive Protestant debate on the hermeneutical problem is of particular relevance to the discussion of doctrinal change. See below, pp. 82-86.

> the Protestant has difficulties explaining the authority of these post-biblical developments because for him the authority of the bible [sic] is unrestricted and unqualified ... The problem, in short, is to maintain the *sola scriptura* while still finding a place for development.[72]

Thus, at the heart of the problem of doctrinal development lies the question of "how to reconcile the historical facts of development with the claim of substantial immutability" of revealed truth.[73] On the one hand, Catholic theologians struggle to harmonize the apparent conflict between the infallible dogmas of the church and the fixed body of divine revelation contained in the apostolic deposit of faith. Protestants, on the other hand, must relate their authoritative confessional statements as well as the contemporary expressions of the faith to the claim of the sole authority of Scripture. In a sense, then, and because of their different starting points,

> the Protestant problematic is the reverse of the Catholic one. The Catholic starts with highly authoritative developments going far beyond what is explicitly in the bible [sic], and must then explain how this is reconcilable with the primacy of scripture ... The Protestant, beginning with the *sola scriptura,* needs to interpret the *sola* in such a way as not to exclude the development of doctrinal traditions possessing some degree of effective authority.[74]

The problem of doctrinal development is, therefore, a universal one applying to virtually all churches and confessional families within the Christian tradition. "Not only the Roman Catholic and the Eastern Orthodox Churches have to face it, but Protestants and Anglicans too."[75] Indeed, all Christian denominations must come to grips with the tension between the essential immutability of the normative revelation in Jesus Christ and what seem to be significant doctrinal developments and changes.

The Complex Nature of the Issue

Traditionally, Christians have believed in the finality and unsurpassable character of the divine revelation in Jesus Christ as recorded in the Scriptures. Yet the understanding of the content and meaning of this revelation has developed through the centuries since the beginning of the Christian era. It is this fact that gives the problem

---

72 George A. Lindbeck, "The Problem of Doctrinal Development and Contemporary Protestant Theology," in *Man as Man and Believer,* Concilium: Theology in the Age of Renewal, vol. 21, ed. E. Schillebeeckx and B. Willems (New York, and Glen Rock, N.J.: Paulist Press, 1967), 134-135.

73 Walgrave, 46.

74 Lindbeck, "The Problem of Doctrinal Development," 135. Cf. Frederick E. Crowe, "Dogma versus the Self-Correcting Process of Learning," *Theological Studies* 31 (1970): 610-611.

75 Walgrave, 7. Stanley N. Gundry, at the time teaching at the Moody Bible Institute, explicitly included his fellow conservative Protestant evangelicals when he remarked: "We would do well to wrestle more seriously with the problem of continuity and development" ("Rahner on the Development of Dogma," *Journal of the Evangelical Theological Society* 15 [1972]: 213).

of doctrinal development its basic aporistic[76] or antinomic[77] structure. To reconcile the unchanging identity of the faith with its changing forms of understanding and expression is the basic puzzle of doctrinal development.

A closely related paradox and another intricate problem faced by theology concerns the truthfulness and historicity of Christian doctrine. As revelation always occurs in incarnated, human form, doctrinal truth stands in apparent tension with the relativity of dogma. How can historically conditioned formulations be said to express the Christian faith in contemporary forms without faith losing its substance in the process of translation and actualization? This question is the subject matter of theological hermeneutics, which deal with the proper methods of re-expressing revealed truth with the help of contemporary language, concepts, and thought forms.

Closely related to this is the complex issue of revelation, inspiration, and authority as well as the intricate problem of the respective roles of Scripture, tradition, and creeds within the hermeneutical task. Then there is the question of the proper role of the magisterium, of theologians, and of believers in general in the ongoing process of doctrinal development, not forgetting the function of the Holy Spirit in the unfolding and safeguarding of revealed truth. Also to be considered are the nature of faith and knowledge, the function of religious language, the possibilities and limits of theological pluralism in view of the need for the unity of faith, the issue of ecclesiastical authority vs. academic freedom, and the place of creativity within the overall task of theology.

Truly, then, "the problem of the development of doctrine is a very comprehensive and complicated one because it is connected with so many other central problems of theology."[78] This means that an adequate concept of doctrinal development, which both meets the need for doctrinal continuity and faces the reality of

---

76 Cf. Karl Rahner and Karl Lehmann, "Geschichtlichkeit der Vermittlung," in *Mysterium Salutis: Grundriß heilsgeschichtlicher Dogmatik,* ed. Johannes Feiner and Magnus Löhrer, vol. 1, *Die Grundlagen heilsgeschichtlicher Dogmatik* (Einsiedeln, Zurich, Cologne: Benziger, 1965), 727-738. An *aporia* (from the Greek *a-poros,* meaning "no-way") denotes a situation without an alternative or solution (German: "eine ausweglose Situation").

77 Cf. Schulz, 38-45, 291. Objecting to Rahner's use of the term *aporia,* which suggests the impossibility of solving the question of the immutability and simultaneous relativity of dogma, Schulz prefers to speak of the "Antinomie von Entwicklung und Abschluss der öffentlichen Offenbarung" which he thinks can be solved but not dissolved. An antinomy (from the Greek *anti-nomos,* meaning "against law") is a (real or apparent) logically irreducible contradiction between two laws, principles, or conclusions both of which are equally sound and well-based. See H. A. Nielsen, "Antinomy," *NCE,* 1967 ed., 1:621-623; and Arend Kulenkampff, *Antimonie und Dialektik* (Stuttgart: Metzler, 1970).

78 Walgrave, 339. Walgrave lists these as "the nature of revelation, the place of Christ in revelation, the sense of Scripture as God's Word and the special requirements of its true interpretation, the relation between divine truth and its human expression; also, the nature of faith, the way it apprehends its object, the possibilities and means of its progress in the human mind; and the nature of the Church, the way tradition lives in it, the relation between its life as a whole and its doctrinal tradition; the relationship between the hierarchical social institution, expressed in forms of human culture and organization, and the inner supernatural

doctrinal change, must involve an answer to many of the fundamental questions faced by Christian theology. At the same time, as Walgrave has also observed, "if one can grasp firmly the true idea of development and its proper application in the fields of Christian doctrine, one would be on the way to solving the most critical questions of contemporary Christianity."[79]

The Hermeneutical Crux of the Matter

At the heart of the universal and complex problem of doctrinal continuity and change lies the profound question of authenticity. How can a development be regarded as authentic unless it is supported by explicit references to Holy Scripture?[80] The answer to this question involves what may be called the hermeneutical crux of the whole issue; it deals with the criteria of the development of Christian doctrine.

It has already been pointed out that development does not necessarily mean progress, improvement, or regeneration; instead, it may involve decline, distortion, and degeneration. But how can one properly distinguish between sound and constructive developments, on the one hand, and illegitimate or destructive changes, on the other hand, between warranted modifications and adulterating deteriorations?

What is needed is "a suitable methodology for evaluating change,"[81] in other words, valid criteria by which to judge the nature of doctrinal variations. But here lies a third predicament of the development of Christian doctrine, for there is a profound disparity of views among Christians on this point. Apart from the canon of Scripture, the range of possible criteria includes tradition, creeds, prophetic authority, church councils, the ecclesiastical teaching office, theology, science, reason, experience, conscience, and the Holy Spirit.

Because of the inevitable subjective dimension of the theological task, there seem to be no purely objective norms by which these various criteria could, in turn, be evaluated. For, together with all human thought, theology finds itself tied to the so-called hermeneutical circle of understanding.[82] From this, it follows that the

reality of the mystical body; the working of the Spirit who guides the Church into all truth" (ibid.). Cf. Hammans, 3; and Mark Schoof, *A Survey of Catholic Theology 1800-1970* (Paramus, N.J., and New York: Paulist Newman Press, 1970), 159.

79 Walgrave, 16.
80 Cf. Pelikan, *Development of Christian Doctrine*, 19.
81 Avery Dulles, *The Survival of Dogma* (Garden City, N.Y.: Doubleday, 1971), [11].
82 According to it, all human understanding takes place in a circular, or spiral, movement. This means that a proper understanding of the whole requires the knowledge of its parts; whereas the parts can be adequately understood only if one has already grasped the whole. Interpretation is, therefore, no presuppositionless process; instead, it always involves a pre-understanding of the object under investigation. This perception of the whole is then adapted and changed on the basis of insights gained from the study of the parts. Thus, a spiral sets in which enables interpreters to transcend their initial prejudices. For a detailed study of this phenomenon, see John C. Maraldo, *Der hermeneutische Zirkel: Untersuchungen zu*

selection of criteria is influenced by one's overall view of doctrinal development. This view is, in turn, decisively shaped by one's criteriological assumptions.

Thus, the criteriological premises upon which one's judgment about particular doctrinal variations is built are themselves part of one's overall theory of development that is rather hypothetical in nature or, theologically speaking, more a matter of faith than of pure fact. This predicament applies to all models of doctrinal development, no matter which criteria are chosen in evaluating doctrinal change.

For example, whether the modern Marian dogmas[83] represent a proper extension of the revealed deposit of faith or rather an unwarranted accretion to biblical revelation hinges on one's view of the authority of the church vis-à-vis the Scriptures. To regard the church guided by the living magisterium as the infallible arbiter of truth, which guarantees the truthfulness of these dogmatic assertions, is a matter of faith that cannot be demonstrated, nor disproved, on a purely objective basis. To reject these dogmas in view of the apparent lack of support for them in the canonical Scriptures conversely presupposes the acceptance of the *sola scriptura* principle, which regards the Bible as the sole authority and the supreme judge of all doctrinal development.

This observation adds weight to the assessment that the issue of doctrinal development actually represents "the line of demarcation between Protestantism and Catholicism."[84] For, as Pelikan has noted, "the problem of development in doctrine is fundamental among the issues that divide Roman Catholics and Protestants – indeed, fundamental to most of the other issues that divide them."[85] Or, in the words of a Catholic theologian,

> I consider that the parting of the ways between the two Christian communities takes place on the issue of development of doctrine. That development has taken place in both communities cannot possibly be denied. The question is, what is legitimate development, what is organic growth in the understanding of the original deposit of faith, what is warranted extension of the primitive discipline of the Church, and what, on the other hand, is accretion, additive increment, adulteration of the deposit, distortion of true Christian discipline? ... The question is, what are the criteria by which to judge between healthy and morbid development, between true growth and rank excrescense?[86]

Schleiermacher, Dilthey und Heidegger, Symposium, vol. 48 (Freiburg and Munich: Karl Alber, 1974).

83 They are the Dogma of the Immaculate Conception (1854) and the Dogma of the Bodily Assumption of Mary (1950).

84 Pelikan, *Development of Christian Doctrine,* 36.

85 Ibid., 12-13; cf. 1-36. Similarly, Frederick E. Crowe regards "the validity of the development of dogma" as "the very issue on which, it seems to me, Catholics and Protestants are most diametrically opposed" ("Development of Doctrine and the Ecumenical Problem," *Theological Studies* 23 [1962]: 37; cf. ibid., 45-46). See also idem, "Development of Doctrine: Aid or Barrier to Christian Unity?" 1-20.

86 John Courtney Murray, *The Problem of God: Yesterday and Today* (New Haven, Conn.: Yale University Press, 1964), 53; quoted in Pelikan, *Development of Christian Doctrine,* 1.

Summary and Conclusion

The import of three basic pairs of words used in this study has been defined by looking at the history of ideas and by investigating the semantic range of these key terms. It was found that *continuity and change* are contrasting but complementary ideas; *development and progress* represent somewhat analogous but distinct concepts; while *doctrine and theology* can, at times, be seen as more or less equivalent and, thus, interchangeable terms. Likewise, the expression continuity and change can be, and is, used as synonymous to development.

In view of the close relationship between the rise of modern historical consciousness in the eighteenth century and the resulting discovery during the nineteenth century of the nature and extent of the development of Christian doctrines, it appears that the study of history can be of considerable help to theology by demonstrating the possibility and manner of doctrinal change. This may also help to correct erroneous views on the development of doctrine. Thus, history can provide a solid foundation upon which an adequate theological concept regarding doctrinal continuity and change may be built.

More precisely, the problem of doctrinal development seems to involve a threefold dilemma consisting of the following predicaments: (1) it is an issue that Protestants as well as Catholics have to face, though from quite different angles; (2) it is closely related to a number of fundamental and difficult theological and hermeneutical questions; and (3) it is hampered by the difficulty of achieving objectivity in selecting proper criteria for evaluating doctrinal change.

If the Christian church wants to come to grips with the hermeneutical and theological issues involved in the problem of doctrinal development in a thorough-going way, it should do so on the basis of an adequate knowledge of (1) the way this problem has been dealt with by the Christian churches and theologians in the past

---

Conversely, this also means that the ecumenical *rapprochement* between Catholicism and Protestantism must of necessity be accompanied by a convergence of views with regard to the divisive issue of doctrinal development. See John R. Morris's dissertation "The Convergence of Doctrine: Hope of Ecumenism"; Walter Karl Sundberg, Jr., "The Development of Dogma as an Ecumenical Problem: Roman Catholic-Protestant Conflict over the Authority and Historicity of Dogmatic Statements" (Ph.D. dissertation, Princeton Theological Seminary, 1981); Dulles, "Dogma as an Ecumenical Problem," 397-416; Magnus Löhrer, "Überlegungen zur Interpretation lehramtlicher Aussagen als Frage des ökumenischen Gesprächs," in *Gott in Welt. Festgabe für Karl Rahner,* ed. J. B. Metz et al. (Freiburg: Herder, 1964), 2:499-523; Edmund Schlink, "Die Struktur der dogmatischen Aussage als ökumenisches Problem," *Kerygma und Dogma* 3 (1957): 251-306 (ET: "The Structure of Dogmatic Statements as an Ecumenical Problem," in *The Coming Christ and the Coming Church* [Edinburgh: Oliver & Boyd, 1967], 16-84); and Wolfhart Pannenberg, Avery Dulles, and Carl E. Braaten, *Spirit, Faith, and Church* (Philadelphia: Westminster, 1970). In his foreword to the just-mentioned book, Edward P. Echlin expresses the hope of ecumenically minded theology "that a historical view of doctrinal development, along with doctrinal 'pruning' by all traditions, may lead to such convergence (within pluralism) that all Christians may again be one" (10-11).

(chapter 2), and (2) the different options available so far for solving this issue (chapter 3). When this has been done, the ground is sufficiently prepared for developing an adequate theological concept of doctrinal continuity and change.

Chapter 2

Conceptual Models of Doctrinal Development

> Those who refuse to learn from history are compelled to repeat it.
>
> *George Santayana*

> Roman Catholics, like all of us, are tempted to substitute for the shackles of traditionalism not obedience to the revelatory word but subservience to the idols of modernity, relevance, and pragmatic success.
>
> *George Lindbeck*

Introduction

It lies beyond the scope of this study to provide a comprehensive account of the history of the idea of doctrinal development in Christian theology. This has been done elsewhere and is, indeed, a fascinating study on its own.[1] The present chapter is confined, therefore, to a historical *tour d'horizon;* its presentation of the highlights of this stirring history intends to demonstrate mainly two things. First, that there actually exists a striking variety of theories and models of doctrinal development[2] proposed by theologians, particularly during the last two centuries; and second, that in spite of the rather disconcerting diversity of views on this subject, there are, in fact, only three basic approaches which evolved successively in the history of the Christian church. This chapter seeks to foster an awareness of the three main stages in the

1   For detailed historical surveys of the controversy on doctrinal development, see Söll, 70-258, and Walgrave, 45-347. The period from the 16th to the 19th century is covered by Owen Chadwick, *From Bossuet to Newman: The Idea of Doctrinal Development* (Cambridge: Cambridge University Press, 1957). Extensive outlines of the modern Roman Catholic debate during the 19th and 20th centuries are provided by Hammans, Schoof, Schulz, and G. E. Meuleman, *De ontwikkeling van het dogma in de Rooms katholieke theologie* (Kampen: J. H. Kok, 1951). Another helpful survey can be found in Wilken's book, *The Myth of Christian Beginnings.*

2   By "theories" of doctrinal development are meant those conceptual models that are advanced in the attempt to explain the facts of doctrinal change without loss of identity to the Christian faith or the abandonment of its continuity (cf. Walgrave, 4-5). Based on certain deductive premises (philosophical-theological assumptions) as well as inductive observations (empirical evidence), these ideas claim to be more than mere tentative conjectures (hypotheses) but cannot be proven to be true in an objective way. Their only "proof" lies in their ability to provide a meaningful and satisfactory explanation of the facts; this necessarily involves a subjective element, particularly with regard to their underlying presuppositions.

ongoing debate on doctrinal continuity and change and to show how they invariably reflect the influence of contemporaneous scientific and philosophical thought.

To understand how and why the intellectual history of humankind has led theologians to address the issue of doctrinal continuity and change in an increasingly comprehensive and diverse manner is foundational to a critical analysis and appreciation of the various theories that were developed in the attempt to come to grips with the problem of permanence and development, identity and innovation, immutability and change. Thus, the following historical-genetic survey provides the background and basis for the systematic-typological outline of chapter 3, which concludes the introductory delineation of the intricate problem of doctrinal development.[3]

Unvarying Doctrine – The Immobilist-Stationary Approach of Traditional Theology

For most of its history, Christian theology paid little attention to the issue of doctrinal continuity and change. This does not mean that there existed no awareness of the fact of doctrinal development, nor does it imply that no attempts were made to describe the nature of doctrinal variations and to evaluate their import. But the scattered discussions of the issue provided only building blocks for what later would become full-fledged theories of doctrinal continuity and change.

Under the impact of Neoplatonic and Aristotelean philosophy, Western theology until the seventeenth century unanimously regarded reality as being essentially static and ultimately unchangeable while movement and change were seen as signs of human imperfection. The revealed truths of the Christian faith were also thought to participate in the eternal nature of God himself who was envisioned as being beyond time and place, movement and change.

This view was adopted by the Church Fathers, fully embodied by medieval scholasticism, and reflected by Protestant orthodoxy. Later, it was revived by neo-scholasticism and is still held today among the so-called fundamentalists.[4] The common denominator of these diverse approaches to the theological task lies in the idea of static perfection which reflects a punctiform thinking succinctly expressed in the old ecclesiological adage *semper eadem*.[5] It allows for no genuine doctrinal diversity or change but rather postulates the historic continuity, and even identity, of the Christian faith – understood as cognitive belief *(fides quae)* – within its traditional conceptual-linguistic framework. Development, at the most, is limited to

---

3   The three basic approaches are studied diachronically rather than by giving a synchronic account of their rise and development. This contributes to a clearer grasp of the similarities and divergences between the various conceptual models of change.

4   For a definition of fundamentalism, see below, p. 60, n. 21.

5   Latin for "always the same." Punctiform thinking stands in contrast to both linear and circular thought (to be discussed later in this chapter) and maintains the permanence and invariableness of revealed truth.

the subjective and merely quantitative increase of understanding regarding the objective and fixed body of revealed truth *(depositum fidei)*.

To use an analogy, doctrinal development according to this approach is like unpacking the contents of a box (equaling the deposit of revealed truth). Everything is already contained therein and nothing is changed by unpacking it; for doctrine is unvarying in its content and meaning and uncorrupted by any additions or subtractions.

The classic expression of this traditional approach to the development of doctrine came from the pen of Vincent of Lérins whose threefold test of catholicity became "the conventional answer of Christian orthodoxy to the question of doctrinal change."[6] According to his view which was based on Ireneus, "one must take the greatest possible care to believe what has been believed everywhere, always, and by all."[7] There can, thus, be no change *(permutatio)* of the meaning, nor any alteration of the content, of the Christian faith.

At the same time, however, there can be much progress *(profectus)* in religion, that is, considerable growth in the understanding of the one and true faith. While it is possible to express the tradition in a new way *(nove)*, one must take care not to say anything new *(nova)*.[8] To illustrate what he meant by proper development, Vincent employed the metaphor of the biological growth of the human body which develops from the prime of childhood to the maturity of old age without any change of its nature or transformation of its inherent form. In like manner, true faith can grow through the actualization of the latent possibilities contained in the immutable doctrine. This takes place without loss of identity in the gradual and progressive clarification of its unchanging meaning.[9]

There are, in the main, three conceptual models that reflect this immobilist-stationary approach to the problem of doctrinal development. They were developed

6   Pelikan, *Historical Theology,* 4; see also ibid., 4-8.
7   *Commonitorium* 1.2, in *Patrologia Latina,* ed. J. P. Migne, 221 vols. (Paris: J. P. Migne, 1844-1864), 50:640 ("quod ubique, quod semper, quod ab omnibus creditum est"). Universality, antiquity, and consensus are here seen as the marks of the true catholic faith. The "Vincentian canon" later became the catchword of those opposed to the idea of doctrinal change. It was quoted approvingly by Vatican Council I *(DS* 3020). Others, however, took up Vincent's analogy of organic growth and elaborated on it further in the light of 19th-century philosophy. In this way, the *Commonitorium* (434 A.D.) could become "the refuge of both conservatives and progressives" (Walgrave, 89).
8   *Commonitorium* 1, 22-23 *(Patrologia Latina,* Migne, ed., 50:667-668): "Eadem tamen quae didicisti doce, ut cum dicas nove, non dicas nova ... Crescat igitur oportet et multum vehementerque proficiat ... intelligentia, scientia, sapientia, sed in suo dumtaxat genere, in eodem scilicet dogmate, eodem sensu, eademque sententia."
9   The first one to employ an organic analogy in discussing the unfolding of doctrine seems to have been Basil the Great (c. 330-379) who likened the progressive growth of changeless doctrines to the gradual unfolding of a seed. Similarly, Jerome (c. 342-420) compared the development of dogma to the growth of a germ into a tree. For documentation, see Walgrave, 83, 86.

by Patristic and medieval theology, respectively, and further explicate the concept of changeless doctrine.

The Model of Conceptual Completion (The Historical Theory)

In their disputes with the heretics, the Church Fathers denounced the dogmatic innovators for their novel and, therefore, erroneous teachings.[10] Instead, they emphasized the immutable Christian tradition going back in an uninterrupted line to the apostles themselves who – as was commonly believed – had possessed a complete knowledge of revealed truth. Since revelation was thought to have ended with the apostolic age, doctrinal development could, at the most, mean an increasing awareness on the part of believers about the totality of apostolic truths which had been explicitly known, at least by some, all along. Thus, there can be only a quantitative increase of knowledge; for seemingly new truths are not new at all — they were as yet merely hidden from common view. In terms of the analogy used above, development means unpacking that part of the box's content that was until now covered by a blanket.[11]

This model, according to which the Christian faith was conceptually complete from the beginning, is commonly known as the "historical theory" of doctrinal development.[12] Some even claimed that the apostles not only had possessed a better grasp of the truths of faith than the church would ever have but also that they had explicitly known all possible dogmas in propositional form.[13] Yet, the apostles may not have fully conveyed their knowledge to the church;[14] or, perhaps, some truths were tacitly believed and only later explicitly affirmed when they were challenged by

10   In his famous *Ecclesiastical History,* Eusebius (c. 260 - c. 340) defended the Christian faith against those who wanted to discredit it as a recent invention. Instead of being a strange innovation, he argued, Christianity was the most ancient of all religions. It was only the heretics whose desire for novelty caused them to deviate from the eternal and unchanging truth and to introduce new doctrines. For documentation, see Pelikan, *The Christian Tradition,* 1:8; cf. idem, *Historical Theology,* 8-10. The "Eusebian model" of dealing with doctrinal development is described in detail by Wilken, 52-103.

11   Wilken points out that "the appeal to antiquity and tradition was not, in the Greco-Roman world, unique to Christianity. Men breathed the air of traditionalism wherever they turned – in politics, in religion, in law, in morality ... To serve the needs of their age, Christians in the second and third centuries constructed a historical portrait of Christianity whose outstanding characteristics were antiquity, tradition, continuity, and unity" (Wilken, 48, 51).

12   It puts the emphasis on the "historic" faith of the Christian church and denies that any real development has taken place at all.

13   In other words, the *fides explicita* of the apostles was thought to have been more intensive as well as more extensive than that of the later church. Resulting, not from human learning *(scientia acquisita),* but from special divine illumination *(scientia infusa),* it allegedly conveyed to them a supernatural knowledge of the truth.

14   It was surmised that the apostles had passed on certain teachings in either exoteric (i.e., publicly announced) or esoteric (i.e., secretly conveyed) oral tradition that escaped adequate historical documentation.

heretics and infidels. In other instances, doctrines may simply have been lost or forgotten in the course of time. In any event, what looks like doctrinal variation and change is, in reality, nothing but the coming to full view of beliefs explicitly present in the primitive church from the very beginning.

In the time of the Protestant Reformation and its disputes with the Roman Catholic Church, the historical theory was still accepted and defended by both sides. Roman Catholics accused their adversaries of heretical deviations from the traditional faith and justified their own apparent doctrinal novelties by an appeal to oral tradition considered as a second source of revealed truth. Protestants, on the other hand, charged their opponents with having obscured and corrupted biblical faith; they rejected the Catholic appeal to oral and arcane tradition as an illicit expansion of the normative biblical canon of truth. But both sides fully agreed on the invariableness of the true faith and used the appeal to antiquity as a key apologetic weapon.[15]

The champion of the historical theory was the Augustinian Bishop Jacques Bénigne Bossuet (1627-1704) who vehemently opposed the idea of doctrinal development and maintained a completely static concept of tradition. In his rigid conservatism he excluded even the possibility of a deepening understanding of revealed truth. To him, doctrinal progress meant either the spreading of the faith or the mere restatement in different words of the immutable truth without the slightest change of meaning. Thus, novelty (except in a purely formal, i.e., verbal, sense) was an *ipso facto* evidence of doctrinal error.[16]

The historical theory was commonly held by Roman Catholic theologians until the nineteenth century when it began to be eclipsed by other models that were justifying doctrinal change. However, it was still propagated by the distinguished scholar F. Marin-Sola in his comprehensive presentation of the problem of doctrinal

---

15 "Neither side would admit that doctrinal change could be anything but pernicious innovation, and therefore both claimed to stand for the unchangeable teaching of the first several centuries" (Pelikan, *Historical Theology*, 39). It is noteworthy that while the *Commonitorium* was virtually unknown during the Middle Ages, the 16th century saw 22 translations and 35 editions of it. We have already noticed how this argument was used by the early confessional historians like Matthias Flacius and Caesar Baronius (see above p. 38, n. 31). In addition, both the *Magdeburg Centuries* (1559-1574) and Gottfried Arnold's *Unparteiische Kirchen- und Ketzer-Historie* (1699-1700) illustrate how the notions of decay/deformation and reformation/restoration flourished on the soil of the historical theory. However, the former are not chained to the latter as Harnack's version of the model of decay in the form of his theory of Hellenization demonstrates.

16 "The Church's doctrine is always the same ... The Gospel is never different from what it was before. Hence, if at any time someone says that the faith includes something which yesterday was not said to be of the faith, it is always *heterodoxy*, which is any doctrine different from *orthodoxy*. There is no difficulty about recognizing false doctrine: there is no argument about it: it is recognized at once, whenever it appears, merely because it is new" (Bossuet, quoted in Chadwick, 17).

development.[17] Some even applied it in the defense of the *Assumptio* dogma of 1950.[18] Today, however, it is almost universally rejected by Roman Catholics.

On the Protestant side, orthodoxy's static view was defended by the strict confessional Lutherans of the nineteenth and twentieth centuries who rejected the notion of doctrinal development because, to them, Christian doctrine was fully completed in apostolic times, only to be preserved and taught without any change.[19] Development would amount to the destruction or, at least, the mutilation of doctrines.

A similar position was taken by the conservative Presbyterians of Princeton Theological Seminary, who limited doctrinal progress to a clearer understanding and systematization of explicit biblical teachings.[20] Their strict conservatism came to full expression in the fundamentalist movement, which arose early in this century in order to defend orthodox historic Christianity against the attacks of liberals and modernists alike.[21] Upholding biblical teachings in their literal sense, fundamentalist theologians denied that there was any need or justification for accommodating the doctrines of the church to the modern mind.[22] Over against the liberal theologians who seemed to say, "Change or perish," fundamentalists were apt to assert, "Change and perish."[23]

17 F. Marin-Sola, *L'Évolution homogène du dogme catholique,* 2 vols. (Friburg: L'Oeuvre de Saint-Paul, 1924). It was this book which, more than any other, brought the issue of doctrinal change to the attention of Catholic theologians in modern times.

18 So, e.g., Heinrich Lennerz, *De Beata Virgine tractatus dogmaticus* (Rome: Gregorian University Press, 1957). To defend the historical theory today as a Roman Catholic necessitates the assumption that the apostles already knew the papal and Marian dogmas of 1854, 1870, and 1950. It is no surprise, then, that this model has increasingly lost ground even among traditionalists in the Roman Catholic Church. For a list of the leading supporters of the historical theory in church history, see Hammans, 105-107.

19 Among them were E. W. Hengstenberg (1802-1869) and Franz Pieper whose *Repristinationstheologie* called for a consistent return to the confessional writings of Protestant orthodoxy. See Franz Pieper, *Christliche Dogmatik,* rev. ed. (St. Louis, Mo.: Evangelisch-Lutherische Synode, 1946), 63-65.

20 Mention should be made here of Charles Hodge (1797-1878), his son A. A. Hodge, B. B. Warfield (1851-1921), and J. G. Machen (1881-1937).

21 Fundamentalism derived its name from a series of tracts published between 1910 and 1915 in the USA in order to reaffirm the fundamental doctrines of the Christian faith. It was characterized by a strictly conservative approach to theology based on the doctrine of biblical inerrancy. It represented the right wing of conservative Protestantism at the time; its spirit lives on among various conservative Evangelical denominations – including Seventh-day Adventists. See below, pp. 266-271.

22 In a manner reminiscent of Vincent of Lérins, J. I. Packer admitted that there had been "a legitimate and necessary advance" and also a "growth in understanding" in church history; but true development would "not in any way alter" doctrines; for "real progress" comes only by looking back to the New Testament. After all, fundamentalism is "just apostolic Christianity itself" (*"Fundamentalism" and the Word of God* [Grand Rapids: Eerdmans, 1958], 20, 38-39, 89).

23 Philip E. Hughes, "Evolutionary Dogma and Christian Theology," *Westminster Theological Journal* 18 (1955): 47.

The Model of Logical Explication (The Logical Theory)

The second major version of the immobilist-stationary approach to doctrinal development was based on the scholastic method of medieval theology.[24] By discussing the role of logical reasoning in the theological quest for truth, the scholastic theologians provided the first building blocks for what in the nineteenth century became known as the "logical theory" of doctrinal development.[25]

Thomas Aquinas (1225-1274) already recognized doctrinal growth by differentiation. The known objects of faith are progressively better understood in a quantitative way by means of an explicative articulation of their implicit but unchanging and identical meaning.[26] The theology of late scholasticism, then, applied this distinction between *implicite* and *explicite* to the method of drawing logical inferences from the revealed deposit of faith. Through such syllogistic deductions, this method arrived at theological conclusions thought to express the necessary implications of the Christian faith.[27]

By this emphasis on the strictly logical character of theological thought, doctrinal development increasingly became a matter of drawing inevitable conclusions not explicitly found in Scripture or creeds but virtually and implicitly contained therein. In this way, all theological truth could be said to be implicitly contained in, though not explicitly taught by, the deposit of revelation.

---

24 The static worldview of the Middle Ages and its concomitant lack of historical perception contributed to the high regard for tradition, the deep distrust toward doctrinal innovation, and the definition of progress in terms of *reformatio* and *restauratio;* in short, the continuation of the Patristic attitude towards development and change. Cf. Söll, 85-86.

25 Peter Abelard (1079-1142) came closest to recognizing the dilemma of doctrinal development in his famous *Sic et Non.* Still, he attempted to resolve the contradictions among the Church Fathers on a logical rather than a historical basis. He thereby illustrates the apparent inability of scholastic theology to move beyond its literary-grammatical approach to the sources (involving a process of logical reasoning and systematization) to a historical method (which regards doctrinal variations as a result of historical forces).

26 "As regards the substance of the articles of faith, they have not received any increase as time went on, since whatever those who lived later have believed, was contained, albeit implicitly, in the faith of those Fathers who preceded them. But there was an increase in the number of articles believed explicitly, since to those who lived in later times some were known explicitly which were not known explicitly by those who lived before them" (Thomas Aquinas, *Summa Theologica,* 2-2.1,7; quoted in Leslie Dewart, *The Future of Belief: Theism in a World Come of Age* [New York: Herder and Herder, 1966], 77; cf. ibid., 85-90).

27 By syllogistic deduction is meant a process of logical reasoning in which conclusions are drawn that necessarily follow from two premises. In his *Organon,* which was the first logical treatise of Western philosophy, Aristotle had set forth the principles and rules of the deductive method. As defined by him, a syllogism consists of a set of three propositions, two of which (if properly linked by a common middle term) necessitate the validity of the third. However, as Aristotle was fully aware of, the truthfulness of a valid conclusion depends on the accuracy of the premises from which it is derived. See Stumpf, 87-92; cf. D. Elton Trueblood, *General Philosophy* (Grand Rapids: Baker Book House, 1963), 99-107.

In the sixteenth and seventeenth centuries, the Spanish schoolmen wrestled with the question of whether, and under what conditions, a *conclusio theologica* could be defined by the church as a doctrine of faith. Does the immutable revelation completed during the apostolic age allow for later dogmatic definitions which consist of conclusions only partly derived from the deposit of faith? Notwithstanding their conflicting answers, these theologians were agreed in making certain distinctions which (in spite of their involved Latin terminology and their Procrustean bed of logical rigorism) proved to be of lasting value for the ensuing discussion of the problem of doctrinal development.[28]

The Spanish schoolmen had differentiated between formally, explicitly, and distinctly revealed truths and those only virtually, implicitly, or confusedly known. Applying these distinctions to the problem of doctrinal development, the neo-scholastic theologians of the Roman School decisively contributed to the elaboration of the logical theory during the nineteenth century.[29] Their approach was also clearly reflected in the papal and conciliar pronouncements of the time which confirmed the traditional Catholic view of development understood as the clarifying explication of the unchangeable truths of revelation.[30]

Shortly after World War I, the traditional scholastic approach to doctrinal development found its most elaborate expression in the works of three Dominican theologians of the Thomist School who provided a comprehensive presentation of

28   They distinguished between (1) truths that were clearly and explicitly revealed; (2) those that were actually but implicitly revealed and recognizable as such only through logical explication which, however, added no new knowledge or content; and (3) those truths that were practically revealed but yielded new theological knowledge or doctrinal content as the result of logical reasoning and syllogistic deduction. This threefold division resembles the three basic types of doctrinal development recognized by Catholic theology today. See above p. 47, n. 68.

29   The revival of scholastic thought between about 1850 and 1950 was marked by (1) the belief in a metaphysical and, thus, timeless and unchanging system of truth, (2) an apologetic concern for preserving traditional orthodoxy, (3) the rejection of modern philosophical trends, and (4) a negative view of biblical and historical criticism. Among the early leading theologians of the *Collegium Romanum* were its father G. Peronne (1794-1876), the Austrian J. B. Franzelin (1816-1886), and his student M. J. Scheeben (1835-1888).

30   Among them were the bull "Ineffabilis Deus" (1854) which defined the dogma of the Immaculate Conception, the "Syllabus of Errors" (1864), and the two Dogmatic Constitutions proclaimed at the First Vatican Council (1870), viz., "Pastor Aeternis" with its dogma of Papal Infallibility, and "Dei Filius" in which the teaching office of the Roman Catholic Church for the first time directly addressed the problem of doctrinal development. According to Schoof, the Council "marked the culmination of neo-scholastic theology" (p. 38). However, the dogmatic definitions of 1854 and 1870 could not convincingly be presented as mere logical deductions from the revealed deposit of faith. Therefore, the emphasis was placed on the living faith of the contemporary church whose infallible magisterium guaranteed the harmony between divine revelation and Catholic dogma. See also John Jacob Gunther, "Papal Views on Authority and Doctrinal Development" (Ph.D. dissertation, Harvard University, 1963).

the logical theory in its different forms. They all agreed that development, in the main, consists of a strictly rational process by which truths which are contained in the body of propositional revelation are deduced from it with the help of syllogistic reasoning and, subsequently, defined by the church as dogmas of faith.[31]

To pick up the analogy used before, the logical theory defines development as the unpacking of the wrapped-up truths contained in the deposit of faith. Previously hidden in the package and, therefore, only implicitly believed, they now become clearly visible, i.e., explicitly known.[32] Thus, development involves, not the content of doctrines, but merely their verbal form. While it leads to new formulations, it in no way changes the meaning of previously held beliefs in which the new statements are thought to be materially included.[33]

While not adopting the syllogistic ratiocinations of Catholic scholasticism, Protestant orthodoxy nonetheless reflected the intellectualistic approach of the logical theory. This rationalistic tendency also characterized both the Princeton theology and fundamentalism; today, it can still be found among conservative theologians.[34]

The Model of Progressive Revelation (The New Revelation Theory)

Of relatively minor importance in the history of theology but of particular interest for this study is a third model arising out of the immobilist-stationary approach of traditional theology. It was first presented by the famous Jesuit theologian Francisco de Suarez (1548-1617) who taught that a theological inference when it is defined by the magisterium as a truth of faith actually receives, by virtue of such an ecclesiastical decision, the weight of a divine revelation and, thereby, constitutes a kind of completion of the deposit of faith.

31 They differed, however, in that R. M. Schultes (1922) held that only those truths given by formal revelation could be dogmatically defined by the magisterium, while M. Tuyaerts (1919) and F. Marin-Sola (1923) in different ways allowed even virtually revealed truths to become official dogmas. Marin-Sola's extremely influential work has been called "the master-piece of scholastic theology on the question of doctrinal development" (Walgrave, 168).

32 Many supporters of the logical theory also held to the historical theory maintaining that syllogistic deductions from the deposit of faith merely rediscovered what had been explicitly believed in the primitive church in the identical sense. However, the two theories can stand quite independently of each other.

33 According to this view, the *explicatio fidei* is, above all, impelled by human reasoning; other factors (like feeling, intuition, piety, and experience) are either totally ignored or reduced to relative insignificance. For instance, of the three 20th-century champions of the logical theory, Tuyaerts promoted an exclusively intellectualistic view, Schultes regarded the non-rational factors of dogmatic development as being of little, if any, importance, while Marin-Sola ascribed to the *via affectiva* some limited value in arriving at doctrinal truth.

34 For example, Carl F. H. Henry, one of evangelicalism's leading scholars, defined the task of theology in terms of the systematizing presentation of both explicit and implicit biblical truths; in building a theological system, attention must be focused on their inner logical relationship *(God, Revelation, and Authority,* 5 vols. [Waco, Tex.: Word Books, 1976-1983], 1:238-239).

John de Lugo (1583-1660), another Spanish schoolman, proposed a modified version of Suarez' view, asserting that a theological conclusion which is only virtually but not formally revealed would, by means of its definition by the church, be given the status of a formal revelation guaranteed by God and to be held with divine faith. This theory was defended more recently by Fidel G. Martinez, bishop of Sululi, in Spain.[35] A similar position was advanced by Arriga (d. 1677) who taught in effect that a new revelation was needed for defining the true sense of divine revelation.[36]

While both the historical theory and the logical theory regard public revelation as having ended with the apostolic age and, as a consequence, limit the task of theology to "unpacking" the contents of the "box" of the *depositum fidei*, the "new revelation theory" adds new content to it by placing teachings among the collection of revelatory truths which previously were considered mere *theologoumena*. Though doctrines as such remain virtually identical and unchanged, their authority is greatly increased by being considered revealed of God.[37]

In summary, the immobilist-stationary approach of traditional theology either rejects or, at least, severely curtails the idea of doctrinal development through its strong emphasis on the immutability of the Christian tradition and its negative interpretation of doctrinal change as the hallmark of heresy and *eo ipso* distortion of truth.

Developing Doctrine – The Progressivist-Evolutionary Approach of Modern Theology

Up to the seventeenth century, theologians quite unanimously believed in the immutability of Christian doctrine, regarding doctrinal developments as either heretical departures from the faith or, at best, strictly logical explications of the fixed body of revealed truth. The departure from the ahistorical method of scholastic theology that regarded doctrines as timeless expressions of truth was initiated during the Renaissance whose fascination with antiquity and ancient sources brought about a growing awareness both of history and of its impact on human thought. Influenced by the new spirit of inquiry and reflecting humanism's bent toward individuality and subjectivity, the Reformation challenged the objectivist intellectualism of scholastic theology.[38]

---

35 Fidel G. Martinez, *Estudios teológicos. En torno al objeto de la fe y a la evolución del dogma,* 2 vols. (Oña [Burgos]: Sociedad Internacional Francisco Suárez, 1953-1958); see also idem, *Evolución del dogma y regla de fe* (Madrid: Instituto Francisco Suárez, 1962); cf. Hammans, 160-162.

36 On Suarez, Lugo, and Arriga, see Walgrave, 144-153.

37 Similar views may be found today among those appealing to extra-biblical authority in support of doctrines not explicitly taught in the biblical canon. A number of Christian "sects" follow this approach, like the Mormons, Christian Scientists, and Jehovah's Witnesses. On the Adventist version of this view, see below, pp. 272-273.

38 Protestant Orthodoxy, however, soon returned to the intellectualistic methods of Roman Catholic theology. Reacting to such scholasticism, pietism substituted personal surrender for

But it was only the revolution of the Western mind during the eighteenth and nineteenth centuries which led to the realization that the issue of doctrinal development poses a serious historical problem demanding further research and theological reflection.[39] This, in turn, resulted in a different approach to doctrinal change and produced a number of new theories which attempted to come to grips with the historical facts of change without altogether abandoning the notion of doctrinal identity and immutability.[40]

In contrast, and even opposition, to the immobilist-stationary approach of traditional theology, this new way of looking at revealed truth frankly admitted that the doctrines of the church did, indeed, undergo both development and change. While the essence of the faith remains identical, its conceptual-linguistic form gradually evolves undergoing certain permutations in the course of time. This leads to an objective increase of knowledge and understanding of revealed truth.

The catchwords of this linear view are progress and growth. What is given in the original apostolic revelation continuously grows and unfolds; doctrinal advance thereby provides the church with an increasingly better understanding of truth. The treasures of revelation are no longer regarded as being forever stored in a "box." A more appropriate analogy for this progressivist-evolutionary approach may be found in nature. As a seed grows into a tree and thereby actualizes its inherent potential, so the truths of revelation gradually evolve until they are fully developed.[41]

This alternate view likewise led to a number of distinct models of doctrinal development; they differ from each other, among other things, by the degree of change they allow, on the one hand, and their definition of the unchanging essence of faith, on the other. Thus, Protestant liberalism, Catholic romanticism as well as modernism, and Cardinal Newman were all representatives of this new progressivist-evolutionary approach. What united these otherwise conflicting theological programs was the optimistic idea of gradual perfectibility which not only served as their common denominator but also expressed the buoyant spirit of the nineteenth and early-twentieth centuries.

---

doctrinal assent as the hallmark of true faith. By its more subjective and existential approach, which entailed a certain devaluation of orthodoxy, pietism became a direct ancestor of theological liberalism.

39 See above, pp. 37-45.

40 "From the beginning the idea of development was present in the Christian mind. The possibility and the fact of development were generally taken for granted. But as long as there was no difficulty about it, the idea was not carefully examined or analyzed. In recent times, however, the problem arose of how to reconcile the historical facts of development with the claim of substantial immutability. Hence the quest for a theory to explain the facts" (Walgrave, 46). Cf. Schulz, 74: "Problematisch und ausführlich theoretisch wird die Frage nach der Dogmenentwicklung erst im vorigen Jahrhundert gestellt." See also Hammans, [13].

41 Previously, theologians had emphasized the identity between seed and tree; now this same illustration was used to explain the enormous progression possibly involved in doctrinal evolution.

The Model of Unlimited Progress (The Transformistic Theory)

English latitudinarianism of the seventeenth century was the harbinger of theological liberalism's radical departure from the static mentality which up to then had characterized Christendom. Abandoning the traditional appeal to the early church in support of Anglican teachings, the Cambridge Platonists (1633-1688) advocated the idea of progress in religion and theology claiming that the immutable and final revelation embodied in the Scriptures is subject to progressive understanding and deepening insight. As human attempts to express divine revelation in contemporary forms, doctrinal and creedal statements can be reformulated and improved. [42] Latitudinarianism first applied the idea of development and progress which was beginning to shape natural science and secular thought to the realm of theology and doctrine. [43]

Theological liberalism came to fruition among the so-called "neologists" in Germany who influenced Continental theology in the second half of the eighteenth century. Their leading representative was Johann Salomo Semler (1725-1791), the father of liberalism, whose *liberalis theologica* defined revelation as an inner sub-jective experience which developed with the human mind and of which the Bible is merely a time-conditioned and fallible expression. Dogmas, likewise, are neither immutable nor even essential to salvation or faith; belonging to the realm of exterior religion, they are subject to correction, adaptation, and reformulation in the light of contemporary (philosophical as well as scientific) thought. [44]

Of crucial importance for the proper understanding of the liberal conception of doctrinal development is the fact that, since Semler, development and progress were postulated not only for faith and doctrine but even for revelation itself which was regarded as gradually moving toward perfection within human experience.

Shaped by his Pietist background and deeply influenced by romantic idealism, [45] Friedrich Schleiermacher (1768-1834), the *bel ideal* of liberal theology, proposed a

---

42 Development is not seen as uniform progress, however, for there have also been doctrinal corruptions in the history of the church. Later, Harnack expressed the same conviction in his theory of Hellenization. See above, p. 40.

43 "For the first time in Christian history [the English latitudinarians] were asking questions about the relation of an always changing vocabulary to the ideas and doctrines which the language is seeking to represent" (Chadwick, 80). In the 18th century, latitudinarianism became known as deism which was the English counterpart to the rationalist Enlightenment on the Continent.

44 Liberalism openly rejected those parts of the primitive Christian teaching that it considered unacceptable, outdated, or irrelevant for modern man. It searched for the lasting kernel in the Christian tradition by peeling away its doctrinal husk. The latter was regarded as an unessential by-product of non-cognitive revelation expressing humanity's religious consciousness in terms of its culture and time.

45 Beside the rationalistic Enlightenment, it was the burgeoning idealistic philosophy which exerted the strongest influence on classical liberalism; the latter developed from a rationalistic

developmental view of religion that entailed an evolutionary conception of doctrine. According to this view, humanity's unfolding religious experience produces doctrinal expressions, which merely reflect a particular stage of religious self-consciousness and constantly change in harmony with mankind's intellectual growth.

In its classic nineteenth-century mold, theological liberalism found its most distinct expression in the thought of Adolf von Harnack (1851-1930). He located the timeless and unchanging essence of Christianity in the realm of individual faith experience and morality expressed in practical life. Ecclesiastical structures, doctrines, creeds, and rituals, on the other hand, belong only to the exterior aspects of religion and are, thus, subject to constant revision and, possibly, even dissolution.[46]

Liberal theology reflected the *Fortschrittsideologie* of the Enlightenment and applied the idea of constant betterment and advance to the realm of theology and doctrine. The resulting transformistic theory can be illustrated best, perhaps, by the analogous theory of natural evolution. Just as new species were said to result from countless and successive mutations which impel the evolution from the single cell up to *homo sapiens*, so new doctrines were seen as the outgrowth of the constantly changing religious experience of mankind which progresses from primitive beginnings towards its highest fulfillment and goal. In liberalism's transformistic concept, the continuity of doctrine gave way to the continuation of development and change.

The Roman Catholic counterpart of the model of unlimited progress arose toward the end of the nineteenth century out of the modernist movement which aimed at reconciling the church to the intellectual, cultural, and scientific advances of modern times. Accepting the historical and evolutionary outlook of contemporary science and philosophy, the modernist theologians – like their liberal Protestant colleagues by whom they were deeply influenced[47] – looked at doctrines as being merely epiphenomena of common human religiosity and in no way constitutive of revelation or faith. Seeing the essence of Christianity in practical life rather than in an intellectual system of truth, the modernists reduced doctrines to pragmatic postulates devoid of any objective truth content. Their practical value lies in the religious function of symbolizing the ineffable object of faith; as inadequate and time-conditioned pointers to truth, they are subject to continual evolution and adaption to humanity's unfolding religious sense.[48]

---

stage (Semler) to an idealist type (Hegel, Schleiermacher) and, finally, to its positivist version (Harnack).

46 For more information and documentation, see above, p. 40.

47 Schleiermacher's liberal theological views reached French Catholic theologians through L. A. Sabatier (1839-1901) who regarded doctrines as symbolic expressions of religious feelings and interpreted revelation in merely psychological categories.

48 Apart from granting doctrines a symbolic value, the modernists, like the liberals, wanted to preserve the essence of Christianity by separating faith from its time-conditioned and outworn forms (including doctrinal formulations) and recasting it with the help, and in terms, of contemporary thought and experience.

Alfred Loisy (1857-1940), the father of Catholic modernism, George Tyrrell (1861-1909) in England, and the French philosopher Edouard Le Roy (d.1954) were the leading figures in the modernist camp;[49] a moderate version of Roman Catholic liberalism was proposed by Baron Friedrich von Hügel (1852-1925).[50] However, the swift and forceful reaction of the magisterium brought the modernist movement to an end within only a few years.[51]

The Model of Organic Unfolding (The Organistic Theory)

Both the historical and the transformistic theories made use of the notion of decay and decline in order to deal with those theological developments regarded as deviations from the truth of faith. The rise of romantic idealism at the end of the eighteenth century provided another option for those who desired to defend the doctrines of the church against the charge of corruption and distortion of truth.[52] It is not surprising that the model of organic unfolding was not only developed by Roman Catholic theologians but, in a modified form, eventually even became the standard fare of apologetic argumentation in the Roman Catholic Church.

49 According to Jean Rivière, Tyrrell differed from Loisy by regarding revelation as an unchanging experience of divine truth, while Loisy saw revelation itself as a constantly changing intuitive experience of the unchanging divine reality. Both concurred, however, in their evolutionary conception of dogma (Le modernisme dans l'Église [Paris: Letouzey et Ané, 1929], 271-273).

50 Another devout Roman Catholic who was closely associated with the modernist movement without actually being part of it was the French philosopher Maurice Blondel (1861-1949). His view of doctrinal development was based upon the so-called "Philosophy of Action" and offered "Tradition" as the missing link between historical facts and dogmatic truths, between development and immutability.

51 Tyrrell and Loisy were excommunicated in 1907 and 1908, respectively; von Hügel remained loyal to his church. To be distinguished from, as well as opposed to, both Continental Protestant liberalism and Catholic modernism, a liberal Anglo-Catholicism developed in 19th-century England which was influenced by German (romantic) idealism mediated through S. T. Coleridge (1772-1834) and F. D. Maurice (1805-1872). The latter initiated a moderate English version of liberal theology. Later this Anglican modernism found organized expression in the "(Modern) Churchmen's Union" (founded 1898) which defended the legitimacy of doctrinal reformulation, advocated free biblical criticism and regarded personal experience as the criterion of Christian faith. See Arthur Michael Ramsey, From Gore to Temple: The Development of Anglican Theology between Lux Mundi and the Second World War, 1889-1939 (London: Longmans, 1960).

52 Originating with J. G. Fichte (1762-1814), romanticism was further developed by F. W. J. Schelling (1775-1854) whose Identitätsphilosophie was aimed at overcoming the common theory of decay and decline (see Wilhelm Maurer, "Das Prinzip des Organischen in der evangelischen Kirchengeschichtsschreibung des 19. Jahrhunderts," Kerygma und Dogma 8 [1962]: 272). The strongest influence on theology was exerted by F. Schlegel (1772-1829), third in the triad of leading romantic thinkers. In contrast, F. C. Baur (1792-1860), the founder of the (Protestant) Tübingen School, applied Hegelian philosophy (i.e., objective idealism) to the history and development of Christian doctrine.

During the first half of the nineteenth century, the Catholic Tübingen School[53] developed this entirely new approach to the problem of doctrinal change, which the growing historical consciousness had shown to be of considerable magnitude and importance. Seeing the church as a living organism, the development of doctrine was explained as the dynamic unfolding of the germ of divine revelation in living tradition under the infallible guidance of its life-giving inner principle, the Holy Spirit.[54]

Central to the organistic theory of development with its dialectic of substantial identity and real change is the idea that the dynamic tradition of revelation finds its criterion, not in the canonical Scriptures, but rather in the contemporary judgment of the church.[55] The metaphor of the organism allowed theologians to interpret the differences between biblical teachings and church doctrines in terms of the natural growth of a living seed whose identity remains unimpaired in spite of the transformations it necessarily undergoes.[56] In this way, Catholic romanticism provided a viable alternative both to the immobilist-stationary approach to change of traditional theology and to the transformistic theory of theological liberalism and modernism.

On the one hand, the immutability of the content of revelation was clearly affirmed; on the other hand, the inevitable historicity of all human expressions of truth was openly conceded. Their time-conditioned character necessitates the continuous clarification and conceptualization of the inexhaustible content of faith. Doctrinal development, then, involves the progressive apprehension and subsequent formulation of revealed truth. This means that new and different doctrines can arise in the history of the Christian church; however, they are merely previously unknown conceptualizations and formulations of the unchanging object of faith grasped by the immediate perception of faith.

53 The leading thinkers of the Catholic faculty of theology at Tübingen (established 1817) were J. S. Drey (1777-1853), J. A. Möhler (1796-1838), and J. E. Kuhn (1806-1887). Their writings made the issue of doctrinal development a prominent theme of Catholic theology. But only Kuhn provided a coherent and systematic analysis of the process of doctrinal change. His involved and intriguing theory of development went considerably beyond the views of his predecessors. The following summary is largely based on his view.

54 According to this view, the Holy Spirit creates in the church a collective consciousness of the object of faith, that is, a subjective apprehension of divine revelation. This interior faith, which precedes all propositional concretization, is expressed as exterior faith in the assent to the dogmas of the church.

55 This living authority finds visible expression in the common faith of believers and also in the official magisterium. Guaranteed by the Holy Spirit, the legitimacy of doctrinal developments cannot be judged by the individual believer. After all, the Scriptures themselves are only the imperfect and time-conditioned expression of revealed truth. Their substantial content is, however, unfailingly preserved in the consciousness of the church.

56 Over against the model of unlimited progress, which finds its proper analogy in the evolutionary hypothesis *(phylogenesis)*, the model of organic unfolding is well illustrated by the maturation and growth of organic life *(ontogenesis)*. Though making allowance for seemingly radical changes (comparable, perhaps, to the metamorphosis of a tadpole to a frog), the organistic theory is, in fact, opposed to truly radical alterations as they are said to occur, e.g., in genetic macro-mutations leading to entirely new species.

At the heart of this view of doctrinal development lies a dialectic conception of human understanding according to which knowledge proceeds from an immediate apprehension *(Wahrnehmung)* to a mediate, conceptual awareness *(Vorstellung)* and from there to a speculative term *(Begriff)*. Applied to divine revelation and its human understanding, this theory postulates an immediate perception of revealed truth as the basis and starting point of a dialectic process in which the pre-reflective knowledge of faith contained in the act of faith is raised to the level of reflective thought. The latter gradually unfolds the truth inherent in the immediate apprehension of the object of faith. The notional grasp of absolute truth, in turn, leads to the progressive formulation of doctrinal truths which, however, never reach the fullness of the immediate consciousness of reality since they partake of the inevitable historical relativity of all human forms of expression.

Though first developed by Roman Catholic theologians, organistic ideas of development also became widespread among Protestant church historians.[57] Even such a conservative historian of dogma as James Orr (1844-1913) argued for an organic conception of dogmatic evolution. Over against those who either rejected the progressive growth of doctrine (Harnack) or supported dogmatic evolutionism (Sabatier), Orr maintained that biblically based dogmas, though possessing a definite truth content, organically evolved according to the divine purpose working in them. Unavoidably imperfect and affected by their environment, doctrinal systems need to progressively develop – but in such a way as not to subvert the permanent doctrinal accomplishments of the past.[58]

The Model of Ideal Growth (The Psychological Theory)

Substantially in harmony with the organistic conceptions of the theologians of the Tübingen School and yet without any direct dependence upon them, John Henry Newman (1801-1890) advanced an original and creative theory of doctrinal development which exerted a far-reaching influence on Catholic theology and remains of basic importance for any discussion of doctrinal change.[59]

---

57 For more information, see Wolf, 786-792, and Maurer, 265-292.

58 Orr, 1-32. In more recent years, Berkhof also proposed an organic concept of doctrinal development (22-23).

59 As the leading spirit of the Oxford Movement (1833-1845), Newman originally defended the Anglican Church as the true *via media* between liberal Protestantism, on the one hand, and Roman Catholicism, on the other. During the early 1840s, however, he gradually arrived at the conclusion that the Roman Catholic Church was indeed the rightful heir of early Christianity being the most faithful preserver of both its principles and its outward appearance. But was it at all possible to justify the obvious doctrinal changes and apparent corruptions of the Catholic doctrinal system as it had developed over the centuries? It is this theological dilemma, paramount in his thought, which Newman tried to solve with his theory of doctrinal development. Newman tackled this intensely personal question of doctrinal development in his famous *Essay on the Development of Christian Doctrine* (1845) which proffered the theological rationale and defense of his conversion to the Roman Catholic Church. This work,

At the heart of Newman's theory lies the view that revelation is not a set of propositional truths, but rather a living and dynamic idea, i.e., a comprehensive mental image or impression of divine truth. This Christian or Catholic idea is the content and object of a real apprehension of faith by which the mind intuitively grasps the divine reality as a whole. This immediate and all-encompassing awareness is gradually clarified and articulated by way of theological reasoning and discursive thought. However, the conscious notional apprehension never completely expresses, nor exhausts, the real apprehension; it only partially unfolds the innumerable aspects of the one and inexhaustible idea. While the two cannot be separated, they still represent two distinct and irreducible dimensions of the knowledge of truth.[60]

Doctrinal development, then, is the progressive unfolding of the various aspects of the Christian idea; it gradually explicates and expresses the wordless impression of the object of faith possessed by the mind of the believing church. This unfolding takes place both through implicit, unconscious reasoning and through explicit, conscious reflection; the latter gives systematic order and logical form to the former and finds its clearest expression in the dogmas and creeds of the church. According to Newman, doctrinal development involves, therefore, much more than mere logical reasoning and syllogistic deduction.[61]

which has been described as "the classic discussion of doctrinal development" and "the almost inevitable starting point for an investigation of development of doctrine" (Pelikan, *Development of Christian Doctrine*, 13, 3), was the first full-fledged treatise ever to be written on the subject of doctrinal development.

60 Newman saw an analogy between the organism of the church and the individual with regard to the way in which the believing mind could receive an intuitive awareness of divine revelation as a whole that goes beyond the incomplete notional apprehension of this intuition expressed in dogmas and creeds. Basic to this analogy is a cognitional theory according to which the human mind apprehends reality both intuitively in an unconscious and incommunicable but real apprehension and rationally through its subsequent notional apprehension, which never fully exhausts the total intuitive grasp of the known objects. However, this does not make dogmas superfluous or of little relevance. While they constitute only partial and inadequate concretions of the Christian idea, faith would not be possible without them. For they evoke in the mind the image of the divine reality and, thus, mediate the real apprehension of the object of faith. In other words, though the immediate awareness of truth far exceeds the intellectual structure of doctrinal propositions, the real cannot be apprehended apart from the notional.

61 For this reason, it is useless to search for clear and unequivocal biblical support of doctrines that developed during post-biblical times. Though the Scriptures are the inspired and inerrant word of God, they provide only a partial and incomplete expression of the all-encompassing Catholic idea. And as doctrines are notional formulations, not of scriptural teachings as such, but rather of the church's immediate apprehension of divine truth, the Bible cannot be regarded as the final arbiter of doctrinal development. This function is instead given to the "illative sense," the ultimate criterion and infallible guide of doctrinal development. As the mind's intuitive capacity for arriving at certain and concrete knowledge apart from a deliberate intellectual and logical process, this instinct assures the identity of the dogmas of the church with the Catholic idea. The *(con)sensus fidelium* is reflected by the magisterium of the church

Dogmas may expand and become more complete and precise; moreover, even the idea unfolds and develops in order to remain itself. But genuine doctrinal additions or variations unfailingly preserve and faithfully express the original Catholic idea, which is incompletely, but authoritatively, expressed in the dogmas and creeds of the early church. In other words, while dogmas may develop and change, the underlying principles remain identical. The propositions expressed in new dogmas only raise to the level of rational thought what the church has always unconsciously known through its immediate intuitive apprehension of the revelatory idea.[62]

With his psychological theory of doctrinal development[63] Newman accomplished much more than the removal of the intellectual obstacles to his conversion to Roman Catholicism. By offering a well-articulated and unified model of doctrinal continuity and change, he compelled his supporters and critics alike to give more attention to an issue touching on what may be some of the most difficult and complex questions confronting theology in modern times.

With the theologians of the Catholic Tübingen School, Newman was convinced that the historical reality of doctrinal change required a solution differing from the strictly logical approach of scholastic theology. Influenced by the general climate of their time, these thinkers found the answer in an organic understanding of development and a dynamic concept of tradition. This allowed them to freely recognize the doctrinal changes that had taken place in the history of the Christian church; at the

which is the outward warrant of sound doctrinal development and the infallible interpreter of revelation.

62   Newman maintained that the general identity of Christian doctrine throughout its history can be defended on rational grounds. To this effect, he advanced seven tests or notes which were intended to serve as aids rather than compelling proofs in discriminating between authentic developments and doctrinal corruptions. Applying the analogy of natural growth to mental processes, Newman illustrated with these tests (1) how even drastic changes can be in harmony with an underlying identity, (2) how ideas grow by interaction with their environment even assimilating extraneous elements not previously contained in the original idea, (3) how the different aspects of the one idea are coherent with each other, and (4) that development is both inevitable and necessary for the identity of a living organism (R. L. Kinast, "Newman's Notes for Genuine Development as a Criteriological Framework" [Ph.D. dissertation, Emory University, 1977], 232-236).

63   W. C. Hunt has neatly summarized the importance of Newman's personalistic psychology for his theory of development: "The key to understanding Cardinal Newman's theory of doctrinal development is an understanding and appreciation of the role of intuition from beginning to end. The starting point is intuitive knowledge, that is, a direct, full, pre-reflexive, wordless, real apprehension of the divine Object of faith by means of an impression on the Imagination or of an original idea. This intuitive knowledge governs the entire process of doctrinal development and is only gradually reduced to propositional expression in the form of systematic doctrines. The term of the process, the defined doctrine, also depends upon intuition. The ultimate criterion of doctrinal certitude is a certain instinct or feeling for the truth, present throughout the Church under the guidance of the Holy Spirit, which recognizes true expressions of the Christian faith" ("Intuition: The Key to John Henry Newman's Theory of Doctrinal Development" [S.T.D. dissertation, Catholic University of America, 1967], 280).

same time, they could still affirm the essential immutability of the Christian faith as well as the lasting importance of dogmas and creeds. In this way, they offered an intriguing alternative to objectivistic scholasticism, on the one hand, and relativistic liberalism, on the other.

While most reviewers of Newman's *Essay* regarded his theory as unacceptable to Catholics and Protestants alike, a few adopted the idea of the objective development of Christian belief. Among them was the Presbyterian church historian Robert Rainy (1826-1906) who presented "the only full-length, positive treatment of the subject of development to come from the pen of an evangelical in the nineteenth century."[64] He distinguished between the divine truths embodied in the Scriptures and their human formulations contained in dogmas and creeds. Though valid and reliable, the latter are open to continuous development, improvement, and even correction; under the guidance of the Holy Spirit, the church advances in its understanding of biblical truth.[65]

A contemporary counterpart to the Scottish Presbyterian Rainy is the Anglican theologian Peter Toon. Advancing "an evangelical view of development of doctrine," he firmly upholds the unique place of the Scriptures; at the same time, however, he acknowledges the influence of the historical and cultural context on doctrinal statements.[66] Theology is, therefore, more than mere exegesis; its task is to express anew the biblical message in contemporary concepts and terms. It seems that the new evangelicalism of recent years is increasingly giving attention to the hermeneutical function of dogmatic theology.[67]

The Model of Controlled Advance (The Theological Theory)

Attempting to renew Roman Catholic theology with the help of Scripture and the Church Fathers as well as to foster interaction and dialogue with modern philosophy and science, a number of theologians in France also dealt with the issue of doctrinal development in a manner clearly differing from the rather intellectualistic and static approach of neoscholasticism. Flowering from the late 1930s to the early 1950s, this theological trend maintained the immutability of truth without denying the necessity

---

64 Peter Toon, *The Development of Doctrine in the Church* (Grand Rapids: Eerdmans, 1979), 38. Rainy's 1873 Cunningham Lectures on "The Delivery and Development of Christian Doctrine" were published under the same title in the following year (Edinburgh: T. & T. Clark, 1874).

65 Rainy saw no conflict between this position and the Protestant conviction regarding the all-sufficiency, clarity, and normative authority of the Scriptures. However, most conservative Protestant scholars of his time sided with the static view of the Princeton school.

66 Toon, 105-126. See also idem, "Development of Doctrine," *New Dictionary of Theology* (1988), 196. Toon opts for a moderate version of "historical situationalism" that appears to partly exempt the biblical "paradigm" from the relativity of the historical. On the situationist theories, see below, pp. 86-91.

67 Among the leading figures of the more progressive type of evangelicalism are G. C. Berkouwer, G. E. Ladd, H. Thielicke, D. G. Bloesch, J. B. Rogers, and P. K. Jewett.

of terminological or conceptual adjustments in the church's heritage of faith. Led by such scholars as Yves M.-J. Congar, Henri de Lubac, J. Danielou, and M.-D. Chenu, the so-called *nouvelle théologie* distinguished between the absolute and unchanging content of dogmas and their contingent and culturally conditioned form.[68]

Wanting to integrate the insights of the Tübingen School, Newman, Blondel, and others into neoscholasticism, these theologians no longer regarded revelation as the communication of a timeless system of ideas; for them, it involved the personal communion of the believer with the divine reality out of which the necessarily inadequate conceptualizations of the Christian faith grow. As they called for an empirical and historical approach to dogma and its development, these Roman Catholic theologians were soon accused of doctrinal relativism and suspected of heretical modernism.[69] However, their broadened approach to doctrinal development was increasingly taken up by other scholars who also felt uncomfortable with the traditional and still dominant immobilism of neoscholastic theology.

Particularly since the promulgation in 1950 of the Dogma of the Bodily Assumption of Mary, more and more Catholic theologians have abandoned the intellectualistic approach to doctrinal change and have adopted what is frequently called the "theological theory" of doctrinal development.[70] Derived from both the organistic views of Catholic romanticism and the psychological theory of Newman, this model of controlled advance makes room for other than strictly rational factors in the process which leads to new dogmas in the church. The views that can be subsumed under the "theological theory" differ from each other according to the weight that is given to the criteria used in judging the validity of doctrinal developments: divine or human logic, the Holy Spirit, or else the church's magisterium.[71]

---

68 See Ph. J. Donelly, "On the Development of Dogma and the Supernatural," *Theological Studies* 8 (1947): 471-491; idem, "Theological Opinion on the Development of Dogma," ibid., 8:668-699; John J. Galvin, "A Critical Survey of Modern Conceptions of Doctrinal Development," in *Proceedings of the Fifth Annual Meeting*, by the Catholic Theological Society of America (Washington, D.C.: Catholic Theological Society of America, 1950), 45-63; and C. E. Sheedy, "Opinions Concerning Doctrinal Development," *American Ecclesiastical Review* 120 (1949): 19-32.

69 The "orthodox" attack against what was derogatorily called "the new theology" was led by C. Boyer, M.-M. Labourdette, and R. Garrigou-Lagrange. It is also reflected in Pope Pius XII's encyclical *Humani Generis* (1950) which affirmed the objective value and adequacy of dogmatic assertions and concepts *(DS* 3882-3884).

70 It became increasingly clear that the bull *Munificentissimus Deus (DS* 3909) could not be justified as a strictly logical inference of biblical teaching; nor were theologians prone any longer to evoke the historical theory. As a result, "the relation between the Roman Catholic and the Protestant attitudes toward development of doctrine seems to have shifted. The polemicists of the Counter-Reformation, from Eck to Bossuet, charged the Reformers with introducing new and unheard-of doctrines; now this charge is being leveled by Protestant critics of the new dogma" (Pelikan, *Development of Christian Doctrine,* 41).

71 The following is presented in considerable detail by Hammans, 175-287, and Schulz, 171-212.

Development as a Supra-Rational Process

The conservative wing of the proponents of the theological theory still regards development as being essentially a logical unfolding of propositional revelation. But, while these proponents firmly maintain the logical nexus between the deposit of faith and the later dogmas of the church, they also admit that something like a "higher methodology" is needed to bridge the obvious gap between the two. This missing link they think to have found in the postulate of a "divine logic" which supplements human and inferential reasoning. Some demonstrable logical connection between revelation and dogma is still required, but the higher, suprarational logic of God, which is not subject to strict logical controls, elevates the probable and persuasive inferences of theology to the level of certain truths.

Starting from the objective revelation embodied in human statements, this process of development takes place, however, "wholly in the night of faith."[72] It is discerned by the intuitive sense of faith and infallibly judged by the magisterium of the church. This is possible because of the enlightening and guiding role of the divine Spirit in the development of doctrine.

Development as a Supernatural Process

It is this illuminating role of the divine Spirit which is the focus of the progressive wing of the so-called theological theory. Strongly opposed to the intellectualist mentality of scholasticism, it emphasizes the special function of divine grace in providing believers with a supernatural intuition which enables them to discern the truth implicit in the divine revelation.

This prevenient grace *(lumen fidei)* expressed in popular piety *(sensus fidei)* is aided by the special charisma of truth given to the magisterium of the church. Because of this instinctive grasp of truth, the church cannot err; neither does it need any historical or logical proofs for its dogmas of faith. According to this view, other factors involved in, or influencing, the process of doctrinal development are relatively insignificant.[73]

---

72   Charles Journet, *Esquisse du développement du dogme marial* (Paris: Alsatia, 1954), 53-54. See also Cyril Vollert, "Doctrinal Development: A Basic Theory," in *Proceedings of the Twelfth Annual Convention,* by the Catholic Theological Society of America (Philadelphia: Catholic Theological Society of America, 1958), 65, who sees this process as unfolding "entirely in the murky night of faith." Other representatives of this view were L. Charlier, E. Dhanis, C. Dillenschneider, and H. Rondet.

73   This view was defended by Henri de Lubac, M. D. Koster, H. M. Köster, R. Spaemann, F. Taymans, and Hans Urs von Balthasar. Some of them came close to the notion of *revelatio continua* which was typical of the liberal-modernist approach to doctrinal change.

Development as a Magisterially Guaranteed Process

Counteracting the strong emphasis on the intuitive sense of faith, other theologians were stressing the unique role of the church's magisterium in determining doctrinal truth.[74] They, too, regarded historical evidences and logical demonstrations as being, in the final analysis, superfluous; for, irrespective of any logical connection, the teaching authority of the church infallibly guarantees the truth of all doctrinal developments. This means that the magisterial decision as such is sufficient evidence for the correctness of any particular doctrinal change: *quia fecit, potuit.*

Development as a Multilateral Process

Many Roman Catholic theologians have adopted a mediating position which recognizes the validity and interaction of various factors at work in the unfolding of revealed truth. While development is beyond the control of human reason, it still has an inherently logical aspect to it; it is not against logic. But the necessary logical connection can, at times, be seen only intuitively; for the starting point of development is not a certain number of revealed propositions, but rather the pre-reflexive knowledge of truth given in the act of faith.

Although the magisterium is, indeed, the only guarantee and final arbiter of doctrinal development and, thus, its most decisive factor, it can claim no new revelation in support of its decisions. Being formally independent of theology, it must nonetheless materially rely on it; for theology has to muster up historical and rational evidences in support of the infallible decisions of the magisterium.

This mediating version of the theological theory has been endorsed by many Roman Catholic theologians,[75] among them such well-known and influential

---

74 Among them were L. Charlier, R. Draguet, and R. Spaemann.
75 See the bibliography for publications by Frederick Crowe, Leo Scheffczyk, and Jan Hendrik Walgrave. John R. Sheets has attempted to relate Newman's view to Teilhardian evolutionism ("Teilhard De Chardin and the Development of Dogma," *Theological Studies* 30 [1969]: 445-462).

scholars as Bernard J. F. Lonergan[76] and Karl Rahner[77] representing the Jesuit school as well as Edward Schillebeeckx[78] who stands for the Dominican School. Their influence was felt at Vatican Council II (1962-1965), which gave recognition to the

76 Though he neither wrote a book on doctrinal development, nor offered a full-fledged theory on it, the Canadian philosopher-theologian Bernard J. F. Lonergan (1904-1984) discussed the manner in which the immutable truth of revelation becomes apprehended and expressed in varying patterns of consciousness. According to him, a global awareness or intuitive insight of truth logically precedes all doctrinal expressions of it. Reflecting on revelation, divinely illuminated intelligence seeks to understand, define, and communicate truth. Doctrinal development involves a triple (theological, dogmatic, and transcultural) movement which combines the essential continuity of revealed truth and dogma with their changing apprehension and forms of expression. Dogmatic evolution involves, then, a cumulative and progressive understanding as well as the changing conceptualizations and formulations of truth. See Lonergan's *Insight: A Study of Human Understanding* (New York: Philosophical Library, 1957), esp. 431-487; idem, *The Way to Nicea: The Dialectical Development of Trinitarian Theology* (London: Darton, Longman & Todd, 1976), esp. 1-17; and idem, *Method in Theology* (New York: Seabury Press, 1972), esp. 305-307, 319-326, 351-353. Cf. also Charles Bent, *Interpreting the Doctrine of God* (New York: Paulist Press, 1968), 17-20, 325-327; and Robert L. Richard, "Contribution to a Theory of Doctrinal Development," *Continuum* 2 (1964): 505-527.

77 In several articles written over the years, the famous Austrian theologian Karl Rahner (1904-1984) set forth his progressive conception of doctrinal change. Like Lonergan a representative of the school of Transcendental Thomism and a proponent of an evolutionary worldview, this profound Roman Catholic thinker also saw the starting point of doctrinal development in an intuitive, pre-reflexive knowledge or global experience of God which is only inadequately and partly expressed in propositional form. Constituting a beginning rather than an end, doctrinal expressions are open to improvement, reinterpretation, and reconceptualization. The unchanging meaning of the truth of faith is variously articulated in propositional form which communicates more than it verbally expresses but never exhausts the original revelation. Doctrinal language is mystagogical, i.e., leading to a personal encounter with the divine mystery itself; it functions sacramentally by transmitting the divine reality to man. Since Vatican Council II, Rahner has increasingly moved toward the revisionist approach to doctrinal change (see below, p. 88, n. 112) allowing for considerable pluralism, errors, irreconcilable discontinuities, and corrective replacements of historically conditioned formulations. According to the late Rahner, the historicity of truth demands conceptual transformations and creative translations into contemporary thought forms and ways of expression. See Rahner, "Dogmenentwicklung," *LThK,* 3:457-463; idem, "Zur Frage der Dogmenentwicklung," in *Schriften zur Theologie,* 16 vols. (Einsiedeln: Benziger, 1954-1984), 1:49-90; ET: "The Development of Dogma," in *Theological Investigations,* 23 vols. (Baltimore: Helicon Press, 1961-1992), 1:39-77; idem, "Considerations on the Development of Dogma," ibid., 4:3-35; idem, "What Is a Dogmatic Statement?" ibid., 5:42-66; idem, "The Historical Dimension in Theology," *Theology Digest,* Sesquicentennial Issue, 16 (1968): 30-42. Cf. also Bent, 14-17, 322-324; Vance LeRoy Eckstrom, "Development of Dogma and Doctrinal Pluralism" (Th.D. dissertation, Graduate Theological Union, 1971), 61-251; Calvin Jacob Eichhorst, "Dogma and Its Development in Recent German Catholic Theology" (Ph.D. dissertation, Yale University, 1972), 132-169, 193-212; and Mary Elizabeth Hines, "Karl Rahner on Religious and Theological Possibilities of Dogma Today" (Ph.D. dissertation, University of St. Michael's College [Canada], 1984).

pioneering work of the "new theology" by taking note of the historical character of dogmas and intimating a theological approach to the question of development.[79] A more recent magisterial pronouncement has explicitly admitted the historical conditioning of revelation and dogma as well as the possibility of having inadequate formulas replaced by more suitable ones.[80]

The attempt made by Roman Catholic theology in recent decades to avoid what was seen as the pitfalls of both modernist subjectivism and scholastic intellectualism found its Protestant counterpart in neo-orthodoxy, which arose following World War I. Reacting to the optimistic-evolutionary and immanentist approach of liberalism, "dialectic theology" reemphasized the utter transcendence of God, the paradoxical nature of theological truth, the full priority of divine revelation over human reason and experience as well as the centrality and normativity of the word of God as the starting point of all doctrinal development.

78 Opposing modernist agnosticism as well as neoscholastic conceptualism, the Belgian scholar Edward Schillebeeckx (1914-2009) proposed a *via media* which amounted to an early and moderate version of the perspectival view of doctrinal development (see below, p. 88, n. 112). While his earlier essays still reflected the influence of the organic theory and only allowed for the reinterpretation of irreformable dogmatic concepts, after Vatican II, he (like Rahner) moved in the direction of the revisionist approach to doctrinal change making room not only for doctrinal reconceptualization, but even for development through demolition. See Edward Schillebeeckx, *Revelation and Theology* (New York: Sheed and Ward, 1967); idem, *The Concept of Truth and Theological Renewal* (London and Sydney: Sheed and Ward, 1968); idem, "Exegesis, Dogmatics, and the Development of Dogma," in *Dogmatic versus Biblical Theology*, ed. H. Vorgrimler (Baltimore: Helicon, 1964), 115-145; idem, *God, the Future of Man* (New York: Sheed and Ward, 1968), 3-49; and idem, *The Understanding of Faith: Interpretation and Criticism* (New York: Seabury Press, 1974).

79 The tone for the Council was set by the opening speech of Pope John XXIII who called for the *aggiornamento* or renewal of Roman Catholicism to be achieved, in part, by the adaptation of the unchangeable Catholic truth to modern times; in a famous phrase, he distinguished between the substance of the faith and its adaptable form of expression *(Acta Apostolicae Sedis* 54 [1962]: 792; cf. *Gaudium et Spes* 4, 5, 37, 39, 44, 53-62). Although doctrinal development was not discussed explicitly (to this day it remains a *quaestio libera* which has not been settled by a magisterial decision), it still was "the central consideration of the Second Vatican Council" (Bent, 7). Rejecting the neoscholastic draft of the Constitution on Divine Revelation, the Council Fathers recognized doctrinal progress and growth *(Dei Verbum* 8) and admitted the possibility of doctrinal variations, of deficient doctrinal expressions, and of the resulting need for reformulation *(Unitatis Redintegratio* 6, 14, 16, 17). Vatican Council II thereby "opened the way toward the recognition of a certain relativity of dogmatic formulas" (Jan Hendrik Walgrave, "Doctrine, Development of," *NCE,* Supplement, 1974, 16:131). See also Eichhorst, 170-192.

80 The Declaration *Mysterium Ecclesiae* issued by the Sacred Congregation for the Doctrine of the Faith in answer to Hans Küng's challenge to the infallibility dogma *(Acta Apostolicae Sedis* 65 [1973]: 396-408) reflects this important change in Catholic teaching on the question of doctrinal development. See P. DeLetter, "Note on the Re-formability of Dogmatic Formulas," *Thomist* 38 (1974): 747-753; and Brown, 116-117.

To Karl Barth (1886-1968), dogmas only imperfectly express the truth of the word of God and are, thus, open to possible revisions on the basis of divine revelation as testified to by the Holy Scriptures. Rejecting the immobilist-stationary approach of traditional theology, Barth focused fully on the biblical message which becomes a revelation of God to man in the act of God-given faith. Though historically conditioned and subject to critical investigation, the Bible nonetheless is the normative witness to, as well as the source and bearer of, revelation. As the word of God in the words of men, it must not be dissected in the manner of liberal theology into its human husk and divine kernel. Neither are doctrinal formulations dispensable; for faith reaches a real knowledge of the unchangeable divine truth only with the help of its fallible, linguistic expressions in Scripture and creed.[81]

Sharply distinguishing between personal encounter with, and propositional information about, the divine, Emil Brunner (1889-1966) maintained that God could reveal himself even through false doctrines, as he is not imprisoned in human and inadequate concepts and expressions.[82] Other more liberal representatives of neo-orthodoxy were the Niebuhr brothers in the United States and the "left wing" dialectic theologians Rudolf Bultmann and Paul Tillich. This leads one to the third, and most recent, basic approach to the problem of doctrinal development.

In conclusion, it should be noted that because of its rooting in rationalist and idealist thought, the concept of development as used in the progressivist-evolutionary approach is closely allied to a teleological understanding which regards nature and history as being internally controlled and steadily moving toward their final consummation and goal.[83] In addition, the organic conceptions of change (Tübingen School, Newman, Orr) and their derivative (the theological theory as represented, e.g., by Lonergan and Rahner) have considered development as being essentially (1) homogeneous (i.e., in basic continuity with the past), (2) cumulative (i.e., a supplement to, rather than a substitute for, previous doctrines), and (3) irreversible (i.e., a genuine and lasting improvement of theological understanding).

Transmutating Doctrine – The Revisionist-Revolutionary Approach of Contemporary Theology

Viewed from the perspective of political and intellectual history, the twentieth century began when the first global military conflict (1914-1918) engulfed the world in a conflagration of fear and death. It was this cataclysmic event which shattered

---

81   See Colin Gunton, "Karl Barth and the Development of Christian Doctrine," *Scottish Journal of Theology* 25 (1972): 171-180.

82   Emil Brunner, *Truth as Encounter* (Philadelphia: Westminster, 1964).

83   This teleological view of development and change has found its clearest expression in the thought of Pierre Teilhard De Chardin (1881-1955). According to him, the evolutionary ascent of mankind irreversibly and unfailingly moves toward the "Omega Point." For an outline of what a theory of development based on a Teilhardian worldview involves, see Sheets, 445-462.

the optimistic expectations of a humanity presuming to stand at the verge of a golden age ushered in by the steady progress of science and technology.

In theological circles, this confidence in the possibility of unlimited progress had been fully shared by liberalism and modernism. While the modernists were virtually silenced by magisterial fiat around 1910, liberal theology received its decisive blow through the shock of the war and was, for a time, eclipsed by neo-orthodoxy. However, it soon reemerged in a new garb when existentialism began to dominate Protestant thought.[84] Similarly, Roman Catholic theologians increasingly moving away from the scholastic mentality rediscovered the concerns of the modernists who, it appeared, had been condemned but not adequately refuted. Thus, some theologians developed what may be called neomodernist theories of doctrinal development.

It was not only the progressivist dreams of the nineteenth century which suffocated in the smoke rising from the ruins of two world wars. The motif of gradual and homogeneous development which had proved so attractive to scholars in many fields (as, e.g., in science, history, philosophy, and theology) likewise gave way to a new and disconcerting manner of looking at nature and history. In natural science, hypotheses postulating cataclysmic changes in earth's history[85] left just as little room for the romantic idea of harmonious unfolding as did the notion of radical historicity which began to intrigue historians, philosophers, and theologians alike. In this way, the age of homogeneous continuity yielded to the age of heterogeneous discontinuity.[86]

In this situation, the rise of a new and different approach to the problem of doctrinal development was almost inevitable. Rejecting the punctiform idea of static perfection as well as the linear notion of gradual perfectibility, more and more theologians accepted the circular idea of radical historicity. Development was no longer seen as guided by a teleological dynamic which would guarantee the steady progress and continuous advancement of the knowledge of truth; rather it would involve contradictions, reversals, and *culs-de-sac*. After all, nothing predetermined the direction of change or guaranteed that it would lead to a real improvement of understanding.[87]

---

84   See Ulrich Neuenschwander, *Die neue liberale Theologie: Eine Standortbestimmung* (Berne: Verlag Stämpfli & Cie, 1953). For a critical assessment of post-Barthian liberalism, see Klaas Runia, "Dangerous Trends in Modern Theological Thought," *Concordia Theological Monthly* 35 (1964): 331-342.

85   As, for example, the "big bang theory" regarding the origin of the universe, catastrophic models of earth's history, and the assumption of macro-mutations in the evolution of life.

86   See L. Harold DeWolf, "Motifs of Continuity and Discontinuity," *Religion in Life* 32 (1963): 334-350.

87   As a consequence, some contemporary scholars again rejected the very notion of doctrinal development as rather misleading – albeit for quite different reasons than those which Bossuet had advanced in the 17th century. See, e.g., P. Misner, "A Note on the Critique of Dogmas," *Theological Studies* 34 (1973): 690-700; A. O. Dyson, *We Believe* (London and Oxford: Mowbrays, 1977), 12, 144; and W. E. Reiser, "What Calls Forth Heresy? An Essay on the

As nothing in this world can escape the relativity of time and place, doctrinal conceptualizations and formulations necessarily reflect a particular historical situation and cultural context. Thus, there can be no timeless and permanent doctrinal meaning, nor any immutable conceptual truth. In an open and processive world, meaning must constantly be discovered anew from the perspective of one's own culture and worldview. This requires the constant reinterpretation of doctrines and their creative translation into the thought forms and idioms of contemporary humanity. At times, this may even involve a radical reorientation and revision of doctrinal beliefs.[88]

Like the other two basic approaches to doctrinal development, the revisionist-revolutionary view has also given rise to a variety of specific models of change which differ from each other in the degree of radicality which they allow for doctrinal transformation.[89] Their common denominator lies in the conviction of the inevitable historicity of all human thoughts and expressions – including those dealing with divine reality and ultimate truth.[90]

The analogy which perhaps best illustrates the basic concern of this third approach to doctrinal development is history itself which, to many, appears like a ceaseless succession of events which possesses no clear direction and purpose. Being neither static nor appearing to move steadily and homogeneously toward a certain goal, history constantly produces new and previously unheard-of ideas; however, it is often doubtful whether new equals better in any real sense. Thus, while mankind seems to be advancing with almost breathtaking speed, it may, in fact, only be racing around a circular course that constantly opens up new perspectives without, however, bringing humanity any closer to an objective knowledge of religious or ultimate truth.

Development of Dogma within a Heideggerian Context" (Ph.D. dissertation, Vanderbilt University, 1977), 105.

88 "The central theme of contemporary theology is accommodation to modernity. It is the underlying motif that unites the seemingly vast differences between existential theology, process theology, liberation theology, demythologization, and many varieties of liberal theology – all are searching for some more compatible adjustment to modernity" (Thomas C. Oden, *Agenda for Theology* [New York: Harper & Row, 1979], 9).

89 In the pluralistic context of today's world, one can, indeed, expect a multitude of models to exist which are based on this third approach to doctrinal change. Due to the ecumenical *rapprochement* among Christian churches in recent decades, these models are often shared in similar form by Roman Catholic and Protestant theologians alike. So far, there does not yet exist a comprehensive historical survey analyzing these more recent theories of development.

90 This includes even those dogmas said to be infallibly true. Consequently, Roman Catholic theologians who follow this approach have broadened the meaning of the term development of dogma to describe not only the history of theology, which leads towards a dogmatic definition, but also the history of its reception and interpretation in the church after a doctrine has been declared infallible. This is usually discussed under the heading of the hermeneutic of dogma.

Models of Radical Revisionism (Revisionist Theories)

Bultmann's Existential Reinterpretation

With his demythologization program Rudolf Bultmann (1884-1976) attempted to sift out the lasting message of the Christian faith from the obsolete, first-century mold of the New Testament. But, rather than eliminating mythological imagery as classical liberalism had done, he radically reinterpreted biblical "myths" with the help of Heidegger's existential philosophy in order to present their true intent in non-mythological language intelligible and meaningful to contemporary man.

According to Bultmann, the biblical kerygma, which is identical to human self-understanding brought to the text as its necessary *Vorverständnis*, is concerned with authentic existence to be affirmed in the decision of faith. As the revelatory event which occurs only in the act of preaching is void of any doctrinal content, Christian faith has nothing to do with either timeless or historical truths; Bultmann opposed all objectifications of revelation. Neither are revelation and faith subject to change; what develops is only the theological explication of the existential happening.[91]

Bultmann's consistent deliteralization of the New Testament had a strong impact on post-World War II theology including Roman Catholic. It found modified expression, for example, in Tillich's symbolism and the New Hermeneutic; it also gave some impetus to the radical "death of God" theology of the 1960s.

Tillich's Existential Correlation

Criticizing Bultmann for eliminating myth through his existential reinterpretation, Paul Tillich (1886-1965) maintained that all that humans can ever say about God is necessarily mythological, symbolic, or analogous – in other words, pointing beyond itself to ultimate reality. Still, if Christian faith is to be relevant today, its symbols require radical reinterpretation in the context of modern man's culture and worldview. Dogmas do not express propositional truths about God but are occasions for the revelation of the divine in human experience; as symbols they may lose their value and need to be replaced by others. As each generation of believers expresses its experience of the immovable point of reference in different terms, theology requires not the repetition, but rather the transformation of the traditional concepts of the Christian faith. This involves the discontinuous development and transformation of beliefs.

---

91 "What develops is only (1) the conceptual explication of our preunderstanding of revelation; and (2) the theological or conceptual explication of faith's knowledge of itself which has its basis in revelation. In other words, all that develops is simply our way of talking about revelation" (Rudolf Bultmann, *Existence and Faith* [New York: Meridian Books, 1960], 89). See also his programmatic 1941 essay "New Testament and Mythology," in *Kerygma and Myth*, 2 vols., ed. H.-W. Bartsch (London: SPCK, 1957-1962), 1:1-44.

Tillich's attempt at a positive revision of Christian tradition with the help of philosophical theology and ontology is based on the principle of correlation according to which religion (theology) and culture (philosophy) interpret and enlighten each other. Correlating the kerygma (i.e., the unchangeable message and substance of faith) with the contemporary situation (which encompasses man's interpretation of himself and the world at any given time), the task of theology is to answer man's existential questions on the basis of the manifestation of ultimate reality or "God." In short, Tillich's philosophy of religion involves an existential view of revelation and truth, an impersonal concept of God, and a mystical notion of faith.[92]

The New Hermeneutic's Word Event

While affirming Bultmann's demythologization as well as his existential under-standing of the word of God as language-event (i.e., as a divine address without conceptual content), the New Hermeneutic attempted to move beyond, and even correct, Bultmann's subjectivism by shifting the emphasis to a reconsideration of the problem of language. Defining hermeneutics as the *Sprachlehre des Glaubens,* Ernst Fuchs and Gerhard Ebeling were concerned with the movement between the ancient text and its modern interpreters which requires the translation, or transculturation, of the word into the language and thought forms of its hearers. This involves a radical transference of meaning as the immutable word of God needs to be proclaimed in ever-changing linguistic forms of expression.

Today, this transposition of the text into new historical situations requires one to speak of God "god-lessly" in order that the unbelieving people of our time may hear the divine address in their own language — the language they can understand.

---

92 Paul Tillich, *Systematic Theology,* 3 vols. (Chicago: University of Chicago Press, 1951-1963), 1:1-68. A similar view was expressed by Langdon Gilkey who called for a creative synthesis between Christian faith and modernity and denied the permanence of doctrinal structures while locating continuity in the presence of the Spirit who calls forth faith, hope, and love. Doctrines, on the other hand, are open to continual change, subject to fundamental transformations, and marked by basically conflicting perspectives *(Naming the Whirlwind;* see also idem, *Catholicism Confronts Modernity).* On the Catholic side, David Tracy also called for a critical correlation and reconciliation between reinterpreted Christianity and secular culture. The theologian must have a dual commitment both to Christian faith and to secular experience and contemporary consciousness *(Blessed Rage for Order: The New Pluralism in Theology* [New York: Seabury Press, 1975]; and idem, *The Analogical Imagination: Christian Theology and the Culture of Pluralism* [New York: Crossroad, 1981]). Tracy has been joined more recently by Hans Küng who has called for a new basic model or "paradigm" of doing theology. To Küng, post-modern theology has to translate the Christian message into the horizon of humanity's world experience by critically correlating and confronting the historic tradition with the contemporary situation. This involves evolutionary and revolutionary changes in beliefs, values, and methods (Hans Küng and David Tracy, eds., *Theologie – wohin? Auf dem Weg zu einem neuen Paradigma* [Zurich and Cologne: Benziger, 1984; Gütersloh: Gütersloher Verlagshaus Gerd Mohn, 1984], 19-25, 37-75).

The existential encounter with the word illuminates their situation and experience and, thus, mediates a new self-understanding to them. In brief, theological interpretation always combines the identity of revelation and faith with the variability of culture and context.[93]

Radical Theology's Consistent Secularism

Arguing that contemporary humanity could no longer understand traditional Christian concepts and doctrines, some American Protestant scholars, in the 1960s, called for a completely secular reinterpretation of Christian faith as well as a religionless and churchless Christianity. Under the impact of Analytical Philosophy,[94] these theologians rejected all religious God-talk as outdated and meaningless and renounced historic Christianity's attachment to the past (Scripture, tradition, creeds, etc.). Instead, the gospel was to be adapted to the thought forms and values of contemporary society and to be purged of all metaphysical notions. Entirely this-worldly in their orientation, the radical theologians were preoccupied with the struggle for human values in a secular society.

By its denial of an unchanging substance of the Christian faith, its demand for a radical reconstruction of theology, and its iconoclastic procedure,[95] which negated even the belief in the existence of God, the death-of-God theology became one of the most radical expressions of the revisionist-revolutionary approach to doctrinal development. Its leading representatives were W. Hamilton,[96] P. Van Buren,[97] and

93 G. Ebeling, *Word and Faith* (Philadelphia: Fortress Press, 1963; London: SCM, 1963); idem, *The Problem of Historicity in the Church and Its Proclamation* (Philadelphia: Fortress Press, 1967); Ernst Fuchs, *Hermeneutik,* 3d ed. (Stuttgart: R. Müllerschön Verlag, 1963); idem, *Marburger Hermeneutik* (Tübingen: J. C. B. Mohr, 1968). For a Roman Catholic assessment and application of the New Hermeneutic, see Ommen, 144-155; cf. also Piet Schoonenberg, "Geschichtlichkeit und Interpretation des Dogmas," in *Die Interpretation des Dogmas,* ed. P. Schoonenberg (Düsseldorf: Patmos-Verlag, 1969), 58-110.

94 This Anglo-Saxon philosophical trend of the 20th century rejected the metaphysical concerns of traditional philosophy limiting itself instead to an investigation of the logical status and meaning of language. In its early, neopositivist phase (which was known under the name of logical positivism and was connected with the Vienna Circle, the early L. Wittgenstein, A. J. Ayer, A. Flew, and others), Analytical Philosophy regarded all theological assertions as intrinsically meaningless; later linguistic analysis somewhat softened its radical empiricism.

95 See Albert C. Outler, "The New Iconoclasm and the Integrity of the Faith," *Theology Today* 25 (1968): 295-319.

96 W. Hamilton, *The New Essence of Christianity* (New York: Association Press, 1961). Cf. William Hamilton and Thomas J. J. Altizer, *Radical Theology and the Death of God* (Indianapolis: Bobbs-Merrill, 1966).

97 P. Van Buren, *The Secular Meaning of the Gospel Based on an Analysis of Its Language* (New York: Macmillan, 1963); cf. idem, *Theological Explorations* (New York: Macmillan, 1968).

Th. Altizer;[98] other theologians were closely associated with it.[99] While the move did not last beyond the 1960s, several theologians have since pursued similar goals.[100]

Process Theology's Permanent Reconstruction

The relational and processive worldview of Alfred North Whitehead (1861-1947) with its underlying evolutionary perspective provided a new epistemological and ontological foundation for both the progressivist-evolutionary and the revisionist-revolutionary approach to doctrinal development.[101] Whitehead's view according to which religion needs constantly to be modified, adapted, and recast was taken up by process theology, which allowed for unending evolutionary and/or revolutionary transformations of Christian doctrines.[102]

According to W. Norman Pittenger, the reconceptualization in contemporary idioms of the enduring meaning of the Christ-event involves radical revisions and alterations.[103] Eugene C. Bianchi exemplifies this approach with his symbolizing and imaginative reinterpretation of foundational Christian doctrines;[104] the church must

---

98 Th. Altizer, *The Gospel of Christian Atheism* (Philadelphia: Westminster, 1966); cf. idem, ed., *Towards a New Christianity: Readings in Death of God Theology* (New York: Harcourt, Brace & World, 1967).

99 Among them were the Anglican bishop John A. T. Robinson *(Honest to God* [Philadelphia: Westminster, 1963]); Harvey Cox *(The Secular City* [New York: Macmillan, 1965]; Gabriel Vahanian *(The Death of God* [New York: G. Braziller, 1961]; and Rosemary Ruether, *The Church against Itself* [New York: Herder and Herder, 1967]).

100 Here one thinks of various forms of secular theology that have sprung up since the 1960s, among them liberation theology (Gutiérrez, Segundo, Boff), political theology (Metz, Moltmann), and feminist theology (Sölle).

101 In his *Religion in the Making* (New York: Macmillan, 1926), Alfred North Whitehead rejected the Platonic view of static and enduring essences positing instead that change and becoming are the hallmark of all being – including God himself who exists in holistic unity with the world. But, if everything is in constant flux, religious language, too, is changing in accordance with the shifting experiences and consciousness of humankind. Thus, doctrines, which are the symbolic expressions of religious institutions regarding the meaning of existence, cannot remain in a state of fixed orthodoxy (this would lead to dogmatic idolatry) but require constant reformulation and reinterpretation if they are to retain their power to rekindle in others the primary experiences of great religious figures. See also Whitehead's *magnum opus* on process philosophy, *Process and Reality: An Essay in Cosmology* (New York: Macmillan, 1929). Cf. above, p. 30, n. 12.

102 Whitehead himself insisted that there are "permanent elements apart from which there could be no changing world" and that "dogmas have their measure of truth, which is unalterable" *(Religion in the Making,* 8, 140; cf. 119-144). He identified the changeless with the meaning of dogmatic formulas; the truth to which they point remains identical amidst its changing contemporizing expressions.

103 W. Norman Pittenger, "Reconception and Renewal of Christian Faith," *Encounter* 34 (1973): 254-266; see also idem, *Process Thought and Christian Faith* (New York: Macmillan, 1968).

104 Eugene C. Bianchi, "A Holistic and Dynamic Development of Doctrinal Symbols," *Anglican Theological Review* 55 (1973): 148-169.

learn how to cope with radical doctrinal discontinuities, i.e., with changes which even threaten its structural and ideological continuity.[105] And, because of the historicity of all truth, William E. Reiser denies the existence not only of fixed doctrines but even of their alleged permanent meaning.[106] To him, Christianity "is born anew, as it were, from age to age."[107]

Models of Historical Perspectivism (Situationist Theories)

Pointing to the inevitable historicity and provisional character of all theological statements, the situationist theories recognize the validity of the historic doctrinal decisions of the church in view of the particular situations and conditions out of which they arose.[108] At the same time, they maintain that there can be a plurality of valid perspectives on truth succeeding each other or even existing side by side.[109] The

105 Eugene C. Bianchi, "History and Evolution in Roman Catholic Thought," *Religion in Life* 38 (1969): 498-521; esp. 515-521.

106 William E. Reiser, *What Are They Saying about Dogma?* (New York: Paulist Press, 1978).

107 Ibid., 70. Other leading representatives of process thought are Charles Hartshorne (1897-) and John Cobb, Jr.; its influence can also be felt in Schubert Ogden and Avery Dulles. Eugene Fontinell combines pragmatism with a processive worldview resulting in the call for a radical reconstruction of philosophy and theology *(Toward a Reconstruction of Religion: A Philosophical Probe* [Garden City, N.Y.: Doubleday, 1970]). See also Charles E. Winquist, "Reconstruction in Process Theology," *Anglican Theological Review* 55 (1973): 169-181. According to Gerald Thomas Floyd, Whitehead's philosophy of creativity provides a viable alternative to Newman's theory on the development of doctrine. Instead of dogmatic finality and irreversible cumulation, the "Whiteheadian alternative" calls for perpetual contextualization as new teachings take their place within the whole complex of beliefs ("The Creativity of Church Teaching: A Whiteheadian Alternative to the Notion of Development of Doctrine" [Ph.D. dissertation, Graduate Theological Union, 1982]).

108 According to the "decision theory" of doctrinal development, all doctrinal formulations are provisional and, thus, reformable and even replaceable; however, the dogmatic decisions of the church are regarded as irreversible, i.e., as "capable of being given an interpretation which is without actual error or which is reconcilable with the truth" (Lindbeck, "Catholic Dogma and the Word of God," in *The Future of Roman Catholic Theology,* 101).

109 The admission of, and even demand for, theological pluralism is a distinguishing mark of the situationist theories; at the same time, it is a characteristic feature of the contemporary theological climate. As certain doctrinal variations seem to have characterized Christianity from its inception, this study might well have paid close attention to apostolic plurality as an explanation for the doctrinal differences in later Christendom. However, doctrinal development apparently takes place independent of whether its starting point is having either a uniform or a pluriform structure. Moreover, what many perceive as the theological pluralism of the New Testament, in itself, seems to have resulted from some previous growth and advance of the primitive Christian faith. Therefore, I consider the diachronic problem of doctrinal development – both logically and chronologically – foundational to the synchronic issue of doctrinal pluralism. On the issue of pluralism in the New Testament, see Walter Bauer, *Orthodoxy and Heresy in Earliest Christianity,* ed. R. A. Kraft and G. Krodel (Philadelphia: Fortress Press, 1971); John Charlot, *New Testament Disunity: Its Significance*

understanding of faith needs to be constantly adapted, reformulated, and reinterpreted by the church in the light of the ever-changing situations and perspectives. The latter demand a fresh rethinking of the implications of the word of God so that the Christian faith may retain its relevance and intelligibility in a particular time and place. As a result, new dogmatic decisions are required which possibly may stand in a discontinuous, and even contradictory, relationship to the doctrinal formulations of the past.

By thus looking at doctrinal developments in a contextual-sociological light as time-conditioned and inadequate expressions of truth, the situationist theories reject the organistic conception of the gradual and homogeneous unfolding of truth. Instead, doctrinal change is looked upon as a pluriform and heterogeneous process resulting from the creative response of the church to divine truth in view of the demands of a particular intellectual and cultural context.

Arising in the 1950s, the perspectivist theories have become quite influential in both Protestant and Roman Catholic theology thereby contributing to the ecumenical *rapprochement* among Christian scholars of the West.[110] These theories have been especially appealing to Roman Catholic theologians struggling with the controversial claim of their church to dogmatic infallibility.[111] Among the leading Roman Catholic representatives of the situationist theories one may mention Yves M.-J. Congar, Walter Kasper, Hans Küng, Nicholas Lash, Edward Schillebeeckx,

---

for *Christianity Today* (New York: E. P. Dutton & Co., 1970); James D. G. Dunn, *Unity and Diversity in the New Testament: An Inquiry into the Character of Earliest Christianity* (Philadelphia: Westminster, 1977); Ernst Käsemann, "The Canon of the New Testament and the Unity of the Church," in *Essays on New Testament Themes,* Studies in Biblical Theology, No. 41 (London: SCM, 1964), 95-107; Helmut Koester, "[Gnomai Diaphoroi.] The Origin and Nature of Diversification in the History of Early Christianity," *Harvard Theological Review* 58 (1965): 279-318; and H. E. W. Turner, *The Pattern of Christian Truth: A Study in the Relations between Orthodoxy and Heresy in the Early Church* (London: Mowbray, 1954; Naperville, Ill.: Allenson, 1954).

110 Already in the 1960s, Lindbeck sensed an implicit and growing Protestant consensus in favor of "historical situationalism" ("The Problem of Doctrinal Development and Contemporary Protestant Theology," 138; see ibid., 133-149, for an elaboration of the situationalist theory). Lindbeck surmised that this view would become common to Roman Catholic theologians in the future ("Catholic Dogma and the Word of God," 101-102). See ibid., 97-118, for another discussion of the decision theory of doctrinal development; cf. Toon, *The Development of Doctrine in the Church,* 79-83.

111 Historical perspectivism admits that "even an infallible dogma can be poorly balanced or incomplete in its statement. Consequently it might actually be misleading" and such "dogmas can be inopportune, unbalanced, and dangerously misunderstood, perhaps even by those involved in their promulgation" (Lindbeck, "Catholic Dogma and the Word of God," 100, 104). But, while the church must not regard its dogmas as irreformable, it may still make binding doctrinal decisions in order to safeguard the unity of the church. In view of the latter's "indefectibility," such dogmas may need reinterpretation and even correction but are not flatly or irretrievably erroneous (ibid., 103-105).

and the late Karl Rahner.[112] Other Roman Catholic scholars have proposed even more radical versions of the perspectivist theories as the following shows.

Dewart's Doctrinal Dehellenization

As one of the most liberal defenders of historical perspectivism, the Canadian philosopher-theologian Leslie Dewart called for the revolutionary reconstruction of church doctrines and for the integration of Christian belief with contemporary experience and thought. This was to be accomplished through the abandonment of the traditional Hellenistic thought patterns with their emphasis on static and immutable truths, in other words, through the dehellenization of the dogmas of the church. Legitimate and useful at their time, classical theology and traditional doctrines have outlived themselves and become inadequate for today's needs which require a fresh conceptualization of humanity's evolving religious experience. Rejecting the notion of linear and homogeneous development as well as the correspondence theory of truth, Dewart allowed for the radical transformation of beliefs involving discontinuities, errors, and negations in the ongoing experience of faith.

Doctrinal evolution is not only unavoidable and necessary but should be deliberately undertaken and controlled in order to safeguard the continued relevance of Christianity in a constantly changing world. For Dewart, the envisioned creation of "the future of belief" involves an ontological atheism, the denial of the Incarnation, and a pragmatic-existential theory of truth according to which truth is constantly developing with human consciousness.[113]

---

112 Yves M.-J. Congar, "Renewal of the Spirit and Reform of the Institution," in *Ongoing Reform in the Church,* Concilium, vol. 73, ed. A. Müller and N. Greinacher (New York: Herder and Herder, 1972), 47; idem, *Vraie et fausse réforme dans l'Église,* 2d rev. ed. (Paris: Édition du Cerf, 1968); Walter Kasper, *Dogma unter dem Wort Gottes* (Mainz: Matthias-Grünewald Verlag, 1965); idem, "Geschichtlichkeit der Dogmen?" *Stimmen der Zeit* (1967): 401-416; Hans Küng, *The Church* (New York: Sheed and Ward, 1967), 342-343; idem, *Infallible? An Inquiry* (Garden City, N.Y.: Doubleday, 1971); cf. Eichhorst, 58-81; Nicholas Lash, *Change in Focus: A Study of Doctrinal Change and Continuity* (London: Sheed & Ward, 1973); idem, ed., *Doctrinal Development and Christian Unity.* On Rahner, see above, p. 77, n. 77; K. Rahner and R. Lehmann, "Geschichtlichkeit der Vermittlung," 727-787; on Edward Schillebeeckx, see above, p. 78, n. 78; and idem, "A Theological Reflection," in *Truth and Certainty,* Concilium, vol. 83, ed. E. Schillebeeckx and B. van Iersel (New York: Herder and Herder, 1973), 77-94.

113 Dewart, *The Future of Belief.* See also idem, "God and the Supernatural," in *New Theology, No. 5,* ed. Martin E. Marty and Dean G. Peerman (New York: Macmillan, 1968), 142-155; cf. Gregory Baum, ed., *The Future of Belief Debate* (New York: Herder and Herder, 1967). Leslie Dewart reiterated and continued his argumentation in favor of the program of dehellenization in his follow-up study, *The Foundations of Belief* (New York: Herder and Herder, 1969). For an exhaustive and critical analysis of Dewart's position, see Eckstrom, 252-433; and Desmond Connell, "Professor Dewart and Dogmatic Development," *Irish Theological Quarterly* 34 (1967): 309-328; 35 (1968): 33-57, 117-140.

Baum's Corrective Refocusing

Another Canadian scholar, Gregory Baum, may be regarded as an outspoken proponent of the perspectival theory of doctrinal change. Openly rejecting what he considered "the legend of the inerrant Church," he maintained that development, at times, demands basic changes in outlook and attitude, involving the abandonment of erroneous views held in the past as well as the affirmation of new doctrinal positions in the present.[114] In his opinion, Vatican Council II shifted the central message and focal point of the gospel to God's redemptive work in the secular world of today. The adoption of this new perspective or focus demands the reinterpretation and restatement of the church's entire body of teaching in order to harmonize it with the contemporary experience of reality.[115]

According to Baum, startling doctrinal accommodations and changes are required if one wants to communicate the gospel effectively to today's world. The church must discern and answer humanity's deepest questionings by listening to God's word in Scripture, tradition, and, above all, contemporary experience. As a result, the church will see changes with regard to its doctrinal formulations and concepts and also adopt new interests and concerns. In fact, in order to preserve the Christian message, its meaning must be adjusted in the light of God's present revelation to humanity.[116]

Dulles's Creative Adaptation

Similar to Gregory Baum, the Jesuit theologian Avery Dulles has called for the radical transmutation and revision of Christian faith and dogma so that they may correspond with the presuppositions, concerns, and thought forms of the contemporary world. All doctrinal statements are subject to historical relativity; for the unchanging revelatory truth can only be grasped within the perspectives of a particular socio-cultural situation. A discontinuous "quantum leap" is required today to prevent the gospel from losing its impact on contemporary society. This task of modernization involves the creative refocusing of the Christian message in the light of a fully modern understanding of humanity and the world as well as its restatement in terms of the conceptual-linguistic frameworks of our time.[117]

114 Gregory Baum, "Doctrinal Renewal," *Journal of Ecumenical Studies* 2 (1965): 365-381; esp. 375-378.
115 Baum, *Faith and Doctrine*. See also idem, *The Credibility of the Church Today,* 141-176, for an elaboration of Baum's notion of the "refocusing of the Gospel."
116 Gregory Baum has applied this view to theology in his *Man Becoming: God in Secular Experience* (New York: Herder and Herder, 1971).
117 Dulles, *The Survival of Dogma,* esp. 12-13, 117-118, 173, 182-184, 198-203. See also idem, "Official Church Teaching and Historical Relativity," in *Spirit, Faith, and Church,* 51-72; and idem, "Contemporary Understanding of the Irreformability of Dogma," in *Proceedings of the Twenty-Fifth Annual Convention,* by the Catholic Theological Society of America (Bronx, N.Y.: Catholic Theological Society of America, 1971), 111-136.

More recently, Dulles has considerably softened his position and objected to the demands for a radical reinterpretation, revision, or transformation of doctrine. He now calls for innovative reform and renewal, instead of doctrinal reconstruction or re-creation. The church's openness and adaptation to the world must be balanced by fidelity to the historic sources of its faith. Accommodation to, and creative inter-action with, contemporary culture must not be confused with an uncritical accep-tance of modernity, which could mean the loss of the identity of the church.[118]

Wiles's Perspectival Alteration

As one of the few Anglican theologians dealing explicitly with the issue of doctrinal development, historian of dogma Maurice Wiles has aroused a lively debate by his critical appraisal of the process of doctrinal change in the early church. Its once necessary doctrinal formulations and legitimate creedal affirmations have become irrelevant in the light of contemporary philosophy and culture. The effective and creative continuation of the aims and objectives of the Church Fathers in today's world demands doctrinal revisions that may appear revolutionary and destructive.

Rather than anachronistically sticking to allegedly infallible and changeless dog-mas, the church today needs to experience something like a Copernican revolution in theology involving drastic doctrinal reversals, shifts of meaning, and a complete reorientation of thought. Substituting a modern worldview for outdated Greek philosophy as a framework of thought is the only path to constructive advance.[119]

In a follow-up study, Wiles has further elaborated on his radical revisionist theory according to which cultural changes lead to an "alteration of perspective" that results in far-reaching and never-ending doctrinal novelties. As the re-presentation of Christian beliefs in new forms cannot be achieved without altering their substantial content, theology can make no absolute or exclusivist claims, offer no fixed criteria of truth, and set no limits to theological pluralism.[120]

Pannenberg's Proleptic (Re-)Formulation

On the Protestant side, Wolfhart Pannenberg has allowed for the formal contra-diction of traditional doctrines with contemporary theological expressions. Because of humanity's constantly changing experience of reality, doctrinal formulations, which were once adequate for a particular time, remain open to change and further

---

118 Avery Dulles, *The Resilient Church: The Necessity and Limits of Adaptation* (Garden City, N.Y.: Doubleday, 1977). For a Protestant version of moderate situationalism, see Toon, *The Development of Doctrine in the Church*, 105-126; cf. above, p. 73, n. 66.

119 Maurice Wiles, *The Making of Christian Doctrine: A Study in the Principles of Early Doctrinal Development* (Cambridge: Cambridge University Press, 1967).

120 Maurice Wiles, *The Remaking of Christian Doctrine* (London: SCM, 1974); see also idem, "Theology and Unity," *Theology* 77 (1974): 4-6; idem, "The Remaking Defended," *Theology* 78 (1975): 394-397; and idem, *Working Papers in Doctrine* (London: SCM, 1976).

development. Their historical relativity must be recognized; therefore, the church cannot achieve unity of faith by means of dogmatic uniformity in the expressions of ultimate truth.   Being provisional and proleptic in nature, doctrines lack the eschatological fullness of truth.[121]

Summary and Conclusion

Up to the seventeenth century, Christian theology – Catholic and Protestant alike – generally shared the belief in the immutable and perfect character of true doctrine. Influenced by scholastic thought patterns and not yet disturbed by the question of historical relativity, theologians were content with the immobilist-stationary approach to doctrinal development which denied the very possibility of legitimate doctrinal changes. They either maintained that the body of doctrinal truths had been complete from the beginning (the historical theory), or they reduced doctrinal development to a merely explicative unfolding and logical explication of propositional truths (the logical theory). Besides, a few scholars enlisted the help of the church's magisterial authority in defining the growing body of revelatory truths (the new revelation theory).

It was only when the newly developing sense as well as the science of history had left its impact on theology during the eighteenth and nineteenth centuries that the complex nature of the problem of doctrinal change was recognized by a growing number of theologians. It was also then that the first attempts were made to tackle this issue with the help of a dynamic conception of development. Influenced by rationalist and idealist philosophy as well as by evolutionary conceptions, a number of scholars – who admitted the possibility of genuine doctrinal development – defined it either in terms of unlimited progress (the transformistic theory), of organic unfolding (the organistic theory), or of ideal growth (the psychological theory).

In the twentieth century, these progressivist-evolutionary models were further refined and discussed with regard to the controlling norms of doctrinal advance (the theological theory). The twentieth century also experienced the near demise of the static mentality of traditional theology with its immobilist notion of unvarying doctrine; besides, it witnessed the steady decline of the evolutionary optimism of modern theology with its teleological view of history and its progressivist assumption of homogeneous development.

Postulating, in its place, the inevitable and radical historicity of all human expressions of truth, contemporary theology generally favors the revisionist-revolutionary models of doctrinal development which make room for, and even

---

121 Wolfhart Pannenberg, "Was ist eine dogmatische Aussage?" in *Grundfragen systematischer Theologie: Gesammelte Aufsätze* (Göttingen: Vandenhoeck & Ruprecht, 1967), 1:177-180, 159-180; ET: idem, "What Is a Dogmatic Statement?" in *Basic Questions in Theology: Collected Essays* (Philadelphia: Fortress Press, 1970), 206-210, 182-210.   See also Pannenberg, Dulles, and Braaten, *Spirit, Faith, and Church,* 13-31, 108-123. For a survey of some other, less prominent revisionist models of doctrinal development, see appendix 1.

foster, the transmutation and revision of doctrinal statements (revisionist theories). The constantly changing perspectives of humanity on reality and truth, according to this approach, not only justify the discontinuities in the historical development of doctrinal beliefs but also help explain the pluralistic and ecumenical character of contemporary theology (situationist theories).

The growing number of diverse and even contradictory theories of doctrinal development proposed during the past two centuries seems to indicate that an easy solution to this intricate problem and a conclusive answer to the difficult questions raised by the fact of doctrinal change may not exist – if ever one will be found.[122]

In order to see one's way in this plurality of views, one needs an intelligent understanding of the basic structural types to which the numerous models of doctrinal development belong which have been proposed until now. To present such a "typology" of theories of doctrinal development is the purpose of chapter 3.

---

122 "Die fast unübersehbare Vielfalt der Theorien über die D[ogmenentwicklung] bei den katholischen Theologen zeigt, daß eine klare und allseits schon verständliche Lösung noch nicht adäquat gegeben ist" (K. Rahner, "Dogmenentwicklung," *LThK,* 1959 ed., 3:461).

Chapter 3

A Typology of Theories on Doctrinal Development

Les extrêmes se touchent.

French Saying

Hold to the middle if you do not want to lose the mean. The middle ground is safe … Every dwelling place beyond the mean is counted an exile by a wise man.

Bernard of Clairvaux

Introduction

The historical-genetic study of theories of doctrinal development presented in chapter 2 has brought to light a large spectrum of diverging and even contradictory conceptual models which took shape during three successive periods of church history. It is also obvious that there exist, at times, substantial disagreements even among theories that follow the same basic approach.[1] This suggests that there may be yet another and perhaps more appropriate way of differentiating and grouping the numerous theories on development.

As this chapter intends to show, a systematic-typological analysis reveals the existence of three fundamental types of theory on doctrinal development.[2] They encompass virtually all existing and even potential models of change but coincide only partially with the three basic approaches successively developed in church

---

1   This is particularly obvious with the theories following the progressivist-evolutionary approach. Among other things, they differ widely regarding the authority ascribed to dogmas and creeds, Scripture and the teaching office, respectively. For example, Newman's theory of development stands in sharp opposition to the liberal and modernist conceptions – their confusion by his earlier critics notwithstanding.

2   A "type" is the classification for study purposes of a number of individuals or ideas on the basis of certain distinctive characteristics shared by all members of the group. This method, which has been used successfully in the natural sciences (zoology), was applied to the religious realm by Max Weber (1864-1920), whose church-sect typology described various ideal ecclesial types *(Gesammelte Aufsätze zur Religionssoziologie I* [Tübingen: J. C. B. Mohr, 1920]). He was followed by Ernst Troeltsch *(The Social Teachings of the Christian Churches,* 2 vols. [New York: Macmillan, 1931]) and H. Richard Niebuhr *(Christ and Culture* [New York: Harper Torchbooks, 1956]). More recently, Avery Dulles has used the typological method in discussing the doctrines of the church *(Models of the Church* [Garden City, N.Y.: Doubleday, 1974]) and of revelation *(Models of Revelation* [Garden City, N.Y.: Doubleday, 1983]).

history. Historically speaking, a theory of doctrinal continuity and change follows either the traditional immobilist-stationary, the modern progressivist-evolutionary, or the contemporary revisionist-revolutionary approach.[3] But seen from a systematic-typological perspective, one can classify any theory of doctrinal development as belonging to either the "conservative" or "right wing" static type, the "liberal" or "left wing" evolutionary/revolutionary type, or the moderate and mediating dynamic type.[4]

Moving from concrete history to abstract typology inevitably involves some kind of (over)simplification and artificial schematization; after all, all mental abstractions from empirical reality necessarily fail to do full justice to the complex structures of real life. Still, and in spite of its obvious limitations, a typology of theories on doctrinal development, which describes ideal types[5] rather than concrete models, may prove to be useful for a proper understanding and evaluation of the numerous models of doctrinal continuity and change. While there exist no rigid boundaries among them, these basic types are clearly marked off from each other in various important respects. Moreover, in my opinion, they constitute the only and fundamental options available to those who attempt to tackle the problem of doctrinal development, be they theologians or religious communities, scholars or churches – including Seventh-day Adventists.

The Static Type

The static type of theory represents the "conservative" or "right wing" method of dealing with the challenge of doctrinal change. It coincides more or less with the traditional immobilist-stationary approach to doctrinal development which has found expression in the three traditional models of doctrinal development, viz., the historical theory, the logical theory, and the new revelation theory.

Closely connected to a static view of reality, these theories regard the doctrines of the Christian church as being more or less immune to real changes and unaffected by the vicissitudes of human history. The usual designation of these theories as

---

3   It is not altogether unlikely that, in the future, still other basic approaches to doctrinal develop-ment may be conceived on the basis of some new, contemporaneous philosophical trends.

4   I use the terms conservative/right wing and liberal/left wing type, not in any derogatory sense, but simply as descriptive of their strong inclination to either oppose or foster doctrinal trans-mutations.

5   "They do not correspond exactly to real distinctions which are actually found in the world. The world is rarely as pure and tidy as the theorist would like. Ideal types represent not an exact reproduction of the world of reality, but, as it were, caricatures. They picture reality not in its structure but in its tendency, exaggerating its peculiar and its significant features, and attempting to formulate it into a rational whole" (David Nicholls, "Modifications and Movements," *Journal of Theological Studies* 25 [1974]: 395).

"logical,"[6] "intellectualistic,"[7] "rational,"[8] and "objective"[9] is due to their common emphasis on the intellectual side of faith and the objective nature of revelatory truth. They may also be called objectivistic because of their proclivity to strongly emphasize the objective aspects, to the possible neglect of the subjective dimensions of revelation, faith, and the knowledge of truth.

Premises and Assumptions

Basic to the objectivistic theories of doctrinal development is the conviction that revelation consists of propositions that contain objective and invariable truth(s) and communicate rational knowledge to humanity. Accordingly, faith (being the believer's response to divine revelation) means the believing assent to the system of doctrinal truths set forth in the normative revelation.

Objective truth is apprehended intellectually and provides humans with rational knowledge conveyed by means of doctrinal propositions which adequately express metaphysical truth. Thus, the believer is confronted with an extrinsic and un-questionable authority in the form of the Scriptures and, possibly, even tradition, the magisterium, and the church. Dogmas are considered all-important, treated as part of the invariable substance of faith, and often surrounded with an aura of infallibility.

Marks and Features

Resulting from these basic theological premises, the principal characteristic of the objectivistic theories is a strong emphasis on the continuity, self-identity, and doctrinal purity of the Christian faith. While they admit (in varying degrees) to changes in the formulation of doctrines, they are strictly opposed to any variations with regard to their content and meaning. Thus, development is limited to linguistic clarifications and explicative restatements in synonymous terms of the invariable meaning and content of revealed truth. Reformulations or translations into the language of another culture and time may involve only apparent, i.e., verbal, changes. Real modifications that affect the meaning and content of doctrinal assertions are rejected as heretical deviations from the immutable faith.

---

6   Walgrave, 135; Rahner called them "formallogisch" ("Dogmenentwicklung," *LThK*, 1959 ed., 3:459-460).
7   Hammans, 119; cf. Rahner, "Dogmenentwicklung," *LThK*, 1959 ed., 3:459-460.
8   Hammans, 119.
9   Mark G. McGrath, *The Vatican Council's Teaching on the Evolution of Dogma* ([Rome: n.p.], 1960), 9.

Varieties and Representatives

In the past, a number of attempts have been made to justify the idea of doctrinal immutability in the face of seemingly undeniable historical developments and changes. Apparently novel views were either seen as rediscovered beliefs of the primitive church or, at least, of the apostles (the historical theory), understood as the mere logical explication of implicitly held truths (the logical theory), or interpreted as the dogmatic definition of truths previously known by human reason but now regarded as divinely revealed (the new revelation theory).

Outstanding representatives of the objectivistic approach to doctrinal development are Vincent of Lérins, Bossuet, scholasticism and neoscholasticism, Protestant orthodoxy, as well as fundamentalism.

Methods and Criteria

In view of its intellectualistic outlook and absolutist notion of truth, it is not surprising that, according to the static type, rational factors (like the logical stringency of deductive reasoning) and highly authoritative institutions (e.g., an inerrant Bible or a supernaturally guided church endowed with an infallible magisterium) are considered the principal arbiters of doctrinal development. It fits the severely restricted view of change as defined by those theories that the criteria employed in judging the legitimacy of doctrinal development are likewise of a rather restrictive kind.[10]

Strengths and Weaknesses [11]

The critique of the objectivistic theories focuses on their highly hypothetical claims and on the philosophical-theological presuppositions on which they are built and with which they apparently stand or fall.[12]

---

10 Interestingly, the manner of doctrinal changes envisaged by a theory of development corresponds fairly exactly to the principles by which the resulting changes are supposed to be evaluated. In other words, doctrine is tested in the same way in which it develops. This is even reflected in the nomenclature of the various theories. Their designation (as historical, logical, theological, etc.) often expresses this twofold characteristic of any given theory, viz., the supposed nature of doctrinal changes and their corresponding criteria. This points to a certain inevitable circularity in arguing for or against any particular theory of doctrinal development. On the hermeneutical circle of human understanding, see above, pp. 51-52.

11 In describing the respective strengths and weaknesses of the three basic types of theory on doctrinal development, I do not want to forestall the results of a theological evaluation of these types. Rather, I simply want to list what can be said (1) in favor of these types (as seen by their adherents) and (2) against them (usually from the perspective of the other two approaches). While trying to be as objective as I possibly can in describing their respective (dis-)advantages, I am cognizant of my personal preference regarding these types.

12 See, e.g., Hammans, 164-173; Schulz, 73-124 passim, 278-280; and Walgrave, 162-178 passim.

First, the so-called historical theory, as seen by its critics, is archaistic, anachronistic, and anything but historical as it flatly ignores and even contradicts the facts of history;[13] it also fails to provide any historical substantiation for its far-reaching claims.[14] The same criticism applies principally also to the logical theory.[15]

Second, the objectivistic theories tend to use oral tradition (both public and esoteric) as a stopgap in bridging the distance between the Scriptures and later church dogmas. This is questionable on both historical[16] and hermeneutical[17] grounds.

Third, contrary to the intellectualistic assumptions of scholastic epistemology,[18] human thought does not always, or even predominantly, proceed in a syllogistic manner.[19] Neither is Christianity a religion of syllogisms.[20] And if, as may be

13　The study of the history of dogma has shown that various doctrinal developments have, indeed, taken place that resulted in what came to be regarded as orthodox teachings – at least, as seen by most Christian churches.

14　It is also highly improbable on psychological grounds. For what should have prompted the apostles to their alleged secrecy in conveying revealed truths? And if conveyed, how could the latter have been completely kept secret or entirely forgotten by the church?

15　"With the best will in the world it seems impossible to fit the facts into the theory except by frankly Procrustean procedures" (Walgrave, 166). Walter Kasper concurred in this assessment: "Jeder, der die konkrete Dogmengeschichte kennt, weiß, daß die Dogmen nicht nur das Ergebnis eines logischen Deduktionsprozesses sind. Eine solche Konzeption der Dogmengeschichte ist eine Abstraktion, sie stellt bestenfalls eine leidliche nachträgliche Nachkonstruktion dar" (Dogma unter dem Wort Gottes, 132; cf. ibid., 132-134). See also Schulz, 118.

16　Why, e.g., did this esoteric tradition fail to surface after the persecution of Christians ceased in the 4th century? And how is one to interpret the fact that the leading theologians ignored or even contradicted this alleged tradition?

17　As a number of Roman Catholic dogmas cannot be sufficiently supported from Scripture alone, the logical theory is closely allied in Roman Catholic theology with the two-source theory of revelation which places the oral apostolic tradition alongside the New Testament (see Karl Rahner, "Scripture and Tradition," Sacramentum Mundi, 1968 ed., 6:54). However, this is unacceptable to Protestants maintaining the sola scriptura principle.

18　The objectivistic theories have their theological and epistemological foundation in medieval and modern scholasticism.

19　If someone makes an assertion, he does not thereby necessarily endorse all of its logical implications (be they premises or conclusions). While God may be assumed to know all the implications of his word, the Scriptures are expressing divine truth with the help of human language, logic, and thought – which are unavoidably fallible and imperfect.

20　Even when a logical connection can afterwards be shown to exist between two propositions, this does not mean that the development that led from one to the other took place in a purely rational-deductive manner. But if the validity of doctrinal derivations does not rest in the logical rigor of their deduction but rather in the authority of an infallible magisterium (which needs no such proofs in promulgating new doctrines), then the strictly logical nexus becomes altogether hypothetical and loses its practical value. Besides, even the supporters of the logical theory must admit that later doctrines (as, for example, the modern Marian dogmas) cannot always be proven logically or verified conclusively. This, however, would be required if the theory were to stand.

argued, God-talk is paradoxical and analogous rather than syllogistic and unequivocal, then that which follows from a statement logically may not yet be valid theologically.[21]

Fourth, there is a rationalistic element in the assumption that the truths of faith are comprehensible to mere human logic. Because of this intellectualism, the objectivistic theories tend to downgrade the importance of nonrational factors in the development of doctrine.[22] For all practical matters, they disregard the inevitable historicity of all human thought.[23]

Finally, the objectivistic theories possess a one-sided view of revelation, faith, and truth, for they neglect the subjective aspects of God's speaking as well as of man's believing response to revealed truth. As a result, they end up with a reductionistic view of development according to which later dogmas are but the rediscovered, reformulated, or syllogistically explicated beliefs of the primitive church.

On the positive side it may be noted, however, that the objectivistic theories (1) share a deep concern for the continuity, self-identity, and purity of the Christian faith, (2) regard the Scriptures as normative revelation and an objective source of truth, (3) uphold the existence of a logical connection between revelation and later dogmas, (4) ascribe to doctrines an important function for the life of faith, and (5) avoid the twin dangers of dogmatic relativism and subjectivism.[24]

---

21 See Wilfried Joest, "Zur Frage des Paradoxon in der Theologie," in *Dogma und Denkstrukturen,* ed. W. Joest and W. Pannenberg, Festschrift für Edmund Schlink (Göttingen: Vandenhoeck & Ruprecht, 1963), 149-151; and Edmund Schlink, "Der theologische Syllogismus als Problem der Prädestinationslehre," in *Einsicht und Glaube,* Festschrift für Gottlieb Söhngen, ed. J. Ratzinger and H. Fries (Freiburg: Herder, 1962), 299, 318-320.

22 Doctrines, however, are not created in the ivory towers of the theologians-logicians; instead, they arise and develop as the church strives for a deeper or more timely understanding of divine revelation.

23 Insofar as the logic used in the Scriptures is human rather than divine, it shares in the relativity of everything human. Besides, one finds in the Bible various historically grown ideas and perspectives which cannot always be correlated in a strictly logical manner.

24 While the historical theory denies the possibility of legitimate doctrinal change, its proponents may recognize and interpret actual doctrinal changes in terms of aberrations. The application of the concept of decline/deformation (see above, p. 32) and reform/restoration allows them to call for doctrinal revisions regarding views held by an apostate church (the Protestant view) or by heretics who have apostasized from the true church (the Roman Catholic view). In this way, they can maintain the idea of doctrinal immutability regarding divinely revealed doctrines. Restorationism has played an important role in the history of Christianity by calling for faithfulness to biblical/apostolic truth in view of apparent doctrinal deviations and corruptions. To classical Protestantism the restoration of doctrinal purity involved the return to the Holy Scriptures, while Roman Catholicism demanded the submission to the divinely guided church. Cutting across several of the approaches to doctrinal change surveyed in this study (but not being identical to any one of them), restorationism can be found even among representatives of the transformistic theory as is shown by Harnack's *Verfallsidee* and its related concept of *Entdogmatisierung.* To him, the restoration of true Christian faith involved the abandonment of all dogmatic truth. See above pp. 40, 58-60, and 67.

Evolutionary/Revolutionary Type

Diametrically opposed to the intellectualism of the objectivistic theories on doctrinal development are those models that place strong emphasis on the subjective factors of faith, opting for an evolutionary or even revolutionary conception of history which regards far-reaching changes and radical transmutations as characteristic symptoms of human history. The designation of these theories as "transformistic"[25] or subjectivistic[26] indicates their tendency to make rather light of doctrinal continuity as well as of the objective aspects of revelation, faith, and the knowledge of truth. Thus, the evolutionary/revolutionary type of theory on doctrinal development represents the "liberal" or "left wing" method of dealing with doctrinal continuity and change.

Premises and Assumptions

Common to the subjectivistic theories of the evolutionary/revolutionary type is the view that divine revelation consists of an inexpressible subjective experience which is beyond the reach of human language and thought. Consequently, faith is not the believing assent to objective truths, but a feeling arising in response to the encounter with ultimate reality. Truth, therefore, can only be existentially experienced and intuitively known, but it cannot adequately be expressed in conceptual or linguistic form.

To these theories, religious authority is seen as intrinsic and relative to human experience; therefore, the Bible constitutes merely the historic and time-conditioned witness of past generations to their mystical encounter with God. It is not an objectively given body of truths transmitted in written or oral tradition which is normative for faith, but rather humanity's contemporary experience of the divine.

While they may serve as useful pointers to and symbolic representations of revelation, doctrines are not an immutable, essential, or constitutive part of the Christian faith but merely the fallible and rather insignificant objectifications of humankind's religious experiences. After all, they are incapable of adequately expressing the intuitive knowledge of faith. Thus, doctrinal propositions possess no permanent validity, having only provisional and pragmatic value instead.

Marks and Features

Because of these *a prioris,* the subjectivistic theories allow for genuine and substantial changes regarding the doctrinal expressions of the Christian faith. Without denying the need for some underlying continuity and self-identity concerning the essence of

---

25 Walgrave, 179.

26 I prefer this term for the sake of a contrasting parallelism to the first group of theories to which they stand in clear opposition.

Christianity, these theories refuse to count any doctrinal propositions as belonging to the invariable substance of faith. Instead, doctrines are subject to far-reaching transformations analogous to the radical mutations of life forms as assumed by the evolutionary hypothesis of natural science. Moreover, because of the inevitable historicity of all human thought, doctrinal developments may involve even radical discontinuities and revolutionary reconstructions regarding the meaning and content of the doctrinal expressions of the Christian faith.

In correspondence with the gradual evolution of the human consciousness, mankind's ongoing experience of the divine reality needs constantly to be translated into the linguistic and conceptual framework of the surrounding culture. Only in this way may faith retain its relevance and intelligibility in the modern world; otherwise, God-talk will become obsolete and incomprehensible. Faithfulness to the truth requires, therefore, the constant accommodation and adaptation of doctrinal propositions to the experience and thinking of today's world.

In short, doctrinal development involves fundamental revisions even with regard to the substance of dogmas. Continuity, on the other hand, is thought to rest mainly in the never-ending existential encounter with the ineffable mystery of God and in the continuing memory of this experience in the church.[27]

Varieties and Representatives

As Walgrave has observed, "It follows from the very nature of the transformistic theory of doctrinal development that it is itself subject to the law of transformation."[28] Depending on the spirit of the times when they arise, the different theories of the subjectivist type invariably reflect the influence of current philosophical trends – without losing, however, their distinctively common features.[29]

Under the impact of the optimistic spirit of the nineteenth and early twentieth centuries, Protestant liberalism and Catholic modernism proposed the idea of unlimited doctrinal progress (the transformistic theories). When the shock of World War I had dampened humanity's exuberant expectations, neoliberal and neomodernist theologies advanced a revisionist view on doctrinal development (the revisionist theories). Radical theology's consistent secularism represents one of the most extreme forms of this approach to date. More common today is the radical version of historical perspectivism which tolerates and even propagates doctrinal relativism and largescale theological pluralism (the situationist theories).

---

27 On the collective memory of the church as a factor of continuity, see Bianchi, "A Holistic and Dynamic Development," 163, n. 37.
28 Walgrave, 202-203.
29 "To be sure, the basic idea is always the same: A distinction between the essence of Christianity and its changeable accidentals, the latter including all objectifying propositions. The relation between the essence and the accidents can, however, be thought of in different ways. There are also different ways of explaining and justifying the theory" (ibid., 203).

Methods and Criteria

In accordance with its subjectivist view of revelation, its existential notion of faith, and its relativistic concept of truth, the evolutionary/revolutionary type of theory regards contemporary culture (including its science, worldview, and self-understanding) as arbiter of doctrinal truth. All objective religious authorities (like Scripture, tradition, and dogmas as well as the church and its magisterium) are held in low esteem; this corresponds, in turn, to the high value that is placed upon human reason and the contemporary experience and consciousness of humanity.

Strengths and Weaknesses

Like their objectivistic counterparts, the subjectivistic theories fully rest on certain premises that are subject to serious questioning.[30]

First, these theories seem to jeopardize the continuity of the Christian faith by their open disregard of the propositional aspects of revealed truth. Their subjectivism leaves the church without objective ties to the all-decisive and historical self-revelation of God in the person of Jesus Christ which is the most basic tenet of the Christian faith. Theologically speaking, such a loss of self-identity would mean the end of the church as the body of the "faith-ful."

Second, the disregard and, at times, outright denial of the objective side of revelation, faith, and truth amounts to the rejection of any objective truth content of doctrinal assertions. It reduces dogmas to the status of replaceable products of religious experience and non-cognitive symbols of subjective impressions of faith. Through such dogmatic relativism, the subjectivistic theories foster an agnostic view of truth which is contrary to biblical faith.

Third, by their acceptance of modern evolutionary conceptions of history postulating radical mutations and ceaseless transformations, these theories seem to have succumbed to a philosophical perspective which – claims to the contrary not-withstanding – has not been sufficiently substantiated by modern science. This evolutionism, however, appears to put in jeopardy a number of fundamental biblical concepts.[31]

Fourth, the attempt to integrate Christian faith with modern philosophy and culture all too easily ends with the collapse of faith in secular experience. Such modernism will not safeguard or enhance the relevance of the Bible and its teachings. Rather, it leads to a faith void of any content and, thereby, ends with a powerless Christianity which searches for a mission but has lost its message.

Fifth, to use human experience and contemporary philosophical thought as normative guides in the reinterpretation of the Bible is to subject the latter to an extrinsic and fallible authority and, as such, is contrary to the Protestant Scripture

---

30 See above, p. 96, n. 11.
31 Such as the character of God, the nature and destiny of man, the meaning of sin and salvation, human ethics, and eschatology.

principle. As a result, revelation is no longer allowed to function as the judge of reason; for the latter has presumptuously declared itself the arbiter of revealed truth.

Finally, the attempt to separate the outdated form and formulations of the Christian faith from its lasting content and essence easily ends up by retaining the verbal form but discarding its inherent meaning. This, for example, seems to have been the practical outcome of consistent deliteralization (Bultmann) and symbolization (Tillich).

As far as their positive contributions are concerned, the subjectivistic theories may be said to (1) fully admit the possibility, and even necessity, of real doctrinal development, (2) take seriously the historicity that characterizes all human concepts and expressions including biblical teachings and doctrinal views, (3) point to the inevitable subjectivity attached to faith's understanding of divine revelation, (4) strive for a truly contextual theology which relates the Christian message to modern culture and desires to communicate the gospel in terms intelligible and relevant to contemporary man, and (5) avoid the twin errors of dogmatic absolutism and objectivism.

The Dynamic Type

The third basic type of theory on doctrinal development differs from the other two because of the conscious attempt to avoid what may be seen as their respective reductionistic pitfalls without, however, losing their essential and valuable insights. Assuming a theologically moderate stance on the issues involved and also employing a dialectic approach by stressing the need for doctrinal continuity while, at the same time, allowing for authentic doctrinal change, the dynamic type hopes to strike a happy medium between the extremes of dogmatic absolutism and doctrinal relativism. For this reason, the third group of theories on doctrinal development has been labelled "anti-intellectualistic," [32] "metalogical," [33] "organic," [34] or, mostly, "theological." [35]

In using the term dialectic, I want to draw attention to the fact that this supposed *via media* does not favor simply a kind of opportunistic eclecticism which randomly chooses whatever it likes from two different quarries. Rather, it involves a genuine synthesis which purposefully transcends what is perceived as the one-sidedness of

---

32 M. Flick, "Il problema dello sviluppo del dogma nella teologia contemporanea," in *Lo sviluppo del dogma secundo la dottrina cattolica* (Rome: Gregorian University Press, 1953), 5-23 passim.

33 Chirico, "Religious Experience and Development of Dogma," 56-84.

34 Dulles, *The Resilient Church*, 49.

35 R. Draguet, "L'évolution des dogmes," in *Apologetique: Nos raisons de croire. Réponses aux objections*, ed. M. Brillant and M. Nedoncelle, 2d ed. (Paris: Bloud et Gay, 1948), 1097-1122; Meulemann, 51; Hammans, 175; Edward Schillebeeckx, *Offenbarung und Theologie* (Mainz: Matthias-Grünewald-Verlag, 1965), 63; and Walgrave, 278. Schulz has pointed out that the label "theological" implies that doctrinal development can be finally grasped only by faith in God's revelation and with the help of theology (p. 302).

both the objectivistic and the subjectivistic types of theory.[36] With this third type, the assumption of a final and unsurpassable divine revelation in the historic past is coupled with the desire for an ever-deepening understanding of the word of God in the present and future which finds continual expression in doctrinal statements conveying objective truth, albeit in a historically conditioned manner.

While such a "both ... and" attitude to doctrinal development may give the impression of trying to have the cake and eat it, too, it can be regarded as being irrational or sophistical only if strictly logical reasoning is required of a true assertion, on the one hand, and if the existence of theological paradoxes is ruled out, on the other hand. But if reality cannot adequately be explained without the help of seemingly contradictory assertions, then one must take seriously the claim of the dialectical theories to present the most balanced and factual approach to the problem of doctrinal identity and change.

Premises and Assumptions

According to the dialectic theories, revelation is a divine act of self-giving which involves both the communication of objective truth and a subjective encounter with and experience of God. Under the guidance of the Holy Spirit, revelation is crystallized into intellectual concepts and finds, however inadequately, linguistic expression in doctrinal propositions. Culminating in the divine self-communication in Jesus Christ, objective-historical revelation cannot be surpassed by later existential encounters with God. Responding to the divine initiative, faith is a subjective act of implicit trust in the self-revealing God *(fides qua)*, which is inextricably bound up with believing assent to the doctrinal content of the divine word *(fides quae)*.[37]

Correspondingly, truth also possesses a twofold dimension: an objective, propositional one, which is reflected in the doctrinal beliefs of the church, and a subjective, existential one, which is related to the personal experience of the living Truth. As the idealist version of the dialectical approach to doctrinal development assumes, this personal encounter with the divine Reality creates in the believer an intuitive grasp and immediate awareness of truth which, in turn, is expressed in ideas and concepts conveying at least some objective knowledge of the divine mystery.

According to the dynamic type, authority likewise participates in the dual (subjective-objective) dimension of revelation, faith, and truth. Ultimately located

---

36   At times, the intellectualistic theories have also been called dialectical. But in contradistinction to the scholastic sense of the term, which refers to a method of logical reasoning by which to "resolve" contradictory or juxtaposed arguments, I rather employ this expression in accordance with its neo-orthodox usage where the *via dialectica* is distinguished from both the *via dogmatica* and the *via negativa*. Cf. the *Oxford Dictionary of the Christian Church*, 2d ed. (1974), s.v. "Dialectical Theology."

37   Speaking of what he prefers to call the "theological theory," Walgrave points out that "it supposes a conception of revelation and faith that combines intimately a propositional and nonpropositional moment" ("Doctrine, Development of," *NCE*, 1967 ed., 4:942).

in God himself, authority assumes visible form in the Scriptures which are the normative and binding expression of the word of God. Yet insofar as they only imperfectly reflect the divine truth in historically conditioned form(ulations), in the final analysis, their authority rests, not in the (human) words themselves, but in the (divine) message they bear. The latter, however, must be extrapolated from the Bible by the divinely guided human interpreter.[38] Doctrines, then, are propositions authorized by the church as valid and binding expressions of the revealed truth of faith.[39]

Marks and Features

To the dialectic theories, the need for substantial doctrinal continuity rates as equally important as the fundamental openness to genuine doctrinal change. Granting that by reason of their contextual relatedness to a particular time and culture doctrinal formulations are, to some degree, subject to reinterpretation (which is more than the mere reformulation conceded by the objectivistic theories) as well as reconceptualization (which is less than the radical transformation demanded by the subjectivistic approach), the dialectic theories allow for changes that do not jeopardize the essential content of faith. Locating its substance, not in the time-conditioned linguistic and conceptual expressions as such, but rather in their intended meaning, this mediating approach leaves room for changes as regards the non-essential content of doctrines while maintaining the immutability of the essential meaning of revealed truth.

Like the objectivistic theories, the dialectic approach considers doctrinal development as the explication of what is implied in the unchanging divine revelation; but it refuses to define this unfolding in strictly logical terms or to limit it to verbal restatements of doctrinal formulations. On the other hand, it concurs with the subjectivistic theories in admitting the historical conditionality of all doctrinal formulations; however, it denies that this renders the substance of doctrinal truths obsolete and replaceable.[40]

---

38 Roman Catholic theologians include the authority of the ecclesiastical traditions, of the divinely guided church in general, and of the magisterium in particular, as additional criteria in determining the doctrinal content of revelation. Protestant interpreters, on the other hand, point to the self-interpretative function of the Bible and regard human reason, contemporary science and experience as well as the past doctrinal insights of the church as hermeneutical assistants in the interpretative task. Both approaches agree, however, in emphasizing the role of the Holy Spirit in prompting as well as in safeguarding an adequate understanding of revealed truth.

39 According to Roman Catholic teaching, dogmas share, at least in their essential content, in the quality of infallibility which Christ himself is said to have promised to his church. Protestants, on the other hand, allow, in principle, for the possibility that some teachings of the church may turn out to be misleading or erroneous. Still, doctrines are deemed necessary in order to provide faith with an identifiable and communicable content.

40 In a nutshell, one could say that according to the objectivistic theories later doctrines say exactly the same thing as previous ones, though in different words; the dialectic theories allow

The dynamic character of this mediating type is reflected in its openness to the re-presenting actualization of the biblical message for contemporary humanity, which does not, however, subject the gospel to the latest scientific hypothesis or philosophical fad. Its theological dynamics are also seen in the readiness for such doctrinal reformation and renewal as may be demanded by the deepening understanding of revealed truth. In brief, the dynamic type of theory on doctrinal development seems to possess a flexibility lacking to the static approach while, at the same time, attempting to avoid the relativism inherent in many progressivist theories as well as in most revisionist models.

Varieties and Representatives

What the earlier representatives of the dynamic type of theory had in common was the idea of a homogeneous, linear-accumulative, and irreversible development of doctrine, a notion which was derived from the optimistic and progressivist spirit of the nineteenth century. The evolution of dogma was described in terms of the organic unfolding of a seed (the organistic theory), the gradual growth of an idea (the psychological theory), or as the controlled advance of truth (the theological theory). Taking recourse to either vitalistic-pneumatic conceptions or psychological-epistemological hypotheses, these theories considered later church doctrines to be germinally present in primitive beliefs out of which they gradually developed in a continuous and harmonious manner.

Under the impact of twentieth-century philosophy and science, more recent theories belonging to the dynamic type have, in addition, made room for heterogeneous developments which not only supplement but even correct the doctrinal heritage of the Christian church. Adopting a moderate historical perspectivism, various situationist theories[41] allow for a certain discontinuity between earlier and later formulations of a particular doctrine. New insights into the meaning of divine revelation may lead to a reversal of formerly held views that have come to be seen as outdated or simply inappropriate. Alongside with this, moderate revisionism allows for, and openly favors, some kind of doctrinal pluralism as inevitable and even beneficial to the church.

Methods and Criteria

Without excluding other criteria from functioning in a subordinate way, each of the dialectic theories emphasizes its own principal arbiters of doctrinal change.

---

for the same essential truths to be expressed in different concepts; while the subjectivistic theories make room for new truths to be formulated in new concepts – which often have recourse to the old (biblical) words.

41 One might mention Congar, Kasper, Küng, Rahner, Schillebeeckx, as well as the more recent views of Dulles, Pannenberg, and Toon.

With the organistic and psychological theories, the so-called intuitive sense of faith and the ecclesiastical tradition figure large in both determining and revealing the direction which doctrinal changes have taken in the history of the Christian church.

The theological theories, on the other hand, place their confidence variously in either (1) the logical verification of doctrinal derivations and a sound and consistent hermeneutic of the Scriptures, (2) the *(con)sensus fidei* as the church's common instinctive grasp of truth, or (3) the infallible authority of the ecclesiastical teaching office which is believed to guarantee the truth of all dogmas of faith.

The situationist theories, in turn, pay special attention to the cultural context and intellectual trends that once helped to shape, and may now help to explain, the doctrines of the church in the light of a particular historical situation.

All in all, the dialectic theories adopt a mixture of rational and non-rational factors in explaining and evaluating doctrinal change. Commonly, they regard the Holy Scriptures as the fundamental criterion and the Holy Spirit as the ultimate arbiter of doctrinal development.

Strengths and Weaknesses

Though they consciously aim at avoiding the mistakes and weaknesses of both the objectivistic and the subjectivistic theories, the dialectic theories themselves are by no means above reproach.[42]

First, their pretension of approaching the issue of continuity and change in a truly balanced way is countered and relativized by the claim of virtually every theologian (including even the extreme archaist and the radical transformist) to maintain the equilibrium between tradition and renewal, stability and innovation.[43] Besides, the attempt to walk on the narrow ridge between subjectivism and object-ivism fails when a position glides off towards either of the two sides – a danger which constantly besets the dialectic theories. Moreover, the desire to strike a happy medium between right-wing conservatism and left-wing liberalism runs the risk of actually submitting to a foul compromise.

---

42 While I am sympathetic to the dialectic approach to doctrinal development, I do not want to be understood as fully agreeing with the way this approach has taken shape so far in any one of the numerous theories belonging to the dynamic type. The following critique does not, therefore, adequately express my own personal conviction on this matter. This must await another presentation which, however, cannot be provided in the context of this dissertation.

43 One is reminded of Vincent of Lérins who admitted of "much progress" in religion (see above, p. 57). On the other end of the theological spectrum, Fontinell who calls for a radical reconstruction of metaphysics and theology also intends "to take cognizance of both continuity and development and to avoid the polarities of mere repetition and total revolution" *(Toward a Reconstruction of Religion,* 24).

Second, the organistic theories arose with, and are tied to, an "immanentistic, progressive, romantic liberalism";[44] apparently, they fail to do justice to the facts of history as well as to the problem of historicity and hermeneutics.[45] Besides, the analogy of organic growth is of rather questionable value as it has been employed by traditionalists (Vatican Council I) and modernists (Tyrrell) alike indicating that it can obviously be understood in radically divergent ways.[46]

Third, Kuhn's epistemological interpretation as well as Newman's psychological explanation of doctrinal development may be regarded as some kind of idealist versions of the historical theory;[47] in addition, both of these models of doctrinal development involve an abstract and quite hypothetical epistemological postulate.[48]

---

44 Lindbeck, "The Problem of Doctrinal Development," 138. On the same page, the author declares: "Doctrinal development is not a matter of continuous and cumulative growth or explicitation of the Church's knowledge of revelation or – even worse from the Protestant's point of view – of the Church's self-awareness or self-understanding. The deposit of faith does not live in the consciousness of the Church in a partially germinal form and then gradually unfold [sic] into a more completely articulated body of truths." Wilhelm Maurer has shown that the principle of organic growth developed out of Schelling's *Identitätsphilosophie* and stands or falls with it ("Das Prinzip des Organischen," 265, 291; idem, "Der Organismusgedanke bei Schelling und in der Theologie der Katholischen Tübinger Schule," *Kerygma und Dogma* 8 [1962]: 202-211).

45 The history of dogma demonstrates that doctrinal changes were not always merely an organic unfolding of revelation, the harmonious/homogeneous development of truth, or the cumulative growth of previously held beliefs; rather, they also involved erroneous developments, reversals, and discontinuities. "Ebensowenig kann das Bild von der organischen Entfaltung der Eichel zum Baum der geschichtlichen Vielfalt, den Rückschlägen, Antizipationen, den Retardationen und Akzelerationen ... gerecht werden, die den Prozeß der Dogmengeschichte bestimmen" (Kasper, *Dogma unter dem Wort Gottes*, 132). See also Ommen, 33-37, 44-47. Neither can Orr's "law of logic," which alleges a logical sequence in the successive treatment of dogmatic *loci*, be maintained on strictly historical grounds; the same applies to his "law of diminishing returns" according to which one should expect a gradually decreasing number of doctrinal developments. And the "law of the survival of the fittest," which he derived from Darwin's theory of natural evolution, does not neatly fit his conservative and deterministic stance (Orr, 1-32).

46 It can also lead to a problematic devaluation of the authority of the Bible. "During the late nineteenth and early twentieth century, the image of organic growth was sometimes employed in such a way that christian [sic] origins, and in particular the new testament [sic], were thought, in practice, to be of no more than genetic significance" (Lash, *Change in Focus*, 145).

47 According to them, the apostles had possessed a wordless and pre-reflective knowledge of all truths; their holistic grasp of the Christian idea was gradually explicated in and by the church.

48 As regards the alleged existence of a pre-reflective and immediate knowledge of truth, Hammans makes the pertinent observation "daß das unmittelbare Wissen eine Abstraktion ist; es kommt nicht in sich vor, sondern immer nur ausgedrückt in den Vorstellungen und Begriffen des mittelbaren Wissens" (p. 38, n. 75). Faith is, therefore, bound to the apostolic word; its truth content is accessible only in ecclesiastical notions and concepts. Newman himself recognized that the real cannot be apprehended, nor developed, apart from the notional. This necessarily follows from the indivisibility of form and content.

Fourth, the various Roman Catholic versions of the theological theory are, in the final analysis, unacceptable to Protestants who object to the assumption of a higher methodology operating on the basis of divine logic as well as to the appeal to a supernatural intuition granted to the church. Neither can they admit to an infallible, living magisterium which guides, determines, and guarantees the progressive unfolding of truth, thereby constituting the decisive factor in doctrinal development. Such a demand for implicit confidence in the dogmatic decisions and doctrinal traditions of the church tends towards fideism.[49] It makes any rational proof of their validity superfluous, downplays the function of hermeneutical rules in biblical interpretation, denies to the Holy Scriptures their rightful place as the decisive arbiter of doctrinal truth, and ignores the boundary line between apostolic teachings and post-apostolic traditions.[50]

Fifth, the situationist theories easily play into the hands of an excessively syncretistic and pluralistic theology which allows for a multitude of heterogeneous and mutually contradictory perspectives on truth. They may, thereby, even relapse into an unhistorical approach to the sources by creatively reinterpreting a debatable dogma until, finally, it has lost its objectionable character.[51]

Sixth, as in the case of the evolutionary/revolutionary type, it may be asked how the essential and immutable content of faith is to be distinguished from its time-conditioned and adjustable form. Are there any valid and objective criteria by which one can judge whether the essential meaning of a biblical or doctrinal statement has been defined properly?

Finally, to allow, as is sometimes proposed, certain doctrines to quietly fall into oblivion because they are no longer deemed relevant or comprehensible raises the

49   "The present-day 'theological' approach to development, as successor to the 'historical' and 'logical' theories, is focused on the non-rational factors ... This is one of the main weaknesses of the theological theory as it stands today" (Eckstrom, 163). Though most theologians concede that rational factors do play a role in doctrinal development, few regard them as being of decisive importance for faith.

50   "Andererseits besteht hier aber die Gefahr, daß der Unterschied zwischen konstituierender apostolischer und kontinuierender nachapostolischer Überlieferung eingeebnet wird" (Hammans, 28). Cf. Schulz, 130; and G. Söhngen, "Überlieferung und apostolische Verkündigung," in *Die Einheit in der Theologie* (Munich: K. Zink, 1952), 305-323.

51   How an admittedly poorly balanced, inopportune, misleading, incomprehensible and erroneous dogma can rightly be designated as infallible and irreformable is, indeed, hard to understand. In spite of Lindbeck's disclaimer, it is difficult to avoid the conclusion that such a position threatens "to eviscerate infallibility and make it an empty and hypocritical shibboleth" *(The Future of Roman Catholic Theology,* 104). At least, it seems quite problematic to distinguish a doctrine's potential and alleged infallible sense from its actual and historical erroneous meaning. Such a distinction between an infallible dogmatic decision and its erroneous formulation looks more like a tool of apologetic artistry than a helpful category of historical understanding. For how can a dogmatic decision be considered correct if its teaching content is to be regarded as erroneous and false? Personally, therefore, I agree with Kasper's *caveat* against "a historically untenable, opportunistic reinterpretation" of doctrines *(Dogma unter dem Wort Gottes,* 138).

suspicion that the decisive question regarding their truth content is rather intentionally ignored in order to avoid the open demise of these teachings. But if, on the other hand, doctrinal progress is compared to the development of a building site involving the pulling down of certain old buildings and the construction of new ones in their place,[52] then one has come quite close to the subjectivistic theories with their controversial demand for radical restatements and major doctrinal readjustments.

On the positive side, it is to be noted that the dialectic theories (1) appear to have best maintained the dual concern for continuity and change, development and identity, objective propositions and subjective experience, (2) have successfully avoided a one-sided and reductionistic outlook, (3) follow a dialectic approach which appears to accord with our knowledge of the nature of revealed truth, (4) regard doctrines as important, though not all-important, (5) take both revelation and historicity seriously, and (6) have succumbed neither to dogmatic absolutism nor to agnostic relativism.

Therefore, the dynamic type of theory on doctrinal development may be regarded as offering a genuine alternative to both the static and the evolutionary/ revolutionary type by following what seems to be a less objectionable avenue available in the search for an adequate response to the problem of doctrinal continuity and change.

Summary and Conclusion

The systematic-typological outline of the existing theories of doctrinal development has brought to light three basic types which, by reason of their respective attitudes toward doctrinal change, may be called (1) the static type (encompassing the objectivistic theories), (2) the evolutionary/revolutionary type (including the subjectivistic theories), and (3) the dynamic type (embracing the dialectic theories). Their differences are, in the final analysis, due to their respective underlying presuppositions which, in turn, determine the characteristic features of the theories belonging to each of the three basic types. These types also differ regarding the methods and criteria used in judging the validity of doctrinal novelties.[53]

Weighing their respective strengths and weaknesses, one may conclude that none of the three types of theory on doctrinal development is free from either serious limitations or possible pitfalls and, thus, above reproach. Still, the mediating, dynamic type with its dialectic approach to doctrinal continuity and change appears to offer a

---

52 Toon, *The Development of Doctrine in the Church,* 83.
53 Even among theologians who seriously and in a scholarly manner wrestle with this intricate problem, there will most likely always exist strong disagreements that are due to differing theological premises, diverging theological convictions, varying hermeneutical approaches, and distinct personal preferences.

more balanced and mature view as it consciously seeks to avoid the reductionistic pitfalls into which the others seem to have fallen.[54]

Having completed this preliminary investigation of the problem, of the conceptual models, and of the typology of theories on doctrinal development (Part I), the ground is now sufficiently prepared for a careful historical and critical investigation of the history of theology of the Seventh-day Adventist Church to present, first, what doctrinal developments, if any, have taken place until now and, second, what Adventists have said thus far about the issue of doctrinal continuity and change (Part II). After all, as has been said before, no theory of doctrinal development can be considered adequate which does not take into full account the historical facts or which ignores the accumulated insights of past generations.

Thus, the remaining chapters attempt to present the actual nature and extent as well as the conceptual models of doctrinal developments to be found in the Seventh-day Adventist denomination.

---

54   For a synoptic table of theories of doctrinal development summarizing the contents of chapter 3, see appendix 2.

Summary and Conclusion

> True fidelity to the past includes a readiness to move forward,
> inspired by the example of our predecessors.
>
> *Avery Dulles*

As this study attempts to show, Christian theology finds itself in a dilemma confronting virtually all Christian churches (chapter 1). There are various conceptual models which were developed in the history of Christianity (chapter 2). In fact, there seem to be only three basic types of theory on doctrinal development on which all possible models of doctrinal continuity and change are ultimately based (chapter 3).

While these general conclusions have, in my view, been reasonably established by this study, there are several historical, sociological, and psychological questions, as well as a number of important theological and hermeneutical issues which deserve closer attention by theologians grappling with the problem of doctrinal continuity and change.

The history of denominations, particularly, provides a rich field for studying theological growth; it also raises some intriguing questions regarding the possibilities and limits of theological development. Doctrinal readjustments are not only a historical fact, they also constitute a theological challenge that the Christian church cannot ignore.

Therefore, the problem of doctrinal development requires the serious attention of theologians. The church needs adequate methodological tools for dealing with the historical facts as well as the contemporary challenge of doctrinal change. This study wants to contribute towards this needed reflection on the complex problem of doctrinal continuity and change.

Above all, it is the theological and hermeneutical aspects of the problem of doctrinal continuity and change which demand the attention of Christian scholars. Conclusions need to be based on sound theological reasoning and hermeneutical reflection. Still, some implications may already now be drawn out. They have to do with the general attitude towards doctrinal continuity and change, as well as with the proper criteria for distinguishing the lasting "kernel" from the passing "husk" of the Christian faith.

Traditional churches are faced with the challenge to justify their doctrinal heritage as a legitimate development and a valid expression of biblical revelation. In this, they should remain open to new doctrinal insights arising from their incessant search for truth.[1]   Christians can no longer afford promoting views on doctrinal development that are based on misconceptions and wishful thinking rather than on established historical facts.[2]

It appears that the so-called "dynamic" approach to doctrinal development offers the greatest promise of helping the church gain a timely understanding of the lasting importance of its doctrinal heritage.   Besides, to maintain a fruitful tension between the demand for contemporary relevance and the need for historic continuity will best protect the church against the twin dangers of stiff traditionalism and slack modernism.

A dialectic approach to doctrinal development with its twofold concern for the preservation of church identity and the openness for authentic doctrinal advance may be particularly helpful to theologians in their endeavor to develop a balanced concept of doctrinal continuity and change.

In view of the complexity of the issue, further investigation into the intricate problem of doctrinal development is needed.   Such theological and hermeneutical studies need to pay close attention to (1) the philosophical and theological foundations, (2) the basic structures, (3) the various criteria, and (4) the practical implications of the various concepts of doctrinal continuity and change.

An adequate and timely theory of doctrinal development will also have to address itself to the issue of doctrinal pluralism and unity.   In addition, it needs to pay attention to the cross-cultural communication and contextualization of the gospel.   Truth may be expressed in many different manners and cultural forms, as long as the essence of the gospel is retained.

Change is a fact, and doctrine is no exception to it.   However, as church history shows, constructive doctrinal changes usually happen not in a sudden and revolutionary manner, but are gradual and evolutionary, allowing believers to maintain confidence in the soundness and integrity of Christian beliefs.

But what are the criteria for distinguishing the lasting "kernel" from the passing "husk" of the Christian faith?   How can the identity of its doctrinal heritage be preserved in the midst of change?

According to the historic Protestant position, the Bible holds priority in deciding what is to be believed and taught in and by the church.   Believed to be the Word of God expressed in the words of men, Scripture is regarded as the inspired and

---

1   "Those societies which cannot combine reverence to their symbols with freedom of revision, must ultimately decay either from anarchy, or from the slow atrophy of a life stifled by useless shadows" (Alfred North Whitehead, quoted in Dulles, *The Survival of Dogma*, [7]).

2   Hans Küng has called the willingness to recognize changes in doctrinal matters "a test-case for ecclesial truthfulness."   In his judgment, Christians should never feel ashamed to admit that they have gained new insights, left wrong ways, and have been converted from error to truth.   "For modern man it is not the revision of a position but the negations of a revision which offend against truthfulness" (*Wahrhaftigkeit: Zur Zukunft der Kirche* [Freiburg: Herder, 1968], 168, 162-180; ET [English Translation]: idem, *Truthfulness: The Future of the Church* [(New York: Sheed and Ward, 1968], 127, 130).

authoritative rule of faith, superseding ecclesiastical traditions, creedal statements, church councils, and philosophical speculations. Thus, any teaching regarding Christian faith and practice must prove itself to be in harmony with the Bible.

This platform, if consistently applied, defines the limits of doctrinal change and, at the same time, protects the church against radical revisions which substitute mere human reason or fashionable theories for divine revelation. Seen in this light, the consistently revisionist or radically perspectivist theories appear to lie outside the historical and doctrinal platform on which Christianity has been built. Still, as in the past, some doctrinal *aggiornamento* is likely to happen if the church continues to search the Scriptures and seeks faithfully to interpret it in the context of contemporary experience. In the words of Jesus that have inspired confidence in, and assurance of, the Spirit's leading throughout the ages,

> I have much more to say to you, more than you can now bear. But when he, the Spirit of truth, comes, he will guide you into all truth. He will not speak of his own; he will speak only what he hears, and he will tell you what is yet to come (John 16:12-13 [NIV]).

PART II

CONTINUITY AND CHANGE
IN ADVENTIST TEACHING

Chapter 4

Adventist Theology between Tradition and Renewal: A Survey

> To live is to change, and to be perfect is to have changed often.
>
> *J. H. Newman*

> No serious student of Adventist history can study our past without noting that one constant factor in Adventism has been its willingness to change.
>
> *Neal C. Wilson*

Introduction

The main object of this chapter is to demonstrate that, in spite of the remarkable continuity of Seventh-day Adventist doctrines, development and change have characterized Adventist beliefs to a degree that, over the years, has affected the teachings of the church in a notable way. For this purpose, this chapter analyzes the extent, nature, and direction of the modifications of Adventist doctrinal beliefs. It also briefly discusses the social forces at work in these developments. In order to place the following analysis in its proper historical context, it begins with a survey of the religious background out of which Seventh-day Adventism arose.

No exhaustive presentation of the modifications of Adventist teachings is intended, or feasible, in this chapter. But those discussed demonstrate and illustrate the factuality of such doctrinal changes. In this way, the relevance of the subject matter of doctrinal development and change and its applicability to Adventist theology should become obvious. In addition, such a historical analysis may possibly serve as a useful basis for further theological reflections by Adventist scholars on the intricate problem of doctrinal continuity and change. After all, no concept of doctrinal development is to be considered adequate that does not take account of the results of historical research. To understand how and why Adventist doctrines have developed is foundational to a proper response of the church and its scholars to the theological, philosophical, and hermeneutical questions raised by these changes.

By focusing on incidents of theological development and change rather than on evidences of doctrinal continuity and identity, this study is intentionally selective and may, therefore, be perceived as being even one-sided.[1] This, however, is due, not to an iconoclastic tendency on the part of the author, but to the basic aim of this work, which is to investigate whether, and in what sense, Seventh-day Adventism, like the Christian church in general, does face the problem of doctrinal change.[2] This, in turn, calls for a historical approach, which allows for, and even welcomes, evidences of doctrinal change as contributing to a better grasp of truth. As Wiles has suggested,

> We ought not, therefore, to begin with any preconceived theory concerning the pattern
> of doctrinal development. We can only proceed by a patient study of the historical evi-
> dence. We must trace out as carefully as we can the way in which doctrinal belief actually
> did develop.[3]

Seventh-day Adventist scholars have expressed similar convictions regarding the proper methodology of historical research into the Adventist past. As one of them wrote, "If truth cannot stand the test of historical research, then it is not truth. Our cause has nothing to hide, and nothing ought to be hidden from our cause. There must be a loyal and complete study of all the available material."[4]

The approach that seems best qualified to accomplish this task is the inductive methodology, which reasons from fact to theory, not vice versa. It is with this goal in mind that this study proceeds now to investigate some particular aspects of the doctrinal history of Seventh-day Adventism.[5]

---

1   Pelikan has observed that "the historian of doctrine, like most other historians, tends to be
     more interested in change than in continuity" *(Development of Christian Doctrine,* 49).
     "Historical theology takes its rise from the question of doctrinal change, but it issues in a quest
     for doctrinal continuity" (idem, *Historical Theology,* 156).
2   This is not to say that Adventists face the problem of change in exactly the same manner or to
     the same degree as does, for example, the Roman Catholic Church (see above, pp. 45-52).
     Nor should one ignore the possibility that Seventh-day Adventists have adopted a particular
     approach to the issue of doctrinal continuity and change (see below, chap. 6). On the other
     hand, the mere fact that the church is, indeed, confronted with the question of doctrinal
     development may, in itself, be of considerable significance for this relatively young
     denomination.
3   Wiles, *The Making of Christian Doctrine,* 15.
4   Daniel Walther, "How Shall We Study History?" *Ministry,* August 1939, 12. More recently,
     Richard Hammill asserted that "Adventists should allow no theory to stand in the way of the
     search for truth, for truth is a part of ultimate reality, and our commitment to it must be
     absolute" ("Fifty Years of Creationism: The Story of an Insider," *Spectrum* 15:2 [August
     1984]: 44).
5   For a more elaborate discussion of the various approaches to Adventist history and a further
     explanation of the methodology used in this study, see Pöhler, "The Adventist Historian
     between Criticism and Faith."

Adventist Theology in Historical Perspective: The Religious Background of Seventh-day Adventism

Within less than one and a half centuries since its birth, the Seventh-day Adventist Church has become the most widespread of all Protestant denominations.[6] Its immediate roots lie in the Millerite Adventist movement, which peaked between 1840 and 1844 in the New England states of America. As most followers of William Miller came from Methodist and Baptist churches, this particular form of Adventism had close affinities to the revivalist movements of the day. In addition, the widespread primitivist notions of Christian restorationism had a strong impact on the Sabbatarian Adventists. Being part of the Victorian culture they also reflected certain other characteristics of contemporary American Protestantism. As these roots have markedly influenced the religious and theological sentiments of Seventh-day Adventism, it is advisable to review briefly their main characteristics.[7]

Millerite Apocalypticism

In response to the preaching of the Baptist farmer William Miller (1782-1849), a converted Deist who had intensely studied the prophecies of the Bible and, particularly, of Daniel and Revelation, an apocalyptic revival movement swept through the northeastern states of the Union in the 1840s. Its up to 100,000 followers expected the immediate return of Jesus in the clouds of heaven "about the year 1843" and, when that year passed, on October 22, 1844. As has been shown, Millerism was only the American culmination of the international Advent Awakening of the first half of the nineteenth century.[8] It was marked by pre-millennialism, literalism, and later also by separatism.

---

6   Oosterwal et al., *Servants for Christ,* 1. For a short introduction to Seventh-day Adventism, see Rolf J. Pöhler and H.-Diether Reimer, "Adventisten," *Evangelisches Kirchenlexikon,* 3d rev. ed. (1985), 1:44-47.

7   For general studies on the religious history of North America, see Sydney E. Ahlstrom, *A Religious History of the American People* (New Haven, Conn.: Yale University Press, 1972); Winthrop S. Hudson, *Religion in America: An Historical Account of the Development of American Religious Life,* 2d ed. (New York: Charles Scribner's Sons, 1973); Clifton E. Olmstead, *History of Religion in the United States* (Englewood Cliffs, N.J.: Prentice-Hall, 1960); and H. Shelton Smith, Robert T. Handy, and Lefferts A. Loetscher, *American Christianity: An Historical Interpretation with Representative Documents,* 2 vols. (New York: Charles Scribner's Sons, 1960-1963). Two other surveys particularly geared towards the context in which Adventism arose are Jerome L. Clark, *1844,* 3 vols. (Nashville: SPA, 1968); and Edwin S. Gaustad, ed., *The Rise of Adventism: Religion and Society in Mid-Nineteenth-Century America* (New York: Harper & Row, 1974).

8   LeRoy Edwin Froom, *The Prophetic Faith of Our Fathers,* 4 vols. (Washington, D.C.: RHPA, 1954). Detailed studies on Millerism are also provided by David Tallmadge Arthur, "'Come Out of Babylon': A Study of Millerite Separatism and Denominationalism, 1840-1865" (Ph.D. dissertation, University of Rochester, 1970); Ernest R. Sandeen, *The Roots of*

Miller's theology was conservatively orthodox and moderately Calvinist; his hermeneutic generally followed the biblicist and literalist approach. As regards prophetic interpretation, he was a chiliast and apocalyptic who followed the historicist approach. He rejected the popular postmillennial optimism of his day, which expected a golden age of progress and peace in the near future preceding the second advent of Christ.[9] As the principal exponent of premillennialism in his time, Miller combined pessimism regarding the possibilities of social and cultural progress with the fervent expectation of a new world following the literal and visible return of Jesus Christ to this earth.[10] Though ridiculed by his postmillennial contemporaries for his apocalyptic views regarding the cataclysmic end of history, Miller shared with

Fundamentalism: British and American Millenarianism, 1800-1930 (Chicago and London: University of Chicago Press, 1970); Robert Kievan Whalen, "Millenarianism and Millennialism in America, 1790-1880" (Ph.D. dissertation, State University of New York, 1972); David Leslie Rowe, "Thunder and Trumpets: The Millerite Movement and Apocalyptic Thought in Upstate New York, 1800-1845" (Ph.D. dissertation, University of Virginia, 1974), published as *Thunder and Trumpets: Millerites and Dissenting Religion in Upstate New York, 1800-1850,* American Academy of Religion, Studies in Religion, vol. 38 (Chico, Calif.: Scholars Press, 1985); Gaustad, ed., *The Rise of Adventism* (1974); David Arnold Dean, "Echoes of the Midnight Cry: The Millerite Heritage in the Apologetics of the Advent Christian Denomination, 1860-1960" (Th.D. dissertation, Westminster Theological Seminary, 1976); P. Gerard Damsteegt, *Foundations of the Seventh-day Adventist Message and Mission* (Grand Rapids: Eerdmans, 1977); Clyde E. Hewitt, *Midnight and Morning: An Account of the Adventist Awakening and the Founding of the Advent Christian Denomination, 1831-1860* (Charlotte, N.C.: Venture Books, 1983); Michael Barkun, *Crucible of the Millennium: The Burned-over District of New York in the 1840s* (Syracuse, N.Y.: Syracuse University Press, 1986); Ruth Alden Doan, *The Miller Heresy, Millennialism, and American Culture* (Philadelphia: Temple University Press, 1987); Ronald L. Numbers and Jonathan M. Butler, eds., *The Disappointed: Millerism and Millenarianism in the Nineteenth Century* (Bloomington and Indianapolis: Indiana University Press, 1987); and George R. Knight, *Millennial Fever and the End of the World* (Boise, Idaho: PPPA, 1993). For short introductions, see *SDAE,* 1976 ed., s.v. "Millerite Movement" and "Seventh-Month Movement"; N. Gordon Thomas, "The Second Coming: A Major Impulse of American Protestantism," *Adventist Heritage* 3:2 (1976): 3-9; and Godfrey T. Anderson, "The Great Second Advent Awakening to 1844," in *The Advent Hope in Scripture and History,* ed. V. Norskov Olsen (Washington, D.C., and Hagerstown, Md.: RHPA, 1987), 152-172.

9   Postmillennialism emerged in the 17th and 18th centuries and was greatly enhanced by Daniel Whitby (1638-1726) and Jonathan Edwards (1703-1758). It was more popular in pre-Civil War America than was premillennialism. See *SDAE,* 1976 ed., s.v. "Millennium" and "Premillennialism."

10   Premillennialism (often also called millenarianism) had been the prevailing view among Protestants since Reformation times. It had been eclipsed by postmillennialism since the 17th century but was revived after the French Revolution particularly in England (by Cunningham, Irving, Drummond, and the Albury Park Conference, 1826-1828) and in America (by Miller). It declined again following the 1844 disappointment until it reappeared as futurist dispensationalism (Darbyism) later in the 19th century (Prophetic Conferences, 1878 and following years). Seventh-day Adventists are the principal heirs of the historicist type of premillennialism advanced by Miller himself.

them the firm belief that the millennial kingdom of Rev 20, the utopia of all millennialists, would soon be established on this earth.[11]

Repeatedly, Miller outlined the hermeneutical principles by which he interpreted the Scriptures. His intention was to discover their literal meaning, to systematize the truths they contained into a harmonious system, and to establish the chronology of Bible prophecies.[12] In the attempt to prove empirically the accuracy of the Bible as the inerrant word of God with the help of history and fulfilled prophecy, Miller showed himself indebted to the very deism he wanted to refute.[13] His declared desire to combine the biblical with the rational principle seems to reflect a semi-rationalist approach, which employs logic and common sense as principal arbiters of the possible and true meaning of the Scriptures.[14] For this study, it is important to keep in mind that "the Millerite movement bequeathed a system of prophetic interpretation and biblical literalism which helped shape the character of the Adventism that arose from its ruins."[15]

11 Miller based his expectation on the 2,300-day prophecy of Dan 8:14. "All Protestants expected some grand event about 1843, and no critic from the orthodox side took any serious issue on basic principles with Miller's calculations" (Whitney R. Cross, *The Burned-Over District: The Social and Intellectual History of Enthusiastic Religion in Western New York, 1800-1850* [New York: Harper & Row, 1965], 321).

12 "Mr. Miller's Letters. No. 5," *Signs of the Times*, 15 May 1840, 25-26; cf. Sylvester Bliss, *Memoirs of William Miller* (Boston: Joshua V. Himes, 1853), 68-72.

13 "Reason was accorded high priority in Miller's epistemology, and this was in keeping with the spirit of the age. It was on the basis of reason that he had become a deist, and it was as a rationalist that he returned to traditional Christianity" (Russell L. Staples, "Adventism," in *The Variety of American Evangelicalism*, ed. Donald W. Dayton and Robert K. Johnston (Downers Grove, Ill.: InterVarsity Press, 1991), 58. Speaking of the Millerites, Timothy P. Weber noted that "in their careful and exacting hands, apocalypticism nearly wrapped itself in Enlightenment robes" ("Premillennialism and the Branches of Evangelicalism," ibid., 7, 5-21).

14 On Miller's hermeneutics/apologetics, see Dean, 38-58, and 144-192; esp. 181-192 where the author describes the tension between the "Biblical principle" and the "Rationalistic principle" as "a legacy of Deism in Miller's intellectual life" (p. 182); and Steen R. Rasmussen, "Roots of the Prophetic Hermeneutic of William Miller (M.A. thesis, Newbold College, Bracknell, Berks., England, 1983). For a description of the contemporary and dominant philosophy of common sense realism which assumed that all humans were capable of knowing truth objectively by means of their common sense, see Sydney E. Ahlstrom, "The Scottish Philosophy and American Theology," *Church History* 24 (1955): 257-272; G. M. Marsden, *Fundamentalism and American Culture* (Oxford: Oxford University Press, 1980), 14-16; and Malcolm Bull and Keith Lockhart, *Seeking a Sanctuary: Seventh-day Adventism and the American Dream* (San Francisco: Harper & Row, 1989), 23-26.

15 Everett N. Dick, "The Millerite Movement, 1830-1945," in *Adventism in America: A History,* ed. Gary Land (Grand Rapids: Eerdmans, 1986), 1. A recent Adventist writer has noted that "ever since Enlightenment critics denied the divine origin of the Bible, the battle over Scripture has been waged largely on Enlightenment turf ... While devout believers have sought to defend Scripture, increasingly they have relied on Enlightenment tools to do so, not only citing proofs from science and archeology, but even resorting to probability statistics in

During its first years and by design, Millerism was an anti-separatist, inter-denominational movement, which united Christians in a common faith regarding the immediate return of Christ.[16] Yet it was exactly this fervent eschatological hope that brought them together in an ecumenical spirit of unity which also worked as a catalyst that was soon to separate them from other Christians who would not adopt their particular interpretation of Bible prophecy. When, in 1843, the preaching of "the advent near" led to increasing polarization and opposition within different churches, the Millerite movement became a separatist and sectarian group.[17] The development from an inclusive to an exclusive movement was expedited even more by the ridicule and antagonism, which Adventists experienced after the disap-pointment of 1844. This helps to explain why the group that was to become the nucleus of the Seventh-day Adventist Church began with a rather exclusivist mindset which only gradually opened itself up again to the surrounding religious world.

Methodist Revivalism

Miller's preaching not only set in motion an apocalyptic movement, it also resulted in a spiritual revival movement not unlike those that had swept through the New England states in previous years and decades.[18] A popular and successful preacher, Miller created considerable excitement particularly among Methodists and Baptists who were prone to a deeply personal and also emotional approach to religious matters.[19] Because of the close affinities between Adventist apocalypticism and

defense of prophecy" (Alden Thompson, *Inspiration: Hard Questions, Honest Answers* (Hagerstown, Md.: RHPA, 1991), 260.

16 At first, Millerite Adventism appeared like another one of the many reform movements of the day. Like them, it was an inter-church movement whose members worshipped and fellow-shipped at the different churches to which they belonged.

17 With tensions rising between them, Millerite Adventists found themselves increasingly at a distance from the denominations to which they belonged. Quite a few were expelled while others withdrew from their churches. Millerite separatism was openly expressed by Charles Fitch in an 1843 sermon which was published and widely distributed *("Come Out of Her, My People": A Sermon* [Rochester, N.Y.: J. V. Himes, 1843]). For more information, see Arthur, "'Come Out of Babylon'," 1-83; cf. idem, "Millerism," in *The Rise of Adventism*, ed. Gaustad, 154-172. Millerism's change from ecumenism to exclusivism is also treated by Wayne Judd, "From Ecumenists to Come-Outers: The Millerites, 1831-1845," *Adventist Heritage* 11:1 (1986): 3-12; and Charles Teel, "Bridegroom or Babylon? Dragon or Lamb? Nineteenth-Century Adventists and the American Mainstream," ibid., 13-25.

18 America had experienced great spiritual and postmillennial revivals under the impact of evangelists like George Whitefield (1714-1770) and Jonathan Edwards (1703-1758) as well as during the Second Awakening (with Charles Finney et al.) in the early decades of the 19th century. According to Richard Carwardine, the Second Awakening actually peaked with the Millerite movement in 1843-1844 *(Transatlantic Revivalism: Popular Evangelicalism in Britain and America, 1790-1865* [Westport, Conn.: Greenwood Press, 1978], 52).

19 There were, however, some conspicuous differences between the Millerite movement and other contemporary revivals. In his preaching, Miller consciously attempted to avoid the

Methodist revivalism, one should be aware of some of the latter's characteristic features, viz., Evangelicalism, Arminianism, and perfectionism.[20]

American Methodism was an heir to European Pietism and Puritanism, which emphasized personal conversion, a literal approach to the Bible as the word of God, and a morality founded on the revealed will of God. True revival, therefore, always involved a return to primitive Christianity as described in the New Testament.[21]

In distinction to the Calvinist tradition with its teaching on predestination, the Methodists subscribed to an Arminian theology, which emphasized the free will of humans and their possibility of acting in accordance with the divine requirements. If people failed to keep the commandments of God and to do his will, it was because of their refusal to cooperate with God and not because of any inherent weakness or inability.

Closely related to this conviction – and actually growing out of it – was the perfectionist character of Methodist revivalism. With entire sanctification and the perfecting of holiness as their goal, believers were not to rest content with their present state of sanctification but were rather to strive for perfection itself. Both the Methodist teaching on the "second blessing" and the holiness revivals at Oberlin College contributed to a religious climate in which the perfection of human nature seemed within the reach of genuine believers.

With quite a number of their leaders and followers coming from Methodist churches,[22] Sabbatarian Adventists were deeply affected by the Evangelical, Arminian, and perfectionist approach to religion in vogue at the time. Their fervent expectation

---

heavy emotionalism of the fire-and-brimstone preachers of his time by emphasizing the rational aspects of the Christian faith. For example, he used charts to explain prophetic truths to his hearers. While it is true that there were some outbursts of emotionalism at Millerite camp-meetings and other occasions, there was also a conscious effort to contain and to stay away from it.

20 See Cross, 287-321; Timothy L. Smith, *Revivalism and Social Reform in Mid-Nineteenth-Century America* (New York: Abingdon, 1957); and Jonathan Butler, "Seventh-day Adventism's Legacy to Modern Revivalism," *Spectrum* 5:1 (1973): 89-99.

21 Through their Baptist and Methodist progenitors, Adventists are also related to the radical (Anabaptist) reformers of the 16th century, not merely to the mainline, orthodox (Lutheran and Calvinist) tradition. The theological parallels between Adventism and the continental Radical Reformation have been investigated by several Adventist writers in recent years. See Richard Müller, *Adventisten – Sabbat – Reformation* (Lund: CWK Gleerup, 1979); idem, "Anabaptists: The Reformers' Reformers," *Ministry,* July 1986, 11-13; Bryan W. Ball, *The English Connection: The Puritan Roots of Seventh-day Adventist Belief* (Cambridge: James Clarke, 1981); Walter Leslie Emmerson, *The Reformation and the Advent Movement* (Washington, D.C.: RHPA, 1983); and Charles Scriven, "Radical Discipleship and the Renewal of Adventist Mission," *Spectrum* 14:3 (December 1983): 11-20.

22 Among them were Hiram Edson and Ellen G. White. Several others, like James White and Joseph Bates, came from the Christian Connection, which also tended to be anti-Calvinist and revivalist.

of the coming of Christ would even serve to strengthen, rather than weaken, the desire for biblical faithfulness and the quest for personal holiness.[23]

Christian Restorationism

The strong influence of primitivist and restorationist ideas on Anglo-American religion and culture has often been overlooked by historians and theologians alike. But, as recent studies have shown, "primitivism" and "restorationism" were widely dispersed phenomena in American political and religious history.[24] While there exists no clear-cut definition of these terms, they may be understood as being roughly synonymous, denoting a particular perspective regarding the desired order of things.

Longing to restore church, society, and/or nation to the "first times," i.e., the pristine state prevailing at the beginning of things, restorationists commonly appealed to some kind of sacred origin or ideal past (like creation, the natural order, or the primitive church) as primordial and transcendent norm on which they could base their judgment on the present time as well as their idealized vision of the future.

---

23 Theologians may choose to distinguish between the belief in the potential perfectibility of man and the actual claim of someone to have arrived at character perfection or a state of sinlessness allocating the somewhat derogatory term "perfectionism" to the latter. In this sense, Ellen G. White and her fellow believers were not perfectionists, for they never claimed to have reached a state of sinless perfection. On the close affinities and notable differences between the Methodist and Adventist conceptions of perfection, see Rolf J. Pöhler, "Sinless Saints or Sinless Sinners? An Analysis and Critical Comparison of the Doctrine of Christian Perfection as Taught by John Wesley and Ellen G. White, 1978," TMs, AHC, JWL, AU, Berrien Springs, Mich. Cf. Woodrow W. Whidden, "The Soteriology of Ellen G. White: The Persistent Path to Perfection, 1836-1902" (Ph.D. dissertation, Drew University, 1989).

24 See Richard T. Hughes, ed., *The American Quest for the Primitive Church* (Urbana and Chicago: University of Illinois Press, 1988), containing 16 papers of a 1985 conference at Abilene Christian University on "The Restoration Ideal in American History"; Richard T. Hughes and C. Leonard Allen, *Illusions of Innocence: Protestant Primitivism in America, 1630-1875,* with a Foreword by Robert N. Bellah (Chicago and London: University of Chicago Press, 1988); Mark A. Noll, "Rethinking Restorationism: A Review Article," *Reformed Journal* 39 (November 1989): 15-21; Nathan O. Hatch, *The Democratization of American Christianity* (New Haven and London: Yale University Press, 1989); Richard T. Hughes, "Recovering First Times: The Logic of Primitivism in American Life," in *Religion and the Life of the Nation: American Recoveries,* ed. Rowland A. Sherrill (Urbana and Chicago: University of Illinois Press, 1990), 193-218; and "Primitivism," *Dictionary of Christianity in America* (1990), 940-941. Valuable typological studies of primitivism/ restorationism are offered by Samuel S. Hill, Jr., "A Typology of American Restitutionism: From Frontier Revivalism and Mormonism to the Jesus Movement," *Journal of the American Academy of Religion* 44 (March 1976): 65-76; and Richard T. Hughes, "Christian Primitivism as Perfectionism: From Anabaptists to Pentecostals," in *Reaching Beyond: Chapters in the History of Perfectionism,* ed. Stanley Burgess (Peabody, Mass.: Hendrickson Publ., 1986), 213-255.

Applying the restorationist impulse to Christianity, biblical primitivists regarded the pure apostolic church and the New Testament writings as the perfect standard and normative pattern for all later Christian beliefs and practices – including church ordinances, polity, and liturgy. On this basis, they criticized historic Christendom as apostatized religion and rejected its corrupt doctrines, sectarian divisions, hierarchical institutions, privileged clergy, venerated traditions, and enforced creeds. Conversely, they longed and worked for a Christian community that was free from coercion, united in faith, and obedient to the biblical blueprint. Perfect doctrinal unity would come about when Christians used their right to think for themselves and to discern ultimate truth by impartially studying the Bible – and the Bible only – aided by human reason and common sense. In this way, primitive Christianity would effectively be restored and the millennial age be ushered in.

Inheriting Christian Humanists, Protestant Reformers (of the Reformed tradition), English Puritans, as well as Enlightenment thinkers, restorationists/ primitivists in the "new world" can be found in most Christian denominations.[25] More than that, the restorationist ideal constitutes a central and persistent motif of American cultural identity and national ethos.[26] While the early nineteenth century saw the heyday of primitivism/restorationism, its spirit still continues today.

> Clearly, the restoration ideal has not been the exclusive property of a few eccentric Christian sects. It has informed the fundamental outlook of preachers and presidents, of soldiers and scholars. Indeed, the restoration perspective has been a central feature of American life and thought from the earliest Puritan settlements, and now continues to exercise a profound influence on the thinking and behavior of the American people.[27]

More particularly, the restoration motif was the single most characteristic feature of several early nineteenth-century Christian movements which are commonly subsumed under the heading "Restoration Movement." Founded by James O'Kelly (1793), Abner Jones and Elias Smith (1801), Barton W. Stone (1803), and Alexander Campbell (1809), their followers came to be known simply as "Christians" or "Disciples." When these movements were consolidated, several church families emerged, including the "Christian Connection," the "Churches of Christ," and the "Christian Churches/Disciples of Christ." Until well into the twentieth century, the

---

25 Restorationist sentiments were prevalent among the New England Puritans and in the American Enlightenment. They characterized the early Baptists, Methodists, and Episcopalians; more recently, they appeared in Pentecostalist and Fundamentalist churches. Outside of Protestantism, restorationism turned up among the Mormons and can also be found among Jews and Catholics.

26 The European settlers of the "new world" saw themselves standing at the threshold of a new and unparalleled era fundamentally different from all previous ages. This is illustrated by the great seal of the United States, which carries the telling inscription *novus ordo seclorum* (new order of the ages). Their vision of the future was allied to the idea of an Edenic past to be reproduced in the primordial nation arising on the North American virgin land.

27 Hughes and Allen, *Illusions of Innocence*, 24.

latter was "the largest indigenous American religious body."[28] Many were attracted to the Restoration Movement, which wanted to overcome Christian fragmentation by uniting believers on the plain teachings of the Bible as norm of faith and practice.

Primitivism/restorationism was, and still is, a strong ideological undercurrent that shaped not only American Protestantism in general but also Adventist life and thought in particular.[29] In fact, a sizeable number of Millerites as well as two well-known Seventh-day Adventist leaders came from the Restoration Movement.[30] This helps explain both the basic restorationist impulse common to Adventist theology and some particular doctrinal as well as hermeneutical conceptions held by Seventh-day Adventists in the nineteenth century and, partly, even today.[31]

Interestingly, there seems to be a close connection between restorationism/primitivism and millennialism, both of which appear to be made out of the same fabric.[32] The millennial vision of a radiant future – whether of the premillennial or postmillennial type – frequently draws on humanity's archetypical recollections of a glorious past, defining the coming kingdom of God as "the restoration of all things," i.e., the ultimate reversion to primordial perfection. Origin time *(Urzeit)* becomes

---

28   T. L. Miethe, "Christian Church (Disciples of Christ)," *Dictionary of Christianity in America* (1990), 253, 253-254. See also J. B. North, "Restoration Movement," ibid., 1005-1008; idem, "Christian Connection," ibid., 255; James DeForest Murch, *Christians Only: A History of the Restoration Movement* (Cincinnati, Ohio: Standard Publ., [1962]); and Leroy Garrett, *The Stone-Campbell Movement: An Anecdotal History of Three Churches* (Joplin, Mo.: College Press Publ. Co., 1981). Consult also the sources listed on p. 124, n. 24.

29   See Froom, *The Prophetic Faith of Our Fathers*, 4:30-32, and *Seventh-day Adventists Answer Questions on Doctrine: An Explanation of Certain Major Aspects of Seventh-day Adventist Belief* (Washington, D.C.: RHPA, 1957), 46-49, for some remarks on the Restoration Movement/Christian Connection in relation to SDA beliefs. For additional insights, consult Daniel Kittle, "[A] Study of the Christian Connection and Its Relationship to the Early Advent Movement, 1989," TMs, AHC, JWL, AU, Berrien Springs, Mich.; see also the works on SDA history listed below, p. 128, n. 39.

30   Joshua V. Himes (beside William Miller the most influential leader among the Millerites), as well as James White and Joseph Bates (two of the founders of the Seventh-day Adventist Church), had been members of the Christian Connection, one of the denominations arising out of the Restoration Movement. "Along with two other influential Christian leaders, Joseph Marsh and L. D. Fleming, Himes led scores of Christian Connection churches into the Adventist camp" (Nathan O. Hatch, *The Democratization of American Christianity*, 145).

31   Among these are certain aspects of the SDA teaching on the Trinity, Christology, Anthropology, Soteriology, Ecclesiology, and Eschatology, as well as such familiar notions as "new light," the "landmarks" of faith, or the slogan "No Creed but the Bible!" In addition, the Adventist view on the Bible itself, its authority and interpretation, is reminiscent of quite similar restorationist notions. These SDA teachings and concepts are discussed in this and the following chapter, though their primitivist mooring is not always explicitly mentioned.

32   "The dependence of millennialism on primitivism is a relationship not often noted by scholars, though it has appeared in Christian history with significant regularity" (Hughes and Allen, *Illusions of Innocence*, 98). See also ibid., ix, 2-3, 20; and Hughes, ed., *The American Quest for the Primitive Church*, 12-14.

the beacon of the end time *(Endzeit)*. In this way, primitivism/restorationism turns out to be a correlate and foundation of Adventist premillennialism.

American Protestantism

Arising from the American soil, the Seventh-day Adventist Church not only inherited the apocalyptic and revivalist emphases of Millerism and the primitivist impulse of Christian restorationism, it also shared in other attitudes typical of North-American Protestantism of the mid-nineteenth century as, for example, social activism and anti-Catholicism.

In some way or other, many of the adherents of Millerism had been actively involved in the numerous reform movements of the time whose goal was the improvement and transformation of society and the elimination of those conditions that were detrimental to the achievement of man's personal as well as social well-being. Most prominent among them was the abolitionist movement as well as those groups striving for reforms in the areas of health, temperance, and education.[33] Even a cursory knowledge of the history of Seventh-day Adventism suffices to recognize the continuity existing between the reform ferment at work in the American society in general and the reformatory ideals shaping one of its subcultural strands in particular.

Finally, one must mention the prevalent anti-Catholicism of the time, which was nourished by fears that the increasing influence of Roman Catholicism could eventually jeopardize or even destroy personal as well as religious liberty, which constituted one of America's most precious possessions.[34] Being part of this culture, it was only natural for Seventh-day Adventists to share in these feelings and apprehensions which were strikingly confirmed by the interpretation of certain apocalyptic prophecies dealing with the anti-Christian powers of the last days.[35]

---

33 For details, see Alice Felt Tylor, *Freedom's Ferment* (Minneapolis: University of Minnesota Press, 1944); Henry Steele Commager, *The Era of Reform, 1830-1860* (Princeton, N.J.: Van Nostrand, 1960); and Smith, *Revivalism and Social Reform*.

34 On the growth of American anti-Catholicism during the first half of the 19th century, see Ray Allen Billington, *The Protestant Crusade, 1800-1860: A Study of the Origins of American Nativism* (New York: Macmillan, 1938). It should also be remembered that the memory of perfidy and persecution was still vivid in the minds of Protestants at the time. Besides, until fairly recently, the Roman Catholic Church vehemently and on principle rejected the idea of religious liberty.

35 For a recent Adventist expression of concern over the possible future loss of civil and religious freedom through a Roman Catholic Church that has regained power over the state, see V. Norskov Olsen, *Papal Supremacy and American Democracy* (Loma Linda/ Riverside, Calif.: Loma Linda University Press, 1987). In spite of its warning tone, the book is free of anti-Catholic polemics and refrains from speculative assertions regarding the future development of American democracy.

Adventist Theology in Significant Progression: The Historical Reality of Doctrinal Development

Having briefly described the religious background of Seventh-day Adventism, this study now traces the extent, nature, and direction of the doctrinal modifications to be found in the tradition of this Protestant denomination. As complete coverage is not feasible, the following is limited to a representative spectrum of teachings that underwent significant developments and changes over the years.[36]

It bears repetition to emphasize that these changes neither separately nor collectively put into question the remarkable continuity that has characterized Adventist theology throughout its history. There exists a clearly recognizable identity between the early and contemporary doctrinal expressions of the Adventist faith, at least with respect to their substantial content.[37] And there seems to be little evidence for a drastic departure on the part of contemporary Seventh-day Adventism from its inherited doctrinal traditions.[38]

At the same time, however, the following survey reveals a number of significant changes in the formulation and conceptualization of various aspects of Adventist doctrine. They do not merely touch lightly on a few peripheral parts of Adventist theology but noticeably affect Adventism's fundamental and distinctive teachings as well. To describe, analyze, and interpret these developments, albeit not comprehensively, is the purpose of the following section.[39]

36 Concentrating attention on dogmatic theology, this study ignores developments in personal and social ethics (including sexual behavior, health reform, dietary laws, stewardship, race relations, social responsibility, and church-state relations), church organization and ordinances (ordination, liturgy, and the Eucharist), mission and ecumenism as well as science and faith. In addition, and because of their rather complex nature, no attempt is made to fully discuss the developments with regard to the doctrines of the heavenly sanctuary and of righteousness by faith. With these, this study is limited to a few selected aspects capable of brief presentation.

37 To verify this statement for themselves, readers are invited to turn to appendix 3 and to compare the three major declarations of Seventh-day Adventist beliefs presented there. They are listed in parallel columns so as to facilitate a detailed comparative analysis.

38 The book *Seventh-day Adventists Believe ...: A Biblical Exposition of 27 Fundamental Doctrines* (Washington, D.C.: Ministerial Association, General Conference of SDAs, 1988), which was hailed as an authoritative and "epoch-making" explanation of Adventist beliefs ("Seventh-day Adventists Believe," *Ministry,* July 1988, 4-5), may serve to illustrate this point. Providing a rather traditional summary of Adventist beliefs, the book described the doctrinal heritage of the church in the spirit and phraseology of the writings of Ellen White, making no special effort to rethink this tradition in the light of recent scholarship or to reconsider its meaning for contemporary humanity. An attempt in this direction had previously been made, however, by Richard Rice in an Adventist college textbook, which called for "a variety of interpretations to display the rich texture" of the Adventist faith *(The Reign of God: An Introduction to Christian Theology from a Seventh-day Adventist Perspective* [Berrien Springs, Mich.: AU Press, 1985], xvii).

39 To date, there exists no study that traces these doctrinal developments collectively and in detail. The best available general surveys of the history of Adventist theology are given by C.

Yet, before one can meaningfully do so, an important question must be addressed, which might otherwise be brought forward as a fundamental criticism of the basic approach of this dissertation. In what sense, if at all, is it possible to speak of a development of Adventist doctrines when the church has consistently refused to formulate a creed and when the earliest official document that could possibly be used in such a sense dates only from the year 1931?[40]

To answer this question, one needs a clear definition of what is meant by the term "doctrine." On the basis of what is said above in this study,[41] doctrinal developments include not only the officially recognized teachings of the church but also the theological views frequently advanced by leading Adventist writers in church publications as expressive of the common belief of Seventh-day Adventists. In other words, and "broadly speaking, doctrine is whatever Christians say when they speak or write about beliefs with a sense of doing so on behalf of the body to which they belong."[42]

Mervyn Maxwell, *Tell It to the World: The Story of Seventh-day Adventists* (Mountain View, Calif.: PPPA, 1976; rev. ed. 1977); R[ichard] W. Schwarz, *Light Bearers to the Remnant* (Mountain View, Calif.: PPPA, 1979); Gary Land, ed., *Adventism in America: A History* (Grand Rapids: Eerdmans, 1986); and Bull and Lockhart, *Seeking a Sanctuary: Seventh-day Adventism and the American Dream* (1989), part 1. A detailed chronicle of the early development of SDA doctrine (which, however, refrains from any critical interpretation of its findings) is offered by Damsteegt in his *Foundations of the Seventh-day Adventist Message and Mission.* Another useful tool covering the same period is the fourth volume of Froom's monumental study on *The Prophetic Faith of Our Fathers* (1954), 855-1173, which is confined, however, to the issue of prophetic interpretation. Less reliable is Froom's *Movement of Destiny* (Washington, D.C.: RHPA, 1971) which provides something like a partisan's history focusing especially on Christological and soteriological issues.

40 See appendix 3. On this issue, Froom formulated "a basic principle," viz., that "no doctrinal teaching can be said to be a 'denominational' position unless and until it is held generally, or is definitely adopted by common consent and acceptance. Not until then can it rightly be called a 'testing truth' of the Advent Faith" *(MOD,* 197). Thus, it is of great importance for this study to determine whether a doctrinal view was indeed generally held by the church at any given time. Of course, complete unanimity may never be found in the church on any given teaching. Still, there should be some clear indications that a view was indeed accepted by common consent, if it is to be regarded as representative doctrinal teaching. Incidentally, even the 1931 statement of Fundamental Beliefs itself, recognized by Froom as fully authoritative, was not, apparently, accepted without challenge, his claim to the contrary notwithstanding (cf. ibid., 414 with 422-428).

41 See above, pp. 33-37.

42 John Baker, "'Carried about by Every Wind?' The Development of Doctrine," chap. in *Believing in the Church: The Corporate Nature of Faith* (London: SPCK, 1981), 262. This does not mean that every statement made by Adventist writers or preachers may be regarded as doctrinal. But when prominent leaders are addressing the church or speaking on behalf of it, and when there are clear indications that their views were shared by most, if not practically all, in the community of faith at a given time, it does seem legitimate to regard such positions as the teachings of the church.

In looking for indications of doctrinal development and change, one therefore needs not only to review the different declarations on the fundamental beliefs of Seventh-day Adventists but also to check books, pamphlets, and the leading Adventist journals, which served as the main channels for the communication and dissemination of doctrinal views among the members and friends of the church.[43]

The Extent of Doctrinal Development

For the sake of clarification and systematization, Adventist doctrines can be sub-divided into *peripheral* teachings possessing little relevance for the Adventist system of doctrinal beliefs, *fundamental* doctrines, which touch the very core of the Christian faith, and *distinctive* beliefs, which are central or unique to Adventism's doctrinal heritage.[44] These three categories are now considered in order.

Continuity and Change in *Peripheral* Teachings

Unquestionably, at various times during its history, there occurred a number of doctrinal developments in Adventism that may be considered as rather insignificant. Among them could be mentioned the interpretation of the ten horns in the prophecy of Daniel 7, the view on the daily in Daniel 8, and the question of the law in Galatians 3. Perhaps one could also list the interpretation of the battle of Armageddon and the question of the proper time to begin the celebration of the weekly Sabbath as belonging to these peripheral Adventist teachings.[45]

It should be noted, however, that at the time when these views were live issues within Adventism, they were not infrequently treated as constituting significant teachings, if not indispensable landmarks of the Adventist faith.[46] Besides, however

---

43 This method is endorsed in a *Review & Herald* editorial that opens with the following statement: "Has Adventism changed? One of the best ways to secure an answer to this question is to do what we do frequently – look through old issues of the *Review*" (K. H. Wood, "Adventism Today," *RH,* 11 February 1960, 3). Froom wrote, "Other literature is not to be overlooked, but the *Review* remained the chief medium of early discussion, instruction, and record" *(PFF,* 4:1109).

44 Similarly, Woodrow Whidden has distinguished "nonessential Adventism" ("that which is interesting but not central to Adventist self-understanding") from "Christian verities" or "eternal verities" ("basic doctrines embraced by Adventists and held by most other Christians") and "essential Adventism" ("that which is distinctively Adventist"); in addition, he introduced the term "processive Adventism" for "those issues that are important but still unsettled" ("Essential Adventism or Historic Adventism?" *Ministry,* October 1993, 5, 5-9).

45 Interestingly, Schwarz discusses the issues of the law in Galatians, the deity of Christ [!], the daily, the Eastern question, Armageddon, and the ten horns in a chapter entitled "Debates Over Nonessentials" *(Light Bearers to the Remnant,* 393-407).

46 For substantiation, see below, pp. 157-158, 167-170, and 228-230. This opens the possibility that the landmark doctrines of one generation actually may become the theological side issues of the next. Though one should be careful not to generalize from this observation, it should

one may rate the relative importance or rather insignificance of these views for and within the Seventh-day Adventist doctrinal structure, they do, in fact, commonly touch on either some fundamental or distinctive beliefs held by the church.[47]

It is for this reason that this chapter does not investigate separately these so-called peripheral matters. Rather they are discussed at their proper place within the system of Adventist beliefs. Here attention is directed first toward those fundamental Christian doctrines that Adventists hold in common with other conservative Christian bodies. After that, this chapter takes a closer look at the distinctive beliefs of the Seventh-day Adventist Church, which are not commonly found among evangelical Protestant denominations.

Continuity and Change in *Fundamental* Doctrines

Protestant dogmatics has traditionally subdivided its subject matter into different *loci,* which cover the areas of theology proper, Christology, pneumatology, anthropology and hamartiology, soteriology, ecclesiology, and eschatology. For the sake of convenience, I follow this outline except for the last two items, which will be treated within the context of the distinctive beliefs of the Adventist Church.

Theology proper: The Trinity

Adventists have always believed in the existence of a personal, all-powerful, and eternal God who is humankind's heavenly Father, in his Son Jesus Christ, and in his representative, the Holy Spirit.[48] However, they did not always accept or understand the traditional Christian doctrine of the Trinity, which is shared by Catholic, Orthodox, and most Protestant churches alike.[49]

In fact, between 1846 and 1886, the doctrine of the Trinity was uniformly rejected and firmly opposed by virtually all Adventist writers as being either inconsistent, unscriptural, contrary to reason and plain common sense, unbelievable and unintelligible, contradictory, absurd, preposterous, papal, pagan, or simply anti-

---

make one reluctant to become too dogmatic in defining the exact boundaries of the Adventist landmarks.

47 The fact that Adventists have usually regarded their doctrines as comprising a unified and indivisible whole supports this conclusion. See below, pp. 270-271.

48 See below, app. 3, pp. 336-337.

49 The development of the doctrine of the Trinity within Adventism is discussed by Erwin Roy Gane, "The Arian or Anti-Trinitarian Views Presented in Seventh-day Adventist Literature and the Ellen G. White Answer" (M.A. thesis, Andrews University, 1963); Russell Holt, "The Doctrine of the Trinity in the Seventh-day Adventist Denomination: Its Rejection and Acceptance, 1969," TMs, AHC, JWL, AU, Berrien Springs, Mich.; H. Varmer, "Analysis of the Seventh-day Adventist Pioneer Anti-Trinitarian Position, 1972," TMs, AHC, AU, Berrien Springs, Mich.; and Froom, *MOD,* 170-180, 188-217, 269-299, 322-323.

Christian.[50] There seems to have been not a single voice that disagreed with this negative assessment – Ellen White included.[51] Even the Adventist hymnal reflected the common opposition of the church to Trinitarian faith.[52]

The seemingly unqualified rejection of this time-honored doctrine was partly due to a confusion of Trinitarianism with modalist monarchianism, an early Christian heresy which identified the Father and the Son as a single person. Besides, the term Trinity appeared nowhere in the Scriptures which Adventists wanted to take utterly serious as their only rule of faith. A doctrine not clearly stated in the Bible was simply not acceptable to them.

50 "Letter from Bro. White," *Day-Star,* 24 January 1846, 30; James White, "The Faith of Jesus," *RH,* 5 August 1852, 52; Joseph Bates, *A Vindication of the Seventh-Day Sabbath, and the Commandments of God* (New Bedford, Mass.: By the Author, 1848), 69, 70, 87; Hiram Bingham, "Bro. White," *RH,* 16 September 1851, 31 ("At length I found a people who, like myself, did not believe our blessed Saviour was the Eternal God"); J. B. Frisbie, "The Seventh-day Sabbath Not Abolished," *RH,* 7 March 1854, 50; idem, "The Trinity," *RH,* 12 March 1857, 146; D. W. Hull, "Bible Doctrine of the Divinity of Christ," *RH,* 10-17 November 1859, 193-195, 201-202; "Questions for Brother Loughborough," *RH,* 5 November 1861, 184; M. E. Cornell, "Who Are Mormons?" *RH,* 7 April 1863, 149; J. H. W[aggoner], "The Atonement – Part II," *RH,* 3-10 November 1863, 181-182, 189-190; idem, "Battle Creek Bible Class, April 4, 1868," *RH,* 14 April 1868, 276; idem, *The Atonement* (Battle Creek, Mich.: RHPA, 1884), 173-177; D. M. Canright, "Jesus Christ the Son of God," *RH,* 18 June 1867, 1-3; idem, "The Personality of God," *RH,* 29 August 1878, 73-74; R. F. Cottrell, "The Doctrine of the Trinity," *RH,* 1 June 1869, 180-181; idem, "The Trinity," *RH,* 6 July 1869, 10-11; idem, "'Lying Unity'," *RH,* 22 April 1873, 148; idem, "Bible Terms for Bible Doctrines," *RH,* 22 April 1880, 266; A. J. Dennis, "One God," *ST,* 22 May 1879, 162; W. H. Littlejohn, "Scripture Questions," *RH,* 17 April 1883, 250 (the author explicitly refers to the fundamental principles of SDAs as published in 1872/1874 in order to demonstrate the general opposition of the church to this doctrine); A. T. Jones, "Historical Necessity of the Third Angel's Message," *RH,* 17 June 1884, 387; and Charles W. Stone, *The Captain of Our Salvation* (Battle Creek, Mich.: n.p., 1886), 12-20.

51 In 1871, James White stated that the visions of his wife "do not agree" with the creed of "the trinitarian" ("Mutual Obligation," *RH,* 13 June 1871, 204). Neither did she explicitly reject Trinitarianism in her writings. Thus, a century later, SDAs were prone to assume that Ellen White "never endorsed the anti-Trinitarian view" (Don F. Neufeld, "125 Years of Advancing Light," *RH,* Anniversary Issue, [13 November 1975], 27). However, Neufeld erroneously assumed that the early Adventists "differed" on the doctrine of the Trinity, while, in fact, they were fully agreed – in rejecting it.

52 When Reginald Heber's (1783-1826) masterpiece "Holy, Holy, Holy" was included in the 1886 edition of *Hymns and Tunes* (*Seventh-day Adventist Hymn and Tune Book for Use in Divine Worship* [Battle Creek, Mich.: Review and Herald Publishing House, 1886; Oakland, Calif.: PPPA, 1886, #99), the phrase "God in three persons, blessed Trinity!" appearing at the end of the first (and fourth) stanza was changed to read: "God over all, who rules eternity." This remained so in the *Church Hymnal: Official Hymnal of the Seventh-day Adventist Church* (Takoma Park, Washington, D.C.: RHPA, 1941, #73). Only in 1985, the *Seventh-day Adventist Hymnal* reverted back to the original Trinitarian text (Washington, D.C., and Hagerstown, Md.: RHPA, 1985, #73). Cf. Roy Allan Anderson, "Adventists and the Trinity," *AR,* 8 September 1983, 4-5; and James Joiner, "Two Altered Hymns," *AR,* 5 April 1984, 10.

However, at least some of these writers (like Cottrell, Friesbie, Littlejohn, Waggoner, and White) did possess a fairly accurate understanding of the historic doctrine of the Trinity – and opposed it nonetheless. It seems that their literalist approach to the Bible, supported by what they regarded as plain common sense, would not allow for a doctrine that ultimately defies rational explanation, requires a dialectic conception of truth, and appears to deny the material reality of God.[53] In addition, it was felt that this doctrine would jeopardize the biblical understanding of the atonement because it did not allow the divine nature of Christ to actually suffer and die on the cross.[54]

Late in his life, James White softened his anti-Trinitarianism by pointing to the rather theoretical nature and secondary importance of this issue. Still, he continued to reaffirm the general Adventist opposition to the doctrine of the Trinity.[55] Contrary to what some have assumed, D. M. Canright likewise never deviated from his strong anti-Trinitarianism as long as he remained loyal to the church.[56] And while E. J. Waggoner came closer than any other Adventist writer before him to the orthodox view on the Trinity, even he never became a Trinitarian – Froom's attempt to argue for the contrary notwithstanding.[57]

---

53 This reminds one of Miller's literalist and semi-rationalist leanings. While he himself believed in the historic doctrine of the Trinity, it was, above all, in interpreting biblical prophecies that his way of reasoning sounded, at times, like an echo of rationalism (see above, pp. 120-121).

54 Trinitarianism was perceived as being inextricably bound up with the doctrine of the immortality of the soul and as teaching that only Christ's human body died, while his eternal Deity as well as his immortal soul did not die on Calvary. On this basis, Trinitarianism was thought to downgrade and, actually, deny the atonement of Christ, for a merely human sacrifice could never atone for the sins of the world.

55 James White, "Christian Union," *RH*, 12 October 1876, 116; idem, "Christ Equal with God," *RH*, 29 November 1877, 172; idem, "Seventh-day Baptists and Seventh-day Adventists," *RH*, 20 November 1879, 164. White's anti-Trinitarian view stemmed from his Millerite days when he had belonged to the Christian Connection.

56 In 1877 he listed "the doctrine of the Trinity" among the teachings on which "all Seventh-day Adventists will agree" ("A Plain Talk to Murmurers," *RH*, 12 April 1877, 116-117). That this, in fact, was meant, not as an affirmation of Trinitarianism, but rather as its complete rejection is clear from another article published about a year later in which he maintains that the Bible "clearly denies the doctrine of the trinity" (idem, "The Personality of God," *RH*, 29 August 1878, 73-74). The understandable but total misinterpretation of his 1877 statement dates back, at least, to the 1930s. See William H. Branson, *In Defense of the Faith* (Washington, D.C.: RHPA, 1933), 370; and C. P. B[ollman], "The Holy Spirit a Person," *RH*, 3 August 1933, 3-4.

57 Unfortunately, Froom offers no proof for his assertion that Waggoner believed in the Trinity by the late 1880s; he merely presents some conjectures based on what seems to be a mis-understanding of the sources *(MOD,* 188-299). He assumes that the Trinitarian dogma is a prerequisite to the proper understanding of the doctrine of righteousness by faith. However accurate this may be theologically, it does not invalidate the historical fact that Waggoner remained a semi-Arian in 1888 and beyond *(Christ and His Righteousness* [Oakland, Calif.: PPPA, 1890], 9, 12, 21, 22). Nor is it accurate from a historical point of view to regard the Trinitarian and Christological questions as the underlying bone of contention in 1888 *(MOD,*

The first clear indication that the church was gradually moving toward a Trinitarian position was the publication in 1892 of a small tract on *The Bible Doctrine of the Trinity.*[58] Trinitarian thought seems to have been enhanced in the late 1890s by W. W. Prescott,[59] who was later denounced by some for having introduced this "deadly heresy" into the Seventh-day Adventist Church.[60] The first Trinitarian statements from the pen of Ellen White date from the years 1897 and 1898 when, to the surprise of many of her fellow believers, she called the Holy Spirit "the third person of the Godhead."[61] Others followed suit.[62]

Trinitarianism was clearly affirmed in the 1931 Statement of Fundamental Beliefs, though the church did not, at the time, formally decide in favor of this doctrine – or any other, for that matter.[63] Still, it has ever since been the recognized, albeit not universally acknowledged, teaching of the church whose writers could now maintain that "Seventh-day Adventists are Trinitarians."[64]

271-280, 313-326). For even Froom must admit that during the Minneapolis Conference apparently neither friend nor foe criticized Waggoner for his alleged departure from the common semi-Arian view on the nature of Christ (ibid., 298).

58 Samuel T. Spear, *The Bible Doctrine of the Trinity,* Bible Student's Library, no. 90 (Oakland, Calif.: PPPA, 1892). This 14-page tract was reprinted from the *New York Independent,* 14 November 1889. Adventists frequently published material by non-SDA authors without necessarily agreeing with everything said. However, the title of this pamphlet reveals that a theological change of view was in the making.

59 "In 1896 Prescott had begun to urge the church toward a more Trinitarian doctrinal position" (Gilbert M. Valentine, "W. W. Prescott: Editor Extraordinaire," *RH,* 5 December 1985, 11, 10-12). I have not been able to substantiate the accuracy of this statement.

60 J. S. Washburn, *The Startling Omega and Its True Genealogy* (Philadelphia: By the Author, [1920]), 1-2.

61 Ellen White, Special Testimonies, Series A, No. 10 (1897), 37; published in idem, *Evangelism* (Washington, D.C.: RHPA, 1946; reprint, 1970), 617. The first printed Trinitarian statements appeared a year later in her book *The Desire of Ages* (Mountain View, Calif.: PPPA, 1898; reprint, 1940), 669, 671. For a compilation of Ellen White's Trinitarian statements, see idem, *Evangelism,* 613-617; and *QOD,* 641-646 (appendix A: "Christ's Place in the Godhead"). It was these statements that strongly influenced the denomination in the direction of Trinitarianism. They were later quoted by SDA writers as authority in favor of the latter (see, e.g., George B. Thompson, "The Holy Spirit – No. 7," *RH,* 27 February 1913, 197-198). Thus, it is questionable whether Harry W. Lowe was correct in saying that the Adventist pioneers "almost all had the Bible conception of the Trinity ... prior to Spirit of Prophecy confirmation" ("The Writings of Ellen G. White as Related to Seventh-day Adventist Doctrines and Prophetic Interpretation," *Ministry,* October 1967, 10).

62 See, e.g., R. A. Underwood, "The Holy Spirit a Person," *RH,* 17 May 1898, 310 ("the personality of the Godhead – the Father, Son, and Holy Ghost"); and "Blended Personalities," *RH,* 3 April 1900, 210 ("the blended personalities of our triune God").

63 It was only after 1946 that the General Conference took any official actions regarding the Fundamental Beliefs. See below, pp. 206.

64 Bollman, "The Holy Spirit a Person," 4. Cf. below, app. 3, p. 337. See also Froom, *MOD,* 35-86; *SDAs Believe,* 17-26; and Rice, *The Reign of God,* 88-92. Incidentally, it is surprising how fast the historical circumstances surrounding this significant doctrinal revision fell into

Christology

All developments of their Christology notwithstanding, Seventh-day Adventists have never wavered in their wholehearted confession of Jesus Christ as Lord and Creator, incarnated and risen Son of God, Redeemer of humankind, heavenly Intercessor and soon-coming King.[65] Still, there were some notable changes regarding the Adventist position on the divine nature, the human nature, and the dual nature of Christ.[66] They are discussed now in this order.

Christ's divine nature. While Seventh-day Adventists never had any doubts about the pre-existence and divinity of Jesus, they did not, at first, as a denomination believe in the eternal self-existence and full equality of Christ with God, the Father.

In the early years, at least some leading Adventists regarded Jesus as a created being elevated to divine status.[67] This view was soon abandoned and replaced by an Arian position, which held that though Christ was not a created being, he still had a beginning in time when he was begotten or born of God. This became the standard Adventist view until about the end of the nineteenth century. It implied that Jesus,

---

total oblivion, even among Adventists themselves. Responding to Canright's contention that during the 19th century Adventists had generally opposed the doctrine of the Trinity, General Conference President William H. Branson, in 1933, claimed that while "there were some Seventh-day Adventists who did not believe the doctrine of the Trinity," it was not the church as a whole that denied it, "for in their earlier history the issue was not raised, and when later it was raised, it was decided ... in favor of [the Trinity]" (*In Defense of the Faith*, 370-371). Bollman even asserted that Trinitarianism "has always been recognized" among Adventists ("The Holy Spirit a Person," 4). As to the reasons for these inaccurate statements, see above, p. 133, n. 56. As late as in 1940, J. S. Washburn, a retired minister, denounced the doctrine of the Trinity as "a cruel heathen monstrosity ... an impossible absurd invention ... a blasphemous burlesque ... a bungling, absurd, irreverent caricature" ("The Trinity, [1940]," TMs; quoted in Gilbert M. Valentine, *The Shaping of Adventism: The Case of W. W. Prescott* [Berrien Springs, Mich.: AU Press, 1992], 279-280).

65 See below, app. 3, pp. 336-337.
66 The development of Adventist Christology is discussed by Gane, "The Arian or Anti-Trinitarian Views"; Froom, *MOD*, 148-180, 188-217, 269-299; Paulo Sarli, "Arian Views Held by Some Pioneers in the Seventh-day Adventist Church between 1844 and 1900, 1972," TMs, AHC, JWL, AU, Berrien Springs, Mich.; *SDAE*, 1976 ed., s.v. "Christology"; Gil Gutierrez Fernández, "Ellen G. White: The Doctrine of the Person of Christ" (Ph.D. dissertation, Drew University, 1978); Eric Claude Webster, *Crosscurrents in Adventist Christology* (New York: Peter Lang, 1984; reprint, Berrien Springs, Mich.: AU Press, 1992); Ralph Larson, *The Word Was Made Flesh: One Hundred Years of Seventh-day Adventist Christology, 1852-1952* (Cherry Valley, Calif.: Cherrystone Press, 1986); and Whidden, "The Soteriology of Ellen G. White," 156-238.
67 J. M. Stephenson, *The Atonement* (Rochester, N.Y.: Advent Review Office, 1854); *The Bible Student's Assistant* (n.p., [ca. 1860]), 42-45; [Uriah Smith], "Christ Our Passover," *RH,* 13 October 1859, 164; and idem, *Thoughts, Critical and Practical, on the Book of Revelation* (Battle Creek, Mich.: SDAPA, 1865), 14, 59, 91-92.

as a derived Being, was clearly inferior to his Father, though deserving to be worshipped and honored as Lord and God.[68]

Increasingly, however, any substantial inferiority of the Son to the Father was denied, albeit still in a semi-Arian context. This meant that God had decided to grant his Son full equality to himself.[69] Even E. J. Waggoner, who strongly influenced Adventists in the direction of orthodox Christology by teaching that Christ was of the very nature and "substance" of God possessing life in himself, held that Christ had a beginning and that the divine attributes were his only "by inheritance," i.e., because they had been given to him by Jehovah God.[70]

After the publication in 1898 of Ellen White's *Desire of Ages*, which ascribed to Jesus Christ "life, original, unborrowed, underived," Seventh-day Adventists increasingly adopted a Trinitarian position which regards the Son as equal to the Father in each and every respect.[71] This view was included in the 1931 Statement of Fundamental Beliefs and has been regarded since then as a basic doctrinal tenet of the Seventh-day Adventist Church.[72]

68   Canright, "Jesus Christ the Son of God"; idem, "The Personality of God," 73-74; A. C. Bourdeau, "The Hope That Is in You," *RH,* 8 June 1869, 185-186; J. N. Andrews, "Melchisedek," *RH,* 7 September 1869, 84; John Matteson, "Children of God," *RH,* 12 October 1869, 123; Smith, *Thoughts, Critical and Practical, on the Book of Daniel and the Revelation,* 487; Littlejohn, "Scripture Questions," 250; J. H. Waggoner, *The Atonement;* and Stone, *The Captain of Our Salvation* (1886), 16-17.

69   James White, "Christ Equal with God"; Stone, 7, 11, 32, 33, 40; E. J. Waggoner, "The Divinity of Christ," *ST,* 8 April 1889, 214; idem, *Christ and His Righteousness,* 9, 12, 21, 22, 44; J. P. Henderson, "Is Christ a Created Being?" *RH,* 12 January 1892, 19; W. W. Prescott, "The Christ for Today," *RH,* 14 April 1896, 232; and Uriah Smith, *Looking unto Jesus: Christ in Type and Antitype* (Battle Creek, Mich.: RHPA, 1898), 10, 11-12, 17.

70   E. J. Waggoner, *Christ and His Righteousness,* 12, 22, 23, 44. See also Webster, *Crosscurrents in Adventist Christology,* 177-180, 194. Froom depicts him as an orthodox Trinitarian who a few times lapsed back into unfortunate semi-Arian terminology *(MOD,* 188-217, 269-299). Obviously, however, Waggoner's strong emphasis on the full deity and complete equality of Christ with the Father did not prevent him from teaching also that he was God's unique Son "by birth," who proceeded from the Father "far back in the ages of eternity" *(Christ and His Righteousness,* 9, 12, 21, 22). To call this "a single unfortunate slip" of his pen *(MOD,* 293) is hardly warranted by the facts of the case.

71   Ellen White, *Desire of Ages,* 530. This statement was first published in "Christ the Life-Giver," *ST,* 8 April 1897, 212. Half a century later, M. L. Andreasen recalled some of the initial reactions on the part of church members to this provoking new idea: "I remember how astonished we were when *Desire of Ages* was first published, for it contained some things that we considered unbelievable; among others the doctrine of the Trinity which was not generally accepted by the Adventists then … I was particularly interested in the statement in *Desire of Ages* which at one time caused great concern to the denomination theologically: 'In Christ is life, original, unborrowed, underived.' p. 530. That statement may not seem very revolutionary to you, but to us it was. We could hardly believe it" ("The Spirit of Prophecy" [1948 address], quoted in Holt, 20).

72   The 1931 statement confessed "That Jesus Christ," the second person of the Godhead, "is very God, being of the same nature and essence as the Eternal Father" (#3). In 1980, the

Christ's human nature. No matter what can be said about the human nature of Christ and the source of the temptations he had to overcome, Adventists have never expressed any doubts regarding the perfect sinlessness of the incarnate life of the Son of God. Where they do have sizeable disagreements is on the question of whether and in what sense his human nature was affected or tarnished by sin; in other words, whether he was tempted only from without or also from within by his own human (sinful) flesh. At the present time, this is an unresolved issue in Adventist theology.[73]

The idea that Christ's human nature was free from any propensities to sin making him start where Adam did before the fall was held at least by some church members towards the end of the nineteenth century.[74] However, another conviction became common among Adventists. It holds that during his earthly life Jesus shared in even the sinful tendencies of the fallen human nature, though he never succumbed to any outward or inward temptation because of the divine power available to him in his divine nature and/or by his heavenly Father. He thereby became a perfect example, which every believer can and should strive to emulate.[75]

In recent decades, many Adventists have adopted the view that in sharing our fallen human nature, Christ did not partake of any of its sinful propensities, as this would have made him a sinner himself in need of a savior.[76] In the 1950s, this belief was publicly presented as the one and only Seventh-day Adventist position. However, there was some noticeable dissent, which has continued until today.[77]

---

church declared that "God the eternal Son" is "co-eternal" with the Father and the Holy Spirit (#3) and "forever truly God" (#4). See below, app. 3, pp. 336-337. See also *QOD*, 35-86; and *SDAs Believe*, 37-57.

73 The three major historic declarations of the Adventist faith do not take sides on this issue, thereby seemingly reflecting the unresolved state of the issue among Adventists (see below, app. 3, pp. 336-337). These texts merely state that Jesus Christ "took on him the nature of the seed of Abraham" (1872), "the nature of the human family" (1931), and that he "experienced temptation as a human being, but perfectly exemplified the righteousness and love of God" (1980). However, at least the first of these may inadvertently have omitted what was commonly held, viz., that Christ did indeed possess a sinful human nature.

74 See, e.g., G. W. Morse, "Scripture Question," *RH*, 28 August 1888, 554. Cf. George R. Knight, *From 1888 to Apostasy: The Case of A. T. Jones* (Washington, D.C., and Hagerstown, Md.: RHPA, 1987), 138.

75 See E. J. Waggoner, *Christ and His Righteousness*, 26, 28; A. T. Jones, "The Third Angel's Message. – Nos. 13-14," *General Conference Bulletin 1895*, 230-235, 265-270; *Bible Readings for the Home Circle* (Washington, D.C.: RHPA, 1918), 174 ("in His humanity, Christ partook of our sinful, fallen nature ... God, in Christ, condemned sin ... by coming and living in the flesh, in sinful flesh"); F. D. Nichol, "Four Charges against Seventh-day Adventists," *RH*, 5 March 1931, 3-4; and Knight, *From 1888 to Apostasy*, 138.

76 In the 1940s, the statement quoted in the previous footnote was revised to read: "God, in Christ, condemned sin ... by coming and living in the flesh, and yet without sinning" *(Bible Readings for the Home* [Washington, D.C.: RHPA, 1949; Mountain View, Calif.: PPPA, 1949], 144). Heppenstall became a leading proponent of this view (cf. below, p. 143, n. 108).

77 See *QOD*, 50-65; Robert Hancock, "The Humanity of Christ: A Brief Study of SDA Teachings on the Nature of Christ, 1962," quoted in Moore, *The Theology Crisis*, 435; Ralph

As is quite common in Adventist doctrinal discussions, both sides have appealed to Ellen White in support of their position – and this not without some justification.[78] For, while she repeatedly spoke of Christ's fallen and sinful human nature, she also strongly defended the perfect sinlessness of the Savior, holding that he was free from any evil propensities.[79]

Adventist theologian Norman R. Gulley has attempted to bring about a reconciliation of both viewpoints. Admitting the existence of two divergent streams of thought in "historic Adventism," he analyzes their respective strengths and weaknesses and proposes a dialectic solution. Unity in the church, according to Gulley, can be achieved if the two views are seen as "complementary rather than contradictory."[80] However, as for now, the subject continues to be discussed rather controversially within the Seventh-day Adventist Church.[81]

Larson, *The Word Was Made Flesh;* and Jean R. Zurcher, "The Seventh-day Adventist Teaching on the Human Nature of Christ during Ellen White's Lifetime, 1986," TMs, AHC, JWL, AU, Berrien Springs, Mich. William H. Grotheer decried the church's "state of apostasy" by moving away from "the historic position of the Church" and teaching instead that Christ took upon himself the pre-fall nature of Adam ("An Interpretive History of the Doctrine of the Incarnation as Taught by the Seventh-day Adventist Church, 1972," TMs, JWL, AU, Berrien Springs, Mich.). According to Webster, the book *Questions on Doctrine* was "an important watershed for Adventist Christology"; however, "it has also served to polarize Adventist thinking" *(Crosscurrents in Adventist Christology,* 40).

78 Opposite views were expressed, e.g., by Edward Heppenstall, *The Man Who Is God: A Study of the Person and Nature of Jesus, Son of God and Son of Man* (Washington, D.C.: RHPA, 1977); and Thomas A. Davis, *Was Jesus Really Like Us?* (Washington, D.C.: RHPA, 1979).

79 For a compilation of Ellen White statements on the human nature of Christ, which is heavily geared towards the sinless-nature position, see *QOD,* 647-660 (appendix B, "Christ's Nature during the Incarnation"). A revised edition was published as supplement to *Ministry,* February 1972 ("The Nature of Christ during the Incarnation"). Another collection of quotations is found in Robert W. Olson, comp., *The Humanity of Christ: Selections from the Writings of Ellen G. White* (Boise, Idaho: PPPA, 1989). It is useful to analyze her statements semantically and contextually in order to determine what exactly Ellen White meant by speaking of Christ's sinful or rather sinless nature. See, e.g., Tim Poirier, "Sources Clarify Ellen White's Christology," *Ministry,* December 1989, 7-9. On her use of the term "propensity," see also *SDAs Believe,* 57, n. 22. For an analysis of White's understanding of sin and of human character/nature, see Pöhler, "Sinless Saints or Sinless Sinners? 1978," 76-91, 112-122, 127-128.

80 Norman R. Gulley, "Behold the Man," *AR,* 30 June 1983, 4-8. Cf. idem, "Model or Substitute? Does It Matter How We See Jesus? – Parts 1-6," *Adventist Review,* 18 January - 22 February 1990; and *SDAs Believe,* 46-49. Similarly, Webster concluded his comparative analysis of four Adventist authors by suggesting "that it is possible to have a multi-faceted Christology, drawing on all the New Testament models concerning the person and work of Christ, while also upholding the full divinity and full humanity of Christ without falling into contradiction" *(Crosscurrents in Adventist Christology,* 452). Herman Bauman has tried to solve "the apparent dilemma" by distinguishing Christ's sinless "spiritual nature" from his sinful "physical condition" ("'And the Word Was Made Flesh'," *Ministry,* December 1994, 18-21, 29).

81 See, e.g., Kenneth Gage [H. E. Douglass] and Benjamin Rand [N. R. Gulley], "What Human Nature Did Jesus Take? Unfallen/Fallen," *Ministry,* June 1985, 8-21, 24; "And furthermore

Christ's dual nature. Early Seventh-day Adventists consistently rejected the orthodox two-nature Christology[82] because, in their view, it reduced the death of Christ to a merely human sacrifice and thereby denied the biblical doctrine of the atonement.[83] J. H. Waggoner, for example, argued the following way:

> Trinitarians hold that "Christ" comprehends two natures; one that was merely human; the other, the second person in the trinity, who dwelt in the flesh for a brief period, but could not possibly suffer, or die: that the Christ that died was only the human nature in which the divinity had dwelt ... if the manhood only died the sacrifice was only human.[84]

As late as 1888, Smith maintained that "Christ was not possessed of a dual nature while here upon the earth" and described "the point made by S. D. Adventists" thus:

> If his nature can be separated into human and divine, and only the *human* part died, then the world is furnished with only a *human* sacrifice, not a divine sacrifice, as we contend ...He, the divine Son of God, appeared here upon the earth, *in human nature.*[85]

According to Norman Young, even after 1888 the common one-nature Christology was not immediately abandoned. Under the influence of E. J. Waggoner the emphasis shifted, though, to the soteriological significance of the incarnation of Christ, while previously the focus had been on Christ's divine sacrifice on the cross.[86]

The orthodox view, according to which Christ possessed a twofold, divine-human nature, was held at least by some Adventists after the late 1870s.[87] In later years, it received full support from Ellen White who spoke of "the dual character of

...," *Ministry,* August 1985, 10-11, 23-24; "Letters," *Ministry,* December 1985, 2, 25-28; Thomas A. Davis, "Christ's Human Nature: An Alternate View," *Ministry,* June 1986, 14-17; Larson, *The Word Was Made Flesh* (1986); and Roy Adams, *The Nature of Christ* (Hagerstown, Md.: RHPA, 1994).

82 According to the Council of Chalcedon (451), Jesus Christ was truly God and truly man, possessing two natures, which were both unconfused and undivided. See Leith, ed., *Creeds of the Churches,* 35-36. Though not unchallenged, it became the orthodox Christian view.

83 See Norman H. Young, "Christology and Atonement in Early Adventism, *Adventist Heritage* 9:2 (1984): 30-39. The one-nature Christology was defended, e.g., by Stephenson, *The Atonement* (1854); Frisbie, "The Trinity"; D. W. Hull, "Bible Doctrine of the Divinity of Christ2; J. H. W[aggoner], "The Atonement – Part II"; Canright, "Jesus Christ the Son of God"; and Uriah Smith, "S. D. Adventism not Orthodox," *RH,* 27 March 1888, 200.

84 J. H. Waggoner, "The Atonement – Part II," 181-182.

85 Uriah Smith, "S. D. Adventism not Orthodox," 200.

86 Young, "Christology and Atonement in Early Adventism," 37-38.

87 James White, "Christ Equal with God"; E. J. Waggoner, *Christ and His Righteousness,* 28; S. N. Haskell, "Was Christ Divine?" *RH,* 21 April 1891, 329-330; and A. T. Jones, "The Faith of Jesus," *RH,* 18-25 December 1900, 808, 824.

[Christ's] nature"[88] and affirmed that Christ "has a twofold nature, at once human and divine. He is both God and man."[89] According to her,

> the two natures were mysteriously blended in one person – the man Jesus Christ. In Him dwelt all the fullness of the Godhead bodily. When Christ was crucified, it was his human nature that died. Deity did not sink and die; that would have been impossible.[90]

The two-nature Christology was expressed clearly in the 1931 Statement of Fundamental Beliefs and has remained the official Adventist position ever since.[91]

Pneumatology [92]

The anti-Trinitarian and (semi-)Arian matrix of Seventh-day Adventist theology during the nineteenth century makes it a foregone conclusion that the idea of ascribing to the Spirit of God the marks of individuality and personality was not easily accepted by Adventists. Though the issue was not directly addressed in publications during the early years, the regular use of the impersonal pronoun "it" leaves little doubt as to their opinion on this question.[93]

J. H. Waggoner declined to address this issue because of the difficulties in defining and agreeing on the meaning of the term "person" and "especially as it is

---

88   Ellen White, *The Desire of Ages,* 507 (published 1898). According to Whidden, Ellen White's view was characterized by "numerous problematic, antithetical statements that give her Christology a very profoundly dialectical flavor. This applies to both the relationship between His full deity and humanity and the way His humanity relates to human sinfulness" ("The Soteriology of Ellen G. White," 158).

89   Ellen White, Manuscript 76, 1903; in *Seventh-day Adventist Bible Commentary,* ed. F. D. Nichol, rev. ed. (Washington, D.C.: RHPA, 1976-1980), 6:1074, hereafter cited as *SDABC.* Cf. Ellen White, Letter 5, 1889; in *SDABC,* 7:904 ("The limited capacity of man cannot define this wonderful mystery – the blending of the two natures, the divine and the human").

90   Ellen White, Letter 280, 1904; quoted in *SDABC,* 5:1113. Cf. idem, "The Risen Saviour," *Youth's Instructor,* 4 August 1898; quoted in *SDABC,* 5:1113b ("Humanity died; divinity did not die").

91   "While retaining His divine nature He took upon Himself the nature of the human family" (1931, #3). "Forever truly God, He became also truly man" (1980, #4). See below, app. 3, pp. 336-337. Cf. *QOD,* 50-65, 647-660; *SDAs Believe,* 50-52.

92   The development of the doctrine of the Holy Spirit among Seventh-day Adventists has been investigated by Christy Mathewson Taylor, "The Doctrine of the Personality of the Holy Spirit as Taught by the Seventh-day Adventist Church up to 1900" (B.D. thesis, SDA Theological Seminary, Washington, D.C., 1953). See also Froom, *MOD,* 163-180; and *SDAE,* 1976 ed., s.v. "Holy Spirit."

93   The 1872 statement of Adventist beliefs is a case in point (see app. 3, col. 1, pars. 1, 14, 16). It had no entry on the Holy Spirit but, in talking about God, called him "his representative" (par. 1). As late as 1915, E. M. Adams spoke consistently of "its" identity, help, place, etc. ("The Holy Spirit – No. 3," *RH,* 23 December 1915, 11-12).

not a question of direct revelation."[94] But apparently he never spoke of the Spirit of God other than in terms of a divine energy and mysterious power.[95] Others, however, were quite outspoken in dismissing the traditional Christian view and, like D. M. Canright, firmly declared, "The Holy Spirit is not a person."[96]

The first indication that the church was in the process of rethinking its pneumatology came in 1883 when two articles in the *Review & Herald* left room for a personal dimension of the Holy Spirit.[97] But it was in 1892 that Seventh-day Adventists, for the first time, publicly promoted the belief in the personality of the Holy Spirit.[98] During the next few years, there appeared a number of ambiguous statements on the Holy Spirit indicative of the gradual reorientation that was under way in the church with respect to its view on God, Christ, and the Spirit.[99]

After Ellen White herself, in 1898, had publicly called the Holy Spirit "the third person of the Godhead,"[100] the new teaching was freely promoted among Seventh-day Adventists. The same year, one of them frankly acknowledged,

94 J. H. Waggoner, "The Gifts and Offices of the Holy Spirit – No. 1," *RH,* 23 September 1875, 89; and idem, *The Spirit of God: Its Offices and Manifestations, to the End of the Christian Age* (Battle Creek, Mich.: SDAPA, 1877), 8-9. (This book is a reprint from the series of twelve articles on "The Gifts and Offices of the Holy Spirit" published in the *Review & Herald* between September 23 and December 9, 1875.) Others also expressed themselves in a guarded manner. See, e.g., J. E. Swift, "Our Companion," *RH,* 3 July 1883, 421 ("Just what the Spirit is, is a mooted question among theologians, and we may not hope to give it a positive answer"); and G. C. Tenney, "The Comforter," *RH,* 30 October 1883, 673-674 ("Whether it is … a personal being or a representative influence, it exists").

95 J. H. Waggoner, *The Spirit of God,* 7-9, 13, 17, 20, 140-142; and idem, *The Atonement,* 2d ed., 89. The same was done, e.g., by J. M. Hopkins, "Grieve Not the Spirit," *RH,* 3 July 1883, 417; Charles W. Stone, *The Captain of Our Salvation;* C. P. Bollman, "The Spirit of God," *ST,* 4 November 1889, 663; and Lee S. Wheeler, "The Communion of the Holy Spirit," *RH,* 21 April 1891, 244.

96 D. M. Canright, "The Holy Spirit Not a Person, but an Influence Proceeding from God," *ST,* 25 July 1878, 218. See also [Uriah Smith], "In the Question Chair," *RH,* 28 October 1890, 664; [idem], "In the Question Chair," *RH,* 23 March 1897, 188; idem, *Looking unto Jesus* (1898), 10; and T. R. Williamson, "The Holy Spirit – Is It a Person?" *RH,* 13 October 1891, 627.

97 Swift, "Our Companion" (uses the pronouns "he" and "it" when speaking about the Holy Spirit); and Tenney, "The Comforter" (allows for the possibility that "it" is an "influence" or "a personal being").

98 Spear, *The Bible Doctrine of the Trinity.* The author refused, however, to get involved in any "speculation" regarding whether or not the Holy Spirit has a "consciousness" of his own.

99 See, e.g., T. L. Waters, "The Holy Spirit," *RH,* 28 November 1893, 743 ("this divine One … in its seven offices"); G. C. Tenney, "To Correspondents," *RH,* 9 June 1896, 362 ("he is something more than an emanation from the mind of God … He is spoken of as a personality … a heavenly intelligence"); and Milton C. Wilcox, "The Spirit – Impersonal and Personal," *ST,* 18 August 1898, 518 ("it … comes to the believer as a person, the person of Christ Jesus").

100 Ellen White, *The Desire of Ages,* 669, 671. Cf. idem, Special Testimonies, Series A, No. 10 (1897), 37, published in idem, *Evangelism,* 617; and idem, Manuscript 66, 1899, published

It seems strange to me now, that I ever believed that the Holy Spirit was only an influence, in view of the work he does. But we want the truth because it is truth, and we reject error because it is error, regardless of any views we may formerly have held.[101]

In 1928, the first book about the Holy Spirit as a divine person was published by Adventists.[102] Finally, in 1931, the church publicly went on record as teaching the "third person of the Godhead" view, which, by then, had become the prevailing though not completely unchallenged belief of Seventh-day Adventists.[103]

Anthropology/Hamartiology

Apparently, no significant developments are to be noted with regard to the Adventist understanding of the nature of man and sin.[104] From the beginning, the church has held a conditionalist view of human immortality and has never adopted any official position regarding the teaching of original sin.[105] In fact, Adventists have consistently

in idem, *Evangelism*, 616 ("We need to realize that the Holy Spirit, who is as much a person as God is a person, is walking through these grounds [at the Avondale School]").

101 Underwood, "The Holy Spirit a Person," 310. See also "The God-Man," *RH*, 20 September 1898, 598 ("the person and presence of the Holy Ghost"); "Walking in the Spirit," *RH*, 24 January 1899, 82 ("we must recognize his personality"); [Mrs.] S. M. I. Henry, *The Abiding Spirit* (Battle Creek, Mich.: RHPA, 1899), 271 ("he is a person"); "The Third Person," *RH*, 16 January 1900, 35; and "Blended Personalities," 210 ("his personality").

102 LeRoy Edwin Froom, *The Coming of the Comforter* (Washington, D.C.: RHPA, 1928).

103 See below, app. 3, col. 2, par. 2. In 1980, a new section was added to the Fundamental Beliefs dealing with the work of "God the eternal Spirit" (see below, app. 3, col. 3, par. 5). Cf. *SDAs Believe*, 59-66. Still, until today, there is opposition to this teaching in the church.

104 However, in his autobiography, James White described a little-known incident that is related to the Adventist doctrine of man. It involves "the identical-particles-of-matter-theory" defended by a number of leading Adventists such as Andrews, Loughborough, Smith, and J. H. Waggoner in the 19th century. It held "that the same particles of matter which constitute the mortal man should enter into the immortal being" at the future resurrection from the dead. As for himself, White publicly questioned this theory in 1861 but then kept silent on it for about 16 years until his wife (supported by Dr. J. H. Kellogg who argued from a scientific point of view) openly sided with him in 1877. See James White and Ellen White, *Life Sketches: Ancestry, Early Life, Christian Experience, and Extensive Labors, of Elder James White, and His Wife, Mrs. Ellen G. White* (Battle Creek, Mich.: SDAPA, 1880), 398-400. See also Ellen White, *Desire of Ages*, 605.

105 See LeRoy Edwin Froom, *The Conditionalist Faith of Our Fathers*, 2 vols. (Washington, D.C.: RHPA, 1966); Cosmas Rubencamp, "Immortality and Seventh-day Adventist Eschatology" (Ph.D. dissertation, Catholic University of America, 1968); Jean Zurcher, *The Nature and Destiny of Man* (New York: Philosophical Library, 1969); and Edwin Harry Zackrison, "Seventh-day Adventists and Original Sin: A Study of the Early Development of the Seventh-day Adventist Understanding of the Effects of Adam's Sin on His Posterity" (Ph.D. dissertation, Andrews University, 1984). For brief introductory essays, see *SDAE*, 1976 ed., s.v. "Conditional Immortality," "Man, Doctrine of," and "Sin." See also Tim Crosby, "Conditionalism: A Cornerstone of Adventist Doctrine," *Ministry*, August 1986, 16-

shunned this notion, which, to them, seemed bound up with the theology and practice of infant baptism. Instead, they emphasized actual sins, which could and were to be overcome with the help of God.[106]

Since the 1950s, however, a number of Adventist theologians have adopted a more radical view of sin, defining it as the inherited state of fallen man (sinful nature, broken relationship) and also his mental attitude (sinful desires) rather than merely his outward behavior (sinful acts).[107] Some of them have also begun to make peace with the terminology, if not the concept, of "original sin."[108] As these issues are still debated among Adventists and have not led to clear doctrinal modifications, they are not treated any further here.[109]

18; *SDAs Believe,* 79-96; and Rice, *The Reign of God,* 96-141. For a comparison of leading SDA declarations of fundamental beliefs on anthropology/hamartiology, see app. 3.

106 Uriah Smith distinguished "sin(s)" (acts of disobedience) from "sinfulness" (the "disposition of mind" that leads men to commit sin[s]). According to him, Jesus came to cure man's sinfulness and remove it from the heart thereby enabling man to perfectly obey the law of God ("The Sinner and His Sins," *RH,* 10 February 1891, 88); cf. [idem], "In the Question Chair," *RH,* 19 April 1892, 248-249. On the other hand, L. A. Smith declared that "sin is not an act, but a condition of the heart. The act is the result of the condition. It is a state of separation from God" ("The Nature of Sin," *RH,* 20 June 1893, 394).

107 Already at the 1919 Bible Conference, W. W. Prescott had pointed out that sin is more than transgression of the law. Rather, it "must be taken to extend to the very nature, the very being, and not simply the outward act ... Sin is in the [inner-most] being, and what one is primarily rather than primarily what he does." Synonymous to rebellion and disloyalty, sin involves a broken relationship and is "a question of our attitude toward God" (W. W. Prescott, study on The Person of Christ, 6 July 1919, 6-10, 1919 Bible Conference Transcripts, General Conference Archives, Silver Spring, Md.).

108 See, e.g., Edward Heppenstall, "'Let Us Go on to Perfection'," in Herbert E. Douglass and others, *Perfection: The Impossible Possibility* (Nashville: SPA, 1975), 57-88. According to him, "sin involves both a state or condition of life and acts contrary to the will of God. Man's sinful condition into which all men are born is the self-centeredness and the consequent self-will as a result of our separation from God. From this condition proceed all sinful thoughts, propensities, passions, and actions ... All men are born in a state of separation from God. This is *the original sin,* a state into which all of us enter the world" (ibid., 63-64 [italics mine]). See also Edward Heppenstall, *Salvation Unlimited: Perspectives in Righteousness by Faith* (Washington, D.C.: RHPA, 1974), 7-25; and idem, *The Man Who Is God* (1977), 107-125 ("this state of sin into which all men are born is called original sin – not in the sense of inherited guilt, but of an inherited disposition to sin). Similarly, George R. Knight has defined original sin as "being primarily a condition of the heart and a rebellious attitude toward God," "a state of fallenness" that leads to "sinful acts" *(The Pharisee's Guide to Perfect Holiness: A Study of Sin and Salvation* (Boise, Idaho: PPPA, 1992), 21, 46. Cf. Adams, *The Nature of Christ,* 69-70, 87-98.

109 On the issue of original sin, see Robert W. Olson, "Outline Studies on Christian Perfection and Original Sin," *Ministry,* Supplement, n.d., 24-30 [48-54]; Lee Herbert Fletcher, "The Seventh-day Adventist Concept of Original Sin" (M.A. thesis, SDA Theological Seminary, Washington, D.C., 1960); Kurt Bangert, "Original Sin – An Adventist Approach, 1974," TMs (in my possession); Tim Crosby, "A New Approach to an Adventist Doctrine of Original Sin, 1978," TMs, EGWRC, AU, Berrien Springs, Mich.; Ruben Hernandez, "Original Sin

Soteriology: Atonement

In briefly reviewing the history of the Adventist doctrine of atonement, the main question to be raised is not at what time or for which event of salvation history the term atonement was used by Adventists, but rather whether or not the gradually shifting application of this term reflected a changing understanding of the significance of Christ's death and his ministry in the heavenly sanctuary, respectively.[110]

William Miller regarded the death of Christ only as "the sacrifice for sin" preparatory to "the atonement to be made by the intercession of Jesus Christ, and the sprinkling of his blood in the Holy of Holies, and upon the mercy-seat and people," by which means reconciliation and forgiveness were made available to all men.[111] As an orthodox believer, in the general Protestant sense of the term, Miller had not the least inclination to downgrade the significance of the death of Christ on Calvary. However, the fact that he nonetheless regarded both reconciliation and atonement as present and ongoing rather than objectively concluded realities should make one slow to criticize the views of those Seventh-day Adventists who, following his lead, would later deny that the death of Christ should properly be called an act of atonement.

In his extended study on "The Law of Moses," which was to exert a decisive influence on the developing theology of Seventh-day Adventism, O. R. L. Crosier likewise reserved the term atonement for the high priestly ministry of Christ in the

and Salvation," *Evangelica,* April 1981, 16-21; Daniel Heinz, "Das Problem der 'Erbsünde' aus adventistischer Sicht," *Aller Diener,* 1983, No. 3, 18-23; Norman R. Gulley, "Preliminary Consideration of the Effects and Implications of Adam's Sin," *Adventist Perspectives* 2:2 (1988): 28-44; idem, "Model or Substitute? Does It Matter How We See Jesus? – Part 2," *AR,* 25 January 1990, 12-14; idem, "The Effects of Adam's Sin on the Human Race," *JATS* 5:1 (1994): 196-215; and Knight, *The Pharisee's Guide to Perfect Holiness* (1992), 9-55. For an analysis of Ellen White's view of sin and sinfulness, see Pöhler, "Sinless Saints or Sinless Sinners? 1978," 76-91, 112-122, 127-128.

110 The development of the Seventh-day Adventist understanding of the doctrine of the atonement is traced in a number of studies. See Morton Jerry Davis, "A Study of Major Declarations on the Doctrine of the Atonement in Seventh-day Adventist Literature" (M.A. thesis, Andrews University, 1962); Russell Holt, "A Comparative Study of the Sanctuary and Its Implications for Atonement in Seventh-day Adventist Theology from Uriah Smith to the Present, 1969," TMs, AHC, JWL, AU, Berrien Springs, Mich.; Froom, *MOD,* 160-174, 327-342; *SDAE,* 1976 ed., s.v. "Atonement"; C. Mervyn Maxwell, "Sanctuary and Atonement in SDA Theology: An Historical Survey," in *The Sanctuary and the Atonement,* ed. A. V. Wallenkampf and W. R. Lesher (Washington, D.C.: General Conference of SDAs, 1981), 516-544; and Young, "Christology and Atonement in Early Adventism."

111 This statement is found in Miller's creed of 1822; see Bliss, *Memoirs of Wm. Miller,* 78-79. Cf. Mervin R. Thurber, "Discovered: A Manuscript Letter from William Miller," *RH,* 15 April 1976, 4-6. See also Dalton D. Baldwin, "William Miller's Use of the Word 'Atonement'," in *Doctrine of the Sanctuary: A Historical Survey (1845-1863),* Daniel and Revelation Committee Series, ed. Frank B. Holbrook, vol. 5 (Silver Spring, Md.: Biblical Research Institute, General Conference of SDAs, 1989), 159-170.

heavenly sanctuary.[112] His basic premise, according to which the old covenant system constituted "a simplified model" of redemption in Christ, led him to conclude that the death of Christ could only be the offering of the sacrifice, while the atonement itself was to occur on the day of atonement at the end of human history. Also implied in this premise was the separation, both in time and locality, of Christ's role as sacrificial lamb and as ministering priest, respectively. The latter, in turn, was divided between the "continual intercession" (or daily atonement) in the holy place and "the making of [the yearly] atonement" in the most holy place. This "at-one-ment" was synonymous with reconciliation, collective forgiveness, and the blotting out of sin both from the sanctuary and the people.

This conception, which was intended to explain the disappointment of 1844 and also provided biblical support for the so-called shut-door doctrine,[113] clearly subordinated the death of Christ to his atoning ministry in the heavenly sanctuary. While Calvary had been a necessary prerequisite to the atonement, the attention was focused almost entirely on the events during the "dispensation of the fulness of times" which had begun in the fall of 1844 and was to last for at least one thousand years.

Although the leaders of Sabbatarian Adventism disagreed with Crosier on a number of points, particularly regarding his Age-to-come theory, they fully accepted and endorsed his basic premise, way of reasoning, and major conclusions.[114] Seventh-day Adventists likewise focused their attention predominantly on the events related to the final "cleansing of the sanctuary," the "blotting out of sins" from the lives of God's people (and, soon, also from the heavenly record books), and the immediate appearing of the heavenly Bridegroom and King.

Still, not all Sabbatarian Adventists followed Crosier in rejecting the designation of the death of Christ as an act of atonement. In fact, the very first occurrences of the word atonement in Seventh-day Adventist literature do apply it directly to Calvary.[115] This practice was also followed by Ellen White, who during her lifetime frequently spoke of Calvary as an atonement for sin.[116]

---

112 O. R. L. Crosier, "The Law of Moses," *Day-Star,* 7 February 1846, 37-44.

113 For more information on this notion, see below, p. 194, n. 324.

114 In 1847 Ellen White wrote: "The Lord showed me in vision ... that Brother Crosier had the true light, on the cleansing of the Sanctuary, &c." ([James White and Ellen White], *A Word to the "Little Flock"* [Brunswick, Maine: James White, 1847; facsimile reproduction, Washington, D.C.: RHPA, n.d.], 12).

115 J. N. Andrews called Calvary "the great atonement" for our sins ("The Perpetuity of the Law of God," *RH,* January-February 1851, 34-35, 41). J. M. Stephenson described it as "an atonement for the whole world" whose "benefits" could, however, only be received through faith and obedience *(The Atonement,* 186, 177). James White not only published this book but praised it highly as a work whose "value cannot be estimated" ("New and Important Works," *RH,* 19 September 1854, 44). The book was advertised in the *Review & Herald* until 1861, six years after its author had left the Sabbatarian group by reason of his propagation of the Age-to-come doctrine.

116 The first available reference mentions that after "the great sacrifice" had been made on the cross, Jesus returned to heaven in order to "shed upon his disciples the benefits of his

However, beginning in the late 1850s and continuing for about three decades, almost all Adventist writers followed the precedent set by Miller and Crosier in denying that the death of Christ could rightly be called an atonement. The term was strictly reserved for the cleansing of the heavenly sanctuary and the blotting out of sins which they believed had begun in 1844.[117] This teaching was also clearly set forth in the 1872 statement of Adventist beliefs.[118] There were only a few, though by no means insignificant, authors who still expressed the view held by Stephenson back in 1854.[119]

Two main reasons were given by Adventist writers for their insistence on limiting the atonement to the priestly ministry of Christ in the heavenly sanctuary. On the one hand, they pointed to the Old Testament types as an exact foreshadowing of the gospel system. Thus, the killing of the sacrificial lamb could not *per se* be regarded as an act of atonement, which occurred only when the blood was applied in the tabernacle. On the other hand, they were convinced that to identify Christ's sacrifice

atonement" (Ellen G. White, *Spiritual Gifts*, vol. 1, *The Great Controversy, Between Christ and His Angels, and Satan and His Angels* [Battle Creek, Mich.: James White, 1858], 170). As this phrase is reminiscent to that of Stephenson who spoke of "the reception of the benefits of the atonement" *(The Atonement*, 177), it may indicate a close affinity, if not identity, of meaning. There is no ambiguity, however, in White's statements coming from the early 1860s that explicitly call Calvary "an atonement" ("Phrenology, Psychology, Mesmerism, and Spiritualism," *RH*, 18 February 1862, 94) and "the great atonement" *(Spiritual Gifts*, vol. 3, *Important Facts of Faith, in Connection with the History of Holy Men of Old* [Battle Creek, Mich.: SDAPA, 1864], 46, 47, 228). On the other hand, Ellen White never hesitated to describe the final work of Christ in the heavenly sanctuary as a "special" or "final atonement" *(Spiritual Gifts*, 1:149, 158, 162, 170). For a collection of Ellen White statements on the atonement, see *QOD*, 661-692 (appendix C: "The Atonement"). An analysis of her view on the atonement is found in John W. Wood, "The Mighty Opposites: The Atonement of Christ in the Writings of Ellen G. White, Parts I-II," in *The Sanctuary and the Atonement*, ed. A. V. Wallenkampf and R. W. Lesher, 694-730.

117 *The Bible Student's Assistant* (Battle Creek, Mich.: RH Office, 1858), 11; J. H. Waggoner, "Questions Answered," *RH*, 29 July 1858, 84-85; idem, *The Atonement;* Moses Hull, "The Two Laws, and Two Covenants," *RH*, 13 May 1862, 189; *Scripture References* (n.p., 1863), 5, and ibid. (n.p., 1889), 10; H. A. St. John, "Synopsis of the Atonement. Nos. 1-2," *RH*, 13-20 February 1883, 101-102, 119; Milton C. Wilcox, "Forgiveness, Atonement," *RH*, 25 September 1883, 610; L. A. Smith, "Sin and the Atonement," *RH*, 4 March 1890, 137; Uriah Smith, "The Sanctuary. Thirty-sixth Paper. – The Atonement," *RH*, 19 October 1876, 124-125; idem, *The Sanctuary and Its Cleansing* (Battle Creek, Mich.: RHPA, 1877), 275-280; and idem, *Looking unto Jesus*, 236-239.

118 It declared that the "atonement, so far from being made on the cross, which was but the offering of the sacrifice, is the very last portion of His work as priest" (see below, app. 3, col. 1, par. 2).

119 J. N. Andrews, "Christ as an Atoning Sacrifice," *RH*, 5 October 1869, 120; and R. F. Cottrell, "The Objects of Christ's Death," *RH*, 27 August 1861, 102; but cf. idem, "One and One Make Two," *RH*, 28 July 1863, 69.

with the atonement was to lay "the foundation of many of the peculiar errors of Universalism, ultra-Calvinism [double predestination], and Campbellism."[120]

In other words, it was their determination to avoid a maximalist as well as a minimalist (mis)interpretation of the meaning of the death of Christ that prompted these writers to take exception to the orthodox view on the atonement. Still, the price paid for it was high. For, according to the Adventist teaching, the death of Christ had only limited power and importance. It did not provide the needed satisfaction or appeasement with God,[121] nor could it remove the guilt and condemnation of man.[122] All it did accomplish was to supply conditional forgiveness for past sins (justification) and the means for the at-one-ment to take place in the heavenly sanctuary at the end of time.

In the judgment of Uriah Smith, who (together with J. H. Waggoner) was the most ardent defender of this view, the difference between the Adventist teaching and the traditional orthodox belief on the atonement was so wide that "if men would accept this [Adventist doctrine], the theology of Christendom would be revolutionized."[123] While this may well be an overstatement, it still serves as an indication that the gradual return of Adventism to the traditional Protestant theology of the atonement – though not adopting its leanings toward universalism and predestination – was indeed more than merely a semantic change.

In the mid-1880s the *Signs of the Times* began to publish a number of articles and selections that identified the death of Christ as an act of atonement.[124] Similarly, in 1892, a writer in the *Review & Herald* referred to "the atonement made for your sins through the death of [Jesus Christ].[125]

Another early sign of the broadening view on the atonement requires some explanation. When, in 1888, Uriah Smith revised his "Fundamental Principles of

---

120 J. H. Waggoner, "The Atonement," *RH,* 10 September 1861, 116; idem, *The Atonement,* 1868 ed., 156-157; [Uriah Smith], "The Atonement," *RH,* 16 December 1884, 792; and idem, "S. D. Adventism Not Orthodox." "Campbellism" referred to the teaching of the Scottish theologian John McLeod Campbell (1800-1872) on the assurance of faith and the universality of the atonement.

121 "We stand in the same relation to the great satisfaction to be made to the law that those did who lived under the first covenant, looking forward to the consummation of the atonement" (J. H. Waggoner, "Questions Answered," 85; cf. idem, *The Atonement,* 1872 ed., 121).

122 J. H. Waggoner, *The Atonement,* 1872 ed., 120-122.

123 [Uriah Smith], "The Atonement," 792.

124 "Giving Himself," *ST,* 27 August 1885, 515 ("He gave himself as a perfect atonement"); E. J. Waggoner, "Concealed Infidelity," *ST,* 24 February 1887, 118 ("Christ did die as an atonement for sin"); "The Bridge of Reconciliation," *ST,* 17 March 1887, 162 ("by his atoning death on the cross … Jesus Christ made his full, rich, complete atonement"); "The Atoning Saviour," *ST,* 11 August 1887, 486 ("the doctrine is preached of an atoning Saviour who died in [man's] stead"); and Ellen G. White, "The Cross of Christ," *ST,* 3 November 1887, 657-658 ("the atonement made on Calvary").

125 Wolcott H. Littlejohn, "Justification by Faith," *RH,* 9 August 1892, 499. Admittedly, this statement is still somewhat ambiguous.

Seventh-day Adventists" (1872) for republication,[126] he removed the sentence dealing with the atonement and replaced it by another one that described the final ministry of Christ in the heavenly sanctuary as "the great atonement." In a long footnote, he explained the strong Adventist dissension "from the view that the atonement was made upon the cross." The entire text was again published in the 1889 *Year Book*. When in 1891, the Battle Creek Church printed its membership list together with this statement of Seventh-day Adventist beliefs, it was further revised in some parts. Among other changes, the footnote was deleted, "the great atonement" became "the final atonement," and the word "atoning" was added to the sentence speaking of the pre-1844 heavenly ministry of Christ "where, through the atoning merits of his blood, he secures the pardon and forgiveness of all who penitently come to God through him."[127] In this way, Crosier's view, which had distinguished the daily from the yearly atonement, was, for the first time, given clear expression in an Adventist Statement of Faith. The same declaration was reprinted in 1894.[128]

The early decades of the twentieth century witnessed the gradual advance of Seventh-day Adventists toward a more orthodox view of the atonement made on the cross (though not only there) as expressed repeatedly in the writings of Ellen White.

126 They were reprinted in [Uriah Smith], *A Brief Sketch of the Origin, Progress, and Principles of the Seventh-day Adventists* (Battle Creek, Mich.: RHPA, 1888).

127 *Membership of the Seventh-day Adventist Church of Battle Creek, Mich.* (Battle Creek, Mich.: n.p., 1891), 10-11.

128 *Membership of the Seventh-day Adventist Church of Battle Creek, Mich.* (Battle Creek, Mich.: n.p., 1894), 12. Froom has claimed that this 1894 statement was intended to correct rather than to confirm Crosier's view on the atonement *(MOD,* 327-342). In his judgment, it was an (1) authoritative, (2) epochal, and (3) representative declaration of Seventh-day Adventist beliefs (ibid., 341-342). However, the facts do not seem to support this assessment. In the first place, the 1894 statement claimed no more authority than did Uriah Smith's 1872 declaration which had explicitly denied that the presentation of the fundamental principles of the Adventist faith was intended as an authoritative statement in any sense. Froom seems to misunderstand the function of the 1894 statement by calling it an "authoritative declaration." Secondly, the 1894 statement could hardly have omitted the disputed phrase in order to repudiate its content. For it was just a reprint of the 1891 text which, in turn, was based on Uriah Smith's own rewording of the 1872 declaration. Thus, there is no historical support for the conjectures that led Froom to call it an "epochal" statement. Thirdly, it should be noted that the long footnote on the atonement appeared again in print in 1897 as well as in a tract published at the newly established SDA General Conference headquarters in Washington, D.C., early in this century. It was again omitted in the *Year Book* of 1905 and in all successive editions. Thus, it can hardly be maintained that the omission of the disputed phrase by the Battle Creek Church in 1891 and 1894 was done by a "representative" group of church leaders and that its publication reflected merely the personal views of a dwindling minority in the church. This incident illustrates how the overbearing theological concerns of a researcher may, at times, prevent him from reaching accurate historical conclusions. While Froom was apparently aware of the pitfalls of historical reconstruction (ibid., 364-365), he seems not always to have been able to avoid them.

Since the 1930s Adventist writers quite consistently and with few exceptions[129] have distinguished between three phases of the atonement, viz., Christ's all-sufficient sacrifice on Calvary, his continual intercession, and his final mediatorial work in the heavenly sanctuary. These three dimensions of atonement were regarded as an indivisible unit. In other words, while the atonement had begun on the cross, it was completed only at the end of time.[130] This teaching found official expression during the 1952 Bible Conference, where several speakers presented a three-stage concept of atonement according to which "each part was a finished work, but all three were required to make the atonement complete."[131]

Some minor differences did exist with regard to the emphasis placed by different writers on Christ's sacrifice or on his intercession, respectively. But there seems to have been general agreement at the time in the conviction that the atonement could not have been concluded on the cross. The reason given was exactly the same that had prompted Waggoner and Smith to deny the atoning function of the death of Christ altogether. To believe that "complete and final atonement" had been made on Calvary would lead to Universalism or to "predestination in its worst form."[132]

This equilibrium between the three phases of Christ's atoning work was at least partly disturbed in 1957 when *Questions on Doctrine* placed the emphasis particularly on the atoning death of Christ as the "completely efficacious" sacrifice for sin.[133] Now Seventh-day Adventists were said to believe in a "completed atonement on the cross," and it was firmly denied that they held to "any theory of dual atonement."[134] At the same time, and in apparent conflict with this view, a two-phase concept of the atonement, similar to the common three-phase model, was still maintained. For the "complete atonement" of Calvary was *"actually and ultimately efficacious* for those *only"* who availed themselves of its "benefits."[135] These are

129 See, e.g., Charles Henry Watson, *The Atoning Work of Christ, His Sacrifice and Priestly Ministry* (Washington, D.C.: RHPA, 1934). M. L. Andreasen saw three phases of the atonement in Christ's life, death, and self-reflection in his end-time people. See M. L. Andreasen, *The Sanctuary Service* (Washington, D.C.: RHPA, 1937; and idem, *The Book of Hebrews* (Washington, D.C.: RHPA, 1948), 52-60, 436-437.

130 T. M. French, "Three Phases of Christ's Redemptive Work," *RH,* 23 September 1937, 6-7; F. D. Nichol, *Answers to Objections,* rev. and enl. ed. (Washington, D.C.: RHPA, 1952), 407-409; and idem, "Do Adventists Minimize Christ's Atonement?" *RH,* 24 July 1952, 13.

131 Taylor G. Bunch, "The Atonement and the Cross," in *Our Firm Foundation,* 2 vols. (Washington, D.C.: RHPA, 1953), 1:373, 357-434. See also W. G. C. Murdoch, "The Gospel in Type and Anti-Type," ibid., 1:299-356; and H. L. Rudy, "The Mediatorial Ministry of Jesus Christ," ibid., 2:9-76.

132 Nichol, "Do Adventists Minimize Christ's Atonement?" 13.

133 *QOD,* 357, 341-401. For more details on how this book came about and what it was intended for, see below, pp. 239-242.

134 Ibid., 342, 390. Cf. ibid., 349, where the expression "dual atonement" is defined as the belief that holds that Calvary provided only a partial atonement to be supplemented by the heavenly intercession of Christ.

135 Ibid., 351, 354, 357.

applied by Christ in two successive phases in the heavenly sanctuary where he ascended "in order to fully carry out His purpose for our redemption."[136]

The differences between the position set forth in *Questions on Doctrine* and that of Adventists during the nineteenth century were explained as being "a matter of definition of terms."[137] Still, the authors of the book were fully aware that the shifting terminology also involved "a new emphasis" placed on the atonement on the cross, understood as constituting "the inner heart of Adventism."[138]

This is where the real significance of the changing application of the term atonement in Adventist theology seems to lie. The almost exclusive concentration on "last things" (eschatology) which had characterized Sabbatarian Adventism from its beginning, gradually diminished and was replaced by a growing emphasis on the redemptive significance of the incarnation, life, death, and resurrection of Jesus (Christology/soteriology). To reduce this shift to a matter of semantics and terminology could mean to miss the substantial and, possibly, far-reaching theological implications of this formal change.[139]

The "Fundamental Beliefs of Seventh-day Adventists" voted in Dallas (1980) reflect this new view on the atonement. They even continue the shift of emphasis by making atonement to encompass not only the sacrificial death and high-priestly

136 Ibid., 384. One author of the book noted that for Ellen White each of these aspects of the atonement was "incomplete without the other" and, therefore, required "the indispensable complement of the other" (L. E. Froom, "The Priestly Application of the Atoning Act," *Ministry,* February 1957, 9). Another contributor distinguished four "aspects" of the atonement, viz., the provisional (Calvary), the applied (priestly intercession), the eliminative (investigative judgment), and the retributive (executive judgment) aspect (Roy Allen Anderson, "The Atonement in Adventist Theology," *Ministry,* February 1959, 10-15, 47).

137 *QOD,* 348; cf. Froom, *MOD,* 146, 163.

138 L. E. Froom, "The Atonement the Heart of Our Message," *Ministry,* December 1956, 12-14. Cf. idem, "The Priestly Application of the Atoning Act," 11, and 9: "We shall never be the same again if we permit this great truth of the atonement to take full possession of us."

139 For example, to stress the soteriological significance of Christ's atonement on the cross while allowing his ministry in the heavenly sanctuary to take second place may have significant consequences for the teaching on the assurance of salvation. This appears to be reflected in the 1980 statement of Fundamental Beliefs, which declares that "abiding in Him we become partakers of the divine nature and have assurance of salvation now and in the judgment" (#10). It also maintains that "for those who accept the atonement" the resurrection of Christ "assures their final victory over sin and death" (#9). No corresponding statements can be found in the 1872 and 1931 texts. Instead, these earlier texts point out that justification covers only past sins (1872, #15; 1931, #8), while the ultimate fate of believers will be determined only by the investigative judgment at the close of time (1872, #18; 1931, #16). Conversely, in 1980 it was said that this judgment only "reveals" and "makes manifest" who "are abiding in Christ" and, thus, worthy of eternal life (#23). For an Adventist viewpoint on the doctrine of perseverance and the assurance of salvation, see Frank B. Holbrook, "The Sanctuary and Assurance – 1-2," *AR,* 15-22 July 1982, 4-5, 6-8; and Ivan T. Blazen, "Justification and Judgment – 1-6," *AR,* 21 July-25 August 1983, 4-6, 6-8, 5-6, 7-10, 6-9, 9-12. According to Blazen, "the reality of justification involves the reality of complete and lasting assurance" ("Justification and Assurance," *AR,* 28 July 1983, 7).

ministry of Christ but his earthly life as well. "In Christ's life of perfect obedience to God's will, His suffering, death, and resurrection, God provided the only means of atonement for human sin ... This perfect atonement ... condemns our sin and provides for our forgiveness" (#9). Since his ascension, Christ is "making available to believers the benefits of His atoning sacrifice offered once for all on the cross." In 1844, "He entered the second and last phase of His atoning ministry" (#23).[140]

Another important aspect of the doctrine of atonement, which could profitably be studied, is the Adventist understanding of the meaning of the death of Christ in the light of the historic theories of the atonement.[141] Until now, most theologians of the church have sided with the "objective" view.[142] Still, some Adventist scholars have reasoned from a "subjective" perspective.[143] The Dallas version of Fundamental Beliefs (1980) supports the classic view without denying that the death of Christ exerts a moral influence on those who accept its provisions. It describes Jesus as humanity's "Substitute and Example" (#10), who "suffered and died voluntarily on the cross for our sins and in our place" (#4); his death, therefore, was "substitutionary and expiatory, reconciling and transforming" (#9).[144]

---

140 See below, app. 3, col. 3, pars. 9, 23.
141 See Raoul Dederen, "Atoning Aspects in Christ's Death," in *The Sanctuary and the Atonement,* ed. A. V. Wallenkampf and W. R. Lesher, 292-325; Paul J. Landa, "Medieval Aspects on the Atonement," ibid., 420-451; V. Norskov Olsen, "The Atonement in Protestant Reformation Thought," ibid., 452-463; Cedric Ward, "The Atonement in Wesley's Theology," ibid., 464-477; Richard Rice, "The Atonement in Contemporary Protestant Theology," ibid., 478-499; David Duffie, "Some Contemporary Evangelical Views of the Atonement," ibid., 500-515. For a concise survey and evaluation, see Rice, *The Reign of God,* 172-177.
142 See, e.g., Edward Heppenstall, "Subjective and Objective Aspects of the Atonement," in *The Sanctuary and the Atonement,* ed. A. V. Wallenkampf and W. R. Lesher, 667-693; George R. Knight, *My Gripe with God: A Study in Divine Justice and the Problem of the Cross* (Washington, D.C., and Hagerstown, Md.: RHPA, 1990); George Reid, "Why Did Jesus Die? How God Saves Us," *AR,* 5 November 1992, 10-13; Richard Fredericks, "The Moral Influence Theory – Its Attraction and Inadequacy," *Ministry,* March 1992, 6-10; and *SDAs Believe,* 110-117.
143 See, e.g., Jack W. Provonsha, *God Is with Us* (Washington, D.C.: RHPA, 1974), 126-135; idem, *You Can Go Home Again* (Washington, D.C.: RHPA, 1982); idem, *A Remnant in Crisis* (1993), 115-121; A. Graham Maxwell, *Can God Be Trusted?* (Nashville: SPA, 1977), 75-89; and Charles Scriven, "God's Justice, Yes; Penal Substitution, No," *Spectrum* 23:3 (1993): 31-38.
144 See below, app. 3, col. 3, pars. 4, 9, 10. Samuele Bacchiocchi has defended "both the subjective and objective aspects of Christ's death" *(The Time of the Crucifixion and the Resurrection,* Biblical Perspectives, no. 4 [Berrien Springs, Mich.: By the Author, 1985; new enl. ed., 1991], 12, 116-133), while Richard Rice proposed "a synthetic view of the atonement," arguing that no single perspective allows us to capture fully the meaning of Christ's work *(The Reign of God,* 177). Besides, the SDA concept of the "great controversy" between Christ and Satan is congenial to a moral influence view of the atonement.

Soteriology: Righteousness by Faith

One of the most fascinating and important aspects of doctrinal development among Seventh-day Adventists has to do with the teaching on righteousness by faith which has occupied Adventists time and again for more than a century.[145] Among others, it involves the definition and mutual relationship of justification and sanctification as well as the meaning of Christian perfection.[146] The complexity of this issue renders it impossible to do justice to it within the confines of this work. It deserves a comprehensive treatment of its own.[147] This section, therefore, is limited to a brief discussion of two aspects of this fundamental doctrine.

145 For more information on the historic Minneapolis General Conference of 1888 and its aftermath, see below, pp. 228-230.

146 To give an example: On the basis of Rom 3:25-26 SDAs have traditionally understood justification to deal with past sins only. This can be seen from the statements of fundamental beliefs published in 1872 ("justification from our past offences," #15) and 1931 ("justified by His blood for the sins of the past," #8). In 1980, this narrow definition was replaced by a more inclusive statement ("Through Christ we are justified, adopted as God's sons and daughters, and delivered from the lordship of sin," #10). See below, app. 3, p. 340.

147 The interested reader is referred to those studies that have already dealt with the subject. See, e.g., Norval F. Pease, "Justification and Righteousness by Faith in the Seventh-day Adventist Church before 1900" (M.A. thesis, SDA Theological Seminary, Washington, D.C., 1945); idem, *By Faith Alone* (Mountain View, Calif.: PPPA, 1962); idem, *The Faith That Saves* (Washington, D.C.: RHPA, 1969); Bruno William Steinweg, "Developments in the Teaching of Justification and Righteousness by Faith in the Seventh-day Adventist Church" (M.A. thesis, SDA Theological Seminary, Washington, D.C., 1948); J. Gordon MacIntyre, "An Investigation of Seventh-day Adventist Teaching Concerning the Doctrine of Perfection and Sanctification" (M.A. thesis, SDA Theological Seminary, Washington, D.C., 1949); Robert Haddock, "A History of the Doctrine of the Sanctuary in the Advent Movement, 1800-1905" (B.D. thesis, Andrews University, 1970); Douglass et al., *Perfection: The Impossible Possibility;* Geoffrey J. Paxton, *The Shaking of Adventism* (Wilmington, Del.: Zenith Publ., 1977); Arnold Valentin Wallenkampf, *What Every Christian Should Know about Being Justified* (Washington, D.C., and Hagerstown, Md.: RHPA, 1988); and George R. Knight, *The Pharisee's Guide to Perfect Holiness* (1992). For short introductory articles, see *SDAE,* 1976 ed., s.v. "Righteousness by Faith," "Justification," and "Faith and Works." The soteriological views of Ellen White are analyzed and discussed by Arthur G. Daniells, *Christ Our Righteousness,* 4th ed. (Washington, D.C.: RHPA, 1941); F. W. Bieber, "An Investigation of the Concept of Perfectionism as Taught in the Writings of Ellen G. White" (M.A. thesis, SDA Theological Seminary, 1958); W. Richard Lesher, "Ellen G. White's Concept of Sanctification" (Ph.D. dissertation, New York University, 1970); Rolf J. Pöhler, "Sinless Saints or Sinless Sinners?" (1978); Moore, *Theology in Crisis* (1980); Helmut Ott, *Perfect in Christ: The Mediation of Christ in the Writings of Ellen G. White* (Washington, D.C., and Hagerstown, Md.: RHPA, 1987); Whidden, "The Soteriology of Ellen G. White"; and Ronald Deane Bissell, "The Background, Formation, Development, and Presentation of Ellen White's Concept of Forgiveness from Her Childhood to 1864" (Ph.D. dissertation, Andrews University, 1990).

Law and grace.[148] From the beginning, Seventh-day Adventists have believed that salvation is by grace through faith and not by works of the law. However, because of their special emphasis on the binding claims of the Decalogue and, particularly, the Sabbath commandment,[149] they have not always unmistakably taught that salvation is by grace and faith *alone*. The different declarations of Fundamental Beliefs reflect a growing awareness regarding the decisive, primary importance of divine grace and the subordinate, secondary role of man's obedient response to it.[150]

The new birth. This section deals with a little known and, indeed, forgotten instance of doctrinal development among Seventh-day Adventists. The reason for describing it here is because it illustrates how rapidly and completely doctrinal modifications may be forgotten even by those who were directly involved in them.

In an article taken from another journal and republished in the *Review & Herald* in March, 1856, the authors argued that the "'new birth,'" which the Bible regards as the condition for entering the kingdom of God, refers to the bodily resurrection of believers at the second coming of Christ. Conversion, they reasoned, was merely the act by which humans were "begotten" of God by the truth, receiving the firstfruits of the Spirit. Only resurrected believers, however, could actually be said to be "born again" as only they would be free from the possibility and actuality of sin.[151]

A couple of readers responded, questioning the identification of the new birth with the resurrection. Their objections were rejected by *Review & Herald* editor Uriah Smith who confirmed the position taken in the disputed reprint.[152] About a year later, he flatly asserted:

148 *SDAE,* 1976 ed., s.v. "Law," and "Law and Grace." See also Rolf J. Pöhler, "Die Entwicklung des Gesetzesverständnisses in der Gemeinschaft der Siebenten-Tags-Adventisten," in *Das biblische Gesetzesverständnis: Vergleich und Entwicklung,* Der Adventglaube in Geschichte und Gegenwart, vol. 22 (Darmstadt: Adventistischer Wissenschaftl. Arbeitskreis, 1985), 43-66.

149 "Here is the message, bearing the last great test, and that is the law of God ... Here is the banner of truth, bearing in the very front the law of God" (James White, "Conference Address," *RH,* 20 May 1873, 184). "The light concerning the binding claims of the law of Jehovah is to be presented everywhere. This is the deciding question; it will test and prove the world" (Ellen White, Manuscript 1, 1874; quoted in Damsteegt, 291-292).

150 The 1872 declaration alluded just briefly to man's need for Christ's "grace whereby to render acceptable obedience to his holy law" (#15). The 1931 statement explained further "that one is justified, not by obedience to the law, but by the grace that is in Christ Jesus," making immortality and eternal life "the free gift of God" (#8, 9). In 1980, this crucial aspect of Adventist soteriology was still further clarified. "Salvation is all of grace and not of works, but its fruitage is obedience to the Commandments" (#18). See below, appendix 3.

151 "'Ye Must Be Born Again','" *RH,* 13-20 March 1856, 186-188, 194-195. The authors of this essay, E. R. Pinney and T. F. Barry, had been Millerite Adventists. The same view, which was based on 1 John 3:9, was again expressed in an article taken from a pamphlet by a certain J. Lenfest ("The New Birth," *RH,* 6 November 1856, 5).

152 [Uriah Smith], "'Must Be Born Again,'" *RH,* 10 April 1856, 8; [idem], "Ye Must Be Born Again," *RH,* 8 May 1856, 28-29. See also [idem], "The New Birth," *RH,* 6 November 1856, 5.

> *No Advent believer, however, will be willing to take the ground* that the kingdom of God
> is a spiritual kingdom in the hearts of believers, and was set up at Christ's first advent,
> and *that conversion is the birth of the spirit* by which we become members thereof. This
> is the view that still flourishes under the darkness of modern orthodoxy; but it cannot
> exist in the light of present truth (emphasis supplied).[153]

By the early 1870s, the Adventist teaching on the "second birth" had been somewhat
broadened to include conversion as well as the resurrection which was seen as the
beginning and the end of the process of spiritual rebirth. This view found succinct
expression in the 1872 declaration of Adventist beliefs, which maintained

> that the new birth comprises the entire change necessary to fit us for the Kingdom of
> God, and consists of two parts: first, a moral change, wrought by conversion and a
> Christian life; second a physical change at the second coming of Christ.[154]

The emphasis, however, continued to be placed on the resurrection as the new birth
proper, while conversion and sanctification were likened to the begetting or the birth
pangs of the new existence.[155]

In 1877, General Conference President George I. Butler publicly endorsed the
traditional idea that conversion is properly called the new birth and rejected the
arguments of those who wanted to confine it to the resurrection alone.[156] Although
the earlier Adventist view lingered on for a number of years,[157] the teaching that
conversion, understood as including the transformation and perfection of character,
constituted the new birth soon became common among Seventh-day Adventists.[158]

---

153 [Uriah Smith], "The New Birth," *RH,* 15-22 January 1857, 92; 84, 92-93. See also J. M.
   McLellan, "Born of Water," *RH,* 12 February 1857, 118. Apparently, Smith assumed that the
   traditional, orthodox view implied or would lead to a spiritualizing, non-literal eschatology.
154 See below, app. 3, col. 1, par. 5; cf. ibid., par. 14.
155 Jos. Clarke, "Regeneration; or, the New Birth," *RH,* 11 July 1871, 26; R. F. Cottrell, "Answers
   to Correspondents," *RH,* 11 March 1873, 104; and Uriah Smith, "To Correspondents," *RH,*
   27 July 1876, 40. That this teaching did not substantially differ from the theology of the 1850s
   seems clear from a statement by Uriah Smith who, in 1876, still affirmed that "we are begotten
   at conversion; we are born at the resurrection" ("The New Birth," *RH,* 10 August 1876, 52).
156 George I. Butler, "Is Conversion Ever Called a Birth?" *RH,* 22 February 1877, 57-58. A few
   months later, Uriah Smith conceded that John 3:3 "probably refers to the conversion" ("To
   Correspondents," *RH,* 18 October 1877, 124).
157 G. W. Morse, "Scripture Questions," *RH,* 25 September 1888, 618; and [U. Smith], "In the
   Question Chair," *RH,* 11 November 1890, 696-697.
158 W. H. Littlejohn, "Scripture Questions," *RH,* 3 March 1885, 138; D. M. Canright, "'He
   Cannot Sin,'" *RH,* 15 September 1885, 586; Albert Weeks, "Conversion, or the New Birth,"
   RH, 22-29 March 1887, 178-179, 195-196; Wm. Brickey, "The New Birth," *RH,* 17 May
   1887, 307; E. P. Jones, "'Born of God,'" *RH,* 9 July 1889, 434-435; J. H. Cook, "Necessity
   of the New Birth," *RH,* 14 January 1890, 18; [Mrs.] M. E. Steward, "The New Birth," *RH,*
   1 July 1890, 404; and Wm. Brickey, "New Birth – No Sin," *RH,* 5 December 1893, 759.

The revised statement of Adventist beliefs published by the Battle Creek church in 1891 and 1894 explicitly identified the new birth with conversion and also clearly distinguished it from the life-long process of sanctification. It maintained

> that the new birth, or conversion, comprises the moral change necessary to make us children of God; and that this is to be followed by a Christian life. That no one can be a true child of God except by conversion, which is the work of the Holy Spirit, changing and renewing the carnal heart, which in its natural state is at enmity with God and his law.[159]

Similarly, the latest version of the Fundamental Beliefs adopted in 1980 affirms that "through the Spirit we are born again and sanctified"; it does not specify, however, whether sanctification is to be thought of as an integral part or only as the result of the new birth.[160]

This case study could be regarded as an insignificant incident of doctrinal re-adjustment.[161] What makes it of particular interest for this study is a pamphlet by former Seventh-day Adventist A. McLearn in which he mentioned that as a church member he had believed with his brethren that the new birth was to be experienced only at the future resurrection from the dead. Uriah Smith responded quite indignantly, leaving no doubt that Adventists did not believe "such stuff as this" and that, if they had known McLearn to hold such a view, "they would have been tempted promptly to disfellowship him."[162] Smith seemed to have forgotten that it was his own strong influence and adamant view on this question that had once contributed to lead many, if not most, in the church to believe and teach for about twenty years what he now considered sufficient ground for disfellowshipping.

---

159 *Membership of the Seventh-day Adventist Church of Battle Creek, Mich.,* 1891 ed., 11; cf. ibid., 1894 ed., 13. In the declaration of 1931, the statement on the new birth was revised to read as follows: "That every person in order to obtain salvation must experience the new birth; that this comprises an entire transformation of life and character by the recreative power of God through faith in the Lord Jesus Christ" (see below, app. 3, col. 2, par. 4).

160 See below, app. 3, col. 3, par. 10.

161 After all, the shifting meaning of the expression "new birth" did not affect the firm Adventist conviction that conversion by the Spirit is indeed a prerequisite to final salvation and the resurrection of the righteous. Nor does the teaching that the new birth coincides with conversion imply or deny that the kingdom of God is a future reality, as Smith feared. Thus, it could be argued that this change was mainly a matter of exegesis rather than of theology or even doctrine. For a response to this objection, see below, p. 202, n. 358.

162 Uriah Smith, "Another Attack," *RH,* 12 March 1889, 168. McLearn, whose experience with SDAs was very short-lived, caused serious trouble at Battle Creek College. He had been trained a Seventh Day Baptist.

Continuity and Change in *Distinctive* Beliefs

As their name indicates, Seventh-day Adventists believe in the continuing validity of the Sabbath commandment as given in the Decalogue and practiced both by Jesus and the early Christian church. They also look forward to the second coming of Christ to establish his visible rule and eternal kingdom on this earth. Their eschatological expectation is related to a number of particular interpretations of biblical prophecies dealing with events at the end of time.

In addition to these distinctive but not necessarily unique beliefs, Adventists hold some doctrinal convictions not shared by any other Christian denomination. These are the doctrines of the heavenly sanctuary and of the investigative judgment, the belief regarding the prophetic role and authority of Ellen White as a genuine manifestation of the spirit of prophecy, and the Adventist self-understanding on its unique role and mission as the remnant church. Together with the doctrine of conditional immortality, viz., of the non-immortality of the soul, which has been mentioned already, these teachings comprise what is frequently referred to as the special "landmarks" and "pillars" of the Adventist faith.[163] The following section analyzes some developmental aspects involving these distinctive Adventist doctrines.

The Sabbath

Adventists believe that Christians who are saved by grace through faith in Jesus Christ will gladly express their gratitude to the Savior by observing his commandments which are an expression of God's loving care for the well-being of his people and, in fact, of all humanity.[164] The insight that this includes the Sabbath commandment of the Decalogue sparked Sabbatarianism among pre- and, especially, post-disappointment Millerites. Without this conviction about the biblical Sabbath truth, the Seventh-day Adventist Church would and, possibly, could not exist.[165]

For this reason, one should not expect any decisive changes with regard to this crucial and distinctive doctrinal tenet. Yet, in spite of its outstanding importance for the message, mission, and self-understanding of Seventh-day Adventists, the way this belief was understood and practiced did develop in some notable respects over the years. Two illustrations may suffice to substantiate this.

---

163 See below, pp. 257-259.

164 Since 1872, the Fundamental Beliefs have invariably expressed this conviction regarding the binding claims of the Decalogue upon all humanity, a view that SDAs have shared from the very beginning. See below, app. 3, p. 345.

165 For more information on the development of the Sabbath doctrine in Christian and Adventist history, see *SDAE*, 1976 ed., s.v. "Sabbath"; Richard Müller, *Adventisten - Sabbat - Reformation* (1979); Kenneth Strand, ed., *The Sabbath in Scripture and History* (Washington, D.C.: RHPA, 1982); and Rolf J. Pöhler, "Adventgeschichtliche Ursprünge der Sabbatheiligung," in *Neue Aspekte adventistischer Sabbattheologie*, Der Adventglaube in Geschichte und Gegenwart, vol. 26 (Darmstadt: Adventistischer Wissenschaftlicher Arbeitskreis, 1986), 8-29.

The beginning of the Sabbath. For about ten years after the initial rediscovery of the Sabbath doctrine, Sabbatarian Adventists generally interpreted the biblical expression "even(ing)" as referring to 6 P.M. as the proper time to begin the Sabbath rest. In this, they followed former sea captain Joseph Bates whose nautical experience had obviously influenced his reasoning on this particular question.[166] Still, some Sabbath-keepers personally favored the sunset view – especially those who had come from a Seventh Day Baptist background.[167]

At the request of James White, the issue was finally restudied in 1855 by J. N. Andrews who came to the conclusion that, according to the Bible, "even(ing)" does not refer to a fixed time of the day but rather to the setting of the sun. With only minor resistance, this new view was quickly accepted and became the general teaching of Seventh-day Adventists until today.[168] Some had difficulties adjusting to this reinterpretation because of the assumption that the traditional view had been taught by Ellen White on the basis of her visions.[169]

Though this change dealt with what may seem to be only a minor practical aspect of the Sabbath doctrine, it should be noted that, at the time, it was looked upon as a significant doctrinal revision.[170] Ellen White supported it by saying that when new

166 Joseph Bates, *The Seventh Day Sabbath, a Perpetual Sign* (New Bedford, Mass.: By the Author, 1846), 32, 36, 42; idem, *A Vindication of the Seventh-Day Sabbath, and the Commandments of God,* 80-82; idem, *A Seal of the Living God* (New Bedford, Mass.: By the Author, 1849), 38, 54; and idem, "Time to Commence the Holy Sabbath," *RH,* 21 April 1851, 71-72; reprint, 26 May 1853, 4-5.

167 In the summer of 1848, the issue seemed to have been settled by a higher authority when a Brother Chamberlain, apparently speaking in tongues, supported the 6 P.M. view (see James White to Dear Brother [Howland], 2 July 1848, EGWRC, AU, Berrien Springs, Mich.). Still, the issue kept coming up again and again as it had not yet been decided on a biblical basis in a manner convincing to the whole Sabbatarian Adventist group. See J. N. Andrews, "The Time of the Sabbath," *RH,* 2 June 1851, 92-93; James White, "Remarks," ibid., 93-94; Joseph Bates, "Dear Bro. White," *RH,* 5 August 1851, 6; and James White, "Boylston Meeting," *RH,* 2 September 1852, 72. In 1855, Andrews observed that "a considerable number of our brethren have long been convinced that the Sabbath commences at sunset" ("To the Brethren," *RH,* 4 December 1855, 78).

168 J. N. Andrews, "Time for Commencing the Sabbath," *RH,* 4 December 1855, 76-78; see also James White, "Time of the Sabbath," ibid., 78; and idem, "The Word," *RH,* 7 February 1856, 148-149. It was the vision of November 20, 1855, that helped convince Ellen White herself, Joseph Bates, and possibly others of the new view. According to the 1980 declaration of SDA beliefs, the Sabbath lasts "from evening to evening, sunset to sunset" (see below, app. 3, col. 3, par. 19).

169 James White, "Time of the Sabbath"; and E. R. Seaman, "Bro. Smith," *RH,* 30 October 1856, 207. In 1847, Ellen White had rejected the sunrise view and opted for "even[ing]" which was naturally interpreted – even by herself – as providing support for Bates's position.

170 Andrews himself regarded the subject as being "one of great importance" and pointed to the "duty to correct our errors when we see them" ("To the Brethren," 78). Back in 1849, Bates had even expressed the conviction that failure to "keep the Sabbath holy in its appointed time" was "just as sinful in the sight of God ... as it would be not to keep it at all"; consequently, such people would not be among the 144,000 sealed ones (*A Seal of the Living God,* 38).

understanding ("light") comes, the church "must change."[171] Her husband concurred by expressing his conviction that "God corrected the error" of the Adventist position and led the church to accept "this change."[172]

The meaning of the Sabbath. Of considerably greater importance than the swift readjustment in 1855 of one particular aspect of Adventist Sabbath observance is the gradual development in recent decades with regard to the understanding of the present-day meaning of the Sabbath commandment for the church and, beyond that, for humanity as a whole.

With the increasing sophistication of Adventist theologians there has also grown a desire to explain the meaning of the Sabbath in terms and concepts more readily understandable to people of today's culture and time. As a result, a number of recent works defending and explaining this doctrine have placed less emphasis on arguing about the identity and validity of the biblical Sabbath[173] than on expounding its theological meaning and experiential significance for the contemporary world.[174]

171 Ellen White, vision of 20 November 1855; published in idem, *Testimonies for the Church,* 9 vols. (Mountain View, Calif.: PPPA, 1948), 1:116.

172 James White, "Time to Commence the Sabbath," *RH,* 25 February 1868, 168. This article contains an early eyewitness account of this doctrinal readjustment. The same incident is also treated in some detail by F. D. Nichol, "The Time to Begin the Sabbath," in *Ellen G. White and Her Critics* (Washington, D.C.: RHPA, 1951), 350-355; and Arthur L. White, *Ellen G. White,* 6 vols. (Washington, D.C.: RHPA, 1981-1986), 1:322-326.

173 The classic Adventist approach to the Sabbath doctrine is found, e.g., in J. N. Andrews, *The Perpetuity of the Royal Law; or the Ten Commandments Not Abolished* (Rochester, N.Y.: Advent Review Office, 1854); Uriah Smith, *A Word for the Sabbath; or Fake Theories Exposed,* 3d rev. and enl. ed. (Battle Creek, Mich.: SDAPA, 1875); J. H. Waggoner, *The Nature and Obligation of the Sabbath of the Fourth Commandment* (Oakland, Calif.: PPPA, 1890); and M. L. Andreasen, *The Sabbath: Which Day and Why?* (Washington, D.C.: RHPA, 1942). See also Raymond F. Cottrell, "The Sabbath in the New World," in Strand, ed., *The Sabbath in Scripture and History,* 244-263; and C. Mervyn Maxwell, "Joseph Bates and Seventh-day Adventist Sabbath Theology," ibid., 352-363. For recent scholarly studies by Adventists on the historical and exegetical aspects of the Sabbath, see Samuele Bacchiocchi, *The Sabbath in the New Testament: Answers to Questions,* Biblical Perspectives, no. 5 (Berrien Springs, Mich.: By the Author, 1985); and Strand, ed., *The Sabbath in Scripture and History.*

174 See, e.g., Niels-Erik Andreasen, *Rest and Redemption: A Study of the Biblical Sabbath,* AU Monographs, Studies in Religion, vol. 11 (Berrien Springs, Mich.: AU Press, 1978); idem, *The Christian Use of Time* (Nashville: Abingdon, 1978); Sakae Kubo, *God Meets Man: A Theology of the Sabbath and the Second Advent* (Nashville: SPA, 1978); Charles Scriven, *Jubilee of the World: The Sabbath as a Day of Gladness* (Nashville: SPA, 1978); Samuele Bacchiocchi, *Divine Rest for Human Restlessness: A Theological Study of the Good News of the Sabbath for Today* (Rome: By the Author, 1980); John C. Brunt, *A Day for Healing: The Meaning of Jesus' Sabbath Miracles* (Washington, D.C.: RHPA, 1981); Raoul Dederen, "Reflections on a Theology of the Sabbath," in Strand, ed., *The Sabbath in Scripture and History,* 295-306; Roy Branson, ed., *Festival of the Sabbath* (Takoma Park, Md.: Association of Adventist Forums, 1985); Rice, *The Reign of God* (1985), 354-381; Pöhler, "Neue Aspekte

While these authors have not rejected the traditional view on the Sabbath, they have offered some interesting new perspectives of it.[175]

Parallel to this shift in Adventist Sabbath apologetics, there seems to be less attention given by the same theologians to the apocalyptic-eschatological dimension of the Sabbath doctrine. The latter had furnished their forebears with a unique framework by which their Sabbath proclamation received special urgency and appeal. Instead of elaborating on the mark of the beast, the threatening Sunday laws, and the imminent time of trouble, a number of Adventist authors today prefer rather to discuss the relevance of the Sabbath for both personal and social life, including its practical implications for ecological issues and political affairs.[176]

This trend may not reflect a reorientation of thought on the part of the church in general;[177] nor does it meet the full approval of its thought leaders.[178] Still, it is

der adventistischen Sabbattheologie"; Clifford Goldstein, *A Pause for Peace* (Boise, Idaho: PPPA, 1992); Charles E. Bradford, "The Sabbath and Liberation," *AR,* 16 April 1992, 8-11; and Provonsha, *A Remnant in Crisis* (1993), 78-90.

175 "Traditionally, and almost exclusively until recent years, it has been customary to emphasize observance of the Sabbath as man's proper response to a divine command, as an obligation. God commands; it is our duty to obey. Contemporary literature on the Sabbath, however, emphasizes its positive aspect, as a gracious provision by a wise Creator designed to meet an inherent need of created beings, even in a perfect world" (Cottrell, "The Sabbath in the New World," 259). "We could say that Seventh-day Adventists are in the process of moving from a doctrine of the sabbath to a more comprehensive theology of the sabbath" (Rice, *The Reign of God,* 355).

176 This shift was not lost on observers of the church. "For most of Adventist history, no discussion of the Sabbath was complete without consideration of 'the seal' and 'the mark of the beast.' But although the connection is maintained in some popular writing, it is absent from recent theological studies" (Bull and Lockhart, *Seeking a Sanctuary,* 41).

177 The wide propagation and use of the so-called *Revelation Seminars* in recent Adventist evangelism indicates the continuing attractiveness of the traditional eschatological approach to the Sabbath doctrine especially among the lay members of the church. See also C. Mervyn Maxwell, *God Cares,* vol. 2, *The Message of Revelation for You and Your Family* (Boise, Idaho: PPPA, 1985), 368-399. *SDAs Believe* likewise presents a more traditional interpretation of the Sabbath, which ignores both its social dimension as a symbol of justice and its ecological implications as a sign of stewardship (pp. 249-266).

178 *Adventist Review* editor Don F. Neufeld, for example, warned of the possible negative outcome of such a gradual shift in Seventh-day Adventist Sabbath understanding. "There is danger that we will forget our historical heritage, shift our emphases, and thus become untrue to the pioneers who handed us the torch. It seems that Adventists are talking less and less about the beast, his image, and his mark; likewise less and less about the Sabbath's being the seal of God ... They prefer to speak of the Sabbath philosophically and theologically ... Admittedly, all of these items are important and significant parts of the Sabbath proclamation. But Adventists must never allow an emphasis of these to cause them to downplay that which impelled our spiritual forebears to launch a great movement of Sabbath reform in the proclamation of the third angel's message. They cannot eliminate the eschatological features of our Sabbath message and be true to their trust" ("Adventists' Contribution to the Sabbath Doctrine," *RH,* 13 September 1979, 35-36).

not insignificant that a number of leading first-world Adventist theologians have presented and (re)interpreted the Sabbath – this outstanding and fundamental tenet of the doctrinal heritage of the church – in the light of the new cultural context and changing life situation of the contemporary world.

That Adventists today generally aim at a more positive, less defensive approach to the Sabbath than was common in the past is also suggested by the statement of Fundamental Beliefs adopted by the church in 1980. While its forerunners stressed the duties and requirements of Sabbath observance, the Dallas declaration particularly emphasizes the beneficent character of the weekly foretaste and sign of redemption, which offers delightful communion and calls for joyful celebration.[179]

To what degree these concepts actually characterize the present-day understanding and observance of the Sabbath among Adventists around the world cannot be investigated here. Still, it appears that both in its theological reflections and in its official statements on the "day of rest and gladness," the Seventh-day Adventist Church has consciously attempted to grow beyond some of the more limited aspects of its past thinking to a theologically more mature and appealing approach to this distinctive Adventist belief.

Eschatology

Like the Millerites from whom they inherited their basic eschatological (premillennial) outlook, Seventh-day Adventists believe in the personal, literal, and imminent return of Jesus to establish his visible and worldwide kingdom upon the renewed earth.[180] Preparing for and expecting Christ's *parousia* whose exact time has not been revealed, Adventists have focused their attention on the "time of the end" and the events leading up to the great climax of human history. This has

---

179 See below, app. 3, pp. 345f. "Unfortunately, we Adventists have traditionally presented the Sabbath as an attempt to fulfill the law rather than as rest in the accomplishments of Christ. No wonder fellow Christians who know God's grace have not been overly impressed by Adventist evangelism. Thank God we are repenting of legalism and beginning to preach the truth as it is in Jesus" (Martin Weber, "Why the Sabbath?" *Ministry,* November 1992, 31).

180 On this as well as on the events during and after the millennium, the different statements of Adventist belief agree (see below, app. 3, pp. 350-353). "A study of Seventh-day Adventist literature indicates that there has been no basic change in the concept of the second advent" (Norval F. Pease, "The Second Advent in Seventh-day Adventist History and Theology," in Olsen, ed., *The Advent Hope in Scripture and History,* 173). On Adventist eschatology, see *SDAs Believe,* 332-383; V. Norskov Olsen, ed., *The Advent Hope in Scripture and History* (Washington, D.C., and Hagerstown, Md.: RHPA, 1987); Jonathan Gallagher, "Believing Christ's Return: An Interpretative Analysis of the Dynamics of Christian Hope" (Ph.D. dissertation, University of St. Andrews, Scotland, 1983); and Roy Israel McGarrell, "The Historical Development of Seventh-day Adventist Eschatology, 1884-1895" (Ph.D. dissertation, AU, 1990). For an analysis of Ellen White's eschatological thought in the context of American premillennialism, see Masao Yamagata, "Ellen G. White and American Premillennialism" (Ph.D. dissertation, Pennsylvania State University, 1983).

prompted the formation of specific and precise views regarding the final events to be expected on this earth before the appearing of Christ.[181]

The distinctiveness of the Adventist eschatological schema, which was largely developed during the early years of the movement, is evident even from a cursory reading of the sources. In fact, Adventist literature is replete with terms and phrases intelligible only to those familiar with biblical imagery and Adventist thought. For example, it speaks about "the sealing," "the time of trouble," "the two-horned beast," and "the Eastern question." These expressions may also serve as reminders of some noteworthy, albeit largely forgotten, developments in Adventist eschatology.[182]

The sealing.[183] For about four years after the disappointment of 1844, those who were to become the founding fathers of the Adventist church spoke of the sealing of the 144,000 (Rev 7) as an imminent event which would occur just before the return of Jesus at the beginning of the final "time of trouble."[184] This view was

---

181 On these, the leading declarations of SDA belief are almost silent. In 1872 explicit mention was made of "the papal power, with all its abominations" and of "evil men and seducers [who] wax worse and worse, as the word of God declares" (#8). The 1931 statement referred in general to the "existing conditions in the physical, social, industrial, political, and religious worlds" as signs of the nearness of the coming of Christ (#20). Similarly, the 1980 declaration briefly alludes to "the present condition of the world" as evidence of its imminent end (#24). See below, app. 3, pp. 349-350.

182 The first three of the following four examples discuss changes that took place during the decade following the great disappointment of 1844. At this time, there existed neither a church organization nor a defined body of beliefs. Still, these formative years of Sabbatarian Adventism are of extreme importance for an investigation of doctrinal developments among SDAs. For it was then that virtually all distinctive Adventist doctrines found their original embodiment in the teaching of those who later became the founders of the SDA Church. The fact that some doctrinal changes did take place at such an early stage that they were soon entirely forgotten does not make their analysis negligible. To the contrary, they serve both to complete the historical picture and to illustrate how doctrinal changes actually took place during the early years of the Adventist church.

183 On the meaning and history of this Adventist concept, see *SDAE*, 1976 ed., s.v. "Seal of God"; and Damsteegt, 143-146, 209-213.

184 Possibly the sealing was even thought of as having already begun, only to be completed in the imminent future. See [Ellen G. White], "Letter from Sister Harmon," *DS*, 24 January 1846, 31 ("By this time [i.e., when God will announce the day and hour of Jesus' coming] the 144,000 were all sealed"); idem, "Letter from Sister Harmon," *DS*, 14 March 1846, 7 ("I had a vision of events, all in the future. And I saw the time of [Jacob's] trouble ... Just before we entered it, we all received the seal of the living God"); James White, "Letter from Bro. White," *DS*, 29 November 1845, 35 ("Then will commence the hour of temptation to try all but the 144,000, who by that time have the seal of the living God"); [James White and Ellen White], *A Word to the "Little Flock,"* 3 ("the humble followers of the Lamb ... will be sealed before the plagues are poured out"); Otis Nichols to William Miller, 20 April 1846, EGWRC, AU, Berrien Springs, Mich. ("when [the day of atonement] is finished, the sanctuary will be cleansed, the saints sealed, their sins blotted out ... I am expecting very soon the saints will be sealed"); Joseph Bates, *Second Advent Way Marks and High Heaps* (New Bedford, Mass.: By

possibly derived from some similar Millerite ideas.[185] In any event, it stood in conscious and clear contrast to the position of the extreme shut-door believers, who taught that the 144,000 were all "sealed and safe" since October 1844.[186] In other words, the view that the sealing was not a past event, but rather an impending and, possibly, present process helped to protect the Sabbatarian group from the extreme views held by other post-disappointment Millerites.

In 1848, Joseph Bates, who was the first to relate the eschatological sealing to the newly discovered Sabbath message,[187] described this special safeguarding measure of God on behalf of his menaced people as an event presently going on among Sabbath-keepers.[188] He was soon confirmed in his conviction by a vision Ellen White had in November 1848, according to which the sealing was, in fact, in progress and the "time of trouble" had already begun.[189] From now on, Sabbatarian Adventists regarded the sealing as a present event, very soon to be concluded.[190] The doctrinal

the Author, 1847), 64 ("Says the reader, I thought that [the saints] were sealed and safe. You have no scripture to prove it; but to the contrary").

185 In the summer of 1844, the view that the sealing was presently going on and would be completed before the four angels were to loosen the four winds (Rev 7:1) was embraced among the Millerites in Maine (Editorial, "The Advent Herald," *Advent Herald,* 30 October 1844, 92-93).

186 "Exhortation to Believers," *Jubilee Standard,* 3 April 1845, 28-29; [Enoch Jacobs], "Rev. 22:11, 12," *Day-Star,* 29 April 1845, 46-48; S. S. Snow, "The Confederacy," *Jubilee Standard,* 12 June 1845, 108-109; and Joseph Turner, "Letter from Bro. Joseph Turner," *Jubilee Standard,* 10 July 1845, 137-139. On the shut-door doctrine, see below, pp. 297-298.

187 Already in 1846 Bates had mentioned the Sabbath and the sealing in close proximity *(The Opening Heavens* [New Bedford, Mass.: By the Author, 1846], 35-37) but had not yet explicitly intertwined the two concepts as he did from 1848 onward after Ellen White had identified the Sabbath with the seal of God (see Bates, *A Seal of the Living God,* 24-26; and Ellen G. White, To Those Who Are Receiving the Seal of the Living God, Broadside, 31 January 1849, EGWRC, AU, Berrien Springs, Mich.).

188 Bates, *A Vindication of the Seventh-Day Sabbath,* 58-61 ("if they keep his Sabbath ... they shall be sanctified"), 82-84 ("God's people are now in their trial ... until God roars out of Zion and utters his voice from Jerusalem, then Jerusalem will be *holy,* the atonement will be finished ... God's people be cleansed, sealed"), 92-98 ("the saints will understand when they are sealed or marked ... This sealing process, then, I understand to be going on with the little flock ... and will be completed and approbated by God in the agonizing time of Daniel's trouble and Jacob's trouble, and proclaimed to the world by God's roaring out of Zion, and uttering his voice from Jerusalem ... then their atonement will be finished, the Sanctuary cleansed ... 'the jewels made up' ... which are now to be sealed").

189 Bates reported on this vision in *A Seal of the Living God* (January 1849), 24-26. According to his verbatim transcript, it taught that "the saints are not all sealed. The time of trouble has commenced, it is begun." Bates explicitly affirmed that the 144,000 "are now being sealed" (pp. 2, 36) and that "none but Sabbath keepers and believers can ever be sealed" (p. 38). He interpreted the time of trouble as referring to the political turmoil occurring among the European nations in 1848 (pp. 45-50). For more details, see the following section.

190 Ellen G. White, To Those Who Are Receiving the Seal of the Living God, 31 January 1849 ("the merciful eye of Jesus gazed on the remnant that were not all sealed ... The sealing time

identification of the Sabbath with the seal of God had resulted in a new interpretation of the sealing process, which, however, could be developed and maintained only in the context of the still existing eschatological fervor.

Only about three years later, at the end of the shut-door period, James White first returned to the original view, which regarded both the sealing and the time of trouble as future events – however near these may have been thought to be.[191]

Finally, in 1856, Uriah Smith presented an interpretation that was to resolve the tensions resulting from the previous two positions on the sealing. By distinguishing "the [present] possession of the seal" from "the [future] state of being sealed," both the new teaching on the Sabbath as the seal of God and the concept of an eschatological sealing were combined and retained.[192] This view has become the common Adventist interpretation on the sealing.[193]

is very short, and soon will be over"); idem to the Hastings, 24-30 March 1849, EGWRC, AU, Berrien Springs, Mich.; partly printed as idem, "Dear Brethren and Sisters," *Present Truth*, August 1849, 21-24 ("Satan is now using every device in this sealing time, to keep the minds of God's people from the present, sealing truth ... God has begun to draw this covering over his people, and it will very soon be drawn over all"); idem, Manuscript 5, 1849, EGWRC, AU, Berrien Springs, Mich.; idem to the Hastings, 11 January 1850, EGWRC, AU, Berrien Springs, Mich.; cf. James White to Bro. Hastings, 11 January 1850, EGWRC, AU, Berrien Springs, Mich. ("Ellen says that she thinks it was one half that professed present truth that she saw covered, and written in the angels' rolls"); and Ellen G. White to Brother Hastings, 18 March 1850, EGWRC, AU, Berrien Springs, Mich. ("I saw that [your late wife] was sealed and ... would be with the 144,000").

191 James White, "Angels of Rev. xiv – No. 4," *RH,* 23 December 1851, 69-70 (the loosening of the four winds and the time of trouble will follow the sealing); and [idem], "Remarks in Kindness," *RH,* 2 March 1852, 100-101. According to this article, "the despised Sabbath of the living God will be that very distinguishing sign. But let no one suppose that the 'Review and Herald' teaches that those who embrace the Sabbath are now sealed and sure of heaven, for it teaches no such thing ... May the Lord prepare Sabbath-keepers to stand in that time, and bear the seal of the living God."

192 [Uriah Smith], "The Seal of the Living God," *RH,* 24 April-1 May 1856, 12, 20-21. On behalf of the church, Smith made it quite clear that "we do not take the position that any who are now living, are sealed." Formally, this statement stands in direct contradiction to the view held by virtually all Sabbatarian Adventists in the late 1840s; at the same time, its substantial continuity with the developing Adventist teaching on both the seal and the sealing should not be overlooked.

193 See, e.g., Uriah Smith, "The Visions – Objections Answered," *RH,* 10 July 1866, 42; A. Smith, "The Hundred and Forty-Four Thousand," *RH,* 4 December 1879, 182-183. For a recent presentation on the sealing, see Beatrice S. Neall, "Sealed Saints and the Tribulation," in *Symposium on Revelation: Introductory and Exegetical Studies – Book 1,* Daniel and Revelation Committee Series, ed. Frank B. Holbrook, vol. 6 (Silver Spring, Md.: Biblical Research Institute, General Conference of SDAs, 1992), 245-278. Incidentally, Neall may have sparked – or even reflected – another minor doctrinal change by proposing that, contrary to what SDAs have traditionally taught, the 144,000 and the great multitude of Rev 7 are actually one and the same group. Another recent scholarly study has reconsidered the traditional identification of the Sabbath/Sunday with the seal of God/the mark of the beast.

The time of trouble.[194] According to the general expectation of the early Sabbatarian Adventists, the "time of trouble, such as never was" (Dan 12:1) would begin shortly at the close of human probation, just prior to the second advent of Christ. More precisely, they distinguished (1) "Daniel's time of trouble" expected to come upon the nations of the earth during the seven last plagues from (2) "the time of Jacob's trouble" to be faced by believers after the close of probation when a death decree would threaten their very lives.[195] The idea that the time of trouble had already begun in 1844 was firmly rejected.[196] On the other hand, room was left for a very short time period between the beginning of the time of trouble and the close of probation.[197]

Considering the political turmoil that rapidly seemed to engulf the European nations in 1847 and, particularly, in 1848, it is no surprise that these Adventists, who were fervently hoping to see the heavenly bridegroom appear in the clouds of heaven at almost any time, assumed that the time of trouble was just about to begin and had, in fact, already started in the Old World.[198] In this, they were confirmed by Ellen White who in her vision of November 19, 1848, exclaimed:

See Richard Lehmann, "Le sceau de Dieu et la marque de la bête," in *Études sur l'apocalypse: Signification des messages des trois anges aujourd'hui,* Conférences bibliques Division Euroafricaine (Salève, France: Institut Adventiste du Salève, 1988), 1:187-201.

194 See *SDAE,* 1976 ed., s.v. "Time of Trouble," "Jacob's Trouble, Time of," "Little Time of Trouble"; and Damsteegt, 143-144.

195 Otis Nichols to William Miller, 20 April 1846 ("I am expecting very soon the saints will be sealed, and then a short time of great affliction just before Michael stands up, Dan 12:1, or Jesus come *[sic]* out of the Holy of Holies; see Jer 30:6-11. 'Jacob's trouble'"); Joseph Bates, *The Opening Heavens,* 33, 37; idem, *Second Advent Way Marks and High Heaps,* 49, 52, 79, 80 ("God's judgments ... hurrying us all on to Daniel *[sic]* and Jacob's time of trouble"); idem, *A Vindication of the Seventh-Day Sabbath,* 67-69, 96, 111 ("This [present] sealing process ... will be completed and approbated by God in the agonizing time of Daniel's and Jacob's trouble"); [Ellen G. White], "Letter from Sister Harmon," *Day-Star,* 14 March 1846, 7 ("I had a vision of events, all in the future. And I saw the time of trouble, such as never was, – Jesus told me it was the time of Jacob's trouble"); James White, "The Time of Trouble," in *A Word to the "Little Flock,"* 8-9 ("The trouble that is to come at the time that Michael stands up, is not the trial, or trouble of the saints; but it is a trouble of the nations of the earth, caused by 'seven last plagues'"); idem, "The Time of Jacob's Trouble," ibid., 9-10; Ellen G. White, "To Bro. Eli Curtis," ibid., 11-12; and idem, "Dear Brother Bates," ibid., 18-20.

196 Ellen White, "To Bro. Eli Curtis," in [James White and Ellen White], *A Word to the "Little Flock,"* 11-12. This view was advanced by the extreme shut-door believers who held that Jesus had finished his mediatorial work in October, 1844.

197 In 1847, Ellen G. White declared that "at the commencement of the time of trouble, we were filled with the Holy Ghost as we went forth, and proclaimed the Sabbath more fully ... In the time of trouble, we all fled from the cities and villages, but were pursued by the wicked" (A Vision, Broadside, 7 April 1847, EGWRC, AU, Berrien Springs, Mich.; published in *Early Writings of Ellen G. White* [Washington, D.C.: RHPA, 1945], 33-34). This description implies, and was understood to mean, that probation has not yet ended at the beginning of the time of trouble (cf. ibid., 85-86).

198 In 1847 James White wrote: "We have blown the trumpet to make all ready. The trouble such as never was has begun in Europe. Jesus is ready to ride forth in indignation and trash the

The angels are holding the four winds. It is God that restrains the powers. The angels have not let go, for the saints are not all sealed. *The time of trouble has commenced, it is begun.* The reasons why the four winds have not let go, is because the saints are not all sealed. It's on the increase, and will increase more and more; *the trouble will never end* until the earth is rid of the wicked ... When Michael stands up *this trouble will be all over the earth.* Why they are just ready to blow. There's a check put on because the saints are not sealed ... And when ye get that you will go through the time of trouble (emphasis supplied).[199]

A few weeks later, Ellen White clarified her position by stating,

I saw that Michael had not stood up, and that *the time of trouble, such as never was, had not yet commenced.* The nations are now getting angry ... I saw that the four angels would hold the four winds until Jesus' work was done in the Sanctuary ... and while they had started on their mission to let them go, the merciful eye of Jesus gazed on the remnant that were not all sealed, then ... another angel was commissioned to fly swiftly to the four angels, and bid them hold until the servants of God were sealed ... I saw that the shaking of the powers in Europe is ... the shaking of the angry nations (emphasis supplied).[200]

However, when things did not turn out as expected, the Sabbatarian Adventists reverted back to their original viewpoint.[201] At the end of the shut-door period, the

heathen in anger" (Letter to S. Howland, 14 March 1847, EGWRC, AU, Berrien Springs, Mich.). In January 1849, Joseph Bates publicly expressed the same view: "Now the time of trouble has begun ... the time of trouble is in Europe ... 'The time of trouble such as never was,' Dan. xii:1, *has* began *[sic]* ... giving the world a specimen of what it will be when Dan. xii:1, is fully realized ... when the time of trouble becomes general throughout the earth ... See the state of things in Europe now; only the beginning" *(A Seal of the Living God,* 2, 4, 15-18, 36-53, 62-68).

199 Bates published his verbatim transcript of this vision in *A Seal of the Living God,* 24-26. Already in May 1848, Ellen White had written, "I can see the restraint is being taken off from the wicked, and very soon ... it will be entirely gone" (Letter to the Hastings, 29 May 1848, EGWRC, AU, Berrien Springs, Mich.).

200 Ellen White, To Those Who Are Receiving the Seal of the Living God, Broadside, 1849; published in idem, *Early Writings,* 36, 38, 41. Cf. idem, "Dear Brethren and Sisters," *Present Truth,* September 1849, 31-32 ("the prevailing pestilence ... is but the beginning of ... the judgements of God"); and idem, "To the 'Little Flock,'" *Present Truth,* April 1850, 71-72 ("the mighty shaking has commenced, and will go on").

201 James White, "The Seventh Angel," *RH,* 9 June 1851, 103-104 ("the nations will become angry"); idem, "The Immediate Coming of Christ," *RH,* 20 January 1853, 140-141 ("It was not so much a time of peace and safety, ten years since, as at the present time"); Ellen White, Manuscript 5, 1851, EGWRC, AU, Berrien Springs, Mich. ("I saw that this world was rocked in the cradle of security ... I saw that it must be a time of peace"); idem, Manuscript 1, 1852, EGWRC, AU, Berrien Springs, Mich. ("I saw in Europe just as things were moving to accomplish their desires, there would seemingly be a slacking up once or twice"); B. B. Brigham, "Dear Bro. White," *RH,* 2 September 1851, 23 ("There is general peace among the nations. No present indications of famine, pestilence, or war that alarms the world"); and R. F. Cottrell, "Dear Bro. White," *RH,* 3 February 1852, 87.

time of trouble – including its initial phase, viz., the commencement of the time of trouble – was again expected only at some future point of time.[202] The position taken by the small group of Sabbath-keeping Adventists in the late 1840s, viz., that the time of trouble had already begun, was dropped again and soon forgotten.[203]

The two-horned beast. According to the prophecy of Revelation 13, it is the (second) beast having "two horns like a lamb" that issues the death decree against those who refuse to give homage to the antichrist (the first beast). The early Sabbatarian Adventists were anxious to identify this power from which they expected fierce persecution in the very near future.[204] Between 1847 and 1851, they pointed unanimously to the Protestant churches of North America whom they considered to have become the apocalyptic "Babylon" as the fulfillment of this prophecy. Its two horns were defined as the powers of church (Protestantism) and state (Republicanism) which would soon unite in opposition to the "remnant." Sabbath-keeping Adventists also identified this second beast with the idolatrous image it erects of the other, i.e., the first beast. This composite they used to call the "Image Beast." The cryptic number "666" was understood as referring to the number of Protestant denominations in the USA, which would form the "Image Beast."[205]

In 1851, after J. N. Andrews had restudied this teaching at the request of James White, the Sabbatarian Adventists adopted a different interpretation. Distinguishing

202 In 1851, Ellen White herself placed "the commencement of the time of trouble" – later renamed by Adventists the "little time of trouble" preceding "the great time of trouble" – again in the future. "At that time," she said, "trouble *will be* coming on the earth, and the nations *will be* angry, yet held in check so as not to prevent the work of the third angel" (emphasis supplied) (*Early Writings*, 85-86).

203 See E. S. Walker, "The Time of Trouble," *RH,* 10 September 1861, 117-119; [Uriah Smith], "The Latter Rain and the Refreshing," *RH,* 12 May 1885, 296-297; Ellen G. White, *Spiritual Gifts,* 1:201-204 (also published in *Early Writings,* 282-285); and idem, *The Great Controversy between Christ and Satan: The Conflict of the Ages in the Christian Dispensation* (Mountain View, Calif.: PPPA, 1888/1950), 613-634.

204 The development of this aspect of Seventh-day Adventist prophetic interpretation is discussed in some detail by Froom, "The Two-Horned 'Beast' of Revelation 13," in *PFF,* 4:1093-1108. For an interpretation this "intriguing element" of SDA eschatology in the context of American millennialism, see Bull and Lockhart, 47-49.

205 Ellen White, "Dear Brother Bates," in [James White and Ellen White], *A Word to the "Little Flock,"* 19 ("I saw that the number (666) of the Image Beast was made up"); idem, Manuscript, 23 October 1850, EGWRC, AU, Berrien Springs, Mich. ("The Catholics will give their power to the image of the beast, and the Protestants will work as their mother worked before them, to destroy the saints"); James White, "The Time of [Jacob's] Trouble," in [James White and Ellen White], *A Word to the "Little Flock,"* 8-10; idem, "The Third Angel's Message," *Present Truth,* April 1850, 65-66; idem, "The 144,000," *Advent Review,* September 1850, 56; G. W. Holt, "Dear Brethren," *Present Truth,* March 1850, 64; H. S. Case, "Dear Bro. White," *Present Truth,* November 1850, 85; Elvira Hastings, "My Dear Brother and Sister," *Advent Review,* August 1850, 15-16; and Hiram Edson, *Advent Review Extra,* September 1850, 4-13.

the "beast" from the "image" it erects, they now identified the former with the United States of America, while the latter was thought to denote the corrupt and fallen churches of the land.[206] This new interpretation became the standard Adventist teaching and was even regarded as a "landmark" doctrine when it was challenged by a few in 1865.[207] Soon no one even seemed to remember that the early Sabbatarian Adventists had once held a different doctrinal view.[208]

The Eastern question.[209] Another apocalyptic symbol of apostasy and oppression, which engaged the church in reflection, debate, and readjustment, was the mysterious "king of the north" (Dan 11:40-45) and the related motifs of the "Euphrates" and of the apocalyptic battle of "Armageddon" (Rev 16:12-16). Even today, there is no unanimity among Adventists on this particular aspect of apocalyptic prophecy.

206 J. N. Andrews, "Thoughts on Revelation xiii and xiv," *RH*, 19 May 1851, 81-86. Andrews now related the number 666 to the second beast but retained the traditional view according to which it referred to the number of Protestant churches (Babylon) in the USA. In 1853, J. M. Stephenson suggested that the number 666 properly belonged to the first (papal) beast though he still applied it to the number of existing churches ("The Number of the Beast," *RH*, 29 November 1853, 166). In 1860, James White questioned the validity of the traditional identification of 666 with the number of denominations which was used as argument against his drive for church organization ("Making Us a Name," *RH*, 26 April 1860, 180-182: "Fifteen years since some declared the number 666 to be full – that there was that number of legally organized bodies"). Finally, in 1865, Uriah Smith pointed out that the numerical value of the Latin title *Vicarius Filii Dei* was 666 making it the "most plausible" explanation of this symbol he had seen *(Thoughts, Critical and Practical, on the Book of Revelation,* 225).
207 Uriah Smith, "The Two-horned Beast," *RH*, 9 October-27 November 1866; M. E. Cornell, "Image of the Beast," *RH*, 12 May 1868, 337-341; and J. N. Andrews, "'The United States in the Light of Prophecy,'" *RH*, 26 December 1871, 12. See also below, p. 227.
208 In 1874, J. H. Waggoner who had become a SDA in 1852 wrote: "I have never changed my mind, nor the manner of my preaching, on the two-horned beast … I do not know of any one of our ministers who has changed his views on the two-horned beast" ("[Letter to] W. M.," *RH*, 24 March 1874, 120). Cf. James White, "The Cause Is Onward," *RH*, 21 April 1874, 148 ("Our views of the two-horned beast of Rev. 13, and of the formation of the image, has been before the world for about twenty years"). For a recent study on the two-horned beast, which cautiously goes beyond the traditional Adventist view, see Richard Lehmann, "Le faux prophète et l'image de la bête," in *Études sur l'apocalypse,* 1:168-186.
209 See *SDAE,* 1976 ed., s.v. "Armageddon"; Raymond F. Cottrell, "Pioneer Views on Daniel Eleven and Armageddon, rev. ed., 1951," TMs, AHC, JWL, AU, Berrien Springs, Mich.; Donald E. Mansell, "What Adventists Have Taught on Armageddon and the King of the North," *Ministry,* November-December 1967, 26-29, 30-32; idem, "Armageddon: Changing Views on the Final Battle," *[College and University] Dialogue* 5:3 (1993): 13-16; Schwarz, *Light Bearers to the Remnant,* 400-403; and Hans K. LaRondelle, "Armageddon: History of Adventist Interpretations," in *Symposium on Revelation: Exegetical and General Studies – Book 2,* Daniel and Revelation Committee Series, ed. Frank B. Holbrook, vol. 7 (Silver Spring, Md.: Biblical Research Institute, General Conference of SDAs, 1992), 435-449.

168

In the 1860s, Sabbatarian Adventists commonly identified the papacy as the apocalyptic king of the north.[210] However, with the Roman Catholic Church losing the Papal State in 1870 and in view of the political developments in the Near East, Uriah Smith, in 1871, abandoned the traditional view and proposed Turkey instead as the king of the north of Daniel's prophecy.[211] Smith expected Turkey to remove its capital to Jerusalem after being driven from Europe by Russia. The complete downfall of the Ottoman Empire – thought to be symbolized by the drying up of the Euphrates River – would be a sign to the church that "Michael," i.e., Christ, was standing up to deliver his people who by then would be facing the final and fierce persecution by the apocalyptic beast powers.[212]

Many, if not most, Adventists embraced this view which not only became the standard interpretation for decades to come but also contributed to the continuing sense of the immediacy of the second advent.[213] Still, there were those who warned against basing faith in the nearness of the second coming of Christ on a speculative interpretation of unfulfilled prophecies.[214] James White, e.g., continued to hold to the traditional view, which was rapidly losing support in the church.[215] To him, the new teaching on the Eastern question was in danger of "removing the landmarks fully established in the advent movement." He also feared the consequences that might arise should things not develop the way they were confidently expected to.[216]

---

210 Uriah Smith, "Will the Pope Remove the Papal Seat to Jerusalem?" *RH,* 13 May 1862, 192; idem, "Warning of the Pope's Power," *RH,* 18 April 1865, 157; idem, "Italy and the Papacy," *RH,* 9 January 1866, 45; idem, "The Papacy," *RH,* 11 September 1866, 116; and William C. Gage, "None Shall Help Him," *RH,* 24 September 1867, 236.

211 Uriah Smith, "Thoughts on Daniel," *RH,* 28 March 1871, 117. Cf. idem, *The Prophecies of Daniel and the Revelation* (Nashville: SPA, 1944), 289-299.

212 [Uriah Smith], "The Eastern Question," *RH,* 25 February 1873, 82-83; and idem, "A Bible Reading on the Eastern Question," *RH,* 29 March 1887, 200-201.

213 See, e.g., G. W. Amadon, "Where Are We?" *RH,* 6 May 1873, 164; A. Smith, "The Seven Last Plagues," *RH,* 8 July 1884, 436-437; idem, "Last-Day Tokens – No. 11," *RH,* 6 December 1887, 754-755; idem, "The Eastern Question," *RH,* 3-17 November 1891, 673-674, 690-691, 706-707; D. H. Lamson, "Armageddon," *RH,* 14 April 1885, 227; idem, "Turkey – Its Rise and Fall," *RH,* 21 April 1885, 243; A. T. Jones, *The Eastern Question: What Its Solution Means to All the World* (Battle Creek, Mich.: RHPA, 1896; Oakland, Calif.: PPPA, 1896); and H. E. Robinson, *The Eastern Question in the Light of God's Promises to Israel* (Battle Creek, Mich.: RHPA, 1897; Oakland, Calif.: PPPA, 1897).

214 J. H. Waggoner, "The Eastern Question," *RH,* 2 March 1876, 68-69; and James White, "Unfulfilled Prophecy," *RH,* 29 November 1877, 172.

215 He conceded: "It may be said that there is a general agreement upon this subject, and that all eyes are turned toward the war now in progress between Turkey and Russia as the fulfillment of [Dan 11:44-45]" (James White, "Unfulfilled Prophecy," 172).

216 Ibid.; cf. James White, "Where Are We?" *RH,* 3 October 1878, 116-117. Ellen White counseled her husband not to press his view nor publicly argue with Smith and those who had adopted the new interpretation. She did not consider the issue vital enough, nor belonging to the pillars of the Adventist faith, to risk a division within the church over it (Ellen White, Letter 37, 1887, EGWRC, AU, Berrien Springs, Mich.; publ. in idem, *Counsels to Writers and*

In the years preceding as well as during World War I, Seventh-day Adventists widely assumed that the prophecies relating to the king of the north and the battle of Armageddon were finding fulfillment before their very eyes. In spite of cautious remarks made by some church leaders, the ensuing/ongoing military conflict seemed to fully corroborate their exposition.[217] Adventists continued to defend Smith's new and by now traditional viewpoint even when the outcome of the war led to a situation almost the exact opposite of what they had firmly believed.[218]

Yet, gone was the unanimity among Adventist interpreters on the "Eastern question."[219] Gradually, Smith's "Turkish" view receded from the limelight of prophetic exposition as more and more Adventists either came to favor a spiritual explanation of the war of Armageddon or were attracted to the refocusing of these prophecies on the "yellow peril," viz., the rising Asian nations of China and Japan.[220]

Editors [Nashville: SPA, 1946], 76-77). While not pushing his view, James White continued to hold that "the eleventh chapter of Daniel closes with ... the Roman Empire which comes to its end at the second coming of Christ" ("Time of the End," *ST,* 22 July 1880, 330).

217 W. A. Spicer, "The Gathering for Armageddon," *RH,* 22 October 1903, 6-7; S. N. Haskell, *The Story of Daniel the Prophet* (South Lancaster, Mass.: Bible Training School, 1908), 281-283; M. C. Wilcox, *Have We Come to Armageddon?* (Mountain View, Calif.: PPPA, [1912-1913]); E. E. Andross, *Turkey and Its End* (Washington, D.C.: RHPA, [1912-1913]; Mountain View, Calif.: PPPA, [1912-1913]); L. A. Reed, *Answers to Queries on the Eastern Question* (Washington, D.C.: RHPA, [1912-1913]; Mountain View, Calif.: PPPA, [1912-1913]); Arthur G. Daniells, "Does the History of Turkey and Egypt since 1798 Fulfil the Prophecy of Dan. 11:40-44?" *RH,* 13 March 1913, 5; idem, *The World War: Its Relation to the Eastern Question and Armageddon* (Washington, D.C.: RHPA, 1917). See also *SDAE,* 1976 ed., s.v. "Armageddon"; and Gary Land, "The Peril of Prophesying: Seventh-day Adventists Interpret World War I," *Adventist Heritage* 1:1 (1974): 28-33.

218 By the end of World War I, Turkey had lost its access to Palestine and was confined to its own territory in Asia Minor. *Review & Herald* editor F. M. Wilcox responded by saying: "We see no reason at the present time for departing from the view we have held for years regarding the exposition of Daniel 11. We have seen no new interpretation which in our judgment is superior to the old. We believe that the conclusions held by us from the beginning *[!]* of this movement, that Turkey is represented by the term 'king of the north' in the prophecy, is correct. And because just at this present juncture in the affairs of this world there seems to be no immediate prospect that Turkey will plant her palaces at Jerusalem, is no reason why we should change our view of the question. If we cannot see, then it is best to wait and bide God's time for fuller light, and watch him work things around as we believe his Word reveals that he will" ("A World of Changing Emphasis," *RH,* 30 January 1919, 3-4). See also Land, ed., *Adventism in America,* 163-164.

219 During the 1919 Bible and History Teachers' Conference, the issue was openly and extensively discussed but no agreement was reached. As reported, participants aligned themselves with either the old view, which, as a matter of fact, was the more recent one (Turkey), or the new view, which reclaimed the original position of the pioneers (Roman Catholicism); others spoke of "Babylon" instead. For details, consult the transcripts of this conference located in the Office of Archives and Statistics, General Conference of SDA, Washington, D.C.

220 T. M. French, "Armageddon – Will It Be Only a Spiritual Conflict?" *RH,* 30 January 1936, 5-6; F. D. Nichol, "Modern Turkey and Unfulfilled Prophecy," *RH,* 8 December 1938, 8.

When the outcome of World War II abated the fear of these latest "kings of the East," a number of Adventists began to restudy these prophecies and, particularly, the hermeneutical principles of their exposition. At first in research papers[221] and private undertakings,[222] but then also in official publications,[223] an increasing number of Adventist Bible scholars interpreted the battle of Armageddon again as a religious and spiritual, rather than a military or political, conflict between the powers of good and evil clashing over the issue of allegiance to Christ or to Antichrist. Thus, the original view of the church had, after a long eclipse, finally been restored as the prevailing position taught by most SDA students of Bible prophecy.[224]

Coping with the delay. It appears that the reinterpretation of the prophetic images and symbols just described and probably other doctrinal readjustments in SDA eschatology as well have been caused by the seeming delay of the advent of Christ and the need of the church to cope with it. Over the years, Adventists have experienced a gradually decreasing sense of imminence regarding the parousia without, however, downplaying or even discarding this fundamental tenet of their faith.

For about ten to fifteen years following the disappointment of 1844, Sabbatarian Adventists maintained their intense expectation of the imminent coming of Christ, similar to that which had characterized the Millerite movement before. To them, it could only be a matter of days, weeks, or, at the most, months until the history of this world would reach its dramatic culmination. For this reason, they encouraged

---

221 Raymond F. Cottrell, "The Kings of the East: An Historical Study, 1943," TMs, AHC, JWL, AU, Berrien Springs, Mich.; idem, "Armageddon: A Study of Historical and Prophetic Backgrounds, 1945," TMs, AHC, JWL, AU, Berrien Springs, Mich.; and idem, "Pioneer Views on Daniel Eleven and Armageddon, rev. ed., 1951."

222 Australian Evangelist Louis F. Were was particularly concerned about the need for a Christocentric interpretation of apocalyptic prophecy. Among his books are *The Certainty of the Third Angel's Message* (n.p., [1945]); *The Kings That Come from the Sunrising* (n.p., [1951]); and *The Moral Purpose of Prophecy* (n.p., n.d.). In Germany, G. W. Mandemaker and R. Stahl were to promote quite similar concepts *(Der Versuch einer christozentrischen Auslegung der sechsten und siebenten Plage* [Berlin: By the Authors, 1970]).

223 W. E. Read, "The Closing Events of the Great Controversy," in *Our Firm Foundation* (1953), 2:239-335 (the 1952 Bible Conference was a milestone in SDA history by reaffirming the spiritual view on Armageddon and the identification of the papacy as the king of the north); "Report on the Eleventh Chapter of Daniel," *Ministry,* March 1954, 22-27; George McCready Price, *The Time of the End* (Nashville: SPA, 1967); Roy Allan Anderson, *Unfolding the Revelation,* rev. ed. (Boise, Idaho: PPPA, 1974), 166-168; Kenneth S. Brown, "'Gathering' for Armageddon," *Ministry,* August 1974, 16-18; George McCready Price, "Armageddon," *RH,* 1 January 1976, 4-7; Manfred Böttcher, *Weg und Ziel der Gemeinde Jesu* (Hamburg: Advent-Verlag, [1981], 268-290); Maxwell, *God Cares – Vol. 2,* 434-446.

224 In recent years, Hans K. LaRondelle has become the foremost advocate in the SDA Church of a consistent Christocentric interpretation of biblical prophecy, including the battle of Armageddon. See, e.g., *Chariots of Salvation: The Biblical Drama of Armageddon* (Washington, D.C.: RHPA, 1987); and idem, "Armageddon: Sixth and Seventh Plagues," in Holbrook, ed., *Symposium on Revelation – Book 2,* 373-390.

each other to hold on to their faith just "a few more days."[225] At one time or other, virtually all of them were looking forward to specific dates for the expected appearing of Christ.[226] However, no time setting was supported by any leading Seventh-day Adventist after 1851.[227] Still, they were expecting Christ's "immediate return."[228]

In 1859, however, Ellen White made it clear that "this message would not accomplish its work in a few short months."[229] Thus far, Adventists had taken the position that the "generation" (Matt 24:34) that had seen the end-time signs of 1780 (Dark Day) and 1833 (falling of the stars) would not pass away before Christ's return.[230] Now they tended to confine the final generation of earth's history to those who had at least heard the Millerites preach on these signs of the approaching end and/or had witnessed the events of 1844.[231] This conviction was reinforced by a

225 [James White and Ellen White], *A Word to the "Little Flock,"* 8; Hiram Edson, *The Time of the End* (Auburn, N.Y.: By the Author, 1849), 3, 15, 26; Ellen White to the Hastings, 22-23 March 1849, EGWRC, AU, Berrien Springs, Mich. What was to be done, had to be done quickly. "Ellen has seen in vision that we should go west before the Lord comes" (James White to Elvira Hastings, 22 August – 1 September 1847, EGWRC, AU, Berrien Springs, Mich.). Believers were not to think that because "time has continued on a few years longer than they expected ... it may continue a few years more" (Ellen White, To Those Who Are Receiving the Seal of the Living God, [1849]). There were just "a few months" left to get ready for translation (idem, Vision of 27 June 1850, EGWRC, AU, Berrien Springs, Mich.; published in *Early Writings,* 67). Cf. idem, Manuscript 2, 1854, EGWRC, AU, Berrien Springs, Mich.

226 According to Bates, "about all that believed in the Lord's coming were looking to the fall of 1845" ("Midnight Cry in the Past," *RH,* December 1850, 23). A few years later, Edson settled on 1849-1850 *(The Time of the End,* 3, 11, 13, 15, 26), while Bates looked forward to October 1851 *(An Explanation of the Typical and Anti-Typical Sanctuary* [New Bedford, Mass.: By the Author, 1850], 10-11).

227 Ellen White had taken the lead in opposing any further time calculations. "The Lord showed me the TIME had not been a test since 1844, and that time will never again be a test" ("Dear Brethren and Sisters," *Present Truth,* November 1850, 86-87). Still, popular piety has, at times, engaged in time speculations – until today.

228 James White, "Tracts," *RH,* 9 December 1852, 120; idem, "The Immediate Coming of Christ," *RH,* 20 January 1853, 140-141; and Ellen White, "To the Saints Scattered Abroad," *RH,* 17 February 1853, 155. When he proposed his view on the investigative judgment, Uriah Smith expressed the conviction that "a large proportion" of the time needed for the examination of the records of the dead had already passed ("The Hour of His Judgment Is Come," *RH,* 29 January 1857, 104).

229 Ellen White, vision of 15 July 1859, EGWRC, AU, Berrien Springs, Mich.; published in idem, *Testimonies,* 1:186. Probably, she did not have the third angel's message in mind but the Laodicean message.

230 "Thus we are assured by the testimony of our Lord that a remnant of the very generation that was born nearly eighty years ago will not pass away before they see all these things, and even the literal coming of the Son of man in the clouds of heaven" (Otis Nichols, "The Signs of the End of the World," *RH,* 9 December 1852, 114). See also idem, "This Generation – The Period of Its Application," *RH,* 18 November 1858, 204; cf. D. Hewitt, "The Parable of the Fig Tree," *RH,* 17 January 1856, 123.

231 H. S. Gurney, "This Generation," *RH,* 14 October 1858, 165; [Uriah Smith], "Remarks," *RH,* 18 November 1858, 204; R. F. Cottrell, "This Generation," *RH,* 4 September 1866,

prediction of Ellen White according to which some of the people present at a certain conference in 1856 would still be alive at the coming of Christ.[232]

Thus, by the time the Seventh-day Adventist Church was organized in the early 1860s, the assumption of the extreme nearness of the *parousia* had been modified to accommodate a somewhat longer period of time. Adventists now reckoned with a few years during which they could complete their mission to this world.[233]

During the 1880s, there were some Adventists who expected time to end in 1884, 1891, or else in 1894. Church leaders firmly opposed such views.[234] At least one of them felt certain, however, that Christ would return before the end of the century.[235] But when the continuation of time made the traditional definition of

108; James White, "Our Faith and Hope," *RH,* 10 January 1871, 25-26; "This Generation," *RH,* 17 April 1879, 128; T. M. Lane, "This Generation," *RH,* 26 July 1881, 68; [Uriah Smith], "This Generation," *RH,* 22 March 1887, 182; M. E. Steward, "This Generation," *RH,* 30 August 1887, 548-549; R. F. Cottrell, "How Many Years Is a Generation?" *RH,* 17 January 1888, 36; George B. Thompson, "This Generation," *RH,* 4 September 1888, 564; [Uriah Smith], "In the Question Chair," *RH,* 16 June 1891, 376; [idem], "This Generation," *RH,* 17 November 1891, 712; [idem], "In the Question Chair," *RH,* 5 January 1892, 8; [idem], "In the Question Chair," *RH,* 6 June 1893, 360; Otey James, "One of 'This Generation,'" *RH,* 20 July 1905, 18; and L. A. Smith, "The End of 'This Generation',," *RH,* 2 November 1905, 5.

232 Ellen White, "Testimony for the Church," *RH,* 6 January 1863, 47 (also published in idem, *Testimonies,* 1:131). Ellen White made a similar forecast in 1888: "Some of us who now believe will be alive upon the earth, and shall see the prediction verified, and hear the voice of the archangel" ("Cast Not Away Your Confidence," *RH,* 31 July 1888, 481-482). For an exhaustive study of the tension in her writings between the immediacy and distance of the second advent, see Ralph E. Neall, "The Nearness and Delay of the Parousia in the Writings of Ellen G. White" (Ph.D. dissertation, Andrews University, 1982); and idem, *How Long, O Lord?* (Washington, D.C., and Hagerstown, Md.: RHPA, 1988).

233 D. T. Bourdeau guessed that this task might perhaps be accomplished within three to five years. He also linked the time of the coming of Christ to the fulfillment of the mission of the Adventist church, a line of reasoning that Adventists have since frequently repeated ("Hasting unto the Coming of Christ," *RH,* 14 March 1871, 101).

234 George I. Butler, "The Forty Years," *RH,* 30 October 1883, 681-683; G. W. Amadon, "Fanaticism and Time-Setting," *RH,* 23 September 1884, 624; J. H. Waggoner, "Is There Prophetic Time Longer?" *RH,* 11 November 1884, 713-714; and [Uriah Smith], "No Time to Set," *RH,* 2 December 1884, 760. Ellen G. White wrote in 1891: "You will not be able to say that He will come in one, two, or five years, neither are you to put off His coming by stating that it may not be for ten or twenty years" ("'It Is Not for You to Know the Times and the Seasons'," *RH,* 22 March 1892, 178; publ. in *Selected Messages from the Writings of Ellen G. White* [Washington, D. C.: RHPA, 1958], 1:189). See also idem, Manuscript 32, 1896; publ. in *Selected Messages from the Writings of Ellen G. White* (Washington, D.C.: RHPA, 1958), 2:113-114.

235 J. N. Andrews, "The Great Week of Time," *RH,* 17 July-21 August 1883. Andrews based his belief on the 6,000-year theory. Similar views were still afloat among Adventists in recent years. See D. F. Neufeld, "Is the 6,000 Year Theory Valid?" *RH,* 25 March 1976, 10-11; and Van G. Hurst, "Will Christ Come in A. D. 2000? A Look at the 6,000-Year Theory," *RH,* 9 July 1987, 16-17.

"this generation" untenable, Adventists reinterpreted Matt 24:34 in various ways in order to adjust their theology to their actual experience.[236]

The conclusion seems unavoidable that Adventists have increasingly lost the strong sense of imminence that had characterized their spiritual progenitors in previous decades. A leading Adventist missiologist has observed a number of years ago,

> the Seventh-day Adventist Church was born out of expectation of the soon coming of Christ. For many years this hope has been the creative center of our movement and the most powerful motive of our worldwide mission. It cannot be denied that after 135 years of existence, the Adventist Church has lost much of the urgency of that message and mission, while other aspects of its faith and work have become more dominant.[237]

In response to these developments, some Adventist writers have attempted to reconsider the meaning of the advent hope in the context of biblical eschatology, reinterpreting it in a manner relevant to the world today.[238] In spite of the seeming

---

236 As late as in 1926, C. B. Haynes maintained that "without doubt there will be some living when the Lord comes who saw the falling of the stars in 1833" *(The Return of Jesus* [Washington, D.C.: RHPA, 1926], 293. Four years later, however, Arthur G. Daniells admitted that this interpretation of Matt 24:34 could no longer be sustained; he now regarded it as conditional prophecy ("Is Christ's Coming Being Delayed? If So, Why?" *Ministry,* November 1930, 5-6, 30). See also W. H. Branson, "'This Generation'," in *Our Firm Foundation* (1953), 2:700-704 ("the generation that hears this [threefold] Advent message ... shall not pass until all be accomplished"); C. S. Longacre, "This Generation Shall Not Pass," *RH,* 19 July 1956, 4-5; D. F. Neufeld, "This Generation Shall Not Pass," *RH,* 5 April 1979, 6; Maxwell, *God Cares – Vol. 2,* 43-44 ("this kind of people"); and Jonathan Gallagher, "'This Generation'?" Ministry, December 1989, 4-6. Schwarz looks at the 1919 Bible Conference discussion *(Light Bearers to the Remnant,* 405-406).

237 G. Oosterwal, "The SDA Church in the 1980's, 1980," TMs, 55 (in my possession). Cf. W. B. Quigley, "Imminence – Mainspring of Adventism – Nos. 1-3," *Ministry,* April, June, August 1980, 4-6, 27; 11 13; 18-19. Cf. Bull and Lockhart, *Seeking a Sanctuary,* chaps. 4 and 6.

238 See, e.g., Provonsha, *God Is with Us* (1974), 136-147; Gerhard Rempel, *Ende und Vollendung der Welt* (Hamburg: Advent-Verlag [1977]); Sakae Kubo, *God Meets Man* (1978); Roy Branson, ed., *Pilgrimage of Hope* (Takoma Park, Md.: Association of Adventist Forums, 1986); Samuele Bacchiocchi, *The Advent Hope for Human Hopelessness: A Theological Study of the Meaning of the Second Advent for Today,* Biblical Perspectives, no. 6 (Berrien Springs, Mich.: By the Author, 1986); idem, *Hal Lindsey's Prophetic Jigsaw Puzzle: Five Predictions That Failed,* Biblical Perspectives, no. 3 (Berrien Springs, Mich.: By the Author, 1987); Fritz Guy, "The Future and the Present: The Meaning of the Advent Hope," in *The Advent Hope in Scripture and History,* ed. V. N. Olsen (1987), 211-229; Rolf J. Pöhler, "Hat die Welt noch eine Zukunft? – Nos. 1-4," *Zeichen der Zeit,* April-October 1989; and Jon Paulien, *What the Bible Says about the End-Time* (Hagerstown, Md.: RHPA, 1994). See also Norval F. Pease, "The Second Advent in Seventh-day Adventist History and Theology," in *The Advent Hope in Scripture and History,* ed. V. N. Olsen, 173-190. According to Pease, theological "variations" among SDAs in regard to the second advent "have resulted from the basic fact of the passing of time, from changing conditions in the world and the church, and from continued reflection and evaluation on the part of the church's preachers,

delay [239] of the *parousia* of Christ, Adventists still regard their eschatological perspective on the present and the future as the most appropriate response of the Christian faith both to biblical revelation and to contemporary human experience.[240]

The Sanctuary

Though not prominently expressed in its name, the so-called "sanctuary doctrine" can be regarded as probably the most distinctive teaching of the Seventh-day Adventist Church.[241] In Ellen White's view, it constituted "the foundation and central pillar of the Advent faith."[242] As with the Sabbath, there would never have been a Seventh-day Adventist Church without it. The centrality of this doctrine and the uniqueness of its content have made it a disputed teaching from the beginning, not only between Seventh-day Adventists and their fellow Christians, but also among church members themselves. Attacks on this teaching coming from without as well as critical questions raised from within the church have usually been answered by pointing to the immutability of this foundational pillar of the Adventist faith. What this apologetic approach tends to overlook, however, is the significant modifications that even this doctrine has experienced over the years.[243]

teachers, writers, and laymen." Today, the church is "faced with the absolute necessity of finding a viable explanation for the delay" (ibid., 176-177).

239 For a helpful discussion of this concept, see Arnold Valentin Wallenkampf, *The Apparent Delay* (Hagerstown, Md.: RHPA, 1994).

240 Jonathan Butler, "When Prophecy Fails: The Validity of Apocalypticism," *Spectrum* 8:1 (1976): 7-14; Rolf J. Pöhler, "Naherwartung in der adventistischen Theologie," in "*2000 Jahre Naherwartung – Altert eine Hoffnung?*" Der Adventglaube in Geschichte und Gegenwart, vol. 30 (Darmstadt: Adventistischer Wissenschaftlicher Arbeitskreis, 1989), 47-63; "'And the Trumpet Shall Sound ...'" *AR*, Second Coming Issue [2 January 1992]; and Robert S. Folkenberg, *We Still Believe* (Boise, Idaho: PPPA, 1994).

241 For detailed studies on the development of the Adventist sanctuary doctrine, see C. Mervyn Maxwell, "Sanctuary and Atonement in SDA Theology: An Historical Survey," in *The Sanctuary and the Atonement*, ed. Wallenkampf and Lesher, 516-544; idem, "The Investigative Judgment: Its Early Development," ibid., 545-581; Roy Adams, *The Sanctuary Doctrine: Three Approaches in the Seventh-day Adventist Church*, Andrews University Seminary Doctoral Dissertation Series, vol. 1 (Berrien Springs, Mich.: AU Press, 1981); Paul A. Gordon, *The Sanctuary, 1844, and the Pioneers* (Washington, D.C.: RHPA, 1983); and Holbrook, ed., *Doctrine of the Sanctuary*. For brief introductory articles, see *SDAE*, 1976 ed., s.v. "Sanctuary," "Judgment," and "Investigative Judgment"; cf. Robert D. Brinsmead, "The Development of the Concept of the Investigative or Pre-Advent Judgment," chap. in *1844 Re-Examined*, Institute Syllabus (Fallbrook, Calif.: I.H.I., 1979). Rather unreliable is Robert Haddock, "A History of the Doctrine of the Sanctuary in the Advent Movement, 1800-1905."

242 Ellen White, *The Great Controversy*, 409, 409-432. Cf. idem, *Christ in His Sanctuary* (Mountain View, Calif.: PPPA, 1969).

243 "Considerable history now lies behind us, and part of that history shows that our thinking on the sanctuary doctrine has not been frozen" (Roy Adams, *The Sanctuary: Understanding the Heart of Adventist Theology* [Hagerstown, Md.: RHPA, 1993], 12).

The time of the judgment. Today, Adventists usually regard the "cleansing of the sanctuary" and the "investigative judgment" as virtually synonymous, denoting the heavenly ministry of Christ that began in 1844 and lasts until just before the second coming of Christ. It is not generally known that, at one time, such a synthesis was actually opposed by Sabbatarian Adventists. Originally, they defined the cleansing of the sanctuary not as a judgment but only in terms of an intercessory ministry of Christ for his church upon earth, precluding from it both believers of past ages and the world at large. It took some years until the pioneers of the Seventh-day Adventist Church generally accepted the idea that Christ's present work in the heavenly sanctuary involved a judgment on all believers – the living and the dead.

Ideas regarding a pre-advent phase of the last judgment arose already among the Millerites in 1841.[244] Shortly after the disappointment of 1844, a number of them began to wonder whether the judgment of the living and the dead had not begun on October 22, 1844.[245] Inasmuch as these views were advanced in support of the extreme shut-door doctrine, Sabbatarian Adventists – particularly James White – opposed the idea of a present pre-advent judgment of the dead.[246] Wrote he,

244 Josiah Litch believed that a heavenly trial during which God would examine people and determine their fate would precede the execution of the decrees of this trial at the second coming of Christ. He also surmised that Dan 7:9-10 referred to a judgment on the dead, which had begun in 1798 and would turn to the living at the opening of the seventh seal when probation had ended. See his *An Address to the Public* (Boston: J. V. Himes, 1841), 37-39; and idem, *Prophetic Expositions,* 2 vols. (Boston: J. V. Himes, 1842), 1:49-54. This view was echoed by Apollos Hale *(Herald of the Bridegroom* [Boston: J. V. Himes, 1843], 22-23) and, in the summer of 1844, apparently led some Millerites in Maine to believe "that we were in the Judgment, that the last dividing line was being drawn, and that the servants of God were being sealed" ("Advent Herald," *Advent Herald,* 30 October 1844, 93).

245 E. Jacobs, "The Time," *Western Midnight Cry,* 29 November 1844, 19-20; idem, "Intolerance," *Western Midnight Cry,* 30 December 1844, 30; "Bro. J. B. Cook," *Western Midnight Cry,* 30 January 1845, 45-46; Joseph Turner and Apollos Hale, "Has Not the Saviour Come as the Bridegroom?" *Advent Mirror,* January 1845; "Has the Bridegroom Come?" *Advent Herald,* 26 February 1845, 18; "To the Believers Scattered Abroad," *Day-Star,* 25 March 1845, 21-24; S. S. Snow, "'And the Door Was Shut,'" *Jubilee Standard,* 24 April 1845, 52-54 ("the judgment of the living and the dead must precede the appearing of the Son of man to *execute judgment"*); [E. Jacobs], "Is the Door Shut?" *Day-Star,* 13-20 May 1845, 1-3, 6-8; "The Door of Matt. 25:10; Is Shut," *Day-Star,* 24 June 1845, 28; G. W. Peavey, "'The Hour of His Judgment Is Come,'" *Jubilee Standard,* 19 June 1845, 113-115 (cf. ibid., 120, for editorial remarks by S. S. Snow); and [E. Jacobs], "The Second Coming," *Day-Star,* 24 January 1846, 28-29 ("Judgment has begun at the house of God"). For a brief time, even Miller himself shared such a view. In March 1845 he wrote: "I cannot see that we were wrong in the chronology. That the prophetic numbers did close in 1844, I have but little doubt ... 'The hour of his judgment is come' ... [God is] now in his last judicial character, deciding the cases of all the righteous ... justifying his sanctuary" ("Letter from Bro. Miller," *Jubilee Standard,* 17 April 1845, 41-42).

246 The extreme shut-door doctrine taught that the atoning work of Christ in the heavenly sanctuary had been finished in October 1844, the fate of people been decided, and the saints already been sealed. The idea of a present judgment neatly fitted into this concept. In his

It is not necessary that the final sentence should be given before the first resurrection, as some have taught; for the names of the saints are written in heaven, and Jesus, and the angels will certainly know who to raise, and gather to the New Jerusalem.[247]

There was, however, some disagreement regarding the biblical teaching on "the day of judgment." Apparently, a few Adventists believed that the final judgment on the dead and the living would be held prior to, and executed at, the second coming of Christ.[248] James White strongly opposed this idea as being "certainly without foundation in the word of God."[249] He was supported in this by the visions of his wife.[250]

informative study, Maxwell seems to have overlooked the crucial distinction between this view and that of the Sabbatarian Adventists who defended a moderate version of the shut-door teaching. Thus, he did not recognize that, in the years following 1844, the Sabbatarian Adventists could not and, in fact, did not speak of a present judgment but rather opposed such a view (Maxwell, "The Investigative Judgment: Its Early Development"). That Bates differed on this point from his brethren is probably due to his leanings toward a more extreme version of the shut-door doctrine. For more information on this teaching, see below, p. 194, n. 324.

247 James White, "The Judgment," in [James White and Ellen White], A Word to the "Little Flock," 23-24; this article was later reprinted in the Review & Herald Extra, 21 July 1851, 4. See also J. F. Wardwell, "Letter from Sister J. F. Wardwell," Day-Dawn, 16 April 1847, 10 (commenting on a James White letter published in the same issue). According to Schwarz, "James White at first flatly rejected the idea of an 'investigative' judgment" (Light Bearers to the Remnant, 170).

248 Bates, Second Advent Way Marks and High Heaps (1847), 6 ("respecting 'the hour of God's judgment is come,' [Rev 14: 6-7] there must be order and time, for God in his judicial character to decide the cases of all the righteous"); idem, A Vindication of the Seventh-day Sabbath (1848), 111 ("to execute upon them (the wicked) the judgment written; this honor have all the saints"). See also Otis Nichols to William Miller, 20 April 1846 ("the Ancient of days did change his place ... to the throne of judgment in the Holy of Holies and did sit ... And very soon our great high priest will come out of the Holy of Holies to turn the captivity of Israel and execute the judgment written").

249 James White, "The Day of Judgment," Advent Review, September 1850, 49, 49-51 (he maintains [1] that Rev 14:6-7 "does not prove that the day of judgment ... will come prior to the second advent" and [2] that Rev 1:7 would be fulfilled only after the millennium). See also idem, "Conferences," Advent Review, November 1850, 72 (reporting on the Sutton, Vt., conference of 26-29 September at which "some trial arose in consequence of the introduction of certain views, relative to the Judgment, &c." But before the conference closed, "errors were confessed, and perfect union" was restored).

250 Ellen White, "Dear Brethren and Sisters," Present Truth, November 1850, 86-87. Ellen White likewise maintained that Rev 1:7 as well as the execution of the judgment would be realized only after the millennium. She also warned of "unhappy divisions" resulting from some who advocated new interpretations without first consulting with their brethren. Maxwell surmises that "Nichols – and others among Ellen White's associates – saw in her early visions an endorsement of the pre-advent judgment" ("The Investigative Judgment: Its Early Development," 559). However, Ellen White, at the time, seems to have proposed no such concept. In fact, already in January 1849, she had opposed Bates by saying that "the time to judge the dead" was not now, but in the future (To Those Who Are Receiving the Seal of the Living God). Neither did she exploit the so-called "breastplate-of-judgment" concept according to

Joseph Bates, in particular, had disagreed with his brethren on this issue, maintaining that the judgment of the dead was already now in progress while the living saints were being sealed. Anticipating the later Adventist teaching, he held that

> DANIEL VII: 9, 10, 13, shows how the Bridegroom *came* ... to judge his people, on the 10th day of the 7th month ... How evident that both Father and Son here left the throne in the Holy and moved into the Most Holy, in accordance also with, and close of, the message of the flying angel in Rev. xiv. 6, 7, to sit in judgment; first, to decide who is, and who is not worthy to enter the gates of the holy city ... the judgment is now set and the books open. After this work is accomplished, then comes the Day of Judgment ...[251]

Bates's view was not accepted at the time.[252] The idea of a present judgment simply did not yet sound true to Sabbath-keeping Adventists – to most of them, at least.[253]

which Jesus was said to have borne the names of Israel (the true believers) into the heavenly sanctuary. While other Sabbath-keeping Adventists frequently used this phrase to indicate that atonement was available "for those only whose names are inscribed on the breast-plate of judgement," even they (with the exception of Bates and Nichols) do not appear to have drawn any conclusions regarding a pre-advent judgment of believers from it (see, e.g., David Arnold, "The Shut Door Explained," *Present Truth*, December 1849, 41-46; Hiram Edson, "An Appeal to the Laodicean Church," *Advent Review Extra*, September 1850, 1-3; James White, [Remarks], *RH*, 7 April 1851, 64; idem, "The Parable, Matthew XXV, 1-12," *RH*, 9 June 1851, 102-103; but cf. Otis Nichols to William Miller, 20 April 1846, EGWRC, AU, Berrien Springs, Mich.). Maxwell himself admits that "inasmuch as these visions endorsed James White's millennial concepts and reproved Bates for one of his favorite arguments in support of the pre-advent judgment, White would have been less than human if he had not assumed the visions proved Bates' position on the heavenly pre-advent judgment completely wrong" ("The Investigative Judgment: Its Early Development," 572). Obviously, James White thought so, and most Sabbatarian Adventists did likewise. After all, "in all these statements, Ellen White was plainly in harmony with her brethren" (ibid., 574).

251 Bates, *An Explanation of the Typical and Anti-Typical Sanctuary* (1850), 10; see also idem, *Second Advent Way Marks and High Heaps* (1847), 6; idem, *A Vindication of the Seventh-day Sabbath* (1848), 111; and idem, *A Seal of the Living God* (1849), 38-39 ("the sealing is for the living saints only. The dead saints are now being judged, Rev. 11:18; Rev. xx:12-13"). In my view, Maxwell has misjudged the historical context of this quotation by asserting that its content "became normative for Seventh-day Adventists for a long time" ("The Investigative Judgment: Its Early Development," 565).

252 One reason for it may have been the impression that Bates's view was too closely related to the short-lived time setting theory he advanced in 1850. In the context of discussing the pre-advent judgment, Bates had argued: "The seven spots of blood on the Golden Altar and before the Mercy Seat, I fully believe represents the duration of the judicial proceedings on the living saints in the Most Holy, all of which time they will be in their affliction, even seven years ... Six last months of this time, I understand, Jesus will be gathering in the harvest, with his sickle, on the white cloud" *(An Explanation of the Typical and Anti-Typical Sanctuary*, 10-11). Incidentally, in 1852, Bates was among the last to abandon the shut-door teaching which had affected his beliefs more than that of the other leading Sabbatarian Adventists.

253 James White, "The Seventh Angel" ("The Second Advent introduces the judgment of quick and dead ... which will occupy the period of 1000 years"); J. N. Andrews, "Review of O. R.

However, the Sabbatarian Adventists did agree that Jesus was presently engaged in examining his people and blotting out their confessed sins in the sanctuary above.[254] Gradually, since 1854, they had come to describe this high-priestly ministry of Jesus in terms of a process of judgment upon his people living on earth.[255]

It took another year or two until the Sabbatarian Adventists also began to argue in favor of a present judgment of the dead – albeit limited to those who had once

L. Crosier on Rev. xiv, 1-13," *RH,* 9 December 1851, 60-61 ("It does not read, the judgment has come, – but THE HOUR of his judgment is come; implying that a brief space in which mercy yet lingered, remained to the unprepared"); James White, "The Immediate Coming of Christ," 140-141 (Dan 7 shows that "the judgment is the next event, and should now be expected"); idem, "Signs of the Times," *RH,* 13 September 1853, 75 (according to Rev 14:6-7 "the period has come for the Judgment to be expected"); and idem, "The Angels of Revelation xiv," *RH,* 29 November 1853, 164 ("the period to expect the judgment 'is come.' And the proclamation of the coming of Christ to judge the quick and dead, that has been given, the last fifteen years, is a perfect fulfillment of the first angel's message. Rev. xiv, 6, 7"). These statements should make one reluctant to give too much weight to the fact that James White, in the fall of 1851, republished two articles by Apollos Hale, both dating from 1845, in which the author referred to "the judiciary *trial* [and decision] which precedes the execution, (the judgment which begins at the house of God,)" ("'Call to Remembrance the Former Days,'" *RH,* 16 September-7 October 1851, 27, 25-28, 33-34) and exclaimed, "*The Judgment is here!*" ("Duties and Trials of Our Position," *RH,* 25 November 1851, 49-50).

254 In regard to the parable of Matt 22:1-14, James White explained that "the third angel's message is such a test, by which the guests are now being examined." However, to him, this was not a heavenly assize but an earthly test of loyalty to God ("The Parable, Matthew XXV, 1-12," 102-103). Cf. G. W. Holt, "The Day of the Lord," *RH,* 23 March 1852, 105-108 ("The sins of the righteous go beforehand to the Sanctuary and are blotted out by the High Priest ... but the sins and evil deeds of the wicked remain unforgiven, and go to judgment afterwards"). At about the same time, Ellen White expressed this idea in a slightly different form: "The sins of Israel must go to judgment beforehand. Every sin must be confessed at the sanctuary" (Manuscript 1, 1852). It seems that this was the first time that Ellen White used the word judgment in writing, albeit only in an allusion to 1 Tim 5:24, in a contemporary sense regarding the work of Christ in the heavenly sanctuary.

255 E. Everts, "Review of the New Time Theory," *RH,* 10 January 1854, 201-202 ("Light on the Sanctuary shows that the judgment commenced on [22 October 1844] ... and our High Priest commenced cleansing the Sanctuary"); and J. N. Loughborough, "The Hour of His Judgment Come," *RH,* 14 February 1854, 29-30. Loughborough pointed out that the Millerites "supposed that judgment did not set until Jesus' second advent." In his own view, however, "the hour of God's judgment" denotes "the cleansing of the sanctuary" which is "a work of judgment" that "must begin at the house of God" (1 Pet 4:17). A few weeks later, James White somewhat reluctantly began to follow suit. Quoting Rev 11: 15-18, he explained: "That judgment has begun at the house of God, that this is, in a certain sense, a period of judgment and decision, we freely admit; but *the* judgment, *the day* of judgment, *the time* of the dead that they should be judged, is, evidently, in the future" ("The Seventh Angel," *RH,* 7 March 1854, 52). A few months later, White again reprinted an article by Hale that maintained that "the trial must precede the execution" of the judgment ("The Kingdom of God," *RH,* 13 June 1854, 153-155). See also J. N. Loughborough, "Is the Soul Immortal?" *RH,* 11 December 1855, 81-83 ("the judgment of the saints must be prior to their resurrection").

belonged to the household of God. Now the heavenly examination was thought to involve not only the character of God's people living on earth but also the life records of the dead saints. At first, these two functions may have been seen as contemporaneous events;[256] but, since 1857, the judgment of the dead was explicitly said to take place before it would pass on to the living.[257]

According to the doctrine of the "investigative judgment" as it was called from then on, the sins of the "living saints" were now to be "blotted out" of their lives, but they would be removed from the heavenly records only during the closing phase of the heavenly trial.[258] Therefore, there was "a special call to the remnant, and a special work to be performed by them, and for them, preparatory to the decisions of the judgment in regard to them."[259] This preparatory call and work they found in the letter to the church at Laodicea (Rev 3).

It appears that the reapplication of the "Laodicean message" to their own group gave a strong impetus to the unfolding and acceptance of the doctrine of the investigative judgment among Seventh-day Adventists.[260] Conversely, it was this new doctrine that helped Seventh-day Adventists to become responsive to the urgent

---

256 "The closing up of the ministration of the heavenly Sanctuary ... must embrace the examination of individual character; and we conclude that the lives of the children of God, not only those who are living, but all who have ever lived, whose names are written in the Lamb's book of life, will during this time pass in final review before that great tribunal" (Uriah Smith, "The Cleansing of the Sanctuary," *RH,* 2 October 1855, 52-53). See also J. N. Andrews, "The Sanctuary and Its Cleansing," *RH,* 30 October 1855, 68-69 ("the sins of the whole church for 6000 years may be disposed of as individual cases, and all the while that the great work is being accomplished, the blood of Jesus still may avail for us in the presence of God").

257 James White, "The Judgment," *RH,* 29 January 1857, 100-101: "In the order of heaven, we must look for their [i.e., the living saints'] judgment to follow that of the dead, and to occur near the close of their probation" (cf. [idem], "The Judgment!" *RH,* 8 April 1858, 164). As set forth by James White in this influential essay, the intercessory ministry of Jesus involves "the blotting out of the forgiven sins of all the just"; in other words, "the judgment of those who died subjects of the grace of God has been going on, while Jesus has been offering his blood for the blotting out of their sins" as well as of the sins of "the living saints." The first reference by Ellen White to the doctrine of the investigative judgment says, "While JESUS had been ministering in the Sanctuary, the judgment had been going on for the righteous dead, and then for the righteous living" *(Spiritual Gifts,* 1:198 [1858]; cf. *Early Writings,* 280).

258 The term "investigative judgment" seems to have been coined by Elon Everts and popularized by James White. See "Communication from Bro. Everts [17 December 1856]," *RH,* 1 January 1857, 72 ("the righteous dead have been under investigative judgment since 1844"); and James White, "The Judgment," *RH,* 29 January 1857, 100-101 (this article uses the phrase "the investigative judgment" three times).

259 James White, "The Judgment," *RH,* 29 January 1857, 100.

260 James White, "The Seven Churches," *RH,* 16 October 1856, 188-189, 192; idem, "The Judgment," *RH,* 29 January 1857, 100-101; and E. Everts, "Communication from Bro. Everts," *RH,* 1 January 1857, 72.

call for spiritual reform raised in view of the approaching end of probation and of the final decision regarding the eternal destiny of humanity.[261]

Thus, Seventh-day Adventists had finally come to accept a teaching that apparently most of them had once firmly opposed.[262] Their seeming about-face regarding a pre-advent judgment became possible after its original shut-door implications no longer posed a threat to their faith. As time went on, this new doctrine appealed to them as it helped both to keep their sense of urgency alive and also to explain the increasing time gap between the entrance of Christ into the most holy place of the heavenly sanctuary in 1844 and the consummation of his priestly work there in the near, though not immediate, future.[263]

The nature of the judgment. When the doctrine of the investigative judgment was developed among Seventh-day Adventists, it was generally understood to imply that the object of the investigation of the life records of God's professed people was to decide their eternal destiny.[264] This belief was expressed in no uncertain terms in the 1872 Statement of Faith, according to which the heavenly court was "to determine who ... are worthy of a part in the first resurrection" (#18). This threefold task of investigation, determination, and final decision meant the settling of a question that had not yet been decided up to this particular point of time.[265]

261 "Report of Conferences," *RH,* 12 March 1857, 152 ("The overwhelming conviction seemed to rest upon the minds there generally, that judgment is about beginning 'at the house of God' among the living saints"); J. N. Loughborough, "Judgment," *RH,* 19 November 1857, 9-11 ("The judgment of the dead saints is fast being brought to a close ... Our suit is pending. We know not how soon it may be investigated").

262 While some Adventist scholars have concluded that the Sabbatarian Adventists "retained and amplified" the concept of a pre-advent judgment inherited from the Millerites (*Doctrine of the Sanctuary,* ed. Holbrook, 119), the results of this study suggest that, after some years of opposition to it, they regained and modified this concept.

263 Interestingly, like other recent publications, the book *SDAs Believe* does not address the question of whether and when the "investigative judgment" will pass from the dead to the living. It seems that the distance between the year 1844 and the present time renders this notion less and less meaningful. This illustrates the possibility that a doctrinal view gradually disappears by losing its power both to explain present experience and to energize believers.

264 In the view of Uriah Smith, the difference between the pre-advent investigative judgment on believers and the investigative judgment on the wicked during the millennium was the following: While the former was "to decide one question, and that is, who are to be saved when Christ appears," there was no need during the latter "to ascertain whether they are to be saved or not, for that question is at that time already settled," leaving only "the degrees of their punishment" to be meted out by the heavenly court ("In the Question Chair," *RH,* 26 April 1892, 264-265).

265 "God has not seen fit to decide by his own omniscience who are worthy of immortality, but has left the determination of that question to the investigation and decision of the Judgment, that an intelligent universe may be able to understand for themselves the righteousness of his doings" (Uriah Smith, "The Judgment of Rev. 14:7," *RH,* 13 January 1874, 36).

This teaching had been accepted and elaborated on by Ellen White[266] and was again expressed in the 1931 Statement of Fundamental Beliefs (#16). Still, it appears that it left quite a number of Seventh-day Adventists rather apprehensive at the thought of having their names come up for review next in the heavenly assize.[267]

Since the 1950s, there has been a gradual but marked change in the way Seventh-day Adventists have described the nature and function of the investigative judgment. While still speaking of the "decisions" of the heavenly court and the "complete and thorough check" it was to make "of all the candidates for eternal life," the book *Questions on Doctrine* cautiously adopted a different tone:

> The great judgment scene of heaven will clearly reveal those who have been growing in grace and developing Christlike characters ... The child of God, with his title clear to heaven, need entertain no fear of any judgment day.[268]

In 1972, Heppenstall offered a non-traditional interpretation of the pre-advent judgment, defining it as the final vindication before the entire universe of God as well as of his government, character, and people. His concept was free of the rather perfectionistic overtones often connected to it.[269] To him, also, there was "nothing to fear," for the judgment "does not mean uncertainty but triumph."[270] This new emphasis on the assurance of faith found official recognition by the denomination in

---

266 Ellen White, *The Great Controversy,* 479-491. For a detailed analysis of her concept of the last judgment including its pre-Advent investigative phase, see Jairyong Lee, "Faith and Works in Ellen G. White's Doctrine of the Last Judgment" (Ph.D. dissertation, Andrews University, 1985).

267 Walter R. Martin, a well-informed observer and critic of the Seventh-day Adventist Church, even surmised that this doctrine was intended "to discipline Christians by the threat of impending judgment" *(The Kingdom of the Cults,* rev. and enl. ed. [Minneapolis, Minn.: Bethany House, 1985], 473). Though the intentionality of this effect may be questioned, it is difficult to deny that some pedagogical influence may, indeed, have been at work here.

268 *QOD,* 417, 419; see also ibid., 421-442 passim. In a similar way, C. Mervyn Maxwell argued in 1981 that the pre-advent judgment was to "disclose" God's faithful people *(God Cares,* vol. 1, *The Message of Daniel for You and Your Family* [Boise, Idaho: PPPA, 1981]), 242-245.

269 M. L. Andreasen, for example, had linked the cleansing of the sanctuary to "God's vindication" through a final generation of believers that would become "victorious over every sin" and "demonstrate that it is possible to live without sin." For "through the last generation of saints God stands finally vindicated ... The cleansing of the sanctuary in heaven is dependent upon the cleansing of God's people on earth" *(The Sanctuary Service,* 2d rev. ed., 299-321). Similarly, G. D. Keough advanced the view that "the cleansing [justification] of the sanctuary is the vindication [justification] of God in the judgment ... through the completion of a perfect character" ("The Cleansing of the Sanctuary," *Ministry,* January 1962, 30-33).

270 Edward Heppenstall, *Our High Priest: Jesus Christ in the Heavenly Sanctuary* (Washington, D.C.: RHPA, 1972), 80, 98-100, 121-124, 188-189, 206-207. In a later essay, Heppenstall again emphasized that "the pre-Advent judgment is *in favor of* the saints ... [and] not a scheme of retribution because God has doubts about His people. It is a true revelation of their standing before God as they are found to be in Christ. No judgment from His sanctuary can put the saints in jeopardy" ("The Pre-Advent Judgment," *Ministry,* December 1981, 12-15).

1980 when it was included in the Fundamental Beliefs of the Seventh-day Adventist Church.[271] It has received widespread support since.[272] Echoing some of James White's early arguments, Seventh-day Adventists today affirm that

> the investigative judgment is not when God finally decides to accept or reject us. All those written in heaven have already been accepted by God (Eph. 1:6). Instead, the judgment merely finalizes our choice to keep or reject Him ... Antagonists unfairly depict the doctrine as God scrutinizing the books in order to decide who is saved or lost. 'The Lord knows those who are his' (2 Tim. 2:19). An omniscient God doesn't need the investigative judgment; the onlooking universe, however, does.[273]

Still more recently, some Adventist writers have even further departed from the historic understanding of the pre-advent judgment (1) by questioning the appropriateness of the traditional notions of an "investigative judgment"[274] and of a "pre-Advent judgment,"[275] (2) by conceding that Dan 8 actually speaks not of "penitential"

271 "Abiding in Him we ... have the assurance of salvation now and in the judgment" (#10). "The investigative judgment reveals ... who among the dead ... are deemed worthy [of eternal life] ... [It also] makes manifest who ... are ready for translation" (#23). For the full text, see below, app. 3, col. 3, pars. 10, 23.

272 See, e.g., Ivan T. Blazen, "Justification and Judgment," in *The Seventy Weeks, Leviticus, and the Nature of Prophecy,* Daniel and Revelation Committee Series, ed. Frank B. Holbrook, vol. 3 (Silver Spring, Md.: Biblical Research Institute, General Conference of SDAs, 1986), 339-388. According to Blazen, the pre-advent judgment tests and attests the believers' saving relationship with Christ and affirms their justification by faith alone. Therefore, it does not rob Christians of the assurance of faith. Likewise, the "Consensus Document" of the Sanctuary Review Committee (1980) affirms that the pre-advent judgment "reveals our relationship to Christ." Thus, "for the child of God, knowledge of Christ's intercession in the judgment brings assurance, not anxiety" ("Christ in the Heavenly Sanctuary," in *Doctrine of the Sanctuary,* ed. Holbrook, 225-233). See also Tim Crosby, "Conditionalism," 16-18; Richard M. Davidson, "The Good News of Yom Kippur," *JATS* 2:2 (1991): 4-27; Samuele Bacchiocchi, "The Good News of the Judgment," *Adventists Affirm* 6:2 (1992): 37-44, 48; Martin Weber, "Heaven on Our Side: Looking at the Pre-Advent Judgment," *AR,* 26 March 1992, 8-11; and Norman R. Gulley, "Focusing on Christ, Not Ourselves," *Ministry,* October 1994, 28-30.

273 Clifford Goldstein, "Investigating the Investigative Judgment," *Ministry,* February 1992, 8, 6-9.

274 "The purpose of this pre-advent judgment is not, as our challengers erroneously assume, to determine 'whether a person shall be saved or not' ... Possibly the term investigative judgment is infelicitous since it may connote that decisions as to a person's destiny are being made during it. But such is not the case. Probably it might more correctly be called an audit ... The audit is just confirmatory" (Arnold V. Wallenkampf, "A Brief Review of Some of the Internal and External Challengers to the Seventh-day Adventist Teachings on the Sanctuary and the Atonement," in *The Sanctuary and the Atonement,* ed. Wallenkampf and Lesher, 597). See also idem, *What Every Christian Should Know about Being Justified,* 112-124; and Adams, *The Sanctuary,* 117-129 (favoring the term "pre-Advent judgment" as a substitute).

275 "'Investigative judgment' is not the same thing as 'pre-Advent judgment' and is based on other premises. I am simply rejecting out-of-hand the idea suggested by pre-Advent judgment.

but rather of "sacrilegious" defilement/desecration,[276] (3) by extending the scope of the pre-advent judgment so as to include the unbelieving world and the divine retribution upon it,[277] and (4) by reducing the judgment on the living to a brief moment at the close of humankind's probationary time.[278]

While these views cannot be said to reflect the common belief of the church, the fact that they were expressed by respected theologians, printed in leading Adventist journals, and published in denominational books indicates the state of flux that seems to exist regarding the interpretation of the sanctuary doctrine in recent years.[279]

There is no pre-advent judgment except in the mind of God, where it is eternal, universal, and rhymes with divine discernment" (Provonsha, *A Remnant in Crisis,* 120).

276 Adams, *The Sanctuary,* chap. 6. "In Daniel 8 the focus is on an entity in open rebellion against God, and what we see there is *rebellious* or *sacrilegious defilement ...* It is on this point that the Seventh-day Adventist interpretation of Daniel 8:14 has been called into question. For historically we have seen in the text the antitypical cleansing of the sanctuary from the sins of God's people, whereas the fact of the matter is that clearly the emphasis in Daniel 8 is on the sins of the 'little horn' ... [Sacrilegious defilement] involves God's apostate people and the nations of the world in judgment, leading to condemnation and damnation" (ibid., 89, 102).

277 "This judgment is a divine process in which both God and His people, as well as their enemies, are included ... We have usually taught that its scope is ... limited to the saints ... The judgment in and from the heavenly sanctuary is not a private affair between God and the remnant church. It also has its counterpart on earth in judgments that are poured out upon the wicked as depicted in the seals, the trumpets, and the plagues of the Apocalypse" (Heppenstall, "The Pre-Advent Judgment," 12-15). Heppenstall's view may not exactly coincide with the official Adventist position; still, in authorized publications the church has recognized that "this heavenly assize will involve all persons (of whatever communion) who profess a relationship to God" (William H. Shea, *Selected Studies on Prophetic Interpretation,* Daniel and Revelation Committee Series, vol. 1 [Washington, D.C.: RHPA, 1982], 125). According to Adams, "the 'little horn' is a major target of the judgment" *(The Sanctuary,* 126); see also Gulley, "Focusing on Christ." This view is a long way off the position of the early SDAs who had limited the ministry of Christ since 1844, first, to "the righteous living" and, then, to them and "the righteous dead" (Ellen White, *Spiritual Gifts,* 1:198 [1858]; cf. idem, *Early Writings,* 280). In the late 1840s and the 1850s, the living saints would have included the faithful Millerite "Philadelphians," the lukewarm Sabbathkeeping "Laodiceans," and also some other "honest souls"; but, by definition, it excluded "nominal Christians" who were reckoned as part of fallen "Babylon." Thus, it can be said that even the official Adventist understanding of the pre-advent judgment has changed significantly over the years.

278 Douglas Bennett, "The Good News about the Judgment of the Living," *AR,* 16 June 1983, 14-15 ("It appears that instead of judging each person individually over a period of time prior to the close of probation, God will judge all the righteous living at the same time ... It seems appropriate to suggest that the close of probation will occur for all the living simultaneously").

279 The book *SDAs Believe* placed the traditional notion of investigation/determination and the recent concepts of revelation, ratification, and affirmation/confirmation side by side – irrespective of their possibly quite diverging implications (pp. 313-331). This reflected the overall tendency of the book which was to summarize rather than analyze Adventist theology as it has developed over the years. On the other hand, the recent publications on the sanctuary doctrine issued by the Daniel and Revelation Committee seem to have been geared toward defending the traditional understanding of the church while, at the same time, exploring

The place of the judgment. Central to the sanctuary doctrine was the belief that on October 22, 1844, Christ had moved from the first apartment of the heavenly sanctuary into the second apartment, the most holy place of the heavenly temple. Regardless of whether this change of locality was visualized in terms of going from one room to the next or was thought of as involving much larger space,[280] there was full agreement as to the existence in heaven of a literal, three-dimensional sanctuary, including its two apartments. Consequently, the decisive event of 1844 involved "the entrance of the high priest into the most holy place" of the heavenly temple.[281]

Intentionally or not, the 1931 statement of Adventist beliefs slightly reformulated this phrase speaking only of "the entrance of Christ as the high priest upon the judgment phase of His ministry in the heavenly sanctuary" (#14). The de-emphasis on the local aspect in favor of the temporal side of the heavenly ministry of Christ was hardly accidental in *Questions on Doctrine* and *Movement of Destiny,* which both simply affirmed the "reality" of the sanctuary in heaven but refrained from using the two-apartment scheme in setting forth the Adventist doctrinal view.[282]

Echoing the 1931 declaration, the 1980 statement of Seventh-day Adventist faith merely affirms that in 1844 Christ "entered the second and last phase of His atoning ministry" (#23).[283] In like manner, some recent church publications have spoken of the "two-phased priestly ministry" of Christ, avoiding discussion of two

possible new avenues of presenting this distinctive Adventist doctrine. See the seven volumes issued by the Biblical Research Institute of the General Conference of SDAs in 1982-1992. They were edited by Frank Holbrook and are listed in the bibliography. For vol. 1, see Shea, *Selected Studies on Prophetic Interpretation.*

280 Ellen White, *Early Writings,* 42, 55.

281 *A Declaration of the Fundamental Principles,* 1872, #10 (see below, app. 3, pp. 348-349). On Adventism's traditional literalistic approach to the Bible, see below, pp. 195-204.

282 See *QOD* (1957), 365-368, 384-386; and L. E. Froom, *MOD* (1971), 544, 545, 559. Dependence on overly literal conceptions of the heavenly sanctuary was explicitly rejected by Heppenstall who maintained that "the realities do not reside in places, materials, or architectural design, but in the divine activity" *(Our High Priest,* 20).

283 Delegates to the General Conference expressed themselves on both sides of the issue; the omission of the word "place" was both welcomed and deplored ("Twelfth Business Meeting," *RH,* 27 April 1980, 14-16). In addition to voting the new statement of Fundamental Beliefs, the Dallas Conference also amended and voted the section of the *Church Manual* on "Doctrinal Instruction for Baptismal Candidates" which still affirms that "Upon his ascension Christ began his ministry as high priest in the holy place of the heavenly sanctuary ... a work of investigative judgment began as Christ entered the second phase of His ministry, in the Most Holy Place" ("Fifth Business Meeting," *AR,* 21 April 1980, 20-21, 27). In 1984, the Annual Council recommended to delete this "Outline of Doctrinal Beliefs" from the *Church Manual* ("Actions of General Interest from the Annual Council – 1," *AR,* 20 December 1984, 17). However, the 1985 General Conference decided to postpone taking an action on this issue ("Eleventh Business Meeting," *AR,* 5 July 1985, 21-22).

apartments or rooms.[284] These publications have also carefully distinguished between the objective reality of the heavenly sanctuary, on the one hand, and a literalistic view of its structure, on the other.[285] It seems that Adventists have become somewhat reluctant to express the sanctuary doctrine in terms of heavenly architecture or geography, preferring to speak of a change of function in Christ's priestly ministry.[286]

The Spirit of Prophecy

Movements that make an impact on the world do not only live on great ideas, they also depend on great people. Insofar as the Seventh-day Adventist Church has become such a movement, it is to be expected that it cherishes not only distinctive beliefs but also some distinguished people. Among them, the unchallenged place of honor belongs to Ellen White, who left an indelible impression on the church she loved, criticized, and built up for almost seventy years of her life.

Inclined as they were to see their world through the eyes of biblical prophecy, the Adventist pioneers also interpreted Ellen White's ministry in this light. This helps to understand why they came to regard "the testimony of Jesus" and "the spirit of prophecy" (Rev 19:10) as a synonym for her voluminous writings. But this view, too, took time to develop over the years.

At first, Sabbatarian Adventists defined "the faith of Jesus" (Rev 14:12) and "the testimony of Jesus" (Rev 12:17) quite comprehensively as denoting the sum total of

---

284 Frank B. Holbrook, ed. *Issues in the Book of Hebrews,* Daniel and Revelation Committee Series, vol. 4 (Silver Spring, Md.: Biblical Research Institute, General Conference of SDAs, 1989). See also the 1980 "Consensus Document" of the Sanctuary Review Committee ("Christ in the Heavenly Sanctuary," in *Doctrine of the Sanctuary,* ed. Holbrook, 225-233).

285 William G. Johnsson, "The Heavenly Cultus in the Book of Hebrews – Figurative or Real," in *The Sanctuary and the Atonement,* ed. Wallenkampf and Lesher, 362-379; reprinted as "The Heavenly Sanctuary – Figurative or Real?" in *Issues in the Book of Hebrews,* ed. Holbrook, 35-51.

286 Adams has argued in some detail against "extreme literalism," i.e., "a literalistic conceptualization" which looks for a "one-on-one correspondence between the earthly type and the heavenly reality"; instead, their relationship should be seen "primarily on a deeper functional and theological level" involving a "functional correspondence." To Adams, the "reality" of the heavenly sanctuary does not necessitate a physical, compartmentalized building. In his view, even the author of Hebrews shows no interest in "celestial geography" *(The Sanctuary,* 43-82, 105-115). Other publications, however, continue to emphasize the literal and spatial character of the heavenly sanctuary. "The Bible is explicit: a literal, physical sanctuary exists in heaven. Attempts have been made to undermine the investigative judgment doctrine by denying the reality of the heavenly sanctuary and emphasizing Christ's *work* in heaven at the expense of the location of that work ... [But] only by understanding that the sanctuary is literal can one truly grasp Christ's ministry in it" (Goldstein, *False Balances,* 102). In like manner, *SDAs Believe* argued that the heavenly sanctuary is "a real place" with two apartments and "furnishings" (p. 314). Cf. Maxwell, *God Cares,* 1:241 (in 1844, Jesus traveled "from one part of heaven to another").

the teachings of Jesus and his apostles as expressed in the New Testament canon.[287] This conviction was generally shared, and frequently expressed, between 1847 and 1857.[288] Only rarely "the testimony of Jesus" was related to "the spirit of prophecy" (Rev 19:10), but no implications were drawn from this.[289] Beginning in 1858 – and ever since – these terms were specifically and more and more exclusively applied to the subject of "spiritual gifts" and, particularly, to the prophetic ministry of Ellen White.[290] Though the identification of the testimony of Jesus with the spirit of prophecy working through Ellen White was criticized by some in the 1880s[291] and also later on,[292] it was fully accepted and defended by the church at large.

In recent years, however, Adventists have come to rethink the meaning and usage of the phrase "testimony of Jesus" as well as "spirit of prophecy." On the basis of the

---

287 To them, this included such diverse aspects as the parables of Jesus dealing with their past "advent experience" and the "shut-door" doctrine (Matt 25:1-10), the command to pray for the sick and to wash one another's feet, the doctrine of repentance, faith, and sanctification, the three angels' messages, and the statements concerning the life, death, resurrection, ascension, and second coming of Christ. For references, see the following footnote.

288 Bates, *The Seventh Day Sabbath,* 52; idem, *Second Advent Way Marks,* 68-72; James White, "The Third Angel's Message," 66-67; Ellen White to Bro. Pierce, 1851, EGWRC, AU, Berrien Springs, Mich.; [James White], "Angels of Rev. xiv – No. 4," *RH,* 23 December 1851, 71; idem, "The Faith of Jesus," *RH,* 5 August 1852, 52-53; idem, "The Faith of Jesus," *RH,* 28 February-7 March 1854, 44, 53-54; idem, "The Faith of Jesus," *RH,* 20 February 1855, 180-182; idem, "An Appeal: To Those Who Profess the Third Angel's Message," *RH,* 20 November 1856, 20-21; and Ellen White to S. Pierce, 1857, EGWRC, AU, Berrien Springs, Mich.

289 James White, "The Testimony of Jesus," *RH,* 18 December 1855, 92-93; and idem, "The Testimony of Jesus," *RH,* 11 December 1856, 45.

290 R. F. Cottrell, "Spiritual Gifts," preface to Ellen White, *Spiritual Gifts* (1858), 1:15-16; idem, "Spiritual Gifts," *RH,* 25 February 1858, 125-126; Isaac Sanborn, "To the Law and Testimony," *RH,* 20 October 1863, 161-162; James White, preface to Ellen White, *Spiritual Gifts* (1864), 3:26; J. N. Andrews, "The Testimony of Jesus," *RH,* 3 March 1868, 177-178; J. H. Waggoner, "'The Law and the Testimony,'" *RH,* 20 July 1869, 27; and Milton C. Wilcox, "'Despise Not Prophesyings,'" *RH,* 29 March 1881, 196.

291 W. H. Littlejohn, "Seventh-day Adventists and the Testimony of Jesus Christ," *RH,* 8-22 May 1883, 290, 307-308, 322-323 ("[since 1844] they have had in their midst the spirit of prophecy," i.e., "the gift of prophecy"); idem, "The Testimony of Jesus the Same as the Spirit of Prophecy: Objections Answered," *RH,* 31 July 1883, 481-483 (Littlejohn's SDA objector-friend defends the traditional SDA position); and idem, "The Testimony of Jesus Again," ibid., 488-489 (Littlejohn here mentions that the first article had "evoked considerable adverse criticism" concerning his approach to this SDA "tenet of faith").

292 In 1970, Richard B. Lewis decried the deeply entrenched use of the phrase "Spirit of Prophecy" as a synonym for Ellen White and the writings of the Adventist prophet. To him, the Holy Spirit himself was the Spirit of Prophecy, which inspired "the literary products of all inspired writers." He called on Adventists to simply speak of "the writings of Ellen White," in order not to give the false impression as if the "spirit of prophecy" had "exclusive reference to a modern prophet" ("The 'Spirit of Prophecy'," *Spectrum,* 2:4 (1970): 69-72). However, it seems that this call faded away largely unnoticed.

biblical data, Adventist scholars have concluded that "the testimony of Jesus" has reference, first, to the prophetic message of the Apocalypse itself and, then, also to inspired writings in general, including – as Adventists believe – those of Ellen White.[293] On the other hand, the "spirit of prophecy" designates the Holy Spirit himself, who inspires the prophets. The spirit of prophecy or the prophetic gift, Seventh-day Adventists affirm, has been manifested also through Ellen White.[294]

The new understanding and use of the phrase "spirit of prophecy" in the mid-1850s was also an indication of the different role that the church was about to give to Ellen White. Up until that time, Sabbatarian Adventists had held to and practiced a strict form of the Protestant *sola scriptura* principle. Viewing the Bible as their only rule of faith and practice, they had developed and defended all of their doctrinal and ethical teachings by an appeal to the Scriptures alone. While treating her visions as corroborative evidence concerning questions of biblical interpretation, Ellen White was not looked upon as a norm of Adventist doctrine or lifestyle.[295] Until the autumn of 1855, the Sabbatarian Adventists could claim that they had never referred to their prophet as an "authority on any point."[296]

By the end of 1855, the uncompromising position of James White concerning the visions of his wife met with the displeasure of those who felt that it slighted the prophet's proper authority.[297] During a conference in Battle Creek, in November, a statement was voted that, for the first time, declared Ellen White's prophetic

---

293 Jean Zurcher, "Le témoignage de Jésus est l'esprit de la prophétie," in *Études sur l'Apocalypse*, 1:230-250. Similarly, Gerhard Pfandl defined the testimony of Jesus as "the testimony born by Jesus Himself, either in His own life and ministry, or by the working of the Holy Spirit inspiring His servants the prophets." According to SDA belief, "Christ's selfdisclosure through the prophets" includes the ministry and writings of Ellen White ("The Remnant Church and the Spirit of Prophecy," in *Symposium on Revelation – Book 2*, ed. Holbrook, 295-333).

294 Pfandl, "The Remnant Church and the Spirit of Prophecy."

295 As early as 1847 James White declared that "the bible *[sic]* is a perfect, and complete revelation. It is our only rule of faith and practice ... True visions are given to lead us to God, and his written word; but those that are given for a new rule of faith and practice, separate from the bible *[sic]*, cannot be from God, and should be rejected" ([James White and Ellen White], *A Word to the "Little Flock,"* 13). Ellen White fully concurred with this belief (see *Early Writings*, 78, 87-88). A few years later, James White elaborated on the practical implications of this view. "Every Christian is therefore in duty bound to take the Bible as a perfect rule of faith and duty. He should pray fervently to be aided by the Holy Spirit in searching the Scriptures for the whole truth, and for his whole duty. He is not at liberty to turn from them to learn his duty through any of the gifts. We say that the very moment he does, he places the gifts in a wrong place, and takes an extremely dangerous position" ("The Gifts of the Gospel Church," *RH*, 21 April 1851, 70).

296 James White, "A Test," *RH*, 16 October 1855, 61.

297 Hiram Bingham, "Dear Bro. White," *RH*, 14 February 1856, 158; and James White, "Note," ibid. See also James White, "The Gifts. – Their Object," *RH*, 28 February 1856, 172.

utterances to be indeed "a test or rule" for Adventists – albeit subject to the Bible as "the great rule."[298] This was, indeed, "a turning point in SDA history."[299]

Still, in the 1872 statement of Adventist beliefs, no reference was made to Ellen White. Writers in the Adventist journals did not refer to or quote the prophet in support of their views. Questions directed to the editors were consistently answered from the Bible alone. In the 1880s, biblical questions were, for the first time, answered by referring to what Ellen White previously had written on the subject.[300] However,

> the views we hold on the question of the Sanctuary were not suggested by any vision from sister White, and in all our investigations of the subject we never appeal to any of her writings, but rest the argument wholly upon the Scriptures, taking the ground on this, as upon all other subjects, that whatever is not sustained by the Bible must fall.[301]

In 1951, a statement on Ellen White was, for the first time, inserted in the list of Fundamental Doctrines of Seventh-day Adventists.[302] The 1980 revision of the Fundamental Beliefs added the thought that "her writings are a continuing and authoritative source of truth," though they must still be tested by the Scriptures (#17).[303] It seems that the trend of enhancing the authority of Ellen White in the church that had begun in 1855 has continued until today.

---

298 "Address," *RH,* 4 December 1855, 78-79.

299 Arthur L. White, *Ellen G. White,* 1:326-330. White was satisfied with this turn of events, which provided her with new opportunities to share her views with believers through the pages of the *Review & Herald,* in numerous pamphlets, and through a growing number of books ("Dear Brethren and Sisters," *RH,* 10 January 1856, 118). However, in later years, she warned against the misuse of her writings as a shortcut to Bible truth. "The Testimonies are not to take the place of the Word ... Let all prove their position from the Scriptures and substantiate every point they claim as truth from the revealed Word of God" *(Evangelism,* 256). "If you are in doubt upon any subject you must first consult Scripture" *(Testimonies,* 5:512).

300 W. H. Littlejohn was one of the first to use this approach ("Scripture Questions," *RH,* 17 April 1883, 250).

301 [Uriah Smith], "J. W. Morton and the Sanctuary Question," *RH,* 2 August 1887, 489. Cf. L. A. Smith, "The Nature of Our Work," *RH,* 15 November 1887, 712. This position was reaffirmed in 1957 when it was declared that "while Adventists hold the writings of Ellen G. White in high esteem, yet these are not the source of our expositions. We base our teachings on the Scriptures, the only foundation of all true Christian doctrine" *(QOD,* 93).

302 The added statement reads, "That the gift of the Spirit of prophecy is one of the identifying marks of the remnant church ... [SDAs] recognize that this gift was manifested in the life and ministry of Ellen G. White" *(SDAY* [Washington, D.C.: RHPA, 1972], 6 [#19]).

303 In 1986, the General Conference of SDAs adopted a document that provided guidelines on how to study the Bible. Commenting on the writings of Ellen White, it said: "Seventh-day Adventists believe that God inspired Ellen G. White. Therefore, her expositions on any given biblical passage offer an inspired guide to the meaning of texts without exhausting their meaning or preempting the task of exegesis." According to the document, her writings should be consulted even before turning "to various commentaries and secondary helps such as scholarly works to see how others have dealt with the passage" ("Methods of Bible Study," *Ministry,* April 1987, 23, 22-24).

The (Remnant) Church[304]

As has been shown, in addition to their fundamental doctrines that they share with other Christian denominations, Seventh-day Adventists also advocate a number of distinctive teachings. Together these form a particular body of beliefs providing Adventists with a special sense of their message and mission. From this, a unique self-understanding naturally follows which finds prominent expression in the denomination's preferred self-designation as the "remnant church" (Rev 12:17).[305]

At the outset, it is rather to be expected that shifting views on fundamental or distinctive Adventist doctrines may also, to a degree, affect the self-understanding of the church. Already during its initial, shut-door phase (1844-1851), the Sabbatarian group had a pronounced sense of particularism.[306] Convinced of their peculiar role in salvation history, these Adventists continued to hold quite distinctive views about themselves.

304 Only two particular aspects of Adventist ecclesiology are treated in this section. Other important ecclesiological issues include the foundation and authority of the church, the marks of the church (unity, catholicity, apostolicity, holiness), its organization, offices, ordinances, and mission as well as its relationship to Israel, to other churches, to society, and to the state. SDAs have consistently sought to build their views on the New Testament, but no major work has been written on Adventist ecclesiology to date. In recent years, there seems to be a growing interest within the church on questions of ecclesiology. In the past, SDAs have experienced major changes in their views on church organization (see below, p. 217, n. 417), the theology of mission (see below, p. 216, n. 413), and open/closed communion (see below, p. 269, n. 224). More recently, their relationship to other churches and to society in general has been undergoing certain notable developments (see below, pp. 208-213). On the whole, however, the remarkable stability of SDA ecclesiological thinking should not be overlooked.

305 One of Ellen White's first publications was the 1846 Broadside entitled "To the Little Remnant Scattered Abroad"; it contained her first visions and was addressed to those Adventists who continued to hold to the prophetic significance of 1844. Since 1849, the term was used regularly for and by Sabbath-keeping Adventists. "Seventh-day Adventists," wrote George I. Butler in 1874, "have everywhere claimed to be the 'remnant' church for the last twenty-five years" ("Visions and Prophecy," *RH,* 2 June 1874, 193). In 1942, a "Baptismal Vow" was included in the *Church Manual,* which contained the following question: "Do you believe that the Seventh-day Adventist Church constitutes the remnant church?" *(SDACM,* 1942 ed., 87). In 1970, it was revised to read: "… is the remnant church of Bible prophecy?" *(SDACM,* 1971 ed., 61). At the 1952 Bible Conference, SDAs identified themselves with the 144,000 and "the Remnant Church" of the Apocalypse (T. H. Jemison, "The Companions of the Lamb," in *Our Firm Foundation,* 2:403-424; and W. R. Beach, "The Gospel Commission and the Remnant Church," ibid., 2:425-462). See also *SDAE,* 1976 ed., s.v. "Remnant Church."

306 "I saw that we are the only people upon earth from whom God is to get glory … The only company who can praise and honor God, I saw, are those who are keeping the commandments of God and have the faith of Jesus" (Ellen G. White, "To the Church in Your Place," Manuscript 5a, 1850, EGWRC, AU, Berrien Springs, Mich.). Contextually, this statement deals with the Sabbatarian manner of divine worship which, at that time, involved loud singing and shouting to the glory of God.

Just as Noah's ark was the only place of safety, of salvation, for the people of the antediluvian world, "the remnant church," the Seventh-day Adventist Church, is the only visible place or organization that God has designated as the place of safety, of salvation, for the people of our day.[307]

At other times, however, Adventists expressed themselves more guardedly, using less exclusive language in describing their relationship to fellow believers and other Christian churches. In 1870, for example, when someone asked whether Adventists claimed to constitute "the only true church on earth," church leaders responded by saying that "the Seventh-day Adventists have never put forth this claim. We attach great importance to the doctrines which we cherish; but we have ever held that God has true people wherever men are found who are obeying what light they have."[308]

Especially since the 1950s, Adventists have tended to describe themselves in less particularistic terms.[309] In 1982, the *Adventist Review* editorialized that "Adventists are not the only people through whom God is working, but He *is* working through us."[310] Observers of the church have noted in statements of this kind a trend towards a more functional ecclesiology among Seventh-day Adventists.[311]

Along with this, there seems to exist today, at times, a certain reluctance on the part of Adventists to identify themselves fully and unreservedly with the "remnant church" of Bible prophecy.[312] Some feel more comfortable seeing the Adventist

307 W. W. Fordham, "The Remnant Church," *Ministry,* June 1970, 61.

308 J. N. Andrews and J. H. Waggoner, "The Articles of Eld. T. M. Preble," *RH,* 15 February 1870, 60. In 1887, Uriah Smith surmised that "even Seventh Day Baptists, if they are saved" would help compose the last generation remnant ("J. W. Morton and the Sanctuary Question").

309 The book *Questions on Doctrine* stated that "millions of devout Christians of all faiths throughout all past centuries, as well as those today who are sincerely trusting in Christ ... are unquestionably saved" (p. 184); for "God has a precious remnant ... in every church" (p. 192) who are living up to the light they have. However, "God has brought the Seventh-day Adventist movement into being to carry His special message to the world at this time" (p. 190). See *QOD,* 177-202. This change, in 1957, from presenting SDAs as *the* remnant church of Bible prophecy to their being only a part of it appears to have been a conscious move on the part of the authors of the book. In the view of a recent observer of the church, *Questions on Doctrine* "reflected a sense of change in how Adventists viewed themselves – and others" (Kenneth R. Samples, "The Recent Truth About Seventh-day Adventism," *Christianity Today,* 5 February 1990, 19).

310 W. G. Johnsson, "The Review in Your Future," *AR,* 9 December 1982, 9, 3, 9-10. Cf. idem, "Uplift Christ," *Ministry,* February 1982, 7: "This is the people of God. I am not saying that we are the only people of God, for God has other people outside this fold. But I believe that he has raised up this people to give a particular message at this particular time of earth's history, and I believe He is working a miracle in the world that no other church can match." See also Rolf J. Pöhler, "Wie sehen die Adventisten ihr Verhältnis zu anderen Kirchen? *Adventecho,* September 1988, 10-11.

311 See, e.g., Hans-Dieter Reimer, "Adventistische Theologie," *Materialdienst* 40:9 (1977): 236-244.

312 Interestingly, the Dallas Declaration of Fundamental Beliefs (1980) only cautiously identifies the SDA Church with the apocalyptic remnant. Its statements on ecclesiology consistently

church as part of God's (present or future) remnant, which is made up of all true believers from various denominations. Or, stressing their "solidarity with historic Christianity," they may describe themselves in more general terms as "an authentic church" possessing "the four classical marks of the biblical church," i.e., as "an authentic expression of the body of Christ."[313]

Some scholars have cautiously reflected on or even redefined the historic self-understanding of Adventists and their mission as the "remnant church."[314] Others, noting the shift of meaning regarding the remnant concept in first-world Adventism during the past forty years, are strongly reaffirming the traditional identification of Seventh-day Adventists as the only true and final end-time "Remnant Church."[315] It remains to be seen what long-range impact these recent discussions will have on the church as a whole.

Seventh-day Adventists have once before experienced a significant readjustment of their ecclesiology. For about ten years after 1844, they identified themselves with

employ biblical concepts and phrases. "The universal church" consists of "the faithful of all the ages," while the eschatological "remnant" is "called out" to proclaim God's end-time message and remain faithful to him in midst of "widespread apostasy." Only in referring to the gift of prophecy – manifested in Ellen White – does the declaration speak of "the remnant church" (see app. 3, col. 3, pars. 11-13, 17). Thus, intentionally or not, the careful wording of this text leaves room for a more theological rather than a strictly confessional interpretation of its statements on the church/remnant. Such an approach seems to be reflected, e.g., by Santo Calarco, "God's Universal Remnant," *Ministry,* August 1993, 5-7, 30, who describes the eschatological remnant church as open and universal, rather than as exclusive, separatist, parochial, and sectarian.

313 "The Church of God: Its Nature, Function, and Authority," *AR,* 1 October 1992, 27, 22-27. This article is an abbreviated version of a position paper on the church commissioned by the North American Division of SDAs. The four classical marks of the church are: holiness, catholicity (universality), apostolicity, and unity.

314 See, e.g., the carefully worded conclusion in Richard Lehmann's essay presented at the 1993 Bible Conferences of the Euro-Africa Division of SDAs ("L'Eglise du reste," in *L'Église de Jesus-Christ: Sa mission et son ministère dans le monde,* Études en Ecclésiologie Adventiste, vol. 2, ed. Comité de recherche biblique, Conférences bibliques de la Division euroafricaine 1993 [Dammarie-lès-Lys Cedex, France: Editions Vie et Santé, 1995], 92); cf. Kit Watts, "The Remnant Is as the Remnant Does," *AR,* 3 September 1992, 5 ("if we don't act like the remnant, we aren't the remnant"). For some less traditional reflections on the remnant motif, see Jack W. Provonsha, "The Church as a Prophetic Minority," *Spectrum* 12:1 (1981): 18-23; idem, *A Remnant in Crisis* (1993), 37-72, 152-153, 161-169; Branson, "Covenant, Holy War, and Glory: Motifs in Adventist Identity" (1983); Charles Scriven, "The 'Remnant' and the Church: A Reconsideration, 1984," TMs, AHC, JWL, AU, Berrien Springs, Mich.; idem, "The Real Truth About the Remnant," *Spectrum* 17:1 (1986): 6-13; Rice, *The Reign of God* (1985), 230-232; and Bruce C. Moyer, "Love in Practice: A Portrait of God's Final Remnant," *AR,* 29 March 1990, 11-12.

315 See, e.g., *Adventists Affirm* 2:2 (1988); Gerhard F. Hasel, "Who Are the Remnant?" *Adventists Affirm* 7:2 (1993): 5-13, 31; and Clifford Goldstein, *The Remnant* (Boise, Idaho: PPPA, 1994). The book *SDAs Believe* (1988) likewise affirmed the concept of SDAs as "the remnant church" of biblical prophecy (pp. 133-179, 216-229).

the "Philadelphia" phase of the church (Rev 3:7-13) and described the "nominal Adventists" as lukewarm "Laodiceans."[316] As early as 1851, Ellen White reapplied the counsel to the Laodicean church (Rev 3:14-22) to Sabbatarian Adventists.[317] Her husband and others followed suit.[318] However, it was James White who, in the fall of 1856, first identified Seventh-day Adventists with the Laodicean church of Rev 3.[319] This reinterpretation sparked a spiritual revival at the time; beyond that, it also served to protect the church against ecclesiastical triumphalism, which seems to threaten any religious movement holding a high view of its particular calling, message, and mission.

The Nature of Doctrinal Development

Having investigated a number of notable doctrinal developments and illustrated the various kinds of doctrinal changes that took place even in the relatively short history of Seventh-day Adventism, it may be useful now to consider a number of questions arising from these findings. For example, how did new doctrinal insights relate to previous beliefs? What impact did these doctrinal developments have on the character of Seventh-day Adventism as a whole? Which forces from within or without the church have contributed to these developments?

This section addresses itself to these three issues. To this end, the nature of the doctrinal changes observed is discussed first, followed by some considerations about the direction they have apparently taken. Finally, a few remarks are offered regarding the social forces that seem to have been at work at it.

Homogeneous Developments

A large portion of the doctrinal modifications described above (and there are others) can be defined as homogeneous developments. This means that essentially they have provided new doctrinal insights, deepened the understanding of faith, and refined

316 Hiram Edson, "An Appeal to the Laodicean Church," *Advent Review Extra*, September 1850, 1; Joseph Bates, "The Laodicean Church," *RH*, November 1850, 7-8; idem, "Our Labor in the Philadelphia and Laodicean Churches," *RH*, 19 August 1851, 13-14; James White, "Who May Hear the Truth?" *RH*, 17 February 1852, 94; idem, "The Immediate Coming of Christ," *RH*, 17 February 1853, 156; and idem, "The 144,000," *RH*, 3 July 1856, 76-77.

317 Ellen White to Bro. Pierce, Letter 2, 1851, EGWRC, AU, Berrien Springs, Mich.; idem, "To the Brethren and Sisters," *RH*, 10 June 1852, 21; and idem, *Testimonies*, 1:126.

318 James White, "The Faith of Jesus," *RH*, 19 August 1852, 60-61; idem, "Eastern Tour," *RH*, 14 October 1852, 96; idem, "Gospel Order," *RH*, 6 December 1853, 173; and N. W. Rockwell, "From Brother Rockwell," *RH*, 8 September 1853, 71.

319 James White, "Watchman, What of the Night?" *RH*, 9 October 1856, 184. Here, and in successive articles, White called for revival and spiritual reformation; the response in the church was quick and positive. For more information, see Felix A. Lorenz, Sr., "A Study of Early Adventist Interpretations of the Laodicean Message with Emphasis on the Writings of Mrs. Ellen G. White" (B.D. thesis, SDA Theological Seminary, Washington, D.C., 1951).

theological interpretations regarding existing beliefs – without, however, involving the revision or abandonment of previously held doctrinal views. In this way, a number of Adventist doctrines have attained deeper significance or developed new connotations, implications, or applications.

Among the Adventist teachings whose theological significance has increased over the years, the doctrine of the atonement of Christ on the cross is a prime example. Other beliefs have gradually gained more practical relevance in the life of the church, such as the doctrine of righteousness by faith, the authority and function of the writings of Ellen White, or the meaning of the Sabbath in a world marked by human restlessness, social injustice, and political oppression. Then there are teachings that have become particularly important at a time when cultural forces tended to further their neglect in the church. This is reflected, e.g., in the statements on intra-church relations as well as on marriage and the family which, in 1980, were added to the list of Fundamental Beliefs.[320]

There are other doctrines held by Adventists that outwardly and verbally remained more or less identical but whose meaning was still adapted in certain respects over the years. These include, e.g., the changing connotations of the belief that the *parousia* of Christ will occur "soon," the role of obedience to the law of God in view of the doctrine of salvation by grace through faith alone, the proper meaning of the "blotting out" of sins from the sanctuary in heaven,[321] the social dimensions of the Sabbath as a day of rest and freedom, and the perceived ecological implications of the doctrine of creation.[322]

At times, Seventh-day Adventists have also come to apply certain biblical concepts in new ways, which either have enlarged their traditional views or focused attention on some particular aspects of these theological concepts. This is the case, e.g., with the meaning of the "law" in Galatians,[323] the scope of the "pre-advent judgment," and the interpretation of both "the testimony of Jesus" and "the spirit of prophecy." All of these developments have contributed to the rather harmonious unfolding of the body of Adventist doctrinal beliefs.

Heterogeneous Developments

Of considerably greater significance for the present study are those doctrinal changes that involved some revisions and corrections of traditional views. Rather than merely

---

320 See below, app. 3, col. 3, pars. 13, 22. Already in 1970, the inclusion of a statement on human (race) equality into the Doctrinal Instruction for Baptismal Candidates and the Baptismal Vow was indicative of this burning social issue, particularly as seen from a North American perspective (see *SDACM,* 1971 ed., 54, 61 [#6, 13]).

321 One could also mention the shifting views regarding the local/spatial or temporal character of the final cleansing of the heavenly sanctuary.

322 On the latter, see app. 3, col. 3, pars. 6-7, which were added to the statement of Fundamental Beliefs in 1980.

323 For details, see below, pp. 297-306.

expanding or amplifying Adventist beliefs, they apparently required at least a partial reversal and abandonment of previous teachings. These doctrinal modifications have likewise affected the church's perception of the relative significance of certain Adventist teachings and have also modified some of their connotations, implications, and applications.

A prime example of the virtual disappearance of a teaching that had lost its significance and could no longer be harmonized with the present understanding and experience of Adventists is the shut-door doctrine, which had been unanimously shared by Sabbatarian Adventists for a number of years.[324] Yet, rather than simply discarding inadequate doctrinal views, they usually modified and revised them.

A number of doctrinal readjustments among Adventists involved the reinterpretation of biblical expressions that gradually came to be seen in a new and different light. These include phrases like "son of God" (Was Jesus born or begotten of the Father?), "even/ing" (Does it denote 6 P.M. or sundown?), "investigative judgment" (Will it decide, determine, and evaluate or rather audit, reveal, and vindicate something/someone?), "Holy Spirit" (Does this term imply personality or simply energy?), and "this generation" (Matt 24:34).

Other doctrinal reversals came about when there was a change of view regarding the possible or inevitable implications of a particular teaching. This led Seventh-day Adventists to accept certain historic Christian doctrines whose seeming or real implications they previously may have wanted to avoid. This was the case with the doctrine of the Trinity (does it reflect a monarchianist heresy and a devaluation of the divine sacrifice on the cross?), the sinless human nature of Christ (can we reach character perfection?), the combined divine and human natures of Christ (was his death only a human sacrifice?), the atonement on the cross (does it lead to universalism or predestination?), and of the new birth (Has the kingdom of God already come?).

Still other doctrinal views were adopted or reinterpreted when certain implications of doctrinal tenets were discovered – implications that may not have been in harmony with traditional positions. Here one could mention the "open-door" view (Christ still serves as high priest for all who call on him), the Trinity (Jesus Christ is fully divine and the Holy Spirit acts in a personal way), and the confirmatory, rather than exploratory, function of the investigative judgment (we can have assurance and need not be afraid of the heavenly assize).

Particularly in the realm of prophetic interpretation, a number of biblical symbols and phrases were reapplied and reinterpreted over the years. As a result, Adventist eschatology – while retaining its basic identity and essential continuity – has been

---

324 See Rolf J. Pöhler, "'… And the Door Was Shut.' Seventh-day Adventists and the Shut-Door Doctrine in the Decade after the Great Disappointment, 1978," TMs, AHC, JWL, AU, Berrien Springs, Mich., 152-154. See also Ingemar Lindén, *1844 and the Shut Door Problem,* Acta Universitatis Upsaliensis, Studia Historico-Ecclesiastica Upsaliensis, vol. 35 (Uppsala: By the Author, 1982); and Robert W. Olson, "*The 'Shut Door' Documents"* (Washington, D.C., Ellen G. White Estate, 1982). See also below, pp. 297-298.

corrected and revised in several important respects. These doctrinal modifications are tied to phrases like "the sealing," "the time of trouble," "the two-horned beast," "the Laodicean church," "the king of the north," "the ten horns," "the daily," and "the battle of Armageddon." With them, development, at times, meant a disharmonious progression of beliefs.

Hermeneutical Readjustments

Experience and common sense indicate that the roads on which one travels determine the destination one will eventually reach. In the context of theology, this means that the methods employed to interpret the Bible invariably affect the theological and doctrinal conclusions reached. As Gerhard F. Hasel has observed:

> The history of any church body is also the history of its interpretation of Scripture. By implication a shift or change in the method used for interpretation of Scripture by a church, its scholars, or others within it inevitably would be accompanied by a shift or change in its course, doctrines, self-understanding, purpose, and mission.[325]

A look at the historic development of Adventist doctrines confirms this insight. In fact, it appears that a number of changes in the Adventist body of beliefs have become possible or even mandatory because of some hermeneutical readjustments on the part of the leading Bible expositors in the church.

That Seventh-day Adventists have applied the literal method of Bible interpretation in a rather strict way is due not only to the lasting influence of Miller's own hermeneutics[326] but also to the strong opposition by the early Sabbatarian Adventists to "spiritualizing" views common among certain groups of disappointed Millerites after 1844.[327] Not wanting to lose their faith in the immediate, personal, and visible coming of Christ to this earth, the Adventist pioneers emphasized the material reality of God as well as the literalness of both the heavenly sanctuary with its two apartments and the Holy City "with all its minute descriptions and measurement."[328]

---

325 Hasel, *Biblical Interpretation Today*, 1.

326 See above, pp. 120-121.

327 According to some observers, it was "the influence of spiritualism ... which impelled Adventists to use literal concepts to the virtual exclusion of spiritual understanding. The early Adventists felt an urgent need to distinguish themselves from spiritualists ... The sanctuary doctrine explained the Great Disappointment, and its emphasis on the literal details of celestial geography and personnel provided a further bulwark against spiritualistic interpretations of the divine realm" (Bull and Lockhart, *Seeking a Sanctuary*, 59, 61). For a vivid description of "Adventism's radical fringe" and the "disentanglement" from it of the founders of Sabbatarian Adventism, see Knight, *Millennial Fever*, chaps. 12 and 14.

328 James White, "How Inconsistent," *RH*, 5 March 1857, 141; cf. Ellen White, *Early Writings*, 77 (opposing "Spiritualism" and asserting that the Father has a bodily form exactly like Jesus); J. B. F[risbie], "The Trinity," *RH*, 12 March 1857, 146 (rejecting the "orthodox" belief according to which God is "without body or parts"); J. N. Andrews, "The Sanctuary," *RH*, 3 February 1853, 148, 145-149 ("believing in a literal sanctuary in heaven, consisting of two

Their determination "to take the word of God as it reads"[329] also confirmed them in the strong opposition to the doctrine of the Trinity and the two-nature Christology, which did not seem to fit with the literalist approach.

In spite of the recognized positive effects of this literalism,[330] Adventists increasingly abandoned its crasser features in favor of a more moderate position. The church was thereby enabled to adopt the "orthodox" Trinitarian view on the God-head. In recent years, Adventist theologians have also become more reticent to make specific assertions about the particulars of heavenly realities.[331]

Influenced by the semi-rationalist philosophy of their times, Seventh-day Adventists, like the Millerites before them, were convinced that the accuracy of the Bible could be objectively proved and conclusively verified with the help of its predictive prophecies which yielded a "mathematical demonstration to the truth."[332] Today, some Adventist authors tend to place less emphasis on these rational "proofs"

real holy places"); [James White], *The Personality of God* (Battle Creek, Mich.: SDAPA, [1861]; asserting that man is God's physical as well as moral image and that God has a human-like body, form, and shape); Cornell, "Who Are Mormons?" (implying that SDAs oppose the idea of "an immaterial God"); Wm. S. Ingraham, "God a Being and Heaven a Place," *RH,* 25 June 1867, 17-18; Canright, "The Personality of God," 81-82 ("God is a real person, having a body, form, and local habitation"); and W. H. Littlejohn, "Heaven: Is It a Place, or Merely a Condition?" *RH,* 12 February 1884, 97-99 (defends the "literality," "locality," and "materiality" of heaven).

329 James White, "Our Present Position," *RH,* January 1851, 29.

330 It not only protected the church against the fanaticism and spiritualism common among shut-door believers in the late 1840s (see Arthur L. White, *Ellen G. White,* 1:79-81; and R. D. Brinsmead, *1844 Re-Examined,* 33-34) but also shielded it against the threat of pan(en)theism that arose at the turn of the century (see Arthur L. White, *Ellen G. White,* 5:280-306).

331 See above, pp. 184-185. Adventist writers today no longer unequivocally assert that "we believe that everything is material" – God included (D. M. Canright, *Matter and Spirit* [Battle Creek, Mich.: RHPA, 1882], 12). According to a recent SDA author, "God himself is not essentially physical," but he may assume a bodily form when revealing himself to his creatures (Rice, *The Reign of God,* 73-74). In regard to a hermeneutic that interprets the Bible "in a literalistic way," John C. Brunt has pointed out that "Seventh-day Adventists long ago decided not to interpret Scripture this way" ("Ordination of Women: A Hermeneutical Question," *Ministry,* September 1988, 12-14). Provonsha has called the heavenly symbols and rituals "'and language'" and "celestial metaphors" and the terms used in describing the investigative judgment "somewhat naive in their anthropomorphic literalism" *(A Remnant in Crisis,* 120-121, 135). However, the book *SDAs Believe* was marked by strongly literalistic views. It upheld a "Scripture chronology" placing creation at about 4,000 B.C., located God "in some distant corner of the universe" (69-77), ascribed to him a bodily form and physical features (85), and emphasized the "physical attributes" of the New Jerusalem with its literal walls, houses, and golden streets (375-377).

332 R. F. Cottrell, "The Firm Foundation of Faith," *RH,* 22 December 1885, 794. Cf. *An Appeal to Men of Reason and Common Sense* (Battle Creek, Mich.: SDAPA, 1859); Moses Hull, *The Bible from Heaven: Or a Dissertation on the Evidences of Christianity* (Battle Creek, Mich.: SDAPA, 1863), 128-164; and D. M. Canright, "Proof of the Inspiration of the Bible," *RH,* 6 October 1885, 611-612.

of the Bible as they have come to recognize more clearly the decisive role of the subjective factors involved in a person's decision of faith.[333]

Closely related to the literal approach to the Scriptures, the so-called proof-text method takes biblical statements at their face value without subjecting them to historical and critical scrutiny.[334] Throughout its history and until today, the church has supported and applied this method.[335] Based on the assumption that words retain their meaning in different contexts,[336] Adventists have explained and justified

---

333 "In the final analysis, however, inspiration cannot be proved – neither of the Bible nor of Ellen White's writings. Inspiration is known in the inner being: as we read we hear God speak to us, and we know that these words of man are the Word of God" (William G. Johnsson, "Reflections on Ellen White's Inspiration," *RH*, 27 November 1980, 13). See also Edward V. H. Vick, "Faith and Evidence," *Andrews University Seminary Studies* 5 (1967): 181-199; idem, *Speaking Well of God* (Nashville: SPA, 1979), 177-183; Richard Rice, "The Knowledge of Faith," *Spectrum* 5:2 (1973): 19-32; and idem, *Reason and the Contours of Faith* (Riverside, Calif.:   La Sierra University Press, 1991).

334 As they frequently quoted the Old Testament in support of their views, Jesus and the apostles may be said to have already used this method.   In a more scholarly setting, the proof-text method was applied by 17th-century Protestant orthodoxy in its attempt to arrive at the truths of faith with the help of clear biblical statements *(dicta probantia)* from which theological conclusions were derived yielding the doctrines of the Christian faith.

335 In 1884, Isaac Morrison defended this approach by referring to Isa 28:9-10; in his judgment, this (proof-)text does indeed allow interpreters to "pick out only a verse here and a verse there from different chapters of the Bible" ("'Here a Little and There a Little,'" *RH*, 9 September 1884, 580). For ample illustrations of the systematic use of the proof-text method by SDAs, see *Bible Readings for the Home [Circle]*, rev. ed.; William H. Granger, *Bible Footlights for the Pilgrim's Path* (Washington, D.C.: RHPA, 1907); Walter O. Edwards, *Great Fundamentals of the Bible* (Mountain View, Calif.: PPPA, 1938); and Walter Leslie Emmerson, *The Bible Speaks: Scripture Readings Systematically Arranged* (Mountain View, Calif.: PPPA, 1967).

336 According to a writer in the *Review,* each word represents a definite, unchangeable idea; therefore, in the Bible, the same terms always convey the same ideas (E. Goodrich, "Language Confounded," *RH,* 25 August 1859, 105-106). According to E. J. Waggoner, "Terms used in one place in the Bible, with a certain signification, must have the *same meaning* attached to them *in every other place* where they occur, provided the same subject is under consideration" (E. J. Waggoner, "A Few Principles of Interpretation," *ST,* 6 January 1887, 8). A similar approach was used by Gerhard F. Hasel who argued that the terminological and conceptual links between Dan 8 and Lev 16, particularly the nouns *peshaᶜ* ("sin, transgression") and *qodesh* ("sanctuary") strongly support the interpretation of Dan 8:14 in terms of the Levitical cultic-judicial cleansing of the sanctuary on the day of atonement, even though the crucial verb *nisdaq* ("shall … be justified/vindicated restored/cleansed"), describing what will happen to God's holy place, nowhere appears in Lev 16 ("The 'Little Horn,' the Saints, and the Sanctuary in Daniel 8," in *The Sanctuary and the Atonement,* ed. Wallenkampf and Lesher, 177-227, esp. 200-206; cf. idem, "The 'Little Horn,' the Heavenly Sanctuary and the Time of the End: A Study of Daniel 8:9-14," in *Symposium on Daniel: Introductory and Exegetical Studies,* Daniel and Revelation Committee Series, ed. Frank B. Holbrook, vol. 2 [Washington, D.C.: Biblical Research Institute, General Conference of SDAs, 1986], 426-461). "Similar terminology presupposes similar concepts. Both the prophecy of Daniel 8 and

doctrines by drawing together statements from the entire Bible, at times paying little and possibly insufficient attention to their respective historical and literary settings.

In more recent years, some Adventist scholars have called for a reconsideration and refinement of this method, criticizing its inclination to neglect certain well-established exegetical rules. In their judgment, Adventist interpreters, like all Bible scholars, should consistently study and consider the historical and literary context of biblical statements.[337]

With the increase of higher education among Adventists, scholars trained in modern research methods began applying these tools to the history and theology of their own church. Many academically trained Adventist theologians have called for and adopted a historical and theological approach to the Bible that seeks to uphold the authority of the inspired writings as well as to determine its original meaning and the truth content of its assertions.[338] In this circumscribed sense, a meticulous "historical" and even "critical" investigation of the Scriptures likely belongs to the hand tools of most Adventists scholars.[339]

Leviticus deal with the concept and reality of the sanctuary. In order to understand Daniel's use of sanctuary terms, it is necessary to go back to Leviticus and the sanctuary ritual for their proper explanation" (W. Richard Lesher and Frank B. Holbrook, "Daniel and Revelation Committee: Final Report," in *Symposium on Revelation – Book 2*, ed. Holbrook, 456).

337 See D. F. Neufeld, "What's Wrong with the Proof-Text Method?" *RH*, 11 March 1976, 10-11; and Raymond F. Cottrell, "Smoothing the Way to Consensus – Nos. 1-3," *AR*, 31 March-14 April 1977, 18, 17-18, 12-13.

338 As early as 1954, the principle of "sanctified skepticism" was defended in an official church publication *(Problems in Bible Translation* [Washington, D.C.: General Conference of SDA, 1954], 89). In 1971, the *Ministry* told its readers that the application of higher criticism to the Bible was valid and necessary as long as it did not detract from the authenticity of the Bible (Edward A. Parker, "Does the Seventh-day Adventist Minister Need to Consider Intellectual Honesty?" *Ministry*, June 1971, 21-23). See also "'Lower' and 'Higher' Biblical Criticism," in *SDABC*, 5:134-189; Raymond F. Cottrell, "A Church in Crisis – Nos. 1-6," *AR*, 13 January-17 February 1977; idem, "The Historical Method of Interpretation," *AR*, 7 April 1977, 17-18; and idem, "A Subtle Danger in the Historical Method," *AR*, 14 April 1977, 12.

339 Jerry Gladson, "Taming Historical Criticism: Adventist Biblical Scholarship in the Land of the Giants," *Spectrum* 18:4 (1988): 19-34. "Eine historische Erforschung der Bibel darf nicht nur, sie muß sogar betrieben werden ... Auch das Wort 'kritisch' (vom griech. *krinein* = unterscheiden, prüfen) hat nicht von Haus aus einen negativen Beigeschmack. Ein Urteil fällen heißt nicht, etwas zu zerstören. Wenn Geschichte nicht zu Geschichten werden soll, muß sie immer kritisch betrieben werden" (H. Heinz, "Die historisch-kritische Methode und die Verkündigung des Evangeliums," *Adventecho*, November 1986, 8-9). "The purpose of the discipline [called 'biblical criticism'] is not to destroy our confidence in the Bible, as people sometimes suspect; rather, it is to help us understand the history of its contents. The fact that it was written by human beings justifies a critical study of the Bible" (Rice, *The Reign of God*, 35). A moderate historical-critical approach to the Bible is used, e.g., by John C. Brunt, "A Parable of Jesus as a Clue to Biblical Interpretation," *Spectrum* 13:2 (1982): 35-43; Larry G. Herr, "Genesis One in Historical-Critical Perspective," ibid., 51-62; and George E. Rice, *Luke, A Plagiarist?* (Mountain View, Calif.: PPPA, 1983).

However, in its official statements and leading publications, the church has tended to repeat the negative assessment of L. A. Smith who, in 1891, maintained that "the vagaries of 'higher' Scripture criticism, have no place in connection with the third angel's message."[340]

The question of the proper methodology for interpreting the Bible was extensively discussed in 1981 at Consultation II, a meeting of nearly 200 Adventist theologians and church administrators. The conference tended toward a moderate position, avoiding the wholesale rejection of all forms of historical criticism as well as the advocacy of its free and indiscriminate use.[341]

More recently, however, the General Conference has adopted a document offering rather restrictive guidelines on "Methods of Bible Study." It not only rejects the historical-critical method, its presuppositions and deductions "as classically formulated," but also asserts that "even a modified use of this method that retains the principle of criticism, which subordinates the Bible to human reason, is unacceptable to Adventists." Still, and in spite of its rejection of "the usual techniques of historical research," the document calls for the careful literary, historical, and contextual analysis of the Bible.[342]

Does such a methodology allow for the recognition of any mistakes, inconsistencies, or discrepancies in the Bible?[343] A review of Adventist history indicates that the majority of Adventists believed that inspiration implied infallibility as well as

---

340 L. A. Smith, "A Defensive Message," *RH,* 4 August 1891, 487. See also M. C. Wilcox, *The Bible, Its Inspiration and Importance* (Oakland, Calif.: PPPA, 1889); [Uriah Smith], "The Higher Criticism," *RH,* 8 November 1892, 696; Earle Albert Rowell, *The Bible in the Critics' Den: Or Modern Infidelity Challenged and Refuted* (Mountain View, Calif.: PPPA, 1917); L. E. Froom, "Secularized History Seeks Admittance," *Ministry,* April 1938, 23; idem, "Encroachments of Secularized History," *Ministry,* August-October 1938; idem, "Two Concepts of Scholarship," *Ministry,* March 1940, 21; idem, "The Spirit and Goal of True Research," *Ministry,* March 1944, 21; idem, *MOD,* 39; F. D. Nichol, "The Historical Foundations of Christianity – Parts 1-2," *RH,* 5-12 September 1963, 14-15, 13; Gordon M. Hyde, ed., *A Symposium on Biblical Hermeneutics* (Washington, D.C.: General Conference of SDA, 1974); E. Edward Zinke, "A Conservative Approach to Theology," *Ministry,* Supplement [October 1977]; and Hasel, *Biblical Interpretation Today.*

341 See Neal C. Wilson, "Together for a Finished Work," *AR,* 17 December 1981, 4-5; Alden Thompson, "Theological Consultation II," *Spectrum* 12:2 (1981): 40-52; and J. Robert Spangler, "Why Consultation II?" *Ministry,* February 1982, 26-29.

342 "Methods of Bible Study," *Ministry,* April 1987, 22-24. The document was voted at the 1986 General Conference Annual Council. Following the same line of reasoning, *SDAs Believe* affirmed "the absolute [doctrinal] authority of the Bible" which "must not be subjected to human norms" or judgment (p. 13). Moreover, the book views the "critical methodology" of contemporary scholarship as a crucial issue in the "great controversy," the cosmic battle between good and evil, God and Satan (p. 103).

343 The document "Methods of Bible Study" admits only "minor errors of copyists" as well as "minor dissimilarities in detail that may be irrelevant to the main and clear message of the passage. In some cases judgment may have to be suspended until more information and better evidence are available to resolve a seeming discrepancy" (ibid., 24). Cf. *SDAs Believe,* 11.

inerrancy. This left virtually no room for any error or contradiction in what a prophet had said or written under the influence of the Holy Spirit.[344]

When Protestant Fundamentalism became an active and controversial movement in the 1920s, Adventists described themselves unhesitatingly as fundamentalists.[345] They even outdid their evangelical brethren by calling themselves "the real Fundamentalists,"[346] "the chief of Fundamentalists,"[347] "fundamentalists of the Fundamentalists,"[348] "absolute Fundamentalists,"[349] "the only true Fundamentalists today,"[350] or "fundamentalism itself." [351]   Observers of the church concurred in this assessment.[352]

344 "Perfection of the Bible," *RH,* 15 September 1859, 134; Hull, *The Bible from Heaven;* "Inspiration," *RH,* 26 February 1880, 139; L. A. Smith, "Demands of 'Enlightened' Orthodoxy," *RH,* 7 June 1887, 368; M. C. Wilcox, *The Bible: Its Inspiration and Importance;* F. D. Nichol, "Modern Apostasy in Christendom," *RH,* 8-15 June 1933, 3-4, 5-6; and G. Burnside, "Our Infallible Bible," *Ministry,* January 1970, 5-7. According to Froom, the basic issue involved in the fundamentalist-modernist controversy was the question of "scriptural inerrancy." On this, he maintained, "we as Adventists stand as a Fundamentalist unit" (L. E. Froom, "Apostasy Marches On," *Ministry,* May 1937, 11, 22).

345 Cf. above, p. 60, n. 21 and 22. See also C. B. Haynes, *Christianity at the Crossroads* (Nashville: SPA, 1924); William George Wirth, *The Battle of the Churches: Modernism or Fundamentalism, Which?* (Mountain View, Calif.: PPPA, 1924); and Milton C. Wilcox, "Fundamentalism or Modernism – Which?" *RH,* 15 January-2 April 1925. From its inception in 1928 and for about two decades, the *Ministry* frequently carried articles and editorials on the contemporary modernist-fundamentalist controversy. The authors invariably aligned themselves with the fundamentalists in their struggle against the errors of liberalism and in defending creationism, a supernatural approach to the Bible, and the historic Protestant faith. In spite of this common ground, Adventists stood aloof from the fundamentalist movement (1) because of certain doctrinal differences, (2) because of their unique self-understanding, and (3) because they were not (yet) considered as brethren by the other fundamentalist evangelicals. See also Land, ed., *Adventism in America,* 167-169.

346 F. D. Nichol, "Modernism's Inadequacy Is Our Opportunity," *Ministry,* February 1936, 14, 22.

347 F. M. Wilcox, "Forsaking the Foundations of Faith," *RH,* 28 November 1929, 13-14.

348 W. H. Branson, "Loyalty in an Age of Doubt," *Ministry,* October 1933, 3.

349 W. H. Branson, *In Defense of the Faith* (1933), 28.

350 F. M. Wilcox, "God's Message for Today," *RH,* 2 June 1938, 5.

351 W. A. Spicer, "The Message That Answers the Need," *RH,* 4 July 1929, 11.

352 F. M. Wilcox, "The World's Estimate of Seventh-day Adventists," *RH,* 9 August 1923, 8; F. E. Meyer, *The Religious Bodies of America,* 2d ed. (St. Louis: Concordia Publ. House, 1956), 435-436; John H. Gerstner, *The Theology of the Major Sects* (Grand Rapids: Baker, 1960), 13; Booton Herndon, "A Look at Adventists," *RH,* Centenary Issue, 1861-1961 [8 June 1961], 8; Gabriel Hebert, *Fundamentalism and the Church of God* (London: SCM Press, 1957), 22; and James Barr, *Fundamentalism* (Philadelphia: Westminster, 1977/1978), 7, 53.

Since the 1950s, however, Adventists gradually disassociated themselves from the fundamentalist movement[353] and later also from its inerrantist view on inspiration.[354] Still, questions regarding the actual ramifications and implications of the Adventist view on revelation and inspiration have continued to flare up, from time to time, in the church, causing vigorous discussions on what it means to confess Scripture as "the written Word of God, given by divine inspiration," "the infallible revelation of His will," "the authoritative revealer of doctrines, and the trustworthy record of God's acts in history."[355] There is general agreement, though, among Adventist scholars that one cannot engage in biblical exegesis or theological reflection without some kind of hermeneutic. Therefore, the careful elaboration and consistent application of proper methods of interpretation are of utmost importance for the discovery and preservation of revealed truth.

353 Carl Walter Daggy, "A Comparative Study of Certain Aspects of Fundamentalism with Seventh-day Adventism" (M.A. thesis, Washington, D.C., SDA Theological Seminary, 1955; located at JWL, AU, Berrien Springs, Mich.); Wilbur K. Nelson, "Are Adventists Fundamentalists?" *Ministry,* April 1965, 16-17; Parker, "Does the Seventh-day Adventist Minister Need to Consider Intellectual Honesty?" (1971); and *SDAE,* 1976 ed., s.v. "Fundamentalism" ("to a considerable extent, Fundamentalists have ignored or rejected the valid findings of Biblical scholarship" [originally published in 1966]). It should also be noted that the term fundamentalism had gradually assumed a pejorative meaning, connoting religious bigotry, obscurantism, and right-wing political extremism.

354 Raymond F. Cottrell, "The Inerrancy of Scripture – Nos. 1-5," *RH,* 10 February-24 March 1966; Edward Heppenstall, "Doctrine of Revelation and Inspiration," *Ministry,* August 1970, 28-31; K. H. Wood, "The Divine-Human Word," *RH,* 24 June 1976, 2; Raymond F. Cottrell, "A Church in Crisis – Nos. 1-6"; William G. Johnsson, "Are Adventists Fundamentalists?" *AR,* 8 January 1981, 14; and Gerhard Rempel, "Fundamentalismus – Heil oder Gefahr?" *Adventecho,* March 1987, 6-8. Fundamentalism has recently been criticized for showing traditionalist and separatist leanings as well as for its tendency to defend historically untenable, black-and-white positions regarding the inspiration of the Bible. See, e.g., Rolf J. Pöhler, "Fundamentalismus in Geschichte und Gegenwart der Siebenten-Tags-Adventisten," *Zeitlupe,* May 1993, 35-39, also published in *Stufen,* 1 December 1993, 11-13; and Klaus Schmitz, "Ist der Adventismus eine Spielart des Fundamentalismus?," in *Fundamentalismus: Glaube – Angst – Gewißheit,* Der Adventglaube in Geschichte und Gegenwart (Darmstadt: Adventistischer Wissenschaftlicher Arbeitskreis, 1996), pp. 83-113.

355 See below, app. 3, col. 3, par. 1; cf. below, p. 207. The recent debate stirred by Alden Thompson's controversial book on what he called "an incarnational model of inspiration" seems to indicate that SDAs, even today, are less than united on this issue. While *Ministry* magazine editor J. David Newman highly recommended *Inspiration* (1991) as "extremely helpful" and possibly "the most significant book published by an Adventist press in this decade" (cited from the book's flyleaf), others expressed deep concern that it might put in jeopardy "the very authority of the Scriptures and the continued existence of the Seventh-day Adventist people as a Bible-centered, Bible-based movement and church" (Frank Holbrook and Leo Van Dolson, eds., *Issues in Revelation and Inspiration,* Adventist Theological Society Occasional Papers, vol. 1 (Berrien Springs, Mich.: ATS Publications, 1992), 8. See also "Inspiration" (Review), *Ministry,* December 1991, 28-30; and *JATS* 5:1 (1994).

The early Sabbath-keeping Adventists, lacking as they were in formal theological training, could hardly have known all the characteristics of what today may be regarded as sound historical and theological methodology. Actually, it appears rather remarkable how well they succeeded without the benefit of academically trained scholars in their midst.[356] The shortcomings of their approach to the Bible – seen from our perspective, which may have its own deficiencies – should, therefore, not be surprising to anyone today. But, by the same token, neither may the Adventist church be able to afford perpetuating what they did unless it has convincing methodological reasons for doing so.

For example, early Adventists gave apparently little thought to the interpretative task of theology. In their view, truth was discovered by simply accepting and consistently applying what the Bible said, without trying to interpret these findings in any particular way.[357] Actually, a theological interpretation of biblical statements appeared to them as an illegitimate attempt to get around the clear, literal meaning of the Scripture.[358] In contrast to their forebears, Adventist theologians today are

356 "Under the circumstances, perhaps they should not be judged too harshly if sometimes they interpreted the Scriptures with a tinge of the naiveté that is often the hallmark of the self-taught" (Provonsha, *A Remnant in Crisis*, 11). Actually, early SDA Bible interpreters did not hesitate to approach their King James Bible in a critical way if it seemed necessary to protect a doctrinal truth. This is illustrated by the long-standing view on the misplaced comma in Jesus's promise to the thief on the cross (see *SDABC* on Luke 23:43) and also by J. N. Loughborough's remark on the Trinitarian interpolation in 1 John 5:7-8 ("Questions for Brother Loughborough"). Ellen White's interpretation of the parable of the rich man and Lazarus in Luke 16:19-31 is another case in point *(Christ's Object Lessons* [Washington, D.C.: RHPA, 1900/1941], 260-271). In fact, her writings on biblical history paid considerable attention to the historical and literary context. See, e.g., *The Desire of Ages* (Mountain View, Calif.: PPPA, 1898; reprint 1940).

357 J. H. Waggoner, *The Kingdom of God* (Battle Creek, Mich.: RH Office, 1859), 5; R. F. Cottrell, "Doctrine," *RH,* 8 January 1875, 10 ("take [the Scriptures] in their most obvious meaning"); idem, "Interpretation," ibid., 12-13 ("abandon interpretations for what the Scriptures say ... Acknowledge and obey God's word as it is, and no longer make it void by baseless interpretations"); idem, "Shall We Have the Bible?" *RH,* 15 April 1875, 125 ("returning to what [the Bible] says, instead of telling what it must mean"); James White, "How Readest Thou?" *RH,* 13 May 1875, 156-157 ("the safe rule of interpretation, that the Scriptures mean what they say"); and J. H. Waggoner, "The Gifts and Offices of the Holy Spirit – No. 1," 89 ("We have a right to be positive in our faith and our statements only when the words of Scripture are so direct as to bring the subject within the range of positive proof").

358 This fact should be kept in mind when dealing with doctrinal development in the Adventist church. From the perspective of current theological scholarship, many doctrinal changes in Adventist history may seem to have been merely a matter of biblical exegesis rather than of dogmatic theology. To the early Adventists, however, this distinction would not have made much sense. For to them, true doctrines could be nothing but the clear and literal teachings of the Scriptures. Anything going beyond that was to be rejected as speculative and erroneous. A study of the different declarations of Fundamental Beliefs reveals the large extent to which Adventist doctrines are simply a restatement or paraphrase of Bible texts, especially with regard to eschatology (see below, app. 3). Therefore, the reinterpretation of a single Bible verse may

trained to think that it does not suffice simply to ascertain and repeat what a biblical writer has said; rather one needs to reflect carefully on what he meant by what he said and, consequently, what this could actually mean for the church today.[359]

In their direct approach to the Bible, ignoring, for all practical matters, the gap between biblical and later times, early Adventists treated large portions of the New Testament as predictive prophecies primarily geared to their own times, "the time of the end."[360] They did this not only with the Apocalypse but also with the Gospels, the book of Acts, and the Letters – with all genres of New Testament writings.[361] Actually, their "prophetic" hermeneutic led early Adventists, at times, to a kind of allegorical interpretation, which makes their strict literalism appear in a somewhat different light. In any event, today SDA scholars in general no longer use this method in biblical exegesis. Consequently, their historical-contextual approach may lead them to somewhat different conclusions from those reached a century ago.[362]

Inasmuch as Seventh-day Adventists have focused their attention particularly on the apocalyptic prophecies of the Bible, it is interesting to investigate the impact that hermeneutical principles have had on the teachings based on these prophecies. The

---

indeed have involved a noteworthy doctrinal development. The definition of the law in Galatians, e.g., was considered not merely a matter of exegesis, but rather one of doctrine (George I. Butler, *The Law in the Book of Galatians* [Battle Creek, Mich.: RHPA, 1886], 6). See also below, chap. 6, pp. 300-303. Cf. above, p. 155, n. 161.

359 See, e.g., Raymond F. Cottrell, "Rightly Dividing the Word of Truth," *RH,* 27 July 1961, 10-11; Don F. Neufeld, "Is an Unbiased Bible Translation Possible?" *RH,* 11 February 1971, 15-16; Rice, *The Reign of God,* 39; and Robert K. McIver, "Bible Alive! How to Understand the 'Plain Meaning' of the Bible," *AR,* 13 August 1992, 8-10. For a study of biblical hermeneutics from an Adventist perspective, see Hyde, ed., *A Symposium on Biblical Hermeneutics;* and Gerhard F. Hasel, *Understanding the Living Word of God* (Mountain View, Calif.: PPPA, 1980).

360 "There has never seemed to us any difficulty in that principle of interpretation, which re-presents the prophetic writer as passing down the stream of time, and speaking as if contemporary with the successive events which he predicts, and as if personally present with the people whom his predictions concerned" ([Uriah Smith], "This Generation," *RH,* 17 November 1891, 712). If Scripture consists largely of prophecy, and if "prophecy is history in advance" (James White, "The Time of the End," *RH,* 22 July 1880, 330), then obviously the Bible is addressed directly to those living at the climax of human history.

361 E.g., parables (like the ten virgins in Matt 25:1-10) and apostolic exhortations (like Acts 3:19-21 and Heb 8 and 9) were thought to have been written not from the perspective of their first-century hearers or readers, but primarily with a view to their 19th-century end-time audience. Cf. G. W. Amadon, "Reasons Why the Book of James Especially Applies to the Last Generation of Christians," *RH,* 20 September 1881, 196; "Coming in to See the Guests," *RH,* 1 August 1882, 488 (on Matt 22:1-13 and Luke 14:14-24); and D. T. Bourdeau, "Principles by Which to Interpret Prophecy – No. 3," *RH,* 11 December 1888, 769.

362 Davidson, e.g., notes that "the blotting out of sins," mentioned in Acts 3:19, does indeed refer to "the immediate forgiveness of sin" but "at the same time alludes to the apocalyptic blotting out of sin" at the investigative judgment ("The Good News of Yom Kippur," 10). SDAs today also consistently view the parable of Matt 25:1-10 as relating to the second coming of Christ *(Seventh-day Adventists Believe,* 333, 345).

practice of reading the Bible in the light of political developments and of interpreting it, if possible, in a literal manner led Adventists to their historic positions on the king of the north, the kings of the east, the Euphrates river, the battle of Armageddon, as well as on several other prophetic symbols.

However, in recent decades, an increasing number of Adventist scholars have questioned this approach to prophecy as it tends to make doctrines, in part, dependent on history books and newspaper reports.[363] Instead, they have called for careful exegesis, which interprets prophecy in its biblical context before making applications to current political, social, or natural events. Seeking to let the Bible interpret itself rather than granting secular history hermeneutical control over it, these scholars have attempted to apply the *sola scriptura* principle to the exegesis of biblical prophecy in a practical and consistently Christocentric way.[364]

The Direction of Doctrinal Development

If one looks at the doctrinal modifications within Seventh-day Adventism in a synoptic way, certain conclusions suggest themselves with regard to the general direction into which these changes have led the church up to now. While it is possible and, actually, tempting to further draw out these lines into the future, it seems advisable not to engage in any prognostication regarding the possible development of Adventist doctrines. The purpose here is simply to identify trends that have already manifested themselves clearly in the past.

363 In an *Adventist Review* editorial, Roy Adams called upon the church to "avoid the newspaper approach to the interpretation of prophecy" as it had forced the church several times in the past to abandon its prophetic interpretations ("An Appeal for Caution," *AR*, 16 January 1992, 4). It should be pointed out, however, that the historic SDA interpretations of biblical prophecies were not, in general, built on a cursory, superficial "newspaper approach."

364 The theological and Christological interpretation of prophecy was particularly emphasized in the 1940s by the Australian evangelist Louis F. Were (see idem, *Bible Principles of Interpretation* [n.p., n.d.]; idem, *The Certainty of the Third Angel's Message;* and idem, *The Moral Purpose of Prophecy.* It received official support at the 1952 Bible Conference which declared that "[Jesus Christ] is to be made the center and circumference of our prophetic message to the world" (A. V. Olson, "The Place of Prophecy in Our Preaching," in *Our Firm Foundation,* 2:563, 533-571). See also M. K. Eckenroth, "Christ the Center of All True Preaching," ibid., 1:117-188; cf. [Raymond F. Cottrell], "Role of Israel in Bible Prophecy," *SDABC* (1955), 4:25-38. In the 1970s and 1980s, this approach was widely and effectively promoted by Hans K. LaRondelle (see idem, "Plea for a Christ-Centered Eschatology," *Ministry,* January 1976, 18-20; idem, *The Israel of God in Prophecy,* AU Monographs, Studies in Religion, vol. 13 [Berrien Springs, Mich.: AU Press, 1983]; and idem, *Chariots of Salvation).*

From Flexible/Simple to Fixed/Compound Statements of Faith[365]

From 1851 until well into the twentieth century (1938), the *Review & Herald* carried on its masthead the text of Rev 14:12, which more than any other statement of Scripture has served to express in a nutshell the core of Seventh-day Adventist belief. Firmly opposed to any "other creed than the Word of God," Adventists were united in these great subjects: Christ's immediate, personal Second Advent, and the observance of all the commandments of God, and the faith of his Son Jesus Christ, as necessary to a readiness for his Advent.[366]

In a sense, then, the Sabbatarian Adventists held only two articles of faith, i.e., the commandments of God and the faith of Jesus. However, they were understood quite comprehensively as encompassing virtually the entire New Testament.[367] For a brief time in 1854, the same *Review & Herald* printed on its masthead a list of "Leading Doctrines Taught by the Review," which touched upon (1) the normative basis of Seventh-day Adventist faith (i.e., "the Bible only"), (2) the standard of the Adventist lifestyle (i.e., "the Law of God"), and (3) the center of Adventist hope (i.e., "Advent of Christ," "Earth restored," and "Immortality").[368]

After the dispute on church organization had been settled in favor of "gospel order," it became common for Adventists to sign a pledge when they enrolled as members forming a local congregation. This "church covenant" stipulated that, "We, the undersigned, hereby associate ourselves together, as a church, taking the name Seventh-day Adventists, covenanting to keep the commandments of God, and the faith of Jesus Christ."[369]

Still, the rejection of any kind of creed apart from the Bible did not leave the church without a clear understanding of its beliefs. In 1872, Uriah Smith wrote and published a list of twenty-five "Fundamental Principles" summarizing the faith of the Seventh-day Adventists.[370] It was the first detailed presentation of Adventist doctrines published by the church, and it was repeatedly revised and reprinted in

---

365 See also [Robert W. Olson and Bert Haloviak, comp.], "Who Decides What Adventists Believe: A Chronological Survey of the Sources, rev. ed., 1978," TMs, EGWRC, AU, Berrien Springs, Mich.; SDAE, 1976 ed., s.v. "Doctrinal Statements."

366 James White, "Resolution of the Seventh-day Baptist Central Association," *RH,* 11 August 1853, 52. Cf. "The Babel of Christendom," *RH,* 24 September 1857, 164.

367 See above, pp. 185-186. Cf. R. F. Cottrell, "The Special Aid of the Spirit," *RH,* 1 August 1871, 55.

368 "Leading Doctrines Taught by the Review," *RH,* 15 August-19 December 1854.

369 "Organization of the Michigan Conference," *RH,* 8 October 1861, 148. This pledge was already used during the organizational proceedings of the Michigan State Conference (Committee) held October 4-6, 1861.

370 *A Declaration of Fundamental Principles Taught and Practiced by the Seventh-day Adventists* (Battle Creek, Mich.: SDAPA, 1872).

later years.[371] Yet, in its preamble, the document strongly disclaimed any intention of providing an authoritative or normative expression of Adventist doctrines.[372]

No such "synopsis" of the Adventist faith was published after 1914[373] until it reappeared again in the 1931 *Yearbook* – albeit in a completely revised form written by *Review & Herald* editor F. M. Wilcox. In 1932, it was taken over into the new *Church Manual* and has appeared there ever since.[374] No official action was taken at the time, but the statement seems to have won general approval in the church. It was given *post ex facto* recognition by the 1946 General Conference, who voted "That no revision of this Statement of Fundamental Beliefs, as it now appears in the *Manual,* shall be made at any time except at a General Conference session."[375]

In addition to the "Fundamental Beliefs," which were primarily intended for the public, two other documents were drawn up whose purpose was to aid in the instruction of prospective church members and to standardize the vow taken at baptism.[376] When the "Doctrinal Instruction for Baptismal Candidates" was first presented, it was emphasized that it was "not in any sense intended to be a formation of a creed."[377] Between 1935 and 1971, the three documents were subjected to a number of minor revisions, which tended to gradually assimilate them in content and wording.[378]

371 See, e.g., "Fundamental Principles," *ST,* 4 June 1874, 3; and *Yearbook of the Seventh-day Adventist Denomination,* 1889, 1905-1914.

372 For the full text of the declaration, see below, app. 3, col. 1. A similar disclaimer was added when the list was republished in 1897: "In presenting to the reader the foregoing epitome of the faith of Seventh-day Adventists, it is to be distinctly understood that this tract does not claim to be an authoritative statement, or rule of faith or practice. We recognize no such rule but the word of God. It is the design of Seventh-day Adventists ever to maintain such an attitude toward the light and truth that God is continually bestowing upon his people that they will ever be ready to receive them. And it is their custom to test that which purports to be light and truth, not by any declaration of faith or formulated creed, but by the Bible, the word of God, itself" *(Fundamental Principles of Seventh-day Adventists,* Words of Truth Series, vol. 5 [Battle Creek, Mich.: RHPA, 1897], 14).

373 According to Froom, this was due to the existence of divergent views on a number of doctrines including the Trinity, Christology, and the atonement *(MOD,* 412-413).

374 For the full text, see below, app. 3, col. 2. For more details regarding the background of this declaration, see Froom, *MOD,* 409-419. See also "Faith of Seventh-day Adventists," *RH,* 19 February 1931, 6-7.

375 "Revision of Church Manual," *RH,* 14 June 1946, 197.

376 The original 1932 *Church Manual* presented a 21-point "suggestive outline of the principles to be understood and accepted by candidates for baptism," entitled "Doctrinal Instruction for Baptismal Candidates" *(SDACM,* 1932 ed., 75-78). In 1942, this statement was replaced by a 27-point "brief summary of the fundamental beliefs" of SDAs, immediately followed by an 11-point "baptismal vow" *(SDACM,* 1942 ed., 81-87). In 1951, the latter was enlarged to comprise a total of 13 questions, while the former was renamed "summary of doctrinal beliefs."

377 *SDACM,* 1932 ed., 75, 75-78; cf. ibid., 1942 ed., 81-87. See also Froom, *MOD,* 420-422.

378 In addition, these revisions reveal a growing emphasis on the role and authority of Ellen White, the special Adventist lifestyle, and the multi-racial character of the Adventist church.

In 1976, General Conference leaders felt the need for documents defining in detail certain historic beliefs that otherwise might be gradually undermined by the inroads into the church of current philosophical and scientific concepts. As a result, statements on revelation/inspiration and creation/creationism were drawn up which were supposed to be used in the screening of teachers employed or wanting to be employed in Adventist educational institutions. These statements were looked upon, however, with considerable chagrin and suspicion by many in the Adventist academic community who feared that creedalism was creeping into the church at last.[379]

In late 1978, the General Conference Church Manual Committee was beginning to work on another minor revision of the "Fundamental Beliefs" to be brought to the General Conference session of 1980. The revised document was submitted to a number of theologians for comment and criticism. Surprisingly, the dozen scholars at Andrews University involved in this review completely rewrote the document. After several stages of revision and a number of significant changes recommended by delegates to the General Conference session in Dallas, the new declaration was officially adopted and has thereby replaced the 1931 text.[380]

Thus, the summary confession of the 1850s ("the commandments of God and the faith of Jesus") had been replaced by a systematically arranged, theologically refined, and elaborate declaration of Seventh-day Adventist beliefs. Moreover, the new statement no longer disclaimed to possess any authority within the church, having been voted as an official document setting forth the fundamental and distinctive teachings of the church.[381]

There may be a certain inevitability to this development from flexible and simple to fixed and compound Statements of Faith. Still, the Dallas declaration can be understood and utilized in quite diverse ways. It may be seen as weakening the traditional emphasis on the distinctive doctrines of the church.[382] It can be interpreted as a mature expression of the Adventist faith, carefully to be guarded against

---

379 See "Study Documents on Inspiration and Creation," *RH,* 17 January 1980, 8-11; and "An Adventist Creed?" *Spectrum* 8:4 (1977): 37-59. Cf. Land, ed., *Adventism in America,* 225-228.

380 For the entire text, see below, app. 3, col. 3. For more information about the events leading up to this new Statement of Faith, see Lawrence T. Geraty, "A New Statement of Fundamental Beliefs," *Spectrum* 11:1 (1980): 2-13; and Bernard E. Seton, "Dallas Statement," *Spectrum* 11:3 (1981): 60-61. A perceptive and sympathetic critique of the document from an observer of the church was provided by Hans-Diether Reimer who regarded the Dallas declaration as an indication "dass die Art und Weise des Glaubens und Theologisierens in der Gemeinschaft der STA in einem Wandel begriffen ist" ("Adventisten: Neufassung der adventistischen 'Glaubensgrundsätze,'" *Materialdienst* 44:9 [1981]: 266-267).

381 "The 1980 action made the statement [of Fundamental Beliefs] much more official than anything the church had had previously" (George R. Knight, "Adventists and Change," *Ministry,* October 1993, 14, 10-15).

382 According to P. Gerard Damsteegt, through the rearrangement of the articles of the Fundamental Beliefs, "the Seventh-day Adventist distinctive doctrines lost some of their distinctiveness, because of the usage or superimposition of categories taken from the discipline of

any attempts to diverge from it. But it can also be viewed as an important milestone in the history of the denomination which needs to be further refined and adjusted in accordance with the developing faith of the community. Only time will tell which role this declaration will actually come to play among Seventh-day Adventists.[383]

From Heterodox to Orthodox Doctrines

If one compares the nineteenth-century declarations of Fundamental Beliefs with the Dallas declaration of 1980, the trend away from certain heterodox doctrines and their replacement by orthodox views on the Trinity, Christology, and soteriology is quite obvious. In the 1950s, observers of the church acknowledged that "on these basic fundamentals of the gospel of Jesus Christ, Seventh-day Adventists are solidly in the tradition of historic orthodox Christianity."[384] At the same time, Adventists continued to present and defend their distinctive teachings such as the doctrine of the heavenly sanctuary, conditional immortality, the seventh-day Sabbath, the prophetic role of Ellen White, and the unique self-understanding of the Adventist church.

From Distinctive to Fundamental Truths

Another trend that could be observed during the last several decades was the gradual turning away from an almost exclusive emphasis on the distinctive doctrines of the church. This accentuation had led, at times, to the virtual neglect of the fundamental truths of the Christian faith. Especially since the 1920s, however, there was a

systematic theology ... [This] can lead to an attitude that some doctrines are irrelevant or outdated" ("Seventh-day Adventist Doctrines and Progressive Revelation," *JATS* 2:1 [1991]: 80, 77-92).

383 According to the preamble of the Dallas declaration, "revision of these statements may be expected at a General Conference session when the church is led by the Holy Spirit to a fuller understanding of Bible truth or finds better language in which to express the teachings of God's Holy Word" (see below, p. 334, col. 3). Incidentally, after the Dallas conference more than 100 of the numerous supporting Bible texts were either added or removed from the list of 27 Fundamental Beliefs. This was obviously done in order to strengthen the biblical-theological reasoning of the declaration. Twenty-two times this involves art. 10 ("The Experience of Salvation"), twelve times art. 11 ("The Church"). Of particular interest from a doctrinal point of view is the removal (1) of Mal 3:1 as text supporting the sanctuary doctrine (#23), (2) of Joel 3:9-16 as only Old Testament support text for the second coming of Christ (#24; cf. the 1931 declaration, #20), and (3) of Zech 14:1-14 which mentions the splitting of the Mount of Olives on the day of the Lord (#26; cf. the 1931 declaration, #21). These changes in the body of supportive Bible texts indicate that, while Adventists seek to advance clear biblical support for their doctrines, the latter do not necessarily depend on certain traditional "proof texts" which may be replaced or perhaps simply be dropped.

384 Walter R. Martin, "What Seventh-day Adventists Really Believe," *Eternity*, November 1956, 20. A few years later, the same author attested: "Seventh-day Adventism adheres tenaciously to the fundamental doctrines of Christian theology as these have been held by the Christian church throughout the centuries" (*The Kingdom of the Cults*, 369); cf. *QOD*, 21-25, 29-32.

growing conviction among Adventists that their body of distinctive truths could not be separated from the basic tenets of Christianity, but rather constituted the restoration, consummation, and end-time expression of the everlasting gospel.[385]

In the eyes of Froom, "The old largely negative approach – emphasizing chiefly the things wherein we differ from all other religious groups – is past, definitely past. And that is as it should be."[386] Instead, the emphasis was placed strongly on the Christ-centered nature of all Adventist doctrines,[387] and it was maintained that "the heart of the Advent message is Christ and Him crucified ... *Christianity is a relationship to a person*."[388] This attempt to let the *solo Christo* of the Protestant Reformers govern contemporary Adventist dogmatics was regarded as being in full accord with Ellen White, who had affirmed that "of all professing Christians, Seventh-day Adventists should be foremost in uplifting Christ before the world."[389] More than in times past, SDA theology today strives to live up to the conviction that

> the sacrifice of Christ as an atonement for sin is the great truth around which all other truths cluster. In order to be rightly understood and appreciated, every truth in the Word of God, from Genesis to Revelation, must be studied in the light that streams from the cross of Calvary ... This is to be the foundation of every discourse given by our ministers.[390]

One significant side-effect of this new concentration on the heart of the gospel message was a decreasing apocalyptic thrust of Adventist teaching over the years.[391]

385 W. W. Prescott, "The Fundamentals of the Advent Message," *RH,* 9 June 1926, 6-8; L. E. Froom, "The Message in Verity," *Ministry,* January 1931, 4; idem, "Apostolic and Remnant Messages," *Ministry,* July 1942, 20, 21, 44; and idem, "A Warning Message or a Saving Gospel – Which?" *Ministry,* July-August 1948, 21-22, 22-23, 46.

386 L. E. Froom, "New Approaches Imperative for a New Day," *Ministry,* March 1966, 10-13. According to Froom, "these 'testing truths,' which separated [SDAs] from all other religious bodies, were not at first centered in ... Christ" *(MOD,* 181).

387 W. W. Prescott, *The Doctrine of Christ* (Washington, D.C.: RHPA, 1920); Daniells, *Christ Our Righteousness;* Henry S. Prenier, *Doctrine Centered in Christ: The Fundamentals, the Controversy, Final Things* (n.p., [1926]); and Francis M. Wilcox, *What the Bible Teaches* (Washington, D.C.: RHPA, 1926).

388 *QOD,* 101; cf. ibid., 99-145, 244-251, 613-617, 647-649, 669-672. See also Froom, *MOD,* 375-408. For a more recent Christ- and gospel-centered presentation of distinctive Adventist beliefs, see Morris L. Venden, *The Pillars* (Mountain View, Calif.: PPPA, 1982). *SDAs Believe* likewise intended to provide a thoroughly "Christ-centered exposition of what we believe" (pp. viii, 25).

389 Ellen White, *Evangelism,* 188; cf. ibid., 184-193. When she was asked about the relationship between the Adventist doctrinal landmarks and the new post-1888 emphasis on righteousness by faith, she left no doubt that, in her judgment, "the message of justification by faith ... is the third angel's message in verity" ("Repentance the Gift of God," *RH,* 1 April 1890, 193; published in *Evangelism,* 190).

390 Ellen White, *Evangelism,* 190.

391 This is recognized by Damsteegt who notes that "post-1874 developments ... resulted in a more Christocentric mission theology with a greater non-apocalyptic thrust" *(Foundations,* xiv).

For one thing, the seemingly delayed advent may have tended to weaken this distinctive Adventist emphasis. For the other, a growing realization of the "already – not yet" tension which characterizes New Testament eschatology may also have contributed to a gradual shift of priorities within the Adventist doctrinal system. This seems to be reflected in the major statements of Adventist belief, which have given less space and attention to apocalyptic issues in recent years.[392] While Adventists are aware of the crucial role of apocalyptic prophecy for their theology,[393] they are beginning to show an increasing awareness of the present dimension of the "kingdom of God" as well as of its implications for the faith and practice of the contemporary church.[394]

From Legalism to Evangelicalism

The rediscovery by Adventist theology of some of the fundamental truths of Christianity was paralleled by an apparent departure from certain legalistic tendencies, which naturally threaten any community that holds the law of God in such high esteem as does the Seventh-day Adventist Church.[395] According to Pease, "in its early days, Adventism placed its greatest stress on the distinctive doctrines of the church. The trend of thinking tended to be legalistic." However, there was a growing emphasis upon "evangelical truths" and "evangelical orthodoxy" which "served to correct legalistic positions" held by some.[396]

---

392 A statistical count shows that, in 1872, 8 of 25 paragraphs (1/3) containing 572 of 2410 words (1/4) were devoted to eschatology; in 1931, 7 of 22 articles (1/3) containing 603 of 1794 words (1/3) dealt with this subject; in 1980, only 4 of the 27 entries (1/7) containing 384 of 3675 words (1/10) discussed the Adventist understanding of "the last things." See appendix 3.

393 See Froom, *PFF*, 4:1152-1173.

394 In the *Adventist Review*, Charles Scriven has called for the participation and active involvement of the church in earthly affairs offering the world "a hope for today as well as for tomorrow" (Charles Scriven, "Two Kinds of Hope," *AR*, 31 May 1984, 3-4). See also John Brunt's little book *Now and Not Yet* which addresses contemporary ethical and social issues like poverty, hunger, political oppression, and sexuality from the perspective of "people waiting for the second coming" (Washington, D.C.: RHPA, 1987). In this context, the inclusion of social and environmental concerns (#6, 13, 20) as well as the accent on the family and the church (#11-13, 22) in the 1980 declaration of faith is a noteworthy development (see app. 3, col. 3).

395 "We reject legalism. Yet that charge against us has stuck. Perhaps this is true to a large extent because of our own creation. The world still suspiciously views us as legalists" (M. K. Eckenroth, "Christ the Center of All True Preaching," in *Our Firm Foundation*, 1:136). Staples has pointed out that an "emphasis on law does not necessarily imply legalism" and that "the more Arminian pattern of Adventist thought" contributed to the "impression that Adventists are legalists." In his view, "theologically, Adventists and evangelicals have much in common and also some differences" ("Adventism," 64, 68-69). See also idem, "Understanding Adventism," *Ministry*, September 1993, 19-23; and Marvin Moore, *The Gospel vs. Legalism: How to Deal with Legalism's Insidious Influence* (Hagerstown, Md.: RHPA, 1994).

396 Pease, *By Faith Alone*, 227. Already towards the end of the 19th century, Ellen White, W. W. Prescott, and others had become increasingly Christ-centered in their preaching, teaching, and writing.

As a result, Froom could note, in 1971, that "we are no longer regarded as mere doctrinarians and legalists, but increasingly as true Christians"; he frankly admitted that by the 1880s "many [Adventists] had drifted into formalism and legalism," and that the church had needed, and experienced, a reorientation from law to gospel.[397] Froom himself exemplified the new Adventist emphasis on the Protestant *sola gratia* and *sola fide* by placing the "all-inclusive and all-important" faith of Jesus above the commandments of God.[398]

Summarily, it can be said that over the years Seventh-day Adventist theology has experienced some rapprochement with evangelical Christianity (1) by shedding certain heterodox aspects of its fundamental teachings, (2) by placing increasing weight on the basic doctrines of the Christian faith, and (3) by overcoming certain legalistic tendencies. In this process, Adventists have somewhat softened their particularism and adopted a less separatist attitude towards other Christian churches.[399]

---

397 Froom, *MOD,* 36, 182; cf. ibid., 33-34, 142-143. Froom pointed to an allegorical picture, lithographed and copyrighted in 1876 by James White and entitled "The Way of Life: From Paradise Lost to Paradise Restored" as well as to its revised edition of 1883 ("Christ, the Way of Life: From Paradise Lost to Paradise Restored") as evidence of the crucial role that Ellen White played in this "radical change" from law to gospel *(MOD,* 182-187). However, he wrongly ascribed the revised version, which placed the cross rather than the "Law Tree" more clearly at the center of the picture, to Ellen White, while, in fact, it had been James White himself who, in 1880, decided to make Christ on the cross the single focus of the steel plate engraving (Letter to Ellen White, 31 March 1880, EGWRC, AU, Berrien Springs, Mich.; and idem, Letter to W. C. White, 16 September 1880, EGWRC, AU, Berrien Springs, Mich.). Incidentally, in describing the original lithograph of 1873 on which the one by James White was based, M. G. Kellogg had remarked: "The crucified Christ is made the central figure in the picture." With the cross being placed next to the law tree, located "near the center of the picture," the lithograph was to illustrate "the fact that the law of God and the gospel of Christ run parallel from the fall of man to the end of probation" (M. G. Kellogg, "The Way of Life from Paradise Lost to Paradise Restored," *RH,* 27 May 1873, 192). For more details on this interesting incident, see Ron Graybill, "Picturing the Prophecies," *AR,* 5 July 1984, 11-14, and Woodrow Whidden, "The *Way of Life* Engravings: Harbingers of Minneapolis?" *Ministry,* October 1992, 9-11 ("the changes … were reflective of profound theological shifts in the thought and ministry of James and Ellen White").

398 Froom, *MOD,* 432-440. Upon arriving in Europe in 1874, J. N. Andrews, who was the first official SDA overseas missionary, still defined the Adventist mission as "giving to the world the warning of the near approach of the Judgment, and in setting forth the sacred character of the law of God, as the rule of our lives and of the final Judgment, and the obligation of mankind to keep God's commandments" ("Meeting of Sabbath-Keepers in Neuchatel," *RH,* 24 November 1874, 172).

399 To a considerable degree, these developments were influenced and guided by Ellen White during her lifetime, but they also continued after her death in 1915. For instance, the unmistakably polemical overtones of the 1872 declaration of SDA beliefs (#2, 6, 8, 12, 13, 16) were omitted in the statements of 1931 and 1980 (see app. 3). "Twentieth-century Adventism differs from contemporary evangelicalism in only a few doctrines … The most extreme religious dissent may, with the passing of time, be transformed into orthodoxy or incorporated into the established structures of society" (Bull and Lockhart, *Seeking a Sanctuary,* 85-86).

In addition, the church is showing signs of reducing its traditional isolation from contemporary society and culture[400] and of moving towards greater involvement in sociopolitical and environmental issues[401] – an attitude that is increasingly supported by top leaders of the church.[402] However, as of today, the Seventh-day Adventist

400 *Review & Herald* editor F. D. Nichol expressed the traditional Adventist view succinctly in this way: "If we understand rightly the spirit and objectives of the Advent movement, we cannot go along with what is now a dominant objective of most Christian bodies, to take a major part in trying to reform the world in its secular aspects ... Ours is a task to prepare men for a better world, which we believe is soon to come" ("The Church and Social Reform," *RH,* 15 April 1965, 15). A few years later, however, Herbert E. Douglass opted for a different approach when he declared in the *Review* that SDAs "should be unreservedly committed to environmental control" ("Is Ecology a Legitimate Concern for Adventists? – 1-3," *RH,* 16-30 April 1970, 13, 12, 12-13). Cf. Enoch Oliveira, "Reform or Redemption: Must the Church Choose?" *Ministry,* September 1982, 10-11.

401 In 1981, B. B. Beach maintained that "the church can hardly ignore public affairs," that it does have "a social responsibility" and should "endeavor to improve the world," and that "truth has political implications." He urged Adventists to "exercise some influence and play some role in 'politics'" by "standing for justice, brotherhood, and peace *now"* ("The Church and Sociopolitical Responsibility," *AR,* 3 September 1981, 4-6). See also idem, "Adventists and Disarmament," *AR,* 21 April 1983, 4-5; Rice, *The Reign of God* (1985), 276-282; Charles Scriven, *The Transformation of Culture: Christian Social Ethics after H. Richard Niebuhr* (Scottdale, Pa., and Kitchener, Ont.: Herald Press, 1988); "Hunger and Poverty," *AR,* Special Issue, 5 May 1988; A. Josef Greig, "Our Poisoned Planet: Adventists and the Environment," *AR,* 19 April 1990, 15-18; Rosado, *Broken Walls* (1990); Roger L. Dudley and Edwin I. Hernandez, *Citizens of Two Worlds: Religion and Politics among American Seventh-day Adventists* (Berrien Springs, Mich.: AU Press, 1992), calling the "remnant" to "radical social involvement" and "a radical shift" in its relationship to secular society (p. 305); Steve Daily, "From Womb to Tomb: Christian Concern for the Total Human Predicament," *AR,* 30 April 1992, 14-18; "Who Is My Neighbor?" *AR,* Special Issue [6 May 1993]; Provonsha, *A Remnant in Crisis,* 97-99; and "Who Is My Neighbor?" *AR,* Special Issue, 10 November 1994.

402 Several declarations on political, social, and environmental issues were published by church leaders and councils in recent years. The General Conference assembly of 1975 voted a state-ment on peace ("Good Will and Understanding between All Men," *RH,* 31 July 1975, 13) as did the following one in 1980 ("Session Actions: Peace Message to All People of Good Will," *AR,* 1 May 1980, 19). During the 1985 General Conference, President Neal C. Wilson issued a statement denouncing the "obvious obscenity" of the arms race and the "sin of racism" in-cluding apartheid. He called upon churches and nations to promote "worldwide justice and peace" and to stamp out the drug epidemic. In support, he repeatedly referred to the "Fundamental Beliefs" of the church ("GC President Issues Statements on Racism, Peace, Home and Family, and Drugs," *AR,* 30 June 1985, 2-3). A few months later, Wilson ex-pressed the SDA concern for peace in letters to Ronald Reagan and Mikhail Gorbachev ("GC President Urges End to Arms Race," *AR,* 21 November 1985, 31). The 1985 Annual Council passed a declaration urging all church members to work for peace, human rights, and socio-economic justice as part of their "essential Christian responsibility" ("International Year of Peace 1986," *AR,* 5 December 1985, 19). See also Neal C. Wilson, "Proposal for Peace and Understanding," *Ministry,* May 1987, 23-25. At the 1990 General Conference, church leaders released a number of position statements dealing, e.g., with gun control, pornography, poverty,

Church still maintains a distinctive sense of its divine calling, unique message, and special, spiritual mission to the contemporary world.[403]

Adventist Theology in Cultural Context: The Social Forces of Doctrinal Change

The analysis of the direction that doctrinal developments have taken in Adventist history seems to confirm the conclusion that "the history of the Seventh-day Adventist Church is the story of its transformation from a sect to a Protestant denomination."[404] As is shown here, this assessment is not shared by everyone knowledgeable about Adventists. But there can be little doubt about the presence and operation of various forces that gradually seem to pull the church away from its sectarian roots towards a more denominational stance. This opens up the possibility that doctrinal modifications are related to, and influenced by, the workings of these gravitational pulls. Inasmuch as the church is influenced by its surrounding culture, its doctrines may possibly likewise reflect the impact of society on the community of faith. This section discusses three of these forces, which have been extensively analyzed and convincingly demonstrated by sociologists of religion.[405]

AIDS, drug misuse, and the environment. It was declared that "Seventh-day Adventists should stand at the forefront of the struggle to save the planet … Ecological responsibility and the belief in the imminent Advent are not mutually exclusive. Both must characterize Adventists" (Neal C. Wilson, "GC Leaders Target Concerns for the Adventist Church," *AR,* 2 August 1990, 12, 10-12). The 1992 Annual Council adopted guidelines and position statements covering abortion, temperance, environment, and care for the dying ("Taking a Stand: The Church Responds to Moral Issues Confronting Christians," *AR,* 31 December 1992, 11-15).

403 This appears to be a major reason for the consistent SDA refusal to join the World Council of Churches. It should also be pointed out, however, that almost from the beginning, the Adventist sense of mission to the world has included the active engagement for the well-being of society. This has found expression in numerous and widely recognized activities, particularly in the area of health and temperance, education, welfare and relief work, and religious liberty – areas where ecumenical cooperation is widely sought and practiced.

404 Lowell Tarling, *The Edges of Seventh-day Adventism* (Barragga Bay, Bermagui South, Australia: Galilee, 1982), 1.

405 While theologians have usually focused on the interior (endogenous) factors of doctrinal development, sociologists of religion have carefully analyzed the exterior (exogenous) forces of change. The former include theological controversy and reflection, the need to respond to heresy, the desire to go back *ad fontes,* and the presence of charismatic authorities in the church. In this context, one should also point to the psychological factors that may help explain the views of theologians whose positions have notably shaped the doctrines of their communities. The exterior (exogenous) forces, in turn, deal with the historical, i.e., the social, cultural, political, and economic causes of change. According to Wiles, these non-theological factors play an important part in the doctrinal decision-making of a church, but they do not exert a very significant influence on the actual content of its doctrines *(The Making of Christian Doctrine,* 15-16).

Prophetic Disconfirmation

Students of Adventist history have always been aware of the decisive impact that the non-occurrence of the *parousia* in 1844 had not only upon the Millerite movement as a whole but particularly on those disappointed Adventists who formed the nucleus of the later Seventh-day Adventist Church. As a kind of constitutive experience,[406] the great disappointment greatly aroused the thoughts and feelings of those Millerites who remained convinced of the fundamental accuracy of Miller's exposition of the 2,300 year-days of Dan 8:14.

Due to several theological reinterpretations, the early Sabbatarian Adventists were able to build a new and stable doctrinal edifice upon the remains of their former hope. At the center of their new faith lay the much-needed explanation of the shattering disappointment of 1844.[407] The bridegroom theory of Joseph Turner (1845), the sanctuary typology of O. R. L. Crosier (1846), and the investigative judgment theology (1850s) were significant steps in the attempt of the Sabbatarian Adventists to make sense of their disappointment and to adjust psychologically and intellectually to the new situation. It can even be said that Seventh-day Adventist theology, at heart, consists in the continued search for the meaning of the 1844 experience.

The fact that the apparent failure of the expectation of the Millerites led to a number of doctrinal readjustments suited for safeguarding its basic validity accords precisely with what sociologist Leon Festinger has called the theory of "cognitive dissonance."[408] His analysis of how millennial groups behave when their predictions fail to materialize has revealed three basic responses to this kind of "prophetic disconfirmation." First, there is an attempt to explain the disconfirming experience (rationalization) through a moderate reconstruction of belief (reinterpretation) intended to strengthen faith and deepen conviction; second, there is an increased

---

406 On this point, Adventists and observers of the church are agreed. "Adventist doctrine is rooted in and derives strength from an event which Adventists later referred to as 'the great disappointment' (October 22, 1844)" ("World Council of Churches/Seventh-day Adventist Conversations," *Ecumenical Review* 24 (1972): 201, 200-207; reprinted in *So Much in Common* [Geneva: World Council of Churches, 1973], 106). See also Paul Schwarzenau, *Ein evangelischer Theologe spricht über die Siebenten-Tags-Adventisten* (Laasphe: Wittgenstein-Verlag, 1979), 8-9.

407 Robin Theobald has pointed out that the disappointment of 1844 required some transformation of understanding which was achieved through a reinterpretation of prophecy and "by advances in scriptural exegesis" ("Seventh-day Adventists and the Millennium," in *A Sociological Yearbook of Religion in Britain – No. 7* [London: SCM, 1974], 127, 111-131). Similarly, SDA historian Gary Land has noted that "although Seventh-day Adventists had set no dates for Christ's Second Coming, their unfulfilled expectation of that event's imminence cried out for an explanation as the years passed" *(Adventism in America,* 215).

408 Leon Festinger, *A Theory of Cognitive Dissonance* (Stanford, Calif.: Stanford University Press, 1957). Cf. Leon Festinger, Henry W. Riecken, and Stanley Schachter, *When Prophecy Fails* (Minneapolis, Minn.: University of Minnesota Press, 1956); Neil Weiser, "The Effects of Prophetic Disconfirmation of the Committed," *Review of Religious Research* 16 (1974): 19-30; and Robert P. Carroll, *When Prophecy Failed* (London: SCM, 1979).

missionary fervor and proselytizing activity resulting in a broadening of the social base of the belief shared by the group; and third, there is an increased group commitment and a strengthening of its inner cohesiveness which likewise tends to validate the communal faith. It seems that this is exactly what happened in early Seventh-day Adventist history.[409]

To the degree that doctrine verbalizes religious experiences,[410] it may also be affected by later modifications of such experiences. The historical development of the sanctuary doctrine among Sabbatarian Adventists seems to bear this out. For example, when people were beginning to be converted from the unbelieving world, the restrictive shut-door doctrine was soon abandoned and replaced by an open-door concept. And when time continued longer than first expected, the concept of the investigative judgment helped to explain the apparent delay of the second coming of Christ.[411] In light of this, one may perhaps expect even further readjustments of those segments of the Adventist doctrinal tradition that developed in response to the 1844 experience and its aftermath.[412]

Church Growth and Internationalization

The rapid numerical growth and internationalization of Seventh-day Adventism in recent decades constitutes another important factor that is likely to have a lasting impact on Adventist theology and may possibly affect even the doctrines of the

---

409 It should be noted that this sociological analysis *per se* says nothing about the theological truth value of the particular prophecy believed by the group nor about the validity of its reinterpretation. For "it could be argued that in some cases the arousal of dissonance is a prerequisite for indicating the true nature of the expectation" (Carroll, 106). This is what Seventh-day Adventists have claimed all along regarding the true meaning of Dan 8:14 relating to the year 1844.

410 "Behind all meaningful religious statements lie acts of religious understanding. Behind all acts of religious understanding lie acts of religious experience" (Peter Chirico, "Religious Experience and Development of Dogma," *American Benedictine Review* 23 [1972]: 84). "In all Christian theology, experience precedes thought. That is to say, theology is the attempt to understand experience" (Edward W. H. Vick, *Let Me Assure You* [Mountain View, Calif.: PPPA, 1968], 16). 1 John 1:1-3 seems to support the view that experience may be a valid foundation of Christian doctrine. On the other hand, Adventists have always emphasized that the Scriptures are "the test of experience" (Ellen White, *The Great Controversy,* vii; see also idem, *Testimonies,* 3:71).

411 Though the notion of a pre-Advent judgment was advanced by Josiah Litch as early as 1841 and also became widespread among shut-door believers after the great disappointment of 1844, it was generally accepted by SDAs only in the mid-1850s. See above, pp. 175-180.

412 Chirico makes another pertinent observation that may be applicable to the sanctuary doctrine, which to Sabbatarian Adventists provided new meaning regarding the 1844 disappointment. "Heresy becomes not the rejection of a formula but the rejection of a meaning. In turn, this rejection of meaning implies a non-participation in the corporate experience that gave rise to that meaning" ("Religious Experience and Development of Dogma," 80, n. 17).

church.[413] The global expansion of Adventism with its resulting racial and cultural diversification makes a centralized and strictly uniform approach to matters of theology and church polity less and less feasible.[414]

This is not to say that the church is inevitably gaining speed on the road toward theological pluralism. But the rapid spread of the church brings about an influx of diverse cultural views which will increasingly shape the thought and behavior of Adventists in significant ways.[415] With the number of theological seminaries and other institutions of higher learning multiplying around the world, differences in emphasis and a certain plurality of theological viewpoints are likely to become more pronounced as the church enters upon another century. The internationalization and cross-fertilization of Seventh-day Adventist theology is rather to be expected in a world church engaged in a global mission.[416]

On the other hand, numerical church growth may also inhibit doctrinal change. Successful evangelization may decrease the readiness to reconsider church doctrines that are obviously quite meaningful to people, while lack of growth may stimulate theological reorientation in the attempt to adjust teachings, no longer deemed

413 That church growth constitutes an important factor of change has been pointed out by G. Oosterwal, "Continuity and Change in Adventist Mission," in *Mission Possible: The Challenge of Mission Today* (Nashville: SPA, 1972), 23-41; and Land, ed., *Adventism in America*, 208-210.

414 In 1977, the manual for ministers still noted "a considerable degree of uniformity" in the church services throughout the world and even wanted "to help in fostering this uniformity" *([Seventh-day Adventist] Manual for Ministers* [Takoma Park, Washington, D.C.: Ministerial Association, General Conference of Seventh-day Adventists, 1977], [3]). The new manual, issued in 1992, calls instead for a "unity without uniformity" and emphasizes that "the church must show respect for cultures in which it functions" *(Seventh-day Adventist Minister's Manual* [Silver Spring, Md.: Ministerial Association, General Conference of Seventh-day Adventists, 1992], 14). See also Jon Dybdahl, "How Culture Conditions Our View of Scripture," *Ministry,* January 1988, 7-9; Gottfried Oosterwal, "Mission and Culture: Shedding the Gospel's Western Package," *AR,* 19 October 1989, 18-23; idem, "Gospel, Culture, and Mission," *Ministry,* October 1989, 22-25; Borge Schantz, "One Message – Many Cultures: How Do We Cope?" *Ministry,* June 1992, 8-11 ("contextualization is a must for effective missionary service"); and Rosa Taylor Banks, "One People in Christ: The Challenge of Relationships," *AR,* 1 October 1992, 8-11.

415 The valuable observation of church historian Justo L. González regarding Christendom in general may, thus, also become true of the SDA church in particular. "The geographical expansion in the scope of theology may in the long run prove to be the most significant development of the twentieth century. Theology is no longer a North Atlantic enterprise" *(A History of Christian Thought,* 3:389; see also ibid., 389-393).

416 "By the 1980s a number of voices purported to speak for Adventism" – like traditionalists, liberals, centrists, and charismatics. The church was developing "signs of pluriformity" (Provonsha, *A Remnant in Crisis,* 8). See also Bull and Lockhart, *Seeking a Sanctuary,* 82-84. Today, there are some in the Adventist community who openly call for cultural pluralism, heterogeneous units, and more diversity. See, e.g., Rosado, *Broken Walls.* On the pluralistic situation of the contemporary world and its implications for the church, see Pöhler, "Religious Pluralism," 81-89. Cf. above, p. 19.

relevant, to the changing needs of the time. Besides, first-generation believers rarely question the theology on which they are spiritually fed; it is later generations that may question the theology of their progenitors. The experience of the worldwide Adventist church seems to support these observations.

An inevitable response on the part of Sabbatarian Adventists to the growth and diversification of their movement was the initial organization of the church in the early 1860s, which was followed by various efforts towards administrative restructuring in later years.[417] With it came a trend toward the institutionalization of church activities which raised what sociologist Thomas O'Dea has called "the dilemmas of institutionalization."[418] Among them is "the creedal dilemma" which places a church between the bondage to the letter and the freedom of the spirit. As a worldwide missionary movement, SDAs may want to avoid both the uniformitarian implications of creedalism and the relativizing consequences of pluralism.

Social Adaptation and Acculturation

There are also certain socio-economic forces at work in the church that may likewise have a sizeable and lasting impact on its theology. The upward social mobility of Seventh-day Adventists,[419] the increasing urbanization, and the influence of higher education[420] seem to have a relativizing effect regarding the adherence of church

---

417 See Andrew G. Mustard, *James White and SDA Church Organization: Historical Development, 1884-1881,* AU Theological Seminary Doctoral Dissertation Series, no. 12 (Berrien Springs, Mich.: AU Press, 1988); and Barry David Oliver, *SDA Organizational Structure: Past, Present, and Future,* AU Theological Seminary Doctoral Dissertation Series, no. 15 (Berrien Springs, Mich.: AU Press, 1989).

418 See Thomas O'Dea, "Five Dilemmas in the Institutionalization of Religion," *Journal for the Scientific Study of Religion* 1 (1961): 30-39; reprinted in idem, *Sociology and the Study of Religion* (New York and London: Basic Books, 1970), 240-255; see also idem, "The Five Dilemmas of Institutionalization," chap. in *The Sociology of Religion* (Englewood Cliffs, N.J.: Prentice-Hall, 1966), 90-97. Charles Teel, Jr., has applied these insights to the Adventist church in an essay presented at the 1980 Theological Consultation ("Withdrawing Sect, Accommodating Church, Prophesying Remnant: Dilemmas in the Institutionalization of Adventism, 1980," TMs, AHC, JWL, AU, Berrien Springs, Mich.). In this essay, the author called upon Adventists to be "a prophesying remnant which holds selected sect-church polarities in creative tension" (p. 2). See also George R. Knight, "Adventism, Institutionalism, and the Challenge of Secularization," *Ministry,* June 1991, 6-10, 29.

419 See Gary Schwartz, *Sect Ideologies and Social Status* (Chicago and London: University of Chicago Press, 1970), 134-136, 220-221.

420 "The [Adventist identity] crisis is associated with the relative increase in the educational level of many church members. This could not help modifying the Adventist paradigm or worldview" (Provonsha, *A Remnant in Crisis,* 29, 27-29). "The denomination, in putting great emphasis on education, had inadvertently produced intellectuals who, on the basis of new experiences and new information, were in various ways reformulating Adventism" (Land, ed., *Adventism in America,* 226). Among the characteristics of intellectuals that affect their attitudes towards religious authorities are critical reflection, methodological doubt, rejection

members to the traditional thought patterns and behavioral norms. For years, this development had been foreseen and explicit warnings been expressed.[421] In spite of this, the acculturation and social adaptation of Adventists have manifested themselves both in a lessening commitment on the part of a sizeable number of Adventists to the distinctive teachings of the church and in the accompanying assimilation and accommodation to the ideas and values of the contemporary secular culture.[422]

With the rapid numerical growth of the church deriving largely from developing nations[423] and from lower-middle-class and low-income groups in Western countries,[424] it is impossible to foresee the results of the respective influence that the affluent and well-educated minority, on the one hand, and the economically poor and less-educated majority of Adventists, on the other hand, will exert on the direction of the theology and the further development of the doctrines of the church.[425]

Sect or Denomination?

In his farewell speech as President of the General Conference, Robert H. Pierson, after pointing to the way in which sects typically evolve into established denominations, exclaimed that "this must never happen to the Seventh-day Adventist Church!"[426] Others soon responded by asserting that "much of this has already happened ... the sect has become a church."[427]

of absolutism and dogmatism, openness to change, and the continuous search for truth instead of the claim of possessing it.

421 See, e.g., L. E. Froom, "Perils of Maturity Beset Us Today," *Ministry,* August 1941, 21-22. In 1929, Adventist colleges began to apply for accreditation. In 1937, the first Theological Seminary was established in Washington, D.C. The first universities were founded in 1960 (Andrews University) and 1961 (Loma Linda University), respectively. In 1993, the church supported 81 colleges and universities worldwide.

422 See, e.g., Jonathan Butler, "Perils of the Enchanted Ground: The Acculturation of Seventh-day Adventists on the Pacific Coast, [1978]," TMs (in my possession). A careful and provocative sociological analysis of Adventism is provided by Bull and Lockhart, *Seeking a Sanctuary: Seventh-day Adventism and the American Dream* (1989). An unsparing study written from a Central European perspective of the psychological and sociological processes involved in acculturation and social adaptation is Thomas R. Steininger's, *Konfession und Sozialisation: Adventistische Identität zwischen Fundamentalismus und Postmoderne* (Göttingen: Vandenhoeck & Ruprecht, 1993).

423 By the end of the century, about 80% of all church members will live in the developing countries of the world.

424 Carlos Medley, "The Changing Face of Adventism," *AR,* 19 February 1987, 5.

425 While some see the church threatened by the inroads of theological liberalism and ethical relativism, others are worried about the strong influence of the conservative and fundamentalist segments in the church. See below, pp. 243-251.

426 Robert H. Pierson, "An Earnest Appeal from the Retiring President of the General Conference," *AR,* 26 October 1978, 10.

427 Donald R. McAdams, "The 1978 Annual Council: A Report and Analysis," *Spectrum* 9:4 (1979): 7-8. A recent Adventist study noted: "Seventh-day Adventism is extremely difficult

It should be noted that what is referred to here is not a theological understanding of sect and church[428] but strictly a sociological definition.[429] From a sociologist's perspective, a sect can be defined as a minority protest group whose distinctive lifestyle, teachings, and self-understanding set it apart both from other churches and from society at large. Its desire to restore Christianity to its pristine purity expresses as well as promotes a certain elitism and exclusivism. When such a group de-emphasizes its unique lifestyle, teachings, and self-understanding, minimizes its sectarian practices, beliefs, and commitment, and becomes increasingly tolerant of cultural, theological, and ecumenical trends, it is on the road towards becoming an established denomination or a church. In other words, it is the attitude towards the world in general and to other denominations in particular that is at the heart of the sociological definition of sect and church.[430]

to categorize on the basis of these [sect-denomination-church] typologies. While it manifests definite sectarian tendencies, it is also a good example of a religious movement where the process of denominationalization is well advanced" (Michael Pearson, *Millennial Dreams and Moral Dilemmas: Seventh-day Adventism and Contemporary Ethics* [Cambridge: Cambridge University Press, 1990], 13).

428 Protestants commonly use the threefold *sola* of the 16th-century Reformers as theological criteria for distinguishing sects from churches. Thus, it is asked, does a denomination (1) affirm the *sola scriptura* or recognize extra-biblical sources of revelation as being of equal authority, (2) maintain the *sola gratia* and *sola fide* or deny the free gift of salvation by grace through faith alone, (3) uphold the *solo Christo* or devaluate the unique redemptive work of Jesus? In addition, the separatist exclusiveness or ecumenical openness, respectively, of a denomination is also frequently used as a criterion of its acceptance or rejection. On these counts, Seventh-day Adventists have often been considered as a sect or cult by their fellow evangelical Christians. See, e.g., Gerstner, *The Theology of the Major Sects,* 6-28, 126-130; and Anthony A. Hoekema, *The Four Major Cults* (Grand Rapids: Eerdmans, 1963), 373-388, 388-403. Others, however, have come to recognize SDAs as an essentially evangelical church. See, e.g., Martin, *The Kingdom of the Cults,* 1965 ed., 359-422. For a Roman Catholic assessment of SDAs, see W. J. Whalen, "Sects and Cults, American," *NCE,* 1967 ed., 13:31-34.

429 The sociological approach to religion and its concomitant church-sect typology was first developed by Max Weber (1864-1920) and Ernst Troeltsch (1865-1923) in their epochal studies on the influence of religion on society (Max Weber, *The Protestant Ethic and the Spirit of Capitalism* [London: Allen & Unwin, 1930]; and Ernst Troeltsch, *The Social Teachings of the Christian Churches,* 2 vols. [New York: Macmillan, 1931; New York: Harper & Row, 1960]). H. Richard Niebuhr (1894-1962), in turn, analyzed the impact of social and economic factors on religion and theology/ethics *(The Social Sources of Denominationalism* [New York and London: New American Library, 1929/1957]). Their "ideal type" approach to sect/church was later criticized and refined and is, today, regarded as a limited but useful tool in the scientific study of religion.

430 See Elmer T. Clark, *The Small Sects in America,* rev. ed. (New York and Nashville: Abingdon-Cokesbury, 1949); Bryan R. Wilson, "An Analysis of Sect Development," *American Sociological Review* 24 (February 1959): 3-15; idem, ed., *Patterns of Sectarianism: Organisation and Ideology in Social and Religious Movements* (London: Heinemann, 1967); idem, *Religious Sects: A Sociological Study* (New York and Toronto: McGraw-Hill, 1970);

Observers of Seventh-day Adventism have identified signs of a gradual movement toward a more denominational stance; at the same time, they clearly recognize
its lasting sectarian features.[431] Will the church retain its sense of identity and
mission as a "prophetic minority"[432] while, at the same time, fellowshipping with
other Christians and involving itself in worldly affairs?[433] Adventists may either strive
to maintain a fruitful tension between their more exclusive and inclusive features, or
they may opt for one side – sectarian exclusiveness or ecumenical inclusiveness – to
the neglect of the other. Only time can reveal how the church will understand its
divine calling to be in, but not of the world. In the words of an Adventist scholar,

> the challenge to Adventism is not to resist the evolution from sect to church; such a
> change has already happened. The challenge is to retain the spark, commitment and
> message that gave the sect its original power, while accepting the institutional, structural
> and cultural changes that are the inevitable concomitant of growth in the real world.
> While it is appropriate, indeed obligatory, to oppose heresy, loss of commitment and
> abandonment of moral standards, it is futile to oppose change and attempt to exist
> outside the reality of contemporary culture.[434]

   idem, *Magic and the Millennium* (London: Heinemann, 1973), 22-26; idem, "Sect or
   Denomination: Can Adventism Maintain Its Identity?" *Spectrum* 7:1 (1975): 34-43; J.
   Milton Yinger, *Religion, Society and the Individual* (New York: Macmillan, 1957); and
   Charles Y. Glock and R. Stark, *Religion and Society in Tension* (Chicago: Rand-McNally,
   1965).

431 See Wilson, *Religious Sects,* 93-103, 236-237. Cf. Irmgard Simon, *Die Gemeinschaft der
   Siebenten-Tags-Adventisten in volkskundlicher Sicht* (Muenster: Verlag Aschendorff, 1965);
   Gary Schwartz, *Sect Ideologies and Social Status;* Hans-Diether Reimer, "Endzeitgemeinde
   im Wandel: Wohin bewegt sich der Adventismus?" *Materialdienst* 36:14 (1973): 218-225;
   and idem, "Die Siebenten-Tags-Adventisten und das Problem der zwischenkirchlichen
   Beziehungen," *Materialdienst* 49:9 (1986): 267-275. In spite of the gradual assimilation of
   denominational features and the shedding of other, more sectarian traits, the SDA church has
   not soft-pedaled its distinctive doctrines over the years.

432 See Jack W. Provonsha, "The Church as a Prophetic Minority," *Spectrum* 12:1 (1981): 18-
   23; idem, *God Is with Us,* 49-57; and idem, *A Remnant in Crisis,* 7-72.

433 For a reconsideration of the SDA understanding of the role of the church vis-a-vis the world,
   see Bernhard Oestreich, "Gemeinde in der Welt," in *Die Gemeinde und ihr Auftrag,* Studien
   zur adventistischen Ekklesiologie, vol. 2, ed. Johannes Mager (Hamburg: Saatkorn-Verlag,
   1994), 127-156. The author calls upon Adventists not to withdraw from the world (which
   would betray a "worldly" attitude) but to be fully involved in the affairs of this world (and
   thereby demonstrate their "otherworldliness").

434 McAdams, "The 1978 Annual Council," 8; cf. Land, ed., *Adventism in America,* 228-230.
   For another Adventist analysis written from a sociological perspective, see Andrew G.
   Mustard, "Implications of Troeltsch's Church-Sect Typology for Seventh-day Adventist
   Ecclesiology, 1978," TMs, AHC, JWL, AU, Berrien Springs, Mich. The following *caveat*
   expressed by Bull and Lockhart should also be taken seriously: "From a theological point of
   view, there is little evidence to support the widely held contention that Adventists have moved
   from the margins of society toward the mainstream. Adventist theology has developed in
   parallel with that of the mainstream. It was at its most distinctive during a period of great

Summary and Conclusion

Seventh-day Adventism is an heir to the apocalyptic revival movement that caught hold of the northeastern parts of the United States in the middle of the nineteenth century. Over the years, it experienced several significant doctrinal revisions with regard to both its fundamental and its distinctive beliefs. In part, these homogeneous as well as heterogeneous changes resulted from hermeneutical readjustments. In time, the church developed rather elaborate Statements of Faith. The general direction of doctrinal changes in Adventism is reflected in an increasing emphasis on orthodox and fundamental Christian doctrines. This has led the church towards a closer identification with evangelical Protestantism and a greater involvement in the contemporary world. An analysis of the social forces at work in the denomination sheds additional light on the phenomenon of doctrinal development within the Seventh-day Adventist Church.

Whatever significance may accrue to these developments, the changes that have occurred in the theology and fundamental teachings of the church must be seen in relation to the remarkable continuity that has characterized Adventist beliefs until today. At the same time, there can be little doubt that what has happened in several instances in the history of Seventh-day Adventism was more than and different from the mere refinement of its doctrinal heritage or the harmonious unfolding of its faith. In the words of an informed and believing insider,

> the young faith continually advanced, not only in numbers but also in understanding. It changed its ideas about organization and the ministry, deepened its understanding of the third angel's message of Revelation 14, and revised its interpretations of prophecy. It corrected its understanding of Christ and the Trinity, reclaimed the great truth of salvation by grace through faith, and found much else to learn or to unlearn. But while it corrected, amplified, and reclaimed, it never lost touch with its roots, the "waymarks."
>
> This is the most striking characteristic of Adventism. Without repudiating the past leading of the Lord, it seeks ever to understand better what that leading was. It is always open to better insights and willing to learn – to seek for truth as for hid treasure.[435]

diversity [in the 19th century]; it became fundamentalist in the era of fundamentalism; and it softened with the rise of evangelicalism" (Bull and Lockhart, *Seeking a Sanctuary,* 91).

435 Robert M. Johnston, "A Search for Truth," *AR,* Adventist History Issue [15 September 1983], 8.

Chapter 5

Adventist Conceptions of Doctrinal Development:

An Assessment

> Tradition is the living faith of the dead; traditionalism is the
> dead faith of the living.
>
> *Jaroslav Pelikan*

> Seventh-day Adventists claim to be different from all other
> denominations in this: That they are willing to receive new
> light. Is this so?
>
> *W. C. White*

Introduction

Having described what kind of doctrinal changes had actually occurred in the history
of the Adventist church, this study now proceeds by investigating the various
responses Adventists have given in the past and until now to these developments.

It should be noted at the outset that just like in church history generally, these
changes took place irrespective of whether they were recognized as such or adequately
explained by the church.[1] In fact, for more than a century, Adventists did not address
the issue of doctrinal development other than in sporadic remarks usually occasioned
by some concrete issue at hand. Only in recent years have a few articles appeared
that directly addressed the problem of doctrinal continuity and change.

To help the reader better grasp the significance of these scattered responses to
doctrinal change, they are presented first in their historical context out of which they
grew. Following this, some catchwords are discussed that were and are still commonly used by Adventists whenever the issue of doctrinal development is being

---

[1] During the Patristic era some important doctrinal developments took place that are reflected in
the Trinitarian and Christological dogmas of the 4th and 5th centuries. However, one can
find only a few sporadic statements dealing with the problem of doctrinal change from this
period (see above, pp. 56-58). This coincidence of major doctrinal developments and minimal
reflection on the problem of change was repeated in the history of the Adventist church.
During its formative years and until recently, the church stressed the continuity with its doctrinal past while paying scant attention to the changes that actually took place in its theology.

considered. Finally, various conceptions of doctrinal continuity and change are analyzed and assessed in the light of Adventist history, concepts that were proposed by
scholars who had become more fully aware of the problem of doctrinal change.[2]

Responses to Doctrinal Developments and Disputes in Adventist History

Brief as it is, the history of Seventh-day Adventism can be subdivided into several
smaller units of time for the sake of analysis and clarification. In the following, seven
periods lasting twenty years each are distinguished which constitute major phases in
the history of the Adventist church. For each period, some of the more significant
events and statements related to doctrinal continuity and change are presented and
briefly analyzed in their historical context.[3]

1846-1865

The first phase of Seventh-day Adventist history – the period prior to and ending
with a stable church organization – was a time of theological innovation and doctrinal
reconstruction. Whatever readjustments seemed to be necessary were made possible
by a remarkable openness on the part of the Sabbatarian Adventists to whatever new
truths might present themselves to their minds. The characteristic spirit of this period
is perhaps best expressed by J. N. Andrews' famous exclamation, "I would exchange a
thousand errors for one truth."[4]

---

2   To assess the various Adventist conceptions of doctrinal development in the light of the
     historical facts presented in chapter 4 is not to pass a theological judgment on them. Rather
     it is the historical basis on which a proper hermeneutical evaluation of the various theories of
     doctrinal development may be built. For to assess something "implies a determining of the
     exact value or extent of a thing prior to judging it or to using it as the ground for a decision"
     (Webster's New Dictionary of Synonyms, 1984 ed., s.v. "Estimate").

3   A general knowledge of the historical and theological development of Adventism will help to
     place the following survey in its proper context. Two works that cover the spectrum of
     denominational history including its doctrinal developments are Schwarz, Light Bearers to the
     Remnant, and Land, ed., Adventism in America: A History. Land subdivides SDA history
     between 1846 and 1980 into six periods of unequal length. In a concise survey, George R.
     Knight distinguishes four stages in Adventism's "search for identity" between 1844 and the
     present time ("Adventist Theology 1844 to 1994," Ministry, August 1994, 10-13, 25).

4   Quoted in Ellen G. White, Spiritual Gifts, vol. 2, My Christian Experience, Views and Labors
     in Connection with the Rise and Progress of the Third Angel's Message (Battle Creek, Mich.:
     James White, 1860), 117; also quoted in idem, Life Sketches of Ellen G. White (Mountain
     View, Calif.: PPPA, 1915/1943), 127. On another occasion, Andrews questioned the
     authority of ecclesiastical traditions by saying, "If the Advent body itself were to furnish the
     fathers and the saints for the future church, Heaven pity the people that should live hereafter!
     Reader, we entreat you to prize your Bible" ("Things to Be Considered," RH, 31 January
     1854, 10, 9-10).

Still, making a new beginning was not understood as laying a new foundation. Repeatedly during these early years, the pioneers of the Seventh-day Adventist Church claimed to be the true heirs of the Millerite movement and charged their fellow Millerites with having "backslidden from the Advent faith" by "over-turning one strong point after another of the 'original Advent faith.'"[5] In particular, the time calculation leading to 1844 was looked upon by Sabbatarian Adventists as "the main pillar" of Adventism.[6] James White spoke for them all when he maintained that

> we claim to stand on the original Advent faith … as to the great fundamental doctrines taught by Wm. Miller, we see no reason to change our views. We claim all the light of past time on this glorious theme, and cherish it as from Heaven. And we cheerfully let the providence of God, and plain Bible testimony correct our past view of the Sanctuary, and give us a more harmonious system of truth, and a firmer basis of faith.[7]

5   James White, "My Lord Delayeth His Coming," *RH,* 10 January 1854, 204-205. Cf. idem, "Who Has Left the Sure Word?" *Present Truth,* December 1849, 46-47; partly reprinted in *RH,* 13 January 1852, 74; idem, "Babylon," *RH,* 24 June 1852, 28-29; idem, "The Original Advent Faith," *RH,* 27 October 1859, 182; Uriah Smith, "The Original Advent Faith," *RH,* 18 September 1855, 44; idem, "Seventh-day Adventists," *RH,* 22 November 1864, 204-205; and idem, "Good, Today," *RH,* 4 August 1868, 108. See also *SDAE,* 1976 ed., s.v. "Millerite Movement."

6   James White, "Our Present Position," *RH,* December 1850, 13. See also idem, "Our Present Position," *RH,* January 1851, 27; idem, "To Ira Fancher," *RH,* March 1851, 52; idem, "The Parable, Matthew XXV, 1-12," *RH,* 9 June 1851, 100; [idem], "The 2300 Days," *RH,* 6 December 1853, 172; Joseph Bates, "The Laodicean Church," *RH,* November 1850, 7-8; idem, "Midnight Cry in the Past," *RH,* December 1850, 23; idem, "Thoughts on the Past Work of William Miller," *RH,* 17 February 1853, 156-157; Hiram Edson, "The Sixty-Nine Weeks and 2300 Days," *RH,* March 1851, 49-50; J. N. Andrews, "The Sanctuary," *RH,* 23 December 1852, 123; idem, "Position of the Advent Herald on the Sanctuary Question," *RH,* 12 May 1853, 204-205; idem, "Under the Necessity of Choosing," *RH,* 8 November 1853, 141; and E. R. Seaman, "Removing the Landmarks," *RH,* 9 June 1853, 15. James White quoted Bliss as saying that "by the abandonment of this last item of the 'original advent faith,' its fundamental principle is given up; for the connection of these two periods [i.e., of the 70 weeks and the 2,300 days] was the distinguishing point between Mr. Miller's faith and that entertained by other more common theories on the prophetic periods" ("My Lord Delayeth His Coming," *RH,* 10 January 1854, 205). To reaffirm this belief in the hope of winning back some of their former brethren was the main reason behind the publication in 1850 of five issues of the *Advent Review.*

7   James White, "'We Are the Adventists,'" *RH,* 18 April 1854, 100-101. Many Millerites wanted to maintain continuity with their past after the disappointment of 1844. But they opted for different avenues to achieve it. The invitation to the Albany Conference in the spring of 1845, e.g., was extended to all "who still adhere to the original Advent faith" – except its time calculation (see D. T. Arthur, "After the Great Disappointment: To Albany and Beyond," *Adventist Heritage* 1:1 [1974]: 8, 5-10). The "open-door" believers and the "shut-door" group were sharply divided over the question of whether the error of the Millerites was related to the time calculation itself or only to the events expected to have taken place on October 22, 1844. While the former group severed the connection between Dan 8 and 9, the

If the Sabbatarian Adventists wanted to build on the past, they were equally willing to move forward into an unknown future. This involved the acceptance of new teachings as well as the revision of previous beliefs.[8] While denying that they held a "new position disconnected with the past," they looked upon their faith as "a further development of that true Advent faith."[9] Uriah Smith well expressed the attitude that characterized Sabbatarian Adventists at that time.

> Since 1844 more light has risen upon our pathway ... We have been enabled to rejoice in truths far in advance of what we then perceived. But we do not imagine that we yet have it all, by any means. We trust to progress still, our way growing continually brighter and brighter unto the perfect day. Then let us maintain an inquiring frame of mind, seeking for more light, more truth.[10]

It was this attitude that contributed to the deep-seated fears that a number of Adventists expressed with regard to James White's drive for church organization in 1860. Defining the "Babylonian" error as "sticking a stake and refusing to pull it up and advance" and pointing to the doctrinal changes already made by the Sabbatarian Adventists, M. E. Cornell maintained that "it may well be that we still have other stakes to pull up." Adventists should, therefore, be prepared to give up any "false applications and interpretations" of the Bible "as fast as possible."[11]

latter abandoned the identification of the sanctuary to be cleansed with the church or the earth. In any event, "the more sincere Millerites could only hold to the substance of their faith. There could be no major error, only some slighter misinterpretation attributable to still-fallible human judgment" (Cross, *The Burned-Over District*, 308-309).

8   "We closely adhere to the fundamental doctrines taught by Wm. Miller, because we believe them to be sound; yet we are willing that the march of Time, and the increase of light should convict all the errors in that theory" ([J. White], "The Twenty-three Hundred Days," *RH*, 18 April 1854, 100). The two dozen Sabbath and sanctuary conferences held between April 1848 and December 1850 were the principal means by which the basic features of the SDA doctrinal system were conveyed to and accepted by the scattered believers who became the nucleus of the later Seventh-day Adventist Church. See *SDAE*, 1976 ed., s.v. "Sabbath Conferences"; and A. L. White, *Ellen G. White*, 1:139-15. Cf. also above, pp. 157-158.

9   Uriah Smith, "Why Can We Not Believe in the New Time?" *RH*, 14 February 1854, 29. When Joshua V. Himes claimed that Seventh-day Adventists had added new doctrines to the original Advent faith, Smith admitted this only with regard to the non-immortality of the soul. For, he retorted, all other doctrines – like the ones on the Sabbath, the sanctuary, the third angel's message, and the spirit of prophecy – "are not additions, but only further developments of the same great system of truth" ("A Friendly Word with the Voice of the West," *RH*, 9 August 1864, 84).

10   Uriah Smith, "The True Course," *RH*, 30 April 1857, 205. After they had modified their view on the proper time to begin the Sabbath, James White explained that the Sabbatarian Adventists "would change on other points of their faith if they could see good reason to do so from the Scriptures" ("The Word," *RH*, 7 February 1856, 149).

11   M. E. Cornell, "'Making Us a Name,'" *RH*, 24 May 1860, 8-9. James White fully agreed with this view (see "Business Proceedings of B. C. Conference," *RH*, 23 October 1860, 178, 177-179; and [James White], "Organization," *RH*, 1 October 1861, 140-141).

1866-1885

While the first phase of Seventh-day Adventist history had been marked by the willingness to advance and change in doctrinal matters and by a sensitivity regarding the dangers of traditionalism and creedalism, the following period was characterized both by the consolidation of what had been achieved thus far and by a growing desire to preserve and protect, rather than to progress in, the faith.[12]

When, in 1865, two ministers questioned the identification of the "two-horned beast" of Revelation 13 with the United States of America, they were charged with having surrendered one of the "fundamental principles of present truth." Yet, the *Review & Herald* could inform its readers that most Seventh-day Adventists faithfully continued to "hold onto the old landmarks."[13]

The attitude of Adventists towards doctrinal change became increasingly ambiguous. On the one hand, they continued to speak of "progressive development," "advancing light," and "additional truths."[14] But, on the other hand, they began to regard the permanence and stability of Adventist doctrines as evidence of their accuracy and truth.[15] If doctrinal development was to take place, it would involve only the unfolding and enlargement of past insights, not their reversal or revision.[16]

Seldom did someone conceive of the possibility that Seventh-day Adventists might still have to abandon erroneous positions or to modify some of their teachings as they had done during their formative years.[17] Changes in the religious world –

---

12 For an enlightening analysis of the transformation and consolidation of Millerite and Sabbatarian Adventism of the 1840s into the Seventh-day Adventism of the 1850s and beyond, see Jonathan M. Butler, "The Making of a New Order: Millerism and the Origins of Seventh-day Adventism," in *The Disappointed: Millerism and Millenarianism in the Nineteenth Century*, ed. Numbers and Butler, 189-208. Cf. idem, "From Millerism to Seventh-day Adventism: Boundlessness to Consolidation," *Church History* 55 (1986): 50-64.

13 Wm. S. Ingraham, "Matters in Iowa," *RH*, 23 January 1866, 63; U. Smith, G. W. Amadon, and J. M. Aldrich, "Remarks," ibid.; J. Dorcas, "Meeting in Marion, Iowa," *RH*, 13 February 1866, 86; and "A Good Move in Iowa," *RH*, 20 February 1866, 94-95. For a contextual interpretation of this "intriguing element" of the Adventist eschatological scenario, see Bull and Lockhart, *Seeking a Sanctuary*, 47-49.

14 R. F. Cottrell, "The Gospel Progressive in Development," *RH*, 23 June 1868, 9; D. T. Bourdeau, "How the Different Protestant Denominations Arose," *RH*, 26 November 1872, 189; Wm. Pepper, "Walk in the Light," *RH*, 20 March 1879, 90; D. T. Bourdeau, "Why Was It Not Found out Before?" *RH*, 30 August 1881, 146; "What a Change!" *RH*, 14 March 1882, 168; R. F. Cottrell, "Have We a Message?" *RH*, 25 April 1882, 266; and "Truth Progressive," *RH*, 23 May 1882, 328.

15 George I. Butler, "Stability a Characteristic of Our Work," *RH*, 15 April 1873, 140; idem, "Old-Fashioned Religion," *RH*, 12 August 1873, 65; and [Uriah Smith], "The Opening Year," *RH*, 6 January 1885, 8.

16 R. F. Cottrell, "Evidence of Truth," *RH*, 13 May 1873, 172; and idem, "Advancing Light," *RH*, 31 January 1878, 36.

17 W. H. Littlejohn, "Seventh-day Adventists and Seventh-day Baptists," *RH*, 11 November 1880, 306; cf. idem, "The Church Manual," *RH*, 31 July 1883, 491.

like those brought about by the theory of evolution – would rather lead to an "epochal crisis" in Christianity.[18] Over against those who attached only little value to doctrines, Adventists firmly upheld the vital importance for the church of both biblical teaching and doctrinal preaching.[19]

A moderate attempt by an "Elder R. S. Owen" to introduce a "new exposition" on the "seven trumpets" was rejected by the 1883 General Conference as being "unscriptural" and also because it "would unsettle some of the most important and fundamental points of our faith." The delegates saw "no occasion to change from the views we have formerly entertained."[20]

The next time a "new theory" would be discussed at a General Conference, it could not be as easily put to rest. Rather, it was to stir up heated debates and create deep divisions among the brethren. Yet, in the long run, the "new view" would actually become the accepted position of Adventists and "a foremost turning point in their theological development" which "changed the shape of Adventism."[21]

1886-1905

In sharp contrast to the previous period, the third phase of Seventh-day Adventist history was marked by doctrinal controversies and the questioning of traditional views. They brought about changes and revisions that, in some areas, significantly altered the teachings of the church.[22] No period in Adventist history has witnessed such intense discussions about the doctrines of the church. Among the controverted points of faith were the meaning of the law in Galatians, the exact application of the ten horns of Daniel 7, the practical significance of the righteousness of Christ, the issues of perfection(ism) and pan(en)theism, and the doctrines of the sanctuary and of the investigative judgment.

The conflict had been smoldering since 1886 when E. J. Waggoner published a series of articles in the *Signs of the Times* in which he set forth a position on the law in Galatians that Ellen White – at least in the minds of many – had clearly rejected years ago.[23] The storm finally broke out during the 1888 General Conference session

---

18 [Uriah Smith], "Giving Way," *RH,* 23 October 1883, 664.

19 R. F. Cottrell, "Doctrine," *RH,* 8 January 1875, 10; D. M. Canright, "Doctrine," *RH,* 18 July 1878, 29; "Doctrine and Life," *RH,* 12 April 1881, 228-229; and "Doctrinal Religion," *RH,* 21 June 1881, 389.

20 "General Conference Proceedings," *RH,* 20 November 1883, 733-734; "General Conference Proceedings," *RH,* 27 November 1883, 741; see also "The Seven Trumpets," *RH,* 8 July 1884, 448.

21 George R. Knight, *Angry Saints: Tensions and Possibilities in the Adventist Struggle Over Righteousness by Faith* (Washington, D.C., and Hagerstown, Md.: RHPA, 1989), [11].

22 Knight speaks of "revolutionary developments in Adventist theology in the late 1880s and 1890s" ("Adventists and Change," 14).

23 "As it looks to me, next to the death of Brother White, the greatest calamity that ever befell our cause was when Dr. Waggoner put his articles on the book of Galatians through the *Signs* ... If I was on oath at a court of justice, I should be obliged to testify that to the best of my

and the Bible Institute that preceded it. It revealed deep-seated disagreements among the ministers of the church with regard to the meaning of the law in Galatians in relation to the gospel, the exact identity of the ten horns/kingdoms (Dan 7),[24] and the new emphasis Waggoner and Jones were placing on the righteousness of Christ.

The traditionalists, headed by George I. Butler and Uriah Smith, were convinced that the new ideas undermined the foundations of the faith and constituted a serious threat to the unity, identity and mission of the church. For this reason, they were determined to do everything in their power to protect the church from these heretical innovations (called by some "new light") and to make believers "stand by the old landmarks" which had been preached for about thirty to forty years.

The progressives, on the other side, were led by E. J. Waggoner and A. T. Jones. They were equally positive that certain traditional views were not adequately supported by the Bible and, in fact, did hinder the advance of the church and the fulfillment of its mission. Thus, it was their desire to lead the church into a new and deeper experience of faith and to promote more accurate doctrinal positions.[25]

In the *Review & Herald,* Smith wrote from Minneapolis that "the sentiments of the delegates appeared, from unmistakable indications, to be overwhelmingly on the side of established principles of interpretation, and the old view" regarding the ten horns/kingdoms.[26] In order to prevent the new ideas from being taught at Battle

knowledge and belief ... you said that Brother [J. H.] Waggoner was wrong [about the law in Galatians] ... The position that Brother [E. J.] Waggoner now takes is open to exactly the same objection ... It seems to me contrary to the Scriptures, and secondly, contrary to what you have previously seen" (Uriah Smith, Letter to Ellen White, 17 February 1890, EGWRC, AU, Berrien Springs, Mich.). For more information, see below, pp. 300-303.

24   Delegates were divided between "Huns" defending the old view and "Alemanni" siding with the new interpretation. According to Butler, "the position that the Huns were one of the Ten Kingdoms" was "the position held by all of our writers for forty years, published in all our books treating on the subject" (George I. Butler to Ellen White, 16 December 1886, EGWRC, AU, Berrien Springs, Mich.). The new view was first advanced by A. T. Jones in a series of articles in the *Signs of the Times* between August 1885 and October 1886, and beyond. See A. T. Jones, "The Alemanni," *ST,* 17 June-8 July 1886, 356-357, 372, 388, 404; and idem, "The Ten Kingdoms," *ST,* 30 September-28 October 1886, 596, 612, 628, 644-645.

25   "I do not regard this view which I hold [on the law in Galatians] as a new idea at all. It is not a new theory of doctrine. Everything that I have taught is perfectly in harmony with the fundamental principles of truth which have been held not only by our people, but by all the eminent reformers. And so I do not take any credit to myself for advancing it" (E. J. Waggoner, *The Gospel in the Book of Galatians* [Oakland, Calif.: PPPA, 1888], 70). Waggoner distributed this book at the Minneapolis conference in answer to George I. Butler's *The Law in the Book of Galatians* (Battle Creek, Mich.: RHPA, 1886) which had been handed out to the delegates of the 1886 General Conference. For more information on this disputed point, see Bert Haloviak, "From Righteousness to Holy Flesh: Judgment at Minneapolis, [1988]," ch. 7, TMs, Library, Friedensau Theological Graduate School, Friedensau, Germany.

26   [Uriah Smith], "The Conference," *RH,* 23 October 1888, 664-665. In a letter to his wife, W. C. White noted that "there is almost a craze for orthodoxy" at the conference (William C. White to Mary White, 3 November 1888, EGWRC, AU, Berrien Springs, Mich.).

Creek College, where Jones was slated to teach in 1889, a resolution was proposed which recommended "that persons holding views different from those commonly taught by us as a denomination" should first present them to various committees for approval.[27] Ellen White, however, strongly opposed such a stifling decree because, in her judgment, it would only serve to hinder the progress and advance of truth.[28]

Waggoner's eleven devotional studies on justification by faith and the righteousness of Christ in relation to the law were attacked by many conference delegates who feared that this new emphasis on faith would destroy the law as a foundational pillar of Adventism and, thereby, undermine its strong opposition to antinomianism. In Ellen White's judgment, however, Waggoner reaffirmed old truths, though presenting them in a new light and with a renewed emphasis.[29] Her wholehearted support of Waggoner's message not only gave him a wide hearing in the years to come but also contributed decisively to the growing acceptance in the church of the doctrine of righteousness by faith, even among those who had originally opposed it in 1888.[30]

27   "S. D. Adventist General Conference [Proceedings]," *RH,* 13 November 1888, 714. A similar resolution had been adopted already by the 1886 General Conference saying that "doctrinal views not held by a fair majority" of SDAs should not be taught or published until they had been "examined and approved by the leading brethren of experience" ("General Conference Proceedings," *RH,* 14 December 1886, 779).

28   "When the resolution was urged upon the conference that nothing should be taught in the college contrary to that which has been taught, I felt deeply, for I knew whoever framed that resolution was not aware of what he was doing" (Ellen White, Manuscript 16, 1889, EGWRC, AU, Berrien Springs, Mich.). "Instructors in our schools should never be bound about by being told that they are to teach only what has been taught hitherto. Away with these restrictions. There is a God to give the message His people shall speak. Let not any minister feel under bonds or be gauged by men's measurements. The gospel must be fulfilled in accordance with the messages God sends. That which God gives His servants to speak today would not perhaps have been present truth twenty years ago, but it is God's message for this time" (idem, Manuscript 8a, 1888, EGWRC, AU, Berrien Springs, Mich.). In 1896, White wrote, "The God of heaven sometimes commissions men to teach that which is regarded as contrary to the established doctrines" *(Testimonies to Ministers and Gospel Workers* [Mountain View, Calif.: PPPA, 1923/1962], 69).

29   Ellen White's personal response to the events of 1888 and beyond is found in A. L. White, *Ellen G. White,* 3:385-475; Ellen White, *Selected Messages,* 1:350-400; idem, *Selected Messages from the Writings of Ellen G. White,* book 3 (Washington, D.C.: RHPA, 1980), 156-189; A. V. Olson, *Thirteen Crisis Years, 1888-1901,* rev. ed. (Washington, D.C.: RHPA, 1981), 248-311; and *The Ellen G. White 1888 Materials,* 4 vols. (Washington, D.C.: Ellen G. White Estate, 1987), which contain a comprehensive collection of all her letters and manuscripts relating to the Minneapolis conference. For the recollections and evaluations of her contemporaries, see *Manuscripts and Memories of Minneapolis* (Boise, Idaho: PPPA, 1988).

30   The teaching on righteousness by faith was reemphasized in the 20th century under the influence of Daniells and Froom. See L. E. Froom, "'Righteousness by Faith' Sparked the Ministerial Association," *Ministry,* May-June 1965, 3-7, 41-44. Adventists are still divided over the contemporaneous meaning as well as the contemporary significance of the meetings and message of 1888. See, e.g., Daniells, *Christ Our Righteousness;* Froom, *Movement of Destiny;* Knight, *Angry Saints;* Olson, *Thirteen Crisis Years;* Norval F. Pease, "'The Truth as

At the turn of the century and in the years following, three additional doctrinal controversies arose which challenged the historic teachings of the church in several significant ways. First, in 1899 and until 1901, there was a brief flurry of charismatic fervor and perfectionistic teaching advanced by the "Holy Flesh Movement" in Indiana.[31] Then there were John Harvey Kellogg's panentheistic views on the nature of God which were expressed in his book *The Living Temple* and proved to be as intriguing as influential for some time.[32] Finally, in 1905, Albion F. Ballenger

It Is in Jesus': The 1888 General Conference Session, Minneapolis, Minnesota," *Adventist Heritage* 10:1 (1985): 3-10; [Donald K. Short], *The Mystery of 1888* (Cape Town, South Africa: By the Author, 1974; reprint, Harrisville, N.H.: MMI Press, 1984); Arnold Valentin Wallenkampf, *What Every Adventist Should Know about 1888* (Washington, D.C., and Hagerstown, Md.: RHPA, 1988); "1888-1988. Advance or Retreat?" *Ministry,* February 1988; Robert J. Wieland, *The 1888 Message: An Introduction* (Washington, D.C., and Hagerstown, Md.: RHPA, 1980); and Robert J. Wieland and Donald K. Short, *1888 Re-Examined,* rev. ed. (Meadow Vista, Calif., and Hendersonville, N.C.: By the Authors, 1987). See also David P. McMahon, *Ellet Joseph Waggoner: The Myth and the Man* (Fallbrook, Calif.: Verdict Publ., 1979); Knight, *From 1888 to Apostasy;* Haloviak, "From Righteousness to Holy Flesh: Judgment at Minneapolis, [1988]"; and *A. T. Jones: The Man and the Message: A Book Review* (Uniontown, Ohio: The 1888 Message Study Committee, 1988).

31   Its so-called "cleansing message" centered on the total eradication of sin and the reception of "holy flesh" and "translation faith." Believers who had passed through this experience would sin or die no more. The movement was accompanied by enthusiastic worship services and ecstatic experiences. Its leaders, however, soon renounced their fanaticism. See Jack J. Blanco, "Pentecostal 'Cleansing Message' in the History of Adventism," *Adventist Perspectives* 6:1 (1992): 14-19; Knight, *From 1888 to Apostasy,* 167-171; E. M. Robinson, *S. N. Haskell – Man of Action* (Washington, D.C.: RHPA, 1967), 168-176; Schwarz, *Light Bearers to the Remnant,* 446-448; Tarling, *The Edges of Seventh-day Adventism,* 74-83; and *SDAE,* 1976 ed., s.v. "Holy Flesh Heresy."

32   In distinction to classical pantheism, which identifies God with nature, Adventist panentheism maintained God's personal and literal presence in every part of nature, pervading everyone and everything. God was seen as a creative and sustaining force within, rather than behind, above, or outside of nature and man; and – while not denying God's real existence and personality – it was claimed that there is "a tree-maker in the tree, a flower-maker in the flower." Salvation, then, consisted in living in harmony with the inner divine power that would free humans from all sickness and sin. See J. H. Kellogg, *The Living Temple* (Battle Creek, Mich.: Good Health Pub. Co., 1903); cf. "Kellogg vs. the Brethren: His Last Interview as an Adventist – October 7, 1907," *Spectrum* 20:3 (1990): 46-62; and "Kellogg Snaps, Crackles, and Pops; His Last Interview as an Adventist – Part 2," *Spectrum* 20:4 (1990): 37-61. Kellogg publicly taught this view since 1897; to its sympathizers belonged Prescott, Jones, and Waggoner. For more information, see Norman H. Young, "The Alpha Heresy: Kellogg and the Cross," *Adventist Heritage* 12:1 (1987): 33-42; Jack J. Blanco, "New Age Series – I, Mysticism Confronts Adventism," *Adventist Perspectives* 2:1 (1988): 21-34; Richard W. Schwarz, "John Harvey Kellogg: American Health Reformer" (Ph.D. dissertation, University of Michigan, 1964); idem, *John Harvey Kellogg, M.D.* (Nashville: SPA, 1970; reprint, Berrien Springs, Mich.: AU Press, 1981); idem, "The Kellogg Schism: The Hidden Issues," *Spectrum* 4:4 (1972): 23-39; idem, *Light Bearers to the Remnant,* 282-298; Knight, *From*

presented some divergent teachings on the sanctuary, maintaining that the atonement had been completed on the cross and that Christ had entered the most holy place of the heavenly sanctuary right after his ascension and not in 1844.[33] Whatever interest these doctrinal innovations – particularly Kellogg's teaching – generated, eventually the church firmly opposed them as dangerous heresies undermining the doctrinal pillars of Seventh-day Adventism.[34]

1906-1925

Another doctrinal novelty proposed at that time possibly might have met the same fate. It held that the *tamid*[35] of Daniel's apocalyptic prophecy referred not to the continual abomination of paganism, as was traditionally and unanimously believed by Adventists, but rather to the continual mediation of Christ in the heavenly temple. As "the new doctrine of the Daily" was not only advocated by the foremost theologian (Prescott) and the leading administrator of the church (Daniells) but also buttressed by exegetical and historical evidences, it gradually became the standard Adventist view. However, it met fierce resistance from some ardent defenders of "the glorious, perfect, old time message of Truth," who were determined to protect the church against the dangerous and "deadly heresy" of this infidel and abhorrent "new theology" which would "change the original truth" and "the doctrines of Seventh Day Adventists."[36]

1888 to Apostasy, 211-215; McMahon, *Ellet Joseph Waggoner,* 147-184; and Valentine, *The Shaping of Adventism,* 145-166.

33 He also questioned the inspiration and authority of Ellen White. See Albion F. Ballenger, *Cast Out for the Cross of Christ* (Tropico, Calif.: By the Author, [1911]); and idem, *An Examination of Forty Fatal Errors Regarding the Atonement* (Riverside, Calif.: By the Author, [1913]). For more information on the Ballenger case, see *SDAE,* 1976 ed., s.v. "Ballenger, Albion Fox"; Adams, *The Sanctuary Doctrine,* 95-164; Bert Haloviak, "Pioneers, Pantheists, and Progressives, 1980," TMs, AHC, JWL, AU, Berrien Springs, Mich.; Richard Lesher, "Landmark Truth versus 'Specious Error' – Nos. 1-2," *AR,* 6-13 March 1980, 4-7, 6-7; and Schwarz, *Light Bearers to the Remnant,* 448-450.

34 For Ellen White's decided view on, and decisive reaction to, these doctrinal novelties, see A. L. White, *Ellen G. White,* 5:97-112, 280-306, 398-413; and Ellen White, *Selected Messages,* 2:31-39. As these new teachings were firmly and fully rejected only a few months or years after their rise, and as their main proponents (Ballenger and Kellogg) were disfellowshipped from the church in 1907, there is no need, in this study, to pay further attention to these doctrinal deviations which came to be seen as *culs-de-sac* for the theological growth of the church. Still, they deserve a thorough treatment of their own.

35 Hebrew term, meaning "continual(ly)"; translated as "the daily (sacrifice)" by the King James Version in Dan 8:11-13; 11:31; 12:11.

36 A. O. Johnson, *"The Daily": Is It Paganism?* (College Place, Wash.: By the Author, [1909]); George I. Butler to Ellen White, 3 July 1910, EGWRC, Silver Spring, Md. (Incoming correspondence file); L. A. Smith and F. C. Gilbert, *"The Daily" in the Prophecy of Daniel* (n.p., n.d.); J. S. Washburn, *The Startling Omega and Its True Genealogy;* idem, *An Open*

Between 1909 and 1922, the controversy surrounding "the daily" reached its culmination. The "new view" was denounced, by some, as a Satanic "innovation" and the ultimate "apostasy" – the "*Omega*" – which would destroy the foundation of the Adventist faith and play into the hands of the opponents of the church.[37] Prescott was sharply attacked for having introduced this error and "a brood of new theories" like the "Catholic doctrine of the Trinity" and "Higher Criticism," "false doctrines" which would change "the original truth" taught by the church and replace it with "a flood of new and strange teachings."[38]

In defending himself against these sweeping accusations, Prescott disclosed the attitude that had guided him and those agreeing with his conclusions in their study.

> It should be our sincere aim to know and teach the truth, and we should be prepared to do what we are constantly asking others to do, viz., to accept evidence, and to change our views when they are proved to be incorrect ... It is more important to know the truth than to cling to a traditional teaching ... To rectify a mistake which has been made in the interpretation of the 'daily' does not make any change in a fundamental doctrine of the third angel's message.[39]

Irrevocably, Ellen White's death in 1915 left the Adventist church without the *viva vox* that had guided its affairs and influenced its doctrinal developments on many occasions in the past. It forced the denomination to reflect on the abiding authority and the proper function of what was commonly called "the Spirit of Prophecy."[40]

Letter to Elder A. G. Daniells and an Appeal to the General Conference (n.p., [1922]); and idem, *The Fruit of the "New Daily"* (n.p., [1923]).

37 For sources, see the previous footnote. One critic wrote, "Are we under the embarrassing necessity of having now to revise our position, admitting that we were in error before, and thus place in the hands of our enemies, who are watching to take advantage of us, a weapon of which they can make effective use to hinder our work? ... But we cannot relinquish the fundamental doctrine of the cleansing of the sanctuary; and we must emphatically protest against any teaching which would tend to throw that fundamental doctrine into the background" (Smith and Gilbert, *"The Daily" in the Prophecy of Daniel,* 2, 31).

38 Washburn regarded "the new doctrine of the Daily" as "the heart, the core, the root, the *seed theory* of all our modern Washington new thought, and Adventist new theology." A nephew of George I. Butler, Washburn was convinced that "if [Butler] were to rise from the dead he would stand with me against [Daniells] and Prescott" *(An Open Letter,* 24, 34). Though he could not stem the tide of this "new theology," he, at least, may have succeeded in preventing the re-election of Daniells as president of the General Conference in 1922.

39 W. W. Prescott, *"The Daily": A Brief Reply to Two Leaflets on This Subject* (n.p., n.d.), 1, 23. "The use of this quotation [from Ellen White] for the purpose of forestalling any candid investigation of our teaching does not seem consistent with that spirit of fairness which opens the way for the unprejudiced consideration of Bible truth" (ibid., 13). For more information on this controversy and on Ellen White's view on the "new daily," see below, pp. 303-305.

40 In 1915, Prescott deplored the way Ellen White's writings were handled in and by the church. "There are serious errors in our authrozied *[sic]* books and yet [we] make no special effort to correct them ... We let [the people and our average ministers] go on year after year asserting things which we know to be untrue ... No serious effort has been made to disabuse the minds

An early occasion for such a reflection came at the Bible and History Teachers'
Conference held in Washington, D.C., in 1919.[41] These rather informal meetings
were marked by open discussions of theological issues and a remarkable frankness on
the part of several speakers (like Daniells and Prescott) to address controverted points.
Among other issues, divergences on prophetic interpretation were discussed, such as
the Eastern question, the king of the north, the ten horns/kingdoms, the daily, and
the seven trumpets. Besides, the need was expressed for a more balanced and factual
approach to Ellen White's writings.[42]

However, no agreement could be reached during the conference on these issues,
and no reports or papers were published afterwards. Some who heard news about the
recent "Bible Institute" concluded that it had sowed doubts on Ellen White's inspiration as well as on "many other fundamental truths."[43] Thus, as the Adventist
church moved into the twentieth century, it became more and more obvious that
doctrinal controversies were to be faced not sporadically but rather continually.[44]

of the people of what was known to be their wrong view concerning her writings" (Arthur L.
White, "The Prescott Letter to W. C. White, April 6, 1915, 1981," TMs, pp. [37-38],
EGWRC, AU, Berrien Springs, Mich.). See also idem, "W. W. Prescott and the 1911 Edition
of the *Great Controversy,* 1981," TMs, EGWRC, AU, Berrien Springs, Mich.). According to
White, "the concept of verbal inspiration" was deeply "embedded in the minds and hearts of
our folk" at the time, making it difficult to reeducate them on these matters ("The Prescott
Letter," 33). Among the "errors" he decried, Prescott listed the beginning of the 2,300 year-
days on October 22, 1844 (he opted for a spring date) and the extension of the 1,260 year-
days from 538 to 1798 A.D. (he favored the time period from 533 to 1793).

41 The Bible Conference was held from July 1 to July 21, 1919, and brought together about 50
    selected church leaders, editors, and teachers. It was followed by a meeting of close to 30 Bible
    and history teachers that lasted from July 22 to August 1. See "The Bible Conference of 1919,"
    Spectrum 10:1 (1979): 23-57; Robert W. Olson, "The 1919 Bible Conference and Bible and
    History Teachers' Council, 1979," TMs, EGWRC, AU, Berrien Springs, Mich.; and Bert
    Haloviak, "In the Shadow of the 'Daily': Background and Aftermath of the 1919 Bible and
    History Teachers' Conference, 1979," TMs, AHC, JWL, AU, Berrien Springs, Mich.

42 Differing opinions were expressed on whether or not Ellen White was to be regarded as an
    inspired authority in matters of history, science, health reform, and theology.

43 Washburn dubbed it a "Diet of Doubts" that was "undermining the confidence of our sons and
    daughters in the very fundamentals of our truth" (Washburn, *An Open Letter,* 28-30).

44 In an article in the general church paper, editor F. M. Wilcox proposed a middle course
    between a narrow dogmatism/traditionalism and an innovative modernism/liberalism. He
    decried the prevailing "spirit of changing emphasis" and denied the need for any "change in
    religious thought" that removes "the essential pillars in the Christian faith." He also ques-
    tioned the need to revise the historic Adventist interpretations of prophecy in the absence of
    other, more convincing views. But, at the same time, Wilcox pointed to the progressive nature
    of truth which implies the possibility that the church may have to give up certain old positions.
    Therefore, church members should hold their "minds open always to receive further light and
    instruction" and allow to others "an opinion which differs from their own" on certain "detail"
    (Wilcox, "A World of Changing Emphasis," *RH,* 30 January 1919, 3-4).

1926-1945

This could also be felt during the following period in which two established church teachings – viz., the doctrine of the heavenly sanctuary and of the spirit of prophecy – were vigorously and repeatedly challenged both from within and from without. The publications issued by E. S. Ballenger in America,[45] the defection, in 1930, of W. W. Fletcher in Australia,[46] and the apostasy, in 1932, of L. R. Conradi in Germany[47] were all occasioned by, and focused on, these teachings. While sending some shock waves through the denomination, neither of these men attracted a large following, and the doctrinal edifice of the church remained virtually unscathed.

It was during those years that M. L. Andreasen developed his "final generation" theology according to which the "remnant" will stop sinning completely and, thus, vindicate God by demonstrating that his law can be obeyed perfectly – even in the absence of a heavenly intercessor.[48] This period also witnessed the rising tide of the

---

45   In 1914, Albion F. Ballenger had begun to publish his deviant views on the sanctuary, the investigative judgment, and Ellen White in *The Gathering Call* and various pamphlets. After his death in 1921, his brother E. S. Ballenger became the editor and continued publishing the magazine and other writings throughout the 1920s and 1930s.

46   In 1930, the Australian pastor William Warde Fletcher severed his connection with the church after having changed his views on the sanctuary doctrine and the authority of Ellen White. Like Ballenger before him, Fletcher came to the conclusion that Jesus had entered the most holy place of the heavenly sanctuary at his ascension. Believing that the atonement was completed at the cross, he rejected the concept of the transfer of guilt to the sanctuary and of the final blotting out of sins at an investigative judgment. To him, the gospel left no room for a final atoning work of Christ to have begun in 1844 as taught by Ellen White and the church. Consequently, he also denied that Ellen White had received direct revelations from God and that she was to be considered an inspired authority. Fletcher published his views in a book *(The Reasons for My Faith* [Sydney: William Brooks, 1932]) and in various pamphlets. His positions were evaluated by the church and rejected as unscriptural and unsound. In 1947, F. D. Nichol provided a detailed response in his *Reasons for Our Faith* (Washington, D.C.: RHPA, 1947). See also Alfred S. Jorgensen, "The Fletcher Case, 1980," TMs, AHC, AU, Berrien Springs, Mich.

47   In 1932 at the age of 76, Ludwig Richard Conradi, successful pioneer and long-time leader of the SDA mission in Europe, separated from the church and joined the Seventh Day Baptists. Agreeing with both Ballenger and Fletcher in their criticism of the sanctuary doctrine and the prophetic claims of Ellen White, Conradi attacked the church in general and its prophet in particular in two books entitled *Ist Frau E. G. White die Prophetin der Endgemeinde?* (Hamburg: By the Author, [1933]) and *The Founders of the Seventh-day Adventist Denomination* (Plainfield, N.Y.: By the Author, 1939). See also G. Padderatz, *Conradi und Hamburg* (Hamburg: By the Author, 1978); Daniel Heinz, *Ludwig Richard Conradi: Missionar der Siebenten-Tags-Adventisten in Europa,* Archives of International Adventist History, ed. Baldur Ed. Pfeiffer and Gottfried Oosterwal, no. 2 (Frankfurt, Bern, New York: Peter Lang, 1986); idem, "Ludwig Richard Conradi: Patriarch of European Adventism," *Adventist Heritage* 12:1 (1987): 17-25; and Schwarz, *Light Bearers to the Remnant,* 475-476.

48   M. L. Andreasen, *The Sanctuary Service* (Washington, D.C.: RHPA, 1937; 2d rev. ed., 1947), 299-321.

Fundamentalist movement. Adventists felt quite akin to Fundamentalism in its defense of the basic doctrines of the historic Christian faith over against the onslaughts of theological liberalism and modernism.[49]

In response to these challenges, the church placed strong emphasis on the invariability of the Adventist fundamentals and the immutability of biblical truth.[50] At the same time, the need to follow the advancing light of truth was also expressed repeatedly, though usually with the *caveat* that new insights would not invalidate past beliefs.[51] Only rarely did someone suggest that this could, at times, involve even the modification, revision, or actual change of views.[52] Other Adventist writers denied that "any new light [had] been discovered that would cause us to change our views."[53] The prevailing attitude in mid-century was well expressed in the following way:

> Truth is eternal and unchangeable, but our knowledge of truth cannot be static. It must grow to live. But clearer light never denies former light; it makes earlier light shine brighter all the while ... This light will shine clearly and more clearly, but not a peg or pin of the foundation of the advent fundamentals is to be removed. The message is to be revived, not revised.[54]

---

49 For more information, see above, pp. 200. These developments set the stage for some major doctrinal controversies that were to shake the church in the 2nd half of the 20th century.

50 F. M. Wilcox, "Attacking the Foundations – Nos. 1-2," *RH*, 18 April, 9 May 1929, 3-4, 3-5; J. E. Fulton, "Back to the Old Paths," *RH*, 13 June 1930, 212-214; L. E. Froom, "Cast Not Therefore away Your Confidence," *Ministry*, February 1932, 7-8, 29; F. M. Wilcox, "Contending for the Faith 'Which Was Once Delivered to the Saints,'" *RH*, 3 March 1932, 5-8; Oliver Montgomery, "The Sure Foundation," *Ministry*, September 1932, 3-4, 28-29; C. H. Watson and C. K. Meyers, "Letter to the Church in Europe," *RH*, 24 November 1932, 1-2; W. A. Spicer, "The Truth That Endures," *RH*, 5 January 1933, 3; F. M. Wilcox, "Attacking the Foundations – Nos. 1-5," *RH*, 2 February-2 March 1933; W. H. Branson, "Loyalty in an Age of Doubt," *Ministry*, October 1933, 3-4; "A Repudiation of Charges and a Declaration of Faith," *Ministry*, April 1935, 6-7; T. M. French, "The Immutability of Truth," *RH*, 30 December 1937, 10; F. M. Wilcox, "A Sure Foundation," *RH*, 19 January 1939, 2, 6; F. Lee, "Giving Heed to the Foundations," *RH*, 26 January 1939, 3-4; F. M. Wilcox, "The Foundation of God – Nos. 1-9," *RH*, 15 August-24 October 1940; A. R. Ogden, "Are You Certain of Your Faith?" *RH*, 14 November 1940, 2, 5; and L. E. Froom, "Not a Block to Be Moved nor a Pin Stirred," *Ministry*, November 1944-February 1945, 21-23, 17-20, 20-22, 11-13, 28, 30.

51 F. M. Wilcox, "Walking in the Advancing Light," *RH*, 18 November 1926, 3-7; L. H. Christian, "The Danger of Conservatism – Nos. 1-2," *RH*, 14-21 June 1928, 3-4, 6-8; Carlyle B. Haynes, "Walking in the Light," *RH*, 27 September 1928, 9-10; L. E. Froom, "Irreconcilable Principles," *Ministry*, December 1931, 6; C. P. Bollman, "Ask for the Old Paths," *RH*, 29 December 1932, 3-4; F. M. Wilcox, "The Quest of Truth," *RH*, 10 January 1934, 3-4; F. Lee, "'Launch Out Into the Deep,'" *RH*, 9 February 1939, 3-4; and J. L. McElhany, "The President's Address," *RH*, 27 May 1941, 11.

52 Taylor G. Bunch, "'Prove All Things,'" *Ministry*, March 1930, 9-11; and L. E. Froom, "Two Equally Disastrous Perils," *Ministry*, December 1937, 15.

53 F. Lee, "'Examine Yourself,'" *RH*, 18 November 1943, 7-8.

54 L. H. Christian, *The Fruitage of Spiritual Gifts* (Washington, D.C.: RHPA, 1947), 187, 206.

1946-1965

The same attitude characterized the two decades following World War II. Aware of living in an era of rapid and accelerating change, which affected virtually all areas of life,[55] the church found safety in holding on to the doctrinal heritage of its fathers.[56] In 1952, *Review & Herald* editor F. D. Nichol could exclaim that "in this world of theological change and outright apostasy, we continue to preach the same great truths that have marked the movement from its earliest days ... We have not changed our theology."[57] Neither should the "emphasis in our preaching and in our living" be allowed to change as this would lead to the loss of denominational distinctiveness.[58]

Occasionally, however, Adventist thought leaders balanced this view by challenging church members to be open for doctrinal progress, growth, and even some changes in matters of doctrine.[59] This attitude also characterized the unofficial "Bible Research Fellowship" which flourished for a decade from 1943 to 1952. Organized in 1940, this association of college Bible teachers studied controversial issues of exegesis and theology in a climate of mutual confidence and open dialogue. Intending to reactivate the spirit that, in the 1840s, had led the Adventist pioneers into frank discussions and a prayerful search for truth, the fellowship focused its attention particularly on matters of prophetic interpretation, eschatology, and Christology.[60] It attracted more than 250 teachers, pastors, and church administrators from various parts of the world. However, it failed to receive the support of the church leadership,

---

55 Ernest Lloyd, "Our Unchanging Lord in a Changing World," *RH,* 19 April 1951, 4; idem, "Our Changeless Friend," *RH,* 17 May 1956, 7; A. M. Ragsdale, "The Certainty of Change," *RH,* 14 June 1951, 10-11; R. L. Hubbs, "Our Changing World," *RH,* 28 October 1954, 12-13; H. L. Rudy, "Unchanging Truth in a Changing World," *RH,* 10 March 1960, 6-7; W. R. Beach, "Unchanging Purpose in a Changing World," *RH,* 27 July 1961, 1, 9; and K. H. Wood, "A Changing World – An Unchanging Task," *RH,* 31 May 1962, 12-13.

56 F. D. Nichol, "The Doubtful Value of 'New Light,'" *RH,* 21 December 1961, 8-9; A. V. Olson, "Defenders of the Faith," *RH,* 14 June 1962, 2-3, 7; F. D. Nichol, "Why Defend the Faith – Nos. 1-2," *RH,* 22-29 November 1962, 12-13, 12-13; and K. H. Wood, "Protest against Theological Doubletalk," *RH,* 23 April 1964, 12.

57 F. D. Nichol, "Looking Back on the Bible Conference," *RH,* 23 October 1952, 10. Cf. R. J. Christian, "Adventists Have Not Changed," *RH,* 22 June 1950, 24 ("Old-fashioned Adventism has not changed. The old ways are still our ways").

58 J. L. McElhany, "Changing Our Emphasis," *RH,* 15 January 1953, 11.

59 [Raymond F. Cottrell], "Principles of Biblical Interpretation," chap. in *Problems in Bible Translation* (Washington, D.C.: Committee on Problems in Bible Translation, 1954), 79-81; *QOD,* 9, 29; F. Lee, "Seeking a Deeper Understanding of God's Will," *RH,* 31 January 1957, 8-9; Daniel Walther, "The Message of Reformation," *RH,* 7 August 1858, 11, 26-27; Raymond F. Cottrell, "A Mind to the Task," *Ministry,* December 1958, 6-10; and Harry W. Lowe, "We Can't Have It Both Ways," *Ministry,* September 1962, 48.

60 The Bible Research Fellowship took up issues that had not been resolved at the 1919 Bible and History Teachers' Conference. It can, therefore, be regarded as a kind of unofficial continuation of the dialogue begun and interrupted in 1919.

who may have feared a weakening of the united doctrinal stand of the church.[61] In its place, the General Conference, in the fall of 1952, appointed a standing Committee for Biblical Study and Research, later reorganized and renamed the "Biblical Research Institute."

In the same year, a Bible Conference held at Washington, D.C. – the first since 1919 – brought together church leaders and teachers from all over the world in the declared attempt to strengthen and reaffirm the basic doctrinal teachings of the Seventh-day Adventist Church. In his opening address, General Conference President W. H. Branson called for "absolute unity" on fundamental teachings and the avoidance of petty side issues. He also expressed the conviction that whatever "new and additional light" might be expected at the conference would only "confirm and not destroy the light already given."[62] Another speaker agreed: "New light does not eclipse or extinguish the old."[63] Looking back at the conference, Nichol could joyfully conclude, "The Bible Conference has come and gone, and the pillars of the temple are still standing, unmoved and erect."[64]

61   See Raymond F. Cottrell, "The Bible Research Fellowship: A Pioneering Seventh-day Adventist Organization in Retrospect," *Adventist Heritage* 5:1 (1978): 39-52. Cf. idem, "The Bible Research Fellowship: Its History and Objective, 1950," TMs, AHC, JWL, AU, Berrien Springs, Mich. All in all, about 100 papers were submitted to the fellowship; they are filed in the Adventist Heritage Center at Andrews University, Berrien Springs, Mich. More than 2/3 of these papers deal with matters of prophetic interpretation and eschatology.

62   W. H. Branson, "Objectives of the Bible Conference," *RH,* 25 September 1952, 3-7. With reference to the upcoming conference, F. D. Nichol likewise maintained that the Adventist doctrinal system could be strengthened and enlarged "without disturbing a single supporting pillar or removing one stone from the foundation." While the primary doctrines were fixed, the arguments and illustrations employed in their defense could be improved and even be corrected or revised. Nichol also admitted that there might still exist some errors or "fallacies" on secondary points of faith ("The Bible Conference," *RH,* 28 August 1952, 1, 14). Questions with regard to the identity of Melchisedek and the king of the north, for example, were regarded as side issues on which no strict uniformity was expected or sought. But otherwise, doctrinal unity was upheld as a major asset and objective of the church (W. R. Beach, "The Gospel Commission and the Remnant Church," 2:437).

63   A. V. Olson, "The Place of Prophecy in Our Preaching," 2:551. However, "we must not conclude that we shall never have to abandon any views that we may have held regarding some prophetic passage. The entrance of new light may reveal that we have held views that were not in harmony with the teachings of the Scriptures. If so, we must be willing to surrender these views. Error, though hoary with age, is error still and should be rejected" (ibid., 552).

64   F. D. Nichol, "Looking Back on the Bible Conference," *RH,* 23 October 1952, 10. Don F. Neufeld later recalled that various conference speakers had affirmed that "we have not come here to change Adventist theology, simply to affirm it" ("The *SDA Bible Commentary* in Retrospect, n.d.," TMs, p. 4, AHC, JWL, AU, Berrien Springs, Mich.). In harmony with this object and in contrast to the meetings of 1919, the 1952 Bible Conference provided no opportunity for informal dialogue but only allowed for written questions to be addressed to the speakers. The papers presented at the conference were published in two volumes carrying the revealing title *Our Firm Foundation.*

If only implicitly, the 1952 Bible Conference had encouraged the pursuit of scholarly studies in order to provide a sound and reasonable underpinning for Adventist doctrines challenged within and without the denomination. The publication of the *Seventh-day Adventist Bible Commentary* (1953-1957) disclosed the influence that theological studies were already exerting on the scholars of the church. While presenting the traditional Adventist interpretations and shunning any disagreement with Ellen White's views, the seven-volume commentary also introduced new exegetical views, which, not infrequently, differed both in method and conclusion from the traditional proof-text approach used by Adventists. In this way, it reflected an openness to new insights and a readiness to allow for a certain variety of conclusions on exegetical questions.[65]

That a diversity of viewpoints might extend even to the core of the doctrinal edifice of the church was evident to the participants of the Problems in Daniel Committee, which met sporadically between 1960 and 1966. The discussions revealed a lack of agreement on the appropriate methodology for presenting and defending the historic doctrine of the heavenly sanctuary.[66]

The most significant event of this period with regard to the attitude of the church toward doctrinal development was the rapprochement between Seventh-day Adventists and conservative Protestants set in motion by the discussions in 1955-1956 between several church leaders (Anderson, Froom, Read, Unruh) and some Fundamentalist Evangelicals (Barnhouse, Martin, Cannon). These talks came about when Walter R. Martin, a Southern Baptist, asked to meet with some Adventist leaders in order to get first-hand information preparatory to a book he was writing on the Seventh-day Adventist "cult." During these conversations, Walter R. Martin, D. G. Barnhouse, and G. Cannon came to regard Seventh-day Adventists as true, born-again Christians and genuine Evangelicals.[67]

---

65 In harmony with the editorial policy, which stipulated that the commentary was not to make but to present Adventist theology, the traditional Adventist interpretations were mentioned even when, to the editors, they seemed unsupported by the context itself. See Raymond F. Cottrell, "The Untold Story of the Bible Commentary," *Spectrum* 16:3 (1985): 35-51; and Don F. Neufeld, "The *SDA Bible Commentary* in Retrospect."

66 The disagreement was related to the question of whether the sanctuary doctrine could be defended from the Bible alone or whether it needed the additional authority of the Ellen White writings. Because of its polarized views, no reports were made to the church on the work of this committee. However, its discussions are partly reflected by Harry W. Lowe, "The Writings of Ellen G. White as Related to Seventh-day Adventist Doctrines and Prophetic Interpretation"; and idem, "Doctrinal Development and Prophetic Interpretation," *Ministry*, November 1967, 36-39. See also Desmond Ford, *Daniel 8:14, the Day of Atonement, and the Investigative Judgment* (Casselberry, Fla.: Euangelion Press, 1980), 61-63, A188-A195; and Richard L. Hammill, *Pilgrimage: Memoirs of an Adventist Administrator* (Berrien Springs, Mich.: AU Press, 1992), 186-187.

67 See T. E. Unruh, "The Seventh-day Adventist Evangelical Conferences of 1955-1956," *Adventist Heritage* 4:2 (1977): 35-47; and Froom, *MOD*, 465-492. When Barnhouse told the readers of *Eternity*, a leading evangelical magazine whose editor he was at the time, that

Hoping to convince their Protestant brethren of the biblical and evangelical nature of Seventh-day Adventist beliefs, the Adventist participants in these dialogues emphasized their full agreement with the "fundamentals" of the Christian faith, down-playing, in the eyes of some, the more objectionable and distinctive teachings of the church.[68] To this end, they reformulated these doctrines in common theological parlance. In addition, they disavowed certain historic and unorthodox Adventist beliefs by describing them as the "unofficial" minority views of a "lunatic fringe" in the church. By selectively quoting Ellen White (as, e.g., her sinless-nature statements on Christ), her support for the "official" church doctrines was also assured.

To lend credibility to their way of presenting Adventist beliefs, the questions raised by the Evangelicals together with the answers provided by the Adventists were sent to about 225 church leaders around the world for their review before the material was published as *Seventh-day Adventists Answer Questions on Doctrine.*[69] However, the book led some Adventists to surmise that the leadership of the church had actually downgraded, if not denied, certain traditional teachings that may have seemed unpalatable to Evangelicals but were indispensable to Adventists.[70]

he had come to know Adventists as brethren in Christ rather than as heretical cultists, the magazine initially lost about ¼ of its subscriptions ("Are Seventh-day Adventists Christians? A New Look at Seventh-day Adventism," *Eternity,* September 1956, 6-7, 43-45). See also Walter R. Martin, "The Truth about Seventh-day Adventism," *Eternity,* October 1956-January 1957, 6-7, 38-40; 20-21, 38-43; 12-13, 38-40. Martin later published his findings in *The Truth about Seventh-day Adventism* (Grand Rapids: Zondervan, 1960).

68 For example, with regard to the authority of Ellen White, *Questions on Doctrine* denied that SDAs claimed infallibility/inerrancy or equality to the Bible for her writings; the book also made no direct prophetic claim for her (pp. 89-98). In view of his fundamentalist stand, Martin's assessment of the Adventist position was inevitable: "For Adventists, 'inspiration' in connection with Mrs. White's writings has a rather different meaning from the inspiration of the Bible ... Apparently, they have adopted a qualified view of inspiration as related to her writings ... which emphasizes subjective interpretation as the criterion for determining specifically where in Mrs. White's writings the 'Spirit of prophecy' has decisively spoken" *(The Kingdom of the Cults,* 381).

69 Of the 225 ministers who had received the draft copy, only 7 made suggestions to improve the manuscript. *Ministry* editor Roy Allen Anderson praised "the unanimous and enthusiastic acceptance of the content of the manuscript" which "gave remarkable testimony to the unity of belief that characterizes us as a people" ("Unity of Adventist Belief – No. 1," *Ministry,* March 1958, 28). According to the introduction of the book, its goal was not to present "a new statement of faith" but "to set forth our basic beliefs in terminology currently used in theological circles" *(QOD,* 8).

70 M. L. Andreasen attacked the church leaders for allegedly changing and abandoning the traditional Adventist doctrines of the incarnation and the atonement, particularly with regard to Christ's sinful human nature and his atoning ministry in the heavenly sanctuary. To him, this seriously undermined some specific Adventist teachings, such as the sealing of the last generation of believers who have overcome all sin(ning) and the final blotting out of sins from the heavenly temple *(Letters to the Churches* [Baker, Oreg.: Hudson Printing Co., 1959; reprint, Payson, Ariz.: Leaves-of-Autumn Books, 1980]). This criticism cost him his ministerial credentials, which, however, were given back to him posthumously. Jerry Moon, who has

In response to these accusations,[71] church leaders pointed to those reviewers of the book who had concluded that Adventism had not changed significantly and that it should still be regarded as a "sect" or "cult."[72] It was asserted that "no attempt whatsoever has been made to add to, take from, or change our doctrines, but only to explain" them.[73] While being "expressed in language that could be clearly understood by all both inside and outside Adventist circles,"[74] *Questions on Doctrine* was "not in any sense a modification or alteration" of the church's fundamental beliefs.[75]

analyzed the dispute between Andreasen and his brethren, concluded: "For Andreasen, the issues of the atonement and the humanity of Christ touched the core of old-time Adventism" ("M. L. Andreasen, L. E. Froom, and the Controversy over *Questions on Doctrine*, 1988," TMs, p. 60, EGWRC, AU, Berrien Springs, Mich.). Others likewise attacked the book for allegedly denying the original advent faith for the sake of harmonizing it with evangelical beliefs. See, e.g., Lelia S. Wilkinson, *Truth versus Error* (Trenton, N.J.: Religious Liberty and Temperance Assn., n.d.). "From the publication of *Questions on Doctrine* in 1957 until the 1980s, the atonement, the incarnation, and the nature of salvation have been the subjects of constant debate within the Adventist church" (Bull and Lockhart, *Seeking a Sanctuary*, 69). Thus, the book has even been called "the most controversial Adventist publication of the century" (ibid., 84).

71 An official answer was provided by A. V. Olsen in "An Examination of M. L. Andreasen's Objections to the Book *Seventh-day Adventists Answer Questions on Doctrine*, 1960," TMs, AHC, JWL, AU, Berrien Springs, Mich. F. D. Nichol also rallied to the book's defense in a series of *Review & Herald* editorials ("The Critics and Their Criticism – Nos. 3-8," *RH*, 8 March-12 April 1962).

72 R. R. Figuhr, "The Pillars of Our Faith Unmoved," *RH*, 24 April 1958, 5-6. Figuhr's surprising suggestion that the book might perhaps be "improved by a revision" amounted, however, to a tacit admission that *Questions on Doctrine* had indeed been more than a mere restatement of historic Adventist beliefs (ibid., 6). F. D. Nichol likewise hinted at a possible revision ("A New Day for Adventists," *RH*, 8 May 1958, 9-10). Among those Evangelicals who saw no reason to reevaluate Adventism were Harold Lindsell ("What of Seventh-day Adventism?" *Christianity Today*, 31 March-14 April 1958, 6-8, 13-15) and Herbert Bird ("Another Look at Adventism," *Christianity Today*, 28 April 1958, 14-17).

73 Roy Allen Anderson, "Changing Attitudes Toward Adventism," *Ministry*, December 1956, 15-17. According to Anderson, the required explanations involved the correction of (1) misunderstandings and misinterpretations, (2) misstatements, (3) misinformation, and (4) misplaced emphases relating to Adventist beliefs.

74 Roy Allen Anderson, "Seventh-day Adventists Answer Questions on Doctrine," *Ministry*, June 1957, 24. Elsewhere Anderson explained that the restatement of Adventist belief in *Questions on Doctrine* had served to expound the proper meaning of the "Adventist vocabulary" to non-Adventists, for certain theological expressions could convey different meanings to different people ("Disarming Prejudice," *Ministry*, April 1957, 2). According to Nichol, the book wanted "to express the old truth in more exact language. Mark carefully our words, not that we should express a revised truth in revised words, but the old truth in language that would take in all the theological facts" ("Have We Forsaken the Sanctuary Doctrine? – No. 3," *RH*, 12 April 1962, 13).

75 R. R. Figuhr, "A Non-Adventist Examines Our Beliefs," *RH*, 13 December 1956, 3. According to Harry W. Lowe, the book does not contain "any major doctrinal change" or "essential change" (review of *Questions on Doctrine*, in *Ministry*, June 1958, 36).

Church leaders strongly maintained that "Adventists have certainly not changed their beliefs."[76]

Martin's positive reassessment of Seventh-day Adventism was founded on his conviction that the church had indeed changed in some significant ways.[77] But, on the basis of what he was told and shown by his informants, he came to the conclusion that the "many unfortunate statements concerning doctrinal theology ... published by the Seventh-day Adventists" throughout their history reflected merely the personal opinions of a few within the church while "the overwhelming majority never held to those divergent views."[78] As Martin saw it, Adventists had always "adhered tenaciously to the cardinal doctrines of the Christian faith with but few exceptions."[79]

In the light of what was shown in chapter 4, this conclusion is not in harmony with the historical sources. Thus, it cannot be maintained without qualifications that *Questions on Doctrine* "truthfully represents the theology and doctrine" that Adventists "have always held."[80] Instead, it appears that some of the doctrinal positions defended in the 1950s may have been bolstered up by a revisionist history that interpreted the past in the light of what certain researchers believed and expected to find in the sources. While this may not invalidate the theological positions held by church leaders in the 1950s, it may not allow us today to ignore, as they did, the existence of significant changes and revisions in Adventist doctrinal history.

76   Roy Allen Anderson, "Evangelical Inconsistency," *Ministry*, February 1962, 39, 4-6, 39-40. "Naturally we have been seeking to be understood, and we regret that some have taken this to mean that we have changed our basic beliefs. But in no way have we compromised our doctrines" (ibid., 4).

77   "For over a century Adventism has borne a stigma of being called a non-Christian cult system." However, "the Adventism of 1965 is different in not a few places from the Adventism of 1845, and with that change the necessity of re-evaluation comes naturally." In recent years, its theology was marked by "clarification" and "redefinition" (Martin, *The Kingdom of the Cults*, 359, 365). In a telephone conversation with A. L. Hudson in 1958, D. G. Barnhouse also asserted that the Adventist church leaders had indeed moved away from a number of traditional doctrinal views. See the transcripts of a telephone conversation between A. L. Hudson and D. G. Barnhouse, 16 May 1958, AHC, JWL, AU, Berrien Springs, Mich.

78   Walter R. Martin, "Seventh-day Adventism Today," *Our Hope*, November 1956, 274-275. Among these divergent views, he mentioned the doctrine of atonement, salvation by grace and faith alone, Christology (Arianism and the sinful nature of Christ), Adventist "remnant" exclusivism and Sunday-keeping understood as constituting "the mark of the beast."

79   Ibid., 277. "It cannot be denied from their truly representative literature and their historic positions that they have always as a majority held to the cardinal, fundamental doctrines of the Christian faith which are necessary to salvation" (Martin, "What Seventh-day Adventists Really Believe," 43).

80   Martin, *The Kingdom of the Cults*, 368-369. Already in 1957, an insider surmised that Martin had not gained an accurate picture of the church and its beliefs and that his conclusions were, in fact, based on "a fundamental fallacy" and "certain gross misconceptions about Adventists." See Raymond F. Cottrell, "An Evaluation of Certain Aspects of the Martin Articles," in Moon, "M. L. Andreasen, L. E. Froom, and the Controversy over *Questions on Doctrine*, 1988," app. 2.

1966-1985

The most recent period of Adventist history treated in this survey kept the church engaged in a number of theological disputes comparable, in some respects, to the trying years towards the end of the nineteenth century. Not surprisingly, reactions within the church were similar to those eighty years before. The issues themselves also had a familiar ring: righteousness by faith, Christian perfection, Christology, sanctuary and judgment theology, prophetic authority, etc. Thus, the church was again forcefully confronted with the problem of doctrinal continuity and change.[81]

Observing significant developments in Roman Catholicism, Adventists questioned whether the church of Rome would and, in fact, could radically depart from its own traditions.[82] Time has confirmed that the winds of change did not substantially alter the doctrinal structure of Roman Catholicism, though the latter underwent a number of significant modifications, relating even to doctrinal matters. Yet, in the view of many observers, a conservative and even reactionary trend has manifested itself in recent years under the leadership of Pope John Paul II.

How did the Seventh-day Adventist Church respond when some of its own members, in line with the spirit of the times, began to call for the reinterpretation and updating of the Adventist doctrinal heritage and its adaptation to the needs of the contemporary world? How did the church both rise to the challenge and define the limits of doctrinal renewal and reform? And how did its leaders deal with the conflicting demands of self-styled conservatives and progressives, respectively, intent on faithful preservation and genuine progress, as the case may be?

Predominantly, the church tended to assume a defensive posture, issuing warnings against the danger of compromising and departing from distinctive beliefs. Any alteration of their fundamental tenets would spell disaster for the unique message and mission of Seventh-day Adventists. Therefore, the church must beware of those calling for changes involving any non-negotiable truths.[83]

---

81 As indicated in the introduction of this chapter, this survey of SDA history intends to place the various reactions to doctrinal development in their historical context in order to help readers better understand and interpret them. The following section, likewise, does not want to trace doctrinal trends or changes occurring in recent years. Instead, it discusses some major doctrinal debates as they have prompted various people to express their views on doctrinal continuity and change. Thus, no conclusions should be drawn from this survey regarding the actual or possible direction of doctrinal development in the SDA church.

82 B. B. Beach, "Change in the Church of Rome," *RH,* 21 April 1966, 4-5. The Second Vatican Council lasted from 1959 till 1965.

83 F. Lee, "The Strong Appeal of Popularity," *RH,* 22 June 1967, 1, 7; idem, "The Passion for Change," *RH,* 29 June 1967, 4-5; idem, "The Lure of Intellectualism," *RH,* 6 July 1967, 6-7; W. J. Hackett, "The Church in an Era of Change," *RH,* 16 May 1968, 1, 8-9; Ellen G. White, "Does Adventist Theology Need Changing?" *Ministry,* October 1968, 16-19; Orley M. Berg, "Church under Fire!" *Ministry,* December 1968, 24-27; B. L. Archbold, "Ask for the Old Paths," *RH,* 20 March 1969, 5-6; Robert H. Pierson, "The Old Message Is Always New/True," *RH,* 1 January 1970, 2-3; W. J. Hackett, "Inspiration in a Changing World,"

While these recurring affirmations of Adventist beliefs may have reinforced the confidence of the rank and file of the church in the immutability of the Adventist message, they did not satisfy those inclined to think that a more critical reflection on church doctrines was warranted and even required in order to ascertain their truthfulness vis-à-vis the Scriptures as well as their relevance in the world today.

The founding of the "Association of Adventist Forums" in 1967 was an early indication that the church had entered upon a new phase in its development.[84] Western societies were becoming increasingly secular, pluralistic, and individualistic. Not surprisingly, then, a new generation of Adventists somehow reflected the values and ideals of contemporary culture, such as independence and self-determination, creativity and critical thinking.[85] The influx of academically trained young adults, in particular, paved the way for a new and different manner of relating to the denomination and its past. Implicit faith in the established doctrines of the church gave way to critical evaluation and a desire to participate in a timely formulation of these teachings. With it came an eagerness to explore new ideas, discover new truths, and express divergent viewpoints even on doctrinal questions. No longer content merely to reiterate traditional beliefs, this small but vocal segment of the church wanted to revive the spirit of open dialogue and unhampered investigation of truth, which seemingly had characterized the early years of the Adventist movement.[86]

RH, 12 February 1970, 4-6: J. R. Spangler, "Times Have Changed," *Ministry,* April 1970, 10-11; Robert H. Pierson, "The Same Yesterday, Today, and Forever," *Ministry,* June 1970, 35-40; idem, "I Have Set Thee a Watchman," *Ministry,* November 1970, 24, 57-58; O. B. Kuhn, "Liberalism Endangers the Church," *Ministry,* May 1971, 17; "Landmarks of Truth," *RH,* 7 October 1971, 1-21 (Week of Prayer Readings); R. R. Bietz, "The Peril of Compromise," *RH,* 17 February 1972, 4-6; David C. Whitley, "Clouded Issues," *Ministry,* May 1972, 24-31, 42; Robert H. Pierson, "No Compromise," *RH,* 8 February 1973, 2; W. J. Hackett, "The Church's Terrible Ordeal," *RH,* 23 January 1975, 4-5; Alfred S. Jorgensen, "The 'Omega' of Apostasy," *Ministry,* March 1975, 8-10; Robert H. Pierson, *We Still Believe* (Washington, D.C.: RHPA, 1975), 9-17; W. Duncan Eva, "Changeless Truth in an Age of Change," *RH,* 1 September 1977, 2; Robert H. Pierson, "The Testimony of Jesus," *RH,* 6 October 1977, 6-7; idem, "How Do You Really Feel about Your Church? – Nos. 1-2," *AR,* 9 February, 5 October 1978, 2-3, 18; K. H. Wood, "'Present Truth' Centers in the Most Holy Place," *AR,* 28 September 1978, 10-11; idem, "When a Church Comes 'of Age,'" *AR,* 28 December 1978, 14-15.

84 Also during the 1960s, the "Adventistischer Wissenschaftlicher Arbeitskreis" was formed in Germany, which pursued goals very similar to those of the AAF in North America. In 1972, it started to publish a magazine called *Stufen* as well as a series of booklets containing the papers presented during the biannual conferences of the AWA *(Die Adventgemeinde in Geschichte und Gegenwart).*

85 Cf. the recent analysis by Jon Paulien, *Present Truth in the Real World: The Adventist Struggle to Keep and Share Faith in a Secular Society* (Boise, Idaho: PPPA, 1993), 7-11, 43-68.

86 Roy Branson, "Adventist Forums: Another Bulwark against Indifference and Apostasy," *RH,* 14 May 1970, 16-17; and Richard C. Osborn, "The First Decade: The Establishment of the Adventist Forums," *Spectrum,* 10:4 (1980): 42-58. The main outlet of the Association was

However, to most church members as well as to the leadership of the denomination, this new breed of intellectuals remained quite suspect as their loyalty to the unchanging landmarks of the Adventist faith was less than assured. Their "unnecessary dissent" appeared like "a prostitution of time, skill, and strength"; after all, the major doctrines of the church had been hammered out and established firmly long ago, requiring no re-evaluation or even revision.[87]

On the other hand, Adventist missiologist Gottfried Oosterwal reminded Adventists that the steady growth of the church through the years had stimulated the "reformulation of its message" and gradually "led to a different self-understanding." He also pointed to the "shift of emphasis" towards a more Christ-centered theological approach and the gradually changing "concept of the church and its mission."[88] Jack Provonsha, another Adventist scholar, also attempted to familiarize the church with the idea that "change is an expression of God's continuous creation and is therefore good and to be welcomed." To him, preserving self-identity was not opposed to participating in genuine change.[89]

Since the mid-seventies, a number of church leaders and scholars have supported a dynamic approach, which recognizes both the need for doctrinal progress and change and the demand for the continuity and stability of church teachings.[90]

The AAF journal *Spectrum* carried a number of articles calling for even more decided efforts to rethink and renew Adventist theology. The necessity for the contemporary relevance and intelligibility of the faith would require the constructive reinterpretation and continual re-contextualization of Adventist beliefs. Some doctrinal revisions as well as a moderate theological pluralism would, therefore, be inevitable. At the same time, destructive innovations were to be avoided.[91] It seems, however, that those hoping for considerable changes in the Adventist body of beliefs

---

Spectrum, which became one of the first independent magazines in the church. Since 1982, the AAF has also sponsored a series of National Conferences addressing issues of contemporary relevance to SDA faith.

87   K. H. Wood, "The *Newsweek* Story," *RH,* 1 July 1971, 2.

88   Oosterwal, *Mission Possible,* 30-32.

89   Provonsha, *God Is with Us,* 70, 67-75. See also ibid., 26-28, for a brief analysis of the psychological structure of human resistance to change.

90   W. R. Beach, "In Defense of Stable Motion," *RH,* 16 January 1975, 4-5; Raoul Dederen, "Adventists and Doctrinal Change," *Ministry,* February 1977, 16-19; Jack W. Provonsha, "Can There Be an Innovative Adventism?" *Ministry,* April 1976, 34-35; William G. Johnsson, "Something Old, Something New," *AR,* 5 August 1982, 8; Richard Hammill, "Change and the SDA Church – Nos. 1-2," *AR,* 6-13 January 1983, 6-8, 6-8; Johnston, "A Search for Truth"; Gordon Bietz, "Leadership in Crisis," *Ministry,* December 1983, 20-22.

91   Charles Scriven, "The Case for Renewal in Adventist Theology," *Spectrum* 8:1 (1976): 2-6; Fred Veltman, "Some Reflections on Change and Continuity," ibid., 8:4 (1977): 40-43; Fritz Guy, "The Shaking of Adventism? I. A View from the Outside," ibid., 9:3 (1978): 28-31; Jonathan Butler, "The World of E. G. White and the End of the World," ibid., 10:2 (1979): 2-13; Roy Branson, "A Time for Healing," ibid., 13:2 (1982): 2-3; "Change and Continuity in the Theology of a Church," ibid., 14:1 (1983): 40-41; and Edward W. Vick, "Must We Keep the Sanctuary Doctrine?" ibid., 14:3 (1983): 52-55.

met with relatively few favorable responses. For the most part, their views were either ignored or resisted by the members and leaders of the church.

In the 1970s, the demand for a reconsideration and even revision of certain Adventist beliefs was raised from both within and without the denomination. It caused intense doctrinal discussions, having quite a polarizing effect on the membership of the church.[92]

Since the mid-1950s, Robert D. Brinsmead's perfectionist leanings had created dissensions in, and defections from, the church. His astounding theological about-face in 1970 and the resulting advocacy of a strictly forensic understanding of righteousness by faith led him to become a sharp critic of traditional Adventist soteriology and eschatology.[93] In 1980, he announced "the end of (traditional) Adventism" which he considered thoroughly judged by the New Testament gospel.[94]

Intense discussions on the meaning and implications of justification and sanctification tended to polarize the church. In time, "righteousness by faith" even became an irritant term, which served more to discomfort than to comfort believers. The proponents of the traditional Adventist view (Douglass, Maxwell, Wood) emphasized the possibility of overcoming sin and developing a perfect character. The "Reformationist theologians" (Brinsmead, Ford, Paxton)[95] pointed to the all-pervasive nature of sin and the all-sufficiency of the imputed righteousness of Christ. Others took a mediating position, recognizing the importance of both the objective and the subjective dimensions of salvation (Heppenstall, LaRondelle, Venden).[96]

---

92 For example, the inspiration and authority of Ellen White increasingly became a controversial issue, particularly after the publication of Walter T. Rea's highly critical study on Ellen White's literary indebtedness. See below, p. 290, n. 5.

93 See Schwarz, *Light Bearers to the Remnant,* 456-461.

94 Born and raised in Australia but living in North America, Brinsmead disseminated his views through a journal entitled *Present Truth* (1972-1978) – later renamed *Verdict* (1978-) – as well as through other publications. His criticism of the sanctuary doctrine and of SDA theology in general was forcefully expressed in the Syllabus *1844 Re-Examined* (1979) as well as in the book *Judged by the Gospel: A Review of Adventism* (Fallbrook, Calif.: Verdict Publications, 1980). For a brief analysis and critique of his views, see Rolf J. Pöhler, "Auf dem Prüffeld des Evangeliums: Robert D. Brinsmead erschüttert den Adventismus," *Materialdienst* 45:5 (1 Mai 1982): 126-130; and idem, "Verkürzte Wahrheit – heilsame Häresie: Eine Kritik des soteriologischen und hermeneutischen Ansatzpunkts Robert D. Brinsmeads," *Aller Diener,* Nos. 3-4, 1982, 101-112. Disfellowshipped since 1961, Brinsmead severed his last theological ties to Seventh-day Adventism when, in 1981, he denounced Adventist Sabbath observance as an implicit betrayal of the gospel of Christ ("Sabbatarianism Re-Examined," *Verdict* 4:4 [June 1981]: 1-70). Today, Brinsmead is reported to be no longer a professing Christian of any type.

95 Geoffrey J. Paxton was an Australian Anglican theologian who, in the 1970s, took an active part in the discussions on righteousness by faith. Calling himself "a sympathetic critic," he analyzed Adventism in the light of his understanding of 16th-century Reformation theology. See Paxton, *The Shaking of Adventism* (1977).

96 Among the numerous publications on these issues, see "Righteousness by Faith," *AR,* Special Issue, [16 May 1974]; Douglass, Heppenstall, LaRondelle, and Maxwell, *Perfection;* Paxton,

Between 1973 and 1976, a so-called "Righteousness by Faith Committee" attempted to clear up certain questions relating to it.[97] Nineteen theologians, editors, and administrators meeting at Palmdale, California, April 23-30, 1976, tried to mediate between the different schools of thought by writing up and publishing a consensus statement.[98] However, neither did it end the discordant views nor could it silence the antagonists. Thus, three years later, General Conference president Neal C. Wilson called for a moratorium on public presentations and contentious discussions of the controversial aspects of salvation "until a representative church committee under the guidance of the Holy Spirit can offer helpful and practical direction."[99] When the "Righteousness by Faith Consultation" met in Washington, D.C., October 3-4, 1979, its 145 members produced a detailed and carefully worded document on the contemporary Adventist understanding of salvation.[100]

During these extended discussions on righteousness by faith, Desmond Ford, another Australian theologian, had become a leading and controversial proponent of a strictly forensic understanding of justification. Passionately fighting against perfectionism in any form, he was criticized for weakening the biblical doctrine of sanctification and discarding the traditional Adventist notion of an eschatological perfection of believers. In 1979, however, Ford caused an even larger stir in the church when he openly questioned the validity of the traditional interpretation of the doctrine of the heavenly sanctuary and of the investigative judgment.[101]

The Shaking of Adventism; J. R. Spangler, "Ask the Editor – 1-2," Ministry, August, October 1978, 14-17, 10-12; Hans K. LaRondelle, Christ Our Salvation: What God Does for Us and in Us (Mountain View, Calif.: PPPA, 1980); Moore, Theology in Crisis; Beatrice S. Neall, "The Dragon Fighters," Ministry, June 1980, 14-15; Ott, Perfect in Christ; and Morris Venden, 95 Theses on Righteousness by Faith (Boise, Idaho: PPPA, 1987).

97 "Righteousness by Faith," Ministry, August 1976, 5-9. The work of this committee focused on the 1888 Minneapolis conference and the questions raised by Wieland and Short regarding its significance as understood by the contemporary church. Cf. above, p. 230, n. 30.

98 "Christ Our Righteousness," RH, 27 May 1976, 4-7. The article intentionally evaded the controversial issues regarding the sinful/-less nature of Christ and Christian perfection. It called for unity to replace the theological disputes dividing the church.

99 Neal C. Wilson, "An Open Letter to the Church," AR, 24 May 1979, [4-5]. He thereby wanted to comply with the biblical precedent as recorded in Acts 15. According to it, "all controversy should cease" until the matter was settled and "a final decision" was given by "the highest authority" in the church. This decision "was to be universally accepted by the churches" and, thus, doctrinal unity would be restored.

100 "The Dynamics of Salvation," AR, 31 July 1980, 3-8. Notably, only the short concluding section of the study document is devoted to the controversial, eschatological dimension of sanctification/perfection. It praises "Christ our Advocate, through whom alone we may stand in the judgment, [and] whose love motivates us to holy living" (ibid., 8).

101 With his unorthodox views, Ford said he had hoped to provide an answer to Brinsmead's recent attack on the sanctuary doctrine. But, what was intended as a defensive measure was recognized by others as a severe criticism of this landmark doctrine. For a comprehensive presentation of his views, see Desmond Ford, Daniel 8:14, the Day of Atonement, and the Investigative Judgment. According to Ford, SDA doctrines underwent significant changes

In response to Ford's daring overtures, the church set up a special study committee and held a theological conference for the sole purpose of examining his deviating views. Meanwhile, the *Adventist Review* reaffirmed the distinctive "landmark" doctrines of the sanctuary/judgment (and continued to do so during the following years[102]). That it did repeatedly so even in the months preceding the Sanctuary Review Committee convened at the Glacier View Conference suggests that the latter was possibly not so much intended to reassess the Adventist position as to reassert the traditional view.[103] As Neal C. Wilson, president of the General Conference, made it very clear to the church, "In no way do we expect this restudy of our distinctive truths to weaken the pillars of our message or the foundation of our faith."[104] Not surprisingly, the Sanctuary Review Committee rejected Ford's interpretation and reaffirmed the traditional teaching.[105] At the same time, it tacitly seems to have admitted the validity of some of his insights by incorporating them into the consensus statement "Christ in the Heavenly Sanctuary."[106]

and revisions over the years; the same was true of Ellen White's own theological beliefs (pp. 1-4, 333-390, 406-408). As a church today, we, too, should "cast away our doctrinal swaddling clothes" and go on to the maturity of faith (pp. 328, 368, 404, 413). However, while the doctrinal views of the pioneers cannot be regarded as the final word on any issue (pp. 339, 345), the church must still retain "the essential heart" of its message (pp. 369, 404). For the landmarks, properly defined, will remain (pp. 374-375).

102 L. R. Van Dolson, "Limits," *AR,* 5 March 1981, 13-14; K. H. Wood, "Building Up or Tearing Down?" *AR,* 28 May 1981, 14-15; R. L. Klingbeil, "The Foundation Stands Secure," *AR,* 17 September 1981, 9; Walter R. L. Scragg, "1844," *AR,* 7 January 1982, 7; N. S. Fraser, "Truth Can Stand Investigation," *AR,* 10 June 1982, 6-7; J. R. Spangler, "Does Truth Change?" *Ministry,* October 1982, 24-25; and Neal C. Wilson, "Christ Our Hope," General Conference Bulletin, No. 10, *AR,* 18-25 July 1985, 5-6.

103 Neal C. Wilson, "'Let the Word Go Out,'" *AR,* 13 December 1979, 4-6; K. H. Wood, "A Solid Foundation," *AR,* 17 January 1980, 3; idem, "Satan versus the Church," *AR,* 24 January 1980, 13-14; and Richard Lesher, "Truth Stands Forever," *AR,* 13 March 1980, 6-7.

104 Neal C. Wilson, "Update on the Church's Doctrinal Discussions," *AR,* 3 July 1980, 24.

105 Ford lost his ministerial credentials but remained a member of the church. He formed the "Good News Unlimited Foundation" and continued to work as a public evangelist and lecturer. In the wake of his defrocking, hundreds of Adventists left the church, forming local congregations of "Evangelical Adventists" or joining other denominations. In October 1980, *Evangelica* – calling itself "an evangelical publication for Adventists" – appeared; within only two years, it had completed its "Exodus from Adventism" and was entering mainstream Evangelicalism.

106 "Overview of a Historic Meeting," *AR,* 4 September 1980, 4-7; "Statement on Desmond Ford Document," ibid., 8-11; "Christ in the Heavenly Sanctuary," ibid., 12-15; and "Christ and His High Priestly Ministry," *Ministry,* October 1980. Cf. "Sanctuary Debate," *Spectrum* 11:2 (1980): 1-78. For some valuable background information on the Sanctuary Review Committee and Des Ford, see Hammill, *Pilgrimage,* 183-198. According to Hammill, "Dr. Ford did raise some issues that need more careful, vigorous investigation than has been given them even to this date" (ibid., 198). In the 1980s, the church actually made an elaborate attempt to undertake such an investigation. The resulting seven-volume "Daniel and Revelation Committee Series" (1982-1992) was prepared and published by the Biblical

While Wilson reported, "Our distinctive beliefs ... have not changed! They have only been confirmed!"[107] *Adventist Review* reader Marshall J. Grosboll expressed concern "about a couple of diversions from our historical position" that he had discovered in the consensus statement.[108] Editor K. H. Wood denied that the latter contained any "major theological changes," but admitted that it included "variant views [that] could be harmonized with well-established doctrines."[109] The more than 60 Adventist Bible scholars and theologians attending the second annual meeting of the Andrews Society for Religious Studies in Dallas, November 1980, viewed the consensus statements "as being in significant continuity with traditional under-standings, while incorporating new understandings."[110]

The Glacier View Conference and the events leading up to it had revealed the possibility of a widening gap between church administration, on the one hand, and some college and university teachers, on the other. In order to improve relations and

Research Institute of the General Conference. Its 2,400 pages were the work of a 25-member committee, which had been appointed in 1981 by the General Conference in order to study and refute the views of Desmond Ford (see Lesher and Holbrook, "Daniel and Revelation Committee: Final Report"). For a popularized version of the results of the Daniel and Revelation Committee Series, vols. 1-3, see Clifford Goldstein, *1844 Made Simple* (Boise, Idaho: PPPA, 1988); the content of these volumes is distilled in Angel Manuel Rodriguez, "The Sanctuary and Its Cleansing," *AR,* Supplement, [1] September 1994, 1-16. The series strongly affirmed the biblical accuracy of the SDA teaching on the sanctuary and judgment as well as the hermeneutical adequacy of the historicist interpretation of apocalyptic prophecies. See Richard M. Davidson, "In Confirmation of the Sanctuary Message," *JATS* 2:1 (1991): 93-114; and C. Mervyn Maxwell, "In Confirmation of Prophetic Interpretation," ibid., 139-151.

107 Neal C. Wilson, "A Letter from the President," *Ministry,* October 1980, 3.

108 "Letters," *AR,* 23 October 1980, 2.

109 K. H. Wood, "F. Y. I.," *AR,* 20 November 1980, 3, 11.

110 "Adventist Scholars Meet," *AR,* 27 November 1980, 24. In a paper presented at the Glacier View Conference, Raymond F. Cottrell had noted that "flexibility in perfecting our under-standing of Bible truth in the light of clearer biblical evidence has marked Seventh-day Adventists as a people from the very first. Our first major doctrinal adjustment was abandon-ment of the 'shut door' theory of the heavenly sanctuary explanation of the 1844 dis-appointment ... The time has come for another step in the perfecting process – with respect to our understanding and use of Daniel 8:14. We can take this step with full assurance that we are acting in the best Adventist tradition, with our minds open to Bible truth. Perfecting our understanding of truth is not a denial of faith, but an affirmation of faith on a higher level of understanding. To imagine that our finite understanding of infinite truth at any stage of our experience is perfect, complete, and irreformable is hardly becoming for finite beings. Imperfections do not become sacrosanct with time" ("A Hermeneutic for Daniel 8:14, 1980," TMs, p. 29 [AHC, JWL, AU, Berrien Springs, Mich.]). It should be noted, however, that in Cottrell's judgment the sanctuary doctrine with its traditional interpretation of Dan 8:14 could not be demonstrated and justified on a strictly biblical basis and, thus, ultimately depended on the inspired authority of Ellen White (cf. below, p. 272-273). For Cottrell's analysis of the Glacier View Conference, see "The Sanctuary Review Committee and Its New Consensus," *Spectrum* 11:2 (1980): 2-26.

increase mutual confidence, two Theological Consultations were held in 1980 and 1981 at which scholars and administrators engaged in open and serious dialogue.[111] In a significant paper dealing with "The Theological Task of the Church," Fritz Guy attempted to remove the embarrassment that Adventists might feel at the idea of doctrinal development.[112] In a similar vein, Charles Teel called upon the church to maintain "a truly creative tension" between the old doctrinal landmarks and new light. After all, he argued, "change is indispensable to continuity. The old must continually be renewed."[113]

In summary, while some scholars and intellectuals in the late 60s and throughout the 70s pondered the possibility and even urged the necessity of certain doctrinal revisions, most Adventists either saw no specific biblical warrant for such a move or may have felt uneasy and even apprehensive at such prospects. As this survey shows, the proposal of a "new view" regularly has been accompanied by apprehensions and fears of a "new theology" which would change or abandon the distinctive truths of the Adventist faith.[114] Something similar happened in the 1970s when church leaders and other members became concerned about the rise of a "new theology."[115]

In this context, the 1980 General Conference in Dallas may be seen as an important milestone in the history of the denomination because of its spirited discussion and official vote on a new version of the Fundamental Beliefs of Seventh-day Adventists. It thereby defined the parameters of what, at present, may be regarded as orthodox or mainstream Adventism. In addition, it marked the temporary endpoint of recent doctrinal developments that have been fully accepted and integrated into the Adventist doctrinal belief system. At the same time, however, it not only left room in its preamble for future doctrinal developments but also gave rise to further theological reflections on the meaning and implications of the fundamental Adventist beliefs.[116]

---

111 Lawrence T. Geraty, "First Adventist Theological Consultation between Administrators and Scholars," *AR*, 16 October 1980, 15-17; Warren C. Trenchard, "In the Shadow of the Sanctuary: The 1980 Theological Consultation," *Spectrum* 11:2 (1980): 26-30; Thompson, "Theological Consultation II"; and Wilson, "Together for a Finished Work."

112 Fritz Guy, "The Theological Task of the Church, 1980," TMs (in my possession). For more details, see below, p. 283.

113 Teel, "Withdrawing Sect, Accommodating Church, Prophesying Remnant," 35-37. In his report on Consultation I, Geraty wrote: "In a world where cultures vary, language changes, and knowledge increases, the understanding and expression of eternal truths must necessarily be updated, although the truths themselves remain clear and unshaken" ("First Adventist Theological Consultation between Administrators and Scholars," 15).

114 This was particularly so in the 1880s, 1910s, and 1950s.

115 See, e.g., Robert H. Pierson, "When Will the 'Other Side' Be Heard?" *RH*, 11 March 1976, 2; D. F. Neufeld, "SDA Biblical Scholars Convene," *RH*, 8 January 1976, 3, 12; and Lewis R. Walton, *Omega* (Washington, D.C.: RHPA, 1981).

116 See *General Conference Bulletin – Nos. 1-10*, 17 April-15 May 1980. Cf. below, app. 3, col. 3. The book *Seventh-day Adventists Believe* (1988) offered a detailed commentary on the Dallas declaration. Its "Biblical Exposition of 27 Fundamental Doctrines" presented a synopsis

Looking briefly at the 1980s, it appears that the increasing polarization between so-called "evangelical" Adventists and some "liberal" Adventists (demanding a theological reorientation), on the one hand, and "traditional" Adventists (calling for the restoration of historic Adventism), on the other, made any attempt to move the church in a particular direction prone to a vigorous effort to counterbalance it. With the majority of church members holding, or leaning to, established positions, the leadership of the church likewise appears to have been concerned more with preserving the faith than with exploring its significance in the modern world. It seems that the challenging questions and tentative concepts of the 1960s and 1970s were replaced increasingly with the confirming answers and solid convictions of the 1980s.

That the conservative forces were on the rise within the church seemed to have become evident after 1985, when, within a few years, a number of organizations were founded that all shared essentially the same goal, viz., to unreservedly affirm, and effectively safeguard, the historic faith of the church. To trace the development of these movements lies outside the scope of this survey which ends with the year 1985. It seems safe to say, however, that the representatives of what some consider the "new right," while others regard it as the real and proper "centrist" view, have been ringing in still another phase in the development of the Seventh-day Adventist Church.[117]

of what Adventists traditionally had understood the Bible to teach. Frequently paraphrasing Ellen White, the book was not so much concerned with reflecting on or translating Adventist teachings in view of the contemporary world as it was with describing and summarizing the historic and established doctrines of the church. For a critique of this "first official book of Adventist doctrines," see Glen Greenwalt, "The Gospel According to *Seventh-day Adventists Believe*," *Spectrum* 20:1 (1989): 24-28; cf. Neal C. Wilson, "Project 27," *AR*, 6 October 1988, 4-5; "Seventh-day Adventists Believe ...," *Ministry*, July 1988, 4-5.

117 Among these organizations and publications are to be mentioned:

(1) *Prophecy Countdown:* This is the name of a Florida-based independent television ministry founded by John Osborne in 1985. Calling himself a strict fundamentalist, he opposed "liberalism" and wanted to stick to the old SDA faith. He was disfellowshipped in 1991.

(2) *Our Firm Foundation:* This monthly journal published by "Hope International," a conservative, independent Adventist ministry, was founded in 1985 by Ron Spear in Eatonville, Wash. Wanting to purify the church, he is critical of its perceived theological slant. For an official response to these groups, see *Issues: The Seventh-day Adventist Church and Certain Private Ministries* (n.p.: North American Division of SDAs, [1993]). The following private ministries are loyal to the denomination, but critical of certain trends within it:

(3) *Adventists Affirm:* This magazine affirming Adventist beliefs has been published since 1987 on the campus of Andrews University in Berrien Springs, Mich. It wants to stem the impact of liberalizing trends gradually eroding the beliefs and practices of the church.

(4) *Adventist Perspectives:* Fourteen issues of this religious journal were published by Southern College in Collegedale, Tenn., from 1987 until 1992. Its goal was to comment from a conservative viewpoint on the 27 Fundamental Beliefs of SDAs and other theological issues.

(5) *Adventism Triumphant:* The new quarterly journal of the 1888 Message Study Committee has been published since 1990 in Paris, Ohio. It stands for the message of righteousness by faith "as presented to the church in 1888" by Waggoner and Jones. This teaching is understood as producing a church that has reached perfection by ceasing to sin.

Catchwords of Doctrinal Continuity and Change
in Adventist Phraseology

Traditionally, Seventh-day Adventists have used certain key terms and phrases that
neatly express their prevalent views on the issue of doctrinal continuity and change.
These catchwords reflect the determination to uphold the fundamental doctrines of
the church as well as the readiness to constantly advance in the understanding of
truth. Because of a certain tendency to use these expressions routinely and without
an accurate understanding of their historical meaning or theological implications, the
most common of these catchwords[118] or "shibboleths"[119] are now briefly analyzed.
This sheds further light on the Adventist understanding of doctrinal development.

"Present Truth" and "New Light"

After 1847, Sabbatarian Adventists came to understand the "third angel's message"
of Rev 14:9-12 as the divine charter of their movement.[120] However, their comprehension of the content and scope of this passage and, consequently, of their own
message and mission did change and increase considerably over the years. The
awareness of the progressive nature and dynamic growth of the understanding of

---

(6) *The Adventist Theological Society:* Founded in 1988, this society has received widespread
support from theologians, administrators, pastors, and other members of the church. It
follows a fundamentalist and literalist approach to theology, opposes modernist/liberal trends,
and seeks to preserve and foster the historic beliefs as well as the unique identity of the Adventist church. Membership is conditioned on and renewed annually by signing an affirmation of faith. The ATS organizes worldwide regional chapters, publishes a newsletter and a
theological journal containing the papers presented at the international, biannual conventions,
and sponsors doctoral students, annual scholars' meetings, and various publications (Monograph Series, Dissertation Series, Occasional Papers). The ATS is a thriving organization considering itself as holding to "a centrist position" and being at "the leading edge in Adventist
theology." See J. R. Spangler, "Adventist Theological Society," *Ministry,* December 1989, 24-
25; and idem, "Too Many Theological Societies?" *Ministry,* June 1990, 22-23.

The captivating story of this latest and current phase of Adventist denominational history still
continues and remains yet to be written.

118 *"Catchword* usually applies to a phrase that serves as the formula or identification mark of an
emotionally charged subject" *(Webster's New Dictionary of Synonyms,* 1984 ed., s.v.
"Catchword, Byword, Shibboleth, Slogan").

119 According to Judg 12, thousands of Ephraimites fleeing from the Gileadites were killed when
they could not correctly pronounce the word *shibboleth* (meaning "ear" or "stream") but ren-
dered it instead as *sibboleth,* thus giving away their identity. Based on this story, the term has
come to denote some kind of stock expression "whose employment identifies a person as
belonging to a particular party ... The term basically stresses help in placing a person ... but
may also imply the emptiness and triteness of such usage" (ibid.).

120 [James White and Ellen White], *A Word to the "Little Flock,"* 10-11; Ellen White, *Life
Sketches of Ellen G. White,* 95-96.

revelation was expressed by the phrase "present truth" (2 Pet 1:12), which was applied particularly to the special truths Adventists felt called to preach.

The expression "present truth" originally had been applied by the Millerites to the proclamation of the imminent coming of Christ.[121] Later, it was also used to denote the proclamation of time by the so-called "seventh month movement" in the summer of 1844.[122] After the great disappointment, the phrase was repeatedly employed by shut-door believers to describe the "bridegroom" theory advanced by Joseph Turner and Apollos Hale to explain the delay of the advent of Christ.[123]

Apparently, Joseph Bates was the first to apply the expression to the newly discovered Sabbath truth.[124] The concept was soon enlarged by the Sabbatarian Adventists to include (1) the Sabbath doctrine, (2) the shut-door teaching, and (3) "the commandments of God and the faith of Jesus" – a comprehensive term for the entire third angel's message they were to proclaim.[125] It seems expedient, therefore, that James White called his first journal *The Present Truth.*[126] After they had abandoned the shut-door doctrine in 1851, the pioneers of Seventh-day Adventism described their amended teaching on the heavenly sanctuary as a vital ingredient and, indeed, the foundation of the present truth.[127]

To the early Seventh-day Adventists, present truth was first and foremost prophetic truth. It had to do, in the main, with the apocalyptic passages of the Bible related to "the world's position in the fulfillment of prophecy"; in other words, it

---

121 "Letter from R. Hutchinson," *Midnight Cry,* 24 August 1843, 8.

122 "Present Truth," *Voice of the Truth,* 2 October 1844, 144.

123 E. C. Clemons to Wm. Miller, 17 February 1845 (typewritten MS); "Letter from Bro. Z. Baker," *Jubilee Standard,* 3 April 1845, 27; S. S. Snow, "Visit to Philadelphia," ibid., 28; C. S. M[inor], "The True Manna," ibid., 29; "Letter from Bro. Cook," *Day-Star,* 6 September 1845, 18; and "Letter from Bro. [Otis] Nichols," *Day-Star,* 27 September 1845, 34.

124 Bates, *The Seventh Day Sabbath,* 2, 45; idem, *The Seventh Day Sabbath,* 2d rev. and enl. ed., iii-iv, 56-57; and idem, *A Vindication of the Seventh-Day Sabbath,* 28, 51-58, 65, 86.

125 At that time, the Sabbath doctrine and the shut-door teaching were regarded as inextricably interwoven. See James White to the Hastingses, 26 August 1848, EGWRC, AU, Berrien Springs, Mich.; idem to the Hastingses, 2 October 1848, EGWRC, AU, Berrien Springs, Mich.; idem, "To Our Readers," *RH,* November 1850, 7; Joseph Bates, *A Seal of the Living God,* 2, 17, 20-26, 54-57, 64-65; idem, *An Explanation of the Typical and Anti-Typical Sanctuary,* 4, 16; idem, "Dear Bro. White," *RH,* March 1851, 55-56; Ellen White, "To Those Who Are Receiving the Seal of the Living God"; Ellen White to the Hastingses, 24-30 March 1849; idem, "Beloved Brethren, Scattered Abroad," *Present Truth,* December 1849, 34-35; and idem, *Early Writings,* 63-64.

126 Five issues were published between July 1849 and November 1850 before the paper was merged with *The Advent Review* to become the *Second Advent Review and Sabbath Herald.* For occurrences of the term "present truth" in the journal *The Present Truth,* see pp. 1, 6, 24-25, 28-29, 34-39, 56, 64, 67-75, 84-85, and 88.

127 James White, "The Sanctuary," *RH,* 6 January 1853, 133; idem, "The Sanctuary and 2300 Days," *RH,* 17 March 1853, 172-173; and idem, "Remarks on This Work." Note added to the *Advent Review,* April 1853.

denoted "prophecies in [the] process of fulfillment."[128] Its attractiveness derived from the fact that it allowed believers to interpret their "present experience in the unfolding light of prophecy."[129]

Second, as present truth was derived from "prophecies relating to our times,"[130] it was always contextual and relevant truth. For it dealt with "truth which is especially applicable to the present time,"[131] and "necessary to our present salvation."[132] As new situations were arising constantly in the history of this world, "certain portions of the Word, and certain subjects [were] particularly applicable to any one time more than another."[133] In other words, present truth was "new truth being developed for new generations all along the stream of time, adapted to the new wants of their ever-changing circumstances."[134] This meant that "some truths are called into existence by circumstances"[135] and have "a more local and temporary application."[136] Adventists, therefore, were always to ask themselves, "What is the truth adapted to the state and condition of the world now?"[137]

Third, the gradual unfolding of Bible prophecy on the end time made present truth a progressive and constantly developing truth. "As new events are continually transpiring, so new truths are continually unfolded."[138] Thus, "in every age there is a new development of truth, a message of God to the people of that generation."[139]

128 [James White], "The Head and Front of Present Truth," *RH*, 15 December 1863, 20. Uriah Smith defined it as "truth concerning those scenes in the fulfillment of prophecy to which mankind hold the nearest relation, be they past or future" ("The Bible Preacher," *RH*, 16 October 1855, 62).

129 J. H. Waggoner, "Present Truth," *RH*, 7 August 1866, 76. "The present truth for this generation we conceive to be the closing fulfillments of prophecy" ([Uriah Smith], "Notes and Queries," *RH*, 11 August 1885, 504).

130 D. T. Bourdeau, "Is Present Truth Essential?" *RH*, 27 January 1874, 53.

131 Ibid.; cf. James White, "To Our Readers," *RH*, November 1850, 7.

132 James White, "Our Present Work," *RH*, 19 August 1851, 12. In the view of the Adventists, present truth was, therefore, also pragmatic truth, showing them "the duties which are now especially incumbent upon the church" ([James White], "The Head and Front of Present Truth," *RH*, 15 December 1863, 20). To them, truth and duty were almost synonymous, the one inevitably leading to the other.

133 James White, "Our Present Work," *RH*, 19 August 1851, 12. See also Ivory Colcord, "Present Truth," *RH*, 11 March 1873, 99 ("truths that demand attention now").

134 [Uriah Smith], "Notes and Queries," *RH*, 11 August 1885, 504. See also J. Clarke, "Present Truth," *RH*, 10 July 1866, 45.

135 M. E. Cornell, "Present Truth," *RH*, 6 August 1867, 113-114.

136 D. M. Canright, "The Present Truth," *RH*, 3 June 1873, 197. "The present truth, the third angel's message, is the word of the Lord to this generation, as much as the gospel preached by Paul was to that" (R. F. Cottrell, "The Word of God," *RH*, 26 November 1872, 189).

137 D. P. Curtis, "Present Truth," *RH*, 10 April 1888, 228.

138 Uriah Smith, "The Bible Preacher," *RH*, 16 October 1855, 62.

139 Ellen White, *Christ's Object Lessons* (Washington, D.C.: RHPA, 1900/1941), 127. See also [James White], "The Head and Front of Present Truth," *RH*, 15 December 1863, 20.

Inasmuch as present truth focused on the contemporary fulfillment of apo-calyptic prophecies, the early Seventh-day Adventists did not relate this phrase to the reformulation and reconceptualization of biblical truth. To them, development and progress primarily denoted the process that changed potential, i.e., prophetically announced truths into actual, historically fulfilled truths. Neither theological concepts nor their doctrinal expressions were to advance beyond what was clearly stated in the Scriptures. Rather, it was the progressive fulfillment of prophecies that led to the continual "development" and "progress" of present truth.[140]

In the 1880s, the understanding of present truth was broadened and further developed. When the gospel of justification by faith was perceived to have been a missing ingredient of Adventist preaching and teaching, the Pauline doctrine of righteousness by faith became a much-needed present truth. Adventists discovered that

> the Bible contains no greater and more vital truths than some by which we are not ap-parently in any way distinguished. There are the subjects of justification and right-eousness through Christ ... All these are emphatically present truth, and no less so for us than for any other people in the world. There is, for the most of us, a vast fund of present truth yet to be discovered and appreciated, and it is time that we realized the fact, and began to seek for it with the earnestness which its importance demands.[141]

This new, gospel-centered understanding of present truth (justification by faith) did not ignore but incorporate the distinctive Adventist emphasis on end-time events (prophetic truth).[142]

More recently, the phrase present truth has been used increasingly without any specific links to its prophetic-apocalyptic rooting. Instead, the emphasis was placed on the timeliness, contextuality, and relevance of Adventist teachings. Thus, present

---

140 "As the work of God in the fulfillment of his plan is progressive, so the faith of believers must be progressive; not that they must abandon their former faith, but they must ... walk in the increasing light of truth" (R. F. Cottrell, "Prophecy – Its Use," *RH,* 1 July 1873, 21). This explains why Adventists were so adamant in denying that the three angels' messages had been proclaimed before 1846. To admit it would have unsettled the prophetic chronology of Rev 12-14. When, in 1865, Snook and Brinkerhoff questioned this view, they were charged with having surrendered "fundamental principles of present truth." See above, p. 227.

141 L. A. S[mith], "Present Truth," *RH,* 6 January 1891, 9. In the context of the Minneapolis Conference, Ellen White wrote that "what would not have been truth twenty years ago, may well be present truth now" (Manuscript 15, 1888, EGWRC, AU, Berrien Springs, Mich.). In her view, "the message of justification by faith" was "the third angel's message [i.e., the present truth] in verity" *(Evangelism,* 190); for "the truth for this time embraces the whole gospel" *(Testimonies for the Church,* 6:291).

142 See on this, F. M. Wilcox, "The Message for Today," *RH,* 29 November-27 December 1928; idem, "God's Message for Today," *RH,* 28 July 1932, 2, 5; idem, "Present Truth for Today," *RH,* 13 April 1939, 2, 10; idem, "Present Truth," *RH,* 8 May 1947, 4-5; H. Prenier, "The Everlasting Gospel in 'Present Truth' Setting," *Ministry,* April 1929, 8-9; L. E. Froom, "Meaning of 'Present Truth,'" *Ministry,* May 1932, 25-26; and *QOD,* 616-617.

truth has been described in a rather general way as "truth in its most recent and clearest expression,"[143] "truth that is peculiarly appropriate in the present historical situation,"[144] "truth whose time has come,"[145] and "which is relevant and meaningful to our time and age and in our cultural context and socioeconomic situation."[146] In spite of the changing usage and varying connotations of the phrase, Adventists will probably agree that

> one of the most important elements in our Adventist heritage is the notion of "present truth" – truth that has come newly alive and has become newly understood and significant because of a new experience, a present situation.[147]

The third aspect of the Adventist understanding of present truth described here, viz., its progressive and developing character, has frequently been expressed with the help of another favorite catchword, viz., the idea of "new light." Frequently, when the phrase was used, it was emphasized that new light would not unsettle or contradict "old light."[148] While it may lead the church into a deeper understanding of truth, an enlargement of its vision, a clarification of its teachings, and the discovery of new doctrinal insights, no conflict will ever arise with previous beliefs. In other words, there may be doctrinal development, progress, and growth, but no change, which would imply the rejection or denial of established doctrines.[149]

> No additional gleams of genuine added light will do other than enhance and establish the fundamentals already known and established as foundational. They will but amplify and apply established principles to particulars not perceived in the past.[150]

143 Provonsha, *God Is with Us,* 22.

144 *SDAE,* 1976 ed., s.v. "Present Truth."

145 Guy, "The Theological Task of the Church," 12.

146 Oosterwal, "The SDA Church in the 1980s," 45. See also Paulien, *Present Truth in the Real World,* 36 ("truth that is particularly relevant at a given time and place"); and William G. Johnsson, "Present Truth: Walking in God's Light," *AR,* 6 January 1994, 8-11 ("truth that presses home with specific, contemporary thrust"). In a thoughtful essay, Fritz Guy has emphasized the "timeliness, newness, and urgency" of present truth, which is always both "conservative" and "progressive" ("Truth Our Contemporary," *AR,* 22 August 1991, 12-14).

147 Guy, "The Shaking of Adventism?" 31. Goldstein emphasizes that "these added truths have always rested upon a foundation rooted in antiquity"; they are not "new, innovative truth" but "old ones," not "new light" but "merely advanced light" *(The Remnant,* 85-88).

148 See, e.g., F. M. Wilcox, "'New Light': Preaching Which Discredits Vital Truth," *RH,* 30 April 1931, 9; and idem, "An Unwavering Message," *RH,* 27 April 1939, 2.

149 E. K. Slade, "The Certainty of Truth," *RH,* 29 August 1935, 4; L. E. Froom, "Not a Block to Be Moved, nor a Pin to Be Stirred," 20-22; idem, "Principles for Testing Added Light," *Ministry,* September 1947, 19, 18 *[sic];* W. E. Read, "Walking in the Light," *RH,* 12 February 1953, 5-6; Lesher, "Truth Stands Forever"; and Damsteegt, "Seventh-day Adventist Doctrines and Progressive Revelation."

150 [L. E. Froom], Editorial Note, *Ministry,* November 1944, 2.

Very rarely someone would hint at the possibility that new light might "change the past teachings of this people," though not "in any essential feature."[151] The analysis presented in chapter 4 also lends credibility and justification for the conclusion that, at times, a new doctrinal insight actually "contradicts what the church has always taught."[152] While new light may be said never to contradict old light, it may, however, conflict with certain traditional teachings hitherto assumed to express biblical truth accurately. In speaking of old or new light, it may be advisable, therefore, to indicate whether certain doctrinal views are meant (perceived truth) or the revelatory truths they want to express (actual truth).[153]

Landmarks, Pillars, and Foundations

In spite of their affirmatory statements on present truth and new light, Seventh-day Adventists, for the most part, have paid considerably more attention to the preservation of their teachings than to the elaboration of new doctrinal insights. This concern for protecting Adventist doctrines commonly has been expressed with the help of catchwords like "landmarks," "pillars," and "foundations."[154]

During the early years, Sabbatarian Adventists often pointed to the time calculations leading to 1844 as a basic and non-negotiable landmark of Millerism. Usually strong warnings were added against any attempts to remove these fixed boundaries of the Advent(ist) faith.[155] To indicate the crucial importance and indispensability of this doctrine, they also liked to compare it to the main pillars of a building.[156] Both catchwords – landmarks and pillars – were soon applied to the new and distinctive teachings of Sabbatarian Adventists, which came to be seen as constituting the third angel's message, i.e., the present truth.[157]

---

151 F. M. Wilcox, "The Fundamentals and New Light," *Ministry,* February 1940, 34-36. "There may come a change in some detail. We do not believe now in every detail what we believed once … I believe that for the most part the new light will be confirmatory of the old light, or it will be new spiritual truth" (ibid., 34). See also idem, "New Light," *RH,* 12 September 1940, 7-9.

152 K. H. Wood, "Bible Study, Technology, and Unity," *AR,* 25 May 1978, 3.

153 I am indebted to Gary B. Patterson for the terms "perceived" and "actual" truth ("The Quest for Truth," *AR,* 26 September 1991, 17).

154 These terms were derived from the KJV. See Deut 19:14; Prov 22:28 (landmark), 1 Tim 3:15; Rev 3:12 (pillar), and Ps 11:3; Luke 6:48; 1 Cor 3:10-11; 2 Tim 2:19 (foundation).

155 [James White and Ellen White], *A Word to the "Little Flock,"* 5; Ellen White, "My Dear Brethren and Sisters," *Present Truth,* March 1850, 64; James White, "To Ira Fancher"; Seaman, "Removing the Land-Marks"; and J. H. Waggoner, "Deserting the Land-marks," *RH,* 14 April 1868, 285. A similar phrase was used by Bates in the title of his book *Second Advent Way Marks and High Heaps.*

156 James White, "Our Present Position," *RH,* December 1850, 13; and idem, "The Parable, Matthew XXV, 1-12," 100.

157 James White, "To Ira Fancher."

Since that time, "in SDA thinking the landmarks are doctrines of such vital importance that they cannot be altered without changing the nature of the SDA Church."[158] Usually, whenever the historic teachings of the church were questioned, strong warnings against removing the old landmarks or destroying the foundational pillars of the faith were issued[159] and decided measures were taken against those who were thought to "pull down and destroy those glorious truths which we believe and live."[160] Seventh-day Adventists were agreed that

> in order for us to have a sense of direction, certain unchanging landmarks must be set up ... The waymarks which have been set up through the years are not movable, for they are settled and unchanging.[161]

It proved somewhat more difficult for Adventists to agree on what exactly was to be counted as the non-negotiable pillars of faith. In fact, whenever new and unfamiliar interpretations of the Scriptures were advanced in the church, someone was likely to oppose them as an attack against the old landmarks of Adventism.[162] Even the leadership of the church received its share of such accusations.[163] While Ellen White had circumscribed the landmarks quite strictly,[164] others tended to identify them with the entire list of Fundamental Beliefs held and published by the church.[165]

---

158 *SDAE,* 1976 ed., s.v. "Landmarks."

159 James White, "Unfulfilled Prophecy," *RH,* 29 November 1877, 172; F. M. Wilcox, "Attacking the Foundations – Nos. 1-2," *RH,* 18 April, 9 May 1929, 3-4, 3-5; idem, "Attacking the Foundations – Nos. 1-5," *RH,* 2 February-2 March 1933; Carlyle B. Haynes, "Has the Time Come for Us to Alter Our Standards and Rebuild Our Platform?" *RH,* 1 March 1934, 3-6; O. A. Hall, "The Enduring Foundation," *RH,* 30 April 1936, 3-4; T. M. French, "Maintaining the Foundations," *RH,* 15 April 1937, 7-8; F. M. Wilcox, "Steps in Apostasy," *RH,* 5 September 1940, 2, 18; idem, "The Ancient Landmarks – The Only Safe Guides," *RH,* 5 May 1949, 20-21, 49-50; and Neal C. Wilson, "'Let the Word Go Out,'" *AR,* 13 December 1979, 4-6.

160 "A Good Move in Iowa," *RH,* 20 February 1866, 94-95. This statement was made in relation to the Snook/Brinkerhoff defection in 1865. See above, p. 227-228; cf. above, p. 248, n. 106 (on Desmond Ford).

161 F. Lee, "The Sense of Direction," *RH,* 19 January 1939, 5-6; reprinted *RH,* 17 January 1957, 8. Cf. idem, "Giving Heed to the Foundations," *RH,* 26 January 1939, 3-4.

162 This was the case, e.g., when Smith introduced a new view on the king of the north, when Waggoner promoted his interpretation on the law in Galatians, and when Jones replaced the Alemanni for the Huns in the list of the ten horns in Dan 7. See above, pp. 167-170, 228-230.

163 F. D. Nichol, "Are We Removing the Old Landmarks?" *RH,* 8 March 1962, 12-13; and idem, "The Landmarks Examined," *RH,* 15 March 1962, 12-13.

164 See below, p. 309, n. 118.

165 F. M. Wilcox, "What Constitutes the Fundamentals?" *RH,* 18 January 1945, 4, 13. Knight has warned against the vice of "landmarkianism," which "manufacture[s] new landmarks" that only serve to divide the church and obscure its true identity *(Angry Saints,* 135-137). In 1987, a series of editorials in the *Adventist Review* sought to discover the main thrust of Adventism's landmark doctrines. The editor reinterpreted the doctrinal pillars of the church in terms of their relevance for Adventist living. To him, they taught a particular view about God as well

Another perennial problem relating to the landmarks had to do with the necessity of distinguishing the immovable foundation and the main pillars of the Adventist faith from their superstructure, which could possibly be corrected and changed. [166] Recognizing that some doctrinal views had, indeed, been modified in time, it was often argued that the essential teachings remained untouched by change, while there was room for certain readjustments and revisions with regard to secondary, non-essential matters. The difficulty, of course, lies in determining which is which; for "in the very nature of the case, it will never be possible for finite men always to establish a clear line of distinction between essentials and incidentals in doctrine."[167]

It was particularly L. E. Froom who, since the 1930s, stressed the need to distinguish the essential Adventist doctrines from other, non-essential views.[168] To him, the "essential verities" had to do, first of all, with the basic gospel truths of salvation by faith alone and the personal relationship of believers to Christ and, second, with the distinctive Adventist doctrines relating to the third angel's message. These had to be distinguished from matters of secondary importance, like controversial details on doctrine or prophetic interpretation, which did not affect the fundamentals of the Seventh-day Adventist faith.[169]

---

as loyalty and utter dependence on him in every situation (William G. Johnsson, "The Landmarks of Adventism," *AR,* 1-29 October 1987, 4, 4-5, 4, 4-5).

166 "Architects inform me that it is often possible to beautify, strengthen and enlarge, yes, even modernize, in a sense, a stately, venerable structure without disturbing a single supporting pillar or removing one stone from the foundation" (F. D. Nichol, "Restudying the Doctrines without Destroying the Foundations," *Ministry,* February 1940, 12).

167 Ibid. In the early decades, Adventists had outright dismissed even the very distinction between nonessential and essential matters of faith as an insult to God whose revelation, it was claimed, contained nothing unimportant (R. F. Cottrell, "Essentials and Non-Essentials," *RH,* 10 February 1863, 84-85; idem, "Essentials and Non-Essentials," *RH,* 18 November 1873, 181; and "Non-Essentials and Essentials," *RH,* 28 May 1889, 341). Soon, however, they came to realize the practical necessity of distinguishing between these two categories – if only to adjust to the growing diversity of viewpoints on certain doctrinal questions. Reporting on the 1884 General Conference, Uriah Smith pointed out that SDAs were fully agreed on the perpetuity of the law of God and that "diversity of opinion in any degree exists only on the non-essential questions" ("The Conference," *RH,* 4 November 1884, 696).

168 L. E. Froom, "Essentials and Nonessentials," *Ministry,* September 1931, 4-5; idem, "The Essential Verities," *Ministry,* October 1930, 3, 31; idem, "The Fundamental Emphasis," *Ministry,* January 1932, 9-10; idem, "A Balanced Emphasis Requisite," *Ministry,* August 1932, 9-10; idem, "Essentials and Nonessentials," *Ministry,* August 1932, 20-21; idem, "Distinguish Centralities from Secondaries," *Ministry,* July 1938, 21-22; and idem, "The Platform of Our Message," *Ministry,* August 1939, 20-21.

169 Recently, Whidden has distinguished the basic and distinctive Adventist doctrines (which he named "eternal verities" and "essential Adventism," respectively) from "processive Adventism" denoting "those issues that are important but still unsettled." Among the latter, he listed the humanity of Christ and Christian perfection. These controverted teachings should be studied in a spirit of openness aimed at reconciling theological "divisions within Adventism" through "earnest dialogue" ("Essential Adventism or Historic Adventism?" 5-9).

"No Creed but the Bible!"

Though wanting to preserve and protect their fundamental and distinctive doctrines, Adventists have never seriously attempted to reach this end with the help of a fixed creed drawing an exact line between non-negotiable and peripheral matters.[170] To the contrary, following an axiom held by the Restorationist Movement and confirmed by their experiences in the early years, Sabbatarian Adventists, from the start, decidedly and consistently opposed any creed or rule of faith apart from the Bible itself.[171] They were convinced that if only believers would fully submit to the word of God, theirs would be perfect harmony and complete doctrinal unity.[172]

When James White insisted on the need for church organization, many feared that this would eventually lead to doctrinal fixations and the adoption of a creed. Their concern was memorably expressed by J. N. Loughborough, who described five steps on the way to apostasy and Babylonian darkness.[173] While he considered "church order" an urgent necessity, White agreed with Loughborough on the destructive result of creedalism. "Making a creed is setting the stakes and barring up the way to all future advancement."[174] For more than three decades, Adventists wrote about creeds only in very negative terms. Opposing their use in the interpretation of the Bible, they were determined to evaluate all teachings by the Scriptures alone.[175]

170 On the development of Adventist statements of Fundamental Beliefs, see above, pp. 205-208.

171 "The Christian Connection backgrounds of Joseph Bates and James White undoubtedly reinforced a suspicion of creeds. Early in the nineteenth century this denomination had taken the position that the Bible would be its only creed, Christian character its only test of fellowship" (Schwarz, *Light Bearers to the Remnant,* 167).

172 "We take the Bible, the perfect rule of faith and practice, given by inspiration of God. This shall be our platform on which to stand, our creed and discipline" (James White, "Gospel Order," *RH,* 13 December 1853, 180). Cf. "The Babel of Christendom," *RH,* 24 September 1857, 164. Ellen White likewise affirmed that "the Bible, and the Bible alone, is to be our creed, the sole bond of union; all who bow to this holy word will be in harmony" *(Selected Messages,* 1:416). She always expressed herself in negative terms about creeds (see, e.g., *The Desire of Ages,* 242, and *The Great Controversy,* 379, 383, 595-596). See also Tim Crosby, "A Law without Profit: Ellen White Opposed a Church Creed as Harmful to Growth and Unity," *AR,* 29 May 1986, 9-10.

173 "The first step of apostasy is to get up a creed, telling us what we shall believe. The second is, to make that creed a test of fellowship. The third is to try members by that creed. The fourth to denounce as heretics those who do not believe that creed. And, fifth, to commence persecution against such" ("Doings of the Battle Creek Conference, Oct. 5 & 6, 1861," *RH,* 8 October 1861, 148, 148-149). See also J. N. Loughborough, "Image of the Beast," *RH,* 15 January 1861, 68-69; and idem, "Creeds," *RH,* 29 October 1861, 176.

174 "Doings of the Battle Creek Conference, Oct. 5 & 6, 1861," 148. "When you see a people adopting a human creed sustaining popular fables, and thus putting an end to investigation and reform ... you may safely include that people in the great Babylonian family" (James White, "Organization," *RH,* 1 October 1861, 141, 140-141).

175 R. F. Cottrell, "The Bible Explained by the Creed," *RH,* 25 April 1878, 133. Cf. "Don't Stagnate in Creeds," *RH,* 23 October 1879, 141.

Fears that the church might drift towards the formulation of a creed were re-kindled in the 1880s when, at the recommendation of the 1882 General Conference, W. H. Littlejohn wrote and published a suggested church manual.[176] Though its "simple rules" and "directions" were to be regarded as "suggestions only," in 1883, the General Conference delegates rejected the proposed manual as unnecessary and potentially dangerous because it would likely lead to uniformity in matters of "practice" and might also stiffen the understanding of "faith."[177]

Yet, when various doctrinal controversies raged through the denomination after the mid-1880s, the idea of using the Fundamental Beliefs of the church as an internal measuring rod became increasingly attractive to Adventists.[178] Several articles in the *Review & Herald* pointed out that some kind of creed was, after all, unavoidable and even enjoined by the Bible as a safeguard against error as well as for the instruction of others in the true faith. Still, those calling for an Adventist creed used the term rather loosely, opposing its use as an inflexible rule of faith.[179]

By and large, however, Adventists retained the traditional anti-creedal attitude and rejected all suggestions of devising a creed, in order to remain free for possible doctrinal advances.[180] The church publicly declared that "it is the design of Seventh-

---

176 W. H. Littlejohn, "The S.D.A. Church Manual," *RH,* 5 June-9 October 1883. It was to include "a statement of the fundamental principles held by S. D. Adventists" outlining "the views of our denomination." Still, it was not to be used as "a cast iron creed to be enforced in all of its minor details" (ibid., 5 June 1883, 361). The manual recommended that a pro-spective church member should be "questioned regarding his adoption of the fundamental principles of the Seventh-day Adventist faith" (idem, "The Church Manual," *RH,* 21 August 1883, 537-538). See also idem, "The Church Manual," *RH,* 31 July 1883, 491.

177 "General Conference Proceedings," *RH,* 20 November 1883, 732-733; and G. I. Butler, "No Church Manual," *RH,* 27 November 1883, 745-746. See also *SDAE,* 1976 ed., s.v. "Church Manual."

178 The 1885 General Conference session "*Resolved ...* that no person be ordained ... who is not sound in faith and practice upon all Bible doctrines as held by Seventh-day Adventists" ("General Conference Proceedings," *RH,* 1 December 1885, 744-747). A few weeks later, it was reported that ministers would have to pass an examination at their next State Conference, which was to determine "if they are sound in the faith in all the fundamental doctrines of our people" (D. M. Canright, "Who Is Doing It?" *RH,* 23 March 1886, 192).

179 J. H. Waggoner, "The Church. – No. 15," *RH,* 25 August 1885, 537-538; L. A. Smith, "The Value of a 'Creed,'" *RH,* 10 May 1887, 298-299; idem, "Creeds," *RH,* 6 November 1888, 699; idem, "Revising a Creed," *RH,* 25 February 1890, 120; and "The Use of Creeds," *RH,* 7 January 1890, 5. On the controversy raging at the time regarding a creedal fixation of certain theological points, see Knight, *Angry Saints,* 26, 34, 36, 100-104; and idem, *From 1888 to Apostasy,* 25, 41, 47, 70.

180 "Elder Olsen stated, that, unlike other denominations, we have no written creed. We believe in the commandments of God and the faith of Jesus, and allow of expansion and growth in the development of these subjects; – and it will be much harder to maintain union under such circumstances than where church creeds are formulated and adopted" (Minutes of the General Conference Committee, 7 July 1889, 8, AHC, JWL, AU, Berrien Springs, Mich.). See also W. A. Blakely, "Why Not Have a Creed?" *RH,* 14 January 1890, 19-20; and G. E. Fifield, "Truth and Unity," *RH,* 9 June 1891, 354.

day Adventists ever to maintain such an attitude toward the light and truth that God is continually bestowing upon his people that they will ever be ready to receive them."[181] When friends and foes were wondering whether the Fundamental Principles did not constitute an Adventist creed, Uriah Smith reaffirmed the historic position that the Bible alone was "the ultimate source of appeal" and "the ground of fellowship and discipline." He added, "If in anything it can be shown that what we hold in faith and practice is not according to the Bible, we are ready to modify it accordingly."[182]

As time passed, the ambiguity toward the notion of a creed, existing since the 1880s, increasingly manifested itself in the church. On the one hand, Adventists still opposed the formation of a creed because of the stagnation, rigidity, and fossilization it would produce, hampering the open investigation of and search for truth.[183] On the other hand, they felt the need to define the non-negotiable points of faith no longer deemed open for debate.[184] More and more, the Fundamental Beliefs were looked upon as an official and binding definition of Adventist faith, assent to which was regarded as condition of church membership. Any significant doctrinal dissent would call forth swift and decided reactions from the church.[185]

In the 1970s, Adventists moved closer than ever before towards defining in detail certain points of their faith in order to protect them against the creeping threat of theological liberalism. It went rather unnoticed when, in 1971, W. R. Beach defended the legitimacy of church creeds in producing, preserving, and protecting unity

181 *Fundamental Principles of Seventh-day Adventists* (1897), 14.
182 [Uriah Smith], "In the Question Chair," *RH,* 20 September 1892, 600. Cf. D. M. Canright, *Life of Mrs. E. G. White, Seventh-day Adventist Prophet; Her False Claims Refuted* (Cincinnati, Ohio: Standard Publ. Co., 1919; Nashville: B. C. Goodpasture, 1953), 32.
183 L. E. Froom, "To Creadalize or Not to Creadalize," *Ministry,* October 1931, 7-8. "The purpose of a creed is said to be to defend the true faith, but in actual experience a creed stifles research and fosters petrified doctrines" (Christian, *The Fruitage of Spiritual Gifts,* 185).
184 "Seventh-day Adventists hold to the Bible as their rule of faith. As statements in the Bible are capable of different interpretations, however, and as wrong teachings have from time to time been urged upon our people, it has become necessary to define more particularly our understanding of certain points. As heresies spring up and we are called upon to meet them, we are compelled to define our faith upon the questions at issue. In this way, the Seventh-day Adventist denomination has already passed upon many important points which may no longer be deemed debatable" (M. L. Andreasen, "Theology – The Science of God," *Ministry,* May 1935, 17; cf. ibid., 18, 23). See also idem, "The Authority of Doctrine: I. Relationship of Doctrine to Life," *Ministry,* January 1936, 3-4; and W. H. Branson, "What Are Our Tests of Fellowship?" *Ministry,* October 1951, 12-13.
185 According to the *Church Manual,* "Denial of faith in the fundamentals of the gospel and in the cardinal doctrines of the church or teaching doctrines contrary to the same" is a sufficient reason for disfellowshipping (1951 ed., 224). In the 1950s, observers of the church were told that if those holding divergent views became too vocal "discipline would rapidly be undertaken by the denomination" (Martin, "Seventh-day Adventism Today," 277) and that the church leaders were "determined to put the brakes on any members who seek to hold views divergent from that of the responsible leadership of the denomination" (Barnhouse, "Are Seventh-day Adventists Christians?" 7).

of belief, in securing uniformity of teaching, and in safeguarding the church against erroneous doctrines and practices – functions that Adventists, in times past, had reserved exclusively to the Bible and the spiritual gifts.[186] But, judging from the responses, W. J. Hackett seemed to have hit a raw nerve in the church and, particularly, in its academic community when, in 1977, he spoke of the need to prepare statements on certain fundamental teachings so that

> administrators, church leaders, controlling boards, and leaders at all levels of the church will find it easier to evaluate persons already serving the church, and those hereafter appointed, as to their commitment to what is considered basic Adventism.[187]

Until today, Adventists have strongly disavowed any intention of wanting to adopt a fixed confession of faith.[188] At the same time, however, it seems that the distinction between the twenty-seven Fundamental Beliefs and a full-fledged creed may become blurred and turn out, in the end, to be little more than mere semantics if the former, for all practical matters, are being used as criteria of orthodoxy and looked upon as invariable definitions of faith.[189]

Actually, some Adventist writers have candidly admitted that, "in effect, therefore, these core doctrines are a creed. Thus, the argument is actually not over whether the church has a creed or not, but in what detail a church's basic beliefs should be stated."[190] Besides, it may be argued that Adventists long since have had a creed

---

186 Beach, *The Creed That Changed the World,* 7-11. The book was a study of the so-called "Apostles' Creed." That SDAs are in agreement with the fundamental articles of the Christian faith as set forth in the three ancient symbols was explicitly noticed in the SDA-WCC discussions of 1965-1969 (*So Much in Common,* 107). For another positive assessment of the historic Christian creeds, see Froom, *MOD,* 282-288.

187 W. J. Hackett, "Preserve the Landmarks," *RH,* 26 May 1977, 2. Reader response, critical as well as complementary, lasted for about six months. While many church members agreed on the need to protect the church against the gradual erosion of its Fundamental Beliefs, many others feared that such a policy would move Adventists dangerously close to finally becoming a creedal church. See "An Adventist Creed?" *Spectrum* 8:4 (1977): 37-59. See also Tim Crosby, "Heresy and the Church: A Theology of Creedalism [1978]," TMs, AHC, JWL, AU, Berrien Springs, Mich.

188 "SDA's have no formal creed … SDA's consider the Bible to be their creed" (*SDAE,* 1976 ed., s.v. "Creed"). According to the preamble of the Fundamental Beliefs adopted in 1980, SDAs "accept the Bible as their only creed" and leave room for doctrinal revisions (see app. 3, col. 3, p. 334). Apparently, this preamble "was designed to be a further safeguard against granting the statement [of fundamental beliefs] the status of a creed in the classic sense" (*Issues,* 46). "There have been, however, progressively stronger moves to set Adventist beliefs in 'creedal cement,' but so far those initiatives have been successfully resisted" (Knight, "Adventists and Change," 14).

189 "There are undoubtedly many today who feel that the denomination should have hard-and-fast creedal statements on such varied topics as the human nature of Christ and biblical hermeneutics" (Knight, "Adventists and Change," 15). Cf. above, p. 199.

190 Don F. Neufeld, "The Battle for the Bible," *AR,* 26 July 1979, 14-15. See also Edward Heppenstall, "Creed, Authority, and Freedom," *Ministry,* April 1979, 12-14; and Eugene F. Durand, "Whose Bible?" *AR,* 11 September 1986, 5.

beside the Bible inasmuch as they ascribed to Ellen White and her writings the very functions that they denied to creeds, viz., to interpret the Bible authoritatively, to prevent schisms/heresies, and to secure doctrinal unity in the church.[191] As a result, Adventist doctrines tended to be rather stable and resistant to any radical change.[192]

In summary, it can be said that, while the early Adventists emphasized the descriptive and informative nature of their statements of faith,[193] by now the Fundamental Beliefs have assumed a prescriptive and normative function in the church. This is clear from their present-day use in outlining conditions of church membership,[194] in defining prerequisites to the employment by the denomination of pastors and teachers,[195] and in maintaining doctrinal unity in the church.[196]

191 "In short, their work is to unite the people of God in the same mind and in the same judgment upon the meaning of the Scriptures ... [and to] prevent different and conflicting interpretations of the Scriptures" ([J. N. Andrews], "Our Use of the Visions of Sr. White," *RH,* 15 February 1870, 65). "God's plan is that, instead of a creed, the church should have the divine gifts, especially the gift of prophecy, and thus prevent this conflicting interpretation of the Scriptures" (Christian, *The Fruitage of Spiritual Gifts,* 13). See also James White, "Unity and Gifts of the Church – Nos. 1-4," *RH,* 3 December 1857-7 January 1858; idem, "Organization," *RH,* 1 October 1861, 140-141; idem, "The Great Movement," *RH,* 19 May 1863, 196; idem, preface to Ellen White, *Spiritual Gifts,* 3:29-30; James White, "Spirit of Prophecy," *RH,* 22 January 1880, 50-52; [Uriah Smith], "The Faith of Jesus," *RH,* 2 February 1860, 84; D. M. Canright, "A Plain Talk to Murmurers," *RH,* 19 April 1877, 125; R. A. Anderson, "Unity of Adventist Belief – Nos. 1-2," 28, 25; Neal C. Wilson, "The Ellen G. White Writings and the Church," *AR,* 9 July 1981, 4; Arthur L. White, "Why Seventh-day Adventists Have No Creed," *AR,* 12 July 1984, 6-8; and idem, "The Certainty of Basic Doctrinal Positions," *AR,* 26 July 1984, 8.

192 "Adventists have proved time and again to be every bit as jealous of their teaching's orthodoxy, and no more eager to modify their teachings in the face of new or alternative views, than were the creedal churches from which they emerged. Adventists have been as resistant to change as any creedal church" (Greenwalt, 24).

193 The preamble of the 1872 declaration of SDA beliefs stated: "We do not put forth this as having any authority with our people, nor is it designed to secure uniformity among them" (see app. 3, col. 1, p. 334). "[SDAs] test that which purports to be light and truth, not by any declaration of faith or formulated creed, but by the Bible, the word of God, itself" (*Fundamental Principles of Seventh-day Adventists* [1897], 14).

194 See *SDACM,* 1986 ed., 41-45.

195 See "Actions of General Interest from the Annual Council," *AR,* 16 December 1982, 12-13, 9-14. "The Church reserves the right to employ only those individuals who personally believe in and are committed to upholding the doctrinal tenets of the church as summarized in the document 'Fundamental Beliefs of Seventh-day Adventists' (1980) ... It is expected that a teacher in one of the Church's educational institutions will not teach as truth what is contrary to ... the fundamental beliefs" ("A Statement on Theological Freedom and Accountability," 1987 Annual Council Action of the General Conference Committee; General Actions of 11 October 1987).

196 "Preserving the Unity of Church and Message," *AR,* General Conference Bulletin No. 7, 5 July 1985, 9. See also Zoral Harold Coberly, "A Study of the Influences Affecting the Unity of Beliefs of Seventh-day Adventists" (M.A. thesis, SDA Theological Seminary, Washington, D.C., 1946).

However, the twenty-seven Fundamental Beliefs officially are regarded, not as definitive and irreformable statements of the Adventist faith, but as "the church's [current] understanding and expression of the teaching of Scripture."[197] As long as the Seventh-day Adventist Church takes the preamble of the 1980 declaration of Fundamental Beliefs seriously and remains willing to update and revise its confession of faith as the need arises, it may rightly claim to be in substantial continuity with its own denominational history and doctrinal tradition.[198]

Concepts of Doctrinal Development in Adventist Theology

In the first part of this book, the historical-genetic study on doctrinal development was followed up by a systematic-typological outline of various models of doctrinal continuity and change. In like manner, this chapter presents an analysis of the ways in which Adventist reactions to the issue of doctrinal continuity and change are related to the three basic approaches available on this question. The historical survey at the beginning of this chapter has already demonstrated that Adventists have responded in a variety of ways to the challenging problem of doctrinal change. To systematize and initially evaluate these responses is the purpose of the following.[199]

Unvarying Doctrine – The Static Approach

Not surprisingly, the overwhelming majority of Adventists have followed the static approach to doctrinal development, just as the Christian church in general did until the seventeenth century. By reason of their fundamentalist leanings, Seventh-day Adventists hardly could have come to any other position. In fact, one finds representatives of all three leading models following the static approach among Adventist writers. Though none of them developed a full-fledged theory on doctrinal continuity and change, enough was said to provide a well-rounded picture of their views.

197 Preamble of the 1980 statement of Fundamental Beliefs; see below, app. 3, col. 3, p. 334.
198 For a brief reflection on the value and limitation of statements of Fundamental Beliefs, see Rolf J. Pöhler, "Die geschichtliche Entwicklung der Glaubensgrundsätze der Siebenten-Tags-Adventisten," in *Adventistische Glaubensgrundsätze im Alltag: Verbindlichkeit und Realisierbarkeit,* Der Adventglaube in Geschichte und Gegenwart, vol. 24 (Darmstadt: Adventistischer Wissenschaftlicher Arbeitskreis, [1986]), 63-68, 46-68.
199 Just as the typological analysis of chapter 3 was based on the historical survey of chapter 2, the following analysis and evaluation of Adventist conceptions of doctrinal change is based on the results of the historical investigation presented in chapter 4. It is not intended as a theological assessment, which requires the use of hermeneutical criteria for evaluating any model of doctrinal development. It should be noted that, in the absence of any full-fledged SDA theories of doctrinal development, these conceptions are, in most cases, only rudimentary.

The Model of Conceptual Completion:
The Historical Theory

Adventists have commonly believed that all true church teachings were revealed by Christ to the prophets and apostles and written down in the Holy Scriptures. In their view, "truth is ready made ... and we only have to receive it just as we find it."[200] Consequently, nothing that goes beyond what is stated in the Bible could be accepted as a doctrine of faith.[201] "The third angel's message calls upon men to forsake all those doctrines, however honored by the Church, which the plain statements of the Bible do not support."[202] Vice versa, "the new teachings of genuine Adventism are all found in the old Bible. We go back to the fountain of truth ... and we content ourselves with repeating those truths which have been true from the beginning."[203]

Therefore, if anything was new, it could not be true.[204] For, "truth is of God, and like God it does not change; but error is constantly changing its form."[205] True, the church was always in need of change and renewal, individually as well as corporately, but only morally and spiritually, not doctrinally. "What we preach and teach is not in need of a change. The needed changes must be made in our lives."[206] Of course, there was always the possibility to better grasp biblical doctrines and even

---

200 R. F. Cottrell, "The Creed of the Opposition," *RH*, 2 September 1884, 563.

201 See above, pp. 202-204. "According to authentic Protestantism and the *sola Scriptura* principle, the formulation of faith (dogma), as it developed, must be identical with the apostolic formulation revealed in Holy Scripture" (V. Norskov Olsen, *Myth and Truth about Church, Priesthood and Ordination* [Riverside: Loma Linda Univ. Press, 1990], 29).

202 L. A. Smith, "The Interpretation of Scripture," *RH*, 29 October 1889, 681. "By [the Bible] all opinions and creeds must be tested, and anything deviating in the minutest particular from its plain utterances, is shown to be spurious" (George B. Thompson, "The Bible, Not Tradition," *RH*, 22 September 1891, 579). See also idem, "Doctrine," *RH*, 18 February 1890, 100.

203 R. F. Cottrell, "Old and New," *RH*, 19 July 1870, 37.

204 "Consequently, while spurious reforms are ever bringing to view something altogether new and strange – something never before revealed to the church in any age, genuine reforms embrace only what is already in that word, and therefore do not reveal new truths, but only remove the rubbish of false theology and superstition from truths which had been revealed and understood ages before" (L. A. Smith, "The Nature of Our Work," 712).

205 R. F. Cottrell, "Old and New," *RH*, 19 July 1870, 37; cf. idem, "Old and New," *RH*, 23 September 1880, 217; and idem, "I Change Not," *RH*, 5 December 1882, 760-761. See also George I. Butler, "Stability a Characteristic of Our Work"; idem, "Old-Fashioned Religion"; and S. M. Swan, "Are Seventh-day Adventists Teaching New Doctrines?" *RH*, 25 November 1880, 341. To the accusation that Adventists were teaching new and unscriptural doctrines, Nichol answered in truly Vincentian fashion, "One of the chief characteristics of our doctrines is their antiquity ... Not Seventh-day Adventists, but popular preachers are the promulgators of new and un-Scriptural doctrines" (*Answers to Objections*, 439-440). Cf. above, pp. 56-58.

206 Eric S. Dillet, "The Seventh-day Adventist Church Is in Need of a Change," *RH*, 3 October 1974, 14-15. See also Geoffrey E. Garne, "The Adventist Church in a Changing World," *RH*, 5 May 1977, 4-7; C. E. Bradford, "Formula for Change," *AR*, 20 April 1980, 11-15; and Walton, *Omega*, 85.

to discover certain truths not seen before.[207] But such a growth of insight and understanding was adding nothing to the explicit teachings of the Bible. At best, these could be restated in words more easily intelligible to contemporary humankind[208] or reinforced with new and convincing arguments by which to defend historic beliefs.[209]

Considering themselves genuine Protestants[210] and "the most evangelical of any church"[211] on account of both their unwavering faithfulness to the Bible and their readiness to receive whatever truth it might contain, Seventh-day Adventists proudly described themselves as "the culmination of the great work of the Reformation."[212] Their mission consisted in the restoration of the original body of undefiled truths and the elimination of all doctrinal corruptions and accretions, which had come about as a result of Christendom's apostasy from its perfect, pristine state.[213] "Seventh-day Adventists are restorationists in doctrine and life style, going back to the faith of the primitive church before apostasy set in."[214] The task was, in the main, completed, for "the truth of God now again shines forth in its original perfection, uncovered from the rubbish of papal error and superstition."[215]

This meant that whatever doctrinal developments and changes had occurred in the history of the Adventist church were, in reality, only "a *rediscovery and restoration* of truth that has always existed!"[216] Genuine progress in matters of faith was

---

207 L. A. Smith, "Search the Scriptures," *RH,* 6 September 1892, 568-569.

208 "The reason for our existence as a denomination is not to give out new doctrines but to restate the old and proved ones and to 'contend for the faith which was once delivered unto the saints'" (Nichol, *Answers to Objections,* 440). See also idem, "Restudying the Doctrines without Destroying the Foundations"; Gordon M. Hyde, "The Adventist Emphasis," *Ministry,* September 1974, 8-10; and John J. Robertson, *The White Truth* (Mountain View, Calif.: PPPA, 1981), 67.

209 F. D. Nichol, "Truth and Trustworthy Evidence," *Ministry,* January 1930, 5-7; idem, "Restudying the Doctrines without Destroying the Foundations," 4; and Froom, *MOD,* 664.

210 D. T. Bourdeau, "Protestantism," *RH,* 4-11 March 1875, 73-74, 81-82.

211 M. E. Kellogg, "Are Seventh-day Adventists Evangelical?" *RH,* 15 March 1892, 170-171.

212 F. D. Starr, "The Reformation Continues," *RH,* 13 March 1883, 164. See also R. F. Cottrell, "Unity of the Third Message," *RH,* 18 September 1855, 44; Carlyle B. Haynes, "The Completion of the Arrested Reformation," *RH,* 3 January 1935, 4-5, 22; F. Lee, "What Makes a Seventh-day Adventist?" *RH,* 4 January 1940, 6-7; F. D. Nichol, "Why Defend the Faith – Concluded," *RH,* 29 November 1962, 12-13; and W. G. Johnsson, "Luther Revisited," *AR,* 3 November 1983, 14. Cf. Paxton, *The Shaking of Adventism,* 18-23.

213 M. Ellsworth Olsen's four-volume *A History of the Origin and Progress of Seventh-day Adventists* (Washington, D.C.: RHPA, 1925) described the church as a restorationist reform movement in the lineage of the 16th-century Reformation. This restoration motif is also found in Uriah Smith, "The Reformation Not Yet Complete," *RH,* 3 February 1874, 60-61; Albert Stone, "The Testimonies," *RH,* 16 January 1883, 34; and Branson, *In Defense of the Faith,* 29, 387-389.

214 D. A. Delafield, "Are Seventh-day Adventists a Cult?" *AR,* 26 April 1979, 15.

215 L. A. Smith, "Present Truth."

216 J. Robert Spangler, "What's So Unique about Adventism? – No. 2," *Ministry,* December 1981, 19.

a *recovery* of the old and established ... *not a discovery* of something new, strange, and untried; a *retention* of the accredited and true, not an invention of the doubtful and fanciful; a *restoration* of the best and the soundest in exposition, *not an innovation,* advancing the questionable and debatable.[217]

In spite of their doctrinal and hermeneutical divergences, both "orthodox" Adventists defending the traditional doctrines and "evangelical" Adventists calling for a revised, gospel-centered theology shared "Adventism's restoration theology."[218] In full agreement with historic Adventism, the so-called "new theology" asserted:

As the witness to God's final and complete revelatory act, the New Testament defines for all time the boundaries of the Christian faith ... Anyone attempting to add to, detract from, or in any way alter the faith and understanding of the apostles must stand under the judgment of God ... If a doctrinal position is not supportable from Scripture and was not held by the apostles, it is not worth defending.[219]

Inasmuch as the congruency of a doctrine with biblical revelation can be determined only hermeneutically, not historically, the model of conceptual completion does not explain but simply claim the identity of church teachings with biblical revelation.

A serious objection to the so-called "historical" theory derives from the observation that to regard change *per se* as evidence of error and apostasy and to insist on the immutability of doctrines tends to make people blind to the very reality of theological modification and doctrinal revision. In fact, the historical theory seems closely related to and fortified by several misconceptions that may actually conceal certain historical facts from the view of a predisposed observer. There are, in the main, three such popular misapprehensions or "myths."[220]

---

217 Froom, *PFF,* 4:1054. Though this statement was made particularly with regard to prophetic interpretation, its author has repeatedly advanced the same view in relation to doctrine in general. See ibid., 1040-1055, 1155-1156, 1161-1162; idem, "Cast Not Therefore away Your Confidence," 29; idem, "Fidelity to Our Commission," *Ministry,* September 1937, 11; and idem, *MOD,* 37, 38, 78. Cf. also *QOD,* 613-617.

218 Spangler, "What's So Unique about Adventism? – No. 2," 19.

219 Bart Willruth, "God's Final Word," *Evangelica,* December 1980, 21-24. See also Ford and Ford, *The Adventist Crisis of Spiritual Identity,* 188; "Ellen G. White Reconsidered," *Evangelica,* November 1981, 25, 42; Brinsmead, *1844 Re-Examined;* idem, *Are the Gospel and the 1844 Theology Compatible?* (Fallbrook, Calif.: Verdict Publ., 1980), 26; and idem, "Sabbatarianism Re-Examined," 6-7, 14-16. In 1983, however, Brinsmead abandoned this view in favor of a more liberal one which defends the "freedom to reinterpret the letter of Scripture to meet new situations" ("The Gospel and the Spirit of Biblicism – Part 2," *The Christian Verdict,* Essay 16, 1984, 5-6) and allows the interpreter to judge and correct Scripture teachings ("The Spirit of Jesus versus Christianity," *The Christian Verdict,* Special Issue 3, 1986, 4, 9, 10). For a critical analysis of the hermeneutical basis of evangelical Adventism, see Pöhler, "Verkürzte Wahrheit – heilsame Häresie," 101-112.

220 George R. Knight has exploited the category of "myth" in analyzing certain misconceptions prevalent among Seventh-day Adventists *(Myths in Adventism* [Washington, D.C.: RHPA,

"We have always believed this"

Adventists have tended to assume that the doctrines of the church have remained virtually unchanged from the beginning. Even among scholars writing on Adventist history, one can detect, at times, a tendency to retroject their present-day views on Adventists of previous generations. Such backward projection reflects a common human tendency and may also result from a lack of meticulous research. But, in addition, it tells something about the difficulties of giving up familiar notions or cherished ideas in exchange for puzzling or perplexing historical facts.

Perhaps this may help explain the forgetfulness of Uriah Smith concerning the teaching on the new birth, which he himself had once introduced and strongly defended in the church.[221] More recently, Froom made a number of statements on doctrinal questions amounting to backward projections of contemporary beliefs.[222] Similarly, Bacchiocchi made some retrojective remarks about the doctrine of the investigative judgment.[223] There seems to be also a common misconception among Adventists about the historic position of the church on what is called "open communion."[224] As this book shows, in quite a number of instances it cannot be claimed on a historical basis that Adventists "have always believed" what they teach today.

1985]). Following his lead, one can perhaps also speak of myths to which the Adventist version of the historical theory possesses close affinity.

221 See above, pp. 153-155.

222 For example, he wrongly assumed that SDAs believed in the doctrine of the investigative judgment since 1848 *(PFF,* 4:1028-1030, 1041, 1047) and that the testimony of Jesus was identified with the spirit of prophecy as applied to Ellen White in the same year (ibid., 1039, 1045-1047). He taught that the Trinitarian and Christological doctrines of the Bible had been suppressed and abandoned by the Roman church while in fact these dogmas were developed under its influence *(MOD,* 42-43). For other examples for such retrojection from his pen, see above, pp. 133, n. 57; p. 148, n. 128; and pp. 239-242.

223 He mistakenly credited the view that the pre-Advent judgment does not merely reveal but actually determine the fate of believers to a misunderstanding on the part of non-SDAs and a misinterpretation of a few "unguarded statements in past Adventist literature" (Bacchiocchi, *The Advent Hope,* 289-290). But as is shown in this book, this notion had been, in fact, the united and explicit teaching of the church for over a century. See above, pp. 180-183.

224 In 1964, K. H. Wood stated that "the Seventh-day Adventist Church has always welcomed Christians of all faiths to take part in its communion service" ("The President and Communion," *RH,* 23 July 1964, 12). This claim was repeated by F. D. Nichol ("From the Editor's Mailbag," *RH,* 29 July 1965, 13) and F. Holbrook ("For Members Only?" *Ministry,* February 1987, 12-14, 30). The truth of the matter is that until the 1880s, SDAs decidedly rejected the idea of "open communion"; the change toward the later position was initiated apparently by Ellen White from Australia in the years 1893 to 1898. See Bruno Ulrich, "Das Abendmahl – eine offene Feier?," in *Abendmahl und Fußwaschung,* Studien zur adventistischen Ekklesiologie, vol. 1 (Hamburg: Saatkorn-Verlag, [1991]), 232-235.

"We have never changed"

Closely related to the first "myth" is another widespread misconception, which denies that any significant doctrinal changes or revisions have ever occurred in the history of the denomination. Prominent Adventists like Butler and Wood have conveyed the impression that the church was moving only in a forward direction and had never held or taught erroneous views on any important Bible doctrine.[225] Contrary to the historical facts as presented in this book, the notion that "we have never changed" was repeatedly affirmed as, e.g., in the following statement by Smith:

> This cause has never had any failures to explain, any misapplications of prophecy to correct, any back track to take on any question. It has taken a uniform position, and borne a uniform testimony from the beginning.[226]

"If anything changes, everything changes"

Unlike the other two, the third prevailing misapprehension makes claims not about the past, but about the future course of the denomination. In the light of the facts presented in this work, it, too, cannot pass the test of history. For, in spite of several doctrinal readjustments and reversals, the Seventh-day Adventist Church has neither radically changed nor has it lost or abandoned its unique blend of doctrines.

What has given that misconception some plausibility is the close-knit structure of SDA teachings. Adventists have commonly looked upon their doctrines as a complete, harmonious, and indissoluble system of truths,[227] an interlocking structure,

---

225 "Not a single theological position have our people, as a whole, ever accepted, that they have been obliged to give up" (George I. Butler, "Stability a Characteristic of Our Work," 140). "Seventh-day Adventists have never taken a stand upon Bible exegesis which they have been compelled to surrender" (idem, A Circular Letter to All State Conference Committees and Our Brethren in the Ministry, 1888, General Conference Archives, Silver Spring, Md.). "It is certainly remarkable that thus far we have not had to change a single position decidedly taken after faithful investigation" (idem, "A Harmonious Faith," *RH,* 1 October 1889, 617). "The Seventh-day Adventist message (not just the old 'landmarks' but even minor beliefs) remains essentially unchanged from what it was in the beginning" and "the pillars of the faith have not been moved even in the slightest particular" (K. H. Wood, "The Old Landmarks," *RH,* 30 March 1961, 3).

226 [Uriah Smith], "The Opening Year" (1885), 8. This statement matched that by L. A. Smith and F. C. Gilbert who claimed that "never in the history of this cause have we been obliged to confess ourselves in error. Never have we been obliged to retract one thing that we have proclaimed to the world as part of this message" (*The 'Daily' in the Prophecy of Daniel,* 2). To the credit of these writers it should be pointed out that several doctrinal changes were either occurring at a later time or were only in the process of taking place. Lacking sufficient historical perspective, these writers should not be faulted for their blurred vision.

227 "God has led us into the most comprehensive, all-inclusive, perfect system of doctrines on earth. It is a golden chain of truth" (J. R. Spangler, "What's So Unique about Adventism?" *Ministry,* October 1981, 24). See also R. F. Cottrell, "Truth Is Harmonious," *RH,* 28 May

which cannot be modified in any particulars without destroying the whole.[228] In the late 1850s, this thought was stated in language abounding in metaphors:

> The present truth is harmonious in all its parts; its links are all connected; the bearings of all its portions upon each other are like clock-work; but break out one cog, and the work is stopped; break one link, and the chain is broken; let down one stitch and we may unravel the whole.[229]

There appears to be, indeed, a close connection among, and a remarkable harmony between, the various Adventist teachings. But the assertion "that they must all stand or fall together" and "that not one point could be removed without destroying the whole"[230] needs to be qualified in the light of Adventist history. After all, the church has neither disappeared nor lost its doctrinal unity. To the contrary, its doctrinal edifice seems even to have been strengthened, rather than weakened, by the doctrinal modifications that occurred in its history.

The Model of Logical Explication:
The Logical Theory

Another version of the static approach is provided by the logical theory, which reduces doctrinal developments to a process of syllogistic reasonings and ratiocinations. This theory finds its counterpart among Adventists when logical inferences and typological explanations are emphasized. Now and then, writers have placed at a premium "truly logical conclusions"[231] and "theological deductions."[232]

W. H. Littlejohn particularly favored the drawing of "logical conclusions" from the Bible as a "legitimate and conclusive" method of arriving at truth, if done in a "proper manner."[233] However, he conceded the possibility that Adventists had

1857, 36; Uriah Smith, "Questions on the Sanctuary," *RH*, 5 August 1875, 44; George I. Butler, "A Harmonious Faith"; and Froom, *PFF*, 4:1031-1032.

228 On this basis, it could then be argued, for example, that to identify the "image of the beast" with Free Masonry would mean to destroy the entire Adventist faith ("The Image of the Beast," *RH*, 16 January 1879, 20).

229 "Are the Seven Last Plagues in the Future?" *RH*, 7 January 1858, 72 (the article was written by Uriah Smith or James White). See also Uriah Smith, "The 1335 Days," *RH*, 27 February 1866, 100-101; idem, "The Two-Horned Beast," 148; W. A. Spicer, "Where One Truth Confirms Every Other," *RH*, 30 December 1948, 5; and Desmond Ford, "Truth's Golden Chain," *RH*, 24 December 1959, 5-7.

230 George I. Butler, "Eld. Canright's Change of Faith," *RH*, 1 March 1887, 138. On this premise Butler and Canright agreed, though they drew opposite conclusions from it.

231 R. F. Cottrell, "Truth Is Harmonious," *RH*, 2 February 1869, 44. See also Uriah Smith, "A Friendly Word with the Voice of the West"; Froom, *PFF*, 4:1051; and idem, *MOD*, 542-543.

232 W. H. Littlejohn, "Seventh-day Adventists and Seventh-day Baptists," *RH*, 4 November 1880, 297.

233 Ibid.

"made mistakes in their theological deductions" and might, on this account, have to give up some "erroneous positions."[234]

Others who also argued along the lines of the historical theory were, however, quite critical of the inferential approach to truth which they compared to speculative assumptions and pious imagination. To them, doctrine must be clearly stated in the Bible and not be inferred from it.[235] Generally speaking, Adventists have been reluctant to use logical extrapolations, particularly in the form of analogous and typological reasoning, prominently in the defense of their doctrines.[236] D. F. Neufeld stated: "Doctrine must never be built on inferences. We should accept as the plain teaching of the Scripture only that which is explicitly stated in the Bible."[237]

The Model of Progressive Revelation:
The New Revelation Theory

In the history of Christianity, the concept of unvarying doctrine was, at times, defended by ascribing to doctrinal developments the character of an additional revelation. In like manner, Seventh-day Adventists have occasionally interpreted the concept of progressive revelation in such a way as to allow for new teachings without having to abandon the traditional notion of doctrinal immutability.

Adventists like to emphasize that revelation is progressive. But they have not always clearly distinguished progressive revelations during the Old Covenant, pointing forward to Jesus Christ and adding to the Canon, from the deepening and progressive understanding during the New Covenant of the final and unsurpassable divine revelation in Christ.[238] This has led some to look upon Ellen White as providing new and additional revelations like the canonical writers, particularly for the

---

234 W. H. Littlejohn, "Seventh-day Adventists and Seventh-day Baptists," *RH*, 11 November 1880, 306.

235 M. E. Kellogg, "Inferences," *RH*, 27 June-4 July 1893, 409, 424-425.

236 "On every Bible doctrine Bible expressions may be found in *plain, direct terms,* that is, such as contain no symbols or figures, or only such figures and forms of speech as are of common use, and easily understood. THESE ARE DECISIVE; and *all our interpretations of prophecy must harmonize with them.* This is 'true *literalism,*' and may not be dispensed with, for any consideration" (J. H. Waggoner, *The Kingdom of God,* 5). Similarly, *Questions on Doctrine* asserted that "we hold to the recognized principle that no cardinal doctrine or belief should be based primarily upon a parable or type, but upon the clear unfigurative statements of Scripture, and understood and defined in the clear light of explicit declarations of gospel realities" (p. 396).

237 D. F. Neufeld, "Footnote to the 6,000-Year Theory," *RH*, 13 May 1976, 10. However, when Desmond Ford insisted on this principle *(Daniel 8:14, the Investigative Judgment, and the Day of Atonement,* 1), Robert W. Olson responded, arguing that "it is legitimate to establish a major doctrine on types and symbols" *(One Hundred and One Questions on the Sanctuary and on Ellen White* [Washington, D.C.: Ellen G. White Estate, 1981], 30).

238 See, e.g., Richard Hammill, "God Speaks through the Scriptures," *RH*, 6 October 1966, 2-5. Historically, Protestants and Catholics agreed that God's revelation in Jesus Christ as shared

remnant church. To them, the Protestant definition of the *sola scriptura* principle appears unnecessarily restrictive and misleading.

Tim Crosby has vigorously defended this view in recent years. According to him, Ellen White provided "authentic later revelations" going beyond clear Bible teachings by offering "new light," that is, "innovative teachings" and novel interpretations "even to the point of apparent contradiction" to the Scriptures themselves. By means of "creative exegesis," the Adventist prophet led the church to "theological progress" and doctrinal advance.[239]

Along similar lines of thought, *Raymond F. Cottrell* has argued that "a new revelation of the divine will and purpose was needed" and, in fact, provided by Ellen White. Certain Adventist doctrines that are based on a reinterpretation of the Bible "rest on the authority of the later inspired writer, not on the former revelation."[240]

This Adventist version of the new revelation theory will have to be evaluated on hermeneutical grounds, for it argues theologically, not historically, by declaring certain doctrinal changes to possess the character of new revelations.[241] From a purely historical perspective, this theory cannot be controverted. It is significant in that it acknowledges the factuality of noteworthy doctrinal changes and modifications in Adventist history. Thus, it confirms the historical analysis of this work and its resulting criticism of the so-called "historical" theory of doctrinal development.

In sum, it appears that, on historical grounds, the static approach to doctrinal development is hardly defensible.[242]

by the apostles allowed only for such additional divine communications that would not add to nor surpass the normative truth content of the divine word conveyed through the apostolic and inspired eyewitnesses.

239 Tim Crosby, "Why I Don't Believe in *Sola Scriptura,*" *Ministry,* October 1987, 11-15.

240 Raymond F. Cottrell, "A Hermeneutic for Daniel 8:14," 20-25. Cf. above, p. 249, n. 110.

241 Historically, however, SDAs have strongly supported the *sola scriptura* principle. Ellen White herself emphasized that "the written testimonies are not to give new light ... Additional truth is not brought out" *(Testimonies for the Church,* 5:665).

242 It also seems to foster a "mythical" view of the past and to involve a kind of collective historical amnesia. Selective memory is a psychological mechanism frequently at work among people individually and collectively, making them "forget" certain unpleasant experiences. With the help of such selective recollection, history can be used in order to buttress preconceived opinions about theological issues. (For these insights, I am indebted to Wilken, *The Myth of Christian Beginnings,* 1-10). "Facts are difficult to deal with when they conflict with theory. And before changing theories most human beings will spend long periods of time pretending that the facts do not exist, hoping that the facts will magically go away, or denying that the facts are important. Only if the facts are very painful and very persistent will they deal with the fundamental inconsistencies in their world views" (Lester C. Thurow, *Newsweek,* 8 August 1983, 66; quoted in Hammill, "Fifty Years of Creationism," 44).

Developing Doctrine – The Dynamic Approach

In recent decades, a number of Adventist writers have adopted a developmental view of Adventist doctrines, rejecting the immobilism of the static approach and acknowledging the possibility of genuine doctrinal progress in the church. Again, these views bear a close resemblance to the various dynamic theories of doctrinal continuity and change as described in Part I of this book.

The Model of Organic Unfolding:
The Organistic Theory

According to the organistic theory, doctrines develop in a gradual, homogeneous, and cumulative way. While there may be additions to and enlargements of the doctrinal system of the church, insights insights are once gained will not have to be abandoned at a later time.[243] The foremost representative of this approach among Adventists was *LeRoy E. Froom*. He recognized that the doctrines of the church were more than just the restoration of the explicit teachings of the primitive church. Though "every truth we hold and proclaim today was held in embryo in the apostolic church," Adventists had "continued and consummated those lost or trampled truths. Added to these are the special truths now due to the world."[244] Particularly with respect to prophetic truth, Seventh-day Adventists were "completing the contribution of the centuries by retention, restoration, and advance."[245]

This position does not go substantially beyond what Adventists have traditionally said about the developing nature of present truth. In Froom's judgment, however,

---

243 On this premise, Uriah Smith had rejected the new view on the law in Galatians in the 1880s: "If the new views proposed were simply some advance on the light we have already received, as was the sanctuary and third message in 1845, I could accept them as gladly as anyone. I am always ready for light in that direction; but when that which is presented as light obliges us to tear up the past ... that is a very different matter" (Uriah Smith to A. T. Robinson, 21 September 1892, General Conference Archives, Silver Spring, Md. [L. E. Froom, Personal Collection 12, Uriah Smith correspondence folder]). "Where the Spirit is will be growth, development, clarification – a newness that does not countermand the old but builds upon it as it brings out the endless beauty of truth ... We believe that these distinctive Adventist doctrines have riches still to be mined, a fullness not yet exhausted" (W. G. Johnsson, "A Distinctive Body of Teaching," *AR*, 27 May 1982, 14). "We humbly confess that there is still much truth to be discovered ... Yet as we find new facets of God's revelation, they will harmonize perfectly with the united testimony of the Scriptures" (*SDAs Believe*, vii). Cf. Damsteegt, "Seventh-day Adventist Doctrines and Progressive Revelation."

244 Froom, *MOD*, 28; cf. ibid., 31-32, 73, 86.

245 Froom, *PFF*, 4:853; see ibid., 4:855-1173; esp. 1049-1054, 1152-1154, and 1171-1172. Froom's view, which may be described as "organic restorationism," is shared by many SDAs. It bears repeating that restorationism is not inextricably tied to the historical theory (static approach). In its different forms, it may be found also among organistic and theological theories (dynamic approach) and even among adherents of the transformistic theory (revolutionary approach). See above, pp. 40-41, 58-60, 66-67, 98, n. 24, and 267-268.

this "progressive development of prophetic exposition"[246] provides "an even deeper meaning to many of the doctrinal fundamentals of the evangelical faith" and enables the church "to see great Bible truths in new and luminous perspective."[247] "Thus in the light of prophecy every redemptive truth assumed a fuller significance and took on new beauty and depth of meaning."[248] From this it appears that Froom was making room for some genuine doctrinal advance in the church.[249]

However, Froom's organistic assumptions apparently did not allow him to recognize doctrinal revisions or heterogeneous changes. Instead, he proceeded on the basis of four hypotheses by which he could explain the apparent reversals of church teachings that the historical sources suggest.[250] But, seen from a historical perspective, these conjectures are hardly tenable as is shown by the following.[251]

The notion of doctrinal vagueness

According to this view, during the early decades, Adventists still lacked clear and undisputed beliefs on a number of points. Articles, books, and even statements of Adventist faith, at times, reflected not the official doctrines of the church, but merely the personal convictions of their respective authors. Therefore, it is impossible to state with any precision what the church actually believed and taught on certain issues. Not only prophetic interpretations but even the "eternal verities" themselves were still regarded as kind of "optional" at the time.[252]

---

246 Ibid., 1049.

247 Ibid., 1153, 1164; see also 1164-1173.

248 Ibid., 1167.

249 "LeRoy Edwin Froom was the first to acknowledge and interpret the theological changes that have taken place within Adventism" (Bull and Lockhart, *Seeking a Sanctuary,* 87).

250 The first three of these four conjectures are found in an article by R. A. Anderson: "Prior to that [1888] conference [1] it would have been difficult to declare just what the denominational position was on some of these aspects of truth [like the Trinity, Christology, and the atonement]. Certain positions had been taken, and some of these appeared in published form. [2] While such publications reflected the ideas of the author and perhaps a few others, it could not be maintained that such statements were our settled denominational position, for we were in our formative years. While there was general unity on most of the main lines of prophecy ... [3] our leaders were not yet united. There were differences of opinion on some of these points" ("Unity of Adventist Belief – II," *Ministry,* April 1958, 22-25).

251 There is no intent on my part to single out Froom for criticism. But no one has expressed himself as clearly on this issue as he did. Besides, few authors have so emphatically stated to have presented a "complete and forthright" and "candid portrayal" of SDA history, "fair and faithful to fact," written with "complete honesty" and "without bias" *(MOD,* 17-23, 27, 31, 148). Cf. Roy Allen Anderson, "The Inside Story of Adventism," *Ministry,* November 1970, 10-11. It should be noted that this critique of Froom's assumptions does not deny the valuable aspects of an organic view of change which, if pruned of its misconceptions and philosophical accretions, may well be retained in a sound theory of doctrinal change.

252 Froom, *MOD,* 31, 73-76, 119-120, 142, 332.

As the historical analysis of chapter 4 indicates, there can be little doubt as to the doctrinal beliefs of the early Seventh-day Adventists. Authors usually reflected the views shared by the church in general. The lack of a formal Statement of Faith was no sign of doctrinal vagueness, for unity of faith was based not on a creed but on a common interpretation of the Bible believed to contain an unequivocal delineation of "the commandments of God and the faith of Jesus." Doctrinal agreement with the church, even in seemingly minor matters, was deemed essential to membership.[253]

The notion of doctrinal deviations

Closely related to it is a second notion according to which any heterodox belief held by Adventists in the past was simply "the constricted view of a minority that brought odium over this point upon the whole movement" and deviated "from the general teaching of the denomination."[254] In other words, "those erroneous early personal views" were "neither truly nor representatively Adventist."[255]

Contrary to what this view asserts, a widespread unanimity did, in fact, exist among nineteenth-century Adventists on many doctrinal questions, including those that the collective memory of the church may tend to forget. It was not wishful thinking when the different versions of the Fundamental Beliefs claimed to describe what Adventists believed "with great unanimity" (1872), with "entire unanimity" (1889), reflecting "a very general agreement" (1891). The proponents of this notion have failed to provide historical evidence in its support, while this study has shown that the alleged minority views were actually shared by the church in general.[256]

The notion of doctrinal unification

There is a third misconception arising out of Froom's organistic view of development. It holds that in the early years, there existed notable differences of opinion on various doctrinal points. A considerable "diversity of views" was granted by common consent, which later was replaced by doctrinal "unanimity" when the church gradually clarified its beliefs. As "there was no time for unifying discussions," "fundamental differences" persisted for decades on the Trinity, Christology, and the doctrine of the

---

253 For substantiation, see, e.g., above, pp. 130-131, 155, 157 (n. 170), 227-228, 229 (n. 26); and below 301-302, 304-305.
254 Froom, "New Approaches Imperative for a New Day," 11; idem, *PFF*, 4:1116. See also, *QOD*, 32; and Christian, *The Fruitage of Spiritual Gifts*, 199-203.
255 Froom, *MOD*, 36; cf. 33, 35, 73-76.
256 The only historical argument provided by Froom in support of this notion is the observation that a majority of Millerite ministers and believers had obviously been Trinitarians. But this does not justify the inference that, therefore, "a majority of our own founding fathers were likewise evidently Trinitarian" (*MOD*, 146-147, 167, 286-288). Evidently, they were not. See above, pp. 131-134.

atonement. But "there was, nevertheless, an underlying respect for the conviction of others"[257] and unity of faith was eventually achieved.

Again, this notion is not supported adequately by history. The early Seventh-day Adventists placed strong emphasis on the unanimity of beliefs in the church.[258] An early attempt to allow for a certain plurality on minor doctrinal issues failed miserably.[259] During the 1870s and 1880s, doctrinal uniformity was regarded as essential and the catchphrase "unity in diversity" was condemned as reflecting Babylonian confusion.[260] When doctrinal disunity became an undeniable fact in the 1880s, the church seemed hardly prepared to cope with it.[261]

257 Froom, *MOD*, 35, 73-76, 120, 133-135, 144-145, 168. See also idem, *PFF*, 4:1109, 1118-1119, 1137; *QOD*, 30-31; and *SDAE*, 1976 ed., s.v. "Holy Spirit."

258 For James White, "Nothing is more desirable than union in the church of Christ. And there can be no permanent and scriptural union, without an agreement in views of bible *[sic]* truth" ("Gospel Union," *RH*, 25 November 1851, 56). He also felt that "the system of truth taught by the Seventh-day Adventists is so harmonious, so clear, and so abundantly sustained by the plain testimony of God's word, that there is little chance for believers to differ" ("The Cause," *RH*, 29 October 1861, 172). Uriah Smith agreed that the truth "will admit of no diversity of sentiment" and regarded "conflicting opinions" and "discordant theories" as marks of Babylonian error and confusion ("The Watchmen Shall See Eye to Eye," *RH*, 28 February 1854, 44). Ellen White counseled that believers "should be perfectly united in their views of Bible truth" (Letter to the Howlands, 12 November 1851, EGWRC, AU, Berrien Springs, Mich.) and that "differences of opinion must be yielded" *(Testimonies,* 1:324).

259 The "Eldorado covenant" of June 1854 allowed D. P. Hall and J. M. Stephenson to hold on to, but not to promote, their "age-to-come" teaching. Both sides agreed to avoid public discussions on this disputed point that was seen as neither essential for salvation nor part of present truth. This compromise broke down ten months later with both sides going separate ways. James White then came to regard the "compromise at Eldorado" as an unwise decision because there could be no compromise with error appearing "in sheep's clothing" (James White, "'The Jews' Return,'" *RH*, 12 June 1855, 248; idem, "The Review 'Sectarian,'" *RH*, 4 December 1855, 80; J. H. Waggoner, "The 'Age to Come,'" *RH*, 11 December 1855, 84-85; James White, "The Review 'Sectarian,'" *RH*, 14 February 1856, 160; and idem, "A Sketch of the Rise and Progress of the Present Truth," *RH*, 14 January 1858, 77-78).

260 R. F. Cottrell, "Unity of the Church," *RH*, 18 October 1870, 141; idem, "'Lying Unity,'" *RH*, 22 April 1873, 148; J. H. Waggoner, "The Gifts and Offices of the Holy Spirit – No. 4," *RH*, 14 October 1875, 113-114; Albert Stone, "Cannot Understand Alike," *RH*, 25 January 1877, 26; Maria Mead, "Present Truth," *RH*, 11 December 1879, 186; James White, "Spirit of Prophecy," *RH*, 22 January 1880, 50-52; Ellen White, "Unity of the Church," *RH*, 19 February 1880, 113-114; D. P. Curtis, "Doctrine vs. Doctrines," *RH*, 3 June 1884, 354-355; R. F. Cottrell, "The Creed of the Opposition," *RH*, 2 September 1884, 563-564; A. Smith, "Some Principles Followed by S. D. Adventists," *RH*, 5 July 1887, 419; R. F. Cottrell, "Unity of the Church," *RH*, 29 May 1888, 338-339; [Uriah Smith], "Origin and History of the Third Angel's Message," *RH*, 27 January 1891, 56; Fifield, "Truth and Unity"; and L. A. Smith, "Unity," *RH*, 5 January 1892, 8-9.

261 "We claim to be a united people, and to teach but one doctrine. It has been a great cause of regret for years among our best brethren that this difference of opinion exists among us [on the law in Galatians] … This question which has long been in agitation among us is most unfortunate" (Butler, *The Law in Galatians,* 6, 85).

There is little if any historical evidence supporting the alleged plurality of doctrinal views in the early decades.[262] Instead, until the 1880s, the sources reveal a widespread unanimity among Adventists on doctrinal issues. Moreover, from today's perspective, doctrinal pluralism is not so much a matter of history but rather a contemporary challenge to the Seventh-day Adventist Church.[263]

The notion of doctrinal perfection

A fourth assumption guiding Froom's interpretation of Adventist history holds that in the "formative years" of the church, the "advances" and "transitions" resulting from "intensive study of doctrine and prophecy" – motivated as they were by "the sole objective" of "seeking truth" – were quite "noteworthy," while "subsequent changes were more along the line of correction of minor matters."[264] As a result of this doctrinal development and advance, Adventists now hold "perfected Fundamental Beliefs."[265] "We passed through an initial period of discovering and formulating our doctrines; but they have long been well defined. All we need to do now is to preach them."[266] Froom implied that "doctrinal growing pains" and the constant "searching for light" are becoming more and more a thing of the past as the church was moving forward towards "perfection in doctrine and practice."[267]

Contrary to Froom's expectation, Adventists seem to have been passing through periods of intense "doctrinal growing pains" even after 1931. To interpret Adventist theological history since the 1930s on the basis of a theory of doctrinal perfection makes an acknowledgment of significant developments and changes in recent decades (as well as in the future) increasingly difficult, if not impossible. This, in turn,

---

262 This is not to deny that there existed different and even conflicting views among SDAs on a number of theological issues. As long as they did not affect the "three angels' messages" and their ramifications, divergent opinions could well be tolerated. But when it came to church doctrines that were seen as the "present truth" necessary for salvation, unity of belief was regarded a "must."

263 See above, pp. 131-134.

264 Froom, *PFF,* 4:1070. Cf. *QOD,* 29-32.

265 Froom, *MOD,* 73. Froom presented a periodization of Adventist history which distinguished three stages of theological growth: the initial phase of doctrinal development (1844-1888), followed by the period of clarification, correction, and advance, leading to perfected beliefs (1888-1931), succeeded by the current, final stage of irrevocable commitment to the eternal verities since 1931 (ibid., 73-76).

266 L. E. Froom, "Restudying the Doctrines without Destroying the Foundations," *Ministry,* February 1940, 12.

267 Froom, *MOD,* 38, 145, 177, 334. Already toward the end of the 19th century, leading Adventist thinkers "demanded absolute perfection in theological system as well as in personal life for the last generation that they believed they represented. It was these assumptions that caused the interpretation of the horns/kingdoms issue of Daniel 2 and 7 to assume such gigantic proportions" (Haloviak, "From Righteousness to Holy Flesh," 23; cf. ibid., 2). See above, pp. 229-230.

jeopardizes the objectivity and unbiased character of historical research on the basis of a speculative philosophical premise.[268]

Thus, the two most popular concepts of doctrinal development among Adventists, viz., the historical theory as well as the organistic theory, are based on and supported by a number of assumptions which, on historical grounds alone, appear to be misconceptions fostering inaccurate views of Adventist history and theology.[269]

There are still other versions of the dynamic approach advanced by Adventist scholars that may offer more promising alternatives to the church in its endeavor to come to grips with the perplexing issue of doctrinal continuity and change.

The Model of Controlled Advance: The Theological Theory

Two major versions of the theological theory have appeared thus far in Adventist literature. They both acknowledge that genuine advances in doctrinal positions have occurred in the history of the church; they also emphasize the need for hermeneutical controls to prevent doctrinal modifications from leading the church away from revealed truth rather than towards a deeper understanding of it. They differ, however, in their respective assessment of these theological criteria.

Development as a unilateral process

According to *Gerhard F. Hasel,* the true meaning of Scripture may surpass the understanding of its human writers or the insights of biblical scholars. "The fuller import and deeper meaning" of biblical statements is "intended or implicit" in the Bible, "homogeneous with the literal meaning," and "a development and outgrowth" of it. "No new meaning" must be read into the text; rather its "implications" are to be "unfolded without misapplication, reinterpretation, or superimposing alien meaning upon the original meaning." As a safeguard against human "subjectivity," Hasel emphasized that these implications – relating, e.g., to typological interpretation and fulfilled prophecy – can be identified safely only by "further revelation," i.e., by

---

268 Froom's 4th conjecture appears to involve a departure from the "original Advent faith" which regarded a constant search for truth and openness to new doctrinal insights a *sine qua non* of true, Bible-based Christianity. Froom's hypothesis seems to amount to doctrinal perfectionism, which, like the ethical perfectionism he shunned, confounds the sincerity of intention with the flawlessness of achievement. As the maturation of human character is tied to a deepening sense of one's own imperfection, so a doctrinally maturing church will increasingly realize the inevitable shortcomings of all human formulations and conceptualizations of truth. Froom's hypothesis contains still another remarkable parallel to ethical perfectionism in that it regards doctrinal error as a reason for the delayed *parousia* of Christ (ibid., 561-603).

269 The importance for a discussion on doctrinal development of these misapprehensions lies in the insight that "the Christian attitude toward change ... can be seen most clearly in the way Christians have viewed their past" (Wilken, *The Myth of Christian Beginnings,* x).

"another inspired writer" to whose interpretation the church remains "always bound." Through such "progressive revelation," there occurs "a constant unfolding of truth in harmony with, rather than in contradiction to, earlier inspired writings."[270]

Hasel is in agreement with Adventist tradition by firmly rejecting a mystical, spiritual sense of the Bible that is not rooted in its literal meaning.[271] His view on the deeper meaning of the Scriptures builds upon similar ideas found in the writings of Ellen White.[272] Neither is he alone in suggesting that, in interpreting the Bible, White unfolds the deeper implications of the revealed word of God.[273] However, by making the authoritative definition of these implications the sole prerogative of an inspired prophet, on whose additional revelation the church depends, he and others[274] have come quite close to the new revelation theory already discussed.[275]

Moreover, by insisting on the continuity and homogeneity of later teachings with earlier beliefs, Hasel embraced a characteristic of the organistic theory that, as has been shown, does not always seem to harmonize with the historical facts.[276]

On the other hand, Hasel had emphasized a basic principle of any theological theory of doctrinal development developed from a conservative Protestant perspective, viz., that later truth unfolds the implications of biblical revelation. There may be different opinions among theologians regarding the various factors and persons involved in the discovery and definition of the deeper meaning of Bible truth. Nevertheless, that this process may indeed lead to new doctrinal positions seems to be an important insight of any theological theory of doctrinal development, which, therefore, needs to be controlled by clearly defined criteria.

---

270 Gerhard F. Hasel, "General Principles of Interpretation," in *A Symposium on Biblical Hermeneutics*, ed. Hyde, 163-191; idem, *Understanding the Living Word of God*, 72, 79, 210-218; and idem, *Biblical Interpretation Today*, 108-110.

271 See, e.g., J. H. Waggoner, "The Literal and Spiritual Meaning of Language," *RH*, 2 July 1872, 20-21; idem, "The Literal and Spiritual Meaning of Language," *RH*, 3 February 1885, 74; and J. C. Stevens, "Safe Rules of Bible Interpretation," *RH*, 25 January 1934, 9.

272 According to her, even the prophets "did not fully comprehend the import of the revelations committed to them. The meaning was to be unfolded from age to age" (Ellen White, *The Great Controversy*, 344). "One passage will prove to be a key to unlock other passages, and in this way light will be shed upon the hidden meaning of the word" (idem, *Fundamentals of Christian Education* [Nashville: SPA, 1923], 187).

273 "Is it not reasonable to believe that she gives us, not extra-scriptural teachings, but rather teachings hidden in the Scriptures?" (D. F. Neufeld, "The Editor's Mailbag," *RH*, 13 August 1964, 12). Similarly, Tim Crosby suggests that Ellen White presents "an unfolding of the principles that may be obscurely implicit" in the Bible. "Later inspired writers often find meaning in a canonical text that transcends the original intent of the human author – though not, evidently, that of the divine author" ("Why I Don't Believe in *Sola Scriptura*,"13).

274 See *A Symposium on Biblical Hermeneutics*, ed. Hyde, 134-140, 159-161, 209, 216-217.

275 See above, pp. 272-272. This view seems to maneuver Ellen White in the position of an (infallible?) magisterium, which – for all practical purposes – serves as the final arbiter of whatever authentic doctrinal developments may occur in the church.

276 See above, pp. 274-279, and below, pp. 293-306.

Development as a multilateral process

In 1976, *Raoul Dederen* presented a chapel talk at the Andrews University Theological Seminary, which virtually became the first published statement by an Adventist author on the problem of doctrinal development that consisted of more than a few incidental remarks on the issue. Entitled "Change and the Seventh-day Adventist Church," the essay discussed some important theological and hermeneutical issues involved in doctrinal change.[277] It contained five key thoughts:

1. Revelation, by which God communicates his saving message to man, is mediated through human channels and, thus, always related to the historical context, contemporary culture, and human experience in which it occurs.

2. Still, doctrines are trustworthy expressions of revealed and propositional truth and as such indispensable for sound Christian faith.

3. In order to communicate the gospel adequately to the modern world, it needs to be restated in terms meaningful to its recipients. There are also new implications to be derived from biblical revelation in the light of modern thought and experience.

4. This involves the re-examination and re-interpretation of doctrinal traditions which may even require some revision, if parts of them are found not to be in harmony with biblical revelation or prove inadequate for the needs and concerns of contemporary humanity.

5. However, the church must remain united on the fundamentals of its message, for the needed theological renewal will not uproot the historic Adventist landmarks of faith.[278]

Another important essay on "Adventists and Change" reflecting awareness of the multifaceted nature of doctrinal development, and implying a theological approach to doctrinal continuity and change, appeared in *Ministry,* October 1993. According to George R. Knight, doctrinal "change needs to be viewed as being of at least three distinct types: (1) clarification, (2) progressive development, and (3) contradiction or reversal." The latter may be prompted by the realization of "theological error." Besides, "changing times" may lead to "changing emphases." Pointing to "the dynamic nature of present truth," Knight still maintained that "new present truth must not negate the central doctrinal pillars" of Adventism. But to protect "historic Adventism" by setting it in "'creedal cement'" may "actually kill its living spirit."[279]

Roy Adams, associate editor of the *Adventist Review,* exemplified this dynamic approach to doctrinal development in his book *The Sanctuary.* According to him, because of our human limitedness and shortsightedness, we fail to grasp all that God

277 Raoul Dederen, "Change and the Seventh-day Adventist Church," *[Andrews University] Focus* 13:1 (April-May 1977), Supplement. For an abbreviated version of this article, see idem, "Adventists and Doctrinal Change," *Ministry,* February 1977, 16-19.

278 This essay displayed a considerably deeper grasp of the hermeneutical process involved in doctrinal development than had been manifested by Adventist writers up to that time. Regrettably, the author has not elaborated further on these insights in writing.

279 Knight, "Adventists and Change."

wants to say to us. Theology, therefore, is never static; rather it involves changes in our perception of (unchanging) truth. Today, we should have a clearer doctrinal vision than our pioneers who erred in some of their views. "How disappointed they would be if they should rise from the dead and discover that we had made no theological progress since their time." While "the essence of the truth they were expressing" was correct, we may express the same truth in a better, more refined or precise way "*without altering a single plank of the basic pillars of the faith.*"[280]

Similarly, *William G. Johnsson* defended a "dynamic understanding of truth" which "values the past but makes it contemporary." Because "our grasp of truth will ever be partial," "conditioned by our times," the "thought patterns of our day," and "the context of our experience," our understanding of truth will always be progressive. Still, "new light" does not nullify "old light" but clarifies or amplifies it.[281]

The Model of Historical Perspectivism:
The (Moderate) Situationist Theory

Several articles in *Spectrum,* a journal promoting moderately liberal theological views in an Adventist context, have elaborated on the theological implications of the historical perspectivity and cultural contextuality of all human understanding and formulation of truth.

Charles Scriven made room for some "constructive change" and advance, based on theological criticism and creative reflection, which would involve some doctrinal revision. He opposed "destructive innovation" and "wholesale alterations," without, however, elaborating on the difference between these two approaches.[282]

Fred Veltman called for the reinterpretation of doctrine in the light of contemporary experience both to safeguard continuity with the past and to speak to the needs of the present. This hermeneutical task demanded "an openness to the ongoing revelation of God in our experience" and the "continual development of church doctrine," in brief, "legitimate and responsible change."[283]

---

280 Adams, *The Sanctuary,* 11, 13, 88, 109, 111-113, 122-124, 133.
281 Johnsson, "Present Truth: Walking in God's Light," 8-11. "Adventist beliefs have changed over the years under the impact of 'present truth' ... Through all these changes, however, God was leading His people" (ibid., p. 10-11). W. W. Prescott appears to have been an early representative of the "theological theory" among SDAs. He "believed that the church could change and should change." To him, "doctrine was not static. Clearer concepts of truth must be adopted. Wrong ideas needed to be discarded." For, "to live was to grow and to grow was to change" (Valentine, *The Shaping of Adventism,* ix).
282 Scriven, "The Case for Renewal in Adventist Theology," 2-6. In a more recent essay, Scriven has emphasized the social aspects of Christ's death on the cross as the most important dimension of the biblical teaching on the atonement, rejecting the penal, substitutionary view. However, many SDAs will likely consider this a far-reaching doctrinal innovation, illustrating the danger of "creative" alterations of biblical truth. See Charles Scriven, "God's Justice, Yes; Penal Substitution, No," *Spectrum* 23:3 (1993): 31-38.
283 Veltman, "Some Reflections on Change and Continuity," 40-43.

Jonathan Butler also called for the "continual reapplication of Adventism of new times and places"; church teachings were to be contextualized and recontextualized in order to retain and regain their relevance in the contemporary world.[284]

In 1978, *Fritz Guy* laconically stated that "a certain pluralism is healthy, and change is essential to life."[285] Two years later, in an essay on "The Theological Task of the Church," he further elaborated on this statement. In our continuously and rapidly changing world, "there is no possibility that our theology ... could remain the same." Change – in the form of reformulation, specification, enlargement, and reinterpretation – is therefore inevitable. And "there will always be room for theological growth" because of (1) "the limitation of our knowledge of infinite and eternal truth," (2) the limits placed by sin upon our capacity for grasping truth accurately, and (3) the dual nature of truth which is both fixed and dynamic. "Our theology is not only incomplete; it is also faulty." Therefore, it can always become "more accurate to eternal truth and more adequate to the world."[286]

According to *Richard Rice,* "good theology is creative and constructive"; its task is never completed. While truth itself does not change, our perception of it does develop. For our theology to become contemporary, it is necessary to translate, rather than merely repeat, the truth for our times. Therefore, we need to rethink our beliefs and revise our terminology so as to be understood by our contemporaries.[287]

These are unfamiliar rings to Adventist ears accustomed to assume the immutability of doctrine and to question the validity of theological change. What makes these notions attractive to some, raises suspicion and fear with others. For instance, the use of words like relevance and contextuality, innovation and creativity, may reflect an awareness of the needs of the contemporary world as well as of the task of a theology fitting for these times. But, by the same token, these terms may also become the means for imbibing relativistic concepts inimical to the Adventist understanding of truth. Besides, it does not suffice simply to declare one's disavowal of destructive theological changes without offering and applying workable criteria which effectively serve to avoid such distortions of revealed truth.

The different versions of the "dynamic" approach to doctrinal development presented here provide a variety of perspectives. While the *organistic* theory may be said to ignore the possibility of heterogeneous developments, the *moderate situationist* theory may seem to underrate the importance of doctrinal stability and identity for the church. Proponents of the *theological* theory, in turn, may need to clarify their definition and use of the criteria of doctrinal development. Still, some

284 J. Butler, "The World of E. G. White and the End of the World," 11-12.

285 Guy, "The Shaking of Adventism? I. A View from the Outside," 29.

286 Guy, "The Theological Task of the Church," 7-13. This essay was presented at Consultation I; see above, p. 249-250. Elaborating on the notion of contemporary truth, Guy, in 1991, pointed out that it may be either an expansion/growth, an application, or a modification/revision of the old. In order to become truly contemporary, "inherited truth" must be appropriated and reflected upon ("Truth Our Contemporary," 12-14).

287 Rice, *The Reign of God,* 9-10.

form of the dynamic approach, which reckons with the factuality and possibility of doctrinal change and at the same time respects the necessity of and demand for substantial doctrinal continuity, may perhaps best serve the needs of the church.

Transmutating Doctrine – The Evolutionary/Revolutionary Approach

Adventist teachings are closely tied to a conservative approach to theology, even showing fundamentalist leanings. One can hardly expect, therefore, to find in the church views comparable to the radical revisionary or transformist theories of liberal and modernist theology. But inasmuch as a theological equilibrium is hard to maintain when two opposite forces exert their persistent influence on the church, it should not be surprising if the dynamic approach would, in some cases, lead to an evolutionary or revolutionary attitude toward doctrinal change. The following authors are mentioned here not necessarily for having formally proposed such radical theories. But, compared to other Adventist writers, they seem to have expressed the most far-reaching and liberal views on doctrinal continuity and change to date.

The Model of Unrestrained Change: The Revisionist Theory[288]

In 1976, *Jack W. Provonsha* pointed out that the communication of truth requires creative and innovative ways. The church is not only in need of new insights into, and a deeper understanding of, truth. Also required are "new ways of stating the

---

288 In 1969, *Herold D. Weiss* defined theology as "an attempt at culture translation" which, utilizing contemporary philosophy, verbalizes humanity's experience of revelation in "the intellectual and cultural framework" of the times. As there is no fixed meaning to revealed truth, "some pillars" of the house of faith may "need to be replaced" so that the church may produce a "modern" and "enlightened theology" (Herold D. Weiss, "The Theological Task," *Spectrum* 1:4 [1969]: 13-22). Similarly, *Walter Douglas* expressed the idea that theologians should be engaged in the creative and imaginative transformation of religious views. In order to achieve contextual relevance in the contemporary world, there must be significant changes in Adventist theology. As theological language possesses no fixed and universally applicable meaning, the latter will greatly vary with humanity's changing consciousness and experience (Walter B. T. Douglas, "Reflections on Contextualization as a Theological Necessity, 1982," TMs, AHC, JWL, AU, Berrien Springs, Mich.). The church is facing "a process of intellectual readjustment, revisions of its thinking, and certain conceptions of its nature and structure. It has become increasingly clear that the old truths need to be redefined, and stated with clarity. New truths need to be recognized" (idem, "The Church: Its Nature and Function," in Oosterwal et al., *Servants for Christ*, 57). However, in a recent essay, Douglas appears to have qualified this view. "Doctrinal beliefs and practices hold this church together as a community, not structures and policies. Despite cultural preferences and contextual appropriateness, the essential theology of the church will remain the same everywhere" (Walter Douglas, "The Future Shape of the Church," *AR*, 150-Year Anniversary Issue [6 October 1994], 52).

truth" and a "progressive openness to new ideas." Thus, "there may be progression and development – indeed must be – but not in discontinuity with the past."[289]

In *A Remnant in Crisis,* Provonsha has elaborated on the implications of this view. He agrees with Heraclitus' famous aphorism on change according to which "everything changes. Nothing stays the same." Universal motion is not only self-evident but also good because "God is the author of change. He is a dynamic God." Heaven, too, involves growth and change. At the same time, "*growth and development involve continuity.*" After all, "nothing can exist without continuity of some sort."[290] Therefore, Adventists need to redefine and re-express the "essence" or "central core" of their prophetic message; for "never has it been more important to keep our language and thought forms up-to-date."[291]

This involves, for example, the rejection of the forensic model of the atonement, which, according to Provonsha, possesses no objective truth value. Christ's death on the cross was not required as a substitutionary sacrifice; rather, it was a special self-revelation of God and his love for humankind. In spite of his fairly balanced statements on doctrinal continuity and change, Provonsha's view on the atonement will appear to many Adventists as a "sell-out" of the biblical teaching on the atonement and a radical reinterpretation of the historic Christian faith. The same may apply to Provonsha's innovatively reconceptualized "remnant" theology.[292]

Speaking of the recent controversies surrounding the sanctuary doctrine, *Edward W. Vick,* in 1983, called upon Adventists to reassess, reinterpret, and modify the foundations of even their essential doctrines. Such a reexamination may lead to the rejection of traditional beliefs, for "an old doctrine necessarily undergoes serious changes in meaning as time passes." Rejecting the assumption that there exist certain static and unalterable truths that are expressed in fixed and formal doctrines, Vick felt that it is God's will for Adventists "to change their doctrinal interpretations."[293]

---

289 Provonsha, "Can There Be an Innovative Adventism?" "A vital theology is never merely a restatement of old ideas, but is continually informed by new insights and discoveries … Revelation is progressive, in that God must measure the unfolding of truth to the capacity of man to understand. Wherever genuine progress appears God may be publishing some new aspect of truth about Himself (Provonsha, *God Is with Us,* 18-19; cf. ibid., 20-28, 67-75).
290 Provonsha, *A Remnant in Crisis,* 15-21; cf. above, pp. 28-30.
291 Provonsha, *A Remnant in Crisis,* 62, 66. "The essentials of a set of ideas or propositions remain constant, while the incidental manner of their expression may vary, even fairly radically, from time to time and place to place. It should not surprise us to find Fundamental Beliefs of one prophetic generation being expressed in quite different language and thought forms from another" (ibid., 62). "Truth will continue to develop while it maintains continuity with its roots … This means that each generation can and must take a fresh look at the ways their fathers perceived and expressed things. Above all, a prophetic movement must maintain an openness to new truth" (ibid., 167-168).
292 See Provonsha, *A Remnant in Crisis,* 37-72, 115-121. Cf. above, pp. 150-151. See also James Londis, "*Remnant in Crisis* and a Second Disappointment," *Spectrum* 24:4 (April 1995): 9-16.
293 Vick, "Must We Keep the Sanctuary Doctrine?"

These suggestions hit what is undoubtedly a very sensitive spot of Seventh-day Adventist theology. All during its history, the church has reacted rather defensively to any real or apparent attacks on the sanctuary teaching and has quite frequently reaffirmed the immutability of this "foundational pillar" of its faith. On the other hand, as has been shown, the sanctuary doctrine underwent certain significant modifications and changes, too, some of them in recent years.[294] Thus, the call to review the significance of the historic sanctuary doctrine in new situations can be defended even on historical grounds – to say nothing of the challenge to constantly grow in the understanding of truth and to strive for the continued relevance of any doctrine for practical Christian living.[295]

At the same time, it must be seriously questioned whether the Seventh-day Adventist Church can abandon its search for meaning in the 1844 experience without a resultant loss of its distinctive message or special sense of mission to the world. To continuously reflect on the deeper significance for the contemporary church of that seminal experience may, perhaps, provide an impetus for Adventists in their desire to wait for and hasten unto the day of God (2 Pet 3:12).[296]

In his book *Adventism for a New Generation, Steven G. Daily* has called for the continual reinterpretation and renewal of Adventism. According to him, "religion must be redefined, both individually and corporately by each new generation, if it is to remain dynamic, relevant, and powerful." [297] The much-needed "Adventist *perestroika"* includes redefining the pillar doctrines of Adventism in a rapidly changing world and reapplying Adventist theology both in the church and in daily life. Daily attempts to provide "a model of faith redefinition" for a new generation of Adventists facing the twenty-first century. In his view, critically evaluating, redefining, and reapplying Adventist beliefs and practices will foster a "healthy religion" which transcends fixed doctrines and creeds. It implies an individualized faith in Jesus, a genuine commitment to meeting human needs, and a pluralistic church.

A radical call to consistent revisionism has come from *Thomas R. Steininger* who presented a sociological analysis of Adventism in Germany in the context of post-modern cultural trends in the Western world. In his view, the individualistic,

---

294 See above, pp. 174-185, 247-249.

295 For a recent vindication and interpretation of the sanctuary doctrine that cautiously goes beyond certain traditional thought patterns, see Adams, *The Sanctuary: Understanding the Heart of Adventist Theology* (1993).

296 This may be compared to the perennial task of Christian theology, viz., to reflect on the con-temporary significance of the Christ event, centered on the death and resurrection of Jesus, which led the disciples to their own "great disappointment" but also to a new beginning as well as a new message and mission for the world at large.

297 Steven G. Daily, *Adventism for a New Generation* (Portland/Clackamas, Oreg.: Better Living Publishers, 1993), 1. Instead of rejecting traditional teachings, Daily apparently wants to reassess and retain them, albeit in a refined or revised form. In one of the book's more radical remarks, he claims that Adventist "eschatology has been built on an unsound foundation, and that it has ultimately done us more harm than good" (314). At the same time, he defends many traditional Adventist theological concepts and ethical values.

relativistic, and pluralistic nature of contemporary society produces new and non-dogmatic forms of spirituality, which involve the radical revision of the traditional tenets of the Adventist (and Christian) faith. This requires the abandonment of all objective, propositional truth claims and the openness toward a radically pluralistic and autonomous understanding of faith as well as an individualistic and relativistic notion of truth. Steininger argues on the basis of an evolutionary model of society, which regards postmodern thinking as a lasting and irreversible phenomenon. This conception, which seems problematic from a philosophical and sociological perspective, results in his call for radical changes in Seventh-day Adventism and in his negative assessment of the search for doctrinal continuity, ethical stability, and denominational identity.[298]

Summary and Conclusion

Parallel to the theological history of Christianity, Seventh-day Adventism has only recently addressed itself in some detail to the issue of doctrinal continuity and change.[299] Traditionally, Adventists have tended to stress doctrinal identity and immutability, allowing only for such developments as would not involve the revision of traditional views. Even when doctrinal changes had actually occurred, they were usually explained in such a way as to fit the historic or the organistic theory, respectively, of doctrinal development.[300] In more recent years, however, a growing awareness has developed among Adventist theologians of the intricate nature of the problem of doctrinal development. Some scholars have abandoned the traditional (historic and organistic) models of change replacing them with more progressive (moderately situationist or even revisionist) approaches to change.

In conclusion, it should be pointed out that this historical analysis of Adventist conceptions of doctrinal development both by choice and by necessity had to be a "critical" one. This should not be understood as reflecting any disrespect of or arrogance over against the views of any of the Adventist church leaders or theologians discussed here. As F. M. Wilcox once pointed out, there is a real sense in which these "pioneer" scholars of the church remain worthy examples for later generations to

---

298 Steininger, *Konfession und Sozialisation: Adventistische Identität zwischen Fundamentalismus und Postmoderne* (1993).

299 The rise of critical historical studies on Adventist history served about the same function that *Dogmengeschichte* had for 19th-century theology. For it brought the problem of doctrinal change into the limelight of Adventist thought and called for new answers different from the ones that had been provided so far.

300 The following quote illustrates this approach: "It may appear to some that we have changed our beliefs; it is better to say that we have emerged, that our denominational beliefs have crystallized, and that we have become unified in our declared understanding of truth ... Our doctrines have been increasingly clarified through the years" (Roy Allen Anderson, "Unity of Adventist Belief – II," *Ministry*, April 1958, 25).

emulate even when the posterity has to move beyond the restricted views of their progenitors in order to remain true to their unique vision of Adventism.

> The pioneers in this movement never claimed infallibility, nor do we claim it for them. We do, however, believe in the sincerity of heart and honesty of purpose which prompted their lives. Instead of censuring them for their limitation of vision and their lack of understanding divine revelation, we honor them for their loyalty to the truth as they saw it, for their honesty of heart in renouncing error as it was revealed to them, and for their lives of labor and sacrifice in the promulgation of the cause they espoused.[301]

301 F. M. Wilcox, *The Faith of the Pioneers* (Washington, D.C.: RHPA, [1930]), 30-31.

Chapter 6

Prophetic Authority and Doctrinal Change:
An Analysis

> Take from the altar of the past the fire, not the ashes!
>
> *Jean Juares*
>
> He who rejects or neglects the new does not really possess the old.
>
> *Ellen G. White*

Introduction

The analysis of the development of Seventh-day Adventist teachings and of Adventist concepts of doctrinal continuity and change has not, thus far, paid close attention to Ellen G. White, who was by far the most influential figure in the history of the denomination. In fact, her importance for and lasting impact on the church can hardly be exaggerated.[1] In harmony with the over-all purpose and approach of this study as set forth in the Introduction, this concluding chapter discusses a number of questions that can hardly be ignored in a study on Adventist doctrinal development.

For example, what influence did Ellen White have on the development of Adventists doctrines? Did she shape the teachings of the church in any significant way? To what degree, if any, did she herself experience theological growth and re-adjustments in matters of belief? And did she express herself specifically on the

---

1   Ellen White not only shaped the sense of purpose and mission, contributed to the unity, and influenced the doctrinal structure of the church, but she also gave the decisive impetus to the educational, evangelistic, medical, temperance, publishing, and welfare programs of the church. Through her writings, the ideas, values, and beliefs, as well as the worldview of 19th-century Adventism, have survived remarkably well until today. "More than the statements of faith ... the thought of Ellen White provides an ideological framework for the church's mission, binding together an eclectic array of doctrines into a coherent world view" (Malcolm Bull, "Eschatology and Manners in Seventh-day Adventism," *Archives des Sciences Sociales des Religions* 65 [1988]: 147, 145-159). "Sie [EGW] ist der eigentliche Schlüssel zum Verständnis des Adventismus" (Steininger, 94; cf. 97, 107). For studies on her life and work, see Roy E. Graham, *Ellen G. White: Co-Founder of the Seventh-day Adventist Church*, American University Studies, series 7: Theology and Religion, vol. 12 (New York, Berne, Frankfurt: Peter Lang, 1985); and Arthur L. White, *Ellen G. White.* For the historical background of her life, see Land, ed., *The World of Ellen G. White.*

problem of doctrinal change? Would she possibly favor or rather oppose changes with regard to the established teachings of the Adventist church?

In addressing these issues, this chapter pursues a threefold objective. First, it briefly analyzes Ellen White's role in the development of Adventist doctrines. Second, it takes a look at her personal participation in theological changes and doctrinal revisions. And third, it presents an outline of what appears to be Ellen White's own concept of doctrinal development.[2]

Inasmuch as Seventh-day Adventists have traditionally ascribed to Ellen White an exceptional authority, equaled and surpassed only by the Bible itself, any investigation of her role and writings, visions and views touches on what is central and dear to the Adventist church and its communal identity. Others, within and with-out the denomination, have expressed critical views on the Adventist prophet. As has rightly been said, studies on Ellen White are dealing with "the most sensitive area of research into the Adventist past."[3]

At the outset, it should not be surprising if certain misconceptions regarding Adventist history also involved the person and work of Ellen White.[4] Actually, the discovery of such misapprehensions relating to her writings has been a shattering experience for a number of Adventists who were confronted with the human side of prophecy.[5] In recent years, Adventists have increasingly come to see Ellen White in

---

2   Because of the complex nature of these issues, the following analysis does not claim or intend to be exhaustive in any sense. It does seek, however, to present a fair and accurate picture of Ellen White that serves to round off this investigation of doctrinal development within the SDA historical and theological setting.

3   William G. Johnsson, "Those Moon Men in Long Black Coats," *AR,* 14 July 1983, 14. Books dealing with Ellen White have sometimes appeared to either recklessly attack or anxiously defend her authority and, by extension, the very foundation of Seventh-day Adventism. For more information on the role of apologetics and polemics in Adventist history writing, see Pöhler, "The Adventist Historian between Criticism and Faith." An observer of the church has remarked: "Das Ringen im Adventismus um die Bedeutung E. G. Whites erweist sich je länger, je mehr ... als eine Schicksalsfrage des Adventismus, als ein Ringen um die Zukunft" (Helmut Obst, "Ellen G. White entmythologisieren!" *Materialdienst* 57:1 [1994]: 22, 19-22).

4   "Because her influence was so great and long-lasting in the movement, a natural mythology was created concerning the authority of her writings" (Steve Daily, "Are We a Non-Prophet Organization?" *AR,* 12 October 1989, 9, 8-10).

5   Since the 1970s, historical and critical studies on Ellen White, spearheaded by Ingemar Lindén *(Biblicism, Apocalyptik, Utopi: Adventismes Historika Utforming i USA samt dess Svenska Utveckling Till o. 1939* [Uppsala: University of Uppsala, 1971]) and Ronald L. Numbers *(Prophetess of Health: A Study of Ellen G. White* [New York: Harper & Row, 1976]; cf. idem, *Prophetess of Health: Ellen G. White and the Origins of Seventh-day Adventist Health Reform,* rev. and enl. ed. [Knoxville: University of Tennessee Press, 1992]), described her in terms of the intellectual and social milieu of her time. Some years later, and perhaps even more shocking to the church, Walter T. Rea harshly accused her of rampant plagiarism and literary theft. He wanted to explode the "legend" that, in his view, had been built around Ellen White through the years *(The White Lie* [Turlock, Calif.: M & R Publ., 1982]). Rea was not the first SDA who foundered on the discrepancy between a restricted view of inspiration

the light of careful historical research, enabling them to abandon erroneous views while retaining confidence in the prophet.[6] As a result, the church appears to have come out of the period of the 1970s and 1980s healthier and stronger.

Ellen White's Role in Doctrinal Development

Doctrinal Formation

According to Froom, "no doctrinal truth or prophetic interpretation ever came to this people initially through the Spirit of Prophecy – not in a single case." Ellen White "never ran ahead of the church's discovery of truth directly from the Word." While she "confirmed truth," she "did not initiate truth."[7] However, Graham seems more accurate in concluding that Ellen White also was "ahead of her contemporaries in her denomination theologically."[8] In the 1840s, she introduced a number of new concepts among the Adventist group, for example, on the "time of Jacob's trouble," on the Sabbath as "the seal of God," and on "the open and shut door" in the heavenly sanctuary.[9] Later, she was among the first in the church consistently to call the death

and the discovery of certain historical facts regarding the Adventist prophetess. Similar difficulties had been encountered already by Canright, Ballenger, Conradi, and others. For an analysis of these developments in EGW studies, see Rolf J. Pöhler, "Adventisten auf der Suche nach der wahren Ellen G. White," *Materialdienst* 47:12 (1 December 1984): 372-375. The SDA church's response to these critical studies is found, e.g., in *A Discussion and Review of Prophetess of Health*; Robertson, *The White Truth*; and Fred Veltman, "Summary and Conclusion of the Veltman Report on Ellen White's Use of Literary Sources in Writing The Desire of Ages, [1988]," TMs, EGWRC, AU, Berrien Springs, Mich. Veltman has published a summary of his findings in "The *Desire of Ages* Project: The Data," *Ministry,* October 1990, 4-7; and idem, "The *Desire of Ages* Project: The Conclusions," *Ministry,* December 1990, 11-15. In brief, "the new scholarship had established that the prophet was neither original nor inerrant, neither changeless nor timeless" (Jonathan M. Butler, "Introduction: The Historian as Heretic," in Numbers, *Prophetess of Health,* rev. and enl. ed., LX).

6   Veltman concluded his 2,561-page report by saying that "our faith in Ellen White must rest upon evidence, not upon myth. I think it is very important for the future of Adventism and for Adventist confidence in the ministry of Ellen White that we base our beliefs on our best knowledge of the truth" ("Summary and Conclusion of the Veltman Report," 950). In 1991, Patrick listed several facts that SDAs had come to recognize on the basis of recent studies on Ellen White: Her writings are "historically conditioned to a significant degree," reflecting ideas of her contemporaries and of books she had read; her use of the Bible was not always exegetical; "her doctrinal understandings underwent both growth and change during her lifetime"; "her literary assistants and advisors did have more than a minor mechanical role in the preparation of her writings for publication," contributing to the "literary excellence" of her writings ("Does Our Past Embarrass Us?").

7   Froom, "The Priestly Application of the Atoning Act," 11.

8   Graham, *Ellen G. White,* 415.

9   See [James and Ellen White], *A Word to the "Little Flock,"* 22; Bates, *A Seal of the Living God,* 24-26; and Ellen White, *EW,* 86. In Bates's view "in every instance [her visions] have

of Christ an act of atonement and to reflect a deeper understanding of justification by faith and the righteousness of Christ.[10]

Late in her life, Ellen White herself described the role she had been playing during the late 1840s when many of the fundamental and most of the distinctive teachings of Seventh-day Adventism had been hammered out. As she remembered it,

> In the early days of the message, when our numbers were few, we studied diligently to understand the meaning of many Scriptures. At times it seemed as if no explanation could be given. My mind seemed to be locked to an understanding of the Word; but when our brethren who had assembled for study came to a point where they could go no farther, and had recourse to earnest prayer, the Spirit of God would rest upon me, and I would be taken off in vision, and be instructed in regard to the relation of Scripture to Scripture. These experiences were repeated over and over again. Thus many truths of the third angel's message were established, point by point.[11]

From these statements it appears that Ellen White had assumed a critical function in helping the fledgling movement to settle firmly on a doctrinal platform, which was to become the theological base of Seventh-day Adventists as well as the foundation of their revitalized missionary zeal. In spite of the illumination coming to them through the visions of Ellen White, however, her fellow believers explained and defended their teachings, not on the basis of her visions but solely from the Scriptures themselves.

During their earliest years, Sabbatarian Adventists had applied the Protestant *sola scriptura* principle in a strict way, denying that post-canonical prophets were ever to be granted normative authority in matters of doctrine. Even after these Adventists, in 1855, had come to consider Ellen White as a secondary "test or rule" of truth, subordinate to the Bible, they refrained from using her writings in support of their views. Only during and after the 1880s, the "Spirit of Prophecy" tended to become – to a number of Adventists, at least – a substitute for a strictly biblical approach to truth.[12]

Doctrinal Preservation

For more than a century now, the writings of Ellen White appear to have been the single most important factor contributing to the remarkable doctrinal unity, stability, and continuity of the Seventh-day Adventist Church. Supplemented by other means, such as a centralized organization, an impressive array of educational institutions,

been in accordance with God's word ... leaving the hearers the privilege of searching the scriptures for the proof" (*A Seal of the Living God,* 31).

10 See above, p. 145, and p. 210.

11 Ellen White, *SM,* 2:38 (originally published in 1906). For a similar statement, see Arthur L. White, *Ellen G. White,* 5:410 (1905).

12 See above, pp. 185-188. The use of Ellen White's writings as a convenient short-cut to truth proved a temptation that SDAs have not always been able to resist, particularly when they were convinced that the prophet was on their side of an issue. For illustrations, see below, "Examples of Ellen White's Participation in Doctrinal Change" (esp. on the law in Galatians and the "daily").

and the weekly "Sabbath School," it was particularly the impact of her writings which has helped to preserve and protect the doctrinal identity of the church and also shaped the beliefs and values of Adventists until today.[13]

At times, Ellen White herself consciously used her own writings in the defense of established doctrines when they were seriously questioned by some within the church. For example, when Ballenger advanced his divergent views on the sanctuary and the atonement, Ellen White not only charged him with misapplying the Bible but also rebuked him for contradicting "the light and the Testimonies that God has been giving us for the past half century."[14] Convinced that his doctrinal views were undermining the irremovable landmarks of the Adventist faith, she boldly placed her own revelations over against his novel teachings.[15]

On the other hand, Ellen White's whole-hearted and unwavering support of the *sola scriptura* principle generally prevented her from either using her own writings as a substitute for serious Bible study or allowing them to be used by others in such a way.[16] Apparently, it was only in exceptional circumstances and when she felt the very doctrinal foundation of the church to be acutely jeopardized that she was ready to use her own authority in settling doctrinal disputes.[17]

Doctrinal Revision

In the 1880s and beyond, Ellen White was repeatedly called upon to resolve doctrinal controversies that tended to divide the church on specific theological issues. Those holding traditional views, apparently sanctioned by the prophet herself, pleaded with her to confirm the historic faith of the church and to reject the new views which threatened what they perceived to be Adventism's doctrinal landmarks. Ellen White, however, consistently refused to do so, calling upon the church to seriously restudy

---

13 See Zoral Harold Coberly, "A Study of the Influences Affecting the Unity of the Beliefs of Seventh-day Adventists" (M.A. thesis, SDA Theological Seminary, Washington, D.C., 1946); and Anderson, "Unity of Adventist Belief – Nos. 1-2"; cf. Howard F. Rampton, "The Miracle of Unity," *AR,* 11 September 1980, 8-9.

14 Ellen G. White, Manuscript 59, 1905, EGWRC, AU, Berrien Springs, Mich. See also Arthur L. White, *Ellen G. White,* 5:398-413.

15 According to Adams, "Mrs. White did not specify the particular aspects of his theology that she found offensive." Notwithstanding her "general condemnation of Ballenger's theology," he was correct in at least some particulars, making "positive contributions to the doctrine of the sanctuary" *(The Sanctuary,* 84-88, 107-109, 154).

16 See above, pp. 186-188, and p. 260, n. 172.

17 By way of explanation, Knight suggests that there was "a fundamental difference" between Ballenger's problem over the sanctuary doctrine and the issue of the "daily" and the law in Galatians. "From EGW's perspective, Adventist scholars had already thoroughly studied from the Bible the point at issue, whereas the law in Galatians and the 'daily' still needed more attention when disagreement arose over them. As a result, she related to Ballenger's situation differently than she did in the other cases" *(Angry Saints,* 115, n. 22).

the controverted points and to remain open to new interpretations of Bible texts, additional doctrinal insights, and possible revisions of erroneous views.[18]

The authority Ellen White enjoyed in the church unquestionably contributed to the acceptance of a number of "orthodox" teachings that Sabbatarian Adventists had once firmly opposed. When, toward the end of the nineteenth century, Adventists were beginning to open up to the historic Trinitarian and Christological dogmas, it was Ellen White who took the lead in supporting these new interpretations.[19]

In summary, Ellen White's role in the development of Adventist theology may be described as "formative, not normative."[20] While she contributed significantly to the development, acceptance, preservation, and revision of doctrines, she was not regarded, or made use of, by the church (though, sometimes, by some of her ardent supporters) as the final criterion and arbiter of truth.[21] Neither did she commonly take the sole initiative in introducing new theological concepts to the church.[22]

Ellen White's Participation in Doctrinal Development

Already during her lifetime, some Seventh-day Adventists accorded to Ellen White an authority comparable to that claimed by the magisterium of the Roman Catholic Church. Asserting that an infallible Bible needed to be "infallibly interpreted" in a

18   For details, see above, pp. 228-232, and below, the following section. For examples of how new doctrinal interpretations were being developed among the early SDAs without the initial endorsement by Ellen White or even in seeming conflict with her view, see above, pp. 157-158 (beginning of the Sabbath), and pp. 166-167 (the two-horned beast).
19   See above, pp. 134, 135-136, 139-140, 141-142.
20   Richard Hammill, "Spiritual Gifts in the Church Today," *Ministry,* July 1982, 17.
21   This is still the position of SDAs today. As Robert W. Olson has emphasized, "we cannot use Ellen White as the determinative final arbiter of what Scripture means. If we do that, then she is the final authority and Scripture is not. Scripture must be permitted to interpret itself" ("Olson Discusses the Veltman Study," *Ministry,* December 1990, 17, 16-18).
22   On Ellen White's role in doctrinal development, see also D. M. Canright, *Life of Mrs. E. G. White, Seventh-day Adventist Prophet; Her False Claims Refuted* (Cincinnati, Ohio: Standard Publ. Co., 1919; Nashville: B. C. Goodpasture, 1953), 66-72; L. H. Christian, *The Fruitage of Spiritual Gifts* (Washington, D.C.: RHPA, 1947), 185-206; L. E. Froom, "Our Doctrines Anchored to Scripture," *RH,* 26 August 1948, 6-8; idem, *MOD,* 107-132; Harry W. Lowe, "The Writings of Ellen G. White as Related to Seventh-day Adventist Doctrines and Prophetic Interpretation," *Ministry,* October 1967, 8-11, 13; idem, "Doctrinal Development and Prophetic Interpretation: Their Relationship," *Ministry,* November 1967, 36-39; Arthur L. White, *Ellen G. White: Messenger to the Remnant,* rev. ed. (Washington, D.C.: RHPA, 1969), 34-40; idem, "How Basic Doctrines Came to Adventists," *AR,* 19 July 1984, 4-6; idem, "The Certainty of Basic Doctrinal Positions," *AR,* 26 July 1984, 6-8; Ronald D. Graybill, "Ellen White's Role in the Resolution of [Doctrinal] Conflicts in Adventist History, 1980," TMs, EGWRC, AU, Berrien Springs, Mich.; and Bert Haloviak with Gary Land, "Ellen G. White and Doctrinal Conflict: Context of the 1919 Bible Conference," *Spectrum* 12:4 (1982): 19-34.

way that would mean "settling all disputes,"[23] the "ex cathedra decrees" of the pope were regarded as "Satan's counterfeit of the true, infallible guide that God has placed in his church under the title of the Spirit of Prophecy."[24] Of course, the "final authority"[25] and "absolute truth"[26] of Ellen White's writings allowed no disagreement with anything she had said or written under inspiration.[27] "When the Spirit of prophecy speaks clearly upon a given question, that settles matters and is the end of the controversy for those who accept the declarations of that gift as authoritative."[28]

This view implied that the writings of Ellen White "not once" shared or echoed "faulty views" and "never needed revision" as they had been "kept free from contemporary errors."[29] Consequently, she was never personally involved in theological changes or doctrinal revisions.

This position has been repudiated by others who had either been close to the prophet or become aware of facts that refuted it.[30] As a result, Adventists have come to realize that "Ellen White's understanding of some Scriptures did change." After all, "the Bible writers themselves were wrong at times in their theology and had to be corrected."[31] Still, "even today it is tempting to use her writings as if they contain an

---

23   Roderick S. Owen, "The Source of Final Appeal," *RH,* 3 June 1971, 4-6; the article was originally published in 1910 (not in the *RH).*

24   Claude E. Holmes, *Have We an Infallible 'Spirit of Prophecy'?* (Takoma Park, [Md.]: By the Author, 1920), 10. This view was later echoed by L. E. Froom who called the Catholic doctrine of papal infallibility "a substitute for God's provisions of inerrant, prophetic guidance for His remnant church" ("Papal Traditions versus the Prophetic Gift," *Ministry,* June 1942, 21, 46).

25   Froom, "Papal Traditions versus the Prophetic Gift," 21, 46.

26   Holmes, 8. According to J. R. Spangler, what we find in the Bible and/or Ellen White's writings "has not been mixed with error." It is "pure," "absolute," and "unquestionably truth"; for "the wheat and the tares have been verbally separated" ("Profiting from His Prophet," *Ministry,* May 1973, 2-3).

27   Implicitly or explicitly, the high regard for Ellen White and her writings has often been tied to a fundamentalist view of inspiration. It tends to ascribe to the prophet a *de facto* inerrancy/infallibility and, consequently, to deny theological errors and changes in what the inspired writer says. The possibility of revisions in Ellen White's theology and doctrinal beliefs does not accord well with this traditional and widespread view.

28   L. E. Froom, "The Platform of Our Message," *Ministry,* August 1939, 21.

29   Froom, *MOD,* 73, 74, 119.

30   For example, neither A. G. Daniells, W. W. Prescott, W. C. White, nor F. M. Wilcox regarded Ellen White as an infallible interpreter of the Bible. See "The Bible Conference of 1919," *Spectrum* 10:1 (1979): 23-57. W. C. White admitted that his mother "sometimes shared with her brethren in the acceptance of partial truths or mistaken views of Scripture teaching" ("The Influence of the Prophetic Gift in the Establishment of Church Doctrine," 8; quoted in Ford, *Daniel 8:14, the Day of Atonement, and the Investigative Judgment,* p. A-201).

31   *One Hundred and One Questions on the Sanctuary and on Ellen White,* 53. This fact hardly allows SDAs to use Ellen White's writings as the final word on the meaning of Scripture or the decisive interpretive norm of its teachings. Her role, then, is essentially "formative, not normative" (Ron Graybill, "Ellen White's Role in Doctrine Formation," *Ministry,* October 1981, 7-11 [this is a very helpful and sensible essay on this issue]). See also Herold D. Weiss, "Are Adventists Protestants?" *Spectrum* 4 (Spring 1972): 69-78; Stanley G. Sturges, "Ellen White's

'infallible filter' for separating the wheat from the chaff, truth from error. Ellen White would not wish it to be so."[32] Support for this statement comes from the following analysis of Ellen White's personal involvement in doctrinal development.

Theological Maturation and Growth

As Alden Thompson suggested, Ellen White experienced "significant changes" during her lifetime in her "theological development" by which "her theological understanding grew" with regard to several basic Christian teachings. The general direction of this process seems to have led her from a discouraging, law-centered position ("Sinai") to an encouraging, love-centered attitude ("Golgotha"). In his view, "the transition from fear to love in her experience resulted in a remarkable shift of emphasis."[33] While Thompson's interpretation does not seem to have been without flaws, [34] his underlying assumption that White's perception of truth developed in time accords with her own view. "For sixty years I have been in communication with heavenly messengers, and I have been constantly learning in reference to divine things."[35]

Authority and the Church," *Spectrum* 4:3 (1972): 66-70; "The Role of the Ellen G. White Writings in Doctrinal Matters," *AR,* 4 September 1980, 15; "The Inspiration and Authority of the Ellen G. White Writings," *AR,* 23 December 1982, 9 (also publ. in *Ministry,* February 1983, 24); and Martin Weber, *Who's Got the Truth? Making Sense out of Five Different Adventist Gospels* (Silver Spring, Md.: Home Study International Press, 1994), 187-211.

32   Warren H. Johns, "Ellen G. White: Prophet or Plagiarist?" *Ministry,* June 1982, 18. "If we are faithful to Ellen White's own position, we will avoid placing her on a level with Scripture. In practice, as well as in theory, we will give the Bible the first and last word in religious matters … If Seventh-day Adventists adhere to this important *[sola scriptura]* principle, they will not treat Ellen White as an infallible interpreter of the Bible … They will support every biblical interpretation, including those of Ellen White, by appealing directly to the Bible itself" (Rice, *The Reign of God,* 200-201). On the apparent tension between Ellen White's support of the normative authority of the Scripture and her concomitant claim to interpret it authoritatively, see Ron Graybill, "The Power of Prophecy: Ellen White and the Women Religious Founders of the Nineteenth Century" (Ph.D. dissertation, Johns Hopkins University, 1983), 113-135.

33   Alden Thompson, "From Sinai to Golgotha – Nos. 1-5," *AR,* 3-31 December 1981, 4-6, 8-10, 7-10, 7-9, 12-13. In Thompson's view, this development reflected the changing religious experience of the church as a whole. But, according to Haloviak, Ellen White far surpassed her fellow believers in her understanding of righteousness by faith, avoiding Adventism's traditional legalism as well as the subjectivism of Waggoner and Jones ("From Righteousness to Holy Flesh," chaps. 5-6).

34   See K. H. Wood, "An Explanation," *AR,* 1 July 1982, 3; Geoffrey E. Garne, "Are the Testimonies Legalistic?" ibid., 4-6; Alden Thompson, "The Prodigal Son Revisited," ibid., 7-11; and J. T. McDuffie, "The Prodigal Son Rebutted," ibid., 11-13. Reactions to these articles indicated that the church did not readily accept the idea that Ellen White's theological understanding evolved significantly over the years.

35   Ellen G. White, *This Day with God* (Washington, D.C.: RHPA, 1979), 76. Cf. idem, *Testimonies,* 5:686. "She, herself, was willing to change her views in the light of increased understanding, as in the case of the 'shut door' idea. There was, in this sense, an openness in her theology" (Graham, *Ellen G. White,* 415).

Doctrinal Readjustments and Revisions

George R. Knight has distinguished "three distinct types" of change in Ellen White's writings relating to matters of doctrine and lifestyle. The first involved the "clarification" of vaguely or, perhaps, implicitly held views; in other words, "a change from ambiguity to clarity." The second type refers to the "progressive development" of new positions or changing emphases on doctrinal and other questions. Such change was progressive, not contradictory, in nature and happened "against the background of the ongoing development of present truth."[36]

According to Knight, some changes in the writings of Ellen White even came by "contradiction, or reversal, of her earlier position." This happened, for example, with "Ellen White's changing belief in the shut door" which also involved certain "contradictory aspects," for "her later understanding contradicted that of her earliest years in the post-1844 period." In other words, "Ellen White was capable of both believing error and growing in her understanding" of truth (ibid.).

Examples of Ellen White's Participation in Doctrinal Change

The following incidents of doctrinal change directly involving Ellen White may, from today's perspective, be considered rather insignificant. It should be kept in mind, however, that most of them were, at one time or another, live and, in fact, hot issues among Seventh-day Adventists. These examples illustrate the participation of Ellen White in the doctrinal growth and development of her church.

The Shut-Door Doctrine

For decades, Seventh-day Adventists and their critics were engaged in strong debates over the question of whether or not the Sabbatarian Adventists and, particularly, Ellen White had actually taught this doctrine in the years following the great disappointment. Until recently, apologists and polemicists were at a deadlock as neither side seemed able or willing to recognize the other half of the historical truth. While most Adventist writers denied that Ellen White's visions supported the "shut-door" doctrine, critics accused the church of suppressing the historical truth about the prophet's involvement in this alleged heresy.

Today the issue has been largely settled as both sides have come to see the possibility, if not accuracy, of a mediating view which this writer has presented in 1978.[37] After an exhaustive study of the sources, I then came to the conclusion that

---

36 Knight, "Adventists and Change," 12-13.
37 Robert W. Olson to Rolf J. Pöhler, 8 November 1978, and 19 October 1979; Ingemar Lindén to Rolf J. Pöhler, 7 November 1979, and 16 January 1980 (all letters in my possession); and Brinsmead, *1844 Re-Examined,* 43. See also Rolf J. Pöhler, "Adventism and 1844: Shut Door or Open Mind?" *Spectrum* 19:1 (1988): 58-60.

it is undeniable that EGW was not detached from the time and place in which she lived. Performing her ministry predominantly among those Millerites who had come to accept Turner's mercy-limiting shut-door doctrine, she apparently shared many of their ideas, though she seems to have been very sensitive to the excesses that occurred among them. It is an incontrovertible fact that for years EGW firmly believed that the parable of Mt 25 had been fulfilled – including the shutting of the door. And while it is true that this view was essentially an expression of faith in the Seventh Month movement and the salvation-historical significance of the October date, it is also true that this position had some rather inevitable soteriological implications. (This is confirmed by the fact that not long after the SDA pioneers abandoned their erroneous shut-door notion they also revised their interpretation of Matt 25 by declaring the "door" to be yet wide open.)

The way in which EGW expressed herself during those early years clearly shows that, in her view, the world and the churches were irrevocably excluded from divine mercy; and, though she never taught that only Millerites could be saved, she did not call for efforts on behalf of "sinners" but only for "honest souls." The close relationship between language and thought does not allow us to ignore the terminological changes that occurred in the writings of EGW after the crucial year 1851 ...

That the realization of the inaccuracies in the shut-door view of the SDA pioneers did also involve EGW herself seems clear from a careful investigation of the passages that were deleted in her first book in 1851. Since some of her previous statements no longer accurately expressed the mind of EGW, it was thought best to simply omit them. Whether or not this decision was the best possible one to take, it is clearly an unfair exaggeration to speak of a dishonest cover-up and of suppression, for this ignores the missiological situation of the group which apparently provided the main rationale for the deletions.[38]

In 1981, Robert W. Olson suggested that Ellen White may have "misinterpreted" her visions along "shut-door" conceptions. Apart from the hermeneutical difficulties accruing from such a view,[39] it does recognize "a fundamental change" in Ellen White's understanding of the parable of Matt 25. "Progressive revelation on God's part had been accompanied by progressive understanding on Ellen White's part."[40]

---

38   Rolf J. Pöhler, "'... And the Door Was Shut.' Seventh-day Adventists and the Shut-Door Doctrine in the Decade after the Great Disappointment, 1978," TMs, AHC, JWL, AU, Berrien Springs, Mich., 152-154. See also Ingemar Lindén, *1844 and the Shut Door Problem,* Acta Universitatis Upsaliensis, Studia Historico-Ecclesiastica Upsaliensis, vol. 35 (Uppsala: By the Author, 1982); Robert W. Olson, *"The 'Shut Door' Documents"* (Washington, D.C., Ellen G. White Estate, 1982); Borge Schantz, "The 'Shut Door' – A Providential Opening?" *AR,* 29 January 1987, 18-19; Ford, *Daniel 8:14, the Day of Atonement, and the Investigative Judgment,* 350-363; Patrick, "Does Our Past Embarrass Us?"; Knight, *Millennial Fever and the End of the World,* 233-242, 313; and idem, *Anticipating the Advent: A Brief History of Seventh-day Adventists* (Boise, Idaho: PPPA, 1993), 37-39, 51-54, 81.

39   To say that Ellen White misunderstood some of her visions requires an objective knowledge of what this vision actually meant. This, however, may place the interpreter above and, in a sense, even against the author's own ("literal") understanding of it. In any event, Olson's suggestion implies some divergence between the original and the later meaning of such visions as understood by the prophet herself.

40   Olson, *One Hundred and One Questions on the Sanctuary and on Ellen White,* 57-61.

The Garments of the High Priest

During the same early years, Sabbatarian Adventists also assumed that, on the day of atonement, the Jewish high priest wore his "gorgeous pontifical robes" (Exod 28:40-42; 39:27-29) instead of the "plain, white linen garment" of the common priest (Lev 16:4). Using the typological approach, they concluded that, in 1844, Christ had entered the most holy place of the heavenly sanctuary wearing the "breastplate of judgment" on which were written the names of those (only) for whom mercy was still available.[41]

With her fellow believers, Ellen White assumed that the high priest was wearing his precious garments on the Day of Atonement. During the "shut-door" period, this view provided the assurance that Jesus was still officiating as priest in the heavenly sanctuary for his people, though no longer for the world at large.[42] When Seventh-day Adventists realized that they had been mistaken regarding the Jewish high priest,[43] Ellen White, too, came to accept the idea that the high priest *laid off* his precious garments on the Day of Atonement. Now she understood this act as a typical fore-shadowing of Christ's self-humiliation during the incarnation.[44]

The Two-Horned Beast

Ellen White also shared the original Adventist understanding of Rev 13:11-18, which applied the apocalyptic symbol of the "two-horned beast" to the Protestant churches of the day.[45] This is clear from several visions she had at the time.[46] When Andrews

41 Crosier, "The Law of Moses," 40; and G. W. Peavey, "'The Hour of His Judgment Is Come,'" 113-115. This view was accepted by the Sabbatarians and can be found in the writings of Bates, Edson, Arnold, Uriah Smith, and James White. See also above, p. 181, n. 266.

42 Ellen White, *Early Writings*, 36, 55, 251, 280-281; and idem, *Testimonies*, 2:190, 691; 5:690; 8:315.

43 J. N. Loughborough, "Thoughts on the Day of Atonement," *RH*, 15 August 1865, 81-83; Uriah Smith, *The Visions of Mrs. E. G. White* (Battle Creek, Mich.: SDAPA, 1868), 121-122; and M. L. Andreasen, "The High Priest's Garments: Which Kind Was Worn on the Day of Atonement?" *Ministry*, February 1939, 23-26.

44 Ellen White, *DA*, 25; cf. idem, *Acts of the Apostles* (Mountain View, Calif.: PPPA, 1911), 33. Richard M. Davidson has argued that there is "complete harmony" between the Bible and Ellen White's view. He maintained that the Jewish high priests only exchanged the simple "white linen" for the "fine linen" coat and breeches but continued to wear the breastplate, the apron (ephod), and the upper garment – all made of "fine linen" – on the day of atonement ("The Robes of the High Priest, 1991," TMs, EGWRC, AU, Berrien Springs, Mich.). However, the biblical evidence does not appear as clear-cut as he assumed; besides, what use would there be in merely changing one's underclothing, while still wearing the same "gorgeous pontifical robes" visible to all?

45 See above, pp. 166-167.

46 Ellen White, A Vision, Broadside, 7 April 1847 ["I saw that the number of the Image Beast (666) was made up"]; and idem, Manuscript, 23 October 1850. From 1931 to 1987, it was located in the Apocryphal file; a comparison with other 1850 manuscripts by Ellen White

advanced the new interpretation, relating the "two-horned beast" to the United States, Ellen White likewise adopted it.[47]

The Pre-Advent Judgment

Together with her husband, Ellen White had originally contested Bates's teaching on a present judgment of the dead.[48] However, she came to see the mediatorial work of Christ in the heavenly sanctuary as a time of judgment on believers waiting for the return of their Lord.[49] When the doctrine of the "investigative judgment," according to which the heavenly court investigates the life records of the dead saints to be followed by judicial proceedings on the living ones, was developed in the mid-1850s, Ellen White with all other Sabbath-keeping Adventists also accepted it.

The Law in Galatians

Around 1850, Sabbatarian Adventists seem to have believed that the law in Galatians referred to or, at least, included the moral law.[50] In 1854, J. H. Waggoner promoted the idea that the law in Galatians referred not to the ceremonial but only to the moral law (Decalogue).[51] Another Adventist, Stephen Pierce, disagreed with him,

(e.g., #9, 12, 14, 15, 1850) indicates, however, that it contains a genuine text. In part it reads: "Then the Catholics bid the Protestants to go forward and issue a [death] decree ... The Catholics will give their power to the image of the beast and then Protestants will work ... to destroy the saints." Cf. also idem, Vision of 27 June 1850 (in *EW,* 64-67).

47 See also Ellen White, *The Great Controversy,* 439-450.

48 See above, pp. 175-180. See also Ellen White, To Those Who Are Receiving the Seal of the Living God ("the wrath of God" and "the time to judge the dead" could not come "until Jesus had finished his work in the most holy place"); and idem, "Dear Brethren and Sisters," *Present Truth,* November 1850, 86-87 (opposing Bates's idea that the saints will "execute the judgment written" when Jesus leaves the Sanctuary).

49 Ellen White, Manuscript 1, 1852 ("the sins of Israel must go to judgment beforehand. Every sin must be confessed at the sanctuary"). Already in January 1849, Ellen White had remarked that "Jesus would not leave the most holy place until every case was decided either for salvation or destruction" *(EW,* 36). However, the context indicates that these judicial decisions would involve not the dead (wicked or saints) but the living saints ("Israel"). Their names (only), it was commonly held, had been borne by Jesus on his "breastplate" into the sanctuary. White did not speak, at the time, about heavenly court investigations of the life records of all believers but rather of the continuing priestly intercession of Christ on behalf of his living, sinful people.

50 J. N. Andrews, "Discourse with Brother Carver," *RH,* 16 September 1851, 28; and idem, "Watchman, What of the Night?" *RH,* 27 May 1852, 15. "In the early history of the work, it is probable that quite a majority of [the leading brethren] accepted the view that the moral law was the main subject of Paul's consideration in the book of Galatians" (Butler, *The Law in the Book of Galatians,* 3).

51 J. H. Waggoner, "The Law of God," *RH,* 18 July 1854, 185-186; cf. idem, *The Law of God* (Rochester, N.Y.: Advent Review Office, 1854), 69-83, 108.

maintaining that the "schoolmaster" referred to in Gal 3:24 had reference not to the moral law but to the old covenant "dispensation" with its entire "law-system."[52]

As Uriah Smith recalled quite distinctly, White rejected Waggoner's position.[53] No contemporary record of this episode has survived, but Waggoner's book was withdrawn, and the view that the law in Galatians did not include the moral law but rather denoted the ceremonial law became the accepted Adventist belief.[54]

Beginning in 1884, E. J. Waggoner (son of J. H. Waggoner) again publicly promoted the idea that the law in Galatians had reference not to the ceremonial law but exclusively to the moral law of the Decalogue.[55] Convinced that Waggoner had abandoned a "landmark" doctrine and, thus, threatened the very *raison d'être* of the Adventist church, General Conference president George I. Butler, Uriah Smith, and others vigorously opposed the "new view" through books, articles, and public debates. To them, it was clearly contrary to "the settled view of the body, according to the Scriptures, confirmed by the Spirit of Prophecy, as long ago as 1856."[56]

Butler wrote a long rebuttal of Waggoner's view on the law and had it distributed to the delegates at the 1886 General Conference.[57] However, he could not get them to clearly condemn the "new view" as he had hoped. The issue surfaced again in 1888 when it was hotly debated at the General Conference in Minneapolis.

---

52   Stephen Pierce, "Answer to Bro. Merriam's Question Respecting the Law of Gal. iii, in Review No. 3, Vol. X," *RH,* 8 October 1857, 180-181.

53   Uriah Smith to W. A. McCutchen, 8 August 1901: "Sister White shortly after this had a vision in which this law question was shown her, and she immediately wrote J. H. W. that his position on the law was wrong, and Bro. Pierce was right" (quoted in *Manuscripts and Memoirs of Minneapolis,* 305-306). In a letter to Ellen White, Smith stated that "[E. J. Waggoner] took his position on Galatians, the same which you had condemned in his father ... You *saw* that his position was wrong. And there was only the one issue then under examination: namely, whether the law in Galatians was the ten commandments as Bro. Waggoner claimed, or was the Mosaic law system as Bro. Pierce claimed ... That was the only point then at issue; and on that you said that Bro. Waggoner was wrong" (17 February 1890).

54   See Tim Crosby, "The Law and the Prophet," *AR,* 8 May 1986, 13, n. 5.

55   E. J. Waggoner, "Under the Law," *ST,* 11 September 1884, 553-554; and idem, *The Gospel in the Book of Galatians* (1888), 17, 21, 22, 43. It was particularly a series of articles on this topic in the *Signs of the Times* (8 July-2 September 1886) that drew much criticism from fellow believers. See also above, pp. 228-230.

56   Uriah Smith to A. T. Robinson, 21 September 1892. "Those who stood ... for the old position regarding the law in Galatians, argued long and loud that it would be very detrimental to our work to change our position ... They believed that the old positions had been sanctioned by the Testimonies, and to make a change would unsettle the confidence of our people everywhere in the Testimonies; and this, they regarded as the most serious feature of the whole question" (W. C. White to P. T. Magan, 31 July 1910; quoted in Haloviak, "From Righteousness to Holy Flesh," chap. 9, p. 7).

57   Butler, *The Law in the Book of Galatians.* "Perhaps there has never been a theological question in all the history of our work concerning which there has been so much disagreement among our ministry and leading brethren as this." In Butler's own estimate, "at least two thirds of our ministers" agreed with his position (ibid., 3).

Ellen White realized that the "new view" was not in full harmony with her own previous thought and teaching.[58] Still, to the surprise and chagrin of many of her brethren, she refused to condemn Waggoner and Jones, who supported it, for their new interpretation. Instead, she called for a serious restudy of the issue on biblical grounds, apparently being willing to change her own mind on the question, if need be.[59] Besides, the whole issue appeared to her as a rather unimportant sideline, not deserving the heat it was generating in the church at the time. Wrote she in 1888,

> There is precious light in what [E. J. Waggoner] has said. Some things presented in reference to the Law in Galatians, if I fully understand his position, do not harmonize with the understanding I have had on this subject; but the truth will lose nothing by investigation ... The fact that he honestly holds some views of the Scriptures differing from yours or mine is no reason why we should treat him as an offender, or a dangerous man, and make him the subject of unjust criticism.[60]

> I have not changed my views in reference to the law in Galatians, but ... will not the truth bear to be investigated? Will it totter and fall, if criticized? If so let it fall, the sooner the better. The spirit that would close the door to investigation of points of truth in a Christlike manner is not the spirit from above.[61]

A few years later, while not endorsing Waggoner's either-or position, Ellen White indicated that she clearly leaned towards his interpretation on the law in Galatians.[62] But she refused to limit the application of Gal 3:24 to any particular part of the law of God. To her, valid use could be made of the passage in different ways.[63]

58 In a letter to Waggoner and Jones, Ellen White stated that she had been looking in vain for an article she had "read" to J. H. Waggoner "nearly twenty years ago" regarding the "added law." She recalled "being shown" that "his position in regard to the law was incorrect." However, in her judgment "these questions are not vital points" (Ellen G. White to E. J. Waggoner and A. T. Jones, 18 February 1887; in *The Ellen G. White 1888 Materials,* 21-31).

59 On Ellen White's role vis-à-vis the traditionalists in 1888, see Knight, *Angry Saints,* 104-111. "She never held [her writings] up as a divine commentary on scripture ... nor did she quote her own writings at Minneapolis to decide any of the theological, historical, or biblical issues. Her writings had their purposes, but one of them was apparently not to take a superordinate position to the Bible by providing an infallible commentary" (ibid., 107-108).

60 Ellen G. White, Manuscript 15, 1888; in *The Ellen G. White 1888 Materials,* 163-175. See also idem, *SM,* 3:173-175: "When I plainly stated my faith there were many who did not understand me and they reported that Sister White had changed."

61 Ellen G. White to W. M. Healey, 9 December 1888, in *The Ellen G. White 1888 Materials,* 186-189. She also wrote: "There are errors in the church, and the Lord points them out by His own ordained agencies, not always through the testimonies" (Ellen G. White to Bro. and Sr. Garmire, August 1890, in *The Ellen G. White 1888 Materials,* 697-702).

62 "In this Scripture [Gal 3:24] the Holy Ghost through the apostle is speaking especially of the moral law" (Ellen G. White to Uriah Smith, 6 June 1896; in *SM,* 1:234). See also idem, *SM,* 1:211-215, 340-344; and idem, *DA,* 308.

63 "I am asked concerning the law in Galatians. What is the schoolmaster to bring us to Christ? I answer: Both the ceremonial and the moral code of the ten commandments" (Ellen G. White, Manuscript 87, 1900; in *SM,* 1:233).

Describing this episode in some detail, Tim Crosby concluded that there was "an evolution in Ellen White's understanding of the law in Galatians." In time, she realized "that her previous understanding was incomplete." To Crosby, this incident reveals "how even an inspired prophet must sometimes struggle with a theological issue before achieving full understanding."[64]

"The Daily"

Around the turn of the century, Seventh-day Adventists came to disagree sharply on the meaning of the "daily,"[65] spoken of in relation to the "little horn" power in Daniel (Dan 8:11-13; 11:31; 12:11). Some were particularly adamant to any new view on this question because, to them, it appeared that Ellen White had already settled this issue once and for all.

Among the Millerites, three different positions had been taken on the "daily." Miller himself as well as most of his followers believed that it referred to "the daily sacrifice abomination" of paganism which had been replaced by the papacy.[66] Some years earlier, he had assumed that the "daily sacrifice" referred to "the typical priesthood," i.e., to the Jewish sacrificial system.[67] A few Millerites thought that it referred to the continual mediation of Christ in heaven which was taken away by the papal "horn" power.[68] This position was defended also in 1847 by O. R. L. Crosier.[69] However, it was Miller's "pagan" view which became the accepted SDA teaching.[70]

On the basis of a vision she had on September 23, 1850, Ellen White made a brief public remark on the "daily."

64   Tim Crosby, "The Law and the Prophet," 12-13; idem, "Using the Law to No Profit," *AR*, 15 May 1986, 12-13; idem, "The Law of the Prophet," *AR*, 22 May 1986, 12-13; and idem, "A Law without Profit," *AR*, 29 May 1986, 9-10. See also Arthur L. White, *Ellen G. White*, 3:385-415.

65   See above, pp. 232-233. This incident is discussed by L. E. Froom, "Historical Setting and Background of the Term 'Daily,' 1940," TMs, AHC, JWL, AU, Berrien Springs, Mich.; Schwarz, *Light Bearers to the Remnant*, 396-399; Haloviak, "In the Shadow of the 'Daily'"; idem, "Pioneers, Pantheists, and Progressives," 36-47; Larry J. Hall, "The Daily of Dan 8:11-13: An Historical Look at the Millerite View, 1986," TMs, AHC, JWL, AU, Berrien Springs, Mich.; Arthur L. White, *Ellen G. White*, 6:246-261; and Valentine, *The Shaping of Adventism*, 185-203.

66   William Miller, *Evidences from Scripture and History of the Second Coming of Christ About the Year 1843, Exhibited in a Course of Lectures* (Troy, [N.Y.]: n.p., 1836), 50-51.

67   William Miller, *Evidences from Scripture and History of the Second Coming of Christ About the Year A.D. 1843, and of His Personal Reign of 1000 Years* (Brandon, Vt.: Vermont Telegraph Office, 1833), 15.

68   "The Daily," *Midnight Cry*, 4 October 1843, 52.

69   O. R. L. Crosier, "Remarks to Weston," *Day-Dawn*, 19 March 1847, 2. On the Millerite view of the "daily," see also Damsteegt, *Foundations of the Seventh-day Adventist Message and Mission*, 22, 32-33, 38, 58-59, 65-69, 73, 75, 126.

70   See, e.g., [Uriah Smith], "The Sanctuary – An Objection Considered," *RH*, 1 November 1864, 180-181.

Then I saw in relation to the "daily" (Dan 8:12) that the word "sacrifice" was supplied by man's wisdom, and does not belong to the text, and that the Lord gave the correct view of it to those who gave the judgment hour cry. When union existed, before 1844, nearly all were united on the correct view of the "daily"; but in the confusion since 1844, other views have been embraced, and darkness and confusion have followed.[71]

From this statement it appears that Ellen White supported the "pagan" view of the "daily" against those who attempted to revive the "Jewish" interpretation. The immediate context of this vision as well as certain ideas existing among post-disappointment Millerites suggest that this "Jewish" view was related to particular notions regarding the return of (literal and spiritual) Jews to Palestine, the possible rebuilding of the temple in Jerusalem, and the reinstitution of animal sacrifices in connection with it. This view came to be known among Adventists as the "age-to-come" doctrine.[72]

The controversy among Seventh-day Adventists over the "daily" broke out in 1897-98 when the "new view," which followed Crosier in relating the "daily" to the continual ministration of Christ in the heavenly sanctuary, was first hinted at, and then openly defended, by a number of leading ministers in the church.[73] Others rejected this interpretation, considering it as an attack on "the old original message and the Spirit of Prophecy."[74] In this way, what might otherwise have been regarded as an insignificant issue turned into a prolonged and heated controversy, having quite a polarizing effect upon the church.[75]

71 Ellen White, "Dear Brethren and Sisters," November 1850, 87; also published in *EW,* 74.
72 For a detailed analysis of this teaching in its bearing on Seventh-day Adventists, see the meticulous study by Julia Neuffer, *The Gathering of Israel* (Washington, D.C.: General Conference of SDA, Biblical Research Committee, [n.d.]). It should be noted that in rejecting the "Jewish" view of the "daily" and in supporting the "pagan" interpretation, White had not explicitly denied the "Christian" version of it. However, later readers who were unaware of the original thrust of this statement used it as a "proof text" for their own view.
73 See G. E. Fifield, "Cleansing of the Sanctuary," *RH,* 21 September 1897, 594. L. R. Conradi seems to have been the first prominent defender of this view. He was supported by W. W. Prescott, E. J. Waggoner, and soon also by E. S. Ballenger, A. T. Jones, J. H. Kellogg, F. M. Wilcox, W. C. White, A. G. Daniells, and others.
74 Washburn, *The Startling Omega,* 5. To say that the writings of Ellen White contained any "imperfect statements" and that her views were "changeable" to some degree was regarded as "Higher Criticism" pronouncing and denouncing these writings as "utterly unreliable" (Washburn, *An Open Letter,* 11-14). "This new view of 'the daily,' therefore, squarely contradicts the Spirit of Prophecy." For, inasmuch as "the church of God has always had an infallible interpreter of the Word of God," Ellen White's inspired comment "settles forever" the correct interpretation of the daily. "That a view contradicts the Spirit of Prophecy should, we think, be sufficient condemnation of it in the minds of all Seventh-day Adventists to cause them to drop it at the start" (Smith and Gilbert, "*The Daily" in the Prophecy of Daniel,* 3, 13-17, 23-24, 29). See also Washburn, *The Fruit of the "New Daily."*
75 The debate on the "daily" reached its peak early in the 20th century when the question was publicly discussed at the 1909 General Conference and the "new view" was denounced by Butler and others as a most dangerous "heresy" and "innovation" (George I. Butler to Ellen

Ellen White, for her part, seemed rather unimpressed by the agitation over the "daily." She considered the matter as being of only minor significance and unworthy of a doctrinal dispute. As long as the issue was not publicly debated in a controversial way, a diversity of viewpoints could well be tolerated in the church. Moreover, she was opposed to the use of her writings as an argument in the debate.[76]

Apparently, Ellen White allowed for corrections and changes in doctrinal matters that did not involve teachings essential to the identity of the Seventh-day Adventist Church. However, even after her death, some Adventists considered the "new view" on the "daily" a "deadly heresy" reflecting "unbelief of the Testimonies and actual infidelity."[77] By this, they may have provided a doubtful service to the prophet whose position on doctrinal development was obviously more progressive than some of her ardent defenders could imagine.[78]

The Apocrypha

Last to be mentioned, there is an incident involving a minor *hermeneutical* reorientation on the part of Ellen White and her fellow Adventists.[79]

In the 1840s, Sabbath-keeping Adventists held the Apocrypha in very high regard. Not only did they cite them,[80] they also appeared to regard them as inspired, if not canonical writings.[81] As late as 1871, Canright considered them, at least partly, inspired.[82] However, by 1878, he had come to the conviction that there were "many

White, 3 July 1910). Leon A. Smith and F. C. Gilbert wrote a pamphlet against the "new view" ("The Daily" in the Prophecy of Daniel [about 1910]). Among those opposed to the "new view" were such well-known men as J. N. Loughborough, S. N. Haskell, G. I. Irwin, E. E. Andross, O. A. Johnson, G. B. Starr, I. H. Evans, J. S. Washburn, C. Holmes, and physician D. H. Kress.

76   See Ellen White, *SM*, 1:164-168.

77   Washburn, *The Startling Omega and Its True Genealogy* (1920).

78   Valentine closes his excellent analysis of the theological controversy over "the daily" with the following remark: "'The daily' conflict illustrates perhaps that change in a church's thinking is achieved more by the passing away of a generation than it is by the present generation accepting the change. This 'storm in a teacup' thus highlights the point that conflict is inevitable whenever change is proposed in the area of religion. It also illustrates the fact that, despite taking precaution and waiting for the proper time, there is probably never a time when a church is 'ready' for change" (*The Shaping of Adventism*, 202).

79   See Ron Graybill, "Under the Triple Eagle: Early Adventist Use of the Apocrypha," *Adventist Heritage* 12:1 (1987): 25-32, for details.

80   [James and Ellen White], *A Word to the "Little Flock,"* 13-22.

81   Ibid. See also Bates, *The Opening Heavens*, 5; idem, *A Seal of the Living God*, 66; and J. H. Waggoner, "The Eagle of 2 Esdras XI," *RH*, 5 November 1861, 183. The Apocrypha were advertised in the *Review and Herald* in 1851 (2 June 1851, 96; and 5 August 1851, 8) and even as late as 1869 and were studied because of their familiar apocalyptic symbols. Many English Bibles contained the Apocrypha, including that in the home of the Harmon family which Ellen once held aloft in vision.

82   D. M. Canright, "2 Esdras 2," *RH*, 8 August 1871, 58.

and good reasons" to "reject" the Apocrypha.[83] In the 1880s and 1890s, this became the common and later also the official Adventist position.[84]

Apparently, Ellen White shared the view of the Sabbatarian Adventists. In a vision she had on September 23, 1849, she deplored the increasing neglect of the Apocrypha among Christians in general and exhorted Sabbath-keeping Adventists to carefully study them.[85] Four months later, another vision reaffirmed this view, but also seems to have distinguished the Apocrypha from the canonical Scriptures.[86] Later, however, Ellen White never seems to have referred to them again as being prophetic writings of special importance to the church.

Ellen White's Concept of Doctrinal Development

More than any other of the Adventist pioneers, Ellen White in her writings directly addressed the problem of doctrinal continuity and change. Her remarks were scattered through the years but are partly collected in several books compiled from her writings.[87] To date, her views on this issue have rarely been analyzed,[88] though some well-known statements are frequently quoted.[89]

83   D. M. Canright, *The Bible from Heaven* (Battle Creek, Mich.: SDAPA, 1878), 183-188. Cf. G. W. Morse, "Scripture Questions," *RH,* 21 June 1887, 394.

84   See *SDAE,* 1976 ed., s.v. "Apocrypha."

85   Ellen White, Manuscript 5, 1849. That she herself had done so is suggested by the visions published in *A Word to the "Little Flock"* to which James White had added a number of "scripture references" alluded to in these visions – including some from the Apocrypha.

86   "I saw that the Apocrypha was the hidden book, and that the wise of these last days should understand it. I saw that the Bible was the standard book, that will judge us at the last day" (Ellen G. White, Manuscript 4, 1850 [26-28 January 1850], EGWRC, AU, Berrien Springs, Mich.). On the allusion to a "hidden book," see 2 Esdras 8:37-38.

87   See Ellen G. White, *Counsels to Writers and Editors* (Nashville: SPA, 1946), 28-54; idem, *EW,* 258-261; idem, *SG,* 1:168-173; idem, *SM,* 1:160-162, 185-191, 201-208, 383-388, 401-405, 406-416; ibid., 2:387-391; idem, *Testimonies to Ministers and Gospel Workers* (Mountain View, Calif.: PPPA, 1923/1962), 24-32, 105-111; idem, *Gospel Workers* (Washington, D.C.: RHPA, 1948), 297-310; idem, *COL,* 124-134; and idem, *Testimonies,* 5:698-711. See also Arthur L. White, *Ellen G. White,* 5:398-428. The following summary outline is based mainly on her published writings; references to books give only the abbreviated titles of her works, immediately followed by the respective page numbers.

88   See, e.g., Richard Hammill, "Ellen White and Change," *AR,* 13 January 1983, 6-8; and Damsteegt, "Seventh-day Adventist Doctrines and Progressive Revelation," 83-92.

89   This section offers only a preliminary survey of Ellen White's concept of doctrinal continuity and change, based on statements she made during her long life and ministry. Of course, such a synthesis should be derived from, and supported by, a careful historical analysis, which interprets the different and, at times, apparently conflicting statements of Ellen White in their proper historical and literary setting. Only in this way can their exact meaning and point of reference be determined adequately. This, however, requires an elaborate contextual study of its own, which cannot be presented here. In spite of the obvious methodological shortcomings of this brief survey, it summarizes what, to me, appears to be Ellen White's basic and dialectic approach to the issue of doctrinal development.

The Twofold Nature of Truth

In Ellen White's view, truth is "eternal"[90] and, therefore, "changeless" and "immovable."[91] At the same time, it is "infinite"[92] and "inexhaustible"[93] and, consequently, ever "expanding" and "developing"[94] as well as "unfolding"[95] in its meaning.[96] Because of this "progressive"[97] and "advancing"[98] nature of truth, the church should experience a "continual advancement in the knowledge of the truth."[99] While the church is to teach the "fundamental truths" of the Scriptures,[100] it must also proclaim "present truth," i.e., "doctrines"[101] fit for the times and embracing "the whole gospel."[102] The third angel's message will achieve its purpose, it is "infallible."[103] Its "consistent"[104] and "harmonious"[105] teachings must be "apprehended by the intellect,"[106] for "our faith is not in [subjective] feeling, but in [objective] truth."[107]

The Dialectic between Continuity and Change

According to Ellen White, Seventh-day Adventists must ever remain open and receptive to "new light."[108] Such increasing insight into truth usually will be in

90   *TM* 107, *CWE* 44.
91   *T* 2:490, *T* 4:595, *CWE* 31, *SM* 2:87.
92   "The truth of God is infinite, capable of measureless expansion" (*FE* 196).
93   "Christ is the inexhaustible wellspring of truth" (*T* 7:276). Cf. *COL* 128-134, which points to the incomprehensible and inexhaustible mystery of truth as the decisive, underlying reason for doctrinal growth. See also *T* 5:698-711 for an impressive elaboration of this theme. Here White shown a remarkable depth of insight not generally reached even by trained theologians.
94   *SM* 1:188.
95   *T* 5:703; cf. Ellen G. White, *Medical Ministry* (Mountain View, Calif.: PPPA, 1932/1963), 187.
96   Ellen G. White, *Counsels to Parents, Teachers, and Students Regarding Christian Education* (Mountain View, Calif.: PPPA, 1913/1943), 463. "The meaning of these truths flashed upon their minds as a new revelation" (*AA* 520).
97   *GC* 297, *SDABC* 2:1000.
98   *Ev* 297, *CWE* 33.
99   *T* 1:345; cf. *GC* 298.
100 *MM* 102, *CWE* 79.
101 *T* 2:355.
102 *T* 6:291.
103 *T* 4:495.
104 Ellen G. White, *The Story of Patriarchs and Prophets as Illustrated in the Lives of Holy Men of Old* (Mountain View, Calif.: PPPA, 1958), 114.
105 *T* 3:215, *T* 4:445.
106 *T* 5:272.
107 *SM* 2:157.
108 "We shall never reach a period when there is no increased light for us" (*SM* 1:404). "The truth of God is progressive; it is always onward, going from strength to a greater strength, from light to a greater light. We have every reason to believe that the Lord will send us

addition to previous beliefs, providing "a clearer understanding" of the word of God.[109] At times, however, "new light" will be in conflict with "our expositions of Scripture," with "long-cherished opinions" and "long-established traditions." In other words, though "new light does not contradict old light,"[110] it does collide with erroneous doctrines and our "misinterpretations of God's word."

> The God of heaven sometimes commissions men to teach that which is regarded as contrary to the established doctrines ... Seventh-day Adventists are in danger of closing their eyes to truth as it is in Jesus, because it contradicts something which they have taken for granted as truth but which the Holy Spirit teaches is not truth.[111]

> If ideas are presented that differ in some points from our former doctrines, we must not condemn them without diligent search of the Bible to see if they are true.[112]

> There are errors in the church, and the Lord points them out by His own ordained agencies, not always through the testimonies.[113]

> In closely investigating ... established truth ... we may discover errors in our interpretation of Scripture.[114]

Therefore, we need to carefully examine, candidly investigate, critically test, and constantly review our doctrines in the light of the Scriptures and must discard everything that is not clearly sustained by the Bible, however difficult this may turn out to be for us. On the other hand, satisfaction with the church's present understanding of truth, opposition to a critical and persevering examination of its teachings, avoidance of controversial doctrinal discussions, prejudice against those who present new doctrinal insights, refusal to accept newly discovered truths, and general resistance to theological change betray – according to Ellen White – a "conservative" mind-set which results from spiritual lethargy.[115] Those would-be "guardians of the doctrine" who prevent this needed reexamination for fear of removing the "old landmarks" are, in reality, hampering the cause of truth.[116]

increased truth, for a great work is yet to be done" (Ellen G. White, "Candid Investigation Necessary to an Understanding of the Truth," *ST,* 26 May 1890, 305-307).

109 "We must not for a moment think that there is no more light, no more truth, to be given us ... While we must hold fast to the truths which we have already received, we must not look with suspicion upon any new light that God may send" (*GW* 310).

110 *SM* 1:161.

111 *TM* 70-71.

112 Ellen White, "Candid Investigation Necessary to an Understanding of the Truth," 307.

113 *SM* 2:81.

114 Ellen G. White, "Treasure Hidden," *RH,* 12 July 1898, 438.

115 David Thiele has shown that "although the words *conservative* and *conservatism* occur in Ellen White's published writings some 30 times, they are always used in a negative sense" ("Is Conservatism a Heresy?" *Spectrum* 23:4 [1994]: 12-15).

116 Repeatedly, Ellen White also applied the Laodicean message to those who stood in the way of doctrinal advance. See, e.g., *SM* 1:413, and *CWE* 33, 36.

At the same time, however, the pioneers of Seventh-day Adventism have laid well the doctrinal foundation of the church under the conspicuous guidance of the Holy Spirit. These "fundamental principles" were firmly established in the early years through careful and prayerful Bible study, were confirmed by divine revelation and "based upon unquestionable authority,"[117] have "withstood test and trial" and are, therefore, unmovable, indispensable, unchangeable, and irreplaceable. No interpretations or applications of the Scriptures must be entertained that would undermine or weaken these distinctive doctrines, contradict the special points of our faith, "unsettle faith in the old landmarks," remove the pillars from their foundation, or "move a block or stir a pin" from the three angels' messages. Instead, Adventists are to preserve "the waymarks which have made us what we are," hold firmly to "the fundamental principles" of our faith, and "stand firm on the platform of eternal ["solid, immovable"] truth."[118]

At first glance, Ellen White's statements on doctrinal continuity and change appear somewhat contradictory. The seeming discrepancies are largely due, however, to the different contexts in which she was expressing herself throughout the years. During and after the 1888 General Conference, she called for openness to theological change in order to counter the reluctance of the church to accept the "new light" which Waggoner and Jones were presenting on the subject of righteousness by faith. But when the church seemed threatened by heresy and apostasy (as in the 1850s, 1880s, and 1900s), Ellen White emphasized the doctrinal continuity and identity of the Adventist faith. Thus, her seemingly conflicting statements may be seen as complementary when interpreted in their proper historical setting.

There is another, related reason that may help to explain the seeming contradiction in Ellen White's statements on doctrinal development. To her, the landmark doctrines of Seventh-day Adventism were central to the message, mission, and self-understanding of the church. Any change with regard to these foundational truths

---

117 This point is particularly emphasized in *TM* 24-25, *CWE* 28, 29, 53, and *SM* 1:160-162, 206-208. It stands in apparent tension with Ellen White's usual emphasis on the *sola scriptura* principle and her repeated refusal to let her writings serve as the interpretative norm of Scripture. For a sensible evaluation of this issue, see Graybill, "Ellen White's Role in the Resolution of Conflicts in Adventist History," 10-17.

118 By "landmarks" Ellen White meant the teachings of the Bible in general (*GC* 525, *T* 5:199, *Ev* 362) and the "fundamental principles" of the SDA faith in particular (*CWE* 52, *SM* 1:208, *SM* 2:389, *T* 7:107). She also used other expressions with synonymous meaning such as (1) "the foundations of our faith" (*SM* 1:206-207; *SM* 2:388-390; *GW* 148, 307; *T* 8:297), (2) "the pillars of our faith" (*TM* 107; *SM* 1:201, 207, 208; *SM* 2:25, 387-391; *CWE* 33, 44, 77; *Ev* 224, 610; *MM* 87, 96; *SDABC* 7:985; *T* 4:74; *T* 9:69), (3) "the platform of eternal truth" (*T* 4:17, *SM* 1:199-201, *SM* 2:388, *CWE* 52, *EW* 258-261, *TM* 29) and (4) "the waymarks of truth" (*T* 3:440; *SM* 1:208; *SM* 2:101, 110; *CWE* 52; LS 278; *Ev* 223; *GW* 103). In 1889, she identified the "old landmarks" with the three angels' messages, including the doctrine of the cleansing of the sanctuary, the teaching on the (Sabbath) law, and the belief in the non-immortality of the wicked (*CWE* 30-31). In 1905, she called them "the special points of our faith" (*CWE* 32).

tended, therefore, to jeopardize the very *raison d'être* of the church. Other teachings, however, not directly belonging to the unchangeable platform of Adventist truths were of only secondary importance. Their revision would not constitute a threat to the church. Therefore, they could be openly reinvestigated and possibly even be modified significantly.

However, it should be kept in mind that when such minor doctrinal matters were debated among Adventists, usually there was a strong tendency to see them as closely tied to the "landmarks," making their readjustment look like an attack on the fundamentals themselves. In order to remain true to Ellen White's intention, it seems important, therefore, to distinguish the core teachings of the Adventist faith from other doctrines which are related but not foundational to it.

But, in a certain sense, any authentic doctrinal development may somehow affect either the fundamental or the distinctive truths of Seventh-day Adventism in some, albeit positive, way. Otherwise, the deepening insight into truth would, in the final analysis, be irrelevant and not worth arguing or even talking about. Ellen White, for her part, held no such low view of doctrinal growth. To the contrary, to her, doctrinal advances were of crucial significance for the church.

> Much has been lost because our ministers and people have concluded that we have had all the truth essential for us as a people; but such a conclusion is erroneous and in harmony with the deceptions of Satan, for truth will be constantly unfolding.[119]

As only those doctrinal insights that, in some real sense, are related to the central beliefs of the church can be regarded as "essential," it follows that, for Ellen White, doctrinal development was not merely a superfluous or dangerous process but rather an indispensable aspect of the spiritual growth and theological maturation of the church.[120]

The Twofold Process of Doctrinal Development

An analysis of Ellen White's view on doctrinal development reveals two major aspects, which, to her, were involved in this process. They reflect the balance she was striving at between the need for substantial doctrinal continuity and the demands for authentic doctrinal change. On the one hand, truth develops through restoration and rediscovery, on the other hand, it involves reinterpretation and recontextualization.

---

119 Ellen White, "Candid Investigation Necessary to an Understanding of the Truth," 305-306.
120 Though written in the context of health reform, James White's description of the difficulty his wife was facing in leading the church to a balanced position may perhaps be recontextualized and applied to the dialectic between doctrinal continuity and change: "She makes strong appeals to the people, which a few feel deeply, and take strong positions, and go to extremes ... What she may say to urge the tardy [the conservatives], is taken by the prompt [the progressives] to urge them over the mark. And what she may say to caution the prompt, zealous, incautious ones [the progressives], is taken by the tardy [the conservatives] as an excuse to remain too far behind" ("To a Brother at Monroe, Wisc.," *RH,* 17 March 1868, 220).

Restoration and Rediscovery

For Ellen White, doctrinal development was first and foremost a process in which old truths were rediscovered and restored to the church. "There are old, yet new truths still to be added to the treasures of our knowledge."[121] What appears to be "new light" is, in reality, "precious [old] light that has for a time been lost sight of by the people."[122] After all, no doctrine must be taught in the church that cannot be shown to be "contained in God's Word."[123] But there are many "precious rays of light yet to shine forth from the word of God. Many gems are yet scattered that are to be gathered together to become the property of the remnant people of God."[124] Ellen White liked to describe this perennial task of the church in colorful language.

> Gems of thought are to be gathered up and redeemed from their companionship with error ... Truths of divine origin, are to be carefully searched out and placed in their proper setting, to shine with heavenly brilliancy amid the moral darkness of the world ... Let the gems of divine light be reset in the framework of the gospel. Let nothing be lost of the precious light that comes from the throne of God. It has been misapplied, and cast aside as worthless; but it is heaven-sent, and each gem is to become the property of God's people and find its true position in the framework of truth. Precious jewels of light are to be collected, and by the aid of the Holy Spirit they are to be fitted into the gospel system.[125]

Reinterpretation and Recontextualization

Obviously, then, there is something really new about "new light." While truth itself is eternal and unchangeable, the understanding of its meaning and the realization of its full significance may grow constantly in the church. Taking Christ as the model and norm of theological progress and doctrinal advance, Ellen White repeatedly pointed out that his work basically consisted in recontextualizing[126] and reinterpreting[127] divine revelation. New meanings resulted from placing old truths in

---

121 Ellen G. White, "Need of Earnestness in the Cause of God," *RH*, 25 February 1890, 113, 113-114.

122 *SM* 1:384; cf. ibid., 401.

123 *Ev* 214; cf. *FE* 406, and *AA* 474.

124 *CWE* 35. Ellen White also spoke of "precious jewels of truth that shall be discovered as men turn their attention to the searching of the rich mine of God's word" (ibid., 51).

125 Ellen G. White, "Truth to Be Rescued from Error," *RH*, 23 October 1894, 657. See also idem, "'Be Zealous and Repent,'" *RH Extra*, 23 December 1890, 1-2.

126 "He did not make new revelations to men, but opened to their understanding truths that had long been obscured or misplaced through false teaching of the priests and teachers. Jesus replaced the gems of divine truth in their proper setting, in the order in which they had been given to patriarchs and prophets" (*SM* 1:187). See also *T* 5:710, *DA* 287-288, and *SDABC* 5:1136.

127 "The great themes of the Old Testament were misapprehended and misinterpreted, and Christ's work was to expound the truth which had not been understood by those to whom they had been given ... They did not see the meaning of the truth" (*SM* 1:404).

different and proper settings.[128] "Though His doctrine seemed new to the people, it was in fact not a new doctrine, but the revelation of the significance of that which had been taught from the beginning."[129]

In other words, the true significance of Bible doctrines can, at times, only be seen when they are related to new scriptural contexts or changing situations which make these old truths possibly appear in a different and new light.[130] Correcting misinterpretations of the Bible and properly reinterpreting old truths, new doctrinal insights reveal new facets and the true import of divine revelation.[131]

> Great truths which have been neglected and unappreciated for ages, will be revealed by the Spirit of God, and new meaning will flash out of familiar texts. Every page will be illuminated by the Spirit of truth.[132]

> When the mind is kept open and is constantly searching the field of revelation, we shall find rich deposits of truth. Old truths will be revealed in new aspects, and truths will appear which have been overlooked in the search.[133]

> Some things must be torn down. Some things must be built up. The old treasures must be reset in the framework of truth ... Jesus will reveal to us precious old truths in a new light, if we are ready to receive them.[134]

Summary and Conclusion

Ellen White exerted a significant influence on the development of the Seventh-day Adventist doctrinal edifice, being actively involved in the formation, preservation, and revision of the teachings of the church. In addition, she herself participated in various types of theological change, encompassing not only theological maturation and doctrinal growth but, at times, even doctrinal readjustments and revisions. To a considerable degree, she shared in and fostered the process of theological growth and doctrinal development that the Seventh-day Adventist Church experienced during her lifetime.

---

128 "Christ in His teaching presented old truths ... but He now shed upon them a new light. How different appeared their meaning!" (*COL* 127; cf. ibid., 124-134).

129 *SDABC* 5:1089; cf. *DA* 279.

130 "There is yet much precious truth to be revealed to the people in this time of peril and darkness ... Precious truths that have long been in obscurity are to be revealed ... [so that the word of God] may appear in a light in which we have never before beheld it" (Ellen G. White, *Counsels on Sabbath School Work* [Washington, D.C.: RHPA, 1938], 25). "In Minneapolis God gave precious gems of truth to his people in new settings" (*CWE* 30).

131 "The old truths will be presented, but they will be seen in a new light. There will be a new perception of truth" (*COL* 130).

132 *CSW* 35.

133 Ellen G. White, Manuscript 75, 1897, EGWRC, AU, Berrien Springs, Mich.

134 Ellen G. White, "Minneapolis Talks," 88-89; quoted in Ford, *Daniel 8:14, the Day of Atonement, and the Investigative Judgment*, 347. See also *SM* 1:355, 409.

At the same time, Ellen White's concept of doctrinal development appears to have surpassed that of her fellow believers not only in terms of its depth of under-standing but also in striking a careful balance between the need for theological continuity and substantial identity, on the one hand, and the possibility of theological revisions and doctrinal changes, on the other. Tirelessly, she warned her church against both the careless rejection of precious "old light" and the stubborn resistance to much-needed "new light."

This concept can still provide guidance for the church faced by the perennial dangers of theological immobilism and doctrinal revisionism. Adventists may do well to emulate the example of their prophetess who served both as a strong factor of doctrinal continuity and a constant catalyst of doctrinal change. Her concept of doctrinal development is perhaps best expressed in the following quotation which is worth pondering for its rich implications.

> [Christ] promised that the Holy Spirit should enlighten the disciples, that the word of God should be ever unfolding to them ... The truths of redemption are capable of constant development and expansion. Though old, they are ever new, constantly revealing to the seeker for truth a greater glory and a mightier power.

> In every age there is a new development of truth, a message of God to the people of that generation. The old truths are all essential; new truth is not independent of the old, but an unfolding of it. It is only as the old truths are understood that we can comprehend the new ... But it is the light which shines in the fresh unfolding of truth that glorifies the old. He who rejects or neglects the new does not really possess the old. To him it loses its vital power and becomes but a lifeless form.[135]

135 *COL* 127-128.

Summary and Conclusion

> True fidelity to the past includes a readiness to move forward,
> inspired by the example of our predecessors.
>
> *Avery Dulles*

> We have nothing to fear for the future, except as we shall forget
> the way the Lord has led us, and His teaching in our past
> history.
>
> *Ellen G. White*

As this study has demonstrated, Adventists have experienced a number of noteworthy doctrinal changes over the years (chapter 4). Distinct theological developments can likewise be found in the writings of Ellen White, the Adventist prophet (chapter 6).[1] This study also shows how difficult it proved for Adventists to fully recognize these facts and to come to an adequate understanding of doctrinal development. Traditionally, the church has tended to regard doctrinal change as a threat to its own particular message, mission, and self-understanding, rather than as an opportunity for genuine growth and constructive theological development (chapter 5).[2]

It appears that Adventist theology finds itself in a dilemma similar to that confronting virtually all Christian churches (chapter 1). The answers Adventists have given to the perplexing question of doctrinal change likewise correspond rather closely to the various conceptual models that were developed in the history of Christianity (chapter 2). In fact, there seem to exist only three basic types of theory on doctrinal development on which all possible models of doctrinal continuity and change are ultimately based (chapter 3).

---

1   The same conclusion was reached by George R. Knight: "By now it should be obvious to our readers that Adventism has experienced major theological change across the course of its history and that Ellen White had a role in that change" ("Adventists and Change," 11).
2   "Throughout the history of the Christian Church, believers have found it hard to accept this double-edged principle – that true religion clings to the old that proves to be truth but reaches out also for new, more appropriate understandings" (Hammill, *Pilgrimage*, 233). Thus, it is quite unusual for an official Adventist publication to state that there are "numerous theological wrecks lying on the Adventist doctrinal highway" that "have not stood the test of time and theological scrutiny" (Whidden, "Essential Adventism or Historic Adventism?" 5) and that "most of the founders of Seventh-day Adventism would not be able to join the church today if they had to subscribe to the denomination's Fundamental Beliefs" (Knight, "Adventists and Change," 10).

One of the most typical and enduring marks of Seventh-day Adventism has been the restorationist impulse which characterized its theology from the very beginning until the present time. In fact, just as there are restorationists adhering to all three basic types of theory on doctrinal development, so the notion of restoring truth to its original purity and pristine perfection by means of an uncompromising return to and acceptance of biblical teachings may be found among Adventists following different approaches to doctrinal continuity and change. Traditionally, most Adventists have favored the "static" type; in more recent decades, however, many have followed Froom in a more "dynamic" approach to doctrinal truth. Thus, today, most Adventists may perhaps best be described as organic restorationists.

While these general conclusions have, in my judgment, been reasonably established by this study, there are several historical, sociological, and psychological questions, as well as a number of important theological and hermeneutical issues that deserve closer attention and well-considered answers by those grappling with the problem of doctrinal continuity and change within the context and from the perspective of Seventh-day Adventism.

First, there are a number of Adventist doctrines whose development has not been investigated closely in this study.[3] Then, there are those instances where doctrinal changes, proposed by some within the church, were ultimately rejected by the denomination as a whole.[4] Third, an in-depth analysis of the why and how of doctrinal development should prove quite useful in understanding and evaluating change.[5] Likewise, the exact role of Ellen White in the development of Adventist doctrines deserves a careful investigation of its own.[6]

But, above all, it is the theological and hermeneutical aspects of the problem of doctrinal continuity and change that demand the serious attention of the scholars of

3   These include, e.g., the controversial doctrines of the heavenly sanctuary and of righteousness by faith (soteriology). Besides, there are many aspects of the Adventist teaching on revelation/ inspiration, God, creation, man, the church, and last things, let alone ethical and social issues that have not been analyzed in this study but whose development may profitably be studied.

4   Among them were Kellog's panentheistic teaching and Ballenger's deviant view on the sanctuary and the atonement. A study of the reasons and manners of opposing their new views should provide helpful insights to the church in relating to similar challenges today.

5   It would be profitable, e.g., to study more closely the various causes, modes, and mechanisms involved in doctrinal change. This includes the historical, theological, sociological, and psychological factors influencing doctrinal development in the SDA church. To give a few examples: To what degree were the emerging doctrines of the Sabbatarian Adventists shaped by the teachings of the Christian Connection? What role did deviant (unorthodox or heretical) views play in the shaping of SDA doctrines? To what extent are theological views influenced by the socio-economic status of church members who hold them? What factors lead to the gradual neglect (or revival) of a doctrine? Are some personality types particularly inclined to adopt specific conceptions of doctrinal change?

6   It appears that an Adventist concept of doctrinal development will be largely determined by what the church considers to be in basic agreement with Ellen White's own view of, and personal involvement in, doctrinal change.

the church. Inasmuch as this study is confined to a historical and typological analysis of change in Adventist theology, it provides no sufficient ground for drawing conclusions that need to be based on theological reasoning and hermeneutical reflection. Still, some implications relating to the communal life and doctrinal teaching of the Seventh-day Adventist Church already now may be drawn from this investigation. They have to do with the general attitude towards doctrinal continuity and change, the rising challenge of theological pluralism and unity, and the proper criteria for distinguishing the lasting "kernel" from the passing "husk" of the Adventist faith.[7]

Like other, more traditional churches, Seventh-day Adventists today are faced with the challenge to justify their doctrinal heritage as a legitimate development and a valid expression of biblical revelation. In this, they should remain open to new doctrinal insights arising from their incessant search for truth.[8] The way in which the church handles this task could be of great importance for the hoped-for identification of its young and well-educated members with the values, beliefs, and goals of the denomination.[9] It may also have a notable impact on how Adventists are looked upon by their contemporaries in general and by other Christians in particular.[10] Thus, the long-range success of the missionary thrust of the church might actually depend on it.

Seventh-day Adventists can no longer afford promoting views on doctrinal development that are based on misconceptions and wishful thinking rather than on established historical facts. As is noted in this study, in recent years they have begun to speak more factually and positively about doctrinal development. There also seems to be a growing awareness that

7   The following considerations are inevitably influenced by the author's own theological and hermeneutical perspective. While readers may want to draw other and different conclusions from this study, the ones offered here are believed to be congruent with both the history and the theology of the SDA church.

8   Pointing to Adventism's commitment and passionate concern for truth, Guy adds the following: "If we ever come to value anything – our reputation, our prosperity, our security, our peace of mind – more than we value truth, then we will indeed have betrayed our heritage and given up an absolutely essential component of Adventist faith" ("Truth Our Contemporary," 13).

9   "Those societies which cannot combine reverence to their symbols with freedom of revision, must ultimately decay either from anarchy, or from the slow atrophy of a life stifled by useless shadows" (Alfred North Whitehead, quoted in Dulles, *The Survival of Dogma*, [7]).

10 Hans Küng has called the willingness to recognize changes in doctrinal matters "a test-case for ecclesial truthfulness." In his judgment, Christians should never feel ashamed to admit that they have gained new insights, left wrong ways, and have been converted from error to truth. "For modern man it is not the revision of a position but the negations of a revision which offend against truthfulness" (*Wahrhaftigkeit: Zur Zukunft der Kirche* [Freiburg: Herder, 1968], 168, 162-180; ET: idem, *Truthfulness: The Future of the Church* [(New York: Sheed and Ward, 1968], 127, 130).

Adventism itself does not stand or fall on the basis of a particular reconstruction of the past ... At times the facts that emerge clash with the idealized picture of the pioneers and the early Adventist church that some people entertain ... No doubt further research will call into question other preconceived ideas. How shall we react to such facts? ... Truth can stand investigation. So can the Adventist past.[11]

Moreover, if there have been significant doctrinal changes in the past, there may also well be notable doctrinal developments in the future.[12] Reminiscent of the view held by the early Adventist pioneers, this insight has received official recognition in recent years in the preamble to the 1980 Statement of Fundamental Beliefs. It affirms that

Seventh-day Adventists accept the Bible as their only creed and hold certain fundamental beliefs to be the teaching of the Holy Scriptures. These beliefs, as set forth here, constitute the church's understanding and expression of the teaching of Scripture. Revision of these statements may be expected at a General Conference session when the church is led by the Holy Spirit to a fuller understanding of Bible truth or finds better language in which to express the teachings of God's Holy Word.[13]

To this end, Adventists may want to reflect more deeply on the proper meaning and effective communication of what they call "present truth." In fact, such a reflection is an absolute necessity if Jack Provonsha is correct in saying that "the crisis facing the Adventist prophetic movement can be met only by a rediscovery of and dedication to what God has commissioned this people to say in the world."[14]

It appears, then, that the restorationist principle of faithfulness to the Bible, combined with the so-called "dynamic" approach to doctrinal development, offers

11   Johnsson, "Those Moon Men in Long Black Coats," 14-15.

12   This book does not intend to show that, as doctrinal changes have repeatedly occurred in the past, they should, therefore, be welcomed generally and uncritically by SDAs today. What it does seek to demonstrate, however, is that Adventists need not entertain any fundamental (or paranoid) fear of change, knowing that, in a number of cases, doctrinal revisions appear to have been quite beneficial to the church – even when they involved intense personal struggles and protracted theological debates.

13   See app. 3, col. 3, p. 334. However, Froom's model of historical reconstruction, according to which the SDA church, after experiencing times of doctrinal uncertainty and controversy, has finally entered the period of doctrinal stability and unity, still appeals to many Adventists today. Apart from its historical inaccuracies, this concept involves a problematic hypothesis, which holds that doctrinal development today is limited to minor modifications and corrections of otherwise "perfected Fundamental Beliefs" (see above, pp. 274-279). If understood in such a context, the preamble to the 1980 Statement of Fundamental Beliefs may seem to pay only lip service to the notion of doctrinal "revision." Time will show which interpretation will be given to this preamble.

14   Provonsha, *A Remnant in Crisis*, 59. "Early Adventism was a radical movement. Sabbath observance, health reform, soul sleep, and belief in the imminent return of Jesus represented radical departures from long-held traditions. Conservative Christians were deeply offended by such smashing of traditions! Ellen White would have none of it. The question to her was not 'Is it old or new?' but 'Is it true?' So it should be with us all" (Thiele, "Is Conservatism a Heresy?" 13).

the greatest promise of helping the church gain a timely understanding of the lasting importance of its doctrinal heritage. Besides, to maintain a fruitful tension between the demand for contemporary relevance and the need for historic continuity will best protect the church against the twin dangers of stiff traditionalism and slack modernism. This is recognized increasingly in and by the church today.

> Adventists must know with certainty the enduring truths that God has called them to preach and preserve. But the very task of fulfilling the gospel commission also requires the church to change, to adapt its message to a world of diverse individuals and cultures. Thus, until the Lord returns, the church is called to live in an uncomfortable tension between the enduring and the adaptable, between that which never changes and that which must. In familiar Adventist terms, it is the tension between "landmarks" and "present truth."[15]

Ellen White's dialectic approach to doctrinal development with its twofold concern for preservation of church identity and openness for authentic doctrinal advance (chapter 6) may serve as a kind of model and guide for Adventist theologians in their endeavor to develop an adequate and balanced concept of doctrinal continuity and change. The following analogy aptly illustrates this dual requirement.

> The conservative element gives stability and strength and is thus of tremendous value. It might be compared to the keel of a ship. The progressive element keeps us relevant and brings growth. If conservatism is the keel, progressivism is the sail. Both elements are essential and must be well matched for optimum effectiveness.[16]

In view of the complexity of the issue, a comprehensive analysis of the intricate problem of doctrinal development is urgently needed by the church. Such a theological and hermeneutical study must pay close attention to (1) the philosophical and theological foundations, (2) the basic structures, (3) the various criteria, and (4) the practical implications of an Adventist concept of doctrinal continuity and change.[17]

Contemporary Adventism is characterized by an increasing variety of viewpoints, especially in the Western world. Though the existence of conflicting opinions on doctrinal questions has usually been downplayed, if not negated, it has become too obvious to be ignored any longer.[18] Adventists are beginning to react in new ways

---

15   *Issues,* 35. This publication was issued by the North American Division of Seventh-day Adventists in response to certain dissident movements who consider themselves as the true defenders of "historic Adventism." See above, p. 251, n. 117.

16   Thiele, "Is Conservatism a Heresy?" 14.

17   Cf. above, pp. 49-51. No full-fledged theory of doctrinal development has been advanced by any Adventist theologian to date. My original intent to add a third part to this dissertation, offering hermeneutical reflections on doctrinal continuity and change, likely would have doubled the size of this study and had to be given up. However, it is my hope to tackle the issue in a later work. Thus, this book may be seen as an extended introduction to, and historical foundation of, such a study.

18   See Richard Rice, "Dominant Themes in Adventist Theology," *Spectrum* 10:4 (1980): 58-74; Fritz Guy, "Adventist Theology Today," *Spectrum* 12:1 (1981): 6-14; William G.

to this challenge. "The church must make room for diversity of opinion and genuine dissent. The attempt to impose unity ultimately splinters the church."[19] Time will show how Adventists are going to handle the opportunities and dangers inherent in this new situation, and whether they will attain and maintain "unity in diversity."[20]

An adequate and timely theory of doctrinal development will have to address itself to the issue of doctrinal pluralism and unity. In addition, it needs to pay attention to the cross-cultural communication and contextualization of the gospel. Adventists are beginning to realize that "divine truth can be expressed in many different ways according to cultural forms, and we should be generally accepting as long as the essence of the gospel truth is undisturbed." However, "in our striving to adapt ourselves to the peculiar ideas of the people, we too must retain our identity."[21]

Johnsson, "Seven Factors Fragmenting the Church," *AR,* 5 May 1994, 12-14; Knight, "Adventist Theology 1844 to 1994"; Martin Weber, *Who's Got the Truth?* (1994); and "A Gathering of Adventisms," *Adventist Today,* January-February 1994 [wrongly dated 1993], 4-16, which describes four different "Adventisms" and their respective attitudes towards doctrinal change: *Historic* Adventism (rejecting doctrinal change), *Mainstream* Adventism (accepting doctrinal change rather cautiously), *Evangelical* Adventism (opting for doctrinal change along the lines of a gospel-centered emphasis), and *Progressive* Adventism (calling for major doctrinal changes on the basis of contemporary insights and needs).

19   *Issues,* 50. Similarly, Bj. Christensen allows for "diversity of thought and opinion, perhaps even interpretation." In his view, the church needs all four "Adventisms" (cf. previous footnote) on its spiritual journey and in its quest for theological growth. At the same time, however, it must shun the two extremes produced by "religious pluralism," viz., indifference/relativism and traditionalism/absolutism ("Dialogue or Ballots?" *Adventist Today,* January-February 1994, 15). See also Knight, "Adventist Theology 1844 to 1994" *("the advocates of Adventism's polar positions need each other");* Ralph Martin, "The Church in Changing Times," *AR,* 4 January 1990, 7-9 (regular, traditional, intellectual, and cultural SDAs should appreciate their differences and stay together); J. David Newman, "How Much Diversity Can We Stand?" *Ministry,* April 1994, 5, 26; Caleb Rosado, "United in Christ," *AR,* 22 June 1995, 9-12 ("the principle of diversity in Christian unity should be taught as a 'testing truth' doctrine"); Alden Thompson, "We Need Your Differences," *AR* [2 November 1989], 17-20 (the church urgently needs the input of "liberals" as well as "conservatives"); Martin Weber, *Who's Got the Truth?* 5-13 ("appreciate other viewpoints in the church besides our own"); Myron Widmer, "Will Diversity Divide Us?" *AR,* 13 October 1988, 4 (diversity fosters needed change in the church); Edwin Zackrison, "When Christians Differ," *Ministry,* August 1983, 19-21 (allowing for different perspectives and varying expressions of truth).

20   Ellen White's "references to unity and diversity formed a significant theme in her writings, particularly during the 1890s when diversity was becoming more apparent due to the rapid growth of the church." Her "repeated references regarding the necessity for both unity and diversity to be respected in the church" indicated "an emphasis which appears to have been unique in Adventism to her" (Oliver, *SDA Organizational Structure,* 296-297). See also Ellen White, "Unity in Diversity," *AR,* 17 February 1994, 14-15.

21   Schantz, "One Message – Many Cultures: How Do We Cope?" 10. Cf. Jon Dybdahl, "Cross-Cultural Adaptation," *Ministry,* November 1992, 14-17, who regards contextualization as "an issue of present truth."

Independently of any scholarly reflections on doctrinal continuity and change, the Seventh-day Adventist Church will continue to evolve theologically, though no one can predict the exact direction this development will take.[22] The pioneers of the church saw themselves as the true heirs of the Millerite movement by retaining its essential teachings and concerns while revising other aspects that time had shown to be erroneous. Likewise, the church today may regard itself as being in substantial and authentic continuity with historic Adventism as long as it preserves the core teachings and main intents of Sabbatarian Adventism.

At the same time, the church may still want or need to modify certain aspects of its doctrinal heritage that require readjustment or revision on the basis of a deeper understanding of truth. Change is a fact, and doctrine is no exception to it. However, as Adventist history also shows, constructive doctrinal changes usually happen not in a sudden and revolutionary manner, but are gradual and evolutionary, allowing church members to maintain confidence in the soundness and integrity of the Adventist body of beliefs.

But, what are the criteria for distinguishing the lasting "kernel" from the passing "husk" of the Adventist faith? How can the identity of its doctrinal heritage be preserved in the midst of change?

In the Adventist tradition, doctrinal modifications are officially recognized only by the representatives of the world church assembled at a General Conference session. No theologian, no local church, nor any one person or assembly possesses the ecclesiastical authority to define what Adventists believe. On the other hand, a vote taken by an official assembly of the world church can give only *ex post facto* recognition to new or additional theological insights that have already taken hold of the thinking of a majority of church members. In making such decisions, the church will seek to remain in organic continuity and essential harmony with its doctrinal heritage as summarily expressed in its Fundamental Beliefs.

However, standing firmly in the Protestant tradition, Seventh-day Adventists have always maintained the absolute priority of the Bible in deciding what is to be believed and taught in and by the church. Believed to be the reliable Word of God expressed in the words of men, Scripture was and is regarded as the inspired and authoritative rule of faith, superseding ecclesiastical traditions, creedal statements, church councils, and philosophical speculations. Thus, any teaching regarding

---

22   It has often been noted that there seem to be stages in the life cycle of just about any religious faith and denomination. For example, in Christian history, the age of apologetics was followed by periods of theological controversy, doctrinal stability, new challenges, etc. In addition, each one of these periods was characterized by a particular attitude towards doctrinal development. Similar phenomena have been observed in Protestant history – including Seventh-day Adventism. However, to determine exactly which period of its life cycle the SDA church is currently experiencing would require a foreknowledge of its future development which is not available today. This makes it quite risky to have one's concept of doctrinal continuity and change depend upon a rather hypothetical view. On the other hand, reliable sociological insights may certainly enrich our theological interpretation.

Christian faith and practice must prove itself to be in full harmony with the Bible. In this, Seventh-day Adventists continue to see themselves as "repairers of the breach," consciously following a biblicist approach and upholding the primitivist/restorationist ideal of the recovery of, and return to, biblical truth.

This platform, if consistently applied, defines the limits of doctrinal change and, at the same time, protects the church against radical revisions, which substitute mere human reason or fashionable theories for divine revelation. Seen in this light, the consistently revisionist or radically perspectivist theories appear to lie outside the historical and doctrinal platform on which Adventism has been built. While the "static type" seems to conflict with certain historical facts, the "evolutionary/revolutionary type" of theories on doctrinal development apparently collides with both the ecclesiastical structure and the theological/hermeneutical premises of Seventh-day Adventism.

Still, as in the past, some doctrinal *aggiornamento* is likely to happen if the church continues to search the Scriptures and seeks faithfully to interpret it in the context of contemporary experience.[23] As one of their scholars has said of Seventh-day Adventists,

> They are still pilgrims on a doctrinal journey who do not repudiate the waymarks, but neither do they remain stopped at any of them. They press on in the direction to which they have been pointed, avoiding legalism and permissivism, dogmatism and disunity, fanaticism and formalism. They realize that tradition can be a useful servant but a dreadful master, so they shun traditionalism, ever eager to learn present truth and perform present duty. There shines a light behind them to illumine their way, and a light ahead of them to beckon. It is the same light – the coming of the Lord.[24]

This allusion to the light shining behind and ahead of the Adventists as they travel on their doctrinal journey is taken from the first vision of Ellen Harmon (White), which she had in December 1844, just a few weeks after the Great Disappointment. It was this programmatic vision which not only set in motion her own seventy-year-long prophetic ministry but also gave a number of disappointed Millerites a new and hopeful perspective regarding their future. Because of its seminal influence on the church, this "view" may be regarded as the constitutive visionary experience of Seventh-day Adventism.[25]

---

23 Rosado's insight, though expressed in a different context, may well be applicable to this situation: "To stay relevant, the church must not only respond to change; it must also *anticipate* change, for change challenges leadership to deal more effectively with differences" (*Broken Walls*, 120).

24 Johnston, "A Search for Truth," 8.

25 Steininger has called this vision the "*Urszene*" of SDAs which turned out to be "of extreme importance" for Ellen White and the church (*Konfession und Sozialisation*, 96). Wrote White, "I raised my eyes, and saw a straight and narrow path, cast up high above the world. On this path the Advent people were traveling to the city, which was at the farther end of the path. They had a bright light set up behind them at the beginning of the path, which an angel told me was the midnight cry. This light shone all along the path and gave light for their feet so that

Inspired by this vision, the Seventh-day Adventist church is still on the way to fulfill its divine destiny and commission as it has come to understand it from the earliest days of the movement, viz., to be a pilgrim people, guided by the insights gained in their past religious experience and, at the same time, constantly pressing forward towards their ultimate goal. In this, they are led by Jesus, upon whom their faith and hope are centered and who is providing further enlightenment to them whenever they are in need of it. Perhaps, this is the real genius of Adventism. As one of their leaders has said,

> A movement is not a settlement; a movement is not a theological point of view. A movement, in the strictest sense, is not a denomination. A movement is a pilgrimage, a people on a journey, an expedition.[26]

they might not stumble. If they kept their eyes fixed on Jesus, who was just before them, leading them to the city, they were safe. But soon some grew weary, and said the city was a great way off, and they expected to have entered it before. Then Jesus would encourage them by raising His glorious right arm, and from His arm came a light which waved over the Advent band, and they shouted, 'Alleluia!'" (Ellen White, *Early Writings,* 14-15, 13-20). On the historical context and main content of this vision, see Tim Poirier, "An Encouraging Word," *AR,* 22 December 1994, 14-16.

26   C. E. Bradford, "A Movement Is Born," *AR,* 10 May 1979, 6.

Epilogue

What Next?

Those societies which cannot combine reverence to their symbols with freedom of revision, must ultimately decay either from anarchy, or from the slow atrophy of a life stifled by useless shadows.

Alfred North Whitehead

The mind is like an umbrella – it functions best when open.

Walter Gropius

How will Seventh-day Adventist readers respond to the findings and conclusions of this book? Inasmuch as it deals with sensitive issues touching the very heart of the Adventist identity and self-understanding, it is to be expected that a work of this nature will be studied not only with keen interest but also with critical discernment – and this is how it should be. Apart from that, human nature being what it is, responses to this volume will likely fall – and have in the past already fallen – into one of four categories.

Some readers will be positively surprised by the fact that Seventh-day Adventism is a much more dynamic movement than many church members seem to be aware of. Thus, they may be tempted to use this book to influence or even push the church in the direction of further and more substantial doctrinal changes. While such corrections and revisions are not ruled out by this study, it is not intended to be used as a club against those who are opposed to change. The church has never supported any rash or precipitate action regarding its doctrinal heritage; neither does it have any reason to do so now. As Adventist history shows, constructive doctrinal change happens, not in a sudden and revolutionary way, but in a gradual and evolutionary manner.

Other readers who also have taken note of the evidence presented in this book, may conclude that I have over-emphasized the findings, placing far too much weight on theological change while unduly minimizing the remarkable and substantial continuity of Seventh-day Adventist teachings. To them, this book may seem to make "a mountain out of a molehill" or to rage "like a bull in a china shop." As a result, they may be inclined to downplay the historical evidence of doctrinal change and to evade the implications it may have for the church today. However meager the results of this study may appear to such readers, these findings do not support the widespread contention that Seventh-day Adventist doctrines are immune to significant developments. Doctrinal change is a historical fact, and Adventist beliefs are no exception to it.

Still other readers may even be shocked by the fact that there have been serious revisions even with regard to a number of fundamental and distinctive Adventist teachings. Brought up on the belief that "we have the truth" and therefore need not abandon any erroneous views, they may be tempted to reject the church's claim to doctrinal excellence and superiority altogether. But, while this study should restrain one from making exaggerated claims regarding the Adventist doctrinal heritage, it gives no reason to abandon confidence in the essential soundness and integrity of the Adventist body of beliefs. While all human understanding of truth is relative – absolute truth belongs only to God –, biblically based, time-proven, and relevant church teachings may still be regarded as *truths* of faith.

Hopefully, there will also be those readers who take this book for what it actually intends to be: *firstly*, a challenge to refine and, if need be, revise one's own view of the developments that doctrines actually undergo in history; *secondly*, a call to develop and maintain a mature and balanced concept of doctrinal continuity and change; and *thirdly*, an opportunity to reaffirm one's faith in the past and future divine guidance of the Adventist movement.

As far as I am concerned, the extensive and ongoing research into Adventist history and theology, beginning in 1973 when I became a Master student at Andrews University, has not jeopardized my relationship to the church of my upbringing, let alone my Adventist Christian faith. To the contrary, the more I have become aware of the contingencies of Adventist history and theology, the more I marvel at the hand that guides humans in their search for, and discovery of, DYNAMIC TRUTH.

Appendix 1

Other Revisionist Models of Doctrinal Development

The pluralistic situation of contemporary theology is reflected by the large number of models of doctrinal continuity and change proposed in recent years. This appendix presents and briefly describes some other theories of doctrinal development of the revisionist type that are less well known but still of interest to our study.[1]

The Model of Conceptual Integration

So far, Reformed theology has hardly made any direct contribution to the discussion of doctrinal change.[2] An exception was the Dutch scholar *A. A. van Ruler* who regarded the creative work of the Spirit in doctrinal formation as a kind of new and continued revelation of God in the ever-changing cultural contexts of this world. The unlimited evolution of dogma involves the constant integration of new conceptual elements from the pagan world into the Christian faith; the latter is constantly reordered and renewed by these innovative leaps.[3]

The Model of Dialectic Advance

Attempting to harmonize contradictory assertions through the application of Hegelian dialectic, the American Trappist *Anselm Atkins* proposed a theory of doctrinal development through "dialectic logic" which involves a doctrinal affirmation (thesis), its negation (antithesis), and the self-negation of the negation (synthesis). As a result, even an anathematized proposition may possess a true meaning while a true doctrine may be expressed in an erroneous verbal form. Hoping

---

1   In addition to the models described here, revisionist views of doctrinal development were also expressed, e.g., by *Hellmut Bandt,* "Kontinuität und Veränderlichkeit," *Studia Theologica* 28 (1974): 69-85; A. O. Dyson, *We Believe* (London and Oxford: Mowbrays, 1977); and John Hick, *God and the Universe of Faiths* (New York: St. Martin's Press, 1973).

2   "No theologian of a Reformed tradition has yet produced a satisfactory or generally acceptable explanation of the development of doctrine" (R. P. C. Hanson, "Tradition," *Dictionary of Christian Theology,* 1969 ed., 342).

3   A. A. van Ruler, "The Evolution of Dogma," in *Christianity Divided: Protestant and Roman Catholic Theological Issues,* ed. D. J. Callahan, H. A. Oberman, and D. J. O'Hanlon (New York: Sheed and Ward, 1961), 89-105.

to open up new possibilities for ecumenical theology, this intellectualistic approach allowed for de-development, doctrinal corruptions and radical revisions.[4]

The Model of Successive Structuring

Defining doctrines as intelligible structures and rational frameworks, the French Dominican *Jean-Pierre Jossua* distinguished the *éléments fondamentaux* (i.e., the constant and fundamental, structured elements of faith) from the *éléments structurants* (i.e., the changing cultural and contextual factors that influence doctrine and belief). The former include the Christian kerygma as well as Christianity's fundamental ideas *(idée-force)* which arise from divine revelation and its resulting faith experience. Yet, there exists a tension between the structural stability provided by permanent ideas and the change which results from their successive interpretations in shifting cultural contexts. Opposing the paradigms of homogeneous development and progress, Jossua merely demanded a fundamental fidelity to Christianity's origin while allowing for a wide pluralism of doctrinal expressions.[5]

The Model of Creative Transmutation

Attempting to justify the diversities and discontinuities of doctrinal beliefs as being authorized by the New Testament, *Donald Aaron Milavec* maintained that later developments always transmute the original meaning of Scripture, for the biblical text evokes different perceptions and beliefs in the course of time. Successive generations of disciples are called to creatively sustain their Master's heritage of faith by using Scripture for both conservation and innovation.[6]

---

4   Anselm Atkins, "Religious Assertions and Doctrinal Development," *Theological Studies* 27 (1966): 523-552; and idem, "Doctrinal Development and Dialectic," *Continuum* 6 (1968): 3-23. *Avery Dulles* also defended the application of a kind of Hegelian triad (involving affirmation, qualified negation, and higher resolution) to doctrinal development *(Survival of Dogma,* 197-198). Similarly, *G.-P. Léonard* argued that the historicity of dogmas demand a dialectic of interpretations ("History and Dogma," in *Proceedings of the Twenty-Eighth Annual Convention,* by the Catholic Theological Society of America [Bronx, N.Y.: Catholic Theological Society of America, 1973], 103-123.

5   Jean-Pierre Jossua, "Immutabilité, progrès, ou structurations multiples des doctrines chrétiennes?" *Revue des sciences philosophiques et théologiques* 52 (1968): 173-200; cf. idem, "Rule of Faith and Orthodoxy," *Concilium* 6:1 (1970): 56-67. See also *P. Misner,* "A Note on the Critique of Dogmas," *Theological Studies* 34 (1973): 690-700, who adopted this view.

6   Donald Aaron Milavec, "The Bible as Inspiring and Authorising Incompatible Doctrines and Practices," *Église et Théologie* 7 (1976): 189-218; and idem, "Modern Exegesis, Doctrinal Innovations, and the Dynamics of Discipleship," *Anglican Theological Review* 60 (1978): 55-74.

The Model of Propositional Transference

According to *Jeremy Moiser,* "sometimes doctrine develops by transferring a body of traditional statements from one set of circumstances to another."[7] In this case, doctrinal propositions are not rejected but reinterpreted by being applied to different situations and objects and thereby adjusted to serve new purposes. Through such a "propositional extension," a theological statement is either salved lexically by being adapted semantically or retained in its content by being lexically adjusted, i.e., restated.[8]

---

7   Jeremy Moiser, "Propositional Transference," *Irish Theological Quarterly* 43 (1976): 198, 198-210.

8   A similar view was defended by *Hans Martin Barth* according to whom "the content must vary, but the predicative form of the confession must remain"; while the church must constantly articulate its faith in literary form, there exists no invariable content which could be expressed in dogmas or creeds *(Theorie des Redens von Gott* [Göttingen: Vandenhoeck & Ruprecht, 1972], 118, 117-121).

Appendix 2

Synoptic Tables of Theories of Doctrinal Development

DESIGNATION	STATIC TYPE	DYNAMIC TYPE	(R)EVOLUTIONARY TYPE
	objectivistic intellectualistic	dialectic theological	subjectivistic transformistic
PREMISES & ASSUMPTIONS			
1. Revelation:	objective & propositional	subjective-objective	subjective & existential
2. Faith:	assent (*fides quae*)	assent & trust	trust & feeling (*fides qua*)
3. Truth:	objectivistic	subjective-objective	subjectivistic
	absolutistic timeless	absolute-relative time-related	relativistic timebound
4. Authority:	absolute & extrinsic	intrinsic-extrinsic	relative & intrinsic
5. Dogma:	irreformable highly authoritative all-important	reformable authoritative important	replaceable non-authoritative unimportant

MARKS &
FEATURES

1. Emphasis on:	identity & continuity	continuity & change identity &	change & discontinuity
	immutability	development	
	purity	actualization	mutability
	conservation	reformation	transformation
	preservation	renewal	relevance
	irreformability	re-presentation	accommodation
			innovation

2. Nature of change & continuity:	verbal & apparent formal	true & accidental real & material	radical & essential material & substantial
	explicative	constructive	re-creative
	reformulation	reinterpretation	revision
	restatement	reconceptuali-zation	reconstruction
	same understanding	developing understanding	new understanding
	identical meaning	same basic meaning	different meaning
	identity of content	identity of substantial/ essential content	identity of (the object of) faith, not of content
	continuous	(dis)continuous	discontinuous
	homogeneous	homogeneous & heterogeneous	heterogeneous
	harmonious	(dis)harmonious	disharmonious

3. Analogies:	maturation	growth (ontogenesis)	evolution (phylogenesis)
	from child to adult	*from seed to tree*	*from cell to vertebrate*
	literal translation	dynamic transl.	free translation

	from reactionary & archaic to orthodox & conservative	from moderately conservative to moderately liberal	from liberal & modernist to radical revisionist
VARIETIES & REPRESEN- TATIVES			
	historical theories historic Catholicism & Protestantism Fundamentalism	*organistic theories* Catholic romanticism & orthodox Protestantism	*transformistic theories* Protestant liberalism & Catholic modernism
	logical theories Catholic (neo-) scholasticism & Protestant orthodoxy	*psychological theory* Newman *theological theories* nouvelle theologie & neo-orthodoxy/ -evangelicalism	*revisionistic theories* Protestant neoliberalism & Catholic neomodernism & radical theology & process theology
	new revelation theory Suarez & Martinez Protestant sects	*moderate situationist theories* contemporary Roman Catholic & Protestant theology	*radical perspectivist theories* contemporary Roman Catholic & Protestant theology
METHODS & CRITERIA:	logical analysis syllogistic deduction speculative reasoning	reason & intellect intuition & feeling experience & context	reason & intellect intuition & feeling experience & context

	scripture & tradition magisterium hermeneutic	scripture & tradition magisterium hermeneutic	culture science philosophy
	Holy Spirit	Holy Spirit	Holy Spirit
STRENGTHS & WEAKNESSES	unhistorical intellectualistic traditionalist archaistic anachronistic immobilist	unhistorical fideistic irrational idealistic romantic	historicist empiricist agnostic existentialist modernistic secularistic pluralistic
	absolutistic objectivistic reductionistic one-sided	paradoxical & sophistical compromising syncretistic eclectic	relativistic subjectivistic reductionistic one-sided
	concern for identity & doctrinal purity	concern for identity & intelligibility	concern for relevance & intelligibility
	recognition of objective truth	awareness of the need for a dialectic approach	admission of change & historicity
	opposition to relativism & subjectivism	avoidance of reductionism & one-sidedness	opposition to absolutism & objectivism

Appendix 3

Fundamental Beliefs of Seventh-day Adventists: A Synopsis

A DECLARATION OF THE FUNDAMENTAL PRINCIPLES TAUGHT AND PRACTICED BY THE SEVENTH-DAY ADVENTISTS	FUNDAMENTAL BELIEFS OF SEVENTH-DAY ADVENTISTS	FUNDAMENTAL BELIEFS OF SEVENTH-DAY ADVENTISTS
1872	1931	1980

In presenting to the public this synopsis of our faith, we wish to have it distinctly understood that we have no articles of faith, creed, or discipline, aside from the Bible. We do not put forth this as having any authority with our people, nor is it designed to secure uniformity among them, as a system of faith, but is a brief statement of what is and has been, with great unanimity, held by them. We often find it necessary to meet inquiries on this subject, and sometimes to correct false statements circulated against us, and to remove erroneous impressions which have obtained with those who have not had an opportunity to become acquainted with our faith and practice. Our only object is to meet this necessity.

As Seventh-day Adventists, we desire simply that our position shall

Seventh-day Adventists hold certain fundamental beliefs, the principal features of which, together with a portion of the scriptural references upon which they are based, may be summarized as follows:

Seventh-day Adventists accept the Bible as their only creed and hold certain fundamental beliefs to be the teaching of the Holy Scriptures. These beliefs, as set forth here, constitute the church's understanding and expression of the teaching of Scripture. Revision of these statements may be expected at a General Conference session when the church is led by the Holy Spirit to a fuller understanding of Bible truth or finds better language in which to express the teachings of God's Holy Word.

be understood; and we are the more solicitous for this because there are many who call themselves Adventists, who hold views with which we can have no sympathy, some of which, we think, are subversive of the plainest and most important principles set forth in the word of God.

As compared with other Adventists, Seventh-day Adventists differ from one class in believing in the unconscious state of the dead, and the final destruction of the unrepentant wicked; from another, in believing in the perpetuity of the law of God as summarily contained in the ten commandments, in the operation of the Holy Spirit in the church, and in setting no times for the advent to occur; from all, in the observance of the seventh day of the week as the Sabbath of the Lord, and in many applications of the prophetic scriptures.

With these remarks, we ask the attention of the reader to the following propositions, which aim to be a concise statement of the more prominent features of our faith.

3

That the Holy Scriptures, of the Old and New Testaments, were given by inspiration of God, contain a full revelation of his will to man, and are the only infallible rule of faith and practice.

1

That the Holy Scriptures of the Old and New Testaments were given by inspiration of God, contain an all-sufficient revelation of His will to men, and are the only unerring rule of faith and practice. 2 Tim. 3:15-17.

1

The Holy Scriptures, Old and New Testaments, are the written Word of God, given by divine inspiration through holy men of God who spoke and wrote as they were moved by the Holy Spirit. In this Word, God has committed to man the knowledge necessary for salvation. The Holy Scriptures are the infallible revelation of His will. They are the standard of character, the test of experience, the authoritative revealer of doctrines, and the trustworthy record of God's acts in history. (2 Peter 1:20, 21; 2 Tim. 3:16, 17; Ps. 119:105; Prov. 30:5, 6; Isa. 8:20; John 10:35; 17:17; 1 Thess. 2:13; Heb. 4:12.)

1

That there is one God, a personal, spiritual being, the creator of all things, omnipotent, omniscient, and eternal, infinite in wisdom, holiness, justice, goodness, truth, and mercy; unchangeable, and everywhere present by his representative, the Holy Spirit. Ps. 139:7.

2

That the Godhead, or Trinity, consists of the Eternal Father, a personal, spiritual Being, omnipotent, omnipresent, omniscient, infinite in wisdom and love; the Lord Jesus Christ, the Son of the Eternal Father, through whom all things were created and through whom the salvation of the redeemed hosts will be accomplished; the Holy Spirit, the third person of the Godhead, the great regenerating power in the work of redemption. Matt. 28:19.

2

There is one God: Father, Son, and Holy Spirit, a unity of three co-eternal Persons. God is immortal, all-powerful, all-knowing, above all, and ever present. He is infinite and beyond human comprehension, yet known through His self-revelation. He is forever worthy of worship, adoration, and service by the whole creation. (Deut. 6:4; 29:29; Matt. 28:19; 2 Cor. 13:14; Eph. 4:4-6; 1 Pet. 1:2; 1 Tim. 1:17; Rev. 14:6, 7.

3

God the eternal Father is the Creator, Source, Sustainer, and Sovereign of all creation. He is just and holy, merciful and gracious, slow to anger, and abounding in steadfast love and faithfulness. The qualities and powers exhibited in the Son and the Holy Spirit are also revelations of the Father. (Gen. 1:1; Rev. 4:11; 1 Cor. 15:28; John 3:16; 1 John 4:8; 1 Tim. 1:17; Ex. 34:6, 7; John 14:9.)

2

That there is one Lord Jesus Christ, the Son of the Eternal Father, the one by whom God created all things, and by whom they do consist; that he took on him the nature of the seed of Abraham for the redemption of our fallen race; that he dwelt among men full of

3

That Jesus Christ is very God, being of the same nature and essence as the Eternal Father. While retaining His divine nature He took upon Himself the nature of the human family, lived on the earth as a man, exemplified in His life as our Example the principles of

4

God the eternal Son became incarnate in Jesus Christ. Through Him all things were created, the character of God is revealed, the salvation of humanity is accomplished, and the world is judged. Forever truly God, He became also truly man, Jesus the Christ. He was conceived of the Holy Spirit and born of the virgin Mary. He lived and experienced grace and truth, lived our example, died our sacrifice, was raised for our justification, ascended on high to be our only mediator in the sanctuary in Heaven, where, with his own blood he makes atonement for our sins; which atonement so far from being made on the cross, which was but the offering of the sacrifice, is the very last portion of his work as priest, according to the example of the Levitical priest-hood, which foreshadowed and prefigured the ministry of our Lord in Heaven. See Lev. 16; Heb. 8:4, 5; 9:6, 7; &c.

righteousness, attested His rela-tionship to God by many mighty miracles, died for our sins on the cross, was raised from the dead, and ascended to the Father, where He ever lives to make intercession for us. John 1:1, 14; Heb. 2:9-18; 8:1, 2; 4:14-16; 7:25.

temptation as a human being, but perfectly exemplified the righteousness and love of God. By His miracles He manifested God's power and was attested as God's promised Messiah. He suffered and died voluntarily on the cross for our sins and in our place, was raised from the dead, and ascended to minister in the heavenly sanctuary in our behalf. He will come again in glory for the final deliverance of His people and the restoration of all things. (John 1:1-3, 14; 5:22; Col. 1:15-19; John 10:30; 14:9; Rom. 5:18; 6:23; 2 Cor. 5:17-21; Luke 1:35; Phil. 2:5-11; 1 Cor. 15:3, 4; Heb. 2:9-18; 4:15; 7:25; 8:1, 2; 9:28; John 14:1-3; 1 Pet. 2:21; Rev. 22:20.)

5

God the eternal Spirit was active with the Father and the Son in Creation, incarnation, and redemption. He inspired the writers of Scripture. He filled Christ's life with power. He draws and convicts human beings; and those who respond He renews and trans-forms into the image of God. Sent by the Father and the Son to be always with His children, He extends spiritual gifts to the church, empowers it to bear witness to Christ, and in harmony with the Scriptures leads it into all truth. (Gen. 1:1, 2; Luke 1:35; 2 Pet. 1:21; Luke 4:18; Acts 10:38; 2 Cor. 3:18; Eph. 4:11, 12; Acts 1:8; John 14:16-18, 26; 15:26, 27; 16:7-13; Rom. 1:1-4.)

6

God is Creator of all things, and has revealed in Scripture the authentic account of His creative activity. In six days the Lord made "the heaven and the earth" and all living things upon the earth, and rested on the seventh day of that first week. Thus He established the Sabbath as a perpetual memorial of His completed creative work. The first man and woman were made in the image of God as the crowning work of Creation, given dominion over the world, and charged with responsibility to care for it. When the world was finished it was "very good," declaring the glory of God. (Gen. 1:2; Ex. 20: 8-11; Ps. 19:1-6; 33:6, 9; 104; Heb. 11:3; John 1:1-3; Col. 1:16, 17.)

7

*["spirit": changed from "soul"; cf. SDAY, 1985 ed., p. 5, to SDAY, 1986 ed., p. 5]

Man and woman were made in the image of God with individuality, the power and freedom to think and to do. Though created free beings, each is an indivisible unity of body, mind, and spirit,* dependent upon God for life and breath and all else. When our first parents disobeyed God, they denied their dependence upon Him and fell from their high position under God. The image of God in them was marred and they became subject to death. Their descendants share this fallen nature and its consequences. They are born with weaknesses and tendencies to evil. But God in Christ reconciled the world to Himself and by His Spirit restores in penitent mortals the image of their Maker. Created for the glory of God, they are called to love Him and one another, and to care for their environment. (Gen. 1:26-28; 2:7; Ps. 8:4-8; Acts 17:24-28; Gen. 3; Ps. 51:5; Rom. 5: 12-17; 2 Cor. 5:19, 20.)

8

All humanity is now involved in a great controversy between Christ and Satan regarding the character of God, His law, and His sovereignty over the universe. This conflict originated in heaven when a created being, endowed with freedom of choice, in self-exaltation became Satan, God's adversary, and led into rebellion a portion of the angels. He introduced the spirit of rebellion into this world when he led Adam and Eve into sin. This human sin resulted in the distortion of the image of God in humanity, the disordering of the created world, and its eventual devastation at the time of the worldwide flood. Observed by the whole creation, this world became the arena of the universal conflict, out of which the God of love will ultimately be vindicated. To assist His people in this controversy, Christ sends the Holy Spirit and the loyal angels to guide, protect, and sustain them in the way of salvation. (Rev. 12:4-9; Isa. 14:12-14; Eze. 28:12-18; Gen. 3; Gen. 6-8; 2 Pet. 3:6; Rom. 1:19-32; 5: 12-21; 8: 19-22; Heb. 1:4-14; 1 Cor. 4:9.)

2

9

(That there is one Lord Jesus Christ, the Son of the Eternal Father, ... our only mediator in the sanctuary in Heaven, where, with his own blood he makes atonement for our sins; which atonement so far from being made on the cross, which was but the offering of the sacrifice, is the very last portion of his work as priest, according to the example of the Levitical priesthood, which foreshadowed and prefigured the ministry of our Lord in Heaven. See Lev. 16; Heb. 8:4, 5; 9:6, 7; &c.)

In Christ's life of perfect obedience to God's will, His suffering, death, and resurrection, God provided the only means of atonement for human sin, so that those who by faith accept this atonement may have eternal life, and the whole creation may better understand the infinite and holy love of the Creator. This perfect atonement vindicates the righteousness of God's law and the graciousness of His character; for it both condemns our sin and provides for our forgiveness. The death of Christ is substitutionary and expiatory, reconciling and transforming. The resurrection of Christ proclaims God's triumph over the forces of evil, and for those who accept the atonement assures their final victory over sin and death. It declares the Lordship of Jesus Christ, before whom every knee in heaven and earth will bow. (John 3:16; Isa. 53; 2 Cor. 5:14, 15, 19-21; Rom. 1:4; 3: 25; 4: 25; 8:3, 4; Phil. 2:6-11; 1 John 2:2; 4:10; Col. 2:15.)

5

4

That the new birth comprises the entire change necessary to fit us for the kingdom of God, and consists of two parts: first, a moral change,

That every person in order to obtain salvation must experience the new birth; that this comprises an entire transformation of life and

wrought by conversion and a Christian life; second, a physical change at the second coming of Christ, whereby, if dead, we are raised incorruptible, and if living, are changed to immortality in a moment, in the twinkling of an eye. John 3:3,5; Luke 20:36.

character by the recreative power of God through faith in the Lord Jesus Christ. John 3:16; Matt. 18:3; Acts 2:37-39.

14

That as the natural or carnal heart is at enmity with God and his law, this enmity can be subdued only by a radical transformation of the affections, the exchange of unholy for holy principles; that this transformation follows repentance and faith, is the special work of the Holy Spirit, and constitutes regeneration or conversion.

15

That as all have violated the law of God, and cannot of themselves render obedience to his just requirements, we are dependent on Christ, first, for justification from our past offences, and, secondly, for grace whereby to render acceptable obedience to his holy law in time to come.

8

That the law of ten commandments points out sin, the penalty of which is death. The law can not save the transgressor from his sin, nor impart power to keep him from sinning. In infinite love and mercy, God provides a way whereby this may be done. He furnishes a substitute, even Christ the Righteous One, to die in man's stead, making "Him to be sin for us, who knew no sin; that we might be made the righteousness of God in Him." 2 Cor. 5:21. That one is justified, not by obedience to the law, but by the grace that is in Christ Jesus. By accepting Christ, man is reconciled to God, justified by His blood for the sins of the past, and saved from the power of sin by his indwelling life. Thus the gospel becomes "the power of God unto salvation to every one that believeth." This experience is wrought by the divine agency of the Holy Spirit, who convinces of sin and leads to the Sin-Bearer, inducting the believer into the new covenant relationship, where the law of God is written on his heart, and through the enabling power of the indwelling Christ, his life is

10

In infinite love and mercy God made Christ, who knew no sin, to be sin for us, so that in Him we might be made the righteousness of God. Led by the Holy Spirit, we sense our need, acknowledge our sinfulness, repent of our transgressions, and exercise faith in Jesus as Lord and Christ, as Substitute and Example. This faith which receives salvation comes through the divine power of the Word and is the gift of God's grace. Through Christ we are justified, adopted as God's sons and daughters, and delivered from the lordship of sin. Through the Spirit we are born again and sanctified; the Spirit renews our minds, writes God's law of love in our hearts, and we are given the power to live a holy life. Abiding in Him we become partakers of the divine nature and have the assurance of salvation now and in the judgment. (Ps. 27:1; Isa. 12:2; Jonah 2:9; John 3:16; 2 Cor. 5:17-21; Gal. 1:4; 2:19, 20; 3:13; 4:4-7; Rom. 3:24-26; 4:25; 5:6-10; 8:1-4, 14, 15, 26, 27; 10:7; 1 Cor. 2:5; 15:3, 4; 1 John 1:9; 2:1, 2; Eph. 2:5-10; 3:16-19; Gal 3: 26; John 3:3-8; Matt. 18:3; 1 Pet. 1:23; 2:21; Heb. 8:7-12.)

11

The church is the community of believers who confess Jesus Christ as Lord and Saviour. In continuity with the people of God in Old Testament times, we are called

brought into conformity to the divine precepts. The honor and merit of this wonderful transformation belong wholly to Christ. 1 John 3:4; Rom. 7:7; Rom. 3:20; Eph. 2:8-10; 1 John 2:1, 2; Rom. 5:8-10; Gal. 2:20; Eph. 3:17; Heb. 8:8-12.

out from the world; and we join together for worship, for fellowship, for instruction in the Word, for the celebration of the Lord's Supper, for service to all mankind, and for the worldwide proclamation of the gospel. The church derives its authority from Christ, who is the incarnate Word, and from the Scriptures, which are the written Word. The church is God's family; adopted by Him as children, its members live on the basis of the new covenant. The church is the body of Christ, a community of faith of which Christ Himself is the Head. The church is the bride for whom Christ died that He might sanctify and cleanse her. At His return in triumph, He will present her to Himself a glorious church, the faithful of all the ages, the purchase of His blood, not having spot or wrinkle, but holy and without blemish. (Gen. 12:3; Acts 7:38; Matt. 21:43; 16:13-20; John 20:21, 22; Acts 1:8; Rom. 8:15-17; 1 Cor. 12:13-27; Eph. 1:15, 23; 2:12; 3:8-11, 15; 4:11-15.)

17

15

12

That God, in accordance with his uniform dealings with the race, sends forth a proclamation of the approach of the second advent of Christ; that this work is symbolized by the three messages of Rev. 14, the last one bringing to view the work of reform on the law of God, that his people may acquire a complete readiness for that event.

That God, in the time of the judgment and in accordance with His uniform dealing with the human family in warning them of coming events vitally affecting their destiny (Amos 3:6, 7), sends forth a proclamation of the approach of the second advent of Christ; that this work is symbolized by the three angels of Revelation 14; and that their threefold message brings to view a work of reform to prepare a people to meet Him at His coming.

The universal church is composed of all who truly believe in Christ, but in the last days, a time of widespread apostasy, a remnant has been called out to keep the commandments of God and the faith of Jesus. This remnant announces the arrival of the judgment hour, proclaims salvation through Christ, and heralds the approach of His second advent. This proclamation is symbolized by the three angels of Revelation 14; it coincides with the work of judgment in heaven and results in a work of repentance and reform on earth. Every believer is called to have a personal part in this worldwide witness. (Mark 16:15; Matt. 28:18-20; 24:14; 2 Cor. 5:10; Rev. 12:17; 14:6-12; 18:1-4; Eph. 5:22-27; Rev. 21:1-14.)

13

The church is one body with many members, called from every nation, kindred, tongue, and people. In Christ we are a new creation; distinctions of race, culture, learning, and nationality, and differences between high and low, rich and poor, male and female, must not be divisive among us. We are all equal in Christ, who by one Spirit has bonded us into one fellowship with Him and with one another; we are to serve and be served without partiality or reservation. Through the revelation of Jesus Christ in the Scriptures we share the same faith and hope, and reach out in one witness to all. This unity has its source in the oneness of the triune God, who has adopted us as His children. (Ps. 133:1; 1 Cor. 12: 12-14; Acts 17:26, 27; 2 Cor. 5:16, 17; Gal. 3:27-29; Col. 3: 10-15; Eph. 4:1-6; John 17:20-23; James 2:2-9; 1 John 5:1.)

4

That Baptism is an ordinance of the Christian church, to follow faith and repentance, an ordinance by which we commemorate the resurrection of Christ, as by this act we show our faith in his burial and resurrection, and through that, of the resurrection of all the saints at the last day; and that no other mode fitly represents these facts than that which the Scriptures prescribe, namely, immersion. Rom. 6:3-5; Col. 2:12.

5

That baptism is an ordinance of the Christian church and should follow repentance and forgiveness of sins. By its observance faith is shown in the death, burial, and resurrection of Christ. That the proper form of baptism is by immersion. Rom. 6:1-6; Acts 16:30-33.

14

By baptism we confess our faith in the death and resurrection of Jesus Christ, and testify of our death to sin and of our purpose to walk in newness of life. Thus we acknowledge Christ as Lord and Saviour, become His people, and are received as members by His church. Baptism is a symbol of our union with Christ, the forgiveness of our sins, and our reception of the Holy Spirit. It is by immersion in water and is contingent on an affirmation of faith in Jesus and evidence of repentance of sin. It follows instruction in the Holy Scriptures and acceptance of their teachings. (Matt. 3:13-16; 28:19, 20; Acts 2:38; 16:30-33; 22:16; Rom. 6:1-6; Gal. 3:27; 1 Cor. 12:13; Col. 2:12, 13; 1 Pet. 3:21.)

15

The Lord's Supper is a participation in the emblems of the body and blood of Jesus as an expression of faith in Him, our Lord and Saviour. In this experience of communion Christ is present to meet and strengthen His people. As we partake, we joyfully proclaim the Lord's death until He comes again. Preparation for the Supper includes self-examination, repentance, and confession. The Master ordained the service of foot washing to signify renewed cleansing, to express a willingness to serve one another in Christlike humility, and to unite our hearts in love. The communion service is open to all believing Christians. (Matt 26:17-30; 1 Cor. 11:23-30; 10:16, 17; John 6:48-63; Rev. 3:20; John 13:1-17.)

16

That the Spirit of God was promised to manifest itself in the church through certain gifts, enumerated especially in 1 Cor. 12 and Eph. 4; that these gifts are not designed to supersede, or take the place of, the Bible, which is sufficient to make us wise unto salvation, any more than the Bible can take the place of the Holy Spirit; that in specifying the various channels of its operation, that Spirit has simply made provision for its own existence and presence with the people of God to the end of time, to lead to an understanding of that word which it had inspired, to convince of sin, and work a transformation in the heart and life; and that those who deny to the Spirit its place and

19

That God has placed in His church the gifts of the Holy Spirit, as enumerated in 1 Corinthians 12 and Ephesians 4. That these gifts operate in harmony with the divine principles of the Bible, and are given for the perfecting of the saints, the work of the ministry, the edifying of the body of Christ. Rev. 12:17; 19:10; 1 Cor. 1:5-7.

16

God bestows upon all members of His church in every age spiritual gifts which each member is to employ in loving ministry for the common good of the church and of humanity. Given by the agency of the Holy Spirit, who apportions to each member as He wills, the gifts provide all abilities and ministries needed by the church to fulfill its divinely ordained functions. According to the Scriptures, these gifts include such ministries as faith, healing, prophecy, proclamation, teaching, administration, reconciliation, compassion, and self-sacrificing service and charity for the help and encouragement of people. Some members are called of God and endowed by the Spirit for functions recognized by the church in pastoral, evangelistic, apostolic, and teaching ministries particularly needed to equip the members for service, to build up the church to spiritual maturity, and to foster unity of the faith and

operation, do plainly deny that part of the Bible which assigns to it this work and position.

6

We believe that prophecy is a part of God's revelation to man; that it is included in that scripture which is profitable for instruction, 2 Tim. 3:16; that it is designed for us and our children. Deut. 29:29; that so far from being enshrouded in impenetrable mystery, it is that which especially constitutes the word of God a lamp to our feet and a light to our path, Ps. 119:105, 2 Pet. 2:19; that a blessing is pronounced upon those who study it, Rev. 1:1-3; and that, consequently, it is to be understood by the people of God sufficiently to show them their position in the world's history, and the special duties required at their hands.

7

That the world's history from specified dates in the past, the rise and fall of empires, and chronological succession of events down to the setting up of God's everlasting kingdom, are outlined in numerous great chains of prophecy; and that these prophecies are now all fulfilled except the closing scenes.

knowledge of God. When members employ these spiritual gifts as faithful stewards of God's varied grace, the church is protected from the destructive influence of false doctrine, grows with a growth that is from God, and is built up in faith and love. (Rom. 12:4-8; 1 Cor. 12:9-11, 27, 28; Eph. 4:8, 11-16; 2 Cor. 5:14-21; Acts 6: 1-7; 1 Tim. 2:1-3; 1 Pet. 4:10, 11; Col. 2:19; Matt. 25:31-36.)

17

One of the gifts of the Holy Spirit is prophecy. This gift is an identifying mark of the remnant church and was manifested in the ministry of Ellen G. White. As the Lord's messenger, her writings are a continuing and authoritative source of truth which* provide for the church comfort, guidance, instruction, and correction. They also make clear that the Bible is the standard by which all teaching and experience must be tested. (Joel 2:28, 29; Acts 2:14-21; Heb. 1:1-3; Rev. 12:17; 19:10.)

*["which": replacing the word "and" which was inadvertantly printed here; see "Corrections," AR, 25 September 1980, p. 32.]

11

That God's moral requirements are the same upon all men in all dispensations; that these are summarily contained in the commandments spoken by Jehovah from Sinai, engraven on the tables of stone, and deposited in the ark, which was in consequence called the "ark of the covenant," or testament. Num. 10:33, Heb. 9:4; &c.; that this law is immutable and perpetual, being a transcript of the tables deposited in the ark in the true sanctuary on high, which is also, for the same reason, called the ark of God's testament; for under the sounding of the seventh trumpet we are told that "the temple of God was opened in Heaven, and there was seen in his temple the ark of his testament." Rev. 11:19.

6

That the will of God as it relates to moral conduct is comprehended in His law of ten commandments; that these are great moral, unchangeable precepts, binding upon all men, in every age. Exod. 20:1-17.

18

The great principles of God's law are embodied in the Ten Commandments and exemplified in the life of Christ. They express God's love, will, and purposes concerning human conduct and relationships and are binding upon all people in every age. These precepts are the basis of God's covenant with His people and the standard in God's judgment. Through the agency of the Holy Spirit they point out sin and awaken a sense of need for a Saviour. Salvation is all of grace and not of works, but its fruitage is obedience to the Commandments. This obedience develops Christian character and results in a sense of well-being. It is an evidence of our love for the Lord and our concern for our fellow men. The obedience of faith demonstrates the power of Christ to transform lives, and therefore strengthens Christian witness. (Ex. 20:1-17; Matt. 5:17; Deut. 28:1-14; Ps. 19:7-13; John 14:15; Rom. 8:1-4; 1 John 5:3; Matt. 22: 36-40; Eph. 2:8.)

12

That the fourth commandment of this law requires that we devote the seventh day of each week, commonly called Saturday, to abstinence from our own labor, and to the performance of sacred and religious duties; that this is the only weekly Sabbath known to the Bible, being the day that was set apart before paradise was lost, Gen. 2:2, 3, and which will be observed in paradise restored, Isa. 66:22, 23; that the facts upon which the Sabbath institution is based confine it to the seventh day, as they are not true of any other day;

7

That the fourth commandment of this unchangeable law requires the observance of the seventh day Sabbath. This holy institution is at the same time a memorial of creation and a sign of sanctification, a sign of the believer's rest from his own works of sin, and his entrance into the rest of soul which Jesus promises to those who come to Him. Gen. 2:1-3; Exod. 20: 8-11; 31:12-17; Heb. 4:1-10.

19

The beneficent Creator, after the six days of Creation, rested on the seventh day and instituted the Sabbath for all people as a memorial of Creation. The fourth commandment of God's unchangeable law requires the observance of this seventh-day Sabbath as the day of rest, worship, and ministry in harmony with the teaching and practice of Jesus, the Lord of the Sabbath. The Sabbath is a day of delightful communion with God and one another. It is a symbol of our redemption in Christ, a sign of our sanctification, a token of our allegiance, and a foretaste of our eternal future in God's kingdom. The Sabbath is God's perpetual sign of His eternal covenant between Him

and that the terms, Jewish Sabbath and Christian Sabbath, as applied to the weekly rest-day, are names of human invention, unscriptural in fact, and false in meaning.

13

That as the man of sin, the papacy, has thought to change times and laws (the laws of God), Dan.7:25, and has misled almost all Christendom in regard to the fourth commandment, we find a prophecy of a reform in this respect to be wrought among believers just before the coming of Christ. Isa. 56:1, 2; 1 Pet. 1:5; Rev. 14:12; &c.

18

That the divine principle of tithes and offerings for the support of the gospel is an acknowledgment of God's ownership in our lives, and that we are stewards who must render account to Him of all that He has committed to our possession. Lev. 27:30; Mal. 3:8-12; Matt. 23:23; 1 Cor. 9:9-14; 2 Cor. 9:6-15.

17

That the followers of Christ should be a godly people, not adopting the unholy maxims nor conforming to the unrighteous ways of the world, not loving its sinful pleasures nor countenancing its follies. That the believer should recognize his body as the temple of the Holy Spirit, and that therefore he should clothe that body in neat, modest, dignified apparel. Further, that in eating and drinking and in his entire course of conduct he should shape his life as becometh a

and His people. Joyful observance of this holy time from evening to evening, sunset to sunset, is a celebration of God's creative and redemptive acts. (Gen. 2:1-3; Ex. 20:8-11; 31:12-17; Luke 4:16; Heb. 4:1-11; Deut. 5:12-15; Isa. 56:5, 6; 58:13, 14; Lev. 23:32; Mark 2:27, 28.)

20

We are God's stewards, entrusted by Him with time and opportunities, abilities and possessions, and the blessings of the earth and its resources. We are responsible to Him for their proper use. We acknowledge God's ownership by faithful service to Him and our fellow men, and by returning tithes and giving offerings for the proclamation of His gospel and the support and growth of His church. Stewardship is a privilege given to us by God for nurture in love and the victory over selfishness and covetousness. The steward rejoices in the blessings that come to others as a result of his faithfulness. (Gen. 1:26-28; 2:15; Haggai 1:3-11; Mal. 3:8-12; Matt. 23:23; 1 Cor. 9:9-14.)

21

We are called to be a godly people who think, feel, and act in harmony with the principles of heaven. For the Spirit to recreate in us the character of our Lord we involve ourselves only in those things which will produce Christlike purity, health, and joy in our lives. This means that our amusement and entertainment should meet the highest standards of Christian taste and beauty. While recognizing cultural differences, our dress is to be simple, modest, and neat, befitting those whose true beauty does not consist of outward adornment but in the imperishable ornament of a gentle and quiet

follower of the meek and lowly Master. Thus the believer will be led to abstain from all intoxicating drinks, tobacco, and other narcotics, and the avoidance of every body- and soul-defiling habit and practice. 1 Cor. 3:16, 17; 9:25; 10:31; 1 Tim. 2:9, 10; 1 John 2:6.

spirit. It also means that because our bodies are the temples of the Holy Spirit, we are to care for them intelligently. Along with adequate exercise and rest, we are to adopt the most healthful diet possible and abstain from the unclean foods identified in the Scriptures. Since alcoholic beverages, tobacco, and the irresponsible use of drugs and narcotics are harmful to our bodies, we are to abstain from them as well. Instead, we are to engage in whatever brings our thoughts and bodies into the discipline of Christ, who desires our wholesomeness, joy, and goodness. (1 John 2:6; Eph. 5:1-13; Rom. 12:1, 2; 1 Cor. 6:19, 20; 10:31; 1 Tim. 2:9, 10; Lev. 11:1-47; 2 Cor.7:1; 1 Pet. 3:1-4; 2 Cor.10:5; Phil. 4:8.)

22

Marriage was divinely established in Eden and affirmed by Jesus to be a lifelong union between a man and a woman in loving companionship. For the Christian a marriage commitment is to God as well as to the spouse, and should be entered into only between partners who share a common faith. Mutual love, honor, respect, and responsibility are the fabric of this relationship, which is to reflect the love, sanctity, closeness, and permanence of the relationship between Christ and His church. Regarding divorce, Jesus taught that the person who divorces a spouse, except for fornication, and marries another, commits adultery. Although some family relationships may fall short of the ideal, marriage partners who fully commit themselves to each other in Christ may achieve loving unity through the guidance of the Spirit and the nurture of the church. God blesses the family and intends that its members shall assist each other toward complete maturity. Parents are to bring up their children to love and obey the Lord. By

9

That the mistake of Adventists in 1844 pertained to the nature of the event then to transpire, not to the time; that no prophetic period is given to reach to the second advent, but that the longest one, the two thousand and three hundred days of Dan. 8:14, terminated in that year, and brought us to an event called the cleansing of the sanctuary.

10

That the sanctuary of the new covenant is the tabernacle of God in Heaven, of which Paul speaks in Hebrews 8, and onward, of which our Lord, as great High Priest, is minister; that this sanctuary is the antitype of the Mosaic tabernacle, and that the priestly work of our Lord, connected therewith, is the antitype of the work of the Jewish priests of the former dispensation. Heb. 8:1-5, &c.; that this is the sanctuary to be cleansed at the end of the 2300 days, what is termed its cleansing being in this case, as in the type, simply the entrance of the high priest into the most holy place, to finish the round of service connected therewith, by blotting out and removing from the sanctuary the sins which had been transferred to it by means of the ministration in the first apartment, Heb. 9:22, 23; and that this work, in the antitype, commencing in 1844, occupies a brief but

13

That no prophetic period is given in the Bible to reach to the second advent, but that the longest one, the 2300 days of Dan. 8:14, terminated in 1844, and brought us to an event called the cleansing of the sanctuary.

14

That the true sanctuary, of which the tabernacle on earth was a type, is the temple of God in Heaven, of which Paul speaks in Hebrews 8 and onward, and of which the Lord Jesus, as our great high priest, is minister; and that the priestly work of our Lord is the antitype of the work of the Jewish priests of the former dispensation; that this heavenly sanctuary is the one to be cleansed at the end of the 2300 days of Dan. 8:14; its cleansing being, as in the type, a work of judgment, beginning with the entrance of Christ as the high priest upon the judgment phase of His ministry in the heavenly sanctuary foreshadowed in the earthly service of cleansing the sanctuary on the day of atonement. This work of

their example and their words they are to teach them that Christ is a loving disciplinarian, ever tender and caring, who wants them to become members of His body, the family of God. Increasing family closeness is one of the earmarks of the final gospel message. (Gen. 2:18-25; Deut. 6:5-9; John 2: 1-11; Eph. 5:21-33; Matt. 5:31, 32; 19:3-9; Prov. 22:6; Eph. 6:1-4; Mal. 4:5, 6; Mark 10:11, 12; Luke 16:18; 1 Cor. 7:10, 11.)

23

There is a sanctuary in heaven, the true tabernacle which the Lord set up and not man. In it Christ ministers on our behalf, making available to believers the benefits of His atoning sacrifice offered once for all on the cross. He was inaugurated as our great High Priest and began His intercessory ministry at the time of His ascension. In 1844, at the end of the prophetic period of 2300 days, He entered the second and last phase of His atoning ministry. It is a work of investigative judgment which is part of the ultimate disposition of all sin, typified by the cleansing of the ancient Hebrew sanctuary on the Day of Atonement. In that typical service the sanctuary was cleansed with the blood of animal sacrifices, but the heavenly things are purified with the perfect sacrifice of the blood of Jesus. The investigative judgment reveals to heavenly intelligences who among the dead are asleep in Christ and therefore, in Him, are deemed worthy to have part in the first resurrection. It also makes manifest who, among the living are abiding in Christ, keeping the commandments of God and the faith of Jesus, and in Him, therefore, are ready for translation into His everlasting kingdom. This judgment vindicates the justice of God in saving those who believe in Jesus. It declares that those who have

indefinite space, at the conclusion of which the work of mercy for the world is finished.

18

That the time of the cleansing of the sanctuary (see proposition X), synchronizing with the time of the proclamation of the third message, is a time of investigative judgment, first with reference to the dead, and at the close of probation with reference to the living, to determine who of the myriads now sleeping in the dust of the earth are worthy of a part in the first resurrection, and who of its living multitudes are worthy of translation – points which must be determined before the Lord appears.

8

That the doctrine of the world's conversion and temporal millennium is a fable of these last days, calculated to lull men into a state of carnal security, and cause them to be overtaken by the great day of the Lord as by a thief in the night; that the second coming of Christ is to precede, not follow, the millennium; for until the Lord appears the papal power, with all its abominations, is to continue, the wheat and tares grow together, and evil men and seducers wax worse and worse, as the word of God declares.

judgment in the heavenly sanctuary began in 1844. Its completion will close human probation.

16

That the time of the cleansing of the sanctuary, synchronizing with the period of the proclamation of the message of Revelation 14, is a time of investigative judgment, first with reference to the dead, and secondly, with reference to the living. This investigative judgment determines who of the myriads sleeping in the dust of the earth are worthy of a part in the first resurrection, and who of its living multitudes are worthy of translation. 1 Pet. 4:17, 18; Dan. 7:9, 10; Rev. 14:6, 7; Luke 20:35.

20

That the second coming of Christ is the great hope of the church, the grand climax of the gospel and plan of salvation. His coming will be literal, personal, and visible. Many important events will be associated with His return, such as the resurrection of the dead, the destruction of the wicked, the purification of the earth, the reward of the righteous, the establishment of His everlasting kingdom. The almost complete fulfillment of various lines of prophecy, particularly those found in the books of Daniel and the Revelation, with existing conditions in the physical, social, industrial, political, and religious worlds, indicates that Christ's

remained loyal to God shall receive the kingdom. The completion of this ministry of Christ will mark the close of human probation before the Second Advent. (Heb. 1:3; 8:1-5; 9:11-28; Dan. 7:9-27; 8:13, 14; 9:24-27; Num. 14:34; Eze. 4:6; Mal. 3:1; Lev. 16; Rev. 14:12; 20:12; 22:12.)

24

The second coming of Christ is the blessed hope of the church, the grand climax of the gospel. The Saviour's coming will be literal, personal, visible, and worldwide. When He returns, the righteous dead will be resurrected, and together with the righteous living will be glorified and taken to heaven, but the unrighteous will die. The almost complete fulfillment of most lines of prophecy, together with the present condition of the world, indicates that Christ's coming is imminent. The time of that event has not been revealed, and we are therefore exhorted to be ready at all times. (Titus 2:13; John 14:1-3; Acts 1:9-11; 1 Thess. 4:16, 17; 1 Cor. 15: 51-54; 2 Thess. 2:8; Matt. 24; Mark 13; Luke 21; 2 Tim. 3:1-5; Joel 3:9-16; Heb. 9:28.)

coming "is near, even at the doors." The exact time of that event has not been foretold. Believers are exhorted to be ready, for "in such an hour as ye think not, the Son of man" will be revealed. Luke 21: 25-27; 17:26-30; John 14:1-3; Acts 1:9-11; Rev. 1:7; Heb. 9:28; James 5:1-8; Joel 3:9-16; 2 Tim. 3:1-5; Dan. 7:27; Matt. 24:36, 44.

19

That the grave, whither we all tend, expressed by the Hebrew *sheol,* and the Greek *hades,* is a place of darkness in which there is no work, device, wisdom, or knowledge. Eccl. 9:10.

20

That the state to which we are reduced by death is one of silence, inactivity, and entire unconsciousness. Ps. 146:4; Eccles. 9:5, 6; Dan. 12:2, &c.

21

That out of this prison house of the grave mankind are to be brought by a bodily resurrection; the righteous having part in the first resurrection, which takes place at the second advent of Christ, the wicked in the second resurrection, which takes place a thousand years thereafter. Rev.20:4-6.

9

That God only hath immortality. Mortal man possesses a nature inherently sinful and dying. Immortality and eternal life come only through the gospel, and are bestowed as the free gift of God at the second advent of Jesus Christ our Lord. 1 Tim. 6:15, 16; 1 Cor. 15:51-55.

10

That the condition of man in death is one of unconsciousness. That all men, good and evil alike, remain in the grave from death to the resurrection. Eccles. 9:5, 6; Ps. 146:3, 4; John 5:28, 29.

11

That there shall be a resurrection both of the just and of the unjust. The resurrection of the just will take place at the second coming of Christ; the resurrection of the unjust will take place a thousand years later, at the close of the millennium. John 5:28, 29; 1 Thess. 4:13-18; Rev. 20:5-10.

25

The wages of sin is death. But God, who alone is immortal, will grant eternal life to His redeemed. Until that day death is an unconscious state for all people. When Christ, who is our life, appears, the resurrected righteous and the living righteous will be glorified and caught up to meet their Lord. The second resurrection, the resurrection of the unrighteous, will take place a thousand years later. (1 Tim. 6:15, 16; Rom. 6:23; 1 Cor. 15:51-54; Eccl. 9:5, 6; Ps. 146:4; 1 Thess. 4:13-17; Rom. 8:35-39; John 5:28, 29; Rev. 20:1-10; John 5:24.)

22

That at the last trump, the living righteous are to be changed in a moment, in the twinkling of an eye, and with the resurrected righteous are to be caught up to meet the Lord in the air, so forever to be with the Lord.

23

That these immortalized ones are then taken to Heaven, to the New Jerusalem, the Father's house in which there are many mansions, John 14:1-3, where they reign with Christ a thousand years, judging the world and fallen angels, that is, apportioning the punishment to be executed upon them at the close of the one thousand years; Rev. 20:4; 1 Cor. 6:2, 3; that during this time the earth lies in a desolate and chaotic condition, Jer. 4:20-27, described, as in the beginning, by the Greek term *abussos* (αβυσσος) bottomless pit (Septuagint of Gen. 1:2); and that here Satan is confined during the thousand years, Rev. 20:1, 2, and here finally destroyed, Rev. 20:10; Mal. 4:1; the theater of the ruin he has wrought in the universe, being appropriately made for a time his gloomy prison house, and then the place of his final execution.

24

That at the end of the thousand years, the Lord descends with his people and the New Jerusalem,

21

That the millennial reign of Christ covers the period between the first and the second resurrections, during which time the saints of all ages will live with their blessed Redeemer in Heaven. At the end of the millennium, the Holy City with all the saints will descend to the earth. The wicked, raised in the second resurrection, will go up on the breadth of the earth with Satan at their head to compass the camp of the saints, when fire will come down from God out of Heaven and devour them. In the conflagration which destroys Satan and his host, the earth itself will be regenerated and cleansed from the effects of the curse. Thus the universe of God will be purified from the foul blot of sin. Rev. 20; Zech. 14:1-4; 2 Pet. 3:7-10.

12

That the finally impenitent, including Satan, the author of sin, will, by the fires of the last day, be reduced to a state of non-existence, becoming as though they had not been, thus purging God's universe

26

The millennium is the thousand-year reign of Christ with His saints in heaven between the first and second resurrections. During this time the wicked dead will be judged; the earth will be utterly desolate, without living human inhabitants, but occupied by Satan and his angels. At its close Christ with His saints and the Holy City will descend from heaven to earth. The unrighteous dead will then be resurrected, and with Satan and his angels will surround the city; but fire from God will consume them and cleanse the earth. The universe will thus be freed of sin and sinners forever. (Rev. 20; Zech. 14:1-4; Mal. 4:1; Jer. 4:23-26; 1 Cor. 6; 2 Peter 2:4; Eze. 28:18; 2 Thess. 1:7-9; Rev. 19:17, 18, 21.)

Rev. 21:2, the wicked dead are raised and come up upon the surface of the yet unrenewed earth, and gather about the city, the camp of the saints, Rev. 20:9, and fire comes down from God out of heaven and devour them. They are then consumed root and branch, Mal. 4:1, becoming as though they had not been. Obad. 15, 16. In this everlasting destruction from the presence of the Lord, 2 Thess. 1:9, the wicked meet the everlasting punishment threatened against them, Matt. 25:46. This is the perdition of ungodly men, the fire which consumes them being the fire for which "the heavens and the earth which are now" are kept in store, which shall melt even the elements with its intensity, and purge the earth from the deepest stains of the curse of sin. 2 Pet. 3:7-12.

of sin and sinners. Rom. 6:23; Mal. 4:1-3; Rev. 20:9, 10; Obad. 16.

25

22

27

That a new heavens and earth shall spring by the power of God from the ashes of the old, to be, with the New Jerusalem for its metropolis and capital, the eternal inheritance of the saints, the place where the righteous shall evermore dwell. 2 Pet. 3:13; Ps. 37:11, 29; Matt. 5:5.

That God will make all things new. The earth, restored to its pristine beauty, will become forever the abode of the saints of the Lord. The promise to Abraham, that through Christ he and his seed should possess the earth throughout the end less ages of eternity, will be fulfilled. The kingdom and dominion and the greatness of the kingdom under the whole heaven will be given to the people of the saints of the Most High, whose kingdom is an everlasting kingdom, and all dominions shall serve and obey Him. Christ, the Lord will reign supreme and every creature

On the new earth, in which righteousness dwells, God will provide an eternal home for the redeemed and a perfect environment for everlasting life, love, joy, and learning in His presence. For here God Himself will dwell with His people, and suffering and death will have passed away. The great controversy will be ended, and sin will be no more. All things, animate and inanimate, will declare that God is love; and He shall reign forever. Amen. (2 Peter 3:13; Gen. 17:1-8; Isa. 35; 65:17-25; Matt. 5:5; Rev. 21:1-7; 22:1-5; 11:15.)

which is in heaven and on the earth and under the earth, and such as are in the sea will ascribe blessing and honor and glory and power unto Him that sitteth upon the throne and unto the Lamb forever and ever. Gen. 13:14-17; Rom. 4:13; Heb. 11: 8-16; Matt. 5:5; Isa. 35; Rev. 21:1-7; Dan. 7:27; Rev. 5:13.

A Declaration of the Fundamental Principles Taught and Practiced by the Seventh-day Adventists.	"Fundamental Beliefs of Seventh-day Adventists."	"Session actions: Fundamental Beliefs of Seventh-day Adventists."
	In *Seventh-day Adventist Yearbook,* 377-380.	*Adventist Review,* 1 May 1980, 23-27.
Battle Creek, Mich.: Seventh-day Adventist Publishing Assn., 1872	Washington, D.C.: Review and Herald Pub. Assn., 1931	General Conference of Seventh-day Adventists, 1980

BIBLIOGRAPHY

This bibliography lists general literature on doctrinal development (bibliographies, books, articles, and dissertations) followed by literature by and about Seventh-day Adventists including sociology of religion (books and pamphlets, articles and journals, dissertations and theses, letters and manuscripts). Entries under the same name are given not in alphabetical but in chronological order.

General Literature on Doctrinal Development

Bibliographies

Colombo, Carlo. "Lo sviluppo del dogma: Bibliografia." In *Problemi e orientamenti di teologia dommatica,* 1:381-386. Milan: Marzorati, 1957.

Feiner, Johannes, and Magnus Löhrer, eds. *Mysterium Salutis: Grundriss heilsgeschichtlicher Dogmatik.* Vol. 1, *Die Grundlagen heilsgeschichtlicher Dogmatik,* 783-787. Einsiedeln, Zurich, Cologne: Benziger, 1965.

Hammans, Herbert. *Die neueren katholischen Erklärungen der Dogmenentwicklung,* ix-xxii. Beiträge zur neueren Geschichte der katholischen Theologie, vol. 7. Essen: Ludgerus-Verlag Wingen, 1965.
> Includes Dutch, English, French, German, Italian, Latin, and Spanish publications.
> Provides a cross-section of works on the Marian dogma of 1950.

Rahner, Karl. "Dogmenentwicklung." *Lexikon für Theologie und Kirche.* 2d ed., 1959. 3:462-463.

Schmaus, Michael, Alois Grillmeyer, and Leo Scheffczyk, eds. *Handbuch der Dogmengeschichte.* Vol. 1, pt. 5, *Dogma und Dogmenentwicklung,* by Georg Söll, 219-222. Freiburg, Basle, Vienna, 1971.
> Lists twentieth-century authors in chronological order.

Schulz, Winfried. *Dogmenentwicklung als Problem der Geschichtlichkeit der Wahrheitserkenntnis: Eine erkenntnistheoretisch-theologische Studie zum Problemkreis der Dogmenentwicklung,* xv-xxxi. Analecta Gregoriana, vol. 173. Rome: Gregorian University Press, 1969.
> Good on Italian, Latin, and German publications.

Walgrave, Jan Hendrik. *Unfolding Revelation: The Nature of Doctrinal Development,* 403-412. Philadelphia: Westminster Press, 1972.
> Lists many older works. Includes Dutch, French, German, Italian, Latin, Russian, and Spanish publications.

Books

Aaron, Raymond. *Introduction to the Philosophy of History: An Essay on the Limits of Historical Objectivity.* Boston: Beacon Press, 1962.

Adam, Alfred. *Lehrbuch der Dogmengeschichte.* 2 vols. 2d ed. Gütersloh: Gerd Mohn, 1970.

Altizer, Th. *The Gospel of Christian Atheism.* Philadelphia: Westminster, 1966.

_____, ed. *Towards a New Christianity: Readings in Death of God Theology.* New York: Harcourt, Brace & World, 1967.

Baillie, John. *The Belief in Progress.* New York: Charles Scribner's Sons, 1950.

Baker, John. "'Carried about by Every Wind?' The Development of Doctrine." Chap. in *Believing in the Church: The Corporate Nature of Faith.* London: SPCK, 1981.

Barth, Hans Martin. *Theorie des Redens von Gott.* Göttingen: Vandenhoeck & Ruprecht, 1972.

Bauer, Walter. *Orthodoxy and Heresy in Earliest Christianity.* Edited by R. A. Kraft and G. Krodel. Philadelphia: Fortress Press, 1971.

Baum, Gregory. *The Credibility of the Church Today.* New York: Herder and Herder, 1968.

_____. *Faith and Doctrine: A Contemporary View.* Paramus, N.J.: Newman Press, 1969.

_____. *Man Becoming: God in Secular Experience.* New York: Herder and Herder, 1971.

_____, ed. *The Future of Belief Debate.* New York: Herder and Herder, 1967.

Becker, Carl. *Detachment and the Writing of History.* Ithaca, N.Y.: Cornell, 1958.

Bent, Charles. *Interpreting the Doctrine of God.* New York: Paulist Press, 1968.

Berkhof, Louis. *The History of Christian Doctrines.* London: Banner of Truth, 1937.

Brown, Raymond E. *Biblical Reflections on Crises Facing the Church.* New York, and Paramus, N.J.: Paulist Press, 1975.

Brunner, Emil. *Truth as Encounter.* Philadelphia: Westminster, 1964.

Bultmann, Rudolf. "New Testament and Mythology." In *Kerygma and Myth.* 2 vols. Edited by H.-W. Bartsch, 1:1-44. London: SPCK, 1957-1962.

_____. *Existence and Faith.* New York: Meridian Books, 1960.

Bury, J. B. *The Idea of Progress: An Inquiry into Its Origin and Growth.* New York: Macmillan, 1932; reprint, New York: Dover Publ., 1955.

Chadwick, Owen. *From Bossuet to Newman: The Idea of Doctrinal Development.* Cambridge: Cambridge University Press, 1957.

Charlot, John. *New Testament Disunity: Its Significance for Christianity Today.* New York: E. P. Dutton & Co., 1970.

Collingwood, R. G. *The Idea of History.* Oxford: Clarendon Press, 1946.

Congar, Yves M.-J. *Vraie et fausse réforme dans l'Église.* 2d rev. ed. Paris: Édition du Cerf, 1968.

————. "Renewal of the Spirit and Reform of the Institution." In *Ongoing Reform in the Church.* Concilium, vol. 73. Edited by A. Müller and N. Greinacher, 39-49. New York: Herder & Herder, 1972.

Cox, Harvey. *The Secular City.* New York: Macmillan, 1965.

Crowe, Frederick E. "Development of Doctrine: Aid or Barrier to Christian Unity?" In *Proceedings of the Twenty-First Annual Convention,* by the Catholic Theological Society of America. Yonkers, N.Y.: Catholic Theological Society of America, 1967, 1-20.

Dewart, Leslie. *The Future of Belief: Theism in a World Come of Age.* New York: Herder and Herder, 1966.

————. "God and the Supernatural." In *New Theology, No. 5.* Edited by Martin E. Marty and Dean G. Peerman, 142-155. New York: Macmillan, 1968.

————. *The Foundations of Belief.* New York: Herder and Herder, 1969.

Draguet, R. "L'évolution des dogmes." In *Apologetique: Nos raisons de croire. Réponses aux objections.* 2d ed. Edited by M. Brillant and M. Nedoncelle, 1097-1122. Paris: Bloud et Gay, 1948.

Dulles, Avery. "Official Church Teaching and Historical Relativity." In *Spirit, Faith, and Church.* Edited by Wolfhart Pannenberg, Avery Dulles, and Carl E. Braaten, 51-72. Philadelphia: Westminster, 1970.

————. "Contemporary Understanding of the Irreformability of Dogma." In *Proceedings of the Twenty-Fifth Annual Convention,* by the Catholic Theological Society of America. Bronx, N.Y.: Catholic Theological Society of America, 1971, 111-136.

————. *The Survival of Dogma.* Garden City, N.Y.: Doubleday, 1971.

————. *Models of the Church.* Garden City, N.Y.: Doubleday, 1974.

_____. *The Resilient Church: The Necessity and Limits of Adaptation.* Garden City, N.Y.: Doubleday, 1977.

_____. *Models of Revelation.* Garden City, N.Y.: Doubleday, 1983.

Dunn, James D. G. *Unity and Diversity in the New Testament: An Inquiry into the Character of Earliest Christianity.* Philadelphia: Westminster, 1977.

Dyson, A. O. *We Believe.* London and Oxford: Mowbrays, 1977.

Ebeling, Gerhard. *Word and Faith.* Philadelphia: Fortress Press, 1963; London: SCM, 1963.

_____. *The Problem of Historicity in the Church and Its Proclamation.* Philadelphia: Fortress Press, 1967.

_____. *Studium der Theologie: Eine enzyklopädische Orientierung.* Tübingen: J. C. B. Mohr (Paul Siebeck), 1975.

Edelstein, Ludwig. *The Idea of Progress in Classical Antiquity.* Baltimore: Johns Hopkins Press, 1967.

Flick, M. "Il problema dello sviluppo del dogma nella teologia contemporanea." In *Lo sviluppo del dogma secundo la dottrina cattolica,* 5-23. Rome: Gregorian University Press, 1953.

Fontinell, Eugene. *Toward a Reconstruction of Religion: A Philosophical Probe.* Garden City, N.Y.: Doubleday, 1970.

Fuchs, Ernst. *Hermeneutik.* 3d ed. Stuttgart: R. Müllerschön Verlag, 1963.

_____. *Marburger Hermeneutik.* Tübingen: J. C. B. Mohr, 1968.

Galvin, John J. "A Critical Survey of Modern Conceptions of Doctrinal Development." In *Proceedings of the Fifth Annual Meeting,* by the Catholic Theological Society of America. Washington, D.C.: Catholic Theological Society of America, 1950, 45-63.

Gilkey, Langdon. *Naming the Whirlwind: The Renewal of God-Language.* New York: Bobbs-Merrill, 1969.

_____. *Catholicism Confronts Modernity: A Protestant View.* New York: Seabury Press, 1975.

_____. *Reaping the Whirlwind: A Christian Interpretation of History.* New York: Seabury Press, 1976.

Glasenapp, Helmuth von. *Die nichtchristlichen Religionen.* Frankfurt: Fischer Bücherei, 1957.

González, Justo L. *A History of Christian Thought.* 3 vols. Nashville: Abingdon, 1970-1975.

Gordan, Paulus. "Identitätskrise und Kontinuität." In *Traditio – Krisis – Renovatio aus theologischer Sicht*. Edited by Bernd Jaspert and Rudolf Mohr, 454-462. Festschrift Winfried Zeller zum 65. Geburtstag. Marburg: N. G. Elwert, 1976.

Hamilton, W. *The New Essence of Christianity*. New York: Association Press, 1961.

Hamilton, William, and Thomas J. J. Altizer, *Radical Theology and the Death of God*. Indianapolis: Bobbs-Merrill, 1966.

Handbuch der Dogmen- und Theologiegeschichte. 3 vols. Edited by Carl Andresen. Göttingen: Vandenhoeck & Ruprecht, 1980-1984.

Harnack, Adolf von. *Lehrbuch der Dogmengeschichte*. 3 vols. Freiburg: J. C. B. Mohr, 1886-1890; 2d enl. ed. 1888-1894.

_____. *Das Wesen des Christentums*. Leipzig: T. C. Hinrichs, 1900.

_____. *[Grundriss der] Dogmengeschichte*. 5th ed. Tübingen: J. C. B. Mohr, 1914.

Harvey, Van Austin. *The Historian and the Believer: The Morality of Historical Knowledge and Christian Belief*. New York: Macmillan, 1966.

Heick, Otto W. *A History of Christian Thought*. 2 vols. Philadelphia: Fortress Press, 1965-66.

Henry, Carl F. H. *God, Revelation, and Authority*. 5 vols. Waco, Tex.: Word Books, 1976-83.

Heraclitus. *The Cosmic Fragments*. Edited with an Introduction and Commentary by G. S. Kirk. Cambridge: University Press, 1962.

Heussi, Karl. *Die Krisis des Historismus*. Tübingen: Mohr (Siebeck), 1932.

Hick, John. *God and the Universe of Faiths*. New York: St. Martin's Press, 1973.

Hoffer, Eric. *The Ordeal of Change*. New York: Harper & Row, 1952/1963.

Inge, W. R. *The Idea of Progress*. Oxford: Clarendon Press, 1920.

Jaspert, Bernd. "'Krise' als kirchengeschichtliche Kategorie." In *Traditio – Krisis – Renovatio aus theologischer Sicht*. Edited by Bernd Jaspert and Rudolf Mohr, 24-40. Festschrift Winfried Zeller zum 65. Geburtstag. Marburg: N. G. Elwert, 1976.

Jaspert, Bernd, and Rudolf Mohr, eds. *Traditio – Krisis – Renovatio aus theologischer Sicht*. Festschrift Winfried Zeller zum 65. Geburtstag. Marburg: N. G. Elwert, 1976.

Joest, Wilfried. "Zur Frage des Paradoxon in der Theologie." In *Dogma und Denkstrukturen*. Edited by W. Joest and W. Pannenberg, 149-151. Festschrift für Edmund Schlink. Göttingen: Vandenhoeck & Ruprecht, 1963.

Joest, Wilfried, and Wolfhart Pannenberg, eds. *Dogma und Denkstrukturen.* Festschrift für
    Edmund Schlink. Göttingen: Vandenhoeck & Ruprecht, 1963.

Journet, Charles. *Esquisse du développement du dogme marial.* Paris: Alsatia, 1954.

Käsemann, Ernst. "The Canon of the New Testament and the Unity of the Church." In *Essays
    on New Testament Themes,* 95-107. Studies in Biblical Theology, no. 41. London: SCM,
    1964.

_____. "Zum Thema der Nichtobjektivierbarkeit." In *Exegetische Versuche und
    Besinnungen,* 1:224-236. Göttingen: Vandenhoeck & Ruprecht, 1964.

Kantzenbach, Friedrich Wilhelm. *Evangelium und Dogma: Die Bewältigung des theologischen
    Problems der Dogmengeschichte im Protestantismus.* Stuttgart: Evangelisches Verlagswerk,
    1959.

Kasper, Walter. *Dogma unter dem Wort Gottes.* Mainz: Matthias-Grünewald Verlag, 1965.

_____. "The Relationship between Gospel and Dogma: An Historical Approach." In *Man
    as Man & Believer.* Concilium: Theology in the Age of Renewal, vol. 21. Edited by E.
    Schillebeeckx and B. Willems, 161-163. New York, and Glen Rock, N.J.: Paulist Press,
    1967.

Köhler, Walther. *Dogmengeschichte als Geschichte des christlichen Selbstbewusstseins.* 2 vols.
    Zürich: Max Niehans, 1951.

Küng, Hans. *The Church.* New York: Sheed and Ward, 1967.

_____. *Wahrhaftigkeit: Zur Zukunft der Kirche.* Freiburg, Basle, Vienna: Herder, 1968;
    9th ed., 1978. ET: *Truthfulness: The Future of the Church.* New York: Sheed and Ward,
    1968.

_____. *Infallible? An Inquiry.* Garden City, N.Y.: Doubleday, 1971.

Küng, Hans, and David Tracy, eds. *Theologie – wohin? Auf dem Weg zu einem neuen
    Paradigma.* Zurich and Cologne: Benziger, 1984; Gütersloh: Gütersloher Verlagshaus
    Gerd Mohn, 1984.

Kulenkampff, Arend. *Antinomie und Dialektik.* Stuttgart: Metzler, 1970.

Ladd, George Eldon. *The New Testament and Criticism.* Grand Rapids: Eerdmans, 1967.

Lash, Nicholas. *Change in Focus: A Study of Doctrinal Change and Continuity.* London:
    Sheed & Ward, 1973.

_____, ed. *Doctrinal Development and Christian Unity.* London: Sheed & Ward, 1967.

Lawler, J. G. "The Future of Belief Debate." In *New Theology, No. 5.* Edited by M. E. Marty and D. G. Peerman, 178-180. New York: Macmillan; London: Collier-Macmillan, 1968.

Leith, John H., ed. *Creeds of the Churches.* Rev. ed. Atlanta: John Knox Press, 1973.

Lengsfeld, Peter. *Überlieferung: Tradition und Schrift in der evangelischen und katholischen Theologie der Gegenwart.* Konfessionskundliche und kontroverstheologische Studien, vol. 3. Paderborn: Verlag Bonifacius-Druckerei, 1960.

Lennerz, Heinrich. *De Beata Virgine tractatus dogmaticus.* Rome: Gregorian University Press, 1957.

Léonard, G.-P. "History and Dogma." In *Proceedings of the Twenty-Eighth Annual Convention,* Catholic Theological Society of America. Bronx, N.Y.: Catholic Theological Society of America, 1973, 103-123.

Lindbeck, George A. "The Problem of Doctrinal Development and Contemporary Protestant Theology." In *Man as Man and Believer.* Concilium: Theology in the Age of Renewal, vol. 21. Edited by E. Schillebeeckx and B. Willems, 133-149. New York, and Glen Rock, N.J.: Paulist Press, 1967.

_____. *The Future of Roman Catholic Theology: Vatican II – Catalyst for Change.* Philadelphia: Fortress Press, 1968/1970.

Löhrer, Magnus. "Überlegungen zur Interpretation lehramtlicher Aussagen als Frage des ökumenischen Gesprächs." In *Gott in Welt. Festgabe für Karl Rahner.* Edited by J. B. Metz et al., 2:499-523. Freiburg: Herder, 1964.

Lonergan, Bernard J. F. *Insight: A Study of Human Understanding.* New York: Philosophical Library, 1957.

_____. *Method in Theology.* New York: Seabury Press, 1972.

_____. *The Way to Nicea: The Dialectical Development of Trinitarian Theology.* London: Darton, Longman & Todd, 1976.

Loofs, Friedrich. *Leitfaden zum Studium der Dogmengeschichte.* 6th ed. Edited by Kurt Aland. Tübingen: M. Niemeyer, 1959.

Mananzan, Mary-John. "Crisis as a Necessary Impetus to Spiritual Growth." In *Traditio – Krisis – Renovatio aus theologischer Sicht.* Edited by Bernd Jaspert and Rudolf Mohr, 560-561. Festschrift Winfried Zeller zum 65. Geburtstag. Marburg: N. G. Elwert, 1976.

Maraldo, John C. *Der hermeneutische Zirkel: Untersuchungen zu Schleiermacher, Dilthey und Heidegger.* Symposium, vol. 48. Freiburg and Munich: Karl Alber, 1974.

Marin-Sola, F. *L'Évolution homogPne du dogme catholique.* 2 vols. Friburg: L'Oeuvre de Saint-Paul, 1924.

Martinez, Fidel G. *Estudios teológicos. En torno al objeto de la fe y a la evolución del dogma.*
2 vols. OZa [Burgos]: Sociedad Internacional Francisco Suárez, 1953-1958.

_____. *Evolución del dogma y regla de fe.* Madrid: Instituto Francisco Suárez, 1962.

Marty, M. E., and D. G. Peerman. *New Theology, No. 5.* New York: Macmillan, 1968;
London: Collier-Macmillan, 1968.

McGrath, Mark G. *The Vatican Council's Teaching on the Evolution of Dogma.*
[Rome: n.p.], 1960.

Meinecke, Friedrich. *Die Entstehung des Historismus.* 2 vols. Munich and Berlin:
R. Oldenbourg, 1936.

Meuleman, G. E. *De ontwikkeling van het dogma in de Rooms katholieke theologie.*
Kampen: J. H. Kok, 1951.

Migne, J. P., ed. *Patrologia Latina.* 221 vols. Paris: Migne, 1844-1864.

Murray, John Courtney. *The Problem of God: Yesterday and Today.* New Haven, Conn.:
Yale University Press, 1964.

Neuenschwander, Ulrich. *Die neue liberale Theologie: Eine Standortbestimmung.* Berne:
Verlag Stämpfli & Cie, 1953.

Newman, John Henry (Cardinal). *An Essay on the Development of Christian Doctrine.*
Westminster, Md.: Christian Classics, 1968. (Reprint of the 2d ed., 1878; originally
published 1845.)

Niebuhr, H. Richard. *Christ and Culture.* New York: Harper Torchbooks, 1956.

Nisbet, Robert. *History of the Idea of Progress.* New York: Basic Books, 1980.

Nolte, Josef. *Dogma in Geschichte.* Freiburg, Basle, Vienna: Herder, 1971.

Oden, Thomas C. *Agenda for Theology.* New York: Harper & Row, 1979.

Ommen, Thomas B. *The Hermeneutic of Dogma.* American Academy of Religion
Dissertation Series, no. 11. Missoula, Mont.: Scholars Press, 1975.

Orr, James. *The Progress of Dogma.* London: Hodder and Stoughten, 1901.

Packer, J. I. *"Fundamentalism" and the Word of God.* Grand Rapids: Eerdmans, 1958.

Pannenberg, Wolfhart. "Heilsgeschehen und Geschichte." In *Grundfragen systematischer
Theologie: Gesammelte Aufsätze,* 1:22-78. Göttingen: Vandenhoeck & Ruprecht, 1967.

_____. "Was ist eine dogmatische Aussage?" In *Grundfragen systematischer Theologie: Gesammelte Aufsätze,* 1:159-180. Göttingen: Vandenhoeck & Ruprecht, 1967. ET: "What Is a Dogmatic Statement?" In *Basic Questions in Theology: Collected Essays,* 1:182-210. Philadelphia: Fortress Press, 1970.

Pannenberg, Wolfhart, Avery Dulles, and Carl E. Braaten. *Spirit, Faith, and Church.* Philadelphia: Westminster, 1970.

Pelikan, Jaroslav. *Development of Christian Doctrine: Some Historical Prolegomena.* New Haven and London: Yale University Press, 1969.

_____. *Historical Theology: Continuity and Change in Christian Doctrine.* Philadelphia: Westminster, 1971.

_____. *The Christian Tradition: A History of the Development of Doctrine.* 5 vols. Chicago and London: University of Chicago Press, 1971-1989.

Pieper, Franz. *Christliche Dogmatik.* Rev. ed. St. Louis, Mo.: Evangelisch-Lutherische Synode, 1946.

Pittenger, W. Norman. *Process Thought and Christian Faith.* New York: Macmillan, 1968.

Popper, Karl R. *The Poverty of Historicism.* Boston: Beacon Press, 1957.

Rahner, Karl. *Schriften zur Theologie.* 16 vols. Einsiedeln: Benziger, 1954-1984. ET: *Theological Investigations.* 23 vols. Baltimore: Helicon, 1961-1992; London: Darton, Longman & Todd, 1961-1992.

_____. "Zur Frage der Dogmenentwicklung." In *Schriften zur Theologie,* 1:49-90. Einsiedeln: Benziger, 1954. ET: "The Development of Dogma." In *Theological Investigations,* 1:39-77. Baltimore: Helicon Press, 1961.

_____. "Überlegungen zur Dogmenentwicklung." In *Schriften zur Theologie,* 4:11-50. Einsiedeln: Benziger, 1960. ET: „Considerations on the Development of Dogma." In *Theological Investigations,* 4:3-35. Baltimore: Helicon, 1966.

_____. "Was ist eine dogmatische Aussage?" In *Schriften zur Theologie,* 5:54-81. Einsiedeln: Benziger, 1962. ET: "What Is a Dogmatic Statement?" In *Theological Investigations,* 5:42-66. Baltimore: Helicon, 1966.

Rahner, Karl, and Karl Lehmann. "Geschichtlichkeit der Vermittlung." In *Mysterium Salutis: Grundriß heilsgeschichtlicher Dogmatik.* Edited by Johannes Feiner and Magnus Löhrer. Vol. 1, *Die Grundlagen heilsgeschichtlicher Dogmatik,* 727-738. Einsiedeln, Zurich, Cologne: Benziger, 1965.

Rainy, Robert. *The Delivery and Development of Christian Doctrine.* Edinburgh: T. & T. Clark, 1874.

Ramsey, Arthur Michael. *From Gore to Temple: The Development of Anglican Theology between Lux Mundi and the Second World War, 1889-1939.* London: Longmans, 1960.

Ranke, Leopold von. "Preface to the History of the Latin and Teutonic Nations." In *The Varieties of History.* 2d ed. Edited by F. Stern, 55-62. London: Macmillan, 1970.

Ratzinger, Josef. *Das Problem der Dogmengeschichte in der Sicht der katholischen Kirche.* Cologne/Opladen: Westdeutscher Verlag, 1966.

Reiser, William E. *What Are They Saying about Dogma?* New York: Paulist Press, 1978.

Richardson, Alan. *The Bible in the Age of Science.* Philadelphia: Westminster Press, 1961.

Rienstra, M. Howard. "History, Objectivity, and the Christian Scholar." In *History and Historical Understanding.* Edited by C. T. McIntire and Ronald A. Wells, 69-82. Grand Rapids: Eerdmans, 1984.

Rivière, Jean. *Le modernisme dans l'Église.* Paris: Letouzey et Ané, 1929.

Robinson, John A. T. *Honest to God.* Philadelphia: Westminster, 1963.

Ruether, Rosemary. *The Church against Itself.* New York: Herder and Herder, 1967.

Ruler, A. A. van. "The Evolution of Dogma." In *Christianity Divided: Protestant and Roman Catholic Theological Issues.* Edited by D. J. Callahan, H. A. Oberman, and D. J. O'Hanlon, 89-105. New York: Sheed and Ward, 1961.

Scheffczyk, Leo. *Tendenzen und Brennpunkte der neueren Problematik um die Hellenisierung des Christentums.* Munich: Verlag der Bayerischen Akademie der Wissenschaften, 1982.

Schillebeeckx, Edward. "Exegesis, Dogmatics, and the Development of Dogma." In *Dogmatic versus Biblical Theology.* Edited by H. Vorgrimler, 115-145. Baltimore: Helicon, 1964.

_____. *Offenbarung und Theologie.* Mainz: Matthias-Grünewald-Verlag, 1965.

_____. *Revelation and Theology.* New York: Sheed and Ward, 1967.

_____. *God, the Future of Man.* New York: Sheed and Ward, 1968.

_____. *The Concept of Truth and Theological Renewal.* London and Sydney: Sheed and Ward, 1968.

_____. *Gott – die Zukunft des Menschen.* Mainz: Matthias-Grünewald, 1969.

_____. "A Theological Reflection." In *Truth and Certainty.* Concilium, vol. 83. Edited by E. Schillebeeckx and B. van Iersel, 77-94. New York: Herder and Herder, 1973.

_____. *The Understanding of Faith: Interpretation and Criticism.* New York: Seabury Press, 1974.

Schlink, Edmund. "Der theologische Syllogismus als Problem der Prädestinationslehre." In *Einsicht und Glaube.* Festschrift für Gottlieb Söhngen. Edited by J. Ratzinger and H. Fries, 299-320. Freiburg: Herder, 1962.

_____. "The Structure of Dogmatic Statements as an Ecumenical Problem." In *The Coming Christ and the Coming Church,* 16-84. Edinburgh: Oliver & Boyd, 1967.

Schmaus, Michael. *Katholische Dogmatik.* 6th enl. ed. Munich: Max Hueber, 1960.

Schmaus, Michael, Alois Grillmeyer, and Leo Scheffczyk, eds. *Handbuch der Dogmengeschichte.* 4 vols. Freiburg, Basle, Vienna: Herder, 1951-. Vol. 1, pt. 5, *Dogma und Dogmenentwicklung,* by Georg Söll. Freiburg, Basle, Vienna: Herder, 1971.

Schoof, Mark. *A Survey of Catholic Theology 1800-1970.* Paramus, N.J., and New York: Paulist Newman Press, 1970.

Schoonenberg, Piet. "Geschichtlichkeit und Interpretation des Dogmas." In *Die Interpretation des Dogmas.* Edited by P. Schoonenberg, 58-110. Düsseldorf: Patmos-Verlag, 1969.

Schulz, Winfried. *Dogmenentwicklung als Problem der Geschichtlichkeit der Wahrheitserkenntnis: Eine erkenntnistheoretisch-theologische Studie zum Problemkreis der Dogmenentwicklung.* Analecta Gregoriana, vol. 173. Rome: Gregorian University Press, 1969.

Seeberg, Reinhold. *Lehrbuch der Dogmengeschichte.* 2 vols. Erlangen and Leipzig: A. Deichert, 1895-1898.

_____. *Grundriss der Dogmengeschichte.* 4th rev. ed. Leipzig: A. Deichert, 1919.

Söhngen, G. "Überlieferung und apostolische Verkündigung." In *Die Einheit in der Theologie,* 305-323. Munich: K. Zink, 1952.

Stumpf, Samuel Enoch. *Socrates to Sartre: A History of Philosophy.* 2d ed. New York: McGraw-Hill, 1975.

Thielicke, Helmut. *Der Evangelische Glaube: Grundzüge der Dogmatik.* Vol 1, *Prolegomena: Die Beziehung der Theologie zu den Denkformen der Neuzeit.* Tübingen: J. C. B. Mohr (Paul Siebeck), 1968.

Tillich, Paul. *Systematic Theology.* 3 vols. Chicago: University of Chicago Press, 1951-1963.

Toon, Peter. *The Development of Doctrine in the Church.* Grand Rapids: Eerdmans, 1979.

Toulmin, Stephen, and June Goodfield. *The Discovery of Time.* New York: Harper and Row, 1965.

Tracy, David. *Blessed Rage for Order: The New Pluralism in Theology.* New York: Seabury Press, 1975.
————. *The Analogical Imagination: Christian Theology and the Culture of Pluralism.* New York: Crossroad, 1981.

Troeltsch, Ernst. *The Social Teachings of the Christian Churches.* 2 vols. New York: Macmillan, 1931.

Trueblood, D. Elton. *General Philosophy.* Grand Rapids: Baker, 1963.

Turner, H. E. W. *The Pattern of Christian Truth: A Study in the Relations between Orthodoxy and Heresy in the Early Church.* London: Mowbray, 1954; Naperville, Ill.: Allenson, 1954.

Vahanian, Gabriel. *The Death of God.* New York: G. Braziller, 1961.

Van Buren, P. *The Secular Meaning of the Gospel Based on an Analysis of Its Language.* New York: Macmillan, 1963.

————. *Theological Explorations.* New York: Macmillan, 1968.

Vollert, Cyril. "Doctrinal Development: A Basic Theory." In *Proceedings of the Twelfth Annual Convention,* by the Catholic Theological Society of America. Philadelphia: Catholic Theological Society of America, 1958, 45-70.

Wagar, W. Warren. *Good Tidings: The Belief in Progress from Darwin to Marcuse.* Bloomington, Ind.: University Press, 1972.

————, ed. *The Idea of Progress since the Renaissance.* New York: Wiley, 1969.

Walgrave, Jan Hendrik. *Unfolding Revelation: The Nature of Doctrinal Development.* Philadelphia: Westminster Press, 1972.

Weber, Max. *Gesammelte Aufsätze zur Religionssoziologie I.* Tübingen: J. C. B. Mohr, 1920.

Whitehead, Alfred North. *Religion in the Making.* New York: Macmillan, 1926.
————. *Process and Reality: An Essay in Cosmology.* New York: Macmillan, 1929.

Wiles, Maurice. *The Making of Christian Doctrine: A Study in the Principles of Early Doctrinal Development.* Cambridge: Cambridge University Press, 1967.
————. *The Remaking of Christian Doctrine.* London: SCM, 1974.
————. *Working Papers in Doctrine.* London: SCM, 1976.

Wilken, Robert L. *The Myth of Christian Beginnings: History's Impact on Belief.* Garden City, N.Y.: Doubleday, 1971.

Wolf, Ernst. "'Kerygma und Dogma'? Prolegomena zum Problem und zur Problematik der Dogmengeschichte." In *Antwort: K. Barth zum 70. Geburtstag,* 780-807. Zollikon-Zurich: Evangelischer Verlag, 1956.

Articles

Aland, K. "Dogmengeschichte." *Die Religion in Geschichte und Gegenwart: Handwörterbuch für Theologie und Religionswissenschaft.* 3d ed., 1958. 2:230-234.

Aristotle Dictionary. Edited by Thomas P. Kiernan. New York: Philosophical Library, 1962. S.v. "On Generation and Corruption." and "Metaphysics."

Atkins, Anselm. „Religious Assertions and Doctrinal Development." *Theological Studies* 27 (1966): 523-552.

————. "Doctrinal Development and Dialectic." *Continuum* 6 (1968): 3-23.

Auer. J. "Dogmengeschichte." *Lexikon für Theologie und Kirche.* 2d ed., 1959. 3:463-470.

Bacht, H. "Dogmatische Tatsachen." *Lexikon für Theologie und Kirche.* 2d ed., 1959. 3:456-457.

Bandt, Hellmut. "Kontinuität und Veränderlichkeit." *Studia Theologica* 28 (1974): 69-85.

Baum, Gregory. "Doctrinal Renewal." *Journal of Ecumenical Studies* 2 (1965): 365-381.

Beisser, Friedrich. "Irrwege und Wege der historisch-kritischen Bibelwissenschaft: Auch ein Vorschlag zur Reform des Theologiestudiums." *Neue Zeitschrift für systematische Theologie und Religionsphilosophie* 15 (1973): 192-214.

Bianchi, Eugene C. "History and Evolution in Roman Catholic Thought." *Religion in Life* 38 (1969): 498-521.

————. "A Holistic and Dynamic Development of Doctrinal Symbols." *Anglican Theological Review* 55 (1973): 148-169.

Bruce, F. F. "The Kerygma of Hebrews." *Interpretation* 23:1 (1969): 3-19.

Brugger, Walter. "Development." *Philosophical Dictionary.* Edited by Walter Brugger and Kenneth Baker. Spokane, Wash.: Gonzaga University Press, 1972. 92-93.

Capek, Milic. "Change." *Encyclopedia of Philosophy.* 1967 ed. 2:75-79.

Centore, F. F. "Evolution (Some Philosophical Dimensions)." *New Catholic Encyclopedia.* Supplement, 1974. 16:175-177.

Chirico, Peter. "Religious Experience and Development of Dogma." *American Benedictine Review* 23 (1972): 56-84.

Connell, Desmond. "Professor Dewart and Dogmatic Development." *Irish Theological Quarterly* 34 (1967): 309-328; 35 (1968): 33-57, 117-140.

Crowe, Frederick E. "Development of Doctrine and the Ecumenical Problem." *Theological Studies* 23 (1962): 27-46.

_____. "Dogma versus the Self-Correcting Process of Learning." *Theological Studies* 31 (1970): 610-611.

_____. "Dogmatic Theology." *New Catholic Encyclopedia.* Supplement, 1974. 16:132.

Daecke, S. M. "Entwicklung." *Theologische Realenzyklopädie.* 1982 ed. 9:705-716.

DeLetter, P. "Theology, Influence of Greek Theology On." *New Catholic Encyclopedia.* 1967 ed. 14:51-61.

_____. "Note on the Reformability of Dogmatic Formulas." *Thomist* 38 (1974): 747-753.

DeWolf, L. Harold. "Motifs of Continuity and Discontinuity." *Religion in Life* 32 (1963): 334-350.

A Dictionary of Christian Theology. Edited by Alan Richardson. Philadelphia: Westminster Press, 1969. S.v. "Development, Doctrine of."

Donelly, Ph. J. "On the Development of Dogma and the Supernatural." *Theological Studies* 8 (1947): 471-491.

_____. "Theological Opinion on the Development of Dogma." *Theological Studies* 8 (1947): 668-699.

Dulles, Avery. "Dogma as an Ecumenical Problem." *Theological Studies* 29 (1968): 397-416.

Ebeling, Gerhard. "Die Bedeutung der historisch-kritischen Methode für die protestantische Theologie und Kirche." *Zeitschrift für Theologie und Kirche* 47 (1950): 1-46.

Filson, Floyd V. "Method in Studying Biblical History." *Journal of Biblical Literature* 69 (1950): 1-18.

Gerdes, Egon. "Dogma." *Weltkirchenlexikon.* 1960 ed. Col. 289.

Gilkey, Langdon. "Theology and the Future." *Andover Newton Quarterly* 17 (1977): 250-257.

Grillmeier, A. "Hellenisierung und Judaisierung des Christentums als Deuteprinzipien der Geschichte des kirchlichen Dogmas." *Scholastik* 33 (1958): 321-355, 528-558.

Gundry, Stanley N. "Rahner on the Development of Dogma." *Journal of the Evangelical Theological Society* 15 (1972): 207-213.

Gunton, Colin. "Karl Barth and the Development of Christian Doctrine." *Scottish Journal of Theology* 25 (1972): 171-180.

Hahn, Ferdinand. "Probleme historischer Kritik." *Zeitschrift für die neutestamentliche Wissenschaft und die Kunde der älteren Kirche* 63 (1972): 1-17.

Halton, T. P. "Christianity and Hellenism." *New Catholic Encyclopedia.* 1967 ed. 3:653-654.

Hanson, R. P. C. "Tradition." *A Dictionary of Christian Theology.* Edited by Alan Richardson. Philadelphia: Westminster Press, 1969. 342.

Hengel, Martin. "Historische Methoden und theologische Auslegung des Neuen Testaments." *Kerygma und Dogma* 19 (1973): 85-90.

Henry, Paul. "Hellenism and Christianity." *Sacramentum Mundi.* 1968 ed. 3:10-16.

Hughes, Philip E. "Evolutionary Dogma and Christian Theology." *Westminster Theological Journal* 18 (1955): 34-47.

Jenson, Robert W. "Missouri and the Existential Fear of Change." *Dialog* 14 (1975): 247-250.

Jossua, Jean-Pierre. "Immutabilité, progres, ou structurations multiples des doctrines chrétiennes?" *Revue des sciences philosophiques et théologiques* 52 (1968): 173-200.

_____. "Rule of Faith and Orthodoxy." *Concilium* 6:1 (1970): 56-67.

Käsemann, Ernst. "Vom theologischen Recht historisch-kritischer Exegese." *Zeitschrift für Theologie und Kirche* 64 (1967): 259-281.

Kasper, Walter. "Geschichtlichkeit der Dogmen?" *Stimmen der Zeit* (1967): 401-416.

Koester, Helmut. "[Gnomai Diaphoroi.] The Origin and Nature of Diversification in the History of Early Christianity." *Harvard Theological Review* 58 (1965): 279-318.

Lohse, Bernhard. "Was verstehen wir unter Dogmengeschichte innerhalb der evangelischen Theologie?" *Kerygma und Dogma* 8 (1962): 27-45.

Loofs, Friedrich. "Dogmengeschichte." *Realencyklopädie.* 1898 ed. 4:760-764.

Malina, Bruce. "The Received View and What It Cannot Do: III John and Hospitality." *Semeia* 35 (1986): 171-194.

Maurer, Wilhelm. „Der Organismusgedanke bei Schelling und in der Theologie der Katholischen Tübinger Schule." *Kerygma und Dogma* 8 (1962): 202-211.

_____. "Das Prinzip des Organischen in der evangelischen Kirchengeschichtsschreibung des 19. Jahrhunderts." *Kerygma und Dogma* 8 (1962): 265-292.

Milavec, Donald Aaron. "The Bible As Inspiring and Authorising Incompatible Doctrines and Practices." *Église et Théologie* 7 (1976): 189-218.

_____. "Modern Exegesis, Doctrinal Innovations, and the Dynamics of Discipleship."
  Anglican Theological Review 60 (1978): 55-74.

Misner, P. "A Note on the Critique of Dogmas." *Theological Studies* 34 (1973): 690-700.

Moiser, Jeremy. "Propositional Transference." *Irish Theological Quarterly* 43 (1976): 198-210.

Moltmann, Jürgen. "Christian Theology and Its Problem Today." *Reformed World* 32 (1972-
  1973): 5-16.

Mühle, G., and K. Weyland. "Entwicklung." *Historisches Wörterbuch der Philosophie.*
  Edited by Joachim Ritter. Basle and Stuttgart: Schwabe & Co., 1971-. 2:550-560.

Nicholls, David. "Modifications and Movements." *Journal of Theological Studies* 25 (1974):
  393-417.

Nielsen, H. A. "Antinomy." *New Catholic Encyclopedia.* 1967 ed. 1:621-623.

Outler, Albert C. "The New Iconoclasm and the Integrity of the Faith." *Theology Today*
  25 (1968): 295-319.

The Oxford Dictionary of the Christian Church. Edited by F. L. Cross and E. A. Livingstone.
  2d ed. Oxford: Oxford University Press, 1974.

Pelikan, Jaroslav. "The Past of Belief: Reflections of a Historian of Doctrine on Dewart's
  The Future of Belief." *Theological Studies* 28 (1967): 352-356.

_____. "Theology and Change." *Cross Currents* 19 (1969): 375-384.

Pittenger, W. Norman. "Reconception and Renewal of Christian Faith." *Encounter*
  34 (1973): 254-266.

Rahner, Karl. "Dogmenentwicklung." *Lexikon für Theologie und Kirche.* 2d ed., 1959.
  3:457-463.

_____. "Dogma I. Theological Meaning of Dogma." *Sacramentum Mundi* 1968 ed. 2:95-98.

_____. "Magisterium." *Sacramentum Mundi.* 1968 ed. 3:351-358.

_____. "Scripture and Tradition." *Sacramentum Mundi.* 1968 ed. 6:54.

_____. "The Historical Dimension in Theology." *Theology Digest,* Sesquicentennial Issue,
  16 (1968): 30-42.

Rausch, Thomas P. "Development of Doctrine." *The New Dictionary of Theology.* Edited by
  Joseph A. Komonchak, Mary Collins, and Dermot A. Lane. Wilmington, Del.: Michael
  Glazier, 1987. 280-283.

Richard, Robert L. "Contribution to a Theory of Doctrinal Development." *Continuum* 2 (1964): 505-527.

Richardson, Alan. "History, Problem of." *A Dictionary of Christian Theology.* Edited by Alan Richardson. Philadelphia: Westminster Press, 1969. 156.

Runia, Klaas. "Dangerous Trends in Modern Theological Thought." *Concordia Theological Monthly* 35 (1964): 331-342.

Schlink, Edmund. "Die Struktur der dogmatischen Aussage als ökumenisches Problem." *Kerygma und Dogma* 3 (1957): 251-306.

Schneemelcher, W. "Das Problem der Dogmengeschichte: Zum 100. Geburtstag Adolf von Harnacks." *Zeitschrift für Theologie und Kirche* 48 (1951): 63-89.

Sheedy, C. E. "Opinions Concerning Doctrinal Development." *American Ecclesiastical Review* 120 (1949): 19-32.

Sheets, John R. "Teilhard De Chardin and the Development of Dogma." *Theological Studies* 30 (1969): 445-462.

Stomps, M. "Entwicklung." *Evangelisches Kirchenlexikon.* 2d ed., 1956. 1:1095-1096.

Stroll, Avrum. "Identity." *Encyclopedia of Philosophy.* 1967 ed. 4:121-124.

Stuhlmacher, Peter. "Neues Testament und Hermeneutik: Versuch einer Bestandsaufnahme." *Zeitschrift für Theologie und Kirche* 68 (1971): 121-161.

_____. "Thesen zur Methodologie gegenwärtiger Exegese." *Zeitschrift für die neutestamentliche Wissenschaft und die Kunde der älteren Kirche* 63 (1972): 18-26.

Toon, Peter. "Development of Doctrine." *New Dictionary of Theology.* Edited by Sinclair B. Ferguson and David F. Wright. Downers Grove, Ill., and Leicester, England: InterVarsity Press, 1988. 196.

Vorgrimler, H., K. Rahner, and W. Lohff. "Dogma." *Lexikon für Theologie und Kirche.* 2d ed., 1959. 3:438-446.

Walgrave, Jan Hendrik. "Doctrine, Development of." *New Catholic Encyclopedia.* 1967 ed. 4:942.

_____. "Doctrine, Development of." *New Catholic Encyclopedia.* Supplement, 1974. 16:131.

Webster's New Dictionary of Synonyms. Springfield, Mass.: G. & C. Merriam Co., 1973. S.v. "Development, Evolution"; "Estimate"; "Predicament, Dilemma, [and others]"; and "Progress."

Wegenast, K. "Teach." *The New International Dictionary of New Testament Theology.* Edited
    by Colin Brown. Grand Rapids: Zondervan, 1975-1978. 3:759-775.

Wiles, Maurice. "Theology and Unity." *Theology* 77 (1974): 4-6.

————. "The Remaking Defended." *Theology* 78 (1975): 394-397.

Winquist, Charles E. "Reconstruction in Process Theology." *Anglican Theological Review*
    55 (1973): 169-181.

Dissertations

Eckstrom, Vance LeRoy. "Development of Dogma and Doctrinal Pluralism."
    Th.D. dissertation, Graduate Theological Union, 1971.

Eichhorst, Calvin Jacob. "Dogma and Its Development in Recent German Catholic Theology."
    Ph.D. dissertation, Yale University, 1972.

Floyd, Gerald Thomas. "The Creativity of Church Teaching: A Whiteheadian
    Alternative to the Notion of Development of Doctrine."
    Ph.D. dissertation, Graduate Theological Union, 1982.

Gunther, John Jacob. "Papal Views on Authority and Doctrinal Development."
    Ph.D. dissertation, Harvard University, 1963.

Hines, Mary Elizabeth. "Karl Rahner on Religious and Theological Possibilities
    of Dogma Today."
    Ph.D. dissertation, University of St. Michael's College [Canada], 1984.

Hunt, W. C. "Intuition: The Key to John Henry Newman's Theory of Doctrinal Development."
    S.T.D. dissertation, Catholic University of America, 1967.

Kinast, R. L. "Newman's Notes for Genuine Development as a Criteriological Framework."
    Ph.D. dissertation, Emory University, 1977.

Morris, John R. "The Convergence of Doctrine: Hope of Ecumenism."
    Th.D. dissertation, Graduate Theological Union, 1976.

Reiser, W. E. "What Calls Forth Heresy? An Essay on the Development of Dogma
    within a Heideggerian Context."
    Ph.D. dissertation, Vanderbilt University, 1977.

Sundberg, Walter Karl, Jr. "The Development of Dogma as an Ecumenical Problem: Roman
    Catholic-Protestant Conflict over the Authority and Historicity of Dogmatic Statements."
    Ph.D. dissertation, Princeton Theological Seminary, 1981.

Literature by and about Seventh-day Adventists including Sociology of Religion

Books and Pamphlets

A. T. Jones: The Man and the Message: A Book Review. Uniontown, Ohio: The 1888 Message Study Committee, 1988.

Adams, Roy. *The Sanctuary Doctrine: Three Approaches in the Seventh-day Adventist Church.* Andrews University Seminary Doctoral Dissertation Series, vol. 1. Berrien Springs, Mich.: Andrews University Press, 1981.

_____. *The Sanctuary: Understanding the Heart of Adventist Theology.* Hagerstown, Md.: Review and Herald Pub. Assn., 1993.

_____. *The Nature of Christ.* Hagerstown, Md.: Review and Herald Pub. Assn., 1994.

Ahlstrom, Sydney E. *A Religious History of the American People.* New Haven, Conn.: Yale University Press, 1972.

Anderson, Godfrey T. "The Great Second Advent Awakening to 1844." In *The Advent Hope in Scripture and History.* Edited by V. Norskov Olsen, 152-172. Washington, D.C., and Hagerstown, Md.: Review and Herald Pub. Assn., 1987.

Anderson, Roy Allan. *Unfolding the Revelation.* Rev. ed. Boise, Idaho: Pacific Press Pub. Assn., 1974.

Andreasen, M. L. *The Sanctuary Service.* Washington, D.C.: Review and Herald Pub. Assn., 1937; 2d rev. ed., 1947.

_____. *The Sabbath: Which Day and Why?* Washington, D.C.: Review and Herald Pub. Assn., 1942.

_____. *The Book of Hebrews.* Washington, D.C.: Review and Herald Pub. Assn., 1948.

_____. *Letters to the Churches.* Baker, Oreg.: Hudson Printing Co., 1959; reprint, Payson, Ariz.: Leaves-of-Autumn Books, 1980.

Andreasen, Niels-Erik. *Rest and Redemption: A Study of the Biblical Sabbath.* Andrews University Monographs, Studies in Religion, vol. 11. Berrien Springs, Mich.: Andrews University Press, 1978.

_____. *The Christian Use of Time.* Nashville: Abingdon, 1978.

Andrews, J. N. *The Perpetuity of the Royal Law; or the Ten Commandments Not Abolished.* Rochester, N.Y.: Advent Review Office, 1854.

Andross, E. E. *Turkey and Its End.* Washington, D.C.: Review and Herald Pub. Assn., [1912-1913]; Mountain View, Calif.: Pacific Press Pub. Assn., [1912-1913].

An Appeal to Men of Reason and Common Sense. Battle Creek, Mich.: Seventh-day Adventist Pub. Assn., 1859.

Arthur, David T. "Millerism." In *The Rise of Adventism: Religion and Society in Mid-Nineteenth-Century America.* Edited by Edwin S. Gaustad, 154-172. New York: Harper & Row, 1974.

Bacchiocchi, Samuele. *Divine Rest for Human Restlessness: A Theological Study of the Good News of the Sabbath for Today.* Rome: By the Author, 1980.

_____. *The Sabbath in the New Testament: Answers to Questions.* Biblical Perspectives, no. 5. Berrien Springs, Mich.: By the Author, 1985.

_____. *The Advent Hope for Human Hopelessness: A Theological Study of the Meaning of the Second Advent for Today.* Biblical Perspectives, no. 6. Berrien Springs, Mich.: By the Author, 1986.

_____. *Hal Lindsey's Prophetic Jigsaw Puzzle: Five Predictions That Failed.* Biblical Perspectives, no. 3. Berrien Springs, Mich.: By the Author, 1987.

_____. *The Time of the Crucifixion and the Resurrection.* Biblical Perspectives, no. 4. Berrien Springs, Mich.: By the Author, 1985; new enl. ed., 1991.

Baldwin, Dalton D. "William Miller's Use of the Word 'Atonement'." In *Doctrine of the Sanctuary: A Historical Survey (1845-1863).* Daniel and Revelation Committee Series, vol. 5. Edited by Frank B. Holbrook, 159-170. Silver Spring, Md.: Biblical Research Institute, General Conference of Seventh-day Adventists, 1989.

Ball, Bryan W. *The English Connection: The Puritan Roots of Seventh-day Adventist Belief.* Cambridge: James Clarke, 1981.

Ballenger, Albion F. *Cast Out for the Cross of Christ.* Tropico, Calif.: By the Author, [1911].

_____. *An Examination of Forty Fatal Errors Regarding the Atonement.* Riverside, Calif.: By the Author, [1913].

Barkun, Michael. *Crucible of the Millennium: The Burned-over District of New York in the 1840s.* Syracuse, N.Y.: Syracuse University Press, 1986.

Barr, James. *Fundamentalism.* Philadelphia: Westminster, 1977/1978.

Bates, Joseph. *The Opening Heavens.* New Bedford, Mass.: By the Author, 1846.

_____. *The Seventh Day Sabbath, a Perpetual Sign.* New Bedford, Mass.: By the Author, 1846; 2d rev. and enl. ed, 1847.

_____. *Second Advent Way Marks and High Heaps.* New Bedford, Mass.: By the Author, 1847.

_____. *A Vindication of the Seventh-Day Sabbath, and the Commandments of God.* New Bedford, Mass.: By the Author, 1848.

_____. *A Seal of the Living God.* New Bedford, Mass.: By the Author, 1849.

_____. *An Explanation of the Typical and Anti-Typical Sanctuary.* New Bedford, Mass.: By the Author, 1850.

Beach, W. R. "The Gospel Commission and the Remnant Church." In *Our Firm Foundation,* 2:425-462. Washington, D.C.: Review and Herald Pub. Assn., 1953.

_____. *The Creed That Changed the World.* Mountain View, Calif.: Pacific Press Pub. Assn., 1971.

Bible Readings for the Home. Washington, D.C.: Review and Herald Pub. Assn., 1949; Mountain View, Calif.: Pacific Press Pub. Assn., 1949.

Bible Readings for the Home Circle. Washington, D.C.: Review and Herald Pub. Assn., 1918. Rev. and enl. ed. Mountain View, Calif.: Pacific Press Pub. Assn., 1920.

The Bible Student's Assistant. Battle Creek, Mich.: Review & Herald Office, 1858.

The Bible Student's Assistant. N.p., [ca. 1860].

Billington, Ray Allen. *The Protestant Crusade, 1800-1860: A Study of the Origins of American Nativism.* New York: Macmillan, 1938.

Blazen, Ivan T. "Justification and Judgment." In *The Seventy Weeks, Leviticus, and the Nature of Prophecy.* Daniel and Revelation Committee Series, vol. 3. Edited by Frank B. Holbrook, 339-388. Silver Spring, Md.: Biblical Research Institute, General Conference of Seventh-day Adventists, 1986.

Bliss, Sylvester. *Memoirs of William Miller.* Boston: Joshua V. Himes, 1853.

Böttcher, Manfred. *Weg und Ziel der Gemeinde Jesu.* Hamburg: Advent-Verlag, 1981.

Branson, Roy, ed. *Festival of the Sabbath.* Takoma Park, Md.: Association of Adventist Forums, 1985.

_____, ed. *Pilgrimage of Hope.* Takoma Park, Md.: Association of Adventist Forums, 1986.

Branson, William H. *In Defense of the Faith.* Washington, D.C.: Review and Herald Pub. Assn., 1933.

_____. "'This Generation.'" In *Our Firm Foundation,* 2:700-704. Washington, D.C. Review and Herald Pub. Assn., 1953.

Brinsmead, Robert D. *1844 Re-Examined.* Institute Syllabus. Fallbrook, Calif.: I.H.I., 1979.

_____. *Judged by the Gospel: A Review of Adventism.* Fallbrook, Calif.: Verdict Publications, 1980.

_____. *Are the Gospel and the 1844 Theology Compatible?* Fallbrook, Calif.: Verdict Publications, 1980.

Brunt, John C. *A Day for Healing: The Meaning of Jesus' Sabbath Miracles.* Washington, D.C.: Review and Herald Pub. Assn., 1981.

_____. *Now and Not Yet.* Washington, D.C.: Review and Herald Pub. Assn., 1987.

Bull, Malcolm, and Keith Lockhart. *Seeking a Sanctuary: Seventh-day Adventism and the American Dream.* San Francisco: Harper & Row, 1989.

Bunch, Taylor G. "The Atonement and the Cross." In *Our Firm Foundation*, 1:357-434. Washington, D.C.: Review and Herald Pub. Assn., 1953.

Butler, George I. *The Law in the Book of Galatians.* Battle Creek, Mich.: Review and Herald Pub. Assn., 1886.

Butler, Jonathan M. "The Making of a New Order: Millerism and the Origins of Seventh-day Adventism." In *The Disappointed: Millerism and Millenarianism in the Nineteenth Century.* Edited by Ronald L. Numbers and Jonathan M. Butler, 189-208. Bloomington and Indianapolis: Indiana University Press, 1987.

_____. "Introduction: The Historian as Heretic." In Ronald L. Numbers, *Prophetess of Health: Ellen G. White and the Origins of Seventh-day Adventist Health Reform.* Rev. and enl. ed., XXV-LXVIII. Knoxville: University of Tennessee Press, 1992.

Canright, D. M. *The Bible from Heaven.* Battle Creek, Mich.: Seventh-day Adventist Pub. Assn., 1878.

_____. *Matter and Spirit.* Battle Creek, Mich.: Review and Herald Pub. Assn., 1882.

_____. *Seventh-day Adventism Renounced After an Experience of Twenty-Eight Years by a Prominent Minister and Writer of that Faith.* 2d ed. New York: Fleming H. Revell, 1889; 11th ed. Cincinnati, Ohio: Standard Publ. Co., 1905.

_____. *Life of Mrs. E. G. White, Seventh-day Adventist Prophet; Her False Claims Refuted.* Cincinnati, Ohio: Standard Publ. Co., 1919; Nashville: B. C. Goodpasture, 1953.

Carroll, Robert P. *When Prophecy Failed.* London: SCM, 1979.

Carwardine, Richard. *Transatlantic Revivalism: Popular Evangelicalism in Britain and America, 1790-1865.* Westport, Conn.: Greenwood Press, 1978.

Christian, L. H. *The Fruitage of Spiritual Gifts.* Washington, D.C.: Review and Herald Pub. Assn., 1947.

Church Hymnal: Official Hymnal of the Seventh-day Adventist Church. Takoma Park, Washington, D.C.: Review and Herald Pub. Assn., 1941.

Clark, Elmer T. *The Small Sects in America.* Rev. ed. New York and Nashville: Abingdon-Cokesbury, 1949.

Clark, Jerome L. *1844.* 3 vols. Nashville: Southern Pub. Assn., 1968.

Commager, Henry Steele. *The Era of Reform, 1830-1860.* Princeton, N.J.: Van Nostrand, 1960.

Conradi, Ludwig Richard. *Ist Frau E. G. White die Prophetin der Endgemeinde?* Hamburg: By the Author, [1933].

_____. *The Founders of the Seventh-day Adventist Denomination.* Plainfield, N.Y.: By the Author, 1939.

Cottrell, R. F. "Spiritual Gifts." Preface to Ellen G. White, *Spiritual Gifts.* Vol. 1, *The Great Controversy, between Christ and His Angels, and Satan and His Angels,* 5-16. Battle Creek, Mich.: James White, 1858.

[Cottrell, Raymond F.]. "Principles of Biblical Interpretation." Chap. in *Problems in Bible Translation.* Washington, D.C.: Committee on Problems in Bible Translation, 1954.

[_____]. "Role of Israel in Bible Prophecy." In *Seventh-day Adventist Bible Commentary.* Edited by F. D. Nichol, 4:25-38. Washington, D.C.: Review and Herald Pub. Assn., 1955.

_____. "The Sabbath in the New World." In *The Sabbath in Scripture and History.* Edited by Kenneth Strand, 244-263. Washington, D.C.: Review and Herald Pub. Assn., 1982.

Cross, Whitney R. *The Burned-Over District: The Social and Intellectual History of Enthusiastic Religion in Western New York, 1800-1850.* New York: Harper & Row, 1965.

Daily, Steven G. *Adventism for a New Generation.* Portland/Clackamas, Oreg.: Better Living Publishers, 1993.

Damsteegt, P. Gerard. *Foundations of the Seventh-day Adventist Message and Mission.* Grand Rapids: Eerdmans, 1977.

Daniells, Arthur G. *The World War: Its Relation to the Eastern Question and Armageddon.* Washington, D.C.: Review and Herald Pub. Assn., 1917.

————. *Christ Our Righteousness.* Washington, D.C.: Review and Herald Pub. Assn., 1926; 4th ed. 1941.

Davis, Thomas A. *Was Jesus Really Like Us?* Washington, D.C.: Review and Herald Pub. Assn., 1979.

A Declaration of the Fundamental Principles Taught and Practiced by the Seventh-day Adventists. Battle Creek, Mich.: Seventh-day Adventist Pub. Assn., 1872.

Dederen, Raoul. "Atoning Aspects in Christ's Death." In *The Sanctuary and the Atonement.* Edited by A. V. Wallenkampf and W. R. Lesher, 292-325. Washington, D.C.: General Conference of Seventh-day Adventists, 1981.

————. "Reflections on a Theology of the Sabbath." In *The Sabbath in Scripture and History.* Edited by Kenneth Strand, 295-306. Washington, D.C.: Review and Herald Pub. Assn., 1982.

Dick, Everett N. "The Millerite Movement, 1830-1945." In *Adventism in America: A History.* Edited by Gary Land, 1-35. Grand Rapids: Eerdmans, 1986.

A Discussion and Review of Prophetess of Health. Washington, D.C.: Ellen G. White Estate, General Conference [of Seventh-day Adventists], 1976.

Doan, Ruth Alden. *The Miller Heresy, Millennialism, and American Culture.* Philadelphia: Temple University Press, 1987.

Douglas, Walter B. T. "The Church: Its Nature and Function." In Gottfried Oosterwal, Russell L. Staples, Walter B. T. Douglas, and R. Edward Turner, *Servants for Christ: The Adventist Church Facing the '80s.* Edited by Robert E. Firth, 53-85. Berrien Springs, Mich.: Andrews University Press, 1980.

Douglass, Herbert E., Edward Heppenstall, Hans K. LaRondelle, and C. Mervyn Maxwell. *Perfection: The Impossible Possibility.* Nashville: Southern Pub. Assn., 1975.

Dudley, Roger L., and Edwin I. Hernandez. *Citizens of Two Worlds: Religion and Politics among American Seventh-day Adventists.* Berrien Springs, Mich.: Andrews University Press, 1992.

Eckenroth, M. K. "Christ the Center of All True Preaching." In *Our Firm Foundation,* 1:117-188. Washington, D.C.: Review and Herald Pub. Assn., 1953.

Edson, Hiram. *The Time of the End.* Auburn, N.Y.: By the Author, 1849.

Edwards, Walter O. *Great Fundamentals of the Bible.* Mountain View, Calif.: Pacific Press Pub. Assn., 1938.

The Ellen G. White 1888 Materials. 4 vols. Washington, D.C.: Ellen G. White Estate, 1987.

Emmerson, Walter Leslie. *The Bible Speaks: Scripture Readings Systematically Arranged.* Mountain View, Calif.: Pacific Press Pub. Assn., 1967.

_____. *The Reformation and the Advent Movement.* Washington, D.C.: Review and Herald Pub. Assn., 1983.

Études sur l'Apocalypse: Signification des messages des trois anges aujourd'hui. Conférences bibliques Division Euroafricaine, 2 vols. Salève, France: Institut Adventiste du Salève, 1988.

Festinger, Leon. *A Theory of Cognitive Dissonance.* Stanford, Calif.: Stanford University Press, 1957.

Festinger, Leon, Henry W. Riecken, and Stanley Schachter. *When Prophecy Fails.* Minneapolis, Minn.: University of Minnesota Press, 1956.

Fitch, Charles. *"Come Out of Her, My People": A Sermon.* Rochester, N.Y.: Joshua V. Himes, 1843.

Fletcher, W. W. *The Reasons for My Faith.* Sydney: William Brooks, 1932.

Folkenberg, Robert S. *We Still Believe.* Boise, Idaho: Pacific Press Pub. Assn., 1994.

Ford, Desmond. *Daniel 8:14, the Day of Atonement, and the Investigative Judgment.* Casselberry, Fla.: Euangelion Press, 1980.

Ford, Desmond, and Gillian Ford. *The Adventist Crisis of Spiritual Identity.* Newcastle, Calif.: Desmond Ford Publ., 1982.

Froom, LeRoy Edwin. *The Coming of the Comforter.* Washington, D.C.: Review and Herald Pub. Assn., 1928.

_____. *The Prophetic Faith of Our Fathers.* 4 vols. Washington, D.C.: Review and Herald Pub. Assn., 1954.

_____. *The Conditionalist Faith of Our Fathers.* 2 vols. Washington, D.C.: Review and Herald Pub. Assn., 1966.

_____. *Movement of Destiny.* Washington, D.C.: Review and Herald Pub. Assn., 1971.

"Fundamental Beliefs of Seventh-day Adventists." In *Seventh-day Adventist Yearbook,* 377-380. Washington, D.C.: Review and Herald Pub. Assn., 1931.

Fundamental Principles of Seventh-day Adventists. Words of Truth Series, vol. 5. Battle Creek, Mich.: Review and Herald Pub. Assn., 1897; reprint, Washington, D.C.: Review and Herald Pub. Assn., n.d.

Garrett, Leroy. *The Stone-Campbell Movement: An Anecdotal History of Three Churches.*
Joplin, Miss.: College Press Publ. Co., 1981.

Gaustad, Edwin S., ed. *The Rise of Adventism: Religion and Society in Mid-Nineteenth-
Century America.* New York: Harper & Row, 1974.

Gerstner, John H. *The Theology of the Major Sects.* Grand Rapids: Baker, 1960.

Glock, Charles Y., and R. Stark. *Religion and Society in Tension.* Chicago: Rand-McNally,
1965.

Goldstein, Clifford. *1844 Made Simple.* Boise, Idaho: Pacific Press Pub. Assn., 1988.

_____. *False Balances.* Boise, Idaho: Pacific Press Pub. Assn., 1992.

_____. *A Pause for Peace.* Boise, Idaho: Pacific Press Pub. Assn., 1992.

_____. *The Remnant.* Boise, Idaho: Pacific Press Pub. Assn., 1994.

Gordon, Paul A. *The Sanctuary, 1844, and the Pioneers.* Washington, D.C.: Review
and Herald Pub. Assn., 1983.

Graham, Roy E. *Ellen G. White: Co-Founder of the Seventh-day Adventist Church.*
American University Studies, series 7: Theology and Religion, vol. 12. New York,
Berne, and Frankfurt: Peter Lang, 1985.

Granger, William H. *Bible Footlights for the Pilgrim's Path.* Washington, D.C.: Review
and Herald Pub. Assn., 1907.

Guy, Fritz. "The Future and the Present: The Meaning of the Advent Hope." In *The
Advent Hope in Scripture and History.* Edited by V. Norskov Olsen, 211-229.
Washington, D.C., and Hagerstown, Md.: Review and Herald Pub. Assn., 1987.

Hale, Apollos. *Herald of the Bridegroom.* Boston: Joshua V. Himes, 1843.

Hammill, Richard L. *Pilgrimage: Memoirs of an Adventist Administrator.* Berrien Springs,
Mich.: Andrews University Press, 1992.

Hasel, Gerhard F. "General Principles of Interpretation." In *A Symposium on Biblical
Hermeneutics.* Edited by Gordon M. Hyde, 163-191. Washington, D.C.: General
Conference of Seventh-day Adventists, 1974.

_____. *Understanding the Living Word of God.* Mountain View, Calif.: Pacific Press
Pub. Assn., 1980.

_____. "The 'Little Horn,' the Saints, and the Sanctuary in Daniel 8." In *The Sanctuary
and the Atonement.* Edited by A. V. Wallenkampf and W. R. Lesher, 177-227.
Washington, D.C.: General Conference of Seventh-day Adventists, 1981.

_____. *Biblical Interpretation Today.* Washington, D.C.: Biblical Research Institute, 1985.

_____. "The 'Little Horn,' the Heavenly Sanctuary and the Time of the End: A Study of Daniel 8:9-14." In *Symposium on Daniel: Introductory and Exegetical Studies.* Daniel and Revelation Committee Series, vol. 2. Edited by Frank B. Holbrook, 426-461. Washington, D.C.: Biblical Research Institute, General Conference of Seventh-day Adventists, 1986.

Haskell, S. N. *The Story of Daniel the Prophet.* South Lancaster, Mass.: Bible Training School, 1908.

Hatch, Nathan O. *The Democratization of American Christianity.* New Haven and London: Yale University Press, 1989.

Haynes, C. B. *Christianity at the Crossroads.* Nashville: Southern Pub. Assn., 1924.

_____. *The Return of Jesus.* Washington, D.C.: Review and Herald Pub. Assn., 1926.

Hebert, Gabriel. *Fundamentalism and the Church of God.* London: SCM Press, 1957.

Heinz, Daniel. *Ludwig Richard Conradi: Missionar der Siebenten-Tags-Adventisten in Europa.* Archives of International Adventist History, ed. Baldur Ed. Pfeiffer and Gottfried Oosterwal, no. 2. Frankfurt, Bern, New York: Peter Lang, 1986.

Henry, [Mrs.] S. M. I. *The Abiding Spirit.* Battle Creek, Mich.: Review and Herald Pub. Assn., 1899.

Heppenstall, Edward. *Our High Priest: Jesus Christ in the Heavenly Sanctuary.* Washington, D.C.: Review and Herald Pub. Assn., 1972.

_____. *Salvation Unlimited: Perspectives in Righteousness by Faith.* Washington, D.C.: Review and Herald Pub. Assn., 1974.

_____. *The Man Who Is God: A Study of the Person and Nature of Jesus, Son of God and Son of Man.* Washington, D.C.: Review and Herald Pub. Assn., 1977.

Hewitt, Clyde E. *Midnight and Morning: An Account of the Adventist Awakening and the Founding of the Advent Christian Denomination, 1831-1860.* Charlotte, N.C.: Venture Books, 1983.

Hoekema, Anthony A. *The Four Major Cults.* Grand Rapids: Eerdmans, 1963.

Holbrook, Frank B., ed. *Symposium on Daniel: Introductory and Exegetical Studies.* Daniel and Revelation Committee Series, vol. 2. Washington, D.C.: Biblical Research Institute, General Conference of Seventh-day Adventists, 1986.

_____, ed. *The Seventy Weeks, Leviticus, and the Nature of Prophecy.* Daniel and Revelation Committee Series, vol. 3. Silver Spring, Md.: Biblical Research Institute, General Conference of Seventh-day Adventists, 1986.

_____, ed. *Issues in the Book of Hebrews.* Daniel and Revelation Committee Series, vol. 4. Silver Spring, Md.: Biblical Research Institute, General Conference of Seventh-day Adventists, 1989.

_____, ed. *Doctrine of the Sanctuary: A Historical Survey (1845-1863).* Daniel and Revelation Committee Series, vol. 5. Silver Spring, Md.: Biblical Research Institute, General Conference of Seventh-day Adventists, 1989.

_____, ed. *Symposium on Revelation: Introductory and Exegetical Studies – Book 1.* Daniel and Revelation Committee Series, vol. 6. Silver Spring, Md.: Biblical Research Institute, General Conference of Seventh-day Adventists, 1992.

_____, ed. *Symposium on Revelation: Exegetical and General Studies – Book 2.* Daniel and Revelation Committee Series, vol. 7. Silver Spring, Md.: Biblical Research Institute, General Conference of Seventh-day Adventists, 1992.

Holbrook, Frank, and Leo Van Dolson, eds. *Issues in Revelation and Inspiration.* Adventist Theological Society Occasional Papers, vol. 1. Berrien Springs, Mich.: ATS Publications, 1992.

Holmes, Claude E. *Have We an Infallible "Spirit of Prophecy"?* Takoma Park, [Md.]: By the Author, 1920.

Hudson, Winthrop S. *Religion in America: An Historical Account of the Development of American Religious Life.* 2d ed. New York: Charles Scribner's Sons, 1973.

Hughes, Richard T. "Christian Primitivism as Perfectionism: From Anabaptists to Pentecostals." In *Reaching Beyond: Chapters in the History of Perfectionism.* Edited by Stanley Burgess, 213-255. Peabody, Mass.: Hendrickson Publ., 1986.

_____. "Recovering First Times: The Logic of Primitivism in American Life." In *Religion and the Life of the Nation: American Recoveries.* Edited by Rowland A. Sherrill, 193-218. Urbana and Chicago: University of Illinois Press, 1990.

_____, ed. *The American Quest for the Primitive Church.* Urbana and Chicago: University of Illinois Press, 1988.

Hughes, Richard T., and C. Leonard Allen. *Illusions of Innocence: Protestant Primitivism in America, 1630-1875.* With a Foreword by Robert N. Bellah. Chicago and London: University of Chicago Press, 1988.

Hull, Moses. *The Bible from Heaven: Or a Dissertation on the Evidences of Christianity.* Battle Creek, Mich.: Seventh-day Adventist Pub. Assn., 1863.

Hyde, Gordon M., ed. *A Symposium on Biblical Hermeneutics.* Washington, D.C.: General Conference of Seventh-day Adventists, 1974.

Issues: The Seventh-day Adventist Church and Certain Private Ministries. N.p.: North American Division of Seventh-day Adventists [1993].

Jemison, T. H. "The Companions of the Lamb." In *Our Firm Foundation,* 2:403-424. Washington, D.C.: Review and Herald Pub. Assn., 1953.

Johnson, A. O. " *The Daily": Is It Paganism?* College Place, Wash.: By the Author [1909].

Johnsson, William G. "The Heavenly Cultus in the Book of Hebrews – Figurative or Real." In *The Sanctuary and the Atonement.* Edited by A. V. Wallenkampf and W. R. Lesher, 362-379. Washington, D.C.: General Conference of Seventh-day Adventists, 1981.

_____. "The Heavenly Sanctuary – Figurative or Real?" In *Issues in the Book of Hebrews.* Daniel and Revelation Committee Series, vol. 4. Edited by Frank B. Holbrook, 35-51. Silver Spring, Md.: Biblical Research Institute, General Conference of Seventh-day Adventists, 1989.

Jones, A. T. *The Eastern Question: What Its Solution Means to All the World.* Battle Creek, Mich.: Review and Herald Pub. Assn., 1896; Oakland, Calif.: Pacific Press Pub. Assn., 1896.

Kellogg, J. H. *The Living Temple.* Battle Creek, Mich.: Good Health Pub. Co., 1903.

Knight, George R. *Myths in Adventism.* Washington, D.C.: Review and Herald Pub. Assn., 1985.

_____. *From 1888 to Apostasy: The Case of A. T. Jones.* Washington, D.C., and Hagerstown, Md.: Review and Herald Pub. Assn., 1987.

_____. *Angry Saints: Tensions and Possibilities in the Adventist Struggle Over Righteousness by Faith.* Washington, D.C., and Hagerstown, Md.: Review and Herald Pub. Assn., 1989.

_____. *My Gripe with God: A Study in Divine Justice and the Problem of the Cross.* Washington, D.C., and Hagerstown, Md.: Review and Herald Pub. Assn., 1990.

_____. *The Pharisee's Guide to Perfect Holiness: A Study of Sin and Salvation.* Boise, Idaho: Pacific Press Pub. Assn., 1992.

_____. *Anticipating the Advent: A Brief History of Seventh-day Adventists.* Boise, Idaho: Pacific Press Pub. Assn, 1993.

_____. *Millennial Fever and the End of the World.* Boise, Idaho: Pacific Press Pub. Assn., 1993.

Kubo, Sakae, *God Meets Man: A Theology of the Sabbath and the Second Advent.* Nashville: Southern Pub. Assn., 1978.

Land, Gary, ed. *Adventism in America: A History.* Grand Rapids: Eerdmans, 1986.

_____, ed. *The World of Ellen G. White.* Washington, D.C.: Review and Herald Pub. Assn., 1987.

LaRondelle, Hans K. *Christ Our Salvation: What God Does for Us and in Us.* Mountain View, Calif.: Pacific Press Pub. Assn., 1980.

_____. *The Israel of God in Prophecy.* Andrews University Monographs, Studies in Religion, vol. 13. Berrien Springs, Mich.: Andrews University Press, 1983.

_____. *Chariots of Salvation: The Biblical Drama of Armageddon.* Washington, D.C.: Review and Herald Pub. Assn., 1987.

_____. "Armageddon: Sixth and Seventh Plagues." In *Symposium on Revelation: Exegetical and General Studies – Book 2.* Daniel and Revelation Committee Series, vol. 7. Edited by Frank B. Holbrook, 373-390. Silver Spring, Md.: Biblical Research Institute, General Conference of Seventh-day Adventists, 1992.

_____. "Armageddon: History of Adventist Interpretations." In *Symposium on Revelation: Exegetical and General Studies – Book 2.* Daniel and Revelation Committee Series, vol. 7. Edited by Frank B. Holbrook, 435-449. Silver Spring, Md.: Biblical Research Institute, General Conference of Seventh-day Adventists, 1992.

Larson, Ralph. *The Word Was Made Flesh: One Hundred Years of Seventh-day Adventist Christology, 1852-1952.* Cherry Valley, Calif.: Cherrystone Press, 1986.

Lehmann, Richard. "Le sceau de Dieu et la marque de la bLte." In *Études sur l'apocalypse: Signification des messages des trois anges aujourd'hui,* 1:187-201. Conférences bibliques Division Euroafricaine. Salève, France: Institut Adventiste du Salève, 1988.

_____. "L'Eglise du reste." In *L'Église de Jesus-Christ: Sa mission et son ministère dans le monde.* Études en Ecclésiologie Adventiste, vol. 2. Edited by Comité de recherche biblique, Conférences bibliques de la Division euroafricaine, 1993, 71-96. Dammarie-lès-Lys Cedex, France: Editions Vie et Santé, 1995.

Lesher, W. Richard, and Frank B. Holbrook, "Daniel and Revelation Committee: Final Report." In *Symposium on Revelation: Exegetical and General Studies – Book 2.* Daniel and Revelation Committee Series, vol. 7. Edited by Frank B. Holbrook, 451-460. Silver Spring, Md.: Biblical Research Institute, General Conference of Seventh-day Adventists, 1992.

Lindén, Ingemar. *Biblicism, Apocalyptik, Utopi: Adventismes Historika Utforming i USA samt dess Svenska Utveckling Till o. 1939.* Uppsala: University of Uppsala, 1971.

_____. *1844 and the Shut Door Problem.* Acta Universitatis Upsaliensis, Studia Historico-Ecclesiastica Upsaliensis, vol. 35. Uppsala: By the Author, 1982.

Litch, Josiah. *An Address to the Public.* Boston: Joshua V. Himes, 1841.

————. *Prophetic Expositions.* 2 vols. Boston: Joshua V. Himes, 1842.

Loughborough, J. N. *Rise and Progress of the Seventh-day Adventists with Tokens of God's Hand in the Movement and a Brief Sketch of the Advent Cause from 1831-1844.* Battle Creek, Mich.: General Conference Association of the Seventh-day Adventists, 1892.

Mandemaker, G. W., and R. Stahl. *Der Versuch einer christozentrischen Auslegung der sechsten und siebenten Plage.* Berlin: By the Authors, 1970.

Manuscripts and Memories of Minneapolis. Boise, Idaho: Pacific Press Pub. Assn., 1988.

Marsden, G. M. *Fundamentalism and American Culture.* Oxford: Oxford University Press, 1980.

Martin, Walter R. *The Truth about Seventh-day Adventism.* Grand Rapids: Zondervan, 1960.

————. *The Kingdom of the Cults.* Grand Rapids: Zondervan, 1965; rev. and enl. ed., Minneapolis, Minn.: Bethany House, 1985.

Maxwell, A. Graham. *Can God Be Trusted?* Nashville: Southern Pub. Assn., 1977.

Maxwell, C. Mervyn. *Tell It to the World: The Story of Seventh-day Adventists.* Mountain View, Calif.: Pacific Press Pub. Assn., 1976; rev. ed., 1977.

————. *God Cares.* Vol. 1, *The Message of Daniel for You and Your Family.* Boise, Idaho: Pacific Press Pub. Assn., 1981.

————. "Sanctuary and Atonement in SDA Theology: An Historical Survey." In *The Sanctuary and the Atonement.* Edited. by A. V. Wallenkampf and W. R. Lesher, 516-544. Washington, D.C.: General Conference of Seventh-day Adventists, 1981.

————. "The Investigative Judgment: Its Early Development." In *The Sanctuary and the Atonement.* Edited by A. V. Wallenkampf and W. R. Lesher, 545-581. Washington, D.C.: General Conference of Seventh-day Adventists, 1981.

————. "Joseph Bates and Seventh-day Adventist Sabbath Theology." In *The Sabbath in Scripture and History.* Edited by Kenneth Strand, 352-363. Washington, D.C.: Review and Herald Pub. Assn., 1982.

————. *God Cares.* Vol. 2, *The Message of Revelation for You and Your Family.* Boise, Idaho: Pacific Press Pub. Assn., 1985.

McMahon, David P. *Ellet Joseph Waggoner: The Myth and the Man.* Fallbrook, Calif.: Verdict Publ., 1979.

Membership of the Seventh-day Adventist Church of Battle Creek, Mich. Battle Creek, Mich.:
n.p., 1891.

Membership of the Seventh-day Adventist Church of Battle Creek, Mich. Battle Creek, Mich.:
n.p., 1894.

Meyer, F. E. *The Religious Bodies of America.* 2d ed. St. Louis: Concordia Publ. House, 1956.

Miller, William. *Evidences from Scripture and History of the Second Coming of Christ About
the Year A.D. 1843, and of His Personal Reign of 1000 Years.* Brandon, Vt.: Vermont
Telegraph Office, 1833.

_____. *Evidences from Scripture and History of the Second Coming of Christ About the
Year 1843, Exhibited in a Course of Lectures.* Troy, [N.Y.]: n.p., 1836.

Moore, Arthur LeRoy. *Theology in Crisis: Or Ellen G. White's Concept of Righteousness by
Faith as It Relates to Contemporary SDA Issues.* Corpus Christi, Tex.: Life Seminars, 1980.

Moore, Marvin. *The Gospel vs. Legalism: How to Deal with Legalism's Insidious Influence.*
Hagerstown, Md.: Review and Herald Pub. Assn., 1994.

Mueller, Konrad F. *Die Frühgeschichte der Siebenten-Tags-Adventisten bis zur
Gemeindegründung 1863 und ihre Bedeutung für die moderne Irenik.* Marburg:
N. G. Elwert, 1969.

Müller, Richard. *Adventisten – Sabbat – Reformation.* Lund: CWK Gleerup, 1979.

Murch, James DeForest. *Christians Only: A History of the Restoration Movement.* Cincinnati,
Ohio: Standard Publ., 1962.

Murdoch, W. G. C. "The Gospel in Type and Anti-Type." In *Our Firm Foundation*, 1:299-
356. Washington, D.C.: Review and Herald Pub. Assn., 1953.

Mustard, Andrew G. *James White and SDA Church Organization: Historical Development,
1884-1881.* Andrews University Theological Seminary Doctoral Dissertation Series, no.
12. Berrien Springs, Mich.: Andrews University Press, 1988.

Neall, Beatrice S. "Sealed Saints and the Tribulation." In *Symposium on Revelation:
Introductory and Exegetical Studies – Book 1.* Daniel and Revelation Committee Series,
vol. 6. Edited by Frank B. Holbrook, 245-278. Silver Spring, Md.: Biblical Research
Institute, General Conference of Seventh-day Adventists, 1992.

Neall, Ralph E. *How Long, O Lord?* Washington, D.C., and Hagerstown, Md.: Review
and Herald Pub. Assn., 1988.

Neuffer, Julia. *The Gathering of Israel.* Washington, D.C.: General Conference of SDA,
Biblical Research Committee, [n.d.].

Nichol, F. D. *Reasons for Our Faith.* Washington, D.C.: Review and Herald Pub. Assn., 1947.

_____. *Ellen G. White and Her Critics.* Washington, D.C.: Review and Herald Pub. Assn., 1951.

_____. *Answers to Objections.* Rev. and enl. ed. Washington, D.C.: Review and Herald Pub. Assn., 1952.

Niebuhr, H. Richard. *The Social Sources of Denominationalism.* New York and London: New American Library, 1929/1957.

Numbers, Ronald L. *Prophetess of Health: A Study of Ellen G. White.* New York: Harper & Row, 1976.

_____. *Prophetess of Health: Ellen G. White and the Origins of Seventh-day Adventist Health Reform.* Rev. and enl. ed. Knoxville: University of Tennessee Press, 1992.

Numbers, Ronald L., and Jonathan M. Butler, eds. *The Disappointed: Millerism and Millenarianism in the Nineteenth Century.* Bloomington and Indianapolis: Indiana University Press, 1987.

O'Dea, Thomas. *Sociology and the Study of Religion.* New York and London: Basic Books, 1970.

_____. "The Five Dilemmas of Institutionalization." Chap. in *The Sociology of Religion.* Englewood Cliffs, N.J.: Prentice-Hall, 1966.

Oestreich, Bernhard. "Gemeinde in der Welt." In *Die Gemeinde und ihr Auftrag.* Studien zur adventistischen Ekklesiologie, vol. 2. Edited by Johannes Mager. 127-156. Hamburg: Saatkorn-Verlag, 1994.

Oliver, Barry David. *SDA Organizational Structure: Past, Present, and Future.* Andrews University Theological Seminary Doctoral Dissertation Series, no. 15. Berrien Springs, Mich.: Andrews University Press, 1989.

Olmstead, Clifton E. *History of Religion in the United States.* Englewood Cliffs, N.J.: Prentice-Hall, 1960.

Olsen, M. Ellsworth. *A History of the Origin and Progress of Seventh-day Adventists.* Washington, D.C.: Review and Herald Pub. Assn., 1925; reprint, New York: AMS Press, 1971.

Olsen, V. Norskov. *Papal Supremacy and American Democracy.* Loma Linda/ Riverside, Calif.: Loma Linda University Press, 1987.

_____. *Myth and Truth about Church, Priesthood and Ordination.* Riverside, Calif.: Loma Linda University Press, 1990.

_____, ed. *The Advent Hope in Scripture and History.* Washington, D.C., and Hagerstown, Md.: Review and Herald Pub. Assn., 1987.

Olson, A. V. "The Place of Prophecy in Our Preaching." In *Our Firm Foundation,* 2:533-571. Washington, D.C.: Review and Herald Pub. Assn., 1953.

_____. *Thirteen Crisis Years, 1888-1901.* Rev. ed. Washington, D.C.: Review and Herald Pub. Assn., 1981.

Olson, Robert W. *One Hundred and One Questions on the Sanctuary and on Ellen White.* Washington, D.C.: Ellen G. White Estate, 1981.

_____. *"The 'Shut Door' Documents."* Washington, D.C.: Ellen G. White Estate, 1982.

_____, comp. *The Humanity of Christ: Selections from the Writings of Ellen G. White.* Boise, Idaho: Pacific Press Pub. Assn., 1989.

Oosterwal, G. *Mission Possible: The Challenge of Mission Today.* Nashville: Southern Pub. Assn., 1972.

Oosterwal, Gottfried, Russell L. Staples, Walter B. T. Douglas, and R. Edward Turner. *Servants for Christ: The Adventist Church Facing the '80s.* Edited by Robert E. Firth. Berrien Springs, Mich.: Andrews University Press, 1980.

Ott, Helmut. *Perfect in Christ: The Mediation of Christ in the Writings of Ellen G. White.* Washington, D.C., and Hagerstown, Md.: Review and Herald Pub. Assn., 1987.

Our Firm Foundation. 2 vols. Washington, D.C.: Review and Herald Pub. Assn., 1953.

Padderatz, G. *Conradi und Hamburg.* Hamburg: By the Author, 1978.

Paulien, Jon. *Present Truth in the Real World: The Adventist Struggle to Keep and Share Faith in a Secular Society.* Boise, Idaho: Pacific Press Pub. Assn., 1993.

_____. *What the Bible Says about the End-Time.* Hagerstown, Md.: Review and Herald Pub. Assn., 1994.

Paxton, Geoffrey J. *The Shaking of Adventism.* Wilmington, Del.: Zenith Publ., 1977.

Pearson, Michael. *Millennial Dreams and Moral Dilemmas: Seventh-day Adventism and Contemporary Ethics.* Cambridge: Cambridge University Press, 1990.

_____. "The Problem of Secularism." In *Cast the Net on the Right Side: Seventh-day Adventists Face the "Isms."* Edited by Richard Lehmann, Jack Mahon, and Borge Schantz, 90-101. Newbold College, Bracknell, Berks, England: European Institute of World Mission, 1993.

Pease, Norval F. *By Faith Alone.* Mountain View, Calif.: Pacific Press Pub. Assn., 1962.

_____. *The Faith That Saves.* Washington, D.C.: Review and Herald Pub. Assn., 1969.

_____. "The Second Advent in Seventh-day Adventist History and Theology." In *The Advent Hope in Scripture and History.* Edited by V. Norskov Olsen, 173-190. Washington, D.C., and Hagerstown, Md.: Review and Herald Pub. Assn., 1987.

Pfandl, Gerhard. "The Remnant Church and the Spirit of Prophecy." In *Symposium on Revelation: Exegetical and General Studies – Book 2.* Daniel and Revelation Committee Series, vol. 7. Edited by Frank B. Holbrook, 295-333. Silver Spring, Md.: Biblical Research Institute, General Conference of Seventh-day Adventists, 1992.

Pierson, Robert H. *We Still Believe.* Washington, D.C.: Review and Herald Pub. Assn., 1975.

Pöhler, Rolf J. "Die Entwicklung des Gesetzesverständnisses in der Gemeinschaft der Siebenten-Tags-Adventisten." In *Das biblische Gesetzesverständnis: Vergleich und Entwicklung,* 43-66. Der Adventglaube in Geschichte und Gegenwart, vol. 22. Darmstadt: Adventistischer Wissenschaftlicher Arbeitskreis, 1985.

_____. "Die geschichtliche Entwicklung der Glaubensgrundsätze der Siebenten-Tags-Adventisten." In *Adventistische Glaubensgrundsätze im Alltag: Verbindlichkeit und Realisierbarkeit,* 46-68. Der Adventglaube in Geschichte und Gegenwart, vol. 24. Darmstadt: Adventistischer Wissenschaftlicher Arbeitskreis, [1986].

_____. "Adventgeschichtliche Ursprünge der Sabbatheiligung." In *Neue Aspekte adventistischer Sabbattheologie,* 8-29. Der Adventglaube in Geschichte und Gegenwart, vol. 26. Darmstadt: Adventistischer Wissenschaftlicher Arbeitskreis, 1986.

_____. "Neue Aspekte der adventistischen Sabbattheologie." In *Neue Aspekte adventistischer Sabbattheologie,* 80-93. Der Adventglaube in Geschichte und Gegenwart, vol. 26. Darmstadt: Adventistischer Wissenschaftlicher Arbeitskreis, 1986.

_____. "Naherwartung in der adventistischen Theologie." In *"2000 Jahre Naherwartung – Altert eine Hoffnung?"* 47-63. Der Adventglaube in Geschichte und Gegenwart, vol. 30. Darmstadt: Adventistischer Wissenschaftlicher Arbeitskreis, 1989.

_____. "Religious Pluralism: A Challenge to the Contemporary Church." In *Cast the Net on the Right Side: Seventh-day Adventists Face the "Isms."* Edited by Richard Lehmann, Jack Mahon, and Borge Schantz, 81-89. Newbold College, Bracknell, Berks, England: European Institute of World Mission, 1993.

Prenier, Henry S. *Doctrine Centered in Christ: The Fundamentals, the Controversy, Final Things.* N.p., [1926].

Prescott, W. W. *The Doctrine of Christ.* Washington, D.C.: Review and Herald Pub. Assn., 1920.

_____. *"The Daily": A Brief Reply to Two Leaflets on This Subject.* N.p., n.d.

Price, George McCready. *The Time of the End.* Nashville: Southern Pub. Assn., 1967.

Problems in Bible Translation. Washington, D.C.: General Conference of Seventh-day Adventists, 1954.

Provonsha, Jack W. *God Is with Us.* Washington, D.C.: Review and Herald Pub. Assn., 1974.

_____. *You Can Go Home Again.* Washington, D.C.: Review and Herald Pub. Assn., 1982.

_____. *A Remnant in Crisis.* Hagerstown, Md.: Review and Herald Pub. Assn., 1993.

Rasi, Humberto M., and Fritz Guy, eds. *Meeting the Secular Mind: Some Adventist Perspectives.* Selected Working Papers of the Committee on Secularism of the General Conference of Seventh-day Adventists 1981-1985. 2d ed. Berrien Springs, Mich.: Andrews University Press, 1987.

Rea, Walter T. *The White Lie.* Turlock, Calif.: M & R Publ., 1982.

Read, W. E. "The Closing Events of the Great Controversy." In *Our Firm Foundation,* 2:239-335. Washington, D.C.: Review and Herald Pub. Assn., 1953.

Reed, L. A. *Answers to Queries on the Eastern Question.* Washington, D.C.: Review and Herald Pub. Assn., [1912-1913]; Mountain View, Calif.: Pacific Press Pub. Assn., [1912-1913].

Rempel, Gerhard. *Ende und Vollendung der Welt.* Hamburg: Advent-Verlag, [1977].

Rice, George E. *Luke, A Plagiarist?* Mountain View, Calif.: Pacific Press Pub. Assn., 1983.

Rice, Richard. *The Reign of God: An Introduction to Christian Theology from a Seventh-day Adventist Perspective.* Berrien Springs, Mich.: Andrews University Press, 1985.

_____. *Reason and the Contours of Faith.* Riverside, Calif.: La Sierra University Press, 1991.

Robertson, John J. *The White Truth.* Mountain View, Calif.: Pacific Press Pub. Assn., 1981.

Robinson, E. M. *S. N. Haskell – Man of Action.* Washington, D.C.: Review and Herald Pub. Assn., 1967.

Robinson, H. E. *The Eastern Question in the Light of God's Promises to Israel.* Battle Creek, Mich.: Review and Herald Pub. Assn., 1897; Oakland, Calif.: Pacific Press Pub. Assn., 1897.

Rosado, Caleb. *Broken Walls.* North American Division Series on Church Leadership. Boise, Idaho: Pacific Press Pub. Assn., 1990.

Rowe, David Leslie. *Thunder and Trumpets: Millerites and Dissenting Religion in Upstate New York, 1800-1850.* American Academy of Religion, Studies in Religion, vol. 38. Chico, Calif.: Scholars Press, 1985.

Rowell, Earle Albert. *The Bible in the Critics' Den: Or Modern Infidelity Challenged and Refuted.* Mountain View, Calif.: Pacific Press Pub. Assn., 1917.

Rudy, H. L. "The Mediatorial Ministry of Jesus Christ." In *Our Firm Foundation,* 2:9-76. Washington, D.C.: Review and Herald Pub. Assn., 1953.

Sandeen, Ernest R. *The Roots of Fundamentalism: British and American Millenarianism, 1800-1930.* Chicago and London: University of Chicago Press, 1970.

Schwartz, Gary. *Sect Ideologies and Social Status.* Chicago and London: University of Chicago Press, 1970.

Schwarz, R. W. *John Harvey Kellogg, M.D.* Nashville: Southern Pub. Assn., 1970; reprint, Berrien Springs, Mich.: Andrews University Press, 1981.

_____. *Light Bearers to the Remnant.* Denominational History Textbook for SDA College Classes Prepared by the Department of Education, General Conference of Seventh-day Adventists. Mountain View, Calif.: Pacific Press Pub. Assn., 1979.

Schwarzenau, Paul. *Ein evangelischer Theologe spricht über die Siebenten-Tags-Adventisten.* Laasphe: Wittgenstein-Verlag, 1979.

Scripture References. N.p., 1863.

Scripture References. N.p., 1889.

Scriven, Charles. *Jubilee of the World: The Sabbath as a Day of Gladness.* Nashville: Southern Pub. Assn., 1978.

_____. *The Transformation of Culture: Christian Social Ethics after H. Richard Niebuhr.* Scottdale, Pa., and Kitchener, Ont.: Herald Press, 1988.

Seventh-day Adventist Bible Commentary. Edited by F. D. Nichol. 7 vols. Washington, D.C.: Review and Herald Pub. Assn., 1953-1957; rev. ed. 1976-1980.

Seventh-day Adventist Church Manual. Issued by the General Conference of Seventh-day Adventists, 1932-1993.

Seventh-day Adventist Encyclopedia. Commentary Reference Series, vol. 10. Rev. ed. Washington, D.C.: Review and Herald Pub. Assn., 1976.

Seventh-day Adventist Hymn and Tune Book for Use in Divine Worship. Battle Creek, Mich.: Review and Herald Publishing House, 1886; Oakland, Calif.: Pacific Press Pub. Assn., 1886.

Seventh-day Adventist Hymnal. Washington, D.C., and Hagerstown, Md.: Review and Herald Pub. Assn., 1985.

[Seventh-day Adventist] Manual for Ministers. Takoma Park, Washington, D.C.: Ministerial Association, General Conference of Seventh-day Adventists, 1977.

Seventh-day Adventist Minister's Manual. Silver Spring, Md.: Ministerial Association, General Conference of Seventh-day Adventists, 1992.

Seventh-day Adventist Yearbook. Washington, D.C.: Review and Herald Pub. Assn., 1931-1993.

Seventh-day Adventists Answer Questions on Doctrine: An Explanation of Certain Major Aspects of Seventh-day Adventist Belief. Washington, D.C.: Review and Herald Pub. Assn., 1957.

Seventh-day Adventists Believe ...: A Biblical Exposition of 27 Fundamental Doctrines. Washington, D.C.: Ministerial Association, General Conference of Seventh-day Adventists, 1988.

Shea, William H. *Selected Studies on Prophetic Interpretation.* Daniel and Revelation Committee Series, vol. 1. Washington, D.C.: Review and Herald Pub. Assn., 1982.

[Short, Donald K.]. *The Mystery of 1888.* Cape Town, South Africa: By the Author, 1974; reprint, Harrisville, N.H.: MMI Press, 1984.

Simon, Irmgard. *Die Gemeinschaft der Siebenten-Tags-Adventisten in volkskundlicher Sicht.* Muenster: Verlag Aschendorff, 1965.

Smith, H. Shelton, Robert T. Handy, and Lefferts A. Loetscher. *American Christianity: An Historical Interpretation with Representative Documents.* 2 vols. New York: Charles Scribner's Sons, 1960-1963.

Smith, L. A., and F. C. Gilbert. *"The Daily" in the Prophecy of Daniel.* N.p., n.d.

Smith, Timothy L. *Revivalism and Social Reform in Mid-Nineteenth-Century America.* New York: Abingdon, 1957.

Smith, Uriah. *Thoughts, Critical and Practical, on the Book of Revelation.* Battle Creek, Mich.: Seventh-day Adventist Pub. Assn., 1865.

_____. *The Visions of Mrs. E. G. White.* Battle Creek, Mich.: Seventh-day Adventists Pub. Assn., 1868.

_____. *A Word for the Sabbath; or Fake Theories Exposed.* 3d rev. and enl. ed. Battle Creek, Mich.: Seventh-day Adventist Pub. Assn., 1875.

_____. *The Sanctuary and Its Cleansing.* Battle Creek, Mich.: Review and Herald Pub. Assn., 1877.

_____. *Thoughts, Critical and Practical, on the Book of Daniel and the Revelation.* Battle Creek, Mich.: Review and Herald Pub. Assn., 1882.

[_____]. *A Brief Sketch of the Origin, Progress, and Principles of the Seventh-day Adventists.* Battle Creek, Mich.: Review and Herald Pub. Assn., 1888.

_____. *Looking unto Jesus: Christ in Type and Antitype.* Battle Creek, Mich.: Review and Herald Pub. Assn., 1898.

_____. *The Prophecies of Daniel and the Revelation.* Nashville: Southern Pub. Assn., 1944.

So Much in Common. Geneva: World Council of Churches, 1973.

Spalding, Arthur W. *Origin and History of Seventh-day Adventists.* 4 vols. Washington, D.C.: Review and Herald Pub. Assn., 1961-1962.

Spear, Samuel T. *The Bible Doctrine of the Trinity.* Bible Student's Library, no. 90. Oakland, Calif.: Pacific Press Pub. Assn., 1892.

Staples, Russell L. "Adventism." In *The Variety of American Evangelicalism.* Edited by Donald W. Dayton and Robert K. Johnston, 57-71. Downers Grove, Ill.: InterVarsity Press, 1991.

Steininger, Thomas R. *Konfession und Sozialisation: Adventistische Identität zwischen Fundamentalismus und Postmoderne.* Göttingen: Vandenhoeck & Ruprecht, 1993.

Stephenson, J. M. *The Atonement.* Rochester, N.Y.: Advent Review Office, 1854.

Stone, Charles W. *The Captain of Our Salvation.* Battle Creek, Mich.: n.p., 1886.

Strand, Kenneth, ed. *The Sabbath in Scripture and History.* Washington, D.C.: Review and Herald Pub. Assn., 1982.

Tarling, Lowell. *The Edges of Seventh-day Adventism.* Barragga Bay, Bermagui South, Australia: Galilee, 1982.

Theobald, Robin. "Seventh-day Adventists and the Millennium." In *A Sociological Yearbook of Religion in Britain – No. 7,* 111-131. London: SCM, 1974.

Thompson, Alden. *Inspiration: Hard Questions, Honest Answers.* Hagerstown, Md.: Review and Herald Pub. Assn., 1991.

Troeltsch, Ernst. *The Social Teachings of the Christian Churches.* 2 vols. New York: Macmillan, 1931; reprint, New York: Harper & Row, 1960.

Tylor, Alice Felt. *Freedom's Ferment.* Minneapolis: University of Minnesota Press, 1944.

Ulrich, Bruno. "Das Abendmahl – eine offene Feier? Chap. in *Abendmahl und Fußwaschung.* Studien zur adventistischen Ekklesiologie, vol. 1. Hamburg: Saatkorn-Verlag, [1991].

Valentine, Gilbert M. *The Shaping of Adventism: The Case of W. W. Prescott.* Berrien Springs, Mich.: Andrews University Press, 1992.

Venden, Morris L. *The Pillars.* Mountain View, Calif.: Pacific Press Pub. Assn., 1982.

_____. *95 Theses on Righteousness by Faith.* Boise, Idaho: Pacific Press Pub. Assn., 1987.

Vick, Edward W. H. *Let Me Assure You.* Mountain View, Calif.: Pacific Press Pub. Assn., 1968.

_____. *Speaking Well of God.* Nashville: Southern Pub. Assn., 1979.

Waggoner, E. J. *The Gospel in the Book of Galatians.* Oakland, Calif.: Pacific Press Pub. Assn., 1888.

_____. *Christ and His Righteousness.* Oakland, Calif.: Pacific Press Pub. Assn., 1890.

Waggoner, J. H. *The Law of God.* Rochester, N.Y.: Advent Review Office, 1854.

_____. *The Kingdom of God.* Battle Creek, Mich.: Review and Herald Office, 1859.

_____. *The Atonement.* Battle Creek, Mich.: Seventh-day Adventist Pub. Assn., 1868; 2d ed., Battle Creek, Mich.: Review and Herald Pub. Assn., 1872; 3d ed., Battle Creek, Mich.: Review and Herald Pub. Assn., 1884.

_____. *The Spirit of God: Its Offices and Manifestations, to the End of the Christian Age.* Battle Creek, Mich.: Seventh-day Adventist Pub. Assn., 1877.

_____. *The Nature and Obligation of the Sabbath of the Fourth Commandment.* Oakland, Calif.: Pacific Press Pub. Assn., 1890.

Wallenkampf, Arnold Valentin. *What Every Christian Should Know about Being Justified.* Washington, D.C., and Hagerstown, Md.: Review and Herald Pub. Assn., 1988.

_____. *What Every Adventist Should Know about 1888.* Washington, D.C., and Hagerstown, Md.: Review and Herald Pub. Assn., 1988.

_____. *The Apparent Delay.* Hagerstown, Md.: Review and Herald Pub. Assn., 1994.

Wallenkampf, A. V., and W. R. Lesher, eds. *The Sanctuary and the Atonement.* Washington, D.C.: General Conference of Seventh-day Adventists, 1981.

Walton, Lewis R. *Omega.* Washington, D.C.: Review and Herald Pub. Assn., 1981.

Washburn, J. S. *The Startling Omega and Its True Genealogy.* Philadelphia: By the Author, [1920].
_____. *An Open Letter to Elder A. G. Daniells and an Appeal to the General Conference.* N.p., [1922].

_____. *The Fruit of the "New Daily."* N.p., [1923].

Watson, Charles Henry. *The Atoning Work of Christ, His Sacrifice and Priestly Ministry.* Washington, D.C.: Review and Herald Pub. Assn., 1934.

Weber, Martin. *Who's Got the Truth? Making Sense out of Five Different Adventist Gospels.* Silver Spring, Md.: Home Study International Press, 1994.

Weber, Max. *The Protestant Ethic and the Spirit of Capitalism.* London: Allen & Unwin, 1930.

Webster, Eric Claude. *Crosscurrents in Adventist Christology.* New York: Peter Lang, 1984; reprint, Berrien Springs, Mich.: Andrews University Press, 1992.

Were, Louis F. *The Certainty of the Third Angel's Message.* N.p., [1945].

_____. *The Moral Purpose of Prophecy.* N.p., 1949.

_____. *The Kings That Come from the Sunrising.* N.p., [1951].

_____. *Bible Principles of Interpretation.* N.p., n.d.

White, Arthur L. *Ellen G. White: Messenger to the Remnant.* Rev. ed. Washington, D.C.: Review and Herald Pub. Assn., 1969.

_____. *Ellen G. White.* 6 vols. Washington, D.C.: Review and Herald Pub. Assn., 1981-1986.

White, Ellen G. *Spiritual Gifts.* Vol. 1, *The Great Controversy, between Christ and His Angels, and Satan and His Angels.* Battle Creek, Mich.: James White, 1858.

_____. *Spiritual Gifts.* Vol. 2, *My Christian Experience, Views and Labors in Connection with the Rise and Progress of the Third Angel's Message.* Battle Creek, Mich.: James White, 1860.

_____. *Spiritual Gifts.* Vol. 3, *Important Facts of Faith, in Connection with the History of Holy Men of Old.* Battle Creek, Mich.: Seventh-day Adventist Pub. Assn., 1864.

_____. *The Great Controversy between Christ and Satan: The Conflict of the Ages in the Christian Dispensation.* Mountain View, Calif.: Pacific Press Pub. Assn., 1888; reprint, 1950.

_____. *The Desire of Ages.* Mountain View, Calif.: Pacific Press Pub. Assn., 1898; reprint, 1940.

_____. *Christ's Object Lessons.* Washington, D.C.: Review and Herald Pub. Assn., 1900/1941.

_____. *Acts of the Apostles.* Mountain View, Calif.: Pacific Press Pub. Assn., 1911.

_____. *Counsels to Parents, Teachers, and Students Regarding Christian Education.* Mountain View, Calif.: Pacific Press Pub. Assn., 1913/1943.

_____. *Life Sketches of Ellen G. White.* Mountain View, Calif.: Pacific Press Pub. Assn., 1915/1943.

_____. *Fundamentals of Christian Education.* Nashville: Southern Pub. Assn., 1923.

_____. *Testimonies to Ministers and Gospel Workers.* Mountain View, Calif.: Pacific Press Pub. Assn., 1923/1962.

_____. *Medical Ministry.* Mountain View, Calif.: Pacific Press Pub. Assn., 1932/1963.

_____. *Counsels on Sabbath School Work.* Washington, D.C.: Review and Herald Pub. Assn., 1938.

_____. *Early Writings of Ellen G. White.* Washington, D.C.: Review and Herald Pub. Assn., 1945.

_____. *Counsels to Writers and Editors.* Nashville: Southern Pub. Assn., 1946.

_____. *Evangelism.* Washington, D.C.: Review and Herald Pub. Assn., 1946; reprint, 1970.

_____. *Gospel Workers.* Washington, D.C.: Review and Herald Pub. Assn., 1948.

_____. *Testimonies for the Church.* 9 vols. Mountain View, Calif.: Pacific Press Pub. Assn., 1948.

_____. *Selected Messages from the Writings of Ellen G. White.* Book 1. Washington, D.C.: Review and Herald Pub. Assn., 1958.

_____. *Selected Messages from the Writings of Ellen G. White.* Book 2. Washington, D.C.: Review and Herald Pub. Assn., 1958.

_____. *The Story of Patriarchs and Prophets as Illustrated in the Lives of Holy Men of Old.* Mountain View, Calif.: Pacific Press Pub. Assn., 1958.

_____. *Christ in His Sanctuary.* Mountain View, Calif.: Pacific Press Pub. Assn., 1969.

_____. *This Day with God.* Washington, D.C.: Review and Herald Pub. Assn., 1979.

_____. *Selected Messages from the Writings of Ellen G. White.* Book 3. Washington, D.C.: Review and Herald Pub. Assn., 1980.

[White, James]. *The Personality of God.* Battle Creek, Mich.: Seventh-day Adventist Pub. Assn., [1861].

_____. Preface to Ellen G. White, *Spiritual Gifts.* Vol. 3, *Important Facts of Faith, in Connection with the History of Holy Men of Old,* 9-32. Battle Creek, Mich.: Seventh-day Adventist Pub. Assn., 1864.

[White, James, and Ellen White]. *A Word to the "Little Flock."* Brunswick, Maine: James White, 1847; facsimile reproduction, Washington, D.C.: Review and Herald Pub. Assn., n.d.

_____. *Life Sketches: Ancestry, Early Life, Christian Experience, and Extensive Labors, of Elder James White, and His Wife, Mrs. Ellen G. White.* Battle Creek, Mich.: Seventh-day Adventist Pub. Assn., 1880.

Wieland, Robert J. *The 1888 Message: An Introduction.* Washington, D.C., and Hagerstown, Md.: Review and Herald Pub. Assn., 1980.

Wieland, Robert J., and Donald K. Short. *1888 Re-Examined.* Rev. ed. Meadow Vista, Calif., and Hendersonville, N.C.: By the Author, 1987.

Wilcox, Francis M. *What the Bible Teaches.* Washington, D.C.: Review and Herald Pub. Assn., 1926.

_____. *The Faith of the Pioneers.* Washington, D.C.: Review and Herald Pub. Assn., [1930].

Wilcox, Milton C. *The Bible, Its Inspiration and Importance.* Oakland, Calif.: Pacific Press Pub. Assn., 1889.

_____. *Have We Come to Armageddon?* Mountain View, Calif.: Pacific Press Pub. Assn., [1912-1913].

Wilkinson, Lelia S. *Truth versus Error.* Trenton, N.J.: Religious Liberty and Temperance Assn., n.d.

Wilson, Bryan R. *Religious Sects: A Sociological Study.* New York and Toronto: McGraw-Hill, 1970.

_____. *Magic and the Millennium.* London: Heinemann, 1973.

_____, ed. *Patterns of Sectarianism: Organisation and Ideology in Social and Religious Movements.* London: Heinemann, 1967.

Wirth, William George. *The Battle of the Churches: Modernism or Fundamentalism, Which?* Mountain View, Calif.: Pacific Press Pub. Assn., 1924.

Wood, John W. "The Mighty Opposites: The Atonement of Christ in the Writings of Ellen G. White, Parts I-II." In *The Sanctuary and the Atonement.* Edited by A. V. Wallenkampf and R. W. Lesher, 694-730. Washington, D.C.: General Conference of Seventh-day Adventists, 1981.

Yearbook of the Seventh-day Adventist Denomination. 1889, and 1905-1914.

Yinger, J. Milton. *Religion, Society and the Individual.* New York: Macmillan, 1957.

Zurcher, Jean. *The Nature and Destiny of Man.* New York: Philosophical Library, 1969.

_____. "Le témoignage de Jésus est l'esprit de la prophétie." In *Études sur l'Apocalypse: Signification des messages des trois anges aujourd'hui,* 1:230-250. Conférences bibliques Division Euroafricaine. Salève, France: Institute Adventiste du Salève, 1988.

Articles and Journals

"Actions of General Interest from the Annual Council." *Adventist Review,* 16 December 1982, 9-14.

"Actions of General Interest from the Annual Council – 1." *Adventist Review,* 20 December 1984, 17.

Adams, E. M. "The Holy Spirit – No. 3." *Review and Herald,* 23 December 1915, 11-12.

Adams, Roy, "An Appeal for Caution." *Adventist Review,* 16 January 1992, 4.

"Address." *Review and Herald,* 4 December 1855, 78-79.

"Advent Herald." *Advent Herald,* 30 October 1844, 93.

Advent Review. Auburn, N.Y.; and Paris, Maine., 1850.

Advent Review, Extra. Port Gibson, N.Y., 1850.

Adventism Triumphant. Paris, Ohio, 1990-.

Adventist Currents. An Unauthorized, Free Press Supplement to Official Seventh-day Adventist Publications. Loma Linda, Calif. Vols. 1-2. 1983-1987.

Adventist Heritage. A Journal of Adventist History. Loma Linda/Riverside, Calif., 1974-.

Adventist Perspectives. A Journal of Topics in Religion. Collegedale, Tenn. Vols. 1-6. 1987-1992.

Adventist Review. Washington, D.C., and Silver Spring, Md., 1978-.

"Adventist Scholars Meet." *Adventist Review,* 27 November 1980, 24.

Adventists Affirm. A Publication Affirming Seventh-day Adventist Beliefs. Berrien Springs, Mich., 1987-

"Adventist Colleges Under Siege." *Spectrum* 13:2 (1982): 4-18.

"An Adventist Creed?" *Spectrum* 8:4 (1977): 37-59.

Ahlstrom, Sydney E. "The Scottish Philosophy and American Theology." *Church History* 24 (1955): 257-272.

Amadon, G. W. "Where Are We?" *Review and Herald,* 6 May 1873, 164.

_____. "Reasons Why the Book of James Especially Applies to the Last Generation of Christians." *Review and Herald,* 20 September 1881, 196.

_____. "Fanaticism and Time-Setting." *Review and Herald,* 23 September 1884, 624.

"And furthermore ..." *Ministry,* August 1985, 10-11, 23-24.

"'And the Trumpet Shall Sound ...'" *Adventist Review.* Second Coming Issue [2 January 1992].

Anderson, Roy Allen. "Changing Attitudes Toward Adventism." *Ministry,* December 1956, 15-17.

_____. "Disarming Prejudice." *Ministry,* April 1957, 2.

_____. "Seventh-day Adventists Answer Questions on Doctrine." *Ministry,* June 1957, 24.

_____. "Unity of Adventist Belief – Nos. 1-2." *Ministry,* March-April 1958, 28, 22-25.

_____. "The Atonement in Adventist Theology." *Ministry,* February 1959, 10-15, 47.

_____. "Evangelical Inconsistency." *Ministry,* February 1962, 4-6, 39-40.

_____. "The Inside Story of Adventism." *Ministry,* November 1970, 10-11.

_____. "Adventists and the Trinity." *Adventist Review,* 8 September 1983, 4-5.

Andreasen, M. L. "Theology – The Science of God." *Ministry,* May 1935, 17-18, 23.

_____. "The Authority of Doctrine: I. Relationship of Doctrine to Life." *Ministry,* January 1936, 3-4.

_____. "The High Priest's Garments: Which Kind Was Worn on the Day of Atonement?" *Ministry,* February 1939, 23-26.

Andrews, J. N. "The Perpetuity of the Law of God." *Review and Herald,* January-February 1851, 34-35, 41.

_____. "Thoughts on Revelation xiii and xiv." *Review and Herald,* 19 May 1851, 81-86.

_____. "The Time of the Sabbath." *Review and Herald,* 2 June 1851, 92-93.

_____. "Discourse with Brother Carver." *Review and Herald,* 16 September 1851, 28.

_____. "Review of O. R. L. Crosier on Rev. xiv, 1-13." *Review and Herald,* 9 December 1851, 60-61.

_____. "Watchman, What of the Night?" *Review and Herald,* 27 May 1852, 15.

_____. "The Sanctuary." *Review and Herald,* 23 December 1852, 121-125.

_____. "The Sanctuary." *Review and Herald,* 3 February 1853, 145-149.

_____. "Position of the Advent Herald on the Sanctuary Question." *Review and Herald,* 12 May 1853, 204-205.

_____. "Under the Necessity of Choosing." *Review and Herald,* 8 November 1853, 141.

_____. "Things to Be Considered." *Review and Herald,* 31 January 1854, 9-10.

_____. "The Sanctuary and Its Cleansing." *Review and Herald,* 30 October 1855, 68-69.

_____. "Time for Commencing the Sabbath." *Review and Herald,* 4 December 1855, 76-78.

_____. "To the Brethren." *Review and Herald,* 4 December 1855, 78.

_____. "The Testimony of Jesus." *Review and Herald,* 3 March 1868, 177-178.

_____. "Melchisedek." *Review and Herald,* 7 September 1869, 84.

_____. "Christ as an Atoning Sacrifice." *Review and Herald,* 5 October 1869, 120.

[_____]. "Our Use of the Visions of Sr. White." *Review and Herald,* 15 February 1870, 65.

_____. "'The United States in the Light of Prophecy.'" *Review and Herald,* 26 December 1871, 12.

_____. "Meeting of Sabbath-Keepers in Neuchatel." *Review and Herald,* 24 November 1874, 172.

_____. "The Great Week of Time." *Review and Herald,* 17 July-21 August 1883.

Andrews, J. N., and J. H. Waggoner. "The Articles of Eld. T. M. Preble." *Review and Herald,* 15 February 1870, 60.

Archbold, B. L. "Ask for the Old Paths." *Review and Herald,* 20 March 1969, 5-6.

"Are the Seven Last Plagues in the Future?" *Review and Herald,* 7 January 1858, 72. [This article was written by Uriah Smith or James White.]

Arnold, David. "The Shut Door Explained." *Present Truth,* December 1849, 41-46.

Arthur, D. T. "After the Great Disappointment: To Albany and Beyond." *Adventist Heritage* 1:1 (1974): 5-10.

"The Atoning Saviour." *Signs of the Times,* 11 August 1887, 486.

"The Babel of Christendom." *Review and Herald,* 24 September 1857, 164.

Bacchiocchi, Samuele. "The Good News of the Judgment." *Adventists Affirm* 6:2 (1992): 37-44, 48.

Banks, Rosa Taylor. "One People in Christ: The Challenge of Relationships." *Adventist Review,* 1 October 1992, 8-11.

Barnhouse, D. G. "Are Seventh-day Adventists Christians? A New Look at Seventh-day Adventism." *Eternity,* September 1956, 6-7, 43-45.

Bates, Joseph. "The Laodicean Church." *Review and Herald,* November 1850, 7-8.

_____. "Midnight Cry in the Past." *Review and Herald,* December 1850, 20-24.

_____. "Dear Bro. White." *Review and Herald,* March 1851, 55-56.

_____. "Time to Commence the Holy Sabbath." *Review and Herald,* 21 April 1851, 71-72; reprint, 26 May 1853, 4-5.

_____. "Dear Bro. White." *Review and Herald,* 5 August 1851, 6.

_____. "Our Labor in the Philadelphia and Laodicean Churches." *Review and Herald,* 19 August 1851, 13-14.

_____. "Thoughts on the Past Work of William Miller." *Review and Herald,* 17 February 1853, 156-157.

Bauman, Herman. "'And the Word Was Made Flesh'." *Ministry,* December 1994, 18-21, 29.

Beach, B. B. "Change in the Church of Rome." *Review and Herald,* 21 April 1966, 4-5.

_____. "The Church and Sociopolitical Responsibility." *Adventist Review,* 3 September 1981, 4-6.

_____. "Adventists and Disarmament." *Adventist Review,* 21 April 1983, 4-5.

Beach, W. R. "Unchanging Purpose in a Changing World." *Review and Herald,* 27 July 1961, 1, 9.

_____. "In Defense of Stable Motion." *Review and Herald,* 16 January 1975, 4-5.

Bennett, Douglas. "The Good News about the Judgment of the Living." *Adventist Review,* 16 June 1983, 14-15.

Berg, Orley M. "Church under Fire!" *Ministry*, December 1968, 24-27.

"The Bible Conference of 1919." *Spectrum* 10:1 (1979): 23-57.

Bietz, Gordon. "Leadership in Crisis." *Ministry*, December 1983, 20-22.

Bietz, R. R. "The Peril of Compromise." *Review and Herald*, 17 February 1972, 4-6.

Bingham, Hiram. "Bro. White." *Review and Herald*, 16 September 1851, 31.

————. "Dear Bro. White." *Review and Herald*, 14 February 1856, 158.

Bird, Herbert. "Another Look at Adventism." *Christianity Today*, 28 April 1958, 14-17.

Blakely, W. A. "Why Not Have a Creed?" *Review and Herald*, 14 January 1890, 19-20.

Blanco, Jack J. "New Age Series – I, Mysticism Confronts Adventism." *Adventist Perspectives* 2:1 (1988): 21-34.

————. "Pentecostal 'Cleansing Message' in the History of Adventism." *Adventist Perspectives* 6:1 (1992): 14-19.

Blazen, Ivan T. "Justification and Judgment – 1-6." *Adventist Review*, 21 July-25 August 1983, 4-6, 6-8, 5-6, 7-10, 6-9, 9-12.

"Blended Personalities." *Review and Herald*, 3 April 1900, 210.

Bollman, C. P. "The Spirit of God." *Signs of the Times*, 4 November 1889, 663.

————. "Ask for the Old Paths." *Review and Herald*, 29 December 1932, 3-4.

————. "The Holy Spirit a Person." *Review and Herald*, 3 August 1933, 3-4.

Bourdeau, A. C. "The Hope That Is in You." *Review and Herald*, 8 June 1869, 185-186.

Bourdeau, D. T. "Hasting unto the Coming of Christ." *Review and Herald*, 14 March 1871, 101.

————. "How the Different Protestant Denominations Arose." *Review and Herald*, 26 November 1872, 189.

————. "Is Present Truth Essential?" *Review and Herald*, 27 January 1874, 53.

————. "Protestantism." *Review and Herald*, 4-11 March 1875, 73-74, 81-82.

————. "Why Was It Not Found out Before?" *Review and Herald*, 30 August 1881, 146.

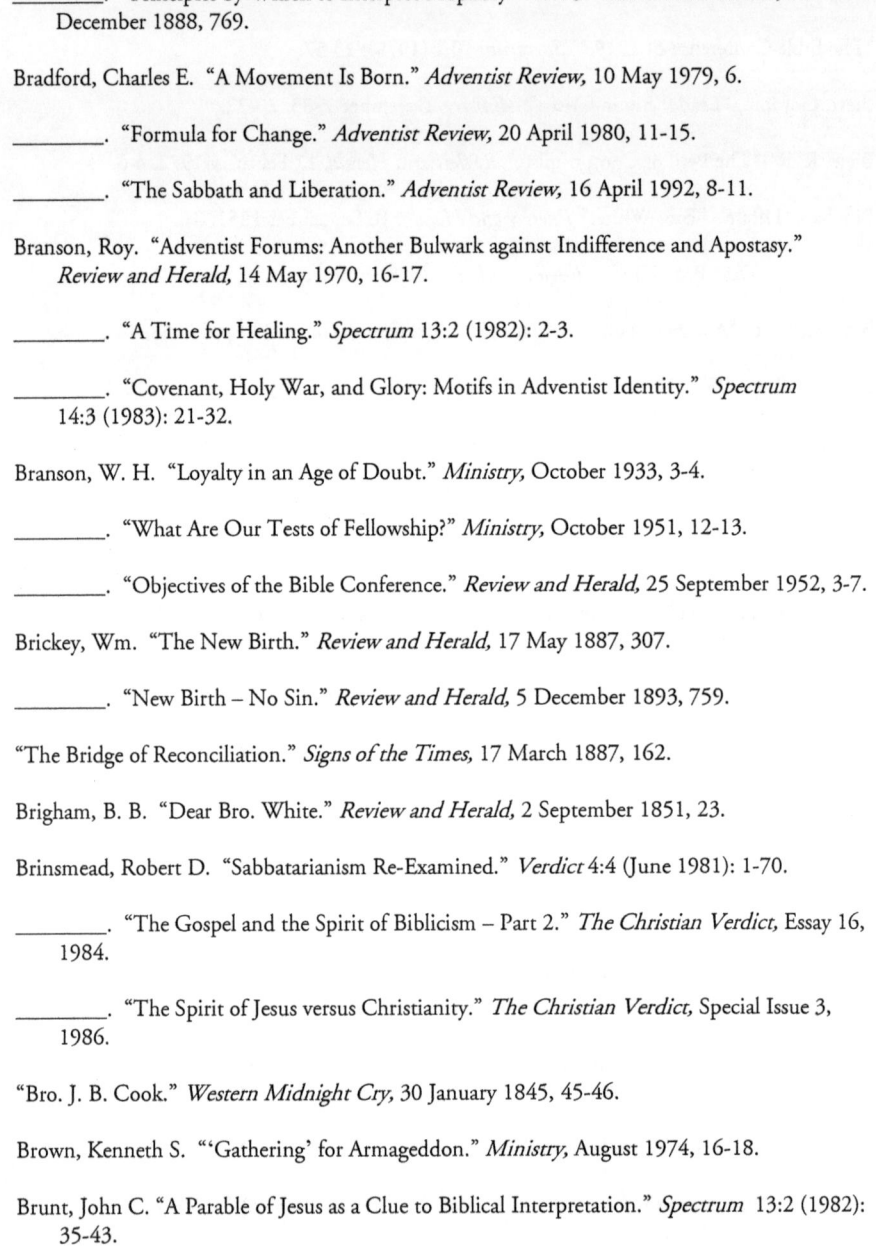

_____. "Principles by Which to Interpret Prophecy – No. 3." *Review and Herald*, 11 December 1888, 769.

Bradford, Charles E. "A Movement Is Born." *Adventist Review*, 10 May 1979, 6.

_____. "Formula for Change." *Adventist Review*, 20 April 1980, 11-15.

_____. "The Sabbath and Liberation." *Adventist Review*, 16 April 1992, 8-11.

Branson, Roy. "Adventist Forums: Another Bulwark against Indifference and Apostasy." *Review and Herald*, 14 May 1970, 16-17.

_____. "A Time for Healing." *Spectrum* 13:2 (1982): 2-3.

_____. "Covenant, Holy War, and Glory: Motifs in Adventist Identity." *Spectrum* 14:3 (1983): 21-32.

Branson, W. H. "Loyalty in an Age of Doubt." *Ministry*, October 1933, 3-4.

_____. "What Are Our Tests of Fellowship?" *Ministry*, October 1951, 12-13.

_____. "Objectives of the Bible Conference." *Review and Herald*, 25 September 1952, 3-7.

Brickey, Wm. "The New Birth." *Review and Herald*, 17 May 1887, 307.

_____. "New Birth – No Sin." *Review and Herald*, 5 December 1893, 759.

"The Bridge of Reconciliation." *Signs of the Times*, 17 March 1887, 162.

Brigham, B. B. "Dear Bro. White." *Review and Herald*, 2 September 1851, 23.

Brinsmead, Robert D. "Sabbatarianism Re-Examined." *Verdict* 4:4 (June 1981): 1-70.

_____. "The Gospel and the Spirit of Biblicism – Part 2." *The Christian Verdict*, Essay 16, 1984.

_____. "The Spirit of Jesus versus Christianity." *The Christian Verdict*, Special Issue 3, 1986.

"Bro. J. B. Cook." *Western Midnight Cry*, 30 January 1845, 45-46.

Brown, Kenneth S. "'Gathering' for Armageddon." *Ministry*, August 1974, 16-18.

Brunt, John C. "A Parable of Jesus as a Clue to Biblical Interpretation." *Spectrum* 13:2 (1982): 35-43.

_____. "Ordination of Women: A Hermeneutical Question." *Ministry,* September 1988, 12-14.

Bull, Malcolm. "Eschatology and Manners in Seventh-day Adventism." *Archives des Sciences Sociales des Religions* 65 (1988): 145-159.

Bunch, Taylor G. "'Prove All Things.'" *Ministry,* March 1930, 9-11.

Burnside, G. "Our Infallible Bible." *Ministry,* January 1970, 5-7.

"Business Proceedings of B. C. Conference." *Review and Herald,* 23 October 1860, 177-179.

Butler, George I. "Stability a Characteristic of Our Work." *Review and Herald,* 15 April 1873, 140.

_____. "Old-Fashioned Religion." *Review and Herald,* 12 August 1873, 65.

_____. "Visions and Prophecy." *Review and Herald,* 2 June 1874, 193.

_____. "Is Conversion Ever Called a Birth?" *Review and Herald,* 22 February 1877, 57-58.

_____. "The Forty Years." *Review and Herald,* 30 October 1883, 681-683.

_____. "No Church Manual." *Review and Herald,* 27 November 1883, 745-746.

_____. "Eld. Canright's Change of Faith." *Review and Herald,* 1 March 1887, 138.

_____. "A Harmonious Faith." *Review and Herald,* 1 October 1889, 617.

Butler, Jonathan M. "Seventh-day Adventism's Legacy to Modern Revivalism." *Spectrum* 5:1 (1973): 89-99.

_____. "When Prophecy Fails: The Validity of Apocalypticism." *Spectrum* 8:1 (1976): 7-14.

_____. "The World of E. G. White and the End of the World." *Spectrum* 10:2 (1979): 2-13.

_____. "From Millerism to Seventh-day Adventism: Boundlessness to Consolidation." *Church History* 55 (1986): 50-64.

Calarco, Santo. "God's Universal Remnant." *Ministry,* August 1993, 5-7, 30.

Canright, D. M. "Jesus Christ the Son of God." *Review and Herald,* 18 June 1867, 1-3.

_____. "2 Esdras 2." *Review and Herald,* 8 August 1871, 58.

_____. "The Present Truth." *Review and Herald,* 3 June 1873, 197.

_____. "A Plain Talk to Murmurers." *Review and Herald*, 12 April 1877, 116-117.

_____. "A Plain Talk to Murmurers." *Review and Herald*, 19 April 1877, 125.

_____. "Doctrine." *Review and Herald*, 18 July 1878, 29.

_____. "The Holy Spirit Not a Person, but an Influence Proceeding from God." *Signs of the Times*, 25 July 1878, 218.

_____. "The Personality of God." *Review and Herald*, 29 August-5 September 1878, 73-74, 81-82.

_____. "'He Cannot Sin.'" *Review and Herald*, 15 September 1885, 586.

_____. "Proof of the Inspiration of the Bible." *Review and Herald*, 6 October 1885, 611-612.

_____. "Who Is Doing It?" *Review and Herald*, 23 March 1886, 192.

Case, H. S. "Dear Bro. White." *Present Truth*, November 1850, 85.

"Change and Continuity in the Theology of a Church." *Spectrum* 14:1 (1983): 40-41.

"Christ and His High Priestly Ministry." *Ministry*, October 1980.

"Christ in the Heavenly Sanctuary." *Adventist Review*, 4 September 1980, 12-15.

"Christ Our Righteousness." *Review and Herald*, 27 May 1976, 4-7.

Christensen, Bj. "Dialogue or Ballots?" *Adventist Today*, January-February 1994, 15.

Christian, L. H. "The Danger of Conservatism – Nos. 1-2." *Review and Herald*, 14-21 June 1928, 3-4, 6-8.

Christian, R. J. "Adventists Have Not Changed." *Review and Herald*, 22 June 1950, 24.

"The Church of God: Its Nature, Function, and Authority." *Adventist Review*, 1 October 1992, 22-27.

Clarke, J[osiah]. "Present Truth." *Review and Herald*, 10 July 1866, 45.

_____. "Regeneration; or, the New Birth." *Review and Herald*, 11 July 1871, 26.

Colcord, Ivory. "Present Truth." *Review and Herald*, 11 March 1873, 99.

"Coming in to See the Guests." *Review and Herald*, 1 August 1882, 488.

Cook, J. H. "Necessity of the New Birth." *Review and Herald*, 14 January 1890, 18.

Cornell, M. E. "'Making Us a Name.'" *Review and Herald,* 24 May 1860, 8-9.

_____. "Who Are Mormons?" *Review and Herald,* 7 April 1863, 149.

_____. "Present Truth." *Review and Herald,* 6 August 1867, 113-114.

_____. "Image of the Beast." *Review and Herald,* 12 May 1868, 337-341.

Cottrell, R. F. "Dear Bro. White." *Review and Herald,* 3 February 1852, 87.

_____. "Unity of the Third Message." *Review and Herald,* 18 September 1855, 44.

_____. "Truth Is Harmonious." *Review and Herald,* 28 May 1857, 36.

_____. "Spiritual Gifts." *Review and Herald,* 25 February 1858, 125-126.

_____. "The Objects of Christ's Death." *Review and Herald,* 27 August 1861, 102.

_____. "Essentials and Non-Essentials." *Review and Herald,* 10 February 1863, 84-85.

_____. "One and One Make Two." *Review and Herald,* 28 July 1863, 69.

_____. "This Generation." *Review and Herald,* 4 September 1866, 108.

_____. "The Gospel Progressive in Development." *Review and Herald,* 23 June 1868, 9.

_____. "Truth Is Harmonious." *Review and Herald,* 2 February 1869, 44.

_____. "The Doctrine of the Trinity." *Review and Herald,* 1 June 1869, 180-181.

_____. "The Trinity." *Review and Herald,* 6 July 1869, 10-11.

_____. "Old and New." *Review and Herald,* 19 July 1870, 37.

_____. "Unity of the Church." *Review and Herald,* 18 October 1870, 141.

_____. "The Special Aid of the Spirit." *Review and Herald,* 1 August 1871, 55.

_____. "The Word of God." *Review and Herald,* 26 November 1872, 189.

_____. "Answers to Correspondents." *Review and Herald,* 11 March 1873, 104.

_____. "'Lying Unity.'" *Review and Herald,* 22 April 1873, 148.

_____. "Evidence of Truth." *Review and Herald,* 13 May 1873, 172.

_____. "Prophecy – Its Use." *Review and Herald,* 1 July 1873, 21.

————. "Essentials and Non-Essentials." *Review and Herald*, 18 November 1873, 181.

————. "Doctrine." *Review and Herald*, 8 January 1875, 10.

————. "Interpretation." *Review and Herald*, 8 January 1875, 12-13.

————. "Shall We Have the Bible?" *Review and Herald*, 15 April 1875, 125.

————. "Advancing Light." *Review and Herald*, 31 January 1878, 36.

————. "The Bible Explained by the Creed." *Review and Herald*, 25 April 1878, 133.

————. "Bible Terms for Bible Doctrines." *Review and Herald*, 22 April 1880, 266.

————. "Old and New." *Review and Herald*, 23 September 1880, 217.

————. "Have We a Message?" *Review and Herald*, 25 April 1882, 266.

————. "I Change Not." *Review and Herald*, 5 December 1882, 760-761.

————. "The Creed of the Opposition." *Review and Herald*, 2 September 1884, 563-564.

————. "The Firm Foundation of Faith." *Review and Herald*, 22 December 1885, 794.

————. "How Many Years Is a Generation?" Review and Herald, 17 January 1888, 36.

————. "Unity of the Church." *Review and Herald*, 29 May 1888, 338-339.

————. "Non-Essentials and Essentials." *Review and Herald*, 28 May 1889, 341.

Cottrell, Raymond F. "A Mind to the Task." *Ministry*, December 1958, 6-10.

————. "Rightly Dividing the Word of Truth." *Review and Herald*, 27 July 1961, 10-11.

————. "The Inerrancy of Scripture – Nos. 1-5." *Review and Herald*, 10 February-24 March 1966.

————. "A Church in Crisis – Nos. 1-6." *Adventist Review*, 13 January-17 February 1977.

————. "Smoothing the Way to Consensus – Nos. 1-3." *Adventist Review*, 31 March-14 April 1977, 18, 17-18, 12-13.

————. "The Historical Method of Interpretation." *Adventist Review*, 7 April 1977, 17-18.

————. "A Subtle Danger in the Historical Method." *Adventist Review*, 14 April 1977, 12.

_____. "The Bible Research Fellowship: A Pioneering Seventh-day Adventist Organization in Retrospect." *Adventist Heritage* 5:1 (1978): 39-52.

_____. "The Sanctuary Review Committee and Its New Consensus." *Spectrum* 11:2 (1980): 2-26.

_____. "The Untold Story of the Bible Commentary." *Spectrum* 16:3 (1985): 35-51.

Crosby, Tim. "The Law and the Prophet." *Adventist Review,* 8 May 1986, 12-13.

_____. "Using the Law to No Profit." *Adventist Review,* 15 May 1986, 12-13.

_____. "The Law of the Prophet." *Adventist Review,* 22 May 1986, 12-13.

_____. "A Law without Profit: Ellen White Opposed a Church Creed as Harmful to Growth and Unity." *Adventist Review,* 29 May 1986, 9-10.

_____. "Conditionalism: A Cornerstone of Adventist Doctrine." *Ministry,* August 1986, 16-18.

_____. "Why I Don't Believe in *Sola Scriptura.* "*Ministry,* October 1987, 11-15.

Crosier, O. R. L. "The Law of Moses." *Day-Star,* 7 February 1846, 37-44.

_____. "Remarks to Weston." *Day-Dawn,* 19 March 1847, 2.

Curtis, D. P. "Doctrine vs. Doctrines." *Review and Herald,* 3 June 1884, 354-355.

_____. "Present Truth." *Review and Herald,* 10 April 1888, 228.

Daily, Steve. "Are We a Non-Prophet Organization?" *Adventist Review,* 12 October 1989, 8-10.

_____. "From Womb to Tomb: Christian Concern for the Total Human Predicament." *Adventist Review,* 30 April 1992, 14-18.

"The Daily." *Midnight Cry,* 4 October 1843, 52.

Damsteegt, P. Gerard. "Seventh-day Adventist Doctrines and Progressive Revelation." *Journal of the Adventist Theological Society* 2:1 (1991): 77-92.

Daniells, Arthur G. "Does the History of Turkey and Egypt since 1798 Fulfil the Prophecy of Dan. 11:40-44?" *Review and Herald,* 13 March 1913, 5.

_____. "Is Christ's Coming Being Delayed? If So, Why?" *Ministry,* November 1930, 5-6, 30.

Davidson, Richard M. "In Confirmation of the Sanctuary Message." *Journal of the Adventist Theological Society* 2:1 (1991): 93-114.

_____. "The Good News of Yom Kippur." *Journal of the Adventist Theological Society* 2:2 (1991): 4-27.

Davis, Thomas A. "Christ's Human Nature: An Alternate View." *Ministry,* June 1986, 14-17.

Dederen, Raoul. "Change and the Seventh-day Adventist Church." *[Andrews University] Focus* 13:1 (April-May 1977), Supplement.

_____. "Adventists and Doctrinal Change." *Ministry,* February 1977, 16-19. [This is a shorter version of the previous entry.]

"A Defensive Message." *Review and Herald,* 4 August 1891, 487.

Delafield, D. A. "Are Seventh-day Adventists a Cult?" *Adventist Review,* 26 April 1979, 15.

Dennis, A. J. "One God." *Signs of the Times,* 22 May 1879, 162.

Dillet, Eric S. "The Seventh-day Adventist Church Is in Need of a Change." *Review and Herald,* 3 October 1974, 14-15.

"Doctrinal Religion." *Review and Herald,* 21 June 1881, 389.

"Doctrine and Life." *Review and Herald,* 12 April 1881, 228-229.

"Doings of the Battle Creek Conference, Oct. 5 & 6, 1861." *Review and Herald,* 8 October 1861, 148, 148-149.

"Don't Stagnate in Creeds." *Review and Herald,* 23 October 1879, 141.

"The Door of Matt. 25:10; Is Shut." *Day-Star,* 24 June 1845, 28.

Dorcas, J. "Meeting in Marion, Iowa." *Review and Herald,* 13 February 1866, 86.

Douglas, Walter. "The Future Shape of the Church." *Adventist Review,* 150-Year Anniversary Issue [6 October 1994], 48-52.

Douglass, Herbert E. "Is Ecology a Legitimate Concern for Adventists? – 1-3." *Review and Herald,* 16-30 April 1970, 13, 12, 12-13.

Durand, Eugene F. "Whose Bible?" *Adventist Review,* 11 September 1986, 5.

Dybdahl, Jon. "How Culture Conditions Our View of Scripture." *Ministry,* January 1988, 7-9.

_____. "Cross-Cultural Adaptation." *Ministry,* November 1992, 14-17.

"The Dynamics of Salvation." *Adventist Review,* 31 July 1980, 3-8.

Editorial. "The Advent Herald." *Advent Herald,* 30 October 1844, 92-93.

Edson, Hiram. "An Appeal to the Laodicean Church." *Advent Review Extra,* September 1850, 1-16.

_____. "The Sixty-Nine Weeks and 2300 Days." *Review and Herald,* March 1851, 49-50.

"Eleventh Business Meeting." *Adventist Review,* 5 July 1985, 21-22.

"Ellen G. White Reconsidered." *Evangelica,* November 1981, 25, 42.

Emmerson, Richard. "The Continuing Crisis." *Spectrum* 12:1 (1981): 40-44.

Eva, W. Duncan. "Changeless Truth in an Age of Change." *Review and Herald,* 1 September 1977, 2.

Evangelica. St. Joseph, Mich. Vols. 1-3. 1980-1982.

Everts, E. "Review of the New Time Theory." *Review and Herald,* 10 January 1854, 201-202.

_____. "Communication from Bro. Everts [17 December 1856]." *Review and Herald,* 1 January 1857, 72.

"Exhortation to Believers." *Jubilee Standard,* 3 April 1845, 28-29.

"Faith of Seventh-day Adventists." *Review and Herald,* 19 February 1931, 6-7.

Fifield, G. E. "Truth and Unity." *Review and Herald,* 2-9 June 1891, 340, 354.

_____. "Cleansing of the Sanctuary." *Review and Herald,* 21 September 1897, 594.

"Fifth Business Meeting." *Adventist Review,* 21 April 1980, 20-21, 27.

Figuhr, R. R. "A Non-Adventist Examines Our Beliefs." *Review and Herald,* 13 December 1956, 3.

_____. "The Pillars of Our Faith Unmoved." *Review and Herald,* 24 April 1958, 5-6.

Ford, Desmond. "Truth's Golden Chain." *Review and Herald,* 24 December 1959, 5-7.

Fordham, W. W. "The Remnant Church." *Ministry,* June 1970, 41-43, 61-62.

Fraser, N. S. "Truth Can Stand Investigation." *Adventist Review,* 10 June 1982, 6-7.

Fredericks, Richard. "The Moral Influence Theory – Its Attraction and Inadequacy." *Ministry,* March 1992, 6-10.

French, T. M. "Armageddon – Will It Be Only a Spiritual Conflict?" *Review and Herald,* 30 January 1936, 5-6.

_____. "Maintaining the Foundations." *Review and Herald,* 15 April 1937, 7-8.

_____. "Three Phases of Christ's Redemptive Work." *Review and Herald,* 23 September 1937, 6-7.

_____. "The Immutability of Truth." *Review and Herald,* 30 December 1937, 10.

Frisbie, J. B. "The Seventh-day Sabbath Not Abolished." *Review and Herald,* 7 March 1854, 50.

_____. "The Trinity." *Review and Herald,* 12 March 1857, 146.

Froom, L. E. "The Essential Verities." *Ministry,* October 1930, 3, 31.

_____. "The Message in Verity." *Ministry,* January 1931, 4.

_____. "Essentials and Nonessentials." *Ministry,* September 1931, 4-5.

_____. "To Creedalize or Not to Creedalize." *Ministry,* October 1931, 7-8.

_____. "Irreconcilable Principles." *Ministry,* December 1931, 6.

_____. "The Fundamental Emphasis." *Ministry,* January 1932, 9-10.

_____. "Cast Not Therefore away Your Confidence." *Ministry,* February 1932, 7-8, 29.

_____. "Meaning of 'Present Truth.'" *Ministry,* May 1932, 25-26.

_____. "A Balanced Emphasis Requisite." *Ministry,* August 1932, 9-10.

_____. "Essentials and Nonessentials." *Ministry,* August 1932, 20-21.

_____. "Apostasy Marches On." *Ministry,* May 1937, 11, 22.

_____. "Fidelity to Our Commission." *Ministry,* September 1937, 11.

_____. "Two Equally Disastrous Perils." *Ministry,* December 1937, 15.

_____. "Secularized History Seeks Admittance." *Ministry,* April 1938, 23.

_____. "Distinguish Centralities from Secondaries." *Ministry,* July 1938, 21-22.

_____. "Encroachments of Secularized History." *Ministry,* August-October 1938.

_____. "The Platform of Our Message." *Ministry,* August 1939, 20-21.

_____. "Restudying the Doctrines without Destroying the Foundations." *Ministry,* February 1940, 12.

_____. "Two Concepts of Scholarship." *Ministry,* March 1940, 21.

_____. "Perils of Maturity Beset Us Today." *Ministry,* August 1941, 21-22.

_____. "Papal Traditions versus the Prophetic Gift." *Ministry,* June 1942, 21, 46.

_____. "Apostolic and Remnant Messages." *Ministry,* July 1942, 20, 21, 44.

_____. "The Spirit and Goal of True Research." *Ministry,* March 1944, 21.

[_____]. Editorial Note. *Ministry,* November 1944, 2.

_____. "Not a Block to Be Moved, nor a Pin [to Be] Stirred." *Ministry,* November 1944-February 1945, 21-23, 17-20, 20-22, 11-13, 28, 30.

_____. "Principles for Testing Added Light." *Ministry,* September 1947, 19, 18 *[sic].*

_____. "A Warning Message or a Saving Gospel – Which?" *Ministry,* July-August 1948, 21-22, 22-23, 46.

_____. "Our Doctrines Anchored to Scripture." *Review and Herald,* 26 August 1948, 6-8.

_____. "The Atonement the Heart of Our Message." *Ministry,* December 1956, 12-14.

_____. "The Priestly Application of the Atoning Act." *Ministry,* February 1957, 9, 11.

_____. "'Righteousness by Faith' Sparked the Ministerial Association." *Ministry,* May-June 1965, 3-7, 41-44.

_____. "New Approaches Imperative for a New Day." *Ministry,* March 1966, 10-13.
Fulton, J. E. "Back to the Old Paths." *Review and Herald,* 13 June 1930, 212-214.

"Fundamental Principles." *Signs of the Times,* 4 June 1874, 3.

"GC President Urges End to Arms Race." *Adventist Review,* 21 November 1985, 31.

Gage, Kenneth [H. E. Douglass], and Benjamin Rand [N. R. Gulley], "What Human Nature Did Jesus Take? Unfallen/Fallen." *Ministry,* June 1985, 8-21, 24.

Gage, William C. "None Shall Help Him." *Review and Herald,* 24 September 1867, 236.

Gallagher, Jonathan. "'This Generation'?" *Ministry*, December 1989, 4-6.

Garne, Geoffrey E. "The Adventist Church in a Changing World." *Review and Herald*, 5 May 1977, 4-7.

_____. "Are the Testimonies Legalistic?" *Adventist Review*, 1 July 1982, 4-6.

"A Gathering of Adventisms." *Adventist Today*, January-February 1994 [erroneously dated 1993], 4-16.

General Conference Bulletin – Nos. 1-10, 17 April-15 May 1980.

"General Conference Proceedings." *Review and Herald*, 20 November 1883, 732-734.

"General Conference Proceedings." *Review and Herald*, 27 November 1883, 741.

"General Conference Proceedings." *Review and Herald*, 1 December 1885, 744-747.

"General Conference Proceedings." *Review and Herald*, 14 December 1886, 777-779.

Geraty, Lawrence T. "A New Statement of Fundamental Beliefs." *Spectrum* 11:1 (1980): 2-13.

_____. "First Adventist Theological Consultation between Administrators and Scholars." *Adventist Review*, 16 October 1980, 15-17.

"Giving Himself." *Signs of the Times*, 27 August 1885, 515.

Gladson, Jerry. "Taming Historical Criticism: Adventist Biblical Scholarship in the Land of the Giants." *Spectrum* 18:4 (1988): 19-34.

"The God-Man." *Review and Herald*, 20 September 1898, 598.

Goldstein, Clifford. "Investigating the Investigative Judgment." *Ministry*, February 1992, 6-9.

"A Good Move in Iowa." *Review and Herald*, 20 February 1866, 94-95.

"Good Will and Understanding between All Men." *Review and Herald*, 31 July 1975, 13.

Goodrich, E. "Language Confounded." *Review and Herald*, 25 August 1859, 105-106.

Graybill, Ron. "The Uses of Adventist History." *Review and Herald*, 8 December 1977, 29-30.

_____. "Ellen White's Role in Doctrine Formation." *Ministry*, October 1981, 7-11.

_____. "Picturing the Prophecies." *Adventist Review*, 5 July 1984, 11-14.

_____. "Under the Triple Eagle: Early Adventist Use of the Apocrypha." *Adventist Heritage* 12:1 (1987): 25-32.

Greenwalt, Glen. "The Gospel According to *Seventh-day Adventists Believe.*" *Spectrum* 20:1 (1989): 24-28.

Greig, A. Josef. "Our Poisoned Planet: Adventists and the Environment." *Adventist Review,* 19 April 1990, 15-18.

Gulley, Norman R. "Behold the Man." *Adventist Review,* 30 June 1983, 4-8.

_____. "Preliminary Consideration of the Effects and Implications of Adam's Sin." *Adventist Perspectives* 2:2 (1988): 28-44.

_____. "Model or Substitute? Does It Matter How We See Jesus? – Parts 1-6." *Adventist Review,* 18 January-22 February 1990.

_____. "The Effects of Adam's Sin on the Human Race." *Journal of the Adventist Theological Society* 5:1 (1994): 196-215.

_____. "Focusing on Christ, Not Ourselves." *Ministry,* October 1994, 28-30.

Gurney, H. S. "This Generation." *Review and Herald,* 14 October 1858, 165.

Guy, Fritz. "The Shaking of Adventism? I. A View from the Outside." *Spectrum* 9:3 (1978): 28-31.

_____. "Adventist Theology Today." *Spectrum* 12:1 (1981): 6-14.

_____. "Truth Our Contemporary." *Adventist Review,* 22 August 1991, 12-14.

Hackett, W. J. "The Church in an Era of Change." *Review and Herald,* 16 May 1968, 1, 8-9.

_____. "Inspiration in a Changing World." *Review and Herald,* 12 February 1970, 4-6.

_____. "The Church's Terrible Ordeal." *Review and Herald,* 23 January 1975, 4-5.

_____. "Preserve the Landmarks." *Review and Herald,* 26 May 1977, 2.

Hale, Apollos. "'Call to Remembrance the Former Days.'" *Review and Herald,* 16 September-7 October 1851, 25-28, 33-34.

_____. "Duties and Trials of Our Position." *Review and Herald,* 25 November 1851, 49-50.

_____. "The Kingdom of God." *Review and Herald,* 13 June 1854, 153-155.

Hall, O. A. "The Enduring Foundation." *Review and Herald,* 30 April 1936, 3-4.

Haloviak, Bert, with Gary Land. "Ellen G. White and Doctrinal Conflict: Context of the 1919 Bible Conference." *Spectrum* 12:4 (1982): 19-34.

Hammill, Richard. "God Speaks through the Scriptures." *Review and Herald,* 6 October 1966, 2-5.

_____. "Spiritual Gifts in the Church Today." *Ministry,* July 1982, 17.

_____. "Change and the SDA Church – Nos. 1-2." *Adventist Review,* 6-13 January 1983, 6-8, 6-8.

_____. "Ellen White and Change." *Adventist Review,* 13 January 1983, 6-8.

_____. "Fifty Years of Creationism: The Story of an Insider." *Spectrum* 15:2 (August 1984): 32-45.

"Has the Bridegroom Come?" *Advent Herald,* 26 February 1845, 18.

Hasel, Gerhard F. "Who Are the Remnant?" *Adventists Affirm* 7:2 (1993): 5-13, 31.

Haskell, S. N. "Was Christ Divine?" *Review and Herald,* 21 April 1891, 329-330.

Hastings, Elvira. "My Dear Brother and Sister." *Advent Review,* August 1850, 15-16.

Haynes, Carlyle B. "Walking in the Light." *Review and Herald,* 27 September 1928, 9-10.

_____. "Has the Time Come for Us to Alter Our Standards and Rebuild Our Platform?" *Review and Herald,* 1 March 1934, 3-6.

_____. "The Completion of the Arrested Reformation." *Review and Herald,* 3 January 1935, 4-5, 22.

Heinz, Daniel. "Das Problem der 'Erbsünde' aus adventistischer Sicht." *Aller Diener,* 1983, No. 3, 18-23.

_____. "Ludwig Richard Conradi: Patriarch of European Adventism." *Adventist Heritage* 12:1 (1987): 17-25.

Heinz, H. "Die historisch-kritische Methode und die Verkündigung des Evangeliums." *Adventecho,* November 1986, 8-9.

Henderson, J. P. "Is Christ a Created Being?" *Review and Herald,* 12 January 1892, 19.

Heppenstall, Edward E. "Doctrine of Revelation and Inspiration." *Ministry,* August 1970, 28-31.

_____. "Creed, Authority, and Freedom." *Ministry,* April 1979, 12-14.

_____. "The Pre-Advent Judgment." *Ministry,* December 1981, 12-15.

Hernandez, Ruben. "Original Sin and Salvation." *Evangelica,* April 1981, 16-21.

Herndon, Booton. "A Look at Adventists." *Review and Herald,* Centenary Issue, 1861-1961,
    [8 June 1961], 8.

Herr, Larry G. "Genesis One in Historical-Critical Perspective." *Spectrum* 13:2 (1982): 51-62.

Hewitt, D. "The Parable of the Fig Tree." *Review and Herald,* 17 January 1856, 123.

Hill, Samuel S., Jr. "A Typology of American Restitutionism: From Frontier Revivalism and
    Mormonism to the Jesus Movement." *Journal of the American Academy of Religion*
    44 (March 1976): 65-76.

Holbrook, Frank B. "The Sanctuary and Assurance – 1-2." *Adventist Review,*
    15-22 July 1982, 4-5, 6-8.

_____. "For Members Only?" *Ministry,* February 1987, 12-14, 30.

Holt, G. W. "Dear Brethren." *Present Truth,* March 1850, 64.

_____. "The Day of the Lord." *Review and Herald,* 23 March 1852, 105-108.

Hopkins, J. M. "Grieve Not the Spirit." *Review and Herald,* 3 July 1883, 417.

Hubbs, R. L. "Our Changing World." *Review and Herald,* 28 October 1954, 12-13.

Hughes, Richard T. "Primitivism." *Dictionary of Christianity in America.* 1990 ed. 940-941.

Hull, D. W. "Bible Doctrine of the Divinity of Christ." *Review and Herald,* 10-17 November
    1859, 193-195, 201-202.

Hull, Moses. "The Two Laws, and Two Covenants." *Review and Herald,* 13 May 1862, 189.

„Hunger and Poverty." *Adventist Review,* Special Issue, 5 May 1988.

Hurst, Van G. "Will Christ Come in A. D. 2000? A Look at the 6,000-Year Theory."
    Review and Herald, 9 July 1987, 16-17.

Hyde, Gordon M. "The Adventist Emphasis." *Ministry,* September 1974, 8-10.

"The Image of the Beast." *Review and Herald,* 16 January 1879, 20.

Ingraham, Wm. S. "Matters in Iowa." *Review and Herald,* 23 January 1866, 63.

_____. "God a Being and Heaven a Place." *Review and Herald,* 25 June 1867, 17-18.

"Inspiration." *Review and Herald,* 26 February 1880, 139.

"Inspiration" (Review), *Ministry,* December 1991, 28-30.

"The Inspiration and Authority of the Ellen G. White Writings." *Adventist Review,* 23 December 1982, 9; also published in *Ministry,* February 1983, 24.

"International Year of Peace 1986." *Adventist Review,* 5 December 1985, 19.

"Into All the World." *Ministry,* November 1992.

Jacobs, E[noch]. "The Time." *Western Midnight Cry,* 29 November 1844, 19-20.

_____. "Intolerance." *Western Midnight Cry,* 30 December 1844, 30.

[_____]. "Rev. 22:11, 12." *Day-Star,* 29 April 1845, 46-48.

[_____]. "Is the Door Shut?" *Day-Star,* 13-20 May 1845, 1-3, 6-8.

[_____]. "The Second Coming." *Day-Star,* 24 January 1846, 28-29.

James, Otey. "One of 'This Generation.'" *RH,* 20 July 1905, 18.

Johns, Warren H. "Ellen G. White: Prophet or Plagiarist?" *Ministry,* June 1982, 18.

Johnsson, William G. "Reflections on Ellen White's Inspiration." *Review and Herald,* 27 November 1980, 13.

_____. "Are Adventists Fundamentalists?" *Adventist Review,* 8 January 1981, 14.

_____. "Uplift Christ." *Ministry,* February 1982, 7.

_____. "A Distinctive Body of Teaching." *Adventist Review,* 27 May 1982, 14.

_____. "Something Old, Something New." *Adventist Review,* 5 August 1982, 8.

_____. "The Review in Your Future." *Adventist Review,* 9 December 1982, 3, 9-10.

_____. "Those Moon Men in Long Black Coats." *Adventist Review,* 14 July 1983, 14.

_____. "Luther Revisited." *Adventist Review,* 3 November 1983, 14.

_____. "The Landmarks of Adventism." *Adventist Review,* 1-29 October 1987, 4, 4-5, 4, 4-5.

_____. "Present Truth: Walking in God's Light." *Adventist Review,* 6 January 1994, 8-11.

_____. "Seven Factors Fragmenting the Church." *Adventist Review,* 5 May 1994, 12-14.

Johnston, Robert M. "A Search for Truth." *Adventist Review,* Adventist History Issue, [15 September 1983], 6-8.

Joiner, James. "Two Altered Hymns." *Adventist Review,* 5 April 1984, 10.

Jones, A. T. "Historical Necessity of the Third Angel's Message." *Review and Herald,* 17 June 1884, 387.

_____. "The Alemanni." *Signs of the Times,* 17 June-8 July 1886, 356-357, 372, 388, 404.

_____. "The Ten Kingdoms." *Signs of the Times,* 30 September-28 October 1886, 596, 612, 628, 644-645.

_____. "The Third Angel's Message. – Nos. 13-14." *General Conference Bulletin 1895.* 230-235, 265-270.

_____. "The Third Angel's Message. – No. 15." *General Conference Bulletin,* 22 February 1895, 298-304.

_____. "The Faith of Jesus." *Review and Herald,* 18-25 December 1900, 808, 824.

Jones, E. P. "'Born of God.'" *Review and Herald,* 9 July 1889, 434-435.

Jorgensen, Alfred S. "The 'Omega' of Apostasy." *Ministry,* March 1975, 8-10.

Journal of the Adventist Theological Society. Collegedale, Tenn., and Berrien Springs, Mich., 1990-

Judd, Wayne. "From Ecumenists to Come-Outers: The Millerites, 1831-1845." *Adventist Heritage* 11:1 (1986): 3-12.

Kellogg, M. E. "Are Seventh-day Adventists Evangelical?" *Review and Herald,* 15 March 1892, 170-171.

_____. "Inferences." *Review and Herald,* 27 June-4 July 1893, 409, 424-425.

Kellogg, M. G. "The Way of Life from Paradise Lost to Paradise Restored." *Review and Herald,* 27 May 1873, 192.

„Kellogg vs. The Brethren: His Last Interview as an Adventist – October 7, 1907." *Spectrum* 20:3 (1990): 46-62.

"Kellogg Snaps, Crackles, and Pops; His Last Interview as an Adventist – Part 2." *Spectrum* 20:4 (1990): 37-61.

Keough, G. D. "The Cleansing of the Sanctuary." *Ministry,* January 1962, 30-33.

Klingbeil, R. L. "The Foundation Stands Secure." *Adventist Review,* 17 September 1981, 9.

Knight, George R. "Adventism, Institutionalism, and the Challenge of Secularization."
     Ministry, June 1991, 6-10, 29.

_____. "Adventists and Change." *Ministry,* October 1993, 10-15.

_____. "Adventist Theology 1844 to 1994." *Ministry,* August 1994, 10-13, 25.

Kuhn, O. B. "Liberalism Endangers the Church." *Ministry,* May 1971, 17.

LaBreque, Alexander. "Adventism in Crisis." *Evangelica,* March 1983, 17-18.

Lamson, D. H. "Armageddon." *Review and Herald,* 14 April 1885, 227.

_____. "Turkey – Its Rise and Fall." *Review and Herald,* 21 April 1885, 243.

Land, Gary. "The Peril of Prophesying: Seventh-day Adventists Interpret World War I."
     Adventist Heritage 1:1 (1974): 28-33.

_____. "Providence and Earthly Affairs: The Christian and the Study of History."
     Spectrum 7:4 (April 1976): 2-6.

_____. "From Apologetics to History: The Professionalization of Adventist Historians."
     Spectrum 10:4 (March 1980): 89-100.

„Landmarks of Truth." Week of Prayer Readings. *Review and Herald,* 7 October 1971, 1-21.

Lane, T. M. "This Generation." *Review and Herald,* 26 July 1881, 68.

LaRondelle, Hans K. "Plea for a Christ-Centered Eschatology." *Ministry,* January 1976, 18-20.

„Leading Doctrines Taught by the Review." *Review and Herald,* 15 August-19 December 1854.

Lee, F. "The Sense of Direction." *Review and Herald,* 19 January 1939, 5-6; reprinted *Review
     and Herald,* 17 January 1957, 8.

_____. "Giving Heed to the Foundations." *Review and Herald,* 26 January 1939, 3-4.

_____. "'Launch Out Into the Deep.'" *Review and Herald,* 9 February 1939, 3-4.

_____. "What Makes a Seventh-day Adventist?" *Review and Herald,* 4 January 1940, 6-7.

_____. "'Examine Yourself.'" *Review and Herald,* 18 November 1943, 7-8.

_____. "Seeking a Deeper Understanding of God's Will." *Review and Herald,* 31 January 1957, 8-9.

_____. "The Strong Appeal of Popularity." *Review and Herald,* 22 June 1967, 1, 7.

_____. "The Passion for Change." *Review and Herald,* 29 June 1967, 4-5.

_____. "The Lure of Intellectualism." *Review and Herald,* 6 July 1967, 6-7.

[Lenfest, J]. "The New Birth." *Review and Herald,* 6 November 1856, 5.

Lesher, Richard. "Principles for Testing Added Light." *Ministry,* September 1947, 19, 18 *[sic].*

_____. "Landmark Truth versus 'Specious Error' – Nos. 1-2." *Adventist Review,* 6-13 March 1980, 4-7, 6-7.

_____. "Truth Stands Forever." *Adventist Review,* 13 March 1980, 6-7.

"Letter from Bro. Cook." *Day-Star,* 6 September 1845, 18.

"Letter from Bro. [Otis] Nichols." *Day-Star,* 27 September 1845, 34.

"Letter from Bro. Z. Baker." *Jubilee Standard,* 3 April 1845, 27.

"Letter from R. Hutchinson." *Midnight Cry,* 24 August 1843, 8.

"Letters." *Adventist Review,* 23 October 1980, 2.

"Letters." *Ministry,* December 1985, 2, 25-28.

Lewis, Richard B. "The 'Spirit of Prophecy'." *Spectrum* 2:4 (1970): 69-72.

Lindsell, Harold. "What of Seventh-day Adventism?" *Christianity Today,* 31 March-14 April 1958, 6-8, 13-15.

Littlejohn, W[olcott]. H. "Seventh-day Adventists and Seventh-day Baptists." *Review and Herald,* 4 November 1880, 297.

_____. "Seventh-day Adventists and Seventh-day Baptists." *Review and Herald,* 11 November 1880, 306.

_____. "Scripture Questions." *Review and Herald,* 17 April 1883, 250.

_____. "Seventh-day Adventists and the Testimony of Jesus Christ." *Review and Herald,* 8-22 May 1883, 290, 307-308, 322-323.

_____. "The S.D.A. Church Manual." *Review and Herald,* 5 June-9 October 1883.

_____. "The S.D.A. Church Manual." *Review and Herald*, 5 June 1883, 361.

_____. "The Testimony of Jesus the Same as the Spirit of Prophecy: Objections Answered." *Review and Herald*, 31 July 1883, 481-483.

_____. "The Testimony of Jesus Again." *Review and Herald*, 31 July 1883, 488-489.

_____. "The Church Manual." *Review and Herald*, 31 July 1883, 491.

_____. "The Church Manual." *Review and Herald*, 21 August 1883, 537-538.

_____. "Heaven: Is It a Place, or Merely a Condition?" *Review and Herald*, 12 February 1884, 97-99.

_____. "Scripture Questions." *Review and Herald*, 3 March 1885, 138.

_____. "Justification by Faith." *Review and Herald*, 9 August 1892, 499.

Lloyd, Ernest. "Our Unchanging Lord in a Changing World." *Review and Herald*, 19 April 1951, 4.

_____. "Our Changeless Friend." *Review and Herald*, 17 May 1956, 7.

Londis, James J. "We Don't All Worship the Same God." *Review and Herald*, 23 October 1969, 5.

_____. "*Remnant in Crisis* and a Second Disappointment." *Spectrum* 24:4 (April 1995): 9-16.

Longacre, C. S. "This Generation Shall Not Pass." *Review and Herald*, 19 July 1956, 4-5.

Loughborough, J. N. "The Hour of His Judgment Come." *Review and Herald*, 14 February 1854, 29-30.

_____. "Is the Soul Immortal?" *Review and Herald*, 11 December 1855, 81-83.

_____. "Judgment." *Review and Herald*, 19 November 1857, 9-11.

_____. "Image of the Beast." *Review and Herald*, 15 January 1861, 68-69.

_____. "Creeds." *Review and Herald*, 29 October 1861, 176.

_____. "Questions for Brother Loughborough." *Review and Herald*, 5 November 1861, 184.

_____. "Thoughts on the Day of Atonement." *Review and Herald*, 15 August 1865, 81-83.

Lowe, Harry W. Review of *Questions on Doctrine,* in *Ministry,* June 1958, 36.

_____. "We Can't Have It Both Ways." *Ministry,* September 1962, 48.

_____. "The Writings of Ellen G. White as Related to Seventh-day Adventist Doctrines and Prophetic Interpretation." *Ministry,* October 1967, 8-11, 13.

_____. "Doctrinal Development and Prophetic Interpretation: Their Relationship." *Ministry,* November 1967, 36-39.

Mansell, Donald E. "What Adventists Have Taught on Armageddon and the King of the North." *Ministry,* November-December 1967, 26-29, 30-32.

_____. "Armageddon: Changing Views on the Final Battle." *[College and University] Dialogue* 5:3 (1993): 13-16.

Martin, Ralph. "The Church in Changing Times." *Adventist Review,* 4 January 1990, 7-9.

Martin, Walter R. "The Truth about Seventh-day Adventism." *Eternity,* October 1956-January 1957, 6-7, 38-40; 20-21, 38-43; 12-13, 38-40.

_____. "What Seventh-day Adventists Really Believe." *Eternity,* November 1956, 20-21, 38-43.

_____. "Seventh-day Adventism Today." *Our Hope,* November 1956, 274-277.

Matteson, John. "Children of God." *Review and Herald,* 12 October 1869, 123.

Maxwell, C. Mervyn. "In Confirmation of Prophetic Interpretation." *Journal of the Adventist Theological Society* 2:1 (1991): 139-151.

McAdams, Donald R. "The 1978 Annual Council: A Report and Analysis." *Spectrum* 9:4 (1979): 7-8.

McArthur, Benjamin. "Where Are Historians Taking the Church? *Spectrum* 10:3 (November 1979): 9-14.

McDuffie, J. T. "The Prodigal Son Rebutted." *Adventist Review,* 1 July 1982, 11-13.

McElhany, J. L. "The President's Address." *Review and Herald,* 27 May 1941, 11.

_____. "Changing Our Emphasis." *Review and Herald,* 15 January 1953, 11.

McIver, Robert K. "Bible Alive! How to Understand the 'Plain Meaning' of the Bible." *Adventist Review,* 13 August 1992, 8-10.

McLellan, J. M. "Born of Water." *Review and Herald,* 12 February 1857, 118.

Mead, Maria. "Present Truth." *Review and Herald,* 11 December 1879, 186.

Medley, Carlos. "The Changing Face of Adventism." *Adventist Review,* 19 February 1987, 5.

"Methods of Bible Study." *Ministry,* April 1987, 23, 22-24.

Miethe, T. L. "Christian Church (Disciples of Christ)." *Dictionary of Christianity in America.* 1990 ed. 253-254.

Miller, William. "Letter from Bro. Miller." *Jubilee Standard,* 17 April 1845, 41-42.

Ministry. Washington, D.C., and Silver Spring, Md., 1928-.

M[inor], C. S. "The True Manna." *Jubilee Standard,* 3 April 1845, 29.

Montgomery, Oliver. "The Sure Foundation." *Ministry,* September 1932, 3-4, 28-29.

Morrison, Isaac. "'Here a Little and There a Little.'" *Review and Herald,* 9 September 1884, 580.

Morse, G. W. "Scripture Questions." *Review and Herald,* 21 June 1887, 394.

————. "Scripture Question." *Review and Herald,* 28 August 1888, 554.

————. "Scripture Questions." *Review and Herald,* 25 September 1888, 618.

Moyer, Bruce C. "Love in Practice: A Portrait of God's Final Remnant." *Adventist Review,* 29 March 1990, 11-12.

"Mr. Miller's Letters. No. 5." *Signs of the Times,* 15 May 1840, 25-26.

Müller, Richard. "Anabaptists: The Reformers' Reformers." *Ministry,* July 1986, 11-13.

"Must the Crisis Continue? *Spectrum* 11:3 (1981): 44-52.

"The Nature of Christ during the Incarnation." *Ministry,* February 1972.

Neall, Beatrice S. "The Dragon Fighters." *Ministry,* June 1980, 14-15.

Nelson, Wilbur K. "Are Adventists Fundamentalists?" *Ministry,* April 1965, 16-17.

Neufeld, Don F. "The Editor's Mailbag." *Review and Herald,* 13 August 1964, 12.

————. "Is an Unbiased Bible Translation Possible?" *Review and Herald,* 11 February 1971, 15-16.

_____. "125 Years of Advancing Light." *Review and Herald,* Anniversary Issue, [13 November 1975], 27.

_____. "SDA Biblical Scholars Convene." *Review and Herald,* 8 January 1976, 3, 12.

_____. "What's Wrong with the Proof-Text Method?" *Review and Herald,* 11 March 1976, 10-11.

_____. "Is the 6,000 Year Theory Valid?" *Review and Herald,* 25 March 1976, 10-11.

_____. "Footnote to the 6,000-Year Theory." *Review and Herald,* 13 May 1976, 10.

_____. "This Generation Shall Not Pass." *Review and Herald,* 5 April 1979, 6.

_____. "The Battle for the Bible." *Adventist Review,* 26 July 1979, 14-15.

_____. "Adventists' Contribution to the Sabbath Doctrine." *Review and Herald,* 13 September 1979, 35-36.

Newman, J. David. "How Much Diversity Can We Stand?" *Ministry,* April 1994, 5, 26.

Nichol, F. D. "Truth and Trustworthy Evidence." *Ministry,* January 1930, 5-7.

_____. "Four Charges against Seventh-day Adventists." *Review and Herald,* 5 March 1931, 3-4.

_____. "Modern Apostasy in Christendom." *Review and Herald,* 8-15 June 1933, 3-4, 5-6.

_____. "Modernism's Inadequacy Is Our Opportunity." *Ministry,* February 1936, 14, 22.

_____. "Modern Turkey and Unfulfilled Prophecy." *Review and Herald,* 8 December 1938, 8.

_____. "Restudying the Doctrines without Destroying the Foundations." *Ministry,* February 1940, 4, 12.

_____. "Do Adventists Minimize Christ's Atonement?" *Review and Herald,* 24 July 1952, 13.

_____. "The Bible Conference." *Review and Herald,* 28 August 1952, 1, 14.

_____. "Looking Back on the Bible Conference." *Review and Herald,* 23 October 1952, 10.

_____. "A New Day for Adventists." *Review and Herald,* 8 May 1958, 9-10.

_____. "The Doubtful Value of 'New Light.'" *Review and Herald,* 21 December 1961, 8-9.

_____. "The Critics and Their Criticism – Nos. 3-8." *Review and Herald*, 8 March-12 April 1962.

_____. "Are We Removing the Old Landmarks?" *Review and Herald*, 8 March 1962, 12-13.

_____. "The Landmarks Examined." *Review and Herald*, 15 March 1962, 12-13.

_____. "Have We Forsaken the Sanctuary Doctrine? – No. 3." *Review and Herald*, 12 April 1962, 13.

_____. "Why Defend the Faith – Nos. 1-2." *Review and Herald*, 22-29 November 1962, 12-13, 12-13.

_____. "The Historical Foundations of Christianity – Parts 1-2." *Review and Herald*, 5-12 September 1963, 14-15, 13.

_____. "The Church and Social Reform." *Review and Herald*, 15 April 1965, 15.

_____. "From the Editor's Mailbag." *Review and Herald*, 29 July 1965, 13.

Nichols, Otis. "The Signs of the End of the World." *Review and Herald*, 9 December 1852, 114.

_____. "This Generation – The Period of Its Application." *Review and Herald*, 18 November 1858, 204.

Noll, Mark A. "Rethinking Restorationism: A Review Article." *Reformed Journal* 39 (November 1989): 15-21.

„Non-Essentials and Essentials." *Review and Herald*, 28 May 1889, 341.

North, J. B. "Christian Connection." *Dictionary of Christianity in America*. 1990 ed. 255.

_____. "Restoration Movement." *Dictionary of Christianity in America*. 1990 ed. 1005-1008.

Obst, Helmut. "Ellen G. White entmythologisieren!" *Materialdienst* 57:1 (1994): 19-22.

O'Dea, Thomas. "Five Dilemmas in the Institutionalization of Religion." *Journal for the Scientific Study of Religion* 1 (1961): 30-39.

Ogden, A. R. "Are You Certain of Your Faith?" *Review and Herald*, 14 November 1940, 2, 5.

Oliveira, Enoch. "Reform or Redemption: Must the Church Choose?" *Ministry*, September 1982, 10-11.

„Olson Discusses the Veltman Study." *Ministry*, December 1990, 16-18.

Olson, Robert W. "Outline Studies on Christian Perfection and Original Sin." *Ministry,* Supplement, n.d., 24-30 [48-54].

Olson, A. V. "Defenders of the Faith." *Review and Herald,* 14 June 1962, 2-3, 7.

Oosterwal, Gottfried. "Mission and Culture: Shedding the Gospel's Western Package." *Adventist Review,* 19 October 1989, 18-23.

_____. "Gospel, Culture, and Mission." *Ministry,* October 1989, 22-25.

„Organization of the Mich. Conference." *Review and Herald,* 8 October 1861, 148.

Osborn, Richard C. "The First Decade: The Establishment of the Adventist Forums." *Spectrum* 10:4 (1980): 42-58.

Our Firm Foundation. Eatonville, Wash., 1985-.

„Overview of a Historic Meeting." *Adventist Review,* 4 September 1980, 4-7.

Owen, Roderick S. "The Source of Final Appeal." *Review and Herald,* 3 June 1971, 4-6.

Parker, Edward A. "Does the Seventh-day Adventist Minister Need to Consider Intellectual Honesty?" *Ministry,* June 1971, 21-23.

Patrick, Arthur N. "Does Our Past Embarrass Us?" *Ministry,* April 1991, 7-10.

Patterson, Gary B. "The Quest for Truth." *Adventist Review,* 26 September 1991, 13-17.

Pease, Norval F. "'The Truth as It Is in Jesus': The 1888 General Conference Session, Minneapolis, Minnesota." *Adventist Heritage* 10:1 (1985): 3-10.

Peavey, G. W. "'The Hour of His Judgment Is Come.'" *Jubilee Standard,* 19 June 1845, 113-115.

Pepper, Wm. "Walk in the Light." *Review and Herald,* 20 March 1879, 90.

"Perfection of the Bible." *Review and Herald,* 15 September 1859, 134.

Pierce, Stephen. "Answer to Bro. Merriam's Question Respecting the Law of Gal. iii, in Review No. 3, Vol. X." *Review and Herald,* 8 October 1857, 180-181.

Pierson, Robert H. "The Old Message Is Always New/True." *Review and Herald,* 1 January 1970, 2-3.

_____. "The Same Yesterday, Today, and Forever." *Ministry,* June 1970, 35-40.

_____. "I Have Set Thee a Watchman." *Ministry,* November 1970, 24, 57-58.

_____. "No Compromise." *Review and Herald*, 8 February 1973, 2.

_____. "When Will the 'Other Side' Be Heard?" *Review and Herald*, 11 March 1976, 2.

_____. "The Testimony of Jesus." *Review and Herald*, 6 October 1977, 6-7.

_____. "How Do You Really Feel about Your Church? – Nos. 1-2." *Adventist Review*, 9 February, 5 October 1978, 2-3, 18.

_____. "An Earnest Appeal from the Retiring President of the General Conference." *Adventist Review*, 26 October 1978, 10.

[Pinney, E. R., and T. F. Barry]. "'Ye Must Be Born Again'." *Review and Herald*, 13-20 March 1856, 186-188, 194-195.

Pöhler, Rolf J. "Auf dem Prüffeld des Evangeliums: Robert D. Brinsmead erschüttert den Adventismus." *Materialdienst* 45:5 (1 Mai 1982): 126-130.

_____. "Verkürzte Wahrheit – heilsame Häresie: Eine Kritik des soteriologischen und hermeneutischen Ansatzpunkts Robert D. Brinsmeads." *Aller Diener*, Nos. 3-4, 1982, 101-112.

_____. "Adventisten auf der Suche nach der wahren Ellen G. White." *Materialdienst* 47:12 (1 December 1984): 372-375.

_____. "Adventism and 1844: Shut Door or Open Mind?" *Spectrum* 19:1 (1988): 58-60.

_____. "Wie sehen die Adventisten ihr Verhältnis zu anderen Kirchen? *Adventecho*, September 1988, 10-11.

_____. "Hat die Welt noch eine Zukunft? – Nos. 1-4." *Zeichen der Zeit*, April-October 1989.

_____. "Fundamentalismus in Geschichte und Gegenwart der Siebenten-Tags-Adventisten." *Zeitlupe*, May 1993, 35-39.

Pöhler, Rolf J., and H.-Diether Reimer. "Adventisten." *Evangelisches Kirchenlexikon*. 3d rev. ed., 1985. 1:44-47.

Poirier, Tim. "Sources Clarify Ellen White's Christology." *Ministry*, December 1989, 7-9.

_____. "An Encouraging Word." *Adventist Review*, 22 December 1994, 14-16.

Prenier, H. "The Everlasting Gospel in 'Present Truth' Setting." *Ministry*, April 1929, 8-9.

Prescott, W. W. "The Christ for Today." *Review and Herald*, 14 April 1896, 232.

_____. "The Fundamentals of the Advent Message." *Review and Herald,* 9 June 1926, 6.

"Present Truth." *Voice of the Truth,* 2 October 1844, 144.

Present Truth. Middletown, Conn.; Oswego, N.Y.; and Paris, Maine, 1849-1850.

"Preserving the Unity of Church and Message." *Adventist Review,* General Conference Bulletin No. 7, 5 July 1985, 9.

Price, George McCready. "Armageddon." *Review and Herald,* 1 January 1976, 4-7.

Provonsha, Jack W. "Can There Be an Innovative Adventism?" *Ministry,* April 1976, 34-35.

_____. "The Church as a Prophetic Minority." *Spectrum* 12:1 (1981): 18-23.

"Questions for Brother Loughborough." *Review and Herald,* 5 November 1861, 184.

Quigley, W. B. "Imminence – Mainspring of Adventism – Nos. 1-3." *Ministry,* April, June, August 1980, 4-6, 27; 11-13; 18-19.

Ragsdale, A. M. "The Certainty of Change." *Review and Herald,* 14 June 1951, 10-11.

Rampton, Howard F. "The Miracle of Unity." *Adventist Review,* 11 September 1980, 8-9.

Read, W. E. "Walking in the Light." *Review and Herald,* 12 February 1953, 5-6.

Reid, George. "Why Did Jesus Die? How God Saves Us." *Adventist Review,* 5 November 1992, 10-13.

Reimer, Hans-Diether. "Endzeitgemeinde im Wandel: Wohin bewegt sich der Adventismus?" *Materialdienst* 36:14 (1973): 218-225.

_____. "Adventistische Theologie." *Materialdienst* 40:9 (1977): 236-244.

_____. "Adventisten: Neufassung der adventistischen 'Glaubensgrundsätze'." *Materialdienst* 44:9 (1981): 266-267.

_____. "Die Siebenten-Tags-Adventisten und das Problem der zwischenkirchlichen Beziehungen." *Materialdienst* 49:9 (1986): 267-275.

Rempel, Gerhard. "Fundamentalismus – Heil oder Gefahr?" *Adventecho,* March 1987, 6-8.

"Report of Conferences." *Review and Herald,* 12 March 1857, 152.

"Report on the Eleventh Chapter of Daniel." *Ministry,* March 1954, 22-27.

"A Repudiation of Charges and a Declaration of Faith." *Ministry,* April 1935, 6-7.

"Revision of Church Manual." *Review and Herald,* 14 June 1946, 197.

Rice, Richard. "The Knowledge of Faith." *Spectrum* 5:2 (1973): 19-32.

_____. "Dominant Themes in Adventist Theology." *Spectrum* 10:4 (1980): 58-74.

"Righteousness by Faith." *Adventist Review,* Special Issue, [16 May 1974].

"Righteousness by Faith." *Ministry,* August 1976, 5-9.

Rockwell, N. W. "From Brother Rockwell." *Review and Herald,* 8 September 1853, 71.

Rodriguez, Angel Manuel. "The Sanctuary and Its Cleansing." *Adventist Review,* Supplement, [1] September 1994, 1-16.

"The Role of the Ellen G. White Writings in Doctrinal Matters." *Adventist Review,* 4 September 1980, 15.

Rosado, Caleb. "United in Christ." *Adventist Review,* 22 June 1995, 9-12.

Rudy, H. L. "Unchanging Truth in a Changing World." *Review and Herald,* 10 March 1960, 6-7.

„S."S. D. Adventist General Conference [Proceedings]." *Review and Herald,* 13 November 1888, 712-714.

St. John, H. A. "Synopsis of the Atonement. Nos. 1-2." *Review and Herald,* 13-20 February 1883, 101-102, 119.

Samples, Kenneth R. "The Recent Truth About Seventh-day Adventism." *Christianity Today,* 5 February 1990, 19.

Sanborn, Isaac. "To the Law and Testimony." *Review and Herald,* 20 October 1863, 161-162.

"Sanctuary Debate." *Spectrum* 11:2 (1980): 1-78.

Schantz, Borge. "The 'Shut Door' – A Providential Opening?" *Adventist Review,* 29 January 1987, 18-19.

_____. "One Message – Many Cultures: How Do We Cope?" *Ministry,* June 1992, 8-11.

Schmitz, K. "Ist der Adventismus eine Spielart des Fundamentalismus? 1993." In *Fundamentalismus: Glaube - Angst - Gewißheit.* Der Adventglaube in Geschichte und Gegenwart. Darmstadt: Adventistischer Wissenschaftlicher Arbeitskreis 1996. 83-113.

Schwarz, Richard W. "The Kellogg Schism: The Hidden Issues." *Spectrum* 4:4 (1972): 23-39.

Scragg, Walter R. L. "1844." *Adventist Review,* 7 January 1982, 7.

Scriven, Charles. "The Case for Renewal in Adventist Theology." *Spectrum* 8:1 (1976): 2-6.

_____. "Radical Discipleship and the Renewal of Adventist Mission." *Spectrum* 14:3 (1983): 11-20.

_____. "Two Kinds of Hope." *Adventist Review,* 31 May 1984, 3-4.

_____. "The Real Truth About the Remnant." *Spectrum* 17:1 (1986): 6-13.

_____. "The Gospel and Global Mission." *Ministry,* May 1992, 16-18.

_____. "God's Justice, Yes; Penal Substitution, No." *Spectrum* 23:3 (1993): 31-38.

Seaman, E. R. "Removing the Land-Marks." *Review and Herald,* 9 June 1853, 15.

_____. "Bro. Smith." *Review and Herald,* 30 October 1856, 207.

[Second] [Advent] Review and [Sabbath] Herald. Paris, Maine; Saratoga Springs, N.Y.; Rochester, N.Y.; Battle Creek, Mich.; and Washington, D.C., 1850-1977.

"Session Actions: Fundamental Beliefs of Seventh-day Adventists." *Adventist Review,* 1 May 1980, 23-27.

"Session Actions: Peace Message to All People of Good Will." *Adventist Review,* 1 May 1980, 19.

Seton, Bernard E. "Dallas Statement." *Spectrum* 11:3 (1981): 60-61.

"The Seven Trumpets." *Review and Herald,* 8 July 1884, 448.

"Seventh-day Adventists Believe ..." *Ministry,* July 1988, 4-5.

Slade, E. K. "The Certainty of Truth." *Review and Herald,* 29 August 1935, 4.

Smith, A. "The Hundred and Forty-Four Thousand." *Review and Herald,* 4 December 1879, 182-183.

_____. "The Seven Last Plagues." *Review and Herald,* 8 July 1884, 436-437.

_____. "Some Principles Followed by S. D. Adventists." *Review and Herald,* 5 July 1887, 419.

_____. "Last-Day Tokens – No. 11." *Review and Herald,* 6 December 1887, 754-755.

_____. "The Eastern Question." *Review and Herald,* 3-17 November 1891, 673-674, 690-691, 706-707.

Smith, L. A. "The Value of a 'Creed.'" *Review and Herald,* 10 May 1887, 298-299.

_____. "Demands of 'Enlightened' Orthodoxy." *Review and Herald,* 7 June 1887, 368.

_____. "The Nature of Our Work." *Review and Herald,* 15 November 1887, 712.

_____. "Creeds." *Review and Herald,* 6 November 1888, 699.

_____. "The Interpretation of Scripture." *Review and Herald,* 29 October 1889, 681.

_____. "Revising a Creed." *Review and Herald,* 25 February 1890, 120.

_____. "Sin and the Atonement." *Review and Herald,* 4 March 1890, 137.

_____. "Present Truth." *Review and Herald,* 6 January 1891, 9.

_____. "Unity." *Review and Herald,* 5 January 1892, 8-9.

_____. "Search the Scriptures." *Review and Herald,* 6 September 1892, 568-569.

_____. "The Nature of Sin." *Review and Herald,* 20 June 1893, 394.

_____. "The End of 'This Generation'." *Review and Herald,* 2 November 1905, 5.

Smith, Uriah. "Why Can We Not Believe in the New Time?" *Review and Herald,* 14 February 1854, 29.

_____. "The Watchmen Shall See Eye to Eye." *Review and Herald,* 28 February 1854, 44.

_____. "The Original Advent Faith." *Review and Herald,* 18 September 1855, 44.

_____. "The Cleansing of the Sanctuary." *Review and Herald,* 2 October 1855, 52-53.

_____. "The Bible Preacher." *Review and Herald,* 16 October 1855, 62.

[_____]. "'Ye Must Be Born Again.'" *Review and Herald,* 10 April 1856, 8.

[_____]. "The Seal of the Living God." *Review and Herald,* 24 April-1 May 1856, 12, 20-21.

[_____]. "Ye Must Be Born Again." *Review and Herald,* 8 May 1856, 28-29.

[_____]. "The New Birth." *Review and Herald,* 6 November 1856, 5.

[_____]. "The New Birth." *Review and Herald,* 15-22 January 1857, 84, 92-93.

_____. "The Hour of His Judgment Is Come." *Review and Herald,* 29 January 1857, 104.

_____. "The True Course." *Review and Herald,* 30 April 1857, 205.

[_____]. "Remarks." *Review and Herald,* 18 November 1858, 204.

[_____]. "Christ Our Passover." *Review and Herald,* 13 October 1859, 164.

[_____]. "The Faith of Jesus." *Review and Herald,* 2 February 1860, 84.

_____. "Will the Pope Remove the Papal Seat to Jerusalem?" *Review and Herald,* 13 May 1862, 192.

_____. "A Friendly Word with the Voice of the West." *Review and Herald,* 9 August 1864, 84.

[_____]. "The Sanctuary – An Objection Considered." *Review and Herald,* 1 November 1864, 180-181.

_____. "Seventh-day Adventists." *Review and Herald,* 22 November 1864, 204-205.

_____. "Warning of the Pope's Power." *Review and Herald,* 18 April 1865, 157.

_____. "Italy and the Papacy." *Review and Herald,* 9 January 1866, 45.

_____. "The 1335 Days." *Review and Herald,* 27 February 1866, 100-101.

_____. "The Visions – Objections Answered." *Review and Herald,* 10 July 1866, 42.

_____. "The Papacy." *Review and Herald,* 11 September 1866, 116.

_____. "The Two-horned Beast." *Review and Herald,* 9 October-27 November 1866.

_____. "Good, To-day." *Review and Herald,* 4 August 1868, 108.

_____. "Thoughts on Daniel." *Review and Herald,* 28 March 1871, 117.

[_____]. "The Eastern Question." *Review and Herald,* 25 February 1873, 82-83.

_____. "The Judgment of Rev. 14:7." *Review and Herald,* 13 January 1874, 36.

_____. "The Reformation Not Yet Complete." *Review and Herald,* 3 February 1874, 60-61.

_____. "Questions on the Sanctuary." *Review and Herald,* 5 August 1875, 44.

_____. "To Correspondents." *Review and Herald,* 27 July 1876, 40.

_____. "The New Birth." *Review and Herald,* 10 August 1876, 52.

_____. "The Sanctuary. Thirty-sixth Paper. – The Atonement." *Review and Herald,* 19 October 1876, 124-125.

_____. "To Correspondents." *Review and Herald,* 18 October 1877, 124.

[_____]. "Giving Way." *Review and Herald,* 23 October 1883, 664.

[_____]. "The Conference." *Review and Herald,* 4 November 1884, 696.

[_____]. "No Time to Set." *Review and Herald,* 2 December 1884, 760.

[_____]. "The Atonement." *Review and Herald,* 16 December 1884, 792.

[_____]. "The Opening Year." *Review and Herald,* 6 January 1885, 8.

[_____]. "The Latter Rain and the Refreshing." *Review and Herald,* 12 May 1885, 296-297.

[_____]. "Notes and Queries." *Review and Herald,* 11 August 1885, 504.

[_____]. "This Generation." *Review and Herald,* 22 March 1887, 182.

_____. "A Bible Reading on the Eastern Question." *Review and Herald,* 29 March 1887, 200-201.

[_____]. "J. W. Morton and the Sanctuary Question." *Review and Herald,* 2 August 1887, 489.

_____. "S. D. Adventism not Orthodox." *Review and Herald,* 27 March 1888, 200.

[_____]. "The Conference." *Review and Herald,* 23 October 1888, 664-665.

_____. "Another Attack." *Review and Herald,* 12 March 1889, 168.

[_____]. "In the Question Chair." *Review and Herald,* 28 October 1890, 664.

[_____]. "In the Question Chair." *Review and Herald,* 11 November 1890, 696-697.

[_____]. "Origin and History of the Third Angel's Message." *Review and Herald,* 27 January 1891, 56.

_____. "The Sinner and His Sins." *Review and Herald,* 10 February 1891, 88.

[_____]. "In the Question Chair." *Review and Herald,* 16 June 1891, 376.

[_____]. "This Generation." *Review and Herald,* 17 November 1891, 712.

[_____]. "In the Question Chair." *Review and Herald,* 5 January 1892, 8.

[_____]. "In the Question Chair." *Review and Herald,* 19 April 1892, 248-249.

[_____]. "In the Question Chair." *Review and Herald,* 26 April 1892, 264-265.

[_____]. "In the Question Chair." *Review and Herald,* 20 September 1892, 600.

[_____]. "The Higher Criticism." *Review and Herald,* 8 November 1892, 696.

[_____]. "In the Question Chair." *Review and Herald,* 6 June 1893, 360.

[_____]. "In the Question Chair." *Review and Herald,* 23 March 1897, 188.

Smith, U., G. W. Amadon, and J. M. Aldrich. "Remarks." *Review and Herald,*
    23 January 1866, 63.

Snow, S. S. "Visit to Philadelphia." *Jubilee Standard,* 3 April 1845, 28.

_____. "'And the Door Was Shut.'" *Jubilee Standard,* 24 April 1845, 52-54.

_____. "The Confederacy." *Jubilee Standard,* 12 June 1845, 108-109.

Spangler, J. Robert. "Times Have Changed." *Ministry,* April 1970, 10-11.

_____. "Profiting from His Prophet." *Ministry,* May 1973, 2-3.

_____. "Ask the Editor – 1-2." *Ministry,* August, October 1978, 14-17, 10-12.

_____. "What's So Unique about Adventism?" *Ministry,* October 1981, 24.

_____. "What's So Unique about Adventism? – No. 2." *Ministry,* December 1981, 19.

_____. "Why Consultation II?" *Ministry,* February 1982, 26-29.

_____. "Does Truth Change?" *Ministry,* October 1982, 24-25.

_____. "Adventist Theological Society." *Ministry,* December 1989, 24-25.

_____. "Too Many Theological Societies?" *Ministry,* June 1990, 22-23.

Spectrum. Journal of the Association of Adventist Forums. Takoma Park, Md., 1968-.

Spicer, W. A. "The Gathering for Armageddon." *Review and Herald,* 22 October 1903, 6-7.

_____. "The Message That Answers the Need." *Review and Herald,* 4 July 1929, 11.

_____. "The Truth That Endures." *Review and Herald,* 5 January 1933, 3.

_____. "Where One Truth Confirms Every Other." *Review and Herald,* 30 December 1948, 5.

Staples, Russell L. "Understanding Adventism." *Ministry,* September 1993, 19-23.

Starr, F. D. "The Reformation Continues." *Review and Herald,* 13 March 1883, 164.

"Statement on Desmond Ford Document." *Adventist Review,* 4 September 1980, 8-11.

Steininger, Thomas. "Adventistische Identität." *Adventecho,* 1 April 1983, 4-5.

Stephenson, J. M. "The Number of the Beast." *Review and Herald,* 29 November 1853, 166.

Stevens, J. C. "Safe Rules of Bible Interpretation." *Review and Herald,* 25 January 1934, 9.

Steward, [Mrs.] M. E. "This Generation." *Review and Herald,* 30 August 1887, 548-549.

_____. "The New Birth." *Review and Herald,* 1 July 1890, 404.

Stone, Albert. "Cannot Understand Alike." *Review and Herald,* 25 January 1877, 26.

_____. "The Testimonies." *Review and Herald,* 16 January 1883, 34.

"Study Documents on Inspiration and Creation." *Review and Herald,* 17 January 1980, 8-11.

Sturges, Stanley G. "Ellen White's Authority and the Church." *Spectrum* 4:3 (1972): 66-70.

Swan, S. M. "Are Seventh-day Adventists Teaching New Doctrines?" *Review and Herald,* 25 November 1880, 341.

Swift, J. E. "Our Companion." *Review and Herald,* 3 July 1883, 421.

"Taking a Stand: The Church Responds to Moral Issues Confronting Christians." *Adventist Review,* 31 December 1992, 11-15.

Teel, Charles. "Bridegroom or Babylon? Dragon or Lamb? Nineteenth-Century Adventists and the American Mainstream." *Adventist Heritage* 11:1 (1986): 13-25.

Tenney, G. C. "The Comforter." *Review and Herald,* 30 October 1883, 673-674.

_____. "To Correspondents." *Review and Herald,* 9 June 1896, 362.

Thiele, David. "Is Conservatism a Heresy?" *Spectrum* 23:4 (1994): 12-15.

"The Third Person." *Review and Herald,* 16 January 1900, 35.

"This Generation." *Review and Herald,* 17 April 1879, 128.

Thomas, N. Gordon. "The Almost Chosen." *Adventist Review*, 14 January 1982, 4.

_____. "The Second Coming: A Major Impulse of American Protestantism." *Adventist Heritage* 3:2 (1976): 3-9.

Thompson, Alden. "Theological Consultation II." *Spectrum* 12:2 (1981): 40-52.

_____. "From Sinai to Golgotha – Nos. 1-5." *Adventist Review*, 3-31 December 1981, 4-6, 8-10, 7-10, 7-9, 12-13.

_____. "The Prodigal Son Revisited." *Adventist Review*, 1 July 1982, 7-11.

_____. "We Need Your Differences." *Adventist Review* [2 November 1989], 17-20.

Thompson, George B. "This Generation." *RH*, 4 September 1888, 564.

_____. "Doctrine." *Review and Herald*, 18 February 1890, 100.

_____. "The Bible, Not Tradition." *Review and Herald*, 22 September 1891, 579.

_____. "The Holy Spirit – No. 7." *Review and Herald*, 27 February 1913, 197-198.

Thurber, Mervin R. "Discovered: A Manuscript Letter from William Miller." *Review and Herald*, 15 April 1976, 4-6.

Thurow, Lester C. *Newsweek*, 8 August 1983, 66. Quoted in Richard Hammill, "Fifty Years of Creationism: The Story of an Insider." *Spectrum* 15:2 (1984): 44.

"To the Believers Scattered Abroad." *Day-Star*, 25 March 1845, 21-24.

Trenchard, Warren C. "In the Shadow of the Sanctuary: The 1980 Theological Consultation." *Spectrum* 11:2 (1980): 26-30.

"Truth Progressive." *Review and Herald*, 23 May 1882, 328.

Turner, Joseph. "Letter from Bro. Joseph Turner." *Jubilee Standard*, 10 July 1845, 137-139.

Turner, Joseph, and Apollos Hale. "Has Not the Saviour Come as the Bridegroom?" *Advent Mirror*, January 1845.

"Twelfth Business Meeting." *Review and Herald*, 27 April 1980, 14-16.

Underwood, R. A. "The Holy Spirit a Person." *Review and Herald*, 17 May 1898, 310.

Unruh, T. E. "The Seventh-day Adventist Evangelical Conferences of 1955-1956." *Adventist Heritage* 4:2 (1977): 35-47.

"The Use of Creeds." *Review and Herald,* 7 January 1890, 5.

Valentine, Gilbert M. "W. W. Prescott: Editor Extraordinaire." *Review and Herald,* 5 December 1985, 10-12.

Van Dolson, L. R. "Limits." *Adventist Review,* 5 March 1981, 13-14.

Veltman, Fred. "Some Reflections on Change and Continuity." *Spectrum* 8:4 (1977): 40-43.

_____. "The *Desire of Ages* Project: The Data." *Ministry,* October 1990, 4-7.

_____. "The *Desire of Ages* Project: The Conclusions." *Ministry,* December 1990, 11-15.

Vick, Edward W. H. "Faith and Evidence." *Andrews University Seminary Studies* 5 (1967): 181-199.

_____. "Must We Keep the Sanctuary Doctrine?" *Spectrum* 14:3 (1983): 52-55.

Waggoner, E. J. "Under the Law." *Signs of the Times,* 11 September 1884, 553-554.

_____. "A Few Principles of Interpretation." *Signs of the Times,* 6 January 1887, 8.

_____. "Concealed Infidelity." *Signs of the Times,* 24 February 1887, 118.

_____. "The Divinity of Christ." *Signs of the Times,* 8 April 1889, 214.

Waggoner, J. H. "The Law of God." *Review and Herald,* 18 July 1854, 185-186.

_____. "The 'Age to Come.'" *Review and Herald,* 11 December 1855, 84-85.

_____. "Questions Answered." *Review and Herald,* 29 July 1858, 84-85.

_____. "The Atonement." *Review and Herald,* 10 September 1861, 116.

_____. "The Eagle of 2 Esdras XI." *Review and Herald,* 5 November 1861, 183.

_____. "The Atonement – Part II." *Review and Herald,* 3-10 November 1863, 181-182, 189-190.

_____. "Present Truth." *Review and Herald,* 7 August 1866, 76.

_____. "Battle Creek Bible Class, April 4, 1868." *Review and Herald,* 14 April 1868, 276.

_____. "Deserting the Landmarks." *Review and Herald,* 14 April 1868, 285.

_____. "'The Law and the Testimony.'" *Review and Herald,* 20 July 1869, 27.

_____. "The Literal and Spiritual Meaning of Language." *Review and Herald*, 2 July 1872, 20-21.

_____. "[Letter to] W. M." *Review and Herald*, 24 March 1874, 120.

_____. "The Gifts and Offices of the Holy Spirit – Nos. 1-12." *Review and Herald*, 23 September-9 December 1875.

_____. "The Eastern Question." *Review and Herald*, 2 March 1876, 68-69.

_____. "Is There Prophetic Time Longer?" *Review and Herald*, 11 November 1884, 713-714.

_____. "The Literal and Spiritual Meaning of Language." *Review and Herald*, 3 February 1885, 74.

_____. "The Church. – No. 15." *Review and Herald*, 25 August 1885, 537-538.

Walker, E. S. "The Time of Trouble." *Review and Herald*, 10 September 1861, 117-119.

"Walking in the Spirit." *Review and Herald*, 24 January 1899, 82.

Walther, Daniel. "How Shall We Study History?" *Ministry*, August 1939, 11-12.

_____. "The Message of Reformation." *Review and Herald*, 7 August 1858, 11, 26-27.

Wardwell, J. F. "Letter from Sister J. F. Wardwell." *Day-Dawn*, 16 April 1847, 10.

Waters, T. L. "The Holy Spirit." *Review and Herald*, 28 November 1893, 743.

Watson, C. H., and C. K. Meyers. "Letter to the Church in Europe." *Review and Herald*, 24 November 1932, 1-2.

Watts, Kit. "The Remnant Is as the Remnant Does." *Adventist Review*, 3 September 1992, 5.

Weber, Martin. "Heaven on Our Side: Looking at the Pre-Advent Judgment." *Adventist Review*, 26 March 1992, 8-11.

_____. "Why the Sabbath?" *Ministry*, November 1992, 4, 31.

Weeks, Albert. "Conversion, or the New Birth." *Review and Herald*, 22-29 March 1887, 178-179, 195-196.

Weiser, Neil. "The Effects of Prophetic Disconfirmation of the Committed." *Review of Religious Research* 16 (1974): 19-30.

Weiss, Herold D. "The Theological Task." *Spectrum* 1:4 (1969): 13-22.

_____. "Are Adventists Protestants?" *Spectrum* 4 (Spring 1972): 69-78.

Whalen, W. J. "Sects and Cults, American." *New Catholic Encyclopedia,* 1967 ed., 13:31-34.

"What a Change!" *Review and Herald,* 14 March 1882, 168.

Wheeler, Lee S. "The Communion of the Holy Spirit." *Review and Herald,* 21 April 1891, 244.

Whidden, Woodrow. "The *Way of Life* Engravings: Harbingers of Minneapolis?" *Ministry,*
    October 1992, 9-11.

_____. "Essential Adventism or Historic Adventism?" *Ministry,* October 1993, 5-9.

White, Arthur L. "Why Seventh-day Adventists Have No Creed." *Adventist Review,* 12 July
    1984, 6-8.

_____. "How Basic Doctrines Came to Adventists." *Adventist Review,* 19 July 1984, 4-6.

_____. "The Certainty of Basic Doctrinal Positions." *Adventist Review,* 26 July 1984, 6-8.

[White, Ellen G]. "Letter from Sister Harmon." *Day-Star,* 24 January 1846, 31.

[_____]. "Letter from Sister Harmon." *Day-Star,* 14 March 1846, 7.

_____. "Dear Brethren and Sisters." *Present Truth,* August 1849, 21-24.

_____. "Dear Brethren and Sisters." *Present Truth,* September 1849, 31-32.

_____. "Beloved Brethren, Scattered Abroad." *Present Truth,* December 1849, 34-35.

_____. "My Dear Brethren and Sisters." *Present Truth,* March 1850, 64.

_____. "To the 'Little Flock'." *Present Truth,* April 1850, 71-72.

_____. "Dear Brethren and Sisters." *Present Truth,* November 1850, 86-87.

_____. "To the Brethren and Sisters." *Review and Herald,* 10 June 1852, 21.

_____. "To the Saints Scattered Abroad." *Review and Herald,* 17 February 1853, 155.

_____. "Dear Brethren and Sisters." *Review and Herald,* 10 January 1856, 118.

_____. "Phrenology, Psychology, Mesmerism, and Spiritualism." *Review and Herald,*
    18 February 1862, 94.

_____. "Testimony for the Church." *Review and Herald,* 6 January 1863, 47.

_____. "Unity of the Church." *Review and Herald,* 19 February 1880, 113-114.

_____. "The Cross of Christ." *Signs of the Times,* 3 November 1887, 657-658.

_____. "Cast Not Away Your Confidence." *Review and Herald,* 31 July 1888, 481-482.

_____. "Need of Earnestness in the Cause of God." *Review and Herald,* 25 February 1890, 113-114.

_____. "Repentance the Gift of God." *Review and Herald,* 1 April 1890, 193.

_____. "Candid Investigation Necessary to an Understanding of the Truth." *Signs of the Times,* 26 May 1890, 305-307.

_____. "'Be Zealous and Repent.'" *Review and Herald Extra,* 23 December 1890, 1-2.

_____. "'It Is Not for You to Know the Times and the Seasons.'" *Review and Herald,* 22 March 1892, 178.

_____. "Truth to Be Rescued from Error." *Review and Herald,* 23 October 1894, 657.

_____. "Christ the Life-Giver." *Signs of the Times,* 8 April 1897, 212.

_____. "Treasure Hidden." *Review and Herald,* 12 July 1898, 438.

_____. "Does Adventist Theology Need Changing?" *Ministry,* October 1968, 16-19.

_____. "Unity in Diversity." *Adventist Review,* 17 February 1994, 14-15.

White, James. "Letter from Bro. White." *Day-Star,* 29 November 1845, 35.

_____. "Letter from Bro. White." *Day-Star,* 24 January 1846, 30.

_____. "Who Has Left the Sure Word?" *Present Truth,* December 1849, 46-47; partly reprinted in *Review and Herald,* 13 January 1852, 74.

_____. "The Third Angel's Message." *Present Truth,* April 1850, 65-69.

_____. "The Day of Judgment." *Advent Review,* September 1850, 49-51.

_____. "The 144,000." *Advent Review,* September 1850, 56.

_____. "Conferences." *Advent Review,* November 1850, 72.

_____. "To Our Readers." *Review and Herald,* November 1850, 7.

_____. "Our Present Position." *Review and Herald,* December 1850, 13-15.

_____. "Our Present Position." *Review and Herald,* January 1851, 27-30.

_____. "To Ira Fancher." *Review and Herald,* March 1951, 52.

_____. [Remarks]. *Review and Herald,* 7 April 1851, 64.

_____. "The Gifts of the Gospel Church." *Review and Herald,* 21 April 1851, 70.

_____. "Remarks." *Review and Herald,* 2 June 1851, 93-94.

_____. "The Parable, Matthew XXV, 1-12." *Review and Herald,* 9 June 1851, 97-104.

_____. "The Seventh Angel." *Review and Herald,* 9 June 1851, 103-104.

_____. "The Judgment." *Review and Herald,* Extra, 21 July 1851, 4.

_____. "Our Present Work." *Review and Herald,* 19 August 1851, 12.

_____. "Gospel Union." *Review and Herald,* 25 November 1851, 56.

[_____]. "Angels of Rev. xiv – No. 4." *Review and Herald,* 23 December 1851, 69-71.

_____. "Who May Hear the Truth?" *Review and Herald,* 17 February 1852, 94.

[_____]. "Remarks in Kindness." *Review and Herald,* 2 March 1852, 100-101.

_____. "Babylon." *Review and Herald,* 24 June 1852, 28-29.

_____. "The Faith of Jesus." *Review and Herald,* 5 August 1852, 52-53.

_____. "The Faith of Jesus." *Review and Herald,* 19 August 1852, 60-61.

_____. "Boylston Meeting." *Review and Herald,* 2 September 1852, 72.

_____. "Eastern Tour." *Review and Herald,* 14 October 1852, 96.

_____. "Tracts." *Review and Herald,* 9 December 1852, 120.

_____. "The Sanctuary." *Review and Herald,* 6 January 1853, 133.

_____. "The Immediate Coming of Christ." *Review and Herald,* 20 January 1853, 140-141.

_____. "The Immediate Coming of Christ." *Review and Herald,* 17 February 1853, 156.

_____. "The Sanctuary and 2300 Days." *Review and Herald,* 17 March 1853, 172-173.

_____. "Remarks on This Work." Note added to the *Advent Review,* April 1853.

_____. "Resolution of the Seventh-day Baptist Central Association." *Review and Herald*, 11 August 1853, 52.

_____. "Signs of the Times." *Review and Herald*, 13 September 1853, 75.

_____. "The Angels of Revelation xiv." *Review and Herald*, 29 November 1853, 164.

[_____]. "The 2300 Days." *Review and Herald*, 6 December 1853, 172.

_____. "Gospel Order." *Review and Herald*, 6 December 1853, 173.

_____. "Gospel Order." *Review and Herald*, 13 December 1853, 180.

_____. "My Lord Delayeth His Coming." *Review and Herald*, 10 January 1854, 204-205.

_____. "The Faith of Jesus." *Review and Herald*, 28 February-7 March 1854, 44, 53-54.

_____. "The Seventh Angel." *Review and Herald*, 7 March 1854, 52.

[_____]. "The Twenty-three Hundred Days." *Review and Herald*, 18 April 1854, 100.

_____. "'We Are the Adventists.'" *Review and Herald*, 18 April 1854, 100-101.

_____. "New and Important Works." *Review and Herald*, 19 September 1854, 44.

_____. "The Faith of Jesus." *Review and Herald*, 20 February 1855, 180-182.

_____. "'The Jews' Return.'" *Review and Herald*, 12 June 1855, 248.

_____. "A Test." *Review and Herald*, 16 October 1855, 61.

_____. "Time of the Sabbath." *Review and Herald*, 4 December 1855, 78.

_____. "The Review 'Sectarian.'" *Review and Herald*, 4 December 1855, 80.

_____. "The Testimony of Jesus." *Review and Herald*, 18 December 1855, 92-93.

_____. "The Word." *Review and Herald*, 7 February 1856, 148-149.

_____. "Note." *Review and Herald*, 14 February 1856, 158.

_____. "The Review 'Sectarian.'" *Review and Herald*, 14 February 1856, 160.

_____. "The Gifts. – Their Object." *Review and Herald*, 28 February 1856, 172.

_____. "The 144,000." *Review and Herald*, 3 July 1856, 76-77.

_____. "Watchman, What of the Night?" *Review and Herald,* 9 October 1856, 184.

_____. "The Seven Churches." *Review and Herald,* 16 October 1856, 188-189, 192.

_____. "An Appeal: To Those Who Profess the Third Angel's Message." *Review and Herald,* 20 November 1856, 20-21.

_____. "The Testimony of Jesus." *Review and Herald,* 11 December 1856, 45.

_____. "The Judgment." *Review and Herald,* 29 January 1857, 100-101.

_____. "How Inconsistent." *Review and Herald,* 5 March 1857, 141.

_____. "Unity and Gifts of the Church – Nos. 1-4." *Review and Herald,* 3 December 1857-7 January 1858.

_____. "A Sketch of the Rise and Progress of the Present Truth." *Review and Herald,* 14 January 1858, 77-78.

[_____]. "The Judgment!" *Review and Herald,* 8 April 1858, 164.

_____. "The Original Advent Faith." *Review and Herald,* 27 October 1859, 182.

_____. "Making Us a Name." *Review and Herald,* 26 April 1860, 180-182.

[_____]. "Organization." *Review and Herald,* 1 October 1861, 140-141.

_____. "The Cause." *Review and Herald,* 29 October 1861, 172.

_____. "The Great Movement." *Review and Herald,* 19 May 1863, 196.

[_____]. "The Head and Front of Present Truth." *Review and Herald,* 15 December 1863, 20.

_____. "Time to Commence the Sabbath." *Review and Herald,* 25 February 1868, 168.

_____. "To a Brother at Monroe, Wisc." *Review and Herald,* 17 March 1868, 220.

_____. "Our Faith and Hope." *Review and Herald,* 10 January 1871, 25-26.

_____. "Mutual Obligation." *Review and Herald,* 13 June 1871, 204.

_____. "Conference Address." *Review and Herald,* 20 May 1873, 184.

_____. "The Cause Is Onward." *Review and Herald,* 21 April 1874, 148.

_____. "How Readest Thou?" *Review and Herald,* 13 May 1875, 156-157.

_____. "Christian Union." *Review and Herald,* 12 October 1876, 116.

_____. "Christ Equal with God." *Review and Herald,* 29 November 1877, 172.

_____. "Unfulfilled Prophecy." *Review and Herald,* 29 November 1877, 172.

_____. "Where Are We?" *Review and Herald,* 3 October 1878, 116-117.

_____. "Seventh-day Baptists and Seventh-day Adventists." *Review and Herald,* 20 November 1879, 164.

_____. "Spirit of Prophecy." *Review and Herald,* 22 January 1880, 50-52.

_____. "The Time of the End." *Signs of the Times,* 22 July 1880, 330.

Whitley, David C. "Clouded Issues." *Ministry,* May 1972, 24-31, 42.

"Who Is My Neighbor?" *Adventist Review,* Special Issue [6 May 1993].

Widmer, Myron. "Will Diversity Divide Us?" *Adventist Review,* 13 October 1988, 4.

Wilcox, F. M. "A World of Changing Emphasis." *Review and Herald,* 30 January 1919, 3-4.

_____. "The World's Estimate of Seventh-day Adventists." *Review and Herald,* 9 August 1923, 8.

_____. "Walking in the Advancing Light." *Review and Herald,* 18 November 1926, 3-7.

_____. "The Message for To-day." *Review and Herald,* 29 November-27 December 1928.

_____. "Attacking the Foundations – Nos. 1-2." *Review and Herald,* 18 April, 9 May 1929, 3-4, 3-5.

_____. "Forsaking the Foundations of Faith." *Review and Herald,* 28 November 1929, 13-14.

_____. "'New Light': Preaching Which Discredits Vital Truth." *Review and Herald,* 30 April 1931, 9.

_____. "Contending for the Faith 'Which Was Once Delivered to the Saints.'" *Review and Herald,* 3 March 1932, 5-8.

_____. "God's Message for Today." *Review and Herald,* 28 July 1932, 2, 5.

_____. "Attacking the Foundations – Nos. 1-5." *Review and Herald,* 2 February-2 March 1933.

_____. "The Quest of Truth." *Review and Herald,* 10 January 1934, 3-4.

_____. "God's Message for Today." *Review and Herald,* 2 June 1938, 5.

_____. "A Sure Foundation." *Review and Herald,* 19 January 1939, 2, 6.

_____. "Present Truth for Today." *Review and Herald,* 13 April 1939, 2, 10.

_____. "An Unwavering Message." *Review and Herald,* 27 April 1939, 2.

_____. "The Fundamentals and New Light." *Ministry,* February 1940, 34-36.

_____. "The Foundation of God – Nos. 1-9." *Review and Herald,* 15 August-24 October 1940.

_____. "Steps in Apostasy." *Review and Herald,* 5 September 1940, 2, 18.

_____. "New Light." *Review and Herald,* 12 September 1940, 7-9.

_____. "What Constitutes the Fundamentals?" *Review and Herald,* 18 January 1945, 4, 13.

_____. "Present Truth." *Review and Herald,* 8 May 1947, 4-5.

_____. "The Ancient Landmarks – The Only Safe Guides." *Review and Herald,* 5 May 1949, 20-21, 49-50.

Wilcox, Milton C. "'Despise Not Prophesyings.'" *Review and Herald,* 29 March 1881, 196.

_____. "Forgiveness, Atonement." *Review and Herald,* 25 September 1883, 610.

_____. "The Spirit – Impersonal and Personal." *Signs of the Times,* 18 August 1898, 518.

_____. "Fundamentalism or Modernism – Which?" *Review and Herald,* 15 January-2 April 1925.

Williamson, T. R. "The Holy Spirit – Is It a Person?" *Review and Herald,* 13 October 1891, 627.

Willruth, Bart. "God's Final Word." *Evangelica,* December 1980, 21-24.

Wilson, Bryan R. "An Analysis of Sect Development." *American Sociological Review* 24 (February 1959): 3-15.

_____. "Sect or Denomination: Can Adventism Maintain Its Identity?" *Spectrum* 7:1 (1975): 34-43.

Wilson, Neal C. "An Open Letter to the Church." *Adventist Review,* 24 May 1979, [4-5].

_____. "'Let the Word Go Out.'" *Adventist Review,* 13 December 1979, 4-6.

_____. "Update on the Church's Doctrinal Discussions." *Adventist Review,* 3 July 1980, 24.

_____. "A Letter from the President." *Ministry,* October 1980, 3.

_____. "The Ellen G. White Writings and the Church." *Adventist Review,* 9 July 1981, 4.

_____. "Together for a Finished Work." *Adventist Review,* 17 December 1981, 4-5.

[_____]. "GC President Issues Statements on Racism, Peace, Home and Family, and Drugs." *Adventist Review,* 30 June 1985, 2-3.

_____. "Christ Our Hope." General Conference Bulletin, No. 10. *Adventist Review,* 18-25 July 1985, 5-6.

_____. "Proposal for Peace and Understanding." *Ministry,* May 1987, 23-25.

_____. "Project 27." *Adventist Review,* 6 October 1988, 4-5.

_____. "GC Leaders Target Concerns for the Adventist Church." *Adventist Review,* 2 August 1990, 10-12.

Wood, K. H. "Adventism Today." *Review and Herald,* 11 February 1960, 3.

_____. "The Old Landmarks." *Review and Herald,* 30 March 1961, 3.

_____. "A Changing World – An Unchanging Task." *Review and Herald,* 31 May 1962, 12-13.

_____. "Protest against Theological Doubletalk." *Review and Herald,* 23 April 1964, 12.

_____. "The President and Communion." *Review and Herald,* 23 July 1964, 12.

_____. "The *Newsweek* Story." *Review and Herald,* 1 July 1971, 2.

_____. "The Divine-Human Word." *Review and Herald,* 24 June 1976, 2.

_____. "Bible Study, Technology, and Unity." *Adventist Review,* 25 May 1978, 3.

_____. "'Present Truth' Centers in the Most Holy Place." *Adventist Review,* 28 September 1978, 10-11.

_____. "When a Church Comes 'of Age.'" *Adventist Review,* 28 December 1978, 14-15.

_____. "Solid Foundation." *Adventist Review,* 17 January 1980, 3.

_____. "Satan versus the Church." *Adventist Review,* 24 January 1980, 13-14.

_____. "F. Y. I." *Adventist Review,* 20 November 1980, 3, 11.

_____. "Building Up or Tearing Down?" *Adventist Review,* 28 May 1981, 14-15.

_____. "An Explanation." *Adventist Review,* 1 July 1982, 3.

„World Council of Churches/Seventh-day Adventist Conversations." *Ecumenical Review* 24 (1972): 200-207.

Young, Norman H. "Christology and Atonement in Early Adventism." *Adventist Heritage* 9:2 (1984): 30-39.

_____. "The Alpha Heresy: Kellogg and the Cross." *Adventist Heritage* 12:1 (1987): 33-42.

Zackrison, Edwin. "When Christians Differ." *Ministry,* August 1983, 19-21.

Zinke, E. Edward. "A Conservative Approach to Theology." *Ministry,* Supplement, [October 1977].

„1888-1988. Advance or Retreat?" *Ministry,* February 1988.

Dissertations and Theses

Arthur, David Tallmadge. "'Come Out of Babylon': A Study of Millerite Separatism and Denominationalism, 1840-1865." Ph.D. dissertation, University of Rochester, 1970.

Bieber, F. W. "An Investigation of the Concept of Perfectionism as Taught in the Writings of Ellen G. White." M.A. thesis, Seventh-day Adventist Theological Seminary, Washington, D.C., 1958.

Bissell, Ronald Deane. "The Background, Formation, Development, and Presentation of Ellen White's Concept of Forgiveness from Her Childhood to 1864." Ph.D. dissertation, Andrews University, 1990.

Coberly, Zoral Harold. "A Study of the Influences Affecting the Unity of Beliefs of Seventh-day Adventists." M.A. thesis, Seventh-day Adventist Theological Seminary, Washington, D.C., 1946.

Daggy, Carl Walter. "A Comparative Study of Certain Aspects of Fundamentalism with Seventh-day Adventism." M.A. thesis, Washington, D.C., Seventh-day Adventist Theological Seminary, 1955.

Davis, Morton Jerry. "A Study of Major Declarations on the Doctrine of the Atonement in Seventh-day Adventist Literature." M.A. thesis, Andrews University, 1962.

Dean, David Arnold. "Echoes of the Midnight Cry: The Millerite Heritage in the Apologetics of the Advent Christian Denomination, 1860-1960." Th.D. dissertation, Westminster Theological Seminary, 1976.

Dick, Everett N. "The Adventist Crisis of 1843-1844." Ph.D. dissertation, University of Wisconsin, 1930.

Fernández, Gil Gutierrez. "Ellen G. White: The Doctrine of the Person of Christ." Ph.D. dissertation, Drew University, 1978.

Fletcher, Lee Herbert. "The Seventh-day Adventist Concept of Original Sin." M.A. thesis, Seventh-day Adventist Theological Seminary, Washington, D.C., 1960.

Gallagher, Jonathan. "Believing Christ's Return: An Interpretative Analysis of the Dynamics of Christian Hope." Ph.D. dissertation, University of St. Andrews, Scotland, 1983.

Gane, Erwin Roy. "The Arian or Anti-Trinitarian Views Presented in Seventh-day Adventist Literature and the Ellen G. White Answer." M.A. thesis, Andrews University, 1963.

Graybill, Ron. "The Power of Prophecy: Ellen White and the Women Religious Founders of the Nineteenth Century." Ph.D. dissertation, Johns Hopkins University, 1983.

Haddock, Robert. "A History of the Doctrine of the Sanctuary in the Advent Movement, 1800-1905." B.D. thesis, Andrews University, 1970.

Lee, Jairyong. "Faith and Works in Ellen G. White's Doctrine of the Last Judgment." Ph.D. dissertation, Andrews University, 1985.

Lesher, W. Richard. "Ellen G. White's Concept of Sanctification." Ph.D. dissertation, New York University, 1970.

Lorenz, Felix A., Sr. "A Study of Early Adventist Interpretations of the Laodicean Message with Emphasis on the Writings of Mrs. Ellen G. White." B.D. thesis, Seventh-day Adventist Theological Seminary, Washington, D.C., 1951.

MacIntyre, J. Gordon. "An Investigation of Seventh-day Adventist Teaching Concerning the Doctrine of Perfection and Sanctification." M.A. thesis, Seventh-day Adventist Theological Seminary, Washington, D.C., 1949.

McGarrell, Roy Israel. "The Historical Development of Seventh-day Adventist Eschatology, 1884-1895." Ph.D. dissertation, Andrews University, 1990.

Neall, Ralph E. "The Nearness and Delay of the Parousia in the Writings of Ellen G. White." Ph.D. dissertation, Andrews University, 1982.

Pease, Norval F. "Justification and Righteousness by Faith in the Seventh-day Adventist Church before 1900." M.A. thesis, Seventh-day Adventist Theological Seminary, Washington, D.C., 1945.

Rasmussen, Steen R. "Roots of the Prophetic Hermeneutic of William Miller." M.A. thesis, Newbold College, Bracknell, Berks., England, 1983.

Rowe, David Leslie. "Thunder and Trumpets: The Millerite Movement and Apocalyptic Thought in Upstate New York, 1800-1845." Ph.D. dissertation, Univ. of Virginia, 1974.

Rubencamp, Cosmas. "Immortality and Seventh-day Adventist Eschatology." Ph.D. dissertation, Catholic University of America, 1968.

Schwarz, Richard W. "John Harvey Kellogg: American Health Reformer." Ph.D. dissertation, University of Michigan, 1964.

Steinweg, Bruno William. "Developments in the Teaching of Justification and Righteousness by Faith in the Seventh-day Adventist Church." M.A. thesis, Seventh-day Adventist Theological Seminary, Washington, D.C., 1948.

Taylor, Christy Mathewson. "The Doctrine of the Personality of the Holy Spirit as Taught by the Seventh-day Adventist Church up to 1900." B.D. thesis, Seventh-day Adventist Theological Seminary, Washington, D.C., 1953.

Whalen, Robert Kievan. "Millenarianism and Millennialism in America, 1790-1880." Ph.D. dissertation, State University of New York, 1972.

Whidden, Woodrow W. "The Soteriology of Ellen G. White: The Persistent Path to Perfection, 1836-1902." Ph.D. dissertation, Drew University, 1989.

Yamagata, Masao. "Ellen G. White and American Premillennialism." Ph.D. dissertation, Pennsylvania State University, 1983.

Zackrison, Edwin Harry. "Seventh-day Adventists and Original Sin: A Study of the Early Development of the Seventh-day Adventist Understanding of the Effects of Adam's Sin on His Posterity." Ph.D. dissertation, Andrews University, 1984.

Letters and Manuscripts

Andreasen, M. L. "The Spirit of Prophecy, [1948 address]". Quoted in Russell Holt. "The Doctrine of the Trinity in the Seventh-day Adventist Denomination: Its Rejection and Acceptance, 1969." 20. TMs. Adventist Heritage Center, James White Library, Andrews University, Berrien Springs, Mich.

Bangert, Kurt. "Original Sin – An Adventist Approach, 1974." TMs (in my possession).

Butler, George I., to Ellen White, 16 December 1886. Ellen G. White Research Center, Andrews University, Berrien Springs, Mich.

_____, A Circular Letter to All State Conference Committees and Our Brethren in the Ministry, 1888. General Conference Archives, Silver Spring, Md.

_____, to Ellen White, 3 July 1910. Ellen G. White Research Center, Silver Spring, Md. (Incoming correspondence file).

Butler, Jonathan. "Perils of the Enchanted Ground: The Acculturation of Seventh-day Adventists on the Pacific Coast [1978]." TMs (in my possession).

[Christ,] The Way of Life: From Paradise Lost to Paradise Restored. Lithograph. 1876; rev. ed., 1883. Ellen G. White Research Center, Andrews University, Berrien Springs, Mich.

Clemons, E. C., to Wm. Miller, 17 February 1845. Typewritten transcript (in my possession).

Cottrell, Raymond F. "The Kings of the East: An Historical Study, 1943." TMs. Adventist Heritage Center, James White Library, Andrews University, Berrien Springs, Mich.

_____. "Armageddon: A Study of Historical and Prophetic Backgrounds, 1945." TMs. Adventist Heritage Center, James White Library, Andrews University, Berrien Springs, Mich.

_____. "The Bible Research Fellowship: Its History and Objective, 1950." TMs. Adventist Heritage Center, James White Library, Andrews University, Berrien Springs, Mich.

_____. "Pioneer Views on Daniel Eleven and Armageddon, rev. ed., 1951." TMs. Adventist Heritage Center, James White Library, Andrews University, Berrien Springs, Mich.

_____. "An Evaluation of Certain Aspects of the Martin Articles, 1957." Quoted in Jerry Moon. "M. L. Andreasen, L. E. Froom, and the Controversy over *Questions on Doctrine*, 1988." app. 2. TMs. Ellen G. White Research Center, Andrews University, Berrien Springs, Mich.

_____. "A Hermeneutic for Daniel 8:14, 1980." TMs. Adventist Heritage Center, James White Library, Andrews University, Berrien Springs, Mich.

Crosby, Tim. "A New Approach to an Adventist Doctrine of Original Sin, 1978." TMs. Ellen G. White Research Center, Andrews University, Berrien Springs, Mich.

_____. "Heresy and the Church: A Theology of Creedalism, [1978]." TMs. Adventist Heritage Center, James White Library, Andrews University, Berrien Springs, Mich.

Davidson, Richard M. "The Robes of the High Priest, 1991." TMs. Ellen G. White Research Center, Andrews University, Berrien Springs, Mich.

Douglas, Walter B. T. "Reflections on Contextualization as a Theological Necessity, 1982."
    TMs. Adventist Heritage Center, James White Library, Andrews University, Berrien
    Springs, Mich.

Froom, L. E. "Historical Setting and Background of the Term 'Daily,' 1940." TMs. Adventist
    Heritage Center, James White Library, Andrews University, Berrien Springs, Mich.

Graybill, Ronald D. "Ellen White's Role in the Resolution of [Doctrinal] Conflicts in Adventist
    History, 1980." TMs. Ellen G. White Research Center, Berrien Springs, Mich.

Grotheer, William H. "An Interpretive History of the Doctrine of the Incarnation as Taught by
    the Seventh-day Adventist Church, 1972." TMs. James White Library, Andrews University,
    Berrien Springs, Mich.

Guy, Fritz. "The Theological Task of the Church, 1980." TMs (in my possession).

Hall, Larry J. "The Daily of Dan 8:11-13: An Historical Look at the Millerite View, 1986."
    TMs. Adventist Heritage Center, James White Library, Andrews University, Berrien
    Springs, Mich.

Haloviak, Bert. "In the Shadow of the 'Daily': Background and Aftermath of the 1919 Bible
    and History Teachers' Conference, 1979." TMs. Adventist Heritage Center, James White
    Library, Andrews University, Berrien Springs, Mich.

_____. "Pioneers, Pantheists, and Progressives, 1980." TMs. Adventist Heritage Center,
    James White Library, Andrews University, Berrien Springs, Mich.

_____. "From Righteousness to Holy Flesh: Judgment at Minneapolis [1988]." TMs.
    Library, Friedensau Theological Graduate School, Friedensau, Germany.

Holt, Russell. "A Comparative Study of the Sanctuary and Its Implications for Atonement in
    Seventh-day Adventist Theology from Uriah Smith to the Present, 1969." TMs. Adventist
    Heritage Center, James White Library, Andrews University, Berrien Springs, Mich.

_____. "The Doctrine of the Trinity in the Seventh-day Adventist Denomination: Its
    Rejection and Acceptance, 1969." TMs. Adventist Heritage Center, James White Library,
    Andrews University, Berrien Springs, Mich.

Hudson, A. L., and D. G. Barnhouse. Transcripts of a telephone conversation, 16 May 1958.
    Adventist Heritage Center, James White Library, Andrews University, Berrien Springs,
    Mich.

Jorgensen, Alfred S. "The Fletcher Case, 1980." TMs. Adventist Heritage Center, James White
    Library, Andrews University, Berrien Springs, Mich.

Kittle, Daniel. "[A] Study of the Christian Connection and Its Relationship to the Early Advent
    Movement, 1989." TMs. Adventist Heritage Center, James White Library, Andrews
    University, Berrien Springs, Mich.

Lindén, Ingemar, to Rolf J. Pöhler, 7 November 1979 (in my possession).

_____ , to Rolf J. Pöhler, 16 January 1980 (in my possession).

Loughborough, J. N. "Some Individual Experience, 1918." TMs. Advent Source Collection, Adventist Heritage Center, James White Library, Andrews University, Berrien Springs, Mich.

Minutes of the General Conference Committee, 7 July 1889, 8. Adventist Heritage Center, James White Library, Andrews University, Berrien Springs, Mich.

Moon, Jerry. "M. L. Andreasen, L. E. Froom, and the Controversy over *Questions on Doctrine*, 1988." TMs. Ellen G. White Research Center, Andrews University, Berrien Springs, Mich.

Mustard, Andrew G. "Implications of Troeltsch's Church-Sect Typology for Seventh-day Adventist Ecclesiology, 1978." TMs. Adventist Heritage Center, James White Library, Andrews University, Berrien Springs, Mich.

Neufeld, Don F. "The *Seventh-day Adventist Bible Commentary* in Retrospect, n.d." TMs. Adventist Heritage Center, James White Library, Andrews University, Berrien Springs, Mich.

Nichols, Otis, to William Miller, 20 April 1846. Ellen G. White Research Center, Andrews University, Berrien Springs, Mich.

Olsen, A. V. "An Examination of M. L. Andreasen's Objections to the Book *Seventh-day Adventists Answer Questions on Doctrine*, 1960." TMs. Adventist Heritage Center, James White Library, Andrews University, Berrien Springs, Mich.

Olson, Robert W., to Rolf J. Pöhler, 8 November 1978 (in my possession).

_____ , to Rolf J. Pöhler, 19 October 1979 (in my possession).

_____ . "The 1919 Bible Conference and Bible and History Teachers' Council, 1979." TMs. Ellen G. White Research Center, Andrews University, Berrien Springs, Mich.

[Olson, Robert W., and Bert Haloviak, comp.]. "Who Decides What Adventists Believe: A Chronological Survey of the Sources, rev. ed., 1978." TMs. Ellen G. White Research Center, Andrews University, Berrien Springs, Mich.

Oosterwal, G. "The Seventh-day Adventist Church in the 1980's, 1980." TMs (in my possession).

Pöhler, Rolf J. "Sinless Saints or Sinless Sinners? An Analysis and Critical Comparison of the Doctrine of Christian Perfection as Taught by John Wesley and Ellen G. White, 1978." TMs. Adventist Heritage Center, James White Library, Andrews University, Berrien Springs, Mich.

_____. "'… And the Door Was Shut.' Seventh-day Adventists and the Shut-Door Doctrine in the Decade after the Great Disappointment, 1978." TMs. Adventist Heritage Center, James White Library, Andrews University, Berrien Springs, Mich.

_____. "The Adventist Historian between Criticism and Faith [1990]." TMs (in my possession).

Prescott, W. W. Study on The Person of Christ, 6 July 1919. 1919 Bible Conference Transcripts. General Conference Archives, Silver Spring, Md.

Rock, Calvin B. "Structures for Renewal, 1980." TMs (in my possession).

Sarli, Paulo. "Arian Views Held by Some Pioneers in the Seventh-day Adventist Church between 1844 and 1900, 1972." TMs. Adventist Heritage Center, James White Library, Andrews University, Berrien Springs, Mich.

Scriven, Charles. "The 'Remnant' and the Church: A Reconsideration, 1984." TMs. Adventist Heritage Center, James White Library, Andrews University, Berrien Springs, Mich.

Smith, Uriah, to Ellen White, 17 February 1890. Ellen G. White Research Center, Andrews University, Berrien Springs, Mich.

_____, to A. T. Robinson, 21 September 1892. General Conference Archives, Silver Spring, Md. (L. E. Froom, Personal Collection 12, Uriah Smith correspondence folder)

_____, to W. A. McCutchen, 8 August 1901. Quoted in *Manuscripts and Memoirs of Minneapolis,* 305-306. Boise, Idaho: Pacific Press Pub. Assn., 1988.

„A Statement on Theological Freedom and Accountability." 1987 Annual Council Action of the General Conference Committee. General Actions of 11 October 1987.

Teel, Charles, Jr. "Withdrawing Sect, Accommodating Church, Prophesying Remnant: Dilemmas in the Institutionalization of Adventism, 1980." TMs. Adventist Heritage Center, James White Library, Andrews University, Berrien Springs, Mich.

Varmer, H. "Analysis of the Seventh-day Adventist Pioneer Anti-Trinitarian Position, 1972." TMs. Adventist Heritage Center, Andrews University, Berrien Springs, Mich.

Veltman, Fred. "Summary and Conclusion of the Veltman Report on Ellen White's Use of Literary Sources in Writing *The Desire of Ages,* [1988]." TMs. Ellen G. White Research Center, Andrews University, Berrien Springs, Mich.

Washburn, J. S. "The Trinity [1940]". TMs. Quoted in Gilbert M. Valentine. *The Shaping of Adventism: The Case of W. W. Prescott,* 279-280. Berrien Springs, Mich.: Andrews University Press, 1992.

White, Arthur L. "The Prescott Letter to W. C. White, April 6, 1915, 1981." TMs. Ellen G. White Research Center, Andrews University, Berrien Springs, Mich.

_____. "W. W. Prescott and the 1911 Edition of the *Great Controversy,* 1981." TMs. Ellen G. White Research Center, Andrews University, Berrien Springs, Mich.

White, Ellen G. To the Little Remnant Scattered Abroad. Broadside, 1846. Ellen G. White Research Center, Andrews University, Berrien Springs, Mich.

_____. A Vision. Broadside, 7 April 1847. Ellen G. White Research Center, Andrews University, Berrien Springs, Mich.

_____, to the Hastingses, 29 May 1848. Ellen G. White Research Center, Andrews University, Berrien Springs, Mich.

_____. To Those Who Are Receiving the Seal of the Living God. Broadside, 31 January 1849. Ellen G. White Research Center, Andrews University, Berrien Springs, Mich.

_____, to the Hastingses, 22-23 March 1849. Ellen G. White Research Center, Andrews University, Berrien Springs, Mich.

_____, to the Hastingses, 24-30 March 1849. Ellen G. White Research Center, Andrews University, Berrien Springs, Mich.

_____. Manuscript 5, 1849. Ellen G. White Research Center, Andrews University, Berrien Springs, Mich.

_____, to the Hastingses, 11 January 1850. Ellen G. White Research Center, Andrews University, Berrien Springs, Mich.

_____. Manuscript 4, 1850 (26-28 January 1850). Ellen G. White Research Center, Andrews University, Berrien Springs, Mich.

_____, to Brother Hastings, 18 March 1850. Ellen G. White Research Center, Andrews University, Berrien Springs, Mich.

_____. Vision of 27 June 1850. Ellen G. White Research Center, Andrews University, Berrien Springs, Mich.

_____. Manuscript, 23 October 1850. Ellen G. White Research Center, Andrews University, Berrien Springs, Mich.

_____. "To the Church in Your Place." Manuscript 5a, 1850. Ellen G. White Research Center, Andrews University, Berrien Springs, Mich.

_____. Manuscript 5, 1851. Ellen G. White Research Center, Andrews University, Berrien Springs, Mich.

_____, to Bro. Pierce, 1851. Ellen G. White Research Center, Andrews University, Berrien Springs, Mich.

_____, to the Howlands, 12 November 1851. Ellen G. White Research Center, Andrews University, Berrien Springs, Mich.

_____. Manuscript 1, 1852. Ellen G. White Research Center, Andrews University, Berrien Springs, Mich.

_____. Manuscript 2, 1854. Ellen G. White Research Center, Andrews University, Berrien Springs, Mich.

_____, to S. Pierce, 1857. Ellen G. White Research Center, Andrews University, Berrien Springs, Mich.

_____. Vision of 15 July 1859. Ellen G. White Research Center, Andrews University, Berrien Springs, Mich.

_____, to E. J. Waggoner and A. T. Jones, 18 February 1887. Quoted in *The Ellen G. White 1888 Materials,* 21-31. Washington, D.C.: Ellen G. White Estate, 1987.

_____. Letter 37, 1887. Ellen G. White Research Center, Andrews University, Berrien Springs, Mich.

_____. Manuscript 8a, 1888. Ellen G. White Research Center, Andrews University, Berrien Springs, Mich.

_____. Manuscript 15, 1888. Ellen G. White Research Center, Andrews University, Berrien Springs, Mich.

_____, to W. M. Healey, 9 December 1888. Quoted in *The Ellen G. White 1888 Materials,* 186-189. Washington, D.C.: Ellen G. White Estate, 1987.

_____. Manuscript 16, 1889. Ellen G. White Research Center, Andrews University, Berrien Springs, Mich.

_____, to Bro. and Sr. Garmire, August 1890. Quoted in *The Ellen G. White 1888 Materials,* 697-702. Washington, D.C.: Ellen G. White Estate, 1987.

_____, to Uriah Smith, 6 June 1896. Quoted in Ellen G. White. *Selected Messages from the Writings of Ellen G. White,* 1:234. Washington, D.C.: Review and Herald Pub. Assn., 1958.

_____. Manuscript 75, 1897. Ellen G. White Research Center, Andrews University, Berrien Springs, Mich.

_____. Manuscript 87, 1900. Quoted in Ellen G. White. *Selected Messages from the Writings of Ellen G. White,* 1:233. Washington, D.C.: Review and Herald Pub. Assn., 1958.

_____. Manuscript 59, 1905. Ellen G. White Research Center, Andrews University, Berrien Springs, Mich.

_____. "Minneapolis Talks." 88-89. Quoted in Desmond Ford. *Daniel 8:14, the Day of Atonement, and the Investigative Judgment,* 347. Casselberry, Fla.: Euangelion Press, 1980.

White, James, to S. Howland, 14 March 1847. Ellen G. White Research Center, Andrews University, Berrien Springs, Mich.

_____, to Elvira Hastings, 22 August-1 September 1847. Ellen G. White Research Center, Andrews University, Berrien Springs, Mich.

_____, to Dear Brother [Howland], 2 July 1848. Ellen G. White Research Center, Andrews University, Berrien Springs, Mich.

_____, to the Hastingses, 26 August 1848. Ellen G. White Research Center, Andrews University, Berrien Springs, Mich.

_____, to the Hastingses, 2 October 1848. Ellen G. White Research Center, Andrews University, Berrien Springs, Mich.

_____, to Bro. Hastings, 11 January 1850. Ellen G. White Research Center, Andrews University, Berrien Springs, Mich.

_____, to Ellen G. White, 31 March 1880. Ellen G. White Research Center, Andrews University, Berrien Springs, Mich.

_____, to W. C. White, 16 September 1880. Ellen G. White Research Center, Andrews University, Berrien Springs, Mich.

White, William C., to Mary White, 3 November 1888. Ellen G. White Research Center, Andrews University, Berrien Springs, Mich.

_____, to P. T. Magan, 31 July 1910. Quoted in Bert Haloviak. "From Righteousness to Holy Flesh: Judgment at Minneapolis [1988]." chap. 9, p. 7. TMs. Library, Friedensau Theological Graduate School, Friedensau, Germany.

_____. "The Influence of the Prophetic Gift in the Establishment of Church Doctrine." Quoted in Desmond Ford. *Daniel 8:14, the Day of Atonement, and the Investigative Judgment.* Casselberry, Fla.: Euangelion Press, 1980. A-201.

Zurcher, Jean R. "The Seventh-day Adventist Teaching on the Human Nature of Christ during Ellen White's Lifetime, 1986." TMs. Adventist Heritage Center, James White Library, Andrews University, Berrien Springs, Mich.

Abbreviations

AA	*The Acts of the Apostles*
AHC	Adventist Heritage Center
AR	*Adventist Review*
ASC	Advent Source Collection
AU	Andrews University
COL	*Christ's Object Lessons*
CSW	*Counsels on Sabbath School Work*
CT	*Counsels to Parents, Teachers, and Students*
CWE	*Counsels to Writers and Editors*
DA	*Desire of Ages*
DS	Denzinger, Henricus, and Schönmetzer, Adolfus, eds., *Enchiridion symbolorum definitionum et declarationum de rebus fidei et morum*
EGWRC	Ellen G. White Research Center
ET	English Translation
Ev	*Evangelism*
EW	*Early Writings*
FE	*Fundamentals of Christian Education*
GC	*The Great Controversy Between Christ and Satan*
GW	*Gospel Workers*
JATS	*Journal of the Adventist Theological Society*
JWL	James White Library

LS	*Life Sketches of Ellen G. White*
LThK	*Lexikon für Theologie und Kirche*
MOD	*Movement of Destiny*
MM	*Medical Ministry*
NCE	*New Catholic Encyclopedia*
PFF	*The Prophetic Faith of Our Fathers*
PP	*The Story of Patriarchs and Prophets*
PPPA	Pacific Press Publishing Association
QOD	*Seventh-day Adventists Answer Questions on Doctrine*
RH	*[Second] [Advent] Review and [Sabbath] Herald*
RHPA	Review and Herald Publishing Association
SDA(s)	Seventh-day Adventist(s)
SDABC	*Seventh-day Adventist Bible Commentary*
SDACM	*Seventh-day Adventist Church Manual*
SDAE	*Seventh-day Adventist Encyclopedia*
SDAPA	Seventh-day Adventist Publishing Association
SDAY	*Seventh-day Adventist Yearbook*
SG	*Spiritual Gifts*
SM	*Selected Messages*
SPA	Southern Publishing Association
ST	*Signs of the Times*
T	*Testimonies for the Church*
TM	*Testimonies to Ministers and Gospel Workers*
TMs	Typewritten Manuscript

Author Index

Subject Index

ADVENTISTICA

Studies in Adventist History and Theology – New Series
Publ. by the Institute of Adventist Studies, Friedensau Adventist University
Editors: Johannes Hartlapp, Daniel Heinz, Stefan Höschele, Rolf J. Pöhler

Volume 01:
Rolf J. Pöhler, ed.
Perceptions of the Protestant Reformation in Seventh-day Adventism (2018)
ISBN Print: 978-3-935480-51-2   (€19.90 | for prices in £ and $, check amazon)
ISBN E-book: 978-3-935480-52-9   (€11.99 | for prices in £ and $, check amazon)

Volume 02:
Stefan Höschele & Chigemezi N. Wogu, eds.
Contours of European Adventism:
Issues in the History of the Denomination on the Old Continent (2020)
ISBN Print: 978-3-935480-53-6   (€19.90 | for prices in £ and $, check amazon)

Volume 03:
Rolf J. Pöhler
Dynamic Truth: A Study of the Problem of Doctrinal Development (2020)
ISBN Print: 978-3-935480-54-3   (€19.90 | for prices in £ and $, check amazon)
ISBN E-book: 978-3-935480-55-0 (€11.99 | for prices in £ and $, check amazon)

Volume 04 (forthcoming):
The Impact of World War I on Seventh-day Adventism:
Prophetic Disconfirmation and Conscientious Cooperation

Volume 05 (forthcoming):
The Impact of World War I on Seventh-day Adventism:
Divergent Perspectives on the Reform Movement

To order, write to ias@thh-friedensau.de,
go to https://www.bod.de/buchshop (GER)
or go to Amazon (GB USA CAN AUS).